Labour Relations in Development

This timely and well-written collection explores the impact of economic reforms in developing and transitional economies across the world. In a first of its kind, this book examines such issues as:

- an in-depth, cross-regional analysis of the pressures for global integration;
- labour costs and their determinants: crucial factors in the success of economic strategies in attracting investment;
- how wage levels, poverty and the important role of workers as part of a civil society are linked with the consequences of global integration.

This important book is essential reading for all those involved in Labour and Development Economics as well as being of great interest to policy-makers.

Alex E. Fernández Jilberto is Senior Lecturer in International Relations at the University of Amsterdam, and **Marieke Riethof** is a researcher at the Amsterdam School for Social Science Research, University of Amsterdam.

Routledge Studies in Development Economics

Labour Relations in Development

Edited by
**Alex E. Fernández Jilberto
and Marieke Riethof**

Routledge
Taylor & Francis Group

NEW YORK AND LONDON

First published 2002
by Routledge

2 Park Square, Milton Park, Abingdon, Oxfordshire OX14 4RN

Simultaneously published in the USA and Canada
by Routledge

711 Third Avenue, New York, NY 10017

Routledge is an imprint of the Taylor & Francis Group, an informa business

Typeset in Baskerville by Taylor & Francis Books Ltd

British Library Cataloguing in Publication Data
A catalogue record for this book is available from the British Library

Library of Congress Cataloging in Publication Data
Labour relations in development/[edited by] Alex E. Fernandez and
Marieke Riethof.
p.cm – (Routledge studies in development economics)
1. Industrial relations – Developing countries. I. Fernández Jilberto, A.E.
(Alex E.) II. Riethof, Marieke, 1974 – III. Series.

HD8943 .L336 2002
331'.09172'4–dc21   2002072624

ISBN 0–415–28707–3

Contents

Illustrations

Figures

Tables

Contributors

Claudia Báez-Camargo is affiliated to the Government and International Studies programme at the University of Notre Dame (USA). She worked as the Department Chief in the Ministry for Social Development (Secretaría de Desarrollo Social), Federal Government of Mexico and as an Associate Researcher at the International Trade Unit of the United Nations' Economic Commission for Latin America and the Caribbean (ECLAC), Mexico City, in research projects dealing with the relationship between international trade and environmental regimes.

Paul Blokker is a researcher at the European University Institute in Florence, Italy. His research project aims to analyse various attempts at modernization in Romania, in a long-term historical perspective. Besides empirical historical research on élites, their modernization strategies and outside pressures for change, the research takes a critical perspective on modernization by criticizing 'transitology' and re-embedding current theories in broader sociological theory.

Antonio Carmona Baez has conducted research on normative structural changes throughout Cuba's post-revolutionary history, labour relations and foreign investment, at the Center for Studies on the Americas (CEA) in Havana, Cuba. He was the author of *Foreign Investment and State Transformation in Cuba: a Revolutionary Response to Globalization* (Amsterdam, 1996) and 'Cuba: reforms and adjustments versus transition', *International Journal of Political Economy*, 30(1) (2001).

Alex E. Fernández Jilberto is Senior Lecturer in International Relations at the University of Amsterdam. He has published various articles and books on the political economy of Latin America and developing countries in general. His most recent publications include (with André Mommen) *Regionalization and Globalization in the Modern World Economy: Perspectives on the Third World and Transitional Economies* (London: Routledge, 1998), 'Special Issue: the political economy of open regionalism in Latin America' (edited with Barbara Hogenboom), *International Journal of Political Economy*, 26(3) (1997) and *Miraculous Metamorphoses: the Neoliberalization of Latin American Populism* (London: Zed Books 2001).

Maarten Keune worked for the International Labour Organization between 1992 and 1999, first in Mexico and then in Hungary, where he was mainly involved in research on labour markets and local development. Currently, his research at the European University Institute in Florence, Italy, focuses on labour market governance in the Czech Republic and Hungary.

Piet Konings is a Senior Researcher at the African Studies Centre, University of Leiden (The Netherlands) and is studying state, labour and class formation in Ghana and Cameroon. He has written and edited several books, including *The State and Rural Class Formation in Ghana* (London: Kegan Paul International, 1986), *Labour Resistance in Cameroon* (London: James Currey, 1993), *Itinéraires d'accumulation au Cameroun* (Paris: Karthala, 1993), *Gender and Class in the Tea Estates of Cameroon* (Aldershot: Avebury, 1995), *Unilever Estates in Crisis and the Power of Organizations in Cameroon* (Hamburg: LIT Verlag, 1998), and *Trajectoires de Libération en Afrique Contemporaine* (Paris: Karthala, 2000).

J. Thomas Lindblad studied economics at Columbia University, New York, and the University of Amsterdam. Since 1975 he has been affiliated to the University of Leiden, at the moment as Senior Lecturer in Economic History and the History of South-east Asia. He has published widely on the modern economic history of Indonesia. His books include *Between Dayak and Dutch: the Economic History of Southeast Kalimantan, 1880–1942* (Dordrecht, Netherlands/Providence, Rhode Island, USA: Foris, 1988) and *Foreign Investment in Southeast Asia in the Twentieth Century* (London: Macmillan, 1998). He is the editor of *New Challenges in the Modern Economic History of Indonesia* (Leiden: Programme of Indonesian Studies, 1993) and *Historical Foundations of a National Economy in Indonesia, 1890s–1990s* (Amsterdam: North-Holland, 1996) as well as co-author of *Coolie Labour in Colonial Indonesia: a Study of Labour Relations in the Outer Islands, c. 1900–1940* (Wiesbaden: Harrassovitz Verlag, 1999).

Andrey S. Makarychev is Professor at the Department of International Relations and Political Science, Nizhny Novgorod Linguistic University. His major fields of research are comparative regionalism and federalism, and international relations of Russia's subnational units. In 2000–3, he is International Policy Fellow at the Open Society Institute, Budapest. He has published articles on the political economy of the Russian Federation, and his recent work includes 'Economic reform and the new patterns of post-Soviet regionalism', in A.E. Fernández Jilberto and A. Mommen, *Regionalization and Globalization in the Modern World Economy* (London: Routledge, 1998).

André Mommen works for the Department of Political Science, University of Amsterdam. In the past, his research has focused on neo-liberal reforms in developing and transitional countries. Currently, he has written on the effects of reforms in both developed and developing countries on the position of trade unions. Among his most recent publications (edited with Alex Fernández Jilberto) is *Regionalization and Globalization in the Modern World Economy: Perspectives on the Third World and Transitional Economies* (London: Routledge, 1998).

Kwame Nimako holds degrees in sociology and economics from the University of Amsterdam, where he teaches International Relations at the Department of Political Science. He worked as a *Tinbergen Fellow* at the Department of Agricultural and Development Economics at the same university. Before that, he was a Lecturer in Race and Ethnic Relations and Development Studies at the Centre for Race and Ethnic Studies (CRES), University of Amsterdam. Among his books are *Beyond Multiculturalisation: Amsterdam Southeast as Strategic Location* (Rotterdam: Gramo de Combinatie, 1998, in Dutch), *Economic Change and Political Conflict in Ghana, 1600–1990* (Amsterdam: Thesis Publishers, 1991), *The Plural Cube: Discourse on Emancipation Models and Minorities Policy* (in Dutch, with C. Mullard and G. Willemsen) (The Hague: Warray, 1990). He is also a contributor to *Liberalization in the Developing World: Institutional and Economic Changes in Latin America, Africa and Asia* (London: Routledge, 1996) edited by A. E. Fernández Jilberto and André Mommen.

Vladimir Popov holds a Ph.D. from the *Institute of the US and Canada* of the Academy of Sciences of the USSR. He is currently Sector Head at the Academy of the National Economy in Moscow and a visiting professor (since 1999) at Carleton University (Ottawa). From 1996 to 1998, he was a Senior Research Fellow in the World Institute for Development Economics Research (WIDER) of the United Nations University in Helsinki, Finland. His most recent publications include: 'Preparing the Russian economy for world market integration' in A.E. Fernández Jilberto and André Mommen (eds) *Regionalization and Globalization in the Modern World Economy* (London: Routledge, 1998), and 'Reform strategies and economic performance of Russia's regions', *World Development*, 9, 2000. A book, co-edited with G.A. Cornia, *Transition and Institutions: The Experience of Late Reformers*, was published by Oxford University Press in 2001; see *http://www.wider.unu.edu/publications/publications.htm* and *http://www.oup.co.uk/ isbn/0-19-924218-6*. For reviews of the book see *Moscow Times*, 10–11 Nov. 2001 at *http://www.themoscowtimes.com/stories/2001/11/10/044.html* and *Wider Angle*, No. 1, 2002 at *http://www.wider.unu.edu/newsletter/newsletter.htm*.

Marieke Riethof is a researcher at the Amsterdam School for Social Science Research, University of Amsterdam. She has done research on the effects of neo-liberal restructuring on labour relations in Chile, at the Programme of Labour Economics (*Programa de Economía del Trabajo*). At present, her research focuses on the responses of Brazilian trade unions to economic reforms, labour flexibilization and privatization. Her publications include 'Labour involvement in national and regional transformation processes: the case of Chile', *Third World Quarterly*, 20(5), 1999 and (with Alex Fernández Jilberto) 'América Latina en el neoliberalismo global: crisis financiera, políticas sociales y reformas laborales', *European Review of Latin American and Caribbean Studies* (17 October 2001, pp. 125–38).

Claudia Sanchez Bajo has done her Ph.D. on the political economy of regionalism and business actors in Mercosur at the Institute of Social Studies in The Hague. She has a 'Licenciatura' in Political Science (El Salvador University, Buenos Aires, 1988) and an MA in Development Studies (ISS, The Hague, 1991). Between 1983 and 1993, she was a researcher and technical adviser to Argentina's Parliament, at the Department of International Studies of the Directorate of Parliamentary Information. Among her publications are 'The European Union and Mercosur: a case of inter-regionalism', *Third World Quarterly* (1999) and 'Mercosur's open regionalism and regulation: the role of business actors. Focusing on the petrochemicals and steel sectors', *Nordic Journal of Latin American and Caribbean Studies*, XXIX(1–2), 1999. She is currently writing a text on technical standards and regionalism.

Diana van Stijn finished her MA in Political Science at the University of Amsterdam. She did research on the effects of globalization in Mali in 2000, which resulted in *The Forces of Globalisation in Africa: the Case of Mali* (Amsterdam, 2001).

Inês Trigo de Sousa obtained her degree in International Relations, at the Instituto de Ciências Sociais e Politicas (ISCSP), Technical University of Lisbon. She obtained a post-graduate degree in International and European Relations (ASIR, University of Amsterdam, 1997–8) and a post-graduate certificate at the Research Centre for International Political Economy (RECIPE, University of Amsterdam, 1998–9). She worked as an independent researcher for the European Legal Affairs Working Group of the Clean Clothes Campaign, The Netherlands, and published a report under the auspices of the Bangladesh People's Solidarity Centre, entitled *Codes of Conduct and Monitoring Systems* (2000). She joined the Amsterdam School for Social Science Research in September 2000.

Hans van Zon is Research Professor in Central and East European Studies, University of Sunderland (UK). He worked as research co-ordinator for the European Commission (DG XII). His recent publications include *The Political Economy of Independent Ukraine* (London: Macmillan, 2000), *Central European Industry in the Information Age* (Aldershot: Ashgate, 2000) and 'Central and Eastern Europe: catching up or marginalization in the European free trade zone', in A.E. Fernández Jilberto and A. Mommen (eds) *Regionalization and Globalization in the Modern World Economy* (London: Routledge, 1998).

Preface

This book examines the adjustment of relations between capital and labour in developing and transitional economies. The relationship between global economic restructuring and labour relations is probably one of the topics that is least considered in studies on globalization, which have been primarily focused on the impact of the substitution of centrally planned economies in Eastern Europe, and of populism and economic nationalism in Latin America, Asia and Africa, on structural adjustment policies and the relationship between the state and civil society. The neo-liberalization of developing and transitional economies shares the common characteristic of the loss of political importance of trade unions, whose interests were represented in the tripartite constructions of transnational Keynesianism and in the party-states that dominated socialist countries. The radical restructuring of labour relations, influenced by neo-liberal globalization, are reflected in the deregulation and flexibilization of labour markets, an increase in precarious work and the informalization of formal labour markets. These developments have weakened the capacity of labour organizations to represent workers. The withdrawal of the state from its regulating role in conflicts between capital and labour, and the transfer of these functions to the market has consolidated the marginality of trade unions in the formulation of economic development policies. The establishment of an 'entrepreneurial society' dominates, subordinating economic and social actors to the logic of the market mechanism.

The accelerated mobility of capital in a globalized world means that developing and transitional economies try to compete with each other on the basis of low labour standards, in order to attract foreign investment flows for economic growth. In this perspective, one of the fundamental objectives of economic policies is the improvement of competitiveness in the global market and domestic stability of macro-economic variables. This can only be achieved through lower salaries and an increase of precarious work. The unions that emerged during the twentieth century are usually considered to be obstacles to economic growth and opponents of the benefits that globalization is expected to bring. Today, falling labour standards often imply the *de facto* suspension of Conventions 87 (freedom of association and protection of the right to organize), 98 (the right to organize and collective bargaining) and 100 (on equal renumeration) of the International Labour Organization. This makes the establishment of a global labour platform more difficult.

It is important to note that the economic and labour reforms implemented in developing and transitional countries have not led to a stable system of capital–labour relations. International financial crises like the Mexican peso crisis in 1995, the Russian moratorium in 1997 and the Asian crisis in 1997–8 have resulted in colossal wage reductions, the deterioration of working conditions and a significant increase in informal labour.

The deterioration of working conditions and the loss of the political influence of trade unions expresses itself in difficulties in creating new social clauses in relations between capital and labour. This is also the result of the political effects of the collapse of socialism in Eastern Europe, of the ideological collapse of *Third-Worldism* in developing countries, and the neo-liberalization of social democracy, as political reference points for workers and trade unions.

The editors of this volume have had the privilege of co-operating with a number of distinguished authors who have contributed their wide-ranging experience on the topic of labour and economic restructuring. They all analyse the position of labour in relation to globalization, from the perspective of the different continents that are incorporated in a fragmented way in the globalization of labour. Every book has its own history, and the authors of this book have always had a critical view on the inequalities generated by the global system. A book that intends to incorporate the study of the global facts that express themselves at the national level is not without its difficulties, but these are solved by the academic excellence of its contributors.

Alex E. Fernández Jilberto
Marieke Riethof
Amsterdam,
November 2001

Acknowledgements

The authors and publishers would like to thank the following for granting permission to reproduce material in this work: Lynne Rienner Publishers, the International Labour Office, the European Bank for Reconstruction and Development, The Haworth Press, the Heritage Foundation and Wendell Cox Consultancy.

Every effort has been made to contact copyright holders for their permission to reprint material in this book. The publishers would be grateful to hear from any copyright holder who is not here acknowledged and will undertake to rectify any errors or omissions in future editions of this book.

1 Labour relations in the era of globalization and neo-liberal reforms

Alex E. Fernández Jilberto and Marieke Riethof

Introduction

Increasing global integration is having a twofold effect on workers. In many cases, it means that they will have to deal with the harsh realities of globalization: the fact that their company may come under foreign ownership, with the concomitant threat of relocation to another country where labour conditions are more favourable, and the limits to which the state can intervene to alleviate the effects of international economic crises. Some groups of workers are able to take advantage of the opportunities offered, for example those with a skill that is in high demand, and some can cope with or welcome increased flexibility in working conditions. Although the opportunities offered and the constraints on workers in a global economy are by no means new, the dynamics of contemporary capitalism increase the interconnectedness of groups of people in different parts of the world.

Global financial crises, from the Latin American debt crisis in 1982 to the Asian crisis in 1997–8, have contributed to a transformation in thinking about economic policies in developing and transitional economies. Changes include structural adjustment programmes promoted by international financial institutions, macro-economic stabilization, state reform and trade liberalization. The relationship between these reforms, economic development and social improvement is still disputed, as levels of poverty, unemployment and real wages do not seem to be changing substantially.

Within this perspective, the chapters in this book aim to study the relationship between the process of globalization and national responses, with a specific focus on the implications of increasing global integration for both the political and economic position of labour. Work and labour are at the centre of the issues outlined above. The labour factor is a central concept in economics, because labour costs and labour productivity are perceived to be key factors in successful economic development. Work in various forms is a central activity for most people in the world, and workers' organizations are of major importance in representing large groups of people and as actors in the process of the determination of wage levels. One can of course argue that trade unions have lost their relevance and power, but this does not deny the social and political importance of issues such as unemployment and labour productivity.

The purpose of the collection of studies in this book is twofold. On the one hand, the chapters discuss the effects of economic reforms on workers and employment. National case studies are used to address the impact of economic reforms, but the dimension of global restructuring is referred to systematically. The case studies illustrate the diversity of national responses to global restructuring, and show how this results in 'varieties of capitalism'. On the other hand, the studies pay attention to the responses of those affected by economic reforms. In this introduction, we give an overview of the way economic reforms can be expected to affect workers and their representative organizations.

The first section of the introduction discusses the general pessimism surrounding the potential role of trade unions in society and the way in which they represent workers' interests. Despite this pessimism, the role of trade unions in democratic transition processes, in alliance with other opposition groups, has led to optimistic conclusions about a genuinely new role for organized labour. This does not mean that these labour movements are not affected by problems similar to those of trade unions in other parts of the world. However, despite these negative developments, there are many initiatives to rethink the role of trade unions.

The second section of the introduction deals with particular reforms that affect the position of workers and trade unions: reform of the state, economic and social policies; labour flexibilization; and privatization. This section provides the necessary framework for the understanding of the context of the reforms implemented in many developing and transitional economies. The denationalization of decision-making processes, the transformation of the role of the state and economic reforms are key aspects of globalization and neo-liberal restructuring that affect the position of workers.

Globalization and labour

The position of the trade unions

Social theorists like Ulrich Beck, Manuel Castells and André Gorz argue that a fundamental transformation is taking place in the nature of work and its relationship to society (Castells 1996 and 1997, Gorz 1999, Beck 2000). Beck (2000) characterizes current changes as a transition from a 'work society', in which paid work is a central category, to a 'world risk society' where categories and activities are more fluid and where the labour market has become more insecure and flexible. In sum:

> paid employment is becoming precarious; the foundations of the social-welfare state are collapsing; normal life-stories are breaking up into fragments; old age poverty is programmed in advance; and the growing demands on welfare protection cannot be met from the empty coffers of local authorities.

> (Beck 2000: 3)

According to André Gorz, today's society is characterized by an ideology that stresses the value of hard work as well as its importance for individual and economic development. However, this work ethic is increasingly being called into question because it is no longer possible to achieve full employment and because an increase in production in some economic sectors is based on reducing the amount of labour used (Gorz 1999: 42; see also Gorz 1982). It does not necessarily follow that this crisis of our work-based society will lead to the demise of the labour movement, but Gorz predicts that it will lead to a rethinking of the role of work in society. Organized labour can overcome this by accepting that other forms of activity (including domestic labour and autonomous activities) will become increasingly important and that full-time work is not the only possible form of work. The labour movement should therefore focus its attention on the possibility that people will work part-time, or will concentrate on leisure and personal development. The task of trade unions is '*to extend its sphere of action beyond the limited defence of workers as workers, in their workplaces*' (Gorz 1999: 48, italics in original).

Manuel Castells supports a nuanced perspective on the future of employment. While arguing that the Information Age is characterized by a decline of industrial and agricultural employment, a shift to employment in the service industries, and the growing importance of knowledge-based productivity and work, Castells also proves that the particular manifestations of this phenomenon differ among developed economies. Therefore, one cannot speak merely of a convergence of employment structures in developed countries (Castells 1996: 128–32). For trade unions, this situation means that organized labour has to deal with an increasingly diversified labour market, in addition to polarization among potential trade-union members. Atypical labour contracts emerge (part-time, temporary, fixed contracts) and workers with different rights and contracts, or even with different employers, can work together in the same company. Castells is quite pessimistic about the possible role of organized labour in the era of globalization, or, in the network society, as he calls it. The nature of the network society clashes with the traditional organization of trade unions:[1]

> The labor movement does not seem fit to generate by itself and from itself a project identity able to reconstruct social control and to rebuild social institutions in the Information Age. Labor militants will undoubtedly be a part of new, transformative social dynamics. I am less sure that labor unions will.
>
> (Castells 1997: 360)

The fragmentation of identities and the decline of traditional forms of identity formation (including collective identities like the working class) present difficulties for trade unions in addressing new members (non-traditional workers) and new issues that have more appeal for the traditional membership of trade unions.

The second chapter of this book provides an overview of reforms and trans-formation processes in Western Europe and the United States. By analysing current experiences in the light of continuities and discontinuities with the past, André Mommen addresses the question of why neo-liberal reforms are now being implemented in all parts of the world. Although the reforms that he anal-yses have features in common, the struggles and conflicts in the national political and economic context are a necessary factor explaining current reform processes. Similarly, Mommen argues that trade unions should be analysed not only as a universal form of worker organization, but as a partial reflection of their national political context and different systems of labour relations. An example of the fundamental changes is the reform of social-security and pension systems. This shows how the role of the state in the economy has been trans-formed in Europe, as well as in developing and transitional countries.

Developing and transitional countries in context

In order to be able to understand the situation in developing and transitional economies, it is necessary to discuss the general differences in the position of workers in these countries as compared with the developed countries such as those in Western Europe and the United States.[2] The existence of a large (agri-cultural) labour surplus in many developing countries puts pressure on the labour market and on wage levels. Instead of a developed welfare state, the informal sector is a labour buffer zone that absorbs the effects of economic shocks and unemployment. Many workers are underemployed, which means that they do not earn enough in their job to make a living. This situation contributes to employment in several (formal and informal) jobs at the same time and to the participation of all family members out of economic need. Because of inadequate social welfare, workers cannot afford not to work and unregulated work becomes a common alternative. Usually called the informal sector, this group consists of a variety of workers, from street vendors and domestic workers, to micro-entrepreneurs and urban marginals (Harrod 1987). The existence of a large informal sector has

> a major impact on the labour market and affects the scope for trade union activism. Its existence limits the possibilities of industrial action since it represents an uncontrolled and competitive group which can influence wage levels and threatens job security.
>
> (Frías and Ruiz-Tagle 1995: 144)

The unprotected workers of the informal sector are marginalized from labour legislation, and this means that the legislative instrument as a way to protect workers becomes less effective.

A characteristic of labour markets in developing and transitional countries is the long-term shift in employment from agriculture to industry and services. In more industrialized developing countries, one can speak of a process of de-industrialization and a decrease in industrial employment. This process can be seen in countries like Brazil, Chile and Indonesia, and in the economies of Eastern Europe. Industry does not become less important in countries like Brazil and South Korea, but capital intensiveness increases. Emphasis on capital intensiveness and global competitiveness decreases the role of industry as a generator of employment, as labour costs and productivity are central. Training and educational levels often do not keep up with the requirements of rapidly changing industrial production and demands. Privatization and restructuring of companies in crisis usually leads to a rationalization of the production process and a reduction in the workforce. In addition, subcontracting and outsourcing, although not new processes, contribute to a fragmentation of tasks in a company and often to more precarious working conditions for the subcontracted workers.

Russia is a country where labour markets are fragmented in many ways. As Andrey Makarychev describes in Chapter 7, sectoral differences correlate with regional differences and specialization in particular economic activities. Regions in which economic activities are concentrated in the metallurgical, automobile, textile and light industries find it hard to deal with the new competitiveness that is now propagated. Other regions are excluded from the dynamics of the more successful regions (a focus on exports, trade and finance is important in these regions). These developments lead to an increase of population movements, both within Russia, and between Russia, the former Soviet republics and neighbouring countries. Although official unemployment figures are low in Russia, real unemployment is higher. Much unemployment is hidden, for example when workers are employed but not paid, because unemployment is an issue that can affect the future of politicians and the legitimacy of governments. For workers, this means that they have to become more 'flexible' themselves, seeking self-employment and other survival strategies outside formal employment.

Labour movements often play an important role in democratization processes, but serious problems appear when post-transition governments introduce economic reforms and macro-economic stabilization policies. Expectations of democratic reforms are high, and social actors expect to be involved in the decision-making process. Even if, based on the example of Western Europe, tripartite consultation institutions are set up, this does not mean that social partners can exercise influence on policy-making. The disillusionment with the results of democratization shows that the installation of democratic rules and institutions does not lead automatically to democratic decisions that satisfy labour movements. Besides, the possibilities for participation of social actors often remain limited. Often given as the reason for this is the perceived fragility of the new regime, with representatives of the old regime often threatening to return. Moreover, economic reforms are generally presented as unavoidable and the only rational way to proceed in times of crisis. There is little room for manoeuvre and alternatives in such a situation. This is the paradox of political and economic liberalization (Starr and Oxhorn 1999).

A common way to regard labour and organized workers' issues in developing countries is to treat them as a potential problem for social order, economic growth (e.g. the way wage demands affect prices and inflation – the wage–price spiral) and political stability. Workers can also be a focus of mobilization and search for political support, as in populism, as well as the basis for the organization of political parties and their strategies. There are several levels on which workers themselves deal with social and economic development issues and respond to and try to influence government policies. Collective bargaining and workers' representation are central activities of trade unions. In some cases, governments consult organized labour about social, economic and labour policy-making. General strikes and demonstrations were usually more effective before and during transition processes, but can affect public opinion and put pressure on employers. Trade-union action increasingly assumes a global dimension, even if it consists simply of information exchange. International and regional institutions are a new framework for the activities of organized labour, containing constraints to union action as well as new possibilities for solidarity and contacts with labour movements in other parts of the world. The activities of organized and non-organized workers are generally aimed at the institutional and social surroundings of their work environment.

These considerations imply that workers cannot be treated simply as a reflection of economic structures, and the chapters in this volume show that there are more issues at work (Adler 1996: 118).[3] For example, in the context of left-wing politics, a radical view on economic and social change is common among workers. In some perspectives on organized labour, unions represent the demands of their members, whose demands and ideas again reflect their material circumstances. Although this might explain the behaviour of trade unions to some extent, it should not exclude the possibility of a broader political view and political action outside the work-place. Trade unions have been involved in democratization processes, in the struggle for the extension of citizenship rights and in community development. It is now increasingly common for unions to broaden their potential membership and to start alliances with other social organizations on issues like human rights, racial and gender equality and environmental improvement. Broader political perspectives and the representation of members' interests can be mutually influencing factors.

As Alex Fernández Jilberto shows in his study of labour relations in Chile in Chapter 12, the expectations of the labour movement were that democratization in the 1990s would allow the reform of the system of restrictive labour legislation,[4] and enable trade unions to play a political role. Chile is unique in the sense that it was the first country to introduce neo-liberal reforms in the mid-1970s. Institutional and political constraints after democratization imply that an open economy, based on exports with low added value and competition on the basis of low labour costs, is maintained. Trade unions played an important role in the long democratization process in Chile. Nevertheless, the legacies of labour legislation introduced during the military regime and flexibilization of labour relations have led to a more problematic position for trade unions and a loss of representativeness. The government has attempted to initiate a form of tripartite negotiations, dealing with the minimum wage level and changes in the labour-relations system.

The Brazilian transition process and the re-emergence of oppositional forces, starting in the early 1970s, provided the context of a significant wave of strikes at the end of the 1970s. These would result in more independent trade unions, whose shop-floor action aimed to transform the labour relations system, something which was also translated into political opposition to the military regime. The labour movement that emerged from this period of change is often called 'new unionism', characterized by attempts to become autonomous from the state, an emphasis on coalitions and alliance with social movements, and a move beyond wage and income issues, towards citizenship rights, community development and democratization.[5]

The case of Argentina is an illuminating example of the confusion and dilemmas that labour movements confront in a time of political and economic transition. First, the Argentinian government has introduced an economic stabilization programme, combined with a call for social cohesion and integration. In Chapter 10 of this book, Claudia Sanchez Bajo argues that even though the labour movement does agree with economic recovery, this process takes place in a framework of severe economic problems and a fundamental transformation of the nature of work and production. Second, there are now cracks appearing in the traditional relationship between Perónist leaders and organized labour. This leads to the undermining of labour institutions in Argentina, with organized labour being discredited as a spent force. At the same time, the official central trade union, CGT (Central General de Trabajadores) now has to compete with several other central union organizations. Third, the financial stabilization plan that pegged the peso to the dollar (introduced by President Carlos Menem), combined with the effects of the Asian crisis and the devaluation of the Brazilian currency, have led to a devastating economic recession, with increasing poverty and unemployment. This crisis does not seem to have an easy solution, and the labour movement finds it difficult to formulate an alternative. The 1990s saw the emergence of a more active opposition of trade unions to neo-liberal policies, but the unions seem to find it difficult to choose between making broader social protests, and sometimes even unorthodox labour actions, and their traditional role as trade unions.

Taking the case of Ghana as an example, in Chapter 15 Konings discusses the responses of African trade unions to structural adjustment programmes. Unfortunately, the consequences for workers have been negative. Workers have been confronted with a combination of problems in the economic and the work sphere. Prices for goods and public services have increased and wage reductions, unemployment and the introduction of flexible labour relations have all undermined the position of Ghanaian workers. Within the logic of structural adjustment, trade unions were seen as beneficiaries of a system in which the state was inefficient, and where they would block retrenchment and initiatives to increase efficiency, but this has not necessarily been the case.

Even though the trade unions in Ghana did not push all the way in the process of democratization, protests started to increase after the implementation of economic reforms in the 1990s. Within the context of a greater degree of democracy, the central trade union, GTUC (Ghana Trades Union Congress), resorted to strikes, legal action against privatization, demonstrations and asserting the right to collective bargaining. In this case, one can speak of a trade-off between certain concessions with regard to reform and the political influence of trade unions.

In addition to Piet Konings' analysis, Kwame Nimako provides (in Chapter 17) a historical context for the Ghanaian working class and trade unions. He describes how decolonization and nationalist development policies have led to a difficult alliance between the labour movement and the government. Structural adjustment and state retrenchment have weakened the position of the GTUC. Unions are not only dependent on the state, because government employees form an important membership base, but also increasingly on foreign NGOs and foreign unions. Nimako calls this the *democratization of dependence*.

The analysis presented in the aforementioned chapters shows how trade unions try to confront new realities. In all four cases, unions are confronted with the legacies of their corporatist past and changes in labour relations that are the result of labour reforms and the introduction of new forms of production organization. In addition, trade unions find it difficult to appeal to their traditional membership base because it has changed significantly. Nevertheless, some trade unions have been able to extend the focus of their activities, and some new forms of protest have emerged.

The role of trade unions

The following paragraphs give an overview of views on the possible roles of trade unions in a globalized world. These views include criticisms on organized labour, but while some critics have lost faith in the labour movement, others try to identify new possibilities and tasks. The following issues can be identified:

- the old and new roles of trade unions
- trade-union representativeness
- trade-union strategies: negotiation and mobilization
- the international dimension of trade-union activities

The context of the debate on the position of trade unions is the perception that globally mobile capital becomes a more and more powerful force, putting pressure on governments to reduce social spending, forcing down wage levels and adversely affecting labour conditions. It is often assumed that states are not able to provide adequate protection for their citizens, including employment and social security. Current discussions emphasize changes in the role of the state that lead to a breakup of old forms of relations between the state and organized labour and a lack of willingness of governments to improve labour and employment conditions and involve organized labour in decision-making. Furthermore, there are tendencies to particularize employment relations at the company level, excluding the role of collective agents like trade unions (Vilas 1997: 31, Catalano 1999: 34–5, Jose 2000: 7).

The first and second debates on the role and representativeness of unions are related to the question of whether trade unions can still function under these conditions. Trade unions are often seen as institutions that cannot adapt to the new environment. On the one hand, unions rely on their relatively privileged position as representatives of large groups of people in society, but are not able to formulate effective alternatives and strategies. On the other hand, unions increasingly represent a minority of people, as the typical worker on which unions are based does not exist any more (Hyman 1999: 1–2). In addition, workers are polarized between those highly skilled, highly paid workers who are not threatened with unemployment, and those who work under precarious circumstances (with part-time contracts or outside the formal sector), who are not adequately skilled for the demands of the global economy. Richard Hyman speaks of an expansion of groups at two extremes:

> those with professional or technical skills who may feel confident of their individual capacity to survive in the labour market; and those with no such resources but whose very vulnerability makes effective collective organization and action difficult to achieve or perhaps even to contemplate.
>
> (Hyman 1999: 3)

The rise of the 'knowledge-based economy' puts a premium on skills and knowledge, or the ability to handle information flows. According to analysts like Manuel Castells (1996, 1997), workers and companies who cannot keep up with information as a new ordering principle of society will lose out.[6]

The challenge for trade unions in developed, developing and transitional countries is to address the differences between these groups on the labour market. An answer to the 'crisis of trade unions' from non-Western countries is a new form of trade-union organization. Emerging from opposition against authoritarian or dictatorial regimes, is a 'social-movement unionism' or 'new unionism'. According to Munck (1999: 9, 12–13), the 'new unions' emphasize internal democracy, acknowledge the limits of traditional notions of unionism and politics and try to be autonomous from the state and party politics. This is a reaction against the trade union as a narrowly productivist, nationally oriented organization, based on male manufacturing workers (Catalano 1999). This new type of unionism addresses issues that are broader than just workplace and wage demands (the economic function of trade unions). They connect these issues to citizenship and democratization and address issues of exclusion and solidarity (Jose 2000: 1–2). Action often takes place in alliance with other social organizations, and this ensures that a certain amount of attention is given to the various groups of working people. This has increased the capacity for collective representation in countries like Brazil, South Africa and South Korea, as:

unions can challenge the authoritarian and hierarchical structures of contemporary employing organizations and can press for an extension of citizenship rights to employment.

(Hyman 1999: 8)

The last two dimensions of trade-union activities that we will discuss here concern the dilemma between negotiation and mobilization and the global dimension of unionism. Francisco Zapata detects a difference

between those national situations where the labor movement has been able to build a strategy that tries to defend workers' interests while accepting most of the 'new economic model' package of measures and those national situations where labor movements have been totally incapable of facing these conditions.

(Zapata 2001: 12)

In the first situation, unions have chosen to participate in changes and reforms as far as institutions allow this. This strategy often clashes with the origin of many new labour movements in developing and transitional countries in opposition and large-scale mobilizations. In this context, some groups in labour movements oppose the strategy of bargaining with governments or employers for benefits. The dilemma between negotiation and confrontation shows the problems that trade unions face when they are confronted with far-reaching reforms in societies with limited possibilities for democratic participation.

The labour movement has always had an international perspective, stressing the common cross-national features of the working class and international solidarity. Recent international activities are a reflection of global restructuring and domestic changes. As the determinants of wage levels and the constraints on economic and social policy-making increasingly lie outside national boundaries, trade unions have focused attention on issues like transnational collective bargaining, influencing international (financial) institutions, global protests and global solidarity initiatives. Widespread availability of information and communication technologies reinforces these tendencies.[7]

International institutions like the World Trade Organization are the target of union attempts to introduce (core) labour standards[8] into the trade agenda, and to include labour and social issues in the structural adjustment programmes of the World Bank and the IMF. Campaigns to promote codes of conduct, and campaigns against child labour, are examples of direct attempts to influence the labour policy of companies. Furthermore, the involvement of trade unions in regional integration initiatives such as NAFTA, the EU and MERCOSUR has resulted in the adoption of more-or-less elaborate social declarations, social policy (regional and social development funds in the case of the EU) and labour-conflict mediation mechanisms. According to some, the offshoot of these activities is the emergence of a new labour internationalism, 'a significant break from the post-war trend of nation-statist unionism' (Munck 2000: 385).

Economic reforms: the state, flexibility and privatization

The changing role of the state

According to the Washington consensus, economic problems in developing and transitional economies are the result of an oversized state and an excess of state intervention.[9] Proponents of neo-liberal policies argue that the crisis of Communist and populist regimes is engendered by the exhaustion of a particular type of state interventionism and protectionism, while the export-led industrialization model proved that state institutions can protect markets from rent-seeking activities and spur economic growth and allocative efficiency.

In Europe and North America, increased competition and subsequent financial and economic liberalization policies opened the way for a transformation of the state and a breakup of the coalition of trade unions, employers and social-democratic parties that supported Keynesian macro-economic policies and expansion of social welfare. Welfare regulations are being revised and the Western European welfare state is being gradually privatized in order to lower its costs and to meet the needs of a growing white-collar middle class.[10] The privatization of the welfare state went hand in hand with the numerical decline of the industrial working class and the breakup of the Fordist organization of production in large factories. In developing countries, the privatization of welfare schemes was the outcome of a crisis of the state system in connection with the fall of import-substituting industrialization projects initiated after the Great Depression of the 1930s.

The Latin American debt crisis of 1982 signified a watershed between the era of state-led development and the neo-liberal revolution. After a decade of stagnation, the Latin American and other developing countries opened up their economies for more foreign competition and liberalized their financial markets. In Africa, where 'progressive' military regimes postponed any reform until the Soviet Union collapsed, the economic situation had been deteriorating since the end of the 1970s. Most of these regimes had carried out their national revolution by adopting a centrally planned economic system. The collapse of Communism proved to many that extreme forms of import substitution and autarchy ('socialism in one country') engendered the same difficulties and inefficiencies. Communism collapsed at the end of the 1980s in a period when the populist regimes in the Third World had exhausted their own resources and prospects for economic growth after a period of economic decline and increased indebtedness *vis-à-vis* the developed capitalist countries and the international financial institutions.

Russia is a key example of a country where reforms have not led to economic growth or the solution of social problems. In the light of current socio-economic problems, in Chapter 3 Vladimir Popov addresses the question of which factors play a role in a possible solution of this situation. In a general overview of the problems that post-Communist countries confront, he stresses the quality of investment and savings as a crucial factor in the improvement of capital productivity. The success of such policies depends on the need to improve the distribution of incomes. He also addresses the role of the state in the case of post-Communist countries. From a state with wide-ranging roles and responsibilities, these countries have swung towards attempts to dramatically reduce the role of the state, but, according to Popov, an effective state is necessary to return to social and economic development.

Even in a country like Cuba, where a 'transition' from Communism has not taken place, the state has introduced certain labour reforms that have led to a more flexible labour relations system. In Chapter 13, Antonio Carmona Baez analyses two such changes in Cuba: the regulation of self-employment and the introduction of a new system of economic management at the enterprise level. The economic difficulties resulting from the collapse of the Soviet Union and the US blockade partly explain this shift. It has become more and more difficult for the Cuban government to provide its population with a high standard of social services, and black-market activities have been growing. Despite regulation of the situation, self-employed workers are expected to pay very high taxes and are subject to strict state control. The position of self-employed workers in Cuba shows how the working class, as it was traditionally defined by the Cuban Communist Party, has become fragmented, although all workers are in the same socio-economic situation. Another reform requires that state-owned enterprises improve their global competitiveness, through modernization of production organization and management. Furthermore, flexibilization of labour contracts, the possibility of wage differentiation and pegging wage levels to productivity should also lead to higher competitiveness.

Governments try to formulate new ways of dealing with economic development, based on an international framework of economic and political reforms promoted by international institutions and developed countries (as well as within the developing and transitional countries themselves). The framework postulates that the workings of market mechanisms should be facilitated by a government that limits itself to essential tasks, such as infrastructure, education and health. Going beyond the minimal tasks of the state is seen as an obstacle to the market mechanism, leading to inefficiency and possibly crisis. Practical reforms include reducing the size of the state, and public expenditure, and the privatizing of state-owned enterprises. Furthermore, countries are recommended to undertake trade and financial liberalization, and to abolish state subsidies and other types of intervention. Another central reform is the flexibilization of the labour market in order to avoid resistance to economic adjustment, related to job protection and social security (Zapata 2001: 1–3).

In his analysis of recent changes in labour market institutions in Hungary, Maarten Keune, in Chapter 4 of this book, emphasizes the importance of an approach to the study of economic reforms and labour that acknowledges the diversity of mechanisms, outcomes and even contradictions with idealized types of reform. These reforms occur

> in one and the same global discursive context, which has by and large set the broad boundaries within which change has moved.

The role of neo-corporatist institutions, whose objective is to co-ordinate socio-economic policy-making with social actors, is limited, but these institutions play an important role in giving trade unions and employers' organizations some legitimacy in collective bargaining and in their new role in post-Communist society. As in most cases studied in this collection, the Hungarian state tries to reduce its role as a major employer, but the labour market institutions still consist of a combination of market mechanisms and state governance. One can speak of a move towards more flexible governance of the labour market, but the extent to which this happens depends on political choices and existing restrictions such as labour legislation.

One could also argue that the perceived effect of globalization poses challenges for governments, as the costs and benefits of adjustment and integration are unevenly distributed among people. Furthermore,

> social polarization is reinforced by state policies, which have abandoned countercyclical measures and operate now in the same direction as the market: they concentrate and strengthen towards the top; they disorganize towards the bottom. Extreme social polarization reduces the range of state policy instruments and their capacity to maintain inequalities within certain limits.
>
> (Vilas 1997: 25)

Other major changes related to global restructuring are shifts in production, towards industrialization and services in developing countries and towards services in developed countries; an increasing internationalization of production processes; and the concentration of flows of capital through multinational corporations.

A shift in economic priorities and the transformation of the state from an active promoter of industrial development to the role as a facilitator of market-driven export-led development, has resulted in the decline of some economic sectors and the rise of others.[11] This process includes shifts in sectoral employment. The increase of external competition as a result of economic liberalization has led to the rationalization and restructuring of the production process. Although this can have positive consequences for some groups of – usually highly skilled – workers, it also means dismissals of workers, outsourcing and subcontracting of production. The expectation is that this will generally lead to an increase in employment in the services sector, based on low wages, low job security and precarious work conditions (Tardanico 1997: 9).

These developments are not generalized across all countries and regions. It is certainly not true that every country benefits or suffers equally. Some countries, like the Latin American and the East Asian Newly Industrializing Countries (NICs) and Eastern European countries have already experienced an industrialization process with significant involvement of capital from abroad. Governments, under pressure from international financial institutions, creditors and domestic groups, try to change the role of the state in the economy. This effort is the result of an ideological shift in favour of the market mechanism over the role of the state. This does not always mean that the purpose of reform is that the state should be relegated to a subsidiary role. The perfect neo-liberal economy does not exist, and a legacy of past macro-economic policies and state intervention usually remains. Most countries represent a mixture of market and state mechanisms, with varying degrees of societal involvement, determining the workings of their economy. Even the rules of the neo-liberal market are the result of political intervention and bargaining. As is shown in the chapters of this book, reforms are not without opposition, and often lead to a politicization of the issues at stake, even though the reforms are claimed to be neutral and technical.

In Chapter 5, Paul Blokker analyses the conflicts and oscillations that occurred in the Romanian political and economic transition. There are many reasons why countries do not implement the 'standard' neo-liberal reform package. Reforms such as privatization and trade liberalization can lead to socio-economic problems that threaten the electoral position of politicians and governments. According to Blokker, it is important to make a careful assessment of continuities and discontinuities with the previous model, instead of arguing for a total rupture or total continuity. The understanding of economic reforms and transition is enhanced when the variety of forms and outcomes of transitions and the factors that cause these differences is acknowledged. In Romania, for example, the introduction of reforms was not just the result of international pressure, but it 'was the outcome of the complex interaction between divided political élites and their inability to formulate a coherent alternative to the global paradigm'. Democratization has led to difficulties in trade unions forming a co-ordinated opposition, as the number of unions has increased rapidly and competition has made effective influence difficult. In general, the labour movement supports the idea that economic reforms can lead to higher wages, but they also criticize the introduction of neo-liberal reforms without regard for the socio-economic consequences.

Developing countries and transitional economies are characterized by fundamental changes in the economic and the political system. The process of change is intended to encompass the whole economic and political system, but continuities with the past often remain. Legacies of past policy-making have to compete with the pressures of international financial institutions and the (perceived) requirements of the global economy. At the same time, the transition process does not change power relations in society overnight. Transition is not just a process in history, but also a conscious policy of factions within governments, groups in society, international institutions and other countries.

The Asian crisis has contributed to a shift in thinking about the role of the state in development, and the fact that the subsidiary state does not necessarily solve problems related to global financial flows.[12] The inefficiency of the banking system or national financial regulation are not the sole causes of failure. The global financial system has its own dynamics, and there is no proof that its systemic effects can be counteracted by a reduction in the role of the state. Even

the World Bank has taken a small step towards acknowledging the possible negative structural impact of the Asian crisis. New perspectives of the World Bank on
the social costs of development, especially poverty, including the notion of social
capital and institution building (Chan 1999, World Bank 1999: 101–10, World
Bank 2001).

The Indonesian case illustrates the devastating social effects of financial
crises. As J. Thomas Lindblad argues in Chapter 9, Indonesia has known a long
process of integration in the global economy, with an increase of export manufacturing and an important role for foreign investment. From the mid-1980s until
1997, economic growth accelerated, and this led to real increases in wages.
When the Asian crisis struck Indonesia, this trend reversed to higher unemployment and declining wages. As a result, labour unrest increased and demands
focused on the effects of reforms and crisis as well as on wage rises. Reforms of
labour legislation after the fall of President Suharto, under President Habibie,
led to the flexibilization of restrictions on the formation of independent trade
unions. As a consequence, the number of trade unions increased at all levels and
in all sectors, also leading to a new commitment to reform among the trade
unions that realized that they had not played a very influential role in the fall of
Suharto.

In Chile, it was impossible to eradicate the heritage (flexible labour, precarious jobs, 'informalization' of the formal sector, and low salaries) of the
dictatorship in an only partially reformed economy. Later, the negative effects of
the Asian crisis (1997–8) confirmed the opinion of the government about labour
flexibilization as a virtuous strategy for intensifying Chile's global economic
competitiveness.

Structural adjustment policies promoted by the World Bank and the IMF
usually impact upon the role of the public sector and the potential role of the
state in the development process. The consequences are a reduction in public-
sector employment, which includes state-owned companies, as a result of
budget reduction and privatization, and, in the private sector, the replacement
of a stable workforce by workers with less-secure contracts. On the basis of an
analysis of one of the poorest countries in the world, Mali, Diana van Stijn
argues, in Chapter 16 of this book, that in societies as poor and underdeveloped as in Africa, workers pay a high price to remain within or to become part
of the integrated global economy. Exploitative labour practices and working
conditions are common practice on the African continent. The position of
labour and the problem of unemployment and low wage levels illustrate the
process of increasing inequality and social injustice. State-owned companies
play an important role in providing employment in Mali. Current economic
common sense suggests that the state should not be involved in the economy,
except for facilitating the way in which economic growth is driven by the
private sector. Still, the question remains as to whether the private sector can
absorb the workers who lose out in the process of privatization. High levels of
unemployment also lead to a questioning of the extent to which the state can
provide social security.

States in developing countries tend to influence the structure of production organization and the labour process in several ways: by negotiating with investors about the terms of investment, and by promoting industrialization or particular economic sectors. First, governments often try to negotiate issues such as technology transfer, the use of local components, locating research and development in the host country, and use of the local labour force. Governments often give concessions to investors in the form of tax exemptions, subsidized loans and land. The second way in which states try to influence their economic future is the promotion of particular domestic sectors. The extensive promotion of economic sectors and state intervention to stimulate industrialization is characteristic of the so-called developmental state.

The implications of foreign direct investment (FDI) for local labour conditions become especially clear in the case of the automobile industry – a highly internationalized industrial sector. The government of Brazil managed to include and strengthen the local components industry, while this is less the case in Mexico. In South Korea and Japan, the government established a national automobile industry without as much TNC involvement as in Mexico and Brazil. Labour standards in the *maquiladora* industrial sites in Mexico, and the repression of the labour force in Korea contributed to the competitiveness of exports and production in both countries (Lee and Cason 1994).[13]

The People's Republic of China shows a new type of labour insertion in the global economy. In Chapter 8, Inês Trigo de Sousa takes the development of cross-border regional economic networks and the integration of two 'different systems', Hong Kong and Macau, into the People's Republic, as an example to illustrate the importance of these changes. Both Hong Kong and Macau are highly integrated in the global economy. Labour-intensive industries such as the garment and footwear industry, which have extensive contacts with suppliers across the border from Macau and Hong Kong in the Special Economic Zones, are characteristic of these regions. The Special Economic Zones are designed to attract investment and to stimulate private activity, but they also function as a trigger for changes in China's labour legislation. The position of trade unions has not been fully liberalized, and labour relations in Macau are traditional, based on patron–client relations, with little regulation of working conditions. This is an attractive situation for foreign investors, but it also leads to workers' protests. Social unrest can seem to be a threat to economic stability in the eyes of reformers, thus further provoking a call for liberalization and modernization of labour relations.

In addition to attracting foreign direct investment and promoting the competitiveness of domestic industry, developing and transitional states tend to reduce welfare budgets and fundamentally reform social legislation in order to reduce public spending and often to increase labour market flexibility. This can lead to a lack of social safety-nets for dismissed workers and an increase in poverty and in informal-sector employment. Structural adjustment programmes, a retrenchment of the public sector and a high debt burden constrain the possibilities for organized labour to struggle for better wages and working conditions.

Deregulation and labour market flexibility

Central in the debate on the impact of post-Fordism on labour relations is the transformation of relations between labour and management, between social actors and the state, and changes in the path and focus of economic development.

Debates on labour flexibility should be seen in the context of the political and economic reforms discussed above, and within the framework of company restructuring. The debates contain several dimensions, all very relevant to the study of the impact of economic reforms on workers. The exigencies of the global economy and the need to be competitive are often used as the rationale to introduce policies that promote adaptability to external economic circumstances. Flexibility relates to both the national institutional framework and to production processes in companies. At the national level, economic and social policies and the legislative framework should facilitate adaptability. In the production process, flexibility should provide companies with possibilities to change aspects of the production process (including the number of workers) in order to maintain a competitive position and to introduce new technologies. The call for adaptability 'also means a redistribution of risks away from the state and the economy towards the individual' (Beck 2000: 3).

The umbrella phrase for this type of transformation in the production process is flexible specialization or lean production.[14] Instead of mass production in large companies, flexible specialization takes place in:

> networks of large and small firms based increasingly on computer networks and close co-operation in technology, quality control, training, investment planning and production planning (just-in-time) etc.
>
> (Nielsen 1991: 5)[15]

The concept of flexible specialization is based on Japanese innovations in production organization ('Toyotism') and it refers to changes in the structure of economic organization, technology and institutions (Hirst and Zeitlin 1991). The so-called Japanese production method is an adaptation of the Fordist mass-production model. Aspects of the model are: just-in-time production (rapid responses to demand and strict organization of supply), total quality management (continuous improvement and solution of mistakes at the assembly line), the integration of design and manufacturing, greater responsibility of workers in the production process and the introduction of team work and self-managed groups of workers.

The purpose of this type of production model is to strengthen the idea of the company as a community:

> There is mutual commitment between management and workers, involving a quid pro quo between effort, on the one hand, and identification with the firm's performance, on the other.
>
> (Sengenberger 1993: 4)

The positive dimensions are that employers make an effort to bind workers to the company in the form of job security. Furthermore, the rotation of tasks and higher responsibilities can increase motivation of workers. Trade unions in this type of company tend to be organized at the company level. The main purpose of such enterprise unions is to contribute to the company as a community, as the model depends on harmonious labour relations. The strength of the unions is mainly derived from the skills of the workers, a situation of relative interdependence between management and employees (Ruigrok and Van Tulder 1995: 84–8).

A negative aspect of lean production is that the Japanese production system is very hierarchical. This means that core firms can provide their workers with job security, but companies in the lower tiers of the supply chain generally pay lower wages and provide less security (Sengenberger 1993: 13). The parallel of this system in developing and transitional economies is the existence of a group of core workers in the formal sector that are highly skilled and highly paid. The companies who employ these workers often subcontract aspects of the production process (e.g. the supply of parts) or services (cleaning, security guards, canteens) to companies that are not able to provide similar wages, or even to workers who fall outside the protection of labour legislation. Unless workers are in a relatively strong position derived from the scarcity of their skills, unions are weak in this system. Labour conflicts are not institutionalized in tripartite negotiations between the state, organized labour and employers' organizations. Because unions are decentralized, it is difficult to establish intra- or inter-sectoral alliances and to address national or even transnational economic and social issues. Hyman characterizes the effects of 'lean production' as follows: it

> has reduced the scope for socialising on the job, diversification of work schedules means increasingly that only a fraction of the workforce is present at any one time, subcontracting entails that workers on a single site may be employees of different companies, and individuals often live a considerable distance from their work.
>
> (1999: 10)

Flexibility can have positive consequences in the sense that it diversifies tasks, increases responsibility in the production process, and increases the commitment of workers. Nevertheless, the down side of flexibility is deregulation of labour legislation, changes in job security, and attempts to reduce indirect labour costs. In many cases, larger companies outsource several activities to small companies in the informal sector. In this way, employers can avoid paying welfare contributions and, because labour standards in the informal sector are less well monitored, this practice can promote the spread of precarious work. Debates on the reduction of employers' contributions to social-security and unemployment funds also reflect attempts to lower labour costs (Cox 1987: 346–7).

Changes in the nature of work, labour flexibility and deregulation do not necessarily result in a generalized worsening of the position of workers. It can strengthen the position of some workers, especially highly skilled ones. Nevertheless, adjustment tends to take place in the labour market (dismissals and changes from the informal to the formal sector) and in terms of labour costs. Ideally, adjustment would also involve changes in the structure of production and increases of labour and capital productivity, but this is usually the result of long-term economic policies and improvement in training (Amadeo and Horton 1997: 16, 25–6). Broadly speaking, one can distinguish between workers who have a protected job situation on the basis of their skills, and workers who are flexible out of necessity and can easily be replaced by others. Post-Fordist production organization and its variants generally lead to a diversification, or fragmentation, of the workforce, 'that is, [fragmentation of] ... workers' interest, demands, and importance for production' (Regini 1992: 7). Segmentation of the labour market and the increase of atypical work forms lead to employers' policies that are aimed at treating workers differently according to their occupational category. 'New forms of flexible decentralised bargaining which match the heterogeneity of the occupational situation' reflect the difficulties that traditional trade unions face in representing their heterogeneous basis (Regini 1992: 11–12).

Privatization

The privatization of state-owned enterprises is an excellent topic for the study of the effects of reforms on workers and trade unions. Privatization can be defined as the transfer of assets, economic and social functions and state tasks to the private sector. Besides the privatization of companies in the public sector, the process includes the transfer of public services to the private sector and the deregulation of public services. Examples of the transfer of public services to the private sector are the privatization of health and education and the establishment of private social-security funds.

The arguments used in the process of privatization provide substantial insight in specific attempts to reform the state sector and in the power relations surrounding the decision to reform the public sector. It becomes clear then that privatization is a central pillar of economic reforms and that the arguments used in favour of privatization partially explain the way that the state is going to be reformed and the role of the state in the economy that politicians prefer. It can also be a political signal, showing that governments are committed to economic reforms and liberalization.

Specific effects of privatization on trade unions and workers are difficult to measure, as the effects are the result of a larger package of reforms. In many cases, privatization means that companies have to be made attractive for investors, so 'privatization usually involves restructuring and changes in management and enterprise behaviour, all with far-reaching effects on employment and labour relations' (Hoeven and Sziraczki 1997: 1). The restructuring process also involves large-scale dismissals, as one of the reasons for privatization is that the large number of employees of many state-owned companies is seen as inefficient (Kikeri 1998: 1).

The argument used to justify privatization and restructuring is that more efficient and internationally competitive companies will be able to generate
high-level employment in the formal sector. The general effect on the economy
would be that a reduction of state spending in non-essential areas would
contribute to economic development and financial resources for the implementation of social policies. There are several problems with these statements. First,
the share of employment in the public sector and in state-owned enterprises
tends to be low in developing countries. Second, privatized companies will probably achieve efficiency by cutting labour costs, which does not allow much space
for employment creation. As Zapata argues,

> productivity increases derive more from control of collective bargaining by
> subordinated unions and the suppression of clauses in collective contracts,
> … than from higher efficiency in production by a stable work force.
>
> (Zapata 2001: 9)

Furthermore, employment creation will probably take place in the more highly
paid and skilled sections of the workforce, and this will not provide a solution for
unskilled workers in the informal sector, as there is a lack of correspondence
between economic and technological modernization (including skill levels). It is
important to note that the public sector plays a very important role in broadening the access to stable, legally regulated jobs in developing countries. In
transitional economies, the public sector used to be the most important
employer, and a transfer to the private sector has had serious consequences for
employment levels and job protection (Tardanico 1997: 7, Zapata 2001: 4–5).

A third issue is the question of popular participation in decision-making
surrounding privatization. In several East European countries, privatization takes
place by issuing vouchers, a process in which all citizens can take part. This is not
automatically translated into more control over investment decisions and social
dimensions of company restructuring. In most other countries, state-owned
enterprises are auctioned or shares are sold on the stock market. This results in a
highly concentrated ownership pattern with a high involvement of foreign
investors. In some cases, trade unions can negotiate participation of their
members in shares of their company. The aim of workers' shares 'is to help forge
a new firm-based identity among workers and to give them an incentive to
increase productivity' (Hoeven and Sziraczki 1997: 14). The ability of unions to
negotiate a say in the restructuring process or to include employment and labour
conditions in the privatization process largely depends on the bargaining power
of a union and is not the result of democratic forms of participation.

The chapters by Marieke Riethof, Hans van Zon and Claudia Báez-Camargo
specifically address the privatization of state-owned enterprises and its social
effects. In the case of Brazil, which Marieke Riethof analyses in Chapter 11, the
labour movement had difficulties in developing a coherent and effective strategy
against the (negative effects of) privatization of state-owned enterprises.
Privatization is one of the central reforms that accompanied the combined stabi-

lization (*Plano Real*)/structural reform package introduced in 1994. Trade unions and other opponents of privatization focused their criticism on the expected positive effects of privatization for the economy and on the direct negative effects of privatization in terms of dismissals. The labour movement that emerged during the opposition against the military regime at the end of the 1970s, also known as 'new unionism', was innovative in its focus on democracy in the workplace and its efforts to move beyond corporatist labour relations. Nevertheless, privatization has provided the labour movement with practical and strategic problems, because many employees of state-owned enterprises decided to buy shares in the newly privatized companies. This clashes with a complete rejection of privatization by other sections of the labour movement. This chapter therefore provides an insight into the dilemmas of unions when dealing with the practical effects of reforms, and into the choices that have to be made between confrontation and negotiation.

In Chapter 14, Claudia Báez-Camargo notes that the main argument used to privatize the electricity and telecommunications sectors in Mexico at the end of the 1990s was that the state did not have sufficient resources to maintain public utilities. Furthermore, privatization as an adjustment measure involved the liberalization of these sectors in order to reduce costs and increase efficiency. The type of regime (more-or-less authoritarian), as well as the internal organizational dynamics of trade unions and their partisan links, can explain the reaction of trade unions and their effectiveness. In the case of the telecommunications company operating during the time of the Salinas government (1988–1994), the political climate was not very conducive to opposition. Through a strategy of support for privatization, the union achieved a guarantee of job security. The electricity privatization, under President Ernesto Zedillo (1994–2000) provoked the establishment of an alliance of unions, political parties, and social organizations, all united in their opposition to the measures. Eventually, this led to a failure to reform the electricity sector. However, unconditional union opposition to privatization can be controversial, as some unions have decided to support privatization and liberalization in exchange for workers' participation in share schemes.

Privatization is expected to affect employment levels, as corporate restructuring precedes the sale of state assets in order to increase the attractiveness of the companies. In the case of privatization in Ukraine (Chapter 6), where state-owned companies provide a large share of employment and many social services for employees, Hans van Zon has noted the disintegration of companies and deterioration of the working environment, while social relations within the enterprise remain petrified. State-owned companies play an important role in the provision of social services (e.g. pension funds, schools, leisure and health facilities), not only for employees, but also for the local community in which the company is based. This role often falls away after privatization, and local governments are not always able to replace these services due to a lack of financial resources. Despite the phenomenon of unpaid leave and spreading part-time work, a labour-hoarding tendency still persists, and is reflected in lower labour productivity and lower intensity of work. Except for some cases in the mining industry, there has been little protest. This is connected with the weak bargaining position of workers, but also with the nature of the state-owned companies in Ukraine, where loyalty of the workforce in the 'company as community' still plays a significant role.

Notes

1 According to Castells, the changes in capitalism that are relevant for labour issues have led to a

> decentralization and networking of firms both internally and in their relationships to other firms; considerable empowering of capital *vis-à-vis* labor, with the concomitant decline of influence of the labor movement.
>
> (Castells 1996: 1)

In addition, the fragmentation of identities and work relations contribute to the demise of movements that are not adapted to the speed of the knowledge-based society and that are based on collective identity and ideals.

2 The so-called 'convergence hypothesis' predicts that a (labour) institutional and policy convergence will take place as a result of globalization, competitiveness and a process of economic and political modernization. Implicit in convergence thinking is the idea that developing and transitional states and economies will eventually converge to one institutional and political form. Another important approach is path dependency, which argues that convergence does not necessarily take place. This approach attempts to explain differentiated development patterns, and state–labour relations often play a significant role in analysis. See Boyer (1996) and Frenkel and Harrod (1995) for a critique of convergence theory. Examples of 'path dependency' approaches that pay attention to the position of workers are Berins Collier (1999), Collier and Collier (1991), Deyo (1990), Kaufman (1990) and Rueschemeyer (1992).

3 This is one of the main problems of a Marxist perspective on workers, and it involves the question about the relative importance of the way that structures constrain workers' activities and of the way that structures make possible the structural change that originates from working-class action. On the other hand, it is necessary to assume that some differences do exist within the working classes and between social and economic groups. These differences are structural but contingent, and do not exclude social change.

4 Legislation on strikes was extremely prohibitive, as were the possibilities for unionization and collective bargaining. Furthermore, the Chilean labour movement suffered as a result of the long period of repression and restrictions.

5 See Adler (1996: 140, note 9), Seidman (1994), Waterman (1999) and Bezuidenhout (2000).

6 Although information seems to be easily available, the ability to use and interpret information (knowledge), is based on access to education and conditions favouring the acquisition of knowledge. A lack of educational funding and social circumstances that prohibit a high level of training limit the possibilities for social mobility. In this sense, there are structural inequalities in access to information and the skills to use it. Access to (new) technology is another example of these structural inequalities.

7 Some titles in the growing literature on this topic are O'Brien (2000), O'Brien *et al.* (2000), Haworth *et al.* (2001) and van Roozendaal (2001).

8 Core labour standards are: freedom of association and collective bargaining; the abolition of forced labour and child labour; non-discrimination; and the right to equal pay. See *http://www.ilo.org/public/english/standards/norm/whatare/ fundam/index.htm* (accessed 26 July 2001).

9 For a discussion of the type of state – the developmental state – that emerged in industrializing developing countries, see Woo-Cumings (1999).
10 It is interesting to note in this respect that the Chilean model of private-pension and social-security funds is used as a model for welfare reform in some European countries.
11 Industrial production for the domestic market declined as compared with production for export of goods or primary materials with a low added value.
12 For the reaction of the International Monetary Fund to the Asian crisis and the transition in the East European countries, see IMF Staff (1998) and Exeter and Fries (1998). See also ECLAC (1998) on the impact of the Asian crisis on Latin America.
13 The South Korean labour movement has become more militant in recent years, and especially so in the wake of the Asian financial crisis. There were many protests against the authoritarian attitude of the government towards labour unions. In June 2001, Korean trade unions mobilized against the sale of the bankrupt Daewoo Motor company to General Motors and Fiat. These protests are linked to widespread criticism of the government's economic and labour policies.
14 See Sengenberger (1993), Frenkel and Harrod (1995), Locke *et al.* (1995) and Hoogvelt (1997: 93–113).
15 On the 'networked' nature of global capitalism, see Castells (1996) and Hoogvelt (1997: 109–13).

References

Adler, G. (1996) 'Global restructuring and labor: the case of the South African trade union movement', in Mittelman, J. (ed.) *Globalization: Critical Reflections*, Boulder, CO: Lynne Rienner.

Amadeo, E.J. and Horton, S. (1997) 'Labour flexibility and productivity: an overview' in E.J. Amadeo and S. Horton (eds) *Labour Flexibility and Productivity*, Basingstoke: Macmillan, pp. 1–35.

Beck, U. (2000) *The Brave New World of Work*, Cambridge: Polity Press.

Berins Collier, R. (1999) *Paths Toward Democracy: the Working Class and Elites in Western Europe and South America*, Cambridge: Cambridge University Press.

Bezuidenhout, A. (2000) *Towards Global Social Movement Unionism? Trade Union Responses to Globalization in South Africa*, Geneva: International Labour Organization/International Institute for Labour Studies.

Boyer, R. (1996) 'The convergence hypothesis revisited: globalization but still the century of nations?', in S. Berger and R. Dore (eds) *National Diversity and Global Capitalism*, Ithaca: Cornell University Press, pp. 29–59.

Castells, M. (1996) *The Information Age: Economy, Society and Culture, Vol. I: The Rise of the Network Society*, Oxford: Basil Blackwell.

—— (1997) *The Information Age: Economy, Society and Culture, Vol. II: The Power of Identity*, Oxford: Basil Blackwell.

Catalano, A.M. (1999) 'The crisis of trade union representation: new forms of social integration and autonomy-construction', in R. Munck and P. Waterman (eds) *Labour Worldwide in the Era of Globalization: Alternative Union Models in the New World Order*, London: Macmillan; New York: St Martin's Press, pp. 27–40.

Chan, C. (1999) 'Globalization's shadow: the East Asian financial crisis', *UN Chronicle*, XXXVI(3): 21–8.

Collier, R.B. and Collier, D. (1991) *Shaping the Political Arena: Critical Junctures, the Labor Movement, and Regime Dynamics in Latin America*, Princeton: Princeton University Press.

Cox, R.W. (1987) *Production, Power and World Order: Social Forces in the Making of History*, New York: Columbia University Press.

Deyo, F.C. (1990) 'Economic policy and the popular sector', in G. Gereffi and D.L. Wyman (eds) *Manufacturing Miracles: Paths of Industrialization in Latin America and East Asia*, Princeton: Princeton University Press, pp. 179–204.

Economic Commission for Latin America and the Caribbean (ECLAC) (1998) *Impact of the Financial Crisis on Latin America*, LC/G.2026, Santiago de Chile: ECLAC.

Exeter, J. and Fries, S. (1998) 'The post-communist transition: patterns and prospects', *Finance and Development*, September: 26–9.

Frenkel, S. and Harrod, J. (eds) (1995) *Industrialization and Labor Relations: Contemporary Research in Seven Countries*, New York: ILR Press.

Frías, P. and Ruiz-Tagle, J. (1995) 'Free market economics and belated democratization: the case of Chile', in H. Thomas (ed.) *Globalization and Third World Trade Unions: the Challenge of Rapid Economic Change*, London and New Jersey: Zed Books.

Gorz, A. (1982) *Farewell to the Working Class: an Essay on Post-Industrial Socialism*, London: Pluto.

—— (1999) 'A new task for the unions: the liberation of time from work', in R. Munck and P. Waterman (eds) *Labour Worldwide in the Era of Globalization: Alternative Union Models in the New World Order*, London: Macmillan; New York: St Martin's Press, pp. 41–63.

Harrod, J. (1987) *Power, Production, and the Unprotected Worker*, New York: Columbia University Press.

Haworth, N., Hughes, S., Stigliani, N.A. and Wilkinson, R. (2001) 'Recasting labor diplomacy: comments and rejoinder', *International Studies Perspectives*, 2(2) May: 207–19.

Hirst, P. and Zeitlin, J. (1991) 'Flexible specialization versus post-fordism: theory, evidence and policy implications', *Economy and Society*, 20(1), February: 1–56.

Hoeven, R. van der and Sziraczki, G. (1997) 'Privatization and labour issues', in R. van der Hoeven and G. Sziraczki (eds) *Lessons from Privatization: Labour Issues in Developing and Transitional Countries*, Geneva: International Labour Organization, pp. 1–19.

Hoogvelt, A. (1997) *Globalisation and the Postcolonial World: the New Political Economy of Development*, London: Macmillan.

Hyman, R. (1999) *An Emerging Agenda for Trade Unions?*, Discussion Papers, Geneva: International Institute for Labour Studies/Labour and Society Programme.

IMF Staff (1998) 'The Asian crisis: causes and cures', *Finance and Development*, June: 18–21.

Jose, A.V. (2000) *The Future of the Labour Movement: Some Observations on Developing Countries*, Geneva: International Institute of Labour Studies.

Kaufman, R.R. (1990) 'How societies change development models or keep them: reflections on the Latin American experience in the 1930s and the postwar world', in G. Gereffi and D.L. Wyman (eds) *Manufacturing Miracles: Paths of Industrialization in Latin America and East Asia*, Princeton: Princeton University Press, pp. 110–38.

Kikeri, S. (1998) *Privatization and Labor: What Happens to Workers When Governments Divest?*, World Bank Technical Paper No. 396, Washington D.C.: World Bank.

Lee, N. and Cason, J. (1994) 'Automobile commodity chains in the NICs: a comparison of South Korea, Mexico and Brazil', in G. Gereffi and M. Korzeniewicz (eds) *Commodity Chains and Global Capitalism*, Westport and London: Praeger: 223–43.

Locke, R., Kochan, T. and Piore, M. (1995) 'Introduction: employment relations in a changing world economy', in R. Locke, T. Kochan, and M. Piore (eds) *Employment Relations in a Changing World Economy*, Cambridge (MA) and London: MIT Press, pp. xiii–xxix.

Munck, R. (1999) 'Labour dilemmas and labour futures' in R. Munck and P. Waterman (eds) *Labour Worldwide in the Era of Globalization: Alternative Union Models in the New World Order*, London: Macmillan; New York: St Martin's Press, pp. 3–23.

—— (2000) 'Review article: labour and globalisation: results and prospects', *Work, Employment and Society*, 14(2): 385–93.

Nielsen, K. (1991) 'Towards a flexible future – theories and policies', in B. Jessop, H. Kastendiek, K. Nielsen and O.K. Pedersen (eds) *The Politics of Flexibility: Restructuring State and Industry in Britain, Germany and Scandinavia*, Aldershot: Edward Elgar, pp. 3–30.

O'Brien, R. (2000) 'Labour and IPE: rediscovering human agency', in R. Palan (ed.) *Global Political Economy: Contemporary Theories*, London and New York: Routledge, pp. 89–99.

O'Brien, R., Goetz, A.M., Scholte, J.A. and Williams, M. (2000) *Contesting Global Governance: Multilateral Economic Institutions and Global Social Movements*, Cambridge: Cambridge University Press.

Regini, M. (ed.) (1992) *The Future of Labour Movements*, London: Sage.

Roozendaal, G. van (2001) *Social Challenges to Trade: Trade Unions and the Debate on International Labour Standards*, unpublished Ph.D. Thesis, University of Amsterdam.

Rueschemeyer, D., Stephens, E.H. and Stephens, J.D. (1992) *Capitalist Development and Democracy*, Cambridge: Polity Press.

Ruigrok, W. and Van Tulder, R. (1995) *The Logic of International Restructuring*, London: Routledge.

Seidman, G.W. (1994) *Manufacturing Militance: Workers' Movements in Brazil and South Africa, 1970–1985*, Berkeley: University of California Press.

Sengenberger, W. (1993) 'Lean production – the way of working and producing in the future?', in International Institute of Labour Studies (ed.) *Lean Production and Beyond: Labour Aspects of a New Production Concept*, Geneva: International Institute for Labour Studies, pp. 1–22.

Starr, P.K. and Oxhorn, P. (1999) 'The problematic relationship between economic reform and political liberalization: some theoretical considerations', in P.K. Starr and P. Oxhorn (eds) *Markets and Democracy in Latin America: Conflict or Convergence?*, Boulder, CO, and London: Lynne Rienner, pp. 13–41.

Tardanico, R. (1997) 'From crisis to restructuring: Latin American transformations and urban employment in world perspective', in R. Tardanico and R.M. Larín (eds) *Global Restructuring, Employment, and Social Inequality in Urban Latin America*, Miami: North–South Center Press, pp. 1–45.

Vilas, C.M. (1997) 'Participation, inequality, and the whereabouts of democracy', in D. Chalmers *et al.* (eds) *The New Politics of Inequality in Latin America: Rethinking Participation and Representation*, Oxford: Oxford University Press, pp. 3–42.

Waterman, P. (1999) 'The new social unionism: a new union model for a new world order', in R. Munck and P. Waterman (eds) *Labour Worldwide in the Era of Globalization: Alternative Union Models in the New World Order*, London: Macmillan; New York: St Martin's Press, pp. 247–64.

Woo-Cumings, M. (1999) *The Developmental State*, Ithaca and London: Cornell University Press.

World Bank (1999) *Global Economic Prospects and the Developing Countries: Beyond Financial Crisis, 1998/1999*, Washington D.C.: World Bank.

—— (2001) *World Development Report 2000/2001: Attacking Poverty*, Washington D.C.: World Bank; New York: Oxford University Press.

Zapata, F. (2001) *Free Markets, Privatization and Latin American Unions*, Paper presented at the Annual Convention of the International Studies Association, Chicago, February 20–4.

2 Labour in the era of globalization

André Mommen

Introduction

Since the 1980s, practically all governments have revised their economies and policies in line with international competitive standards and have implemented institutional reforms when international competition has endangered macro-economic stability. The Keynesian State (KS), created after 1945, was transformed according to the new criteria of individualism, market principles and free choice. After the 1960s, the state-socialist countries lost their international competitiveness, resulting in loan-based modernization programmes, enmeshing them in debt. With the internationalization of capital and production, and the globalization of the means of communication, all economic regimes were exposed to competitive forces, integrating them into a new economic and political world order.

In most cases, the state privatized its control over large segments of industry and finance, deregulated the labour market and reformed the social benefit system. In Eastern Europe, the collapse of the Communist regime was accompanied by a sudden liberalization of the markets, rampant privatization and growing social inequality. Privatization aimed to improve enterprise efficiency, and favoured the creation of a small but wealthy property-owning class in all of these countries. The 'winners' of the transition process from Communism to capitalism became ideologically and politically dominant in Central and Eastern Europe (Ágh 1998). Keynesian Welfare States (KWS) in Western Europe, which used to have highly protective labour standards, had to revise their funding procedures. This came at the expense of women and ethnic minorities and blue-collar workers in traditional industries. In the reforming Third World countries, the emphasis on public-sector-led growth was associated with import-substituting industrialization (ISI) and protectionism (Gavin 1997). The consequence of this process is that in most countries the trade-union movement lost much of its bargaining power, and the welfare state underwent thorough restructuring, under pressure from international capital and a privatization drive affecting the state-pension systems.

Theories of political and economic change

Before discussing the political impact of globalization on national economies and the labour movement, we need to list the different theories of political change or transition politics. The changes in labour and accumulation regimes have to be explained by referring back to the conditions under which they previously existed, as well as the conditions that have caused their disruption. The collapse of the Communist regimes obliged political scientists specializing in comparative politics to revise their analytical tools. New theories emerged, exploring and explaining the transition from authoritarian to democratic rule. As we shall see, the several explanatory theoretical concepts developed by political scientists can be seen as competing with each other. However, most of these theories have neglected the underlying structural and economic changes and necessities that led to the systemic 'earthquake' experienced by most countries at the end of the 1980s and the beginning of the 1990s.

This inability to explain the underlying economic problems responsible for systemic transition is particularly noteworthy in the case of the *functionalist school*. In the 1980s, Philippe C. Schmitter started by focusing on institutionalized forms of transitory regimes in Southern Europe and Latin America. He defined the dynamics of interaction between the international subcontexts of power and influence and the diverse national cases of democratization (Schmitter 1996: 31). However, Schmitter's proposals confined the analysis of regime changes to the political and ideological realm or superstructure by juxtaposing historical and structural elements and perspectives without indicating which elements were predetermining the outcome of a regime's restructuring. Moreover, the functionalist approach paid too much attention to structural determinants and was heavily inclined to the view that regime transformations are predetermined by economic and cultural conditions influencing modernization processes. In reality, Schmitter simply amended the old modernization theory that dominated all debates during the 1960s. When studying Schmitter's four proposals, one has the impression that pure imitation could never have played the very important role of inducing successful political and social transformations of well-established institutional arrangements. Authoritarian regimes based on populist power and corporatist arrangements appeared in Europe in the 1920s. But was it only imitation that inspired Juan Domingo Perón to adopt elements from Mussolini's fascist state?

The post-Marxist scholars of the French *Regulation School* (RS) provide us with a second theory of regime changes. The RS discusses the consequences of growing economic interdependence on regimes and their distinctive social and political structures. RS scholars reject the idea of disappearing national states. Consequently, RS scholar Robert Boyer believes that states and regimes adapt to changing international conditions. Statist and social-democratic regimes are now under reconstruction, while the Communist regimes simply collapsed.

Reformed institutional settings are introduced in order to increase economic efficiency in combination with democratic reforms. Public regulations, associations, private and public hierarchies and markets are supposed to foster a series of dynamic adjustments and economic efficiencies which in turn give birth to new social and political arrangements. These institutional changes mean that various national economies converge if they respond in the same way to foreign competition, unexpected disturbances, internal political crises and economic imbalances (Boyer 1996: 29–35). One may argue that all adjustment policies give birth to more uniformity and convergence under global competition, economic openness and financial liberalization policies in the long run. The RS admits that regime convergence exists and that the choice of social and political arrangements engendering economic efficiencies is not entirely free. Aglietta argues that

> the essential point (...) is that the wage-earning class is involved in a mode of access to labour and a condition of life whose continuity goes far beyond the relations of commodity exchange that are reflected in the costs of reproduction borne by capitalist firms.

He also stresses the fact that capitalist relations of production are promoted by the capitalist state and that imperialism imposed them on today's developing world (Aglietta 1979: 31–3).

Today, everybody admits that capital accumulation is the engine of social, economic and political changes, but global capitalism is still an 'incomplete' regime. Even if global capitalism has come to take precedence over national economies, the political and social functions remain grounded in the sovereign state. Although governments retain the power to interfere in the economy, they have become increasingly subject to the forces of global competition. The global capitalist system consists of many sovereign states with national economies, each with its own policies, but each subject to international competition and capital movements. Although there is nothing new in this combination of a global economy with political arrangements based on the sovereignty of the state, the difference from a century ago is that both states and markets have changed (Soros 2000: 178):

> It is important to note that exchange involves not only goods and services but also the factor of production. (...) As the system expands, the economic function comes to dominate the lives of people and societies. It penetrates areas not previously considered economic – culture, politics, medicine, education, and law.
>
> (Soros 2000: 172)

Regime convergence is certainly boosted by converging economic development, as *Marxist theory* stresses: 'The country that is more developed industrially only shows, to the less developed, the image of its own future', wrote Karl Marx in the preface to Volume 1 of *Capital* (Marx 1954: 9). But history also shows that this generalization is misleading. The emerging European economies of the nineteenth century had the misfortune to face the problem of the Industrial Revolution in a less favourable situation. They had to catch up with Great Britain as the factory of the world, and then with the US. The economic and political regimes that they adopted differed from the liberal regimes in Great Britain and the US. The ideology of free trade and the capitalist ethic was generated in Britain and then adopted in the US. In continental Europe, the bourgeoisie had to emancipate from the semi-absolutist monarchies and the landed interest groups. In France, it took the liberal bourgeoisie about a century to firmly establish a lay republic, but the French bourgeoisie never converted itself to the credo of *laissez faire*.

Most European countries adopted different industrial policies when dealing with the problem of economic growth and social stability. Agricultural interests formed powerful protectionist lobbies in and outside of parliament. Infant industries were protected by tariffs. Soon nation-wide cartels appeared in all European countries. Many of them also established international cartels in order to fix prices and regulate exports of commodities. Pre-1914 liberalism had given birth to imperialism and international cartels based on national monopolies representing the national interests of governments. Instead of trade wars, capitalism established peace and created stability. When liberal members of parliament and governments decided to create and animate international arbitration institutions, optimists were able to interpret this development as a necessary process towards the final elimination of the danger of war. Karl Polanyi thought that this liberal capitalist world system needed peace in order to function, and that the balance of power was made to serve it (Polanyi 1957: 18). He actualized the hypothesis provided by Immanuel Kant, who had once suggested that democratic states were more likely than authoritarian regimes to promote trade instead of war and therefore they could be expected to survive external shocks and wars. Kant's vision of 'perpetual peace' was built on a complex of ideological and institutional conditions:

1   a republican and democratic state;
2   an economy bound to trade, reinforcing liberal institutional structures;
3   international arrangements respecting human rights and the autonomy of the republics.

When defending his point of view that a developing capitalist regime required ever-expanding international trade, and that capitalist expansion would therefore make a world war in the near future improbable, Karl Kautsky espoused Kant's thesis, and he thought that democratic regimes would be the outcome of an ever-expanding capitalist system. Kautsky's thesis was based on the premise that finance capital had become dominant. Because finance capitalists had a direct interest in transforming each national state into a militarized force to support their imperialist expansion, these financial capitalists had to come into conflict with those industrial capitalists interested only in the maintenance of free trade, meaning that the labour movement should move closer to the peace-seeking industrialists. Therefore, capitalism as a system of production could also expand. It was not predetermined that imperialism would necessarily give way to hyper-imperialism and war. Industrialists are mainly interested in making profits not war, and prefer free export markets to protected colonial markets reserved for trading monopolies. Kautsky observed that the United States enjoyed faster economic growth because the other developed capitalist countries had imposed heavy financial burdens on themselves when opting for rearmament (Salvadori 1979: 169–80, Donald 1993: 201–12). Kautsky argued that ultra-imperialism, a joint exploitation of the world by the united finance capital of the great powers, would be forced by the threat that these powers faced from the oppressed colonial nations and from their own proletariat (Brewer 1980: 122–7). When World War I broke out, Kautsky did not change his mind, but now hoped that the outcome would be the creation of a federation of the strongest powers. But his deterministic economic development theory based on Kant's hypothesis received a severe blow in the 1930s and 1940s with the rise of fascism and authoritarianism in Europe and Latin America.

Latin American states were confronted with serious economic problems caused by the fall of world market prices paid for their raw materials and agricultural products and the rise of agrarian protectionism in Europe. These regimes backed the mobilization of the urban masses pressing for better welfare programmes and ISI. Echoing these policy transformations in Latin America, *dependency theory* explained why these regime changes occurred in Latin America and South Africa (Davenport 1987). Regime changes of this authoritarian type were provoked by internal tensions and antagonisms between the vested interests of the exporting landowners, the burgeoning class of industrial entrepreneurs, the organized labouring classes, and the military as the best organized apparatus of a still-backward national state. These regimes were compelled to conform to economic liberalization and political democratization in order to gain mass support for the breakdown of protectionist policies. Latin America, Southern Europe and South Africa (Lipton 1985, Fine and Rustomjee 1996) represent, among others, three different cases of dependent development.

Global capitalism and labour organization

The general wisdom is that the penetration of global capitalism revolutionized social and industrial relations in all developed and developing countries, and that all countries have adapted their institutions and socio-political regimes in accordance with the newly created situation. For instance, new developments in the organization of work – notably the shift from standardized assembly work practices (*Fordism*) to flexible work practices (*Post-Fordism*) – furthered a change in the wage regime and a breakup of the *Fordist* collective bargaining system, toward a much greater diversity between individual companies and a substantial variety in remuneration schemes. In the case of Eastern Europe, we have to discuss these regime changes within the context of the transition from Communism to capitalism. The socialist model, based on state-owned companies and import-substituting industrialization policies was unable to reform and adapt to capitalism as the only way out of economic decay (Lavigne 1995). Developing countries underwent an analogous transformation when authoritarian regimes collapsed, with many of them adopting democratic constitutions. Our problem here is how to conceptualize these changes and the dynamics affecting practically all types of regimes. It is striking that all governments – post-Communist regimes as well as Third World populist governments or social-democratic states in Western Europe – having embarked on a reformist, neo-liberal economic agenda, were heading in surprisingly similar directions. Their reform agenda comprised a set of ten reforms:

- financial discipline to bring down public borrowing and to stop printing money as a solution to their economic problems;
- re-ordering public spending priorities; shifting spending away from politically powerful interest groups toward urgent investment in infrastructures;
- tax reforms in order to broaden the tax base and cut marginal tax rates;
- financial liberalization and competitive allocation of investment funds;
- elimination of multiple exchange rates and ensuring a competitive, broadly stable exchange rate for exporters;
- trade liberalization, i.e. replacing quotas and other quantitative trade restrictions with tariffs, which should be made more uniform and slowly reduced in order to spur domestic efficiency improvements through tougher external competition;
- lifting of the barriers impeding foreign direct investment (FDI) inflows and treating foreign and domestic firms alike;
- privatization of state firms;
- abolishing market-unfriendly regulations in order to encourage greater efficiency and market competition;
- property-rights reforms in order to secure basic property rights for all members of the economy, including workers in the informal sector.

These structural reforms brought the economic rules in line with the rules of a globalizing world economy (Boyer 1996: 29–59). These reforms were also accompanied by institutional changes, and this had much to do with the need to adapt all political and social rules to a rapidly changing economy shifting from a low-level to a high-level technological economy and the development of a service economy.

The philosophy allegedly behind the globalization agenda is that maximizing global economic deregulation will in itself result in broad economic and social benefits (Wallach and Sforza 1999: 9). Therefore, globalization has to be understood as a process of suppressing state influence on the economy and of giving private capital hegemony over any investment decision. Globalization has created wider markets for trade and services and has increased competition between policy regimes. International capital market integration, combined with the volatility of capital flows, is making macro-economic management more complex and makes it necessary to maintain a liberal trade and investment regime combined with macro-economic management that sustains the confidence of capital owners. Globalization appears here as the outcome of lowering trade barriers and freeing capital movements. Promoted by international organizations and financial institutions (GATT/WTO, IMF, World Bank, EBRD), liberal trade and investment regimes have to replace protectionist and ISI regimes and enhance international capital market integration. The overall impression is that globalization has many negative effects and that politicians are powerless to reverse the globalization drive (Fidler 1997: 4). Multinational firms have increased their foreign direct investment and redeployed production according to the principle of comparative advantage (IMF 1997). Flexible firms are still looking for flexible production facilities in low-wage countries, and this means that redeployment from high-wage countries to low-wage countries is still continuing. Financial markets are globalizing even faster than production and sourcing networks, obliging most countries to open up and liberalize their financial markets (Wade 1996: 60–88).

Because of the globalization drive, the world's economy is going through two great changes affecting the way that political regimes shape their economic and social policies. First, industrial production is escaping governmental control by moving from the developed capitalist world to developing countries in Latin America and Asia. A classic example is the flight of the textile industry from the rich to the poor countries. Second, in the developed capitalist countries, the balance of economic activity is swinging from the manufacturing to the service sector. For instance, in Britain and the US, the proportion of workers in manufacturing has declined since 1900, from around 40 per cent to barely half of that today. Even in Germany and Japan, the share of manufacturing in the labour market is now below 30 per cent. The effect of the shift is increased as manufacturing moves from rich countries to developing ones where labour is cheap and unorganized. But the increasing integration of developed economies with developing countries will not occur without creating adjustment costs for industrialized countries, especially for those labour-intensive industries employing low-skilled workers. The reallocation of resources that this structural change entails will generate friction and mobilize people and movements against the globalization drive, which is changing the way that production is organized and the conditions under which goods or services are produced, as well as intensifying the networks of mutual dependency beyond national boundaries (Beck 2000: 22–63). This *glocalization*, as it has been called, has not only changed the outlook of the assembly lines in the Fordist factories of the developed world, but also the trade patterns between the industrialized and industrializing countries. By the early 1990s about a fifth of the total output of US firms was being produced by non-Americans, outside America. Low-cost production of textiles, clothing, shoes, handbags, car seats and electrical wiring migrated from the US to Mexico or further afield.

Twenty years ago, the Western world talked of this phenomenon by making a distinction between sunset and sunrise industries. Sunrise industries, such as electronics, were the future of a 'new economy', sunset industries (steel, chemicals and ship-building) represented the past. One could also note that even the sunrise industries have spread over newly industrializing regions in Asia and Mexico, where wages are lower and profits higher. What remains unnoticed is that a global structure for manufacturing is emerging. The law of supply and demand drives the lowest-value-added part of the supply chain to where wages are lowest (IMF 1997). Multinational firms have equipped themselves with the technologies and management techniques needed to produce even complicated parts efficiently in the most remote areas of the globe, where labour is relatively unskilled. Globalization boosts productivity and promotes increased division of labour between countries, allowing low-wage countries to specialize in labour-intensive production while high-wage countries use workers in higher value-added activities (Soros 2000: 265–329).

Globalization also means a race to the bottom, as countries reduce wages, taxes, welfare benefits and environmental controls to make themselves more competitive. Globalization increases competition from low-wage countries and destroys jobs or pushes down wages in the developed world. Pressure to compete is eroding the ability of governments to set their own economic policies (Haggard and Kaufman 1995). The increased power wielded by the financial markets has caused economic havoc, as the European currency crises of 1992 and 1993, the Mexican crisis in 1994–5 and the South-east Asia and Chinese meltdown in 1997 demonstrated (Lupher 1996, Lardy 1998: 78–88, Tong Whan Park 1998: 1–10, Krugman 1999: 56–94). The crisis that erupted in Asia in 1997 was transmitted to Latin America through the external sector, with the overall result that Latin American export earnings fell by nearly 2 per cent for the first time since 1986 (ECLAC 1999: 12). However, 'the global financial crisis of 1997–1999 is now history' (Soros 2000: 265).

Two driving forces have boosted globalization. The first is technology, which has rapidly reduced the costs of telecommunication and computing, meaning that markets can integrate. The second driving force has been trade liberalization under the aegis of the GATT and as a result of unilateral decisions (Schott and Buurman 1994). Liberalization has proceeded at different speeds in different places. Over the past decade, trade has increased twice as fast as output, FDI three times as fast and cross-border trade in shares ten times as fast. But in the meantime, product markets are still nowhere near as integrated across borders as they are within nations. In theory, free trade should cause price convergence, since it forces high-cost producers to lower their prices. However, large divergences in prices persist for the same goods. This reflects a variety of factors, including consumer tastes, transport costs, differences in taxes, inefficient production lines with concomitant reductions in capacity, thus slowing techno-logical change, inefficient distribution networks, and barriers to imports. Neither are the financial markets truly integrated. In the future, new technology is likely to encourage further integration and to help make markets more transparent, allowing buyers and sellers to compare prices in different countries. So tech-nology will continue to power the globalization drive. This will pose challenges for governments, because the costs and benefits of globalization will be unevenly distributed among people. Unskilled manufacturing workers in rich economies will find the demand for their labour falling as the jobs they used to do are performed more cheaply abroad. The growth of multinational capital makes it harder to erect effective trade barriers. New technologies make it tricky for governments to impose effective capital controls, as well as creating distribution channels that protectionist governments find it hard to block. This implies the end of the era of import-substituting policies implemented in the wake of the international economic crisis of the 1930s. ISI policies were the backbone of the social, political and economic base of the Third World modernizing regimes that replaced the oligarchic regimes based on commodity exports and commercial capital linked with the developed capitalist world (Ianni 1975).

The demise of Keynesian labourism

The process of globalization has a major impact on domestic economic and labour policies. Neo-liberal models acquired credibility and replaced Keynesianism as a source of inspiration for socialist parties in Western Europe and for populist parties in the developing world. However, the prognosis that with the end of Communism social democracy had also come to an end proved to be false. Social-democratic parties were able to renew themselves during the 1990s and re-occupy a substantial part of the terrain of the centre-left spec-trum, although their ideological hegemony over society was broken when the traditional social-democratic electorate split into antagonistic factions as a result of the post-industrial revolution. The number of traditional blue-collar working-class voters diminished to the same extent over the past thirty years as the number of better-educated post-materialist voters increased, while various societal groups with divergent social and economic interests and expectations that had once supported the parties of the Left developed other interests in a period when mass unemployment had given birth to neo-liberal proposals stressing the importance of market forces and supply-side economics. This new middle class rejected Keynesianism as a major source of macro-economic imbalances and slow growth. Government was depicted as the problem, not as the solution. Privatization and liberalization were presented as remedies to public ownership and state control. Market solutions were accepted in combina-tion with a leaner state that could organize the premises for a smoothly working labour market.

A similar ideological change occurred in the Democratic Party of the United States, where the influence of Big Labour had waned after the unsuccessful presidential campaigns of candidates with close links to the trade-union movement. In the early 1990s, the emerging New Democrats were looking for a new policy mix that could entice the voters of an ever-expanding middle class. Job creation through the market, rather than increased state spending, became an attractive solution to most social problems caused by unemployment. In 1992, Clinton's Secretary of Labour, Robert Reich, invented a kind of supply-side labour policy that stressed the importance of education, training and skills for economic growth and full employment. His labour strategy, copied by social-democratic parties of Western Europe, also implied a new balance between the welfare state and the labour market. Meanwhile, the US economy had acquired growing links to the global economy and US corporate profitability had become highly sensitive to events abroad. However, in the 1990s, the US was judged on its stellar economic performance – low inflation, low unemployment, a vanishing budget deficit, a strong currency, a booming stock market and steady growth. In the meantime, the share of US GDP attributable to international trade doubled in the 1990s, to 23 per cent, and today, exports are responsible for 30 per cent of US economic growth. During the 1990s, US jobs supported by exports had doubled, to 16 million. Foreign investors increased their purchase of US Treasury bonds. Nowadays, a huge number of American companies, such as Coca-Cola, General Electric and Microsoft, are expecting foreign markets to provide a huge portion of their revenues, often more than 50 per cent.

The strong position of a globalizing US economy had a positive impact on a Democratic Party now representing the modernizing social and economic forces of the American society. The story of Clinton's Democratic Party may suggest that economic performance based on internationalization and combined with social progress ineluctably engenders political and financial stability (Clinton 1996). This can be true for that part of the capitalist world where expanding export markets also mean faster economic growth and higher profits. But in Latin America, where US exports are growing faster than in any other region, there is some cause for concern, because the region is extremely dependent on incoming capital flows. Any increase in US interest rates would reverse those flows, causing a continent-wide implosion. Therefore, US responsibility for what is going on in Latin America is immense, now that this subcontinent is more than ever under the economic dominance of US capital.

One can argue that this liberalization drive has contributed to the democratization and openness of practically all of the Latin American regimes, but, until now, these regime transformations have added nothing to the well-being of the lowest strata of society. Throughout the Latin American region, millions of people become poorer even as the middle and upper classes prosper and massively back their democratized regimes. In Argentina, 20 per cent of the working class is unemployed. In Mexico 22 million people – 25 per cent of the population – are living in extreme poverty (Kessler 1998: 36–66).

The poor are still a source of instability in all Latin American countries (IDB 1996). Notwithstanding the fact that elections are working as security valves, a social explosion may occur at any moment and destabilize any Latin American or other Third World regime. Formerly sacrosanct populist leaders could be toppled by renewed violence and repression (Philip 1998: 81–97). Even the more stable authoritarian regimes of South Asia have experienced the same social and political shocks until now confined to Latin American countries.

In post-World War II Europe, social-democratic and Christian-democratic parties created neo-corporatist systems – arrangements which constrained market mechanisms, and protected the working classes and the middle classes from market uncertainties (Goodin *et al.* 1999: 56–86). Institutional arrangements had to restrain individualistic wage claims, stressing solidarity and giving the *solidaristic* fronts of workers, peasants and small-business people opportunities to influence governmental policies and regulations limiting free competition, and setting the price of the labour force and many collective goods. This model of interest intermediation is threatened by the drive towards globalization, and explains why in Eastern Europe the transition to democracy and capitalism strengthened the neo-liberal economic dimensions of the regimes that succeeded Communism. In the Third World, similar reforms were set in motion when authoritarian regimes liberalized their economies. The triumph of the market signified the decline of redistribution mechanisms implemented by populist regimes and carried out by the state. In the whole world, increased competition and subsequent financial and economic liberalization policies opened the way for a breakup of the solidaristic fronts of workers and peasants, in order to lower social costs. The privatization of the welfare state went hand in hand with the numerical decline of the industrial working class and the breakup of the Fordist organization of production.

The dismissal of economic models based on public monopolies occurred for the first time in the early 1980s in the US, when pushing forward a broad programme of deregulation that was already under way in the UK. Privatization soon followed world-wide. Privatization schemes were drafted in developing countries (World Bank 1993) and Eastern Europe. Privatization became a key part of economic reform and adjustment policies, and a prime mover of the economic transition in Eastern Europe. Privatization was seen as a response to the failure of ISI strategies and protectionist regimes, and as an instrument of profit maximization. It was also seen as a response to the failure of state-led industrialization, with state-owned companies being kept afloat at the taxpayer's expense, either through explicit government subsidies, such as direct cash grants, or through implicit subsidies, such as subsidized credit, guaranteed sales, government equity injections, or preferential exchange rates. The solution was to subject state-owned enterprises to market discipline, i.e. foreign competition. Privatization was seen as the best means to enforce market discipline and to promote efficiency. The so-called Washington consensus holds that most economic problems stem chiefly from an excess of state control. Hence, privatization also meant that governments would lose control over an essential part of their economy when opening up the market. In many countries, the state still held large shares in oil companies, power stations and electricity distribution infrastructure, coal mines, steel mills, railway companies, ports, telecommunications and airlines. Privatization of all these sectors would mean that the state would wither away and disappear as the anchor of socialist policies. According to János Kornai the way out of this crisis would be to implement the necessary structural adjustments and to develop profitable exports (Kornai 1995: 60).

The demise of trade unionism

Trade unions meet with a general resistance from different public institutions. This resistance is fed by the idea that trade unions are organized only to destroy the existing society and its institutions. In the past, conservatives understood that a new social regime was coming to the fore, with newly created institutions. But on the other hand, they felt a general uneasiness about the rising labour movement. In most developed capitalist countries the voting of emergency laws was forbidden. The ruling class could rely on anti-coalition laws that still forbade trade-union action. During strikes, coalitions that forced anybody at any time to participate or to keep anyone from returning to work were severely repressed because they were contrary to the freedom of work. It was also a penal offence to try to keep anyone from accepting the employment offered. As long as bourgeois parties dominated parliaments, the anti-strike laws were not revised. Around 1900, a new labour regime emerged in most developed countries. Mediation in labour conflicts was the first form of active intervention by the authorities when governments had to face large-scale labour conflicts. The purpose was to name suitable persons as mediators for the benefit of the parties involved. Later on, governments appointed professional mediators who also prevented the outbreak of strikes.

Trade unions became institutionalized bodies negotiating with mediators, government officials and employers, and with an interest in being recognized as representatives of the workforce. Employers still wanted to prevent the rise of strong unions, and they tried to reverse this tendency. Meanwhile, governments feared bitter fights for union rights, and in some cases they intervened in favour of the unions. On the other hand, the authorities repressed unionization of several categories of workers, especially of civil servants and municipal workers. The degree of unionization increased, leading to an increased risk of unexpected conflicts.

Ordinary courts had great difficulties explaining the meaning of collective agreements and in settling labour conflicts. Moreover, the courts were slow and in poor shape to deal with labour conflicts and collective agreements. Collective agreements instituted a new regime regulating agreements between employers and employed. Collective agreements were signed between the trade unions on the labour side in an enterprise or a sector and one or more employers. These collective agreements regulated wage and working conditions and they covered all employed persons. This labour regime came into force in Western Europe and in a modified form in the US after World War I. The creation of special labour courts completed this system. However, the conflict of the rights of the individual in connection with disputes about collective agreements, and society's rights in such cases, remained. In connection with the establishment of collective agreements and their application, outsiders may be adversely affected. The victims are individuals, consumers, unorganized workers, retailers, members of other trade unions, other enterprises and institutions, or society as a whole. Liberals defended the traditional idea that outsiders ought to be protected against undue interference from organizations. On the other hand, the trade-union movement refused to protect strike-breakers.

With the growth of the trade-union movement, employers began to understand that a responsible and well-organized trade-union movement could act as a stabilizing element. Collective agreements could protect employers and society against mass labour unrest. Labour unrest could cripple the vital functions of society and adversely affect public life, and, with the rapid growth of the trade-union movement, every open conflict could harm any sector of the economy. Therefore, the labour movement was confronted with macro-economic policies and the interests of other social classes. Unemployment was the main problem that had to be solved. But the demand for full and stable employment went far beyond the powers of the trade-union movement and anticipated a change in the political regime itself. Only a social-democratic government could be interested in combating unemployment and promise better working conditions under a regime of macro-economic stability and economic growth.

In general, trade unions had been inconsistent in dealing with capitalism. Unions asked for full freedom in relation to the state when dealing with labour problems, but they also asked the state to intervene in questions of social security when some social categories (women and children) needed special protection. In matters of wages and working conditions, trade unions could rely on their own strength. The fact that early factory laws had enacted this dualism reinforced trade unions in their attitude.

Trade unions were still too weak to influence political decisions, and conservative and liberal governments enacted the first protective legislation. These laws were passed thanks to bourgeois reformists in response to the abuse of child labour in factories and mines. Laws regarding occupational accidents were seen as the most that the state could do for workers in large-scale industries. On the whole, most trade unions adopted very liberal programmes, which were later replaced by more socialist demands, that would include compulsory accident, health, and old-age insurance through subsidies from the government and the employers. This also included shortening of the working day to at most ten hours and regulation of Sunday and night-work. Early social legislation for the protection of workers was not very effective and could be ignored without any risk of punishment. It took a long time before effective laws were passed. The real breakthrough only came after 1918, when the labour movement dominated the political scene in Western Europe and socialist parties could participate in government. In the slipstream of the Versailles Treaties, the International Labour Organization (ILO) was founded in order to co-ordinate social legislation at the international level. Leading union leaders and socialist politicians dominated the ILO at a time when important social reforms were realized. In practically all of the advanced capitalist countries, working hours were limited to eight hours a day and 48 hours per week. The last important problems to be solved were health and unemployment insurance. Sickness relief funds belonged to the old labour-movement traditions that went back to the days of workers' guilds. Trade unions used these funds to attract new members. This made them indifferent to government regulation or the nationalization of the health-insurance sector. Important reforms in this sector were only introduced after 1945.

Unemployment insurance was slow to develop. Trade unions had already established a type of compulsory unemployment insurance for their members. They were also pushing for more state intervention and subsidies, because they were meeting serious difficulties in fulfilling their obligations. But the trade unions also feared the intervention of the state. Unemployment funds allowed the trade unions to recruit new members. An eventual nationalization of unemployment funds would allow the government to control the workforce and oblige the unemployed to accept any job at any wage. State interference was accepted when the state subsidized union unemployment funds. Liberal governments favoured and established national pension schemes on a capitalization basis. However, the benefits were limited and insufficient. Some large employers had already introduced gratuity pensions. They wanted to avoid state interference, because their pension funds were used to keep the labour force tied to their enterprises. The labour movement campaigned for a pension paid by the government, as otherwise it was difficult for children to help their parents directly in their old age. Governments in Great Britain (Crossland 1964) and Sweden (Lindbeck 1975, Hinrichs 1988: 569–90) favoured schemes that were completely based on compulsory dues paid by every taxpayer. After 1945, state pensions schemes for all workers were standardized in all developed European countries.

Trade unions affect the functioning of labour and capital markets and the distribution of economic resources. Concentrated union power, in combination with strong social-democratic parties, influence the functioning of the labour market by creating complex labour legislation and by restricting the labour supply. The West European welfare states are based on these legal mechanisms. Unions play a role as channels through which collective nationwide labour contracts are negotiated. Labour power used to be based on solidaristic fronts organizing workers of the same industrial sector. However, today, these solidaristic fronts have lost a good part of their bargaining power.

In the beginning, the trade-union movement was built on the basis of common trades and professions. Workers with the same trades and skills banded together in order to defend their common interests. The first trade unions in all countries were craft unions, and in some cases they still survive as such. Belonging to the same trade was a powerful argument for organizing workers, but quite often this turned out to be detrimental to other groups of workers. Craft unions were able to win better working conditions and higher wages for their members, while these favours were denied to the unskilled non-unionized workers. Organizations based on crafts meant that there were always workers left out of the trade-union movement, and that many different craft unions were represented within every branch of industry. In turn, the employers organized themselves into industrial federations.

When industry expanded and factories became larger, craft unionism became outdated. Labour leaders considered organizing industrial unions. The first industrial or sectoral unions appeared after 1900, when capitalism had already created large-scale industries. In the US, the first industrial unions were created by *syndicalists*, under the flag of the Industrial Workers of the World (IWW). This form of syndicalism did not reach the already well-organized workers in traditional crafts and industries, but only the forest and agricultural workers, miners, river and dock workers, seamen, i.e. relatively unskilled seasonal and migratory workers (De Caux 1978). By 1917, the IWW had reached its highest membership, with about 30,000 lumberjacks, 40,000 metal miners, 24,000 agricultural workers, 15,000 building-trade workers, and about 10,000 in other occupations (Bimba 1927: 258). However, mechanization in these trades would soon cause the decline of the IWW unions in a period when work in factories was on its way to being reorganized. This would create opportunities for a new trade unionism based on industrial occupation instead of crafts. With the introduction of the Fordist organization of factories, the workforce could be treated as a homogeneous mass of semi-skilled interchangeable workers. As a consequence, craft unions had to open their organizations to semi-skilled workers. Thus, they transformed themselves into industrial unions. World War I marked the watershed between old and new unionism in most of the developed countries. After 1918, unions in Western Europe saw the number of their adherents increase explosively as the system of collective bargaining was introduced and favoured by governments in which socialists participated. In most countries, all workers employed by one industry were organized in the same union. Where unions of different ideological background existed, they started to co-operate when dealing with entrepreneurial organizations. In the US, the American Federation of Labour (AFL) remained a federation of craft unions, but in the 1930s, the growth of the competing Congress of Industrial Organization (CIO) obliged the leaders of the craft unions to form one front, and later, in 1954–5, to federate their organizations.

Trade unions play an important role in politics. In the US, their influence is based on the resources that they are able to mobilize, both financially and numerically through campaigns and votes. Ultimately, this influence is rooted in their numerical strength. US trade unions have played an active political role, supporting candidates and lobbying legislatures. But the US unions, while pursuing pressure-group ambitions, do not present themselves as political organizations representing the class interests of labour. The unions accept the existing social system. In Great Britain, the Trades Union Congress (TUC) founded the Labour Party and is still the party's most powerful component. But the labour movement in continental Europe is quite different from that in Great Britain and the US, because in Europe all trade unions were funded/founded by political parties, but all share the same characteristics: unions are based on industrial sectors, not on crafts or single factories. Craft unions have disappeared or only survive in professions. Business or 'yellow' unions never had a chance to compete with the independent unions because the system of collective bargaining superseded the practice of individual labour contracts.

The philosophy of capitalist society is one of open entry. The winner takes the prize. But open entry was always the exception rather than the rule. Factory owners prefer protection from foreign competition at home, and so the law of competition has been softened by cartels, protectionism, and even many governmental favours. When the enterprise was a family affair, family involvement discouraged competition and taking risks. Although the state encouraged industrialization, the great mass of the workers was still employed in small factories. Craftsmen served local markets, rather than industrial producers of consumer goods using advanced techniques. In most countries, crafts were able to survive until the 1950s when Fordist multinationals moved into the market of daily consumer goods. During this post-war period, capitalism could stabilize and grow under the umbrella of Keynesianism and a Fordist (re)organization of production in large factories, attracting a large number of semi-skilled workers from the rural areas and the capitalist periphery, which meant that the industrial unions could easily recruit these workers by pressing for higher wages and better working conditions.

With the retreat of the Fordist system of industrial production in the 1980s, the industrial unions were confronted with a change in the social composition of their membership. Workforces in modern economies had become highly differentiated. This explains the shrinking role of the trade-union movement. The significance of what is happening now to unions is widely recognized. The decay of union power inspired the theory that the significance of class has diminished in favour of individualism, and that Marxist forms of political analysis have become obsolete. Nonetheless, for many, a strong trade-union movement is the cornerstone of a liberal or a social-democratic state system. For others, unions are monopolists which make labour expensive and hinder economic growth. Of course, there is no single model of trade unionism because trade unions operate under a number of very different conditions. In the US, trade unions are locally organized and represent the local interests of the labour force, and the AFL/CIO is nothing more than a very loosely organized voluntary organization of independent unions. US unions are craft unions or organize workers in some industries and occupations. In continental Europe, the emphasis is on links between unions, government and employers, allowing reconciliation in a grand compromise when economic restructuring becomes necessary. In the English-speaking countries, unions are mainly concerned with shop-floor matters, as promoted by a legal system that penalizes violations. Japanese unions organize workers of the same industrial company. In Germany, trade unions are powerful voluntary centralized organizations, while in France trade unions are weak and ideologically and organizationally divided, and they organize not more than 10 per cent of the total labour force. In many countries of Western Europe (Belgium, The Netherlands, France, Spain and Italy), political parties representing trade unions at the political level ideologically dominate them.

A fundamental premise is that trade unions are located in different parts of the world and that they operate under different political regimes. Hence, they have followed different paths of development. In Western Europe, they went through mobilization in the 1960s and early 1970s, corporatism in the late 1970s and early 1980s, and then decentralization, flexibility and decline (Regini 1992). This has usually occurred in the context of social or liberal democracies. Many trade unions from the South, however, were involved in broader struggles for democracy under regimes of labour repression. This form of unionism took on the character of a social movement in South Africa and Brazil (Webster 1985, Seidman 1994). In most Third World countries, trade-union power has been relatively limited because infant industries were regulated and funded by the state. The involvement of South African labour in the struggle against apartheid resulted in the democratization of labour relations institutions and broader social institutions. This democratization process, however, took place in the context of a macro-economic environment that is becoming increasingly hostile to the social regulation of labour relations. The breakup of the ISI regime has facilitated certain pressures towards regulation by the markets, and most employers have resorted to casual labour and the intensification of work. Calls for labour market flexibility have challenged the centralized institutions and minimum labour standards (which had resulted from campaigns started in the 1980s). Thus globalization as an economic force or as an ideology reshaped South Africa's approach to managing its economy (Bezuidenhout 2000: 4–10). Webster and Adler (1998) call this process of political democratization under the conditions of economic liberalization a 'double transition'.

In Bolivia and Argentina, trade unions developed as social movements integrating into nationalist political movements which mixed a modernizing nationalism with touches of Mussolini-style corporatism. But the populist leaders elected by a massive majority of the nation, such as Juan Domingo Perón in Argentina and Victor Paz Estenssoro in Bolivia found themselves squeezed between trade-union demands for more nationalization and higher living standards and the anti-Communism of the armed forces. In Mexico, the leading trade-union confederation is separate from but dominated by the PRI, and operates as part of a corporatist arrangement with the state. In Latin America the dominant model was a Bonapartist state integrating the trade unions into a state–party–syndicate triad. With the breakup of import substitution, the Latin

American trade-union movement lost much of its bargaining power and was itself subjected to market pressures. Rising unemployment favoured individual-istic reactions and a breakup of the old solidaristic fronts.

In the post-Communist countries, the trade-union movement was 'privatized', after having played the role of 'transmission belt' in the state–party–syndicate triad for decades. Under the Soviet model of development, state control over trade unions was vital for the economic system. Trade unions were to serve the interests of the party and the state. Tools for ensuring that this remained the case included the interference of the Communist Party at every level of the state and the enterprises. With the breakup of the Communist systems, the role of the trade unions had to be revised. The rise of the *Solidarity* union in Poland demon-strated that a combination of social discontent and nationalism could give birth to an oppositional movement organized on the shop floor.

The rampant economic crisis in the developed capitalist world meant that trade unions had to revise their relationship with the Keynesian state. This was particularly the case in the US, where the United Automobile Workers (UAW) had come to prominence after 1937, and had extended the concept of collective bargaining well beyond the traditional boundaries of business unionism (Raskin 1986: 3–38). Although full-scale industrial bargaining was introduced in the coal-mining industry in the 1930s, the UAW pioneered institutionalized industry-wide bargaining. The link with the then-triumphant Fordism has to be stressed, because the UAW–General Motors 1950 five-year contract (also called the 'Treaty of Detroit') became an example for other industrial sectors, including steel, rubber, and farm and construction equipment. The last major sector to join this bargaining system was trucking, with the Master Freight Agreement signed between the International Brotherhood of Teamsters (IBT) and almost 10,000 trucking companies employing over 300,000 workers. The food and retail sector followed the IBT. This system established industry-wide patterns of wages, bene-fits, and working conditions, unaffected by competitive conditions in other separate industries and sectors, and lasted until the 1980s. In the mining industry, it had already crumbled, and in other sectors workers began leaving their unions. Industry-wide bargaining patterns lost their predominance and unions started making concessions connected with the profitability of companies. That was notably the case in the steel, auto, airline, and meat-packing industries. This destruction of nation-wide bargaining was a significant indicator of growing union weakness in the US, as a result of growing competition on the domestic market. The crisis in the American automobile industry of Detroit and the appearance of Asian cars on the North American market undermined the UAW's bargaining power. The subsequent anti-labour stance of the Reagan administration was legitimated by the notion that collective bargaining and trade unions were worthless relics of the past that hindered economic expansion. This has not gone unnoticed by union-busters and employers. Reagan's re-election in 1984 gave a green light to union-busting, with the absolute number of unionized workers decreasing for the first time since the 1930s (Goldfield 1987: 3–25). As in other countries, the US unions constituted a political force influencing the

Democratic Party by campaigning for the Democratic candidates. Thus a steadily declining union membership in the private sector weakened the Democratic Party considerably and obliged most Democratic politicians to consider a restructuring of the class alliances supporting them..

Compared with Western Europe, Japan, Australia and Canada, the US trade unions remained rather weak. This explains the weakness of US state influence on social welfare and economic policy. In the US, the ideology of individualism remained particularly strong and the link between work and remuneration prevailed over the principle of solidarity in meeting risks. Private insurance schemes far outweigh public social insurance systems and are the principal forms of contractual saving. The system of collective bargaining did not remain unchallenged after it had been established in the 1930s. The New Deal significantly weakened the conservative–liberal bloc, but after World War II, an anti-labour campaign was launched in order to obtain the revision of the pro-union Wagner Act of 1935 (Plotke 1996). Various states had passed bills prohibiting the closed shop, and the 1946 elections produced a strong conservative majority in Congress. In 1947 Congress passed the Taft–Hartley Act, which obliterated the pro-union provisions of the Wagner Act. The new principle was that union action had to be limited and freedom of exchange secured. The National Labor Relations Board had to control union elections in factories and their legal recognition. Any attempt to establish a closed shop was prohibited. The act prohibited unions from financially supporting any organization except in time of national elections, and deprived employees of the Federal government of the right to strike. The federal government received the right to intervene in labour conflicts endangering the national economy and to suspend a strike for eighty days. In the meantime, the federal government was empowered to influence wages and working conditions, which were closely tied to the decisions of firms regarding prices and investment. The trade-union movement failed to have the Taft–Hartley Act repealed and this contributed to the stagnation of the trade-union movement in the 1950s (Aglietta 1979: 193).

In the US, union density has declined steadily. Two main factors have been put forward to account for the trends in declining union affiliation. The first factor refers to changes in the composition and structure of the labour force. In particular, the decline of heavy industry and coal mining combined with automation in manufacturing has led to a reduction in the number of blue-collar workers and a decreasing membership of the industrial unions. Increasing employment in the service sector has not compensated for this loss of membership of the industrial unions. A second factor explaining the decay of the trade-union movement refers to new legal policies and laws, making it more difficult for unions to organize in the newly industrialized states of the US and the inability of unions to reverse this trend (Goldfield 1986: 2–29).

In Britain, union membership has evolved in a similar manner. In 1998, union membership was 7.1 million (29.6 per cent of all employees), but trade-union membership had been declining steadily over the previous decades. In 1979, 13.3 million people were members of trade unions, and the proportion of employees who were union members stood at 55 per cent. Several reasons for this fall in membership can be invoked:

1   a dramatic fall in the number of jobs in manufacturing industries, where union membership was traditionally high;
2   larger numbers of unemployed people;
3   a fall in traditional full-time employment and an increase in the numbers of part-time and temporary workers, workers who are less likely to join unions;
4   an increase in the proportion of the workforce employed by small companies where it is often difficult to organize unions;
5   hostile legislation – the previous Conservative government introduced laws which make it more difficult for unions to operate and retain their members.

Unions are by far the most powerful and influential force in capitalist countries that strive for the institution of large social welfare programmes. A strong labour movement is often a key factor in extending social legislation. In all developed capitalist countries the labour movement adopted Keynesianism as its economic programme when entering into government. Gösta Esping-Andersen asserts that the tendency of labour movements to seek the institutionalization of social rights that are independent of market mechanisms is universal in capitalist democracies, and that unions are strong supporters of universalistic social legislation (Esping-Andersen 1990). In the US, welfare-state institutions remained modest and the absence of any national health plan is striking, even while this exists in all Western European countries. In the US, unemployment compensation is less automatic, lasts a shorter time than in any European country and covers a smaller percentage of a worker's pay. This partially explains why the trade-union movement is much weaker in the US than in Europe and why centralized collective bargaining patterns were not destroyed in most of the developed capitalist countries. The notable exception was Great Britain where the miners were defeated by the Thatcher government in 1984–5 (Goldfield 1987: 48).

At the outset of the economic crisis (1975–80), the European industrial unions – with the exception of those in France – were influential in decision-making, well organized, hierarchically structured, rich, well connected, conservative, moderate and powerful within the general trade-union movement. Industrial unions ruled over a workforce, which, although occasionally obstreperous and rebellious, accepted leadership mediation that had provided it with a stable, secure and structured job situation, high wages, and a considerable degree of control over personnel levels and work practices. A comfortable and conclusive relationship existed with management. National union leaders restricted demands to wages and immediate working conditions. The industrial unions were able to extract the planning of lay-offs and force companies or the government to suspend or withdraw planned closures. The cost of various social measures was considerable and was met by the firms, national governments and the EC. Spontaneous outbursts of workforce anger – often beyond union control

– were much more effective in frightening governments and pushing management into reluctant generosity. Finally, the industrial unions were pressurized into accepting measures that they found unpalatable or intolerable (Rhodes and Wright 1988: 171–95).

Trade affects wages through the prices of imports and exports. After the opening of the frontiers in the EU and the creation of regional trade areas like NAFTA and MERCOSUR, the bargaining system based on national accords lost much of its impact. But the unions feared chaos. Therefore, they still wanted hands-on involvement in setting national wage and economic policies in order to protect their members' security. Most ex-Communist regimes in Central Europe adopted a German-style tripartite bargaining system at the very moment when this system in Germany had come under intense scrutiny (Frydman *et al.* 1998: 87–97).

With respect to the fall of the Swedish welfare state, Peter Swenson (1991: 381) argues that:

> highly progressive taxes can break the link between nominal and real disposable pay increases, since pay raises can also bring tax rate increases. Pay raises high enough to overcome the effects of 'bracket creep' may bring so much inflation that real wages and/or employment suffer and may tend to push pay in the public sector up in step as well.

A rich country, which has a relatively large proportion of well-educated workers will specialize in making goods that use more brainpower; poor countries will invest in industries that use less brainpower and more lower-skilled workers. The least educated workers in the rich countries may lose their jobs, because the relative prices of the goods that they make are forced down by import competition, and this pushes down their wages too. The import of goods made by low-skilled workers may have the same effect as an increase in the supply of low-skilled workers: they drive down wages. Moreover, trade affects the labour market mainly through the volume of trade, not through prices. The idea is that by importing goods, a country is essentially importing the labour used to make those goods. Thus changes in a country's imports and exports can be used to estimate the effect on the demand for local workers. Trade theorists argue that it is not just the volume of goods imported that affects wages in a certain industry, but the mere threat of foreign competition may be enough to force down prices and wages, whether or not imports are large.

Trade and labour economists agree on the fact that trade has done little to increase inequality and that technology has played a far bigger part. Faced with increased competition from abroad, firms can cut costs by replacing workers with machines. Trade and more competition go hand in hand with technological development. The impact of trade is hard to isolate when considering changes in the composition of an industry's workforce. The clothing industry in the developed world is now employing a higher proportion of designers than in the developing countries. In part, this is a response to foreign competition, but it is also a reaction to the increased purchasing power in the rich countries. The rich countries are buying upgraded and more sophisticated products incorporating a higher portion of design costs (IMF 1997).

Globalization puts workers in competition with each other, which opens up the danger of a 'levelling down' in wages and working conditions. As workers across the globe become more closely linked through common employers, or through the threat of factories relocating to areas where labour is docile and cheap, trade unions have become increasingly aware of the need for a different approach to their campaigns. Recent events, such as the involvement of the International Conference of Free Trade Unions (ICFTU) in social clause campaigns during the Seattle talks of the WTO, have indicated that organized labour understands that national responses to the effects of globalization are not sufficient in themselves (Taylor 1998). However, Lambert (1998: 73) argues that many unions have been responding to globalization through a form of business unionism. Business unionism becomes global business unionism when unions accept the logic of globalization as a reason for their engagement. This form of unionism takes a narrow national focus on an economy that is in practice not only national, but also global. Richard Hyman argues: 'Rather than a crisis of trade unionism, what has occurred is a crisis of a specifically narrow based type of trade unionism' (in Munck 1999: 12). But Lambert argues that an alternative form of unionism has been emerging, a global social movement unionism conscious of the linkage between work-place, civil society, the state and global forces, and is developing a strategy to resist the damaging pressures of globalization by creating a movement linking these spheres (Lambert 1998: 73).

Privatizing the Keynesian welfare state

The dismantling of the welfare state is a relatively new phenomenon accompanying the demise of labourism. The privatization of the welfare state appeared on the political agenda in the 1980s and 1990s, when the continental European welfare states were suffering from high spending deficits. Social security and public pension systems were in deep trouble and in need of fundamental reform. After the demise of Communism, pension funds in Eastern Europe failed to provide adequate incomes to most of their pensioners. As the public pension systems were run on a *pay-as-you-go basis*, they made no contribution to the accumulation of long-term financial assets. The *pay-as-you-go basis* had been introduced just after World War II, and had a universalistic character or had acquired this in the 1950s. Social entitlements, rights to claim a certain level of income and access to health and social services, had become a distinctive part of European modernity (Therborn 1995: 89–97). For the period up to 1960, increased public spending on education, health, training and other social programmes led to measurable improvements in social indicators (Shonfield 1965). After 1960, spending growth was less socially productive than before. The group of countries with 'big governments', spending more than 50 per cent of GDP, did not perform better than 'small governments', spending less than 40 per cent of GDP. Cutting back welfare became an important issue. Reform of pension and health systems would yield considerable budgetary savings in most countries, but most governments decided to postpone thorough reforms. Reformers argued that properly supervised private-sector companies could finance many pension, health and social insurance programmes and that the traditional state-run system had become too costly to be sustainable in the long run. For instance, contribution rates in pension systems in Latin America and the Caribbean average 10.5 per cent, and rates are even higher in some industrial countries. Workers with forty years of service can expect a replacement rate of 80 per cent.

As the national economy becomes more competitive – neo-liberals argue – and as capital and labour become more mobile, countries with big and especially inefficient governments risk falling behind in terms of growth and welfare. The neo-liberal thesis is that as most developing countries and ex-Communist countries are competing for capital inflows, they also have to further economic growth by creating privately owned pension funds, helping them to develop their capital markets. The constraints of international competition may be particularly important for countries where international agreements have eliminated the influence of protectionist interest groups and coalitions and where parties defending expensive welfare programmes are opting for a so-called 'Third Way' (Hay 1997: 234–56, Leys 1997: 17–43, Giddens 1998) and *employability* programmes sponsored by the government (Visser and Hemerijck 1998, Rochon 1999: 219).

The experience of Chile, Singapore and Malaysia showed that once a credible and well-run system is in place, it can accumulate long-term resources at a fast pace. Funded pension schemes can generate substantial financial savings in a short time in countries where labour incomes represent an important percentage of national income. This was especially the case in the US and Great Britain, where contractual savings expanded in the 1980s in relation to GDP as a result of the steep rise of stock-market prices. Hence, pension funds can play a decisive role in a country's financial system, and especially in securities markets, because of their long-term liabilities. In most countries, pension funds found themselves allied with the big banks in order to invest their funds. They also stimulated the security markets and financial innovations as a direct response to the needs of pension funds. The value of pension-fund assets is growing faster than the world economy because more and more people join them. The value of the world's pension assets grew by more than 60 per cent, from just under US$6 trillion in 1992 to US$9.7 trillion in 1997. In America, the average annual growth rate of pension-fund assets between 1992 and 1997 was 10 per cent. In Great Britain, which has the second-biggest pension assets, the annual growth rate was 12 per cent (*The Economist* 13 June 1998: 123). Of course, this increase in funded pension schemes was also connected with stock-market speculation and over-priced real-estate markets in the capitalist world system, which explains why in most continental European countries no strong political pressure for radical and fundamental reform has appeared.

Continental European countries are aware of the danger of overvalued assets owned by pension funds. Therefore, countries with large public pension systems have opted for piecemeal reform, such as increasing the assessment period for the calculation of initial pensions, and tightening the eligibility conditions for early retirement and disability pensions. The reformed public pension system could be based on flat pensions irrespective of career earnings, and these could be subject to means tests. Under a narrow means test, only retired workers with more than a certain high level of income and wealth would be excluded. The reformed public pension system could be based on a two-part structure: a low, flat minimum pension for everybody, combined with private pension schemes. In OECD and in several developing countries a major determinant of the size and growth of private pension funds is the size of the public pension systems, their coverage, the nature of their liabilities, and their investment returns. Pension funds can mobilize savings in a short span of time, but the downsizing of state-financed pension funds in favour of privately managed capital funds also leads to a creeping privatization of the welfare state in one of its most important sectors – e.g. retirement – and has important implications for investment returns, the rate of national savings, corporate governance and the financing of firms.

Defined-occupational pension schemes create a substantial minority of privileged workers. Historically, company schemes tended to define benefit plans, and they were initially conceived as an attraction for skilled workers, rewarding their loyalty and facilitating their retirement. They also punished labour mobility. But large firms were also interested in retaining their workers and in stabilizing their workforce by preventing workers from going elsewhere. The Fordist organization of production and consumption encouraged low labour mobility, and the trade unions backed this management strategy. This was the case in countries with a liberal welfare state with capital-based pension funds. In countries with generous non-capital funded pensions, funded pension schemes were slow to develop. These countries include Germany, Austria, France, Italy, Belgium, and, to a lesser extent, Japan. In countries with modest state-financed pension schemes, private-capital funds and insurance companies moved into the pensions market. They experienced considerable success in the English-speaking countries and South Africa. Several continental European countries saw private pension schemes developing to supplement state-financed pension schemes. The Netherlands and the Scandinavian countries adopted a double-track pension system. In the case of the Netherlands and Switzerland, private pension schemes have wider coverage and larger assets, related to GNP, than in most English-speaking countries, and both offer pensions index-linked to inflation, which require higher funding levels. Adding the assets of life insurance companies, the total assets of contractual savings institutions exceed 100 per cent of GNP. In the developing world, large private pension funds exist in Singapore, Malaysia and Chile, where they are based on defined-contribution plans with individual capitalization accounts. Decentralized, competitive firms subject to state supervision centrally manage Singapore's and Malaysia's pension schemes. In other developing countries, funded pension schemes are mostly company based. Most Latin American countries, the countries of the Middle East, Francophone Africa and East Asia have pay-as-you-go pension systems, making no contribution to the accumulation of financial assets.

Chile's pension reforms during the Pinochet era can be considered as a successful example of a neo-liberal welfare-state reform in a developing country. The pay-as-you-go system run by the government was privatized in the early 1980s, when the state stopped taking new contributions and a dozen new private pension funds started to hold assets. Neo-liberals consider pension fund reform as the key to Chile's economic success. Pension fund reforms improved the functioning of both the capital and the labour markets. They pushed the growth rate of the economy upward from the historical 3 per cent a year to 6.5 per cent on average after 1983. Pensions ceased to be an issue for government, depoliticizing a huge sector of the economy. Today, pension funds hold assets roughly equivalent to 50 per cent of Chile's GDP. This has turned Chile into a nation of small capitalists, and means that the national savings rate could increase from under 3 per cent in 1974 to 24 per cent of GDP today. Chilean workers now receive regular statements of their individual accounts, and if they are not satisfied with the performance of their pension fund, they can switch to another. The funds are now allowed to invest abroad in safe assets such as US Treasury bonds. These reforms were combined with a privatization of state-owned companies and a dramatic scaling back of industrial, agricultural and social subsidies. Resources gained by these cuts in subsidies were used for covering the costs of the old pension system. In the Chilean case, higher public savings have contributed to a phenomenal increase in savings rate, from less than 10 per cent in 1986 to almost 29 per cent in 1996. This has been mostly through an increase in public-sector savings from close to 0.1 per cent of GDP to more than 5 per cent by 1993. It has helped to create a dynamic and modern capital market – insurance companies have increased as a percentage of GDP by more than four times between 1985 and 1995 – and has provided important long-term investment. According to the neo-liberals, pension funds improved the functioning of the labour market, thereby lowering unemployment, by reducing the total rate of payroll taxes and reducing the labour tax component of the retirement system. However, following the establishment of its pension funds, Chile enjoyed economic circumstances that are difficult to replicate elsewhere. From 1985 to 1991, performance was boosted by high real interest rates, while the stock market enjoyed 14 consecutive positive returns (Edwards 1996, Salomon Brothers *Private Pension Funds* 1996) (Table 2.2). Most private Latin American pension funds enjoyed rapid capital gains because of a boom on the stock market caused by monetary stability, and liberalization of the capital market and privatization schemes, enabling capital funds to invest in stocks. Brazil, Chile, Peru, and, to a lesser extent Argentina, saw pension funds acquire some preponderance on their local stock market (*Financial Times* 14 March 1997). But in 1998 Brazil and Argentina were severely affected by the Russian financial crisis, which caused capital outflows in spite of their overvalued currencies and major privatization schemes. These traditional exporters of commodities and agricultural products lost most of the gains that they had acquired in a period when they had presented themselves as emerging markets favouring inflows of foreign capital.

Table 2.1 Private pension funds in Latin America

	Stock-market capital (US$ million)	Assets under mgt 1996 ($ million)	% assets under management in stocks ($ million)	Assets under management, by 2000	% assets under management in stocks, by 2000
Argentina	42,345	5,369	14.8	19,927	20.0
Bolivia	970	–	–	1,543	25.0
Brazil	153,931	71,789	33.0	103,114	35.0
Chile	57,423	29,540	28.5	43,347	35.0
Colombia	14,579	772	0.5	4,736	10.0
Mexico	102,385	–	–	24,228	20.0
Peru	12,385	1,018	23.0	3,080	35.0
Uruguay	2,500	49	0.0	802	25.0
Total	386,518	108,537	30.5	200,777	30.8

Source: *Financial Times*, 14 March 1997, p. iii.

Countries privatizating their pension systems created capital funds. The Chilean case became extremely popular among reformers in other Latin American countries and the post-Communist countries. A succession of Chilean government officials and technocrats visited countries as disparate as Estonia, Albania and Kirgizstan, but only a few Eastern European countries were tempted by a privatization movement based on the Chilean model. Today, the spontaneous generation of pension funds is taking place, with many big companies establishing their own pension funds, sometimes in collaboration with in-house trade unions. In Russia, this model was followed by energy monopolists like Gazprom and by the big Moscow-based banks. Even the Russian Orthodox Church started a private pension fund for its priests. Pension funds can become important players on the domestic capital market, holding the government in check. In Russia, the private pension funds banded together in 1995 when the government intended to force them to buy state securities. The Czech government, led by Václav Klaus removed the legal barriers to the formation of private pension funds, but in the meantime the government was unable to get rid of the pay-as-you-go pension system. The latter system, funded by continued levies on wages, would remain as a social safety-net, expressing the solidarity between old and young. If pensioners want to have an additional pension they must invest their own money in any of the private pension plans competing for their savings (Frydman *et al.* 1998: 241–3).

The welfare model of Europe is known to be unsustainable. As the continent's populations age, large increases in tax rates will be needed to balance the budget. Benefits and labour laws both reduce insecurity, but labour laws are bad for efficiency, and so governments may try to ease regulations while increasing benefits. The preservation of the European welfare state in its present form faces growing difficulties because the search for flexibility in the labour market destabilizes its social base (Castells 2000: 355). Better benefit coverage to more workers with short contribution records could be pursued too, because employment-protection laws concentrate the risk of unemployment on 'outsider' groups such as workers on temporary contracts and the currently unemployed (Boeri *et al.* 2001). Now that all European countries have vowed to maintain economic policies based on sound public finances and because all governments believe in stable fundamental economic indicators, the EU is still pressing its member countries and those applying for membership to continue economic reforms and to activate their workforce. Because European governments have to bring their budgets under control with deficits close to balance (*Financial Times*, 16/17 June 2001: 2), they have become eager to privatize their pension systems.

In Europe, pension funds are still sponsored by the state and even a reform of the pay-as-you-go state pension systems will require a long period of transition. Recent reform proposals introduced by Chancellor Gerhard Schröder of Germany have met resistance in parliament. Like other European countries, Germany faces a demographic time-bomb because of low birth rates, longer life expectancy and a decreasing number of workers to shoulder the tax burden. Germany has opted for a two-track pension system, with a privately funded pension system complementing the old state-supported scheme. However, compulsory contributions to the state scheme, jointly paid by entrepreneurs and employees, are not meant to rise above 22 per cent by 2030 (*The Economist*, 12 May 2001). International institutions and financial experts are pressing the other European Keynesian welfare states to imitate the German example and to study the possibility of a leaner welfare state in combination with a partial privatization of the state pension schemes. This neo-liberal project to transform the basic structure of the European welfare states is still opposed by the trade-union movements, but, as the German case illustrates, entrepreneurs and trade unions may agree on a compromise if the state promises tax breaks and subsidies to encourage workers to contribute into such schemes. Trade unions may be interested in joining the board of the new pension funds and to include them into the collective bargaining regulations.

Conclusions

The nature of systemic changes, combined with a liberalization drive leading to the creation of free-market economies of the type that existed prior to the Great Depression of the 1930s, is now our overriding concern. The trajectory followed by liberalizing regimes suggests that they have returned to early capitalist methods associated with the early British and US model of capital accumulation, with social and economic regulations giving free rein to the private sector with state agencies operating at arm's length. This so-called 'universalistic model' reflects the trajectory of the Anglo-American countries on their way to capitalist development. But we also have the successful emerging economies of East Asia, where state activities have fostered an alternative model of capitalist development. The so-called 'particularistic model' demonstrates that rapid economic growth with the state as a surrogate entrepreneur can be successful. The Communist regimes were highly particularistic, and most populist or Marxist African and Latin American countries adopted policies derived from

Eastern European countries with their stress on quantitative production targets. Central economic planning required state ownership of the means of production and an extreme form of protectionism in order to insulate these economies from world market influences. Political decisions, rather than market forces, were steering the economy until the moment that the foundations of the command economy collapsed, when these countries were unable to shift their policies from import substitution to export-led growth. The outcome was the introduction of capitalism and multi-party regimes trying to connect their economies with the developed capitalist world. The command economy proved to be 'unreformable'. Structural adjustment had to be adopted within a totally new political framework by new social and political forces rejecting autarchy and state-led industrialization schemes. The breakdown of Communism eliminated a competing model that had obliged most Western leaders and capitalism to respect some kind of equilibrium between the worlds of capital and labour. The fall of the Soviet Union and the rapid impoverishment of the countries of the former Socialist Bloc eliminated the non-capitalist development model and created disarray in the Third World. At the same time, the crisis of European Keynesianism undermined labour's idea that the nation-state could operate as the determining force for balancing economic growth and social welfare.

Bibliography

Ágh, A. (1998) *The Politics of Central Europe*, London: Sage.

Aglietta, M. (1979) *A Theory of Capitalist Regulation: the US Experience*, London: New Left Books.

Beck, U. (2000) *What is Globalization?*, Cambridge: Polity Press.

Bezuidenhout, A. (2000) *Towards Global Social Movement Unionism? Trade Union Responses to Globalization in South Africa*, Geneva: International Labour Organization/International Institute for Labour Studies.

Bimba, A. (1927) *The History of the American Working Class*, New York: International Publishers.

Boeri, T., Supan-Börschi, A. and Tabellini, G. (2001) 'Would you like to shrink the welfare state? A survey of European citizens', *Economic Policy*, 32(16), April: 7–50. http://www.economic-policy.org/

Boyer, R. (1996) 'The convergence hypotheses revisited: globalization but still the century of nations?', in S. Berger and R. Dore (eds) *National Diversity and Global Capitalism*, Ithaca and London: Cornell University Press, pp. 29–59.

Brewer, A. (1980) *Marxist Theories of Imperialism: a Critical Survey*, London, Boston and Henley: Routledge & Kegan Paul.

Brown, S.J., Goetzmann, W.N. and Park, J. (1998) *Hedge Funds and the Asian Currency Crisis of 1997*, National Bureau of Economic Research (NBER), Working Paper No. 6427, February.

Castells, M. (2000) *The End of the Millennium*, Vol. 3, *The Information Age: Economy, Society and Culture*, Oxford: Basil Blackwell.

Clinton, B. (1996) *Between Hope and History: Meeting America's Challenges for the 21st Century*, New York: Random House.

Crossland, C.A.R. (1964) *The Future of Socialism*, London: Jonathan Cape.

Davenport, T.R.H. (1987) *South Africa: a Modern History*, Basingstoke, Hampshire: Macmillan.

De Caux, L. (1978) *The Living Spirit of the Wobblies*, New York: International Publishers.

Donald, M. (1993) *Marxism and Revolution: Karl Kautsky and the Russian Marxists 1900–1924*, New Haven and London: Yale University Press.

Economic Commission for Latin America and the Caribbean (ECLAC) (1999) *Economic Survey of Latin America and the Caribbean 1998–1999*, Santiago, Chile: United Nations.

Edwards, S. (1996) *The Chilean Pension Reform: a Pioneering Program*, Working Paper 5811, Cambridge, MA: National Bureau of Economic Research.

Eichengreen, B. and Mathieson, D. (1998) *Hedge Funds and Financial Market Dynamics*, Occasional Paper 166, Washington D.C.: IMF, May.

Esping-Andersen, G. (1990) *The Three Worlds of Welfare Capitalism*, Cambridge: Polity Press.

Fidler, S. (1997) 'Better supervision is needed', *Financial Times*, 14 March, p. 4.

Fine, B. and Rustomjee, Z. (1996) *The Political Economy of South Africa: from Minerals–Energy Complex to Industrialisation*, London: Hurst.

Frydman, R., Murphy, K. and Rapaczynski, A. (1998) *Capitalism with a Comrade's Face: Studies in the Postcommunist Transition*, Budapest: Central University Press.

Gavin, M. (1997) *A Decade of Reform in Latin America: Has it Delivered Lower Volatility?*, Office of the Chief Economist, Washington: Inter-American Development Bank.

Giddens, A. (1998) *The Third Way: the Renewal of Social Democracy*, Cambridge, Polity Press.

Goldfield, M. (1986) 'Labor in American Politics – its current weakness', *Journal of Politics*, 48 (1): 2–29.

Goldfield, M. (1987) *The Decline of Organized Labour in the United States*, Chicago and London: University of Chicago Press.

Goodin, Robert *et al.* (1999) *The Real Worlds of Welfare Capitalism*, Cambridge: Cambridge University Press.

Haggard, S. and Kaufman, R.R. (1995) *The Political Economy of Democratic Transitions*, Princeton, NJ: Princeton University Press.

Hay, C. (1997) 'Anticipating accommodations, accommodating anticipations: the appeasement of capital in the "modernization" of the British Labour Party, 1987–1992', *Politics and Society*, 25(2): 234–56.

Hinrichs, K. (1988) 'Vollbeschäftigung in Schweden. Zu den kulturellen Grundlagen und den Grenzen erfolgreicher Arbeitsmarkt- und Beschäftigungspolitik', *Politische Vierteljahresschrift*, 29(4): 569–90.

Ianni, O. (1975) *La Formación del Estado Populista en América Latina*, Mexico: Serie Popular ERA.

Institute for International Finance (1997) *Capital Flows to Emerging Market Economies*, Washington D.C.: Institute for International Finance.

Inter-American Development Bank (IDB) (1996) *Economic and Social Progress in Latin America*, Washington D.C.: Inter-American Development Bank.

International Monetary Fund (IMF) (1997) *The Effect of Globalization on Wages in the Advanced Economies*, IMF Working Paper, April, Washington D.C.: IMF.

Kaufman, R. and Stallings, B. (1991) 'The political economy of Latin American populism', in R. Dornbusch and S. Edwards (eds) *The Macroeconomics of Populism in Latin America*, Chicago: University of Chicago Press.

Kendall, W. (1975) *The Labour Movement in Europe*, London: Allen Lane.

Kessler, T.P. (1998) 'Political capital: Mexican financial policy under Salinas', *World Politics*, 51(4): 36–66.

Kitschelt, H. (1994) *The Transformation of European Social Democracy*, Cambridge: Cambridge University Press.

Kornai, J. (1995) 'Transformational recession: the example of Hungary', in C.T. Saunders (ed.) *Eastern Europe in Crisis and the Way Out*, London: Macmillan and Vienna Institute for Comparative Economic Studies, pp. 311–42.

Krugman, P. (1998) 'An open letter to Prime Minister Mahathir', September 1. http://www.mit.edu/krugman//mahathir.html.

Krugman, P. (1999) 'The return of depression economics', *Foreign Affairs*, 78(1): 56–74.

Lambert, R. (1998) 'Globalization: can unions resist?', *South African Labour Bulletin*, 22(6): 72–7.

Lardy, N.R. (1998) 'China and the Asian contagion', *Foreign Affairs*, 77(4): 78–88.

Lavigne, M. (1995) *The Economics of Transition: from Socialist Economy to Market Economy*, Basingstoke, Hampshire: Macmillan.

Leys, C. (1997) 'The British Labour Party since 1989', in Donald Sassoon (ed.), *Looking Left: European Socialism after the Cold War*, London and New York: I.B. Tauris Publishers, pp. 17–43.

Lindbeck, A. (1975) *Swedish Economic Policy*, London and Basingstoke, Hampshire: Macmillan.

Lipton, M. (1985) *Capitalism and Apartheid: South Africa, 1910–84*, Aldershot: Gower/Maurice Temple Smith.

Lupher, M. (1996) *Power Restructuring in China and Russia*, Boulder, CO: Westview Press.

Marx, K. (1954) *Capital: a Critical Analysis of Capitalist Production*, Volume 1, Moscow: Foreign Languages Publishing House.

Munck, R. (1999) 'Labour dilemmas and labour futures', in R. Munck and P. Waterman (eds) *Labour Worldwide in the Era of Globalization: Alternative Union Models in the New World Order*, London: Macmillan.

Ortíz Martínez, G. (1998) 'What lessons does the Mexican crisis hold for recovery in Asia?', *Finance and Development*, 35(2): 6–9.

Philip, G. (1998) 'The new populism, presidentialisation and market-orientated reforms in Spanish South America', *Government and Opposition*, 33(1): 81–97.

Plotke, D. (1996) *Building a Democratic Political Order: Reshaping American Liberalism in the 1930s and 1940s*, Cambridge: Cambridge University Press.

Polanyi, K. (1957) *The Great Transformation: the Political and Economic Origins of Our Time*, Boston: Beacon Press.

Punyaratabandhy, S. (1998) 'Thailand in 1997: financial crisis and constitutional reform', *Asian Survey*, 38(1): 161–7.

Raskin, A.H. (1986) 'Labor, a movement in search of a mission', in M.L. Seymour (ed.) *Unions in Transition: Entering the Second Century*, San Francisco: ICS Press, pp. 3–38.

Regini, M. (ed.) (1992) *The Future of Labour Movements*, London: Sage/ISA.

Rhodes, M. and Wright, V. (1988) 'The European steel union and the steel crisis, 1974–84: a study in the demise of traditional unionism', *British Journal of Political Science*, 18: 171–95.

Rochon, T. (1999) *The Netherlands: Negotiating Sovereignty in an Independent World*, Boulder, CO: Westview Press.

Salomon Brothers (1996) *Private Pension Funds in Latin America*, New York: Salomon Brothers.

Salvadori, M. (1979) *Karl Kautsky and the Socialist Revolution 1880–1938*, London: New Left Books.

Schmitter, P.C. (1996) 'The influence of the international context upon the choice of national institutions and policies in neo-democracies', in L. Whitehead (ed.) *The Inter-*

national Dimensions of Democratization: Europe and the Americas, Oxford: Oxford University Press, pp. 26–54.

Schott, J.J., assisted by Buurman, J.W. (1994) *The Uruguay Round: an Assessment*, Washington D.C., Institute for International Economics.

Seidman, G. (1994) *Manufacturing Militance: Workers' Movements in Brazil and South Africa*, Stanford: University of California Press.

Shonfield, A. (1965) *Modern Capitalism: the Changing Balance of Public and Private Power*, Oxford: Oxford University Press.

Soros, G. (2000) *Open Society: Reforming Global Capitalism*, London: Little, Brown & Co.

Swenson, P. (1991) 'Labor and the limits of the welfare state: the politics of intraclass conflict and cross-class alliances in Sweden and West Germany', *Comparative Politics*, 23(4): 379–99.

Taylor, R. (1998) *Trade Unions and Trans-national Industrial Relations*, Geneva: International Institute for Labour Studies.

Therborn, G. (1995) *European Modernity and Beyond: the Trajectory of European Societies 1945–2000*, London: Sage.

Tong Whan Park (1998) 'South Korea in 1997: clearing the last hurdle to political–economic maturation', *Asian Survey*, 30(1): 1–10.

Visser, J. and Hemerijck, A. (1998) *'A Dutch miracle': Job Growth, Welfare Reform and Corporatism in the Netherlands*, Amsterdam: Amsterdam University Press.

Wade, R. (1996) 'Globalization and its limits: reports of the death of the national economy are greatly exaggerated', in S. Berger and R. Dore (eds) *National Diversity and Global Capitalism*, New York: Cornell University Press, pp. 60–88.

Wallach, L. and Sforza, M. (1999) *The WTO: Five Years of Reasons to Resist Corporate Globalization*, New York: Seven Stories Press.

Webster, E. (1985) *Cast in a Racial Mould: Labour Process and Trade Unionism in the Foundries*, Johannesburg: Ravan.

Webster, E. and Adler, G. (1998) *Towards a Class Compromise in South Africa's 'Double Transition': Bargained Liberalization and the Consolidation of Democracy*, Paper presented at the 14th World Congress of Sociology, Montreal, Canada, 26 July–1 August.

World Bank (1993) *Privatizing Public Enterprises and Foreign Investment in Developing Countries 1988–93*, Foreign Investment Advisory Service Occasional Paper 5, Washington D.C.: World Bank.

3 Political economy of growth in Russia

Vladimir Popov

Introduction

After the election of a new Russian president in March 2000, there came a series of predictions that the acceleration of the economic reform process, accompanied by a strengthening of the state, would result in fast economic growth. In this chapter, I will play the role of devil's advocate in order to identify the most important barriers to growth. I will also provide evidence that these barriers are too serious to be eliminated immediately. The last section of this chapter discusses how the barriers might eventually be overcome.

Accounting for economic growth

Hopefully, the lowest point of the decade-long transformational recession in Russia was reached in 1998, when GDP shrank to nearly half of its pre-recession (1989) level. The 4.5 per cent reduction in GDP in 1998 occurred before the August 1998 currency crisis (not after the crisis, as in the East Asian countries), and was the direct result of counterproductive and ultimately futile attempts to hold the exchange rate at an unsustainably high level. The resumption of growth after the crisis – in late 1998 and in 1999 – occurred not because of, but despite, government policies that overvalued the rouble. However, even with the stimulating effect of a cheaper rouble, economic growth only amounted to a modest 3.2 per cent.

If, in 2000, the Russian economy starts to grow at an average rate of 5 per cent a year, it will take fifteen years (up to 2015) to achieve the pre-recession 1989 level of GDP (Figure 3.1). Russian GDP per capita, on a purchasing-power basis comparison, is currently equivalent to some 15 per cent of the US level, and close to the level of China. Assuming 5 per cent average annual growth in Russia and 3 per cent annual growth in the US, Russia's GDP per capita will rise to 20 per cent of the US level.

However, an annual growth rate of 5 per cent may be quite optimistic, since most economies recovering from transformational recession have shown a poorer performance. The crucial prerequisite for steady growth – the solid flow of investment – is almost completely missing from the current Russian economic

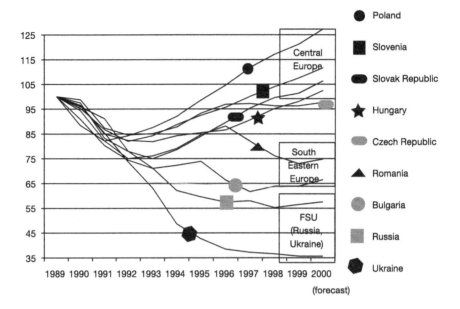

Figure 3.1 Change in GDP in selected transition economies (1989 = 100 per cent)
Source: EBRD (1999)

scene. Russian investment in 1999 was four times lower than in pre-recession 1989, and did not even compensate for the removal of capital stock. In the second half of the 1990s, the Russian investment/GDP ratio fell below even that of many East European countries and Baltic states, where it had increased markedly during recovery, and where the magnitude of restructuring required is somewhat less than in Russia.

For the purposes of this analysis, it is appropriate to classify factors of economic growth into those that depend on the contribution of investment to GDP and those that depend on the efficiency of investment, or marginal capital productivity (MCP).[1]

$$\frac{\text{Change in GDP}}{\text{GDP}} = \frac{\text{Investment}}{\text{GDP}} \times \frac{\text{Change in GDP}}{\text{Investment}} = (\text{Contribution of investment to GDP}) \times (\text{MCP})$$

Thus, the acceleration of growth can come from only two sources – either from increased capital productivity (qualitative sources of growth) or from an increase in the contribution of investment to GDP (a quantitative source of growth). Let us consider both.

Capital productivity and institutions

The prospects for increased capital productivity are bleak. It is common knowledge that losses in allocative efficiency in the centrally planned economies (CPE), as compared with market economies, existed mostly in the form of low capital productivity: specifically, higher capital accumulation ratios in these countries were needed to achieve growth rates similar to those of market economies (Shmelev and Popov 1990). In a sense, CPEs were compensating for the lack of quality (capital productivity) through an abundance of quantity (contribution of investment to GDP).

The expectations that the transition to the market economy would provide a 'marketization dividend' in the form of increased capital efficiency turned out to be right in some post-Communist countries. In China and Vietnam, rates of growth accelerated considerably during the reform period without a great increase in the investment/GDP ratios, whereas Poland has maintained reasonable growth rates with a lower contribution of investment to GDP than before transition. These countries, however, are exactly the ones that managed to preserve strong institutions during transition. The benefits of liberalization thus became noticeable only in economies with strong institutional capacities. On the contrary, in Russia (Commonwealth of Independent States – CIS – and SE Europe as well), the burden of weakened institutions proved to be more damaging for capital productivity than central planning. In terms of the degree of economic liberalization, Russia is in fact very close to China, but the performance of the two economies differs dramatically (Figure 3.2).

The greater magnitude of the Russian recession is associated with long-term structural factors, such as distortions in the industrial structure and trade patterns and, most importantly, with the collapse of state institutions, for which there is no quick fix in the short term. Overcoming distortions inherited from the

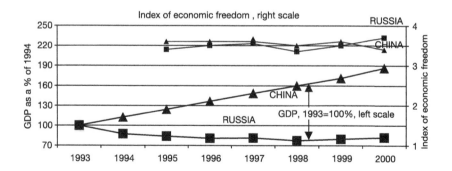

Figure 3.2 Indices of economic freedom and growth in GDP in Russia and China

Source: Heritage Foundation (*http://www.heritage.org/index/execsum.html*)

CPE (industrial restructuring) and creating strong institutions is a task that will obviously require decades rather than years.

In most former Soviet and Balkan countries, the collapse of their institutions is observable in:

- the dramatic increase of the market share of the shadow economy;
- the decline of government revenues as a proportion of GDP;
- the inability of the state to deliver basic public goods and an appropriate regulatory framework;
- the accumulation of tax, trade, wage and bank arrears;
- the demonetization, 'dollarization' and 'barterization' of the economy, as measured by high and growing capital flight;
- the decline of bank financing as a proportion of GDP;
- poor enforcement of property rights, bankruptcies, contracts and law-and-order in general; and
- increased crime rates.

Most of the phenomena mentioned here may be defined quantitatively, with the remarkable result that China and Vietnam in this respect are closer to Eastern European (EE) countries than to the CIS.

One possible general measure is the trust of businesses and individuals in various institutions – here former Soviet states rank much lower than East European countries in all available surveys. In a global survey of firms in sixty-nine countries on the credibility of state institutions, the CIS had the lowest credibility, below that of sub-Saharan Africa (World Bank 1997: 5, 35). Especially striking was the gap between EE and CIS countries: differences in the credibility index between South and South-east Asia and EE were less pronounced than differences between sub-Saharan Africa and the CIS.

Another good proxy for measuring the institutional capacity of the state is the financial strength of the government – the share of state revenues in GDP. Although much has been said about 'big government' and excessive taxes in former socialist countries, by now it is fairly obvious that the downsizing of the government, which occurred in most CIS states during transition, went too far. This argument has nothing to do with the long-term considerations of the optimal size of the government in transition economies – it is true that in most of them, government revenues and expenditure as a share of GDP are still higher than in countries with comparable GDP per capita. But whatever the long-term optimal level of government spending should be, the drastic reduction of such spending (by 50 per cent and more in real terms) cannot lead to anything but institutional collapse.

Before transition in former socialist states, not only were government regulations pervasive, but also the financial power of the state was roughly the same as in European countries (government revenues and expenditure amounted to about 50 per cent of GDP). This allowed the state to provide the bulk of public goods and extensive social transfers. During the transition, tax revenues as a proportion of GDP decreased markedly in most countries. However, the Central European countries and Estonia managed to arrest the decline, while Russia (together with Lithuania, Latvia and several SE European and Central Asian states) experienced the greatest reduction. In Vietnam, the share of government revenues in GDP grew by 1.5 times in 1989–93. Chinese government revenues as a percentage of GDP have fallen more than twofold since the late 1970s, but this looks more like a conscious policy choice rather than a spontaneous process (authoritarian regimes always have better powers to collect tax revenues, if they choose to do so, as did all governments in the CPEs before the transition).

In most CIS states, the reduction in government expenditure occurred in the worst possible way – it proceeded without any coherent plan and did not involve the reassessment of government commitments. Instead of completely shutting down some government programmes and concentrating limited resources on other programmes with the aim of raising their efficiency, the government kept all programmes half-alive, half-financed and barely working.

This led to the slow decay of public education, health care, infrastructure, law-and-order institutions and fundamental R&D. Virtually all services provided by the government – from collecting custom duties to regulating urban traffic – are currently symbolic of a notorious economic inefficiency. There were numerous cases of government failure, which further undermined the credibility of the state, since many government activities that provided public goods were slowly dying and were only partly replaced by private and semi-private businesses.

Three major patterns of change in the share of government expenditure in GDP,[2] which generally coincide with the three major archetypes of institutional developments, and even broader – with three most typical distinct 'models' of transition, are shown in Figure 3.3. Under strong authoritarian regimes (China, for example), cuts in government expenditure have occurred at the expense of defence, subsidies, and budgetary financed investment, while expenditure on 'ordinary government' as a percentage of GDP has remained largely unchanged (Naughton 1997). Under strong democratic regimes (Poland, for example), budgetary expenditure, including that for 'ordinary government', declined only in the pre-transition period, but increased during transition itself. Finally, under weak democratic regimes such as that of Russia, the reduction of the general level of government expenditure did not just lead to the decline in the financing of defence, investment and subsidies, but also to the downsizing of 'ordinary government', which undermined and in many instances even led to the collapse of the institutional capacities of the state.

While in China the total budgetary expenditure and that for 'ordinary government' are much lower than in Russia and Poland, they are sufficient to preserve the functioning of institutions, since the financing of social security from the government budget was traditionally low. In Russia, however, although expenditure for ordinary government does not seem that much lower than in Poland, the pace of its reduction during transition exceeded that of GDP: to put it another way, given the various patterns of GDP dynamics, while in Poland 'ordinary government' finances grew by about one-third in real terms in 1989–95/6 (and

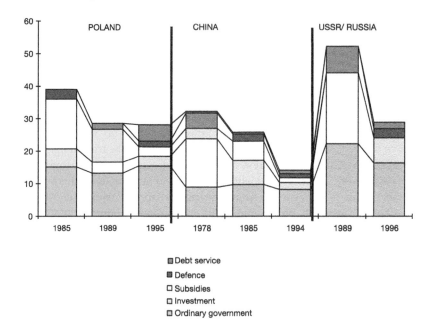

Figure 3.3 Government expenditure (Poland, China, Russia) as a percentage of GDP
Source: Popov (2000)

while in China they nearly doubled), in Russia they fell roughly threefold! The Russian pattern of institutional decay proved to be extremely detrimental for investment and for general economic performance. While Russia's tax rates are not that low as compared with other countries, its tax revenues are fairly low because the shadow economy has expanded dramatically in recent years.[3]

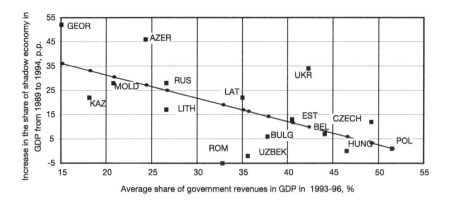

Figure 3.4 Government revenues and the shadow economy; percentage of GDP, 1989–96
Source: Popov (2000)

Normally, there is a positive correlation between the level of taxation, the contribution of government revenues to GDP and the size of the shadow economy in market economies: if taxes are excessive, economic agents tend to avoid taxation through underground activity, including non-reported barter operations (Gardner 1998: 24). In transition economies, the opposite is true: the lower the state revenues the larger the shadow economy (Figure 3.4).[4] In fact, there was a nearly one-to-one crowding-out effect: for every one percentage point of the reduction of the contribution of state revenues to GDP, the contribution of the shadow economy increased by one percentage point. To put it differently, the dynamics of the share of government revenues in GDP in transition economies is a rather accurate measure of the ability of the state to enforce rules and regulations. The decline in government revenues is obviously correlated with performance (Figure 3.5).

There was only one group of transition economies where the share of state revenues in GDP remained relatively stable during transition – Central European countries (Figure 3.6). Outside Central Europe there were only four countries where the share of government revenues in GDP did not fall markedly – Belarus, Estonia, Uzbekistan and Vietnam. The first three are also the top three performers in the former Soviet Union region, whereas Vietnam's performance is second only to that of China. It is noteworthy that Belarus and Uzbekistan, commonly perceived as procrastinators, nevertheless show better results than most more advanced reformers. On the other hand, this is the alternative explanation of the Estonian success in economic transformation as compared with most CIS states and even with neighbouring Baltic states: the usual interpretation focusing on the progress in liberalization may overlook the impact of strong institutions.

According to the EBRD (1999), the quality of governance in transition economies, as it is evaluated by the companies themselves, is negatively correlated with the state capture index (percentage of firms reporting a significant

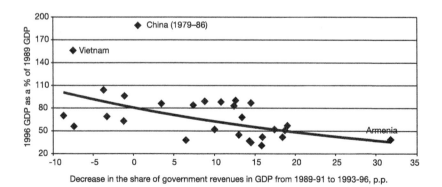

Figure 3.5 Changes in government revenues and GDP

Source: Popov (2000)

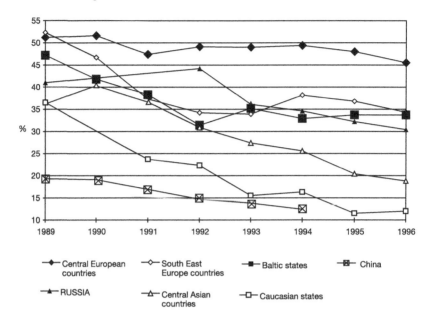

Figure 3.6 Consolidated government revenues as a percentage of GDP
Source: Popov (2000)

impact of bribes to private interests in exchange for parliamentary votes and presidential decrees). The relationship seems to be natural – the less corrupt the government, the better the quality of governance. What is more interesting is that both the quality of governance (positively) and the state capture index (negatively) are correlated with the change in the contribution of state expenditure to GDP, so that countries like Belarus and Uzbekistan fall into the same group as Central European countries and Estonia (a small reduction of state expenditure as a percentage of GDP during transition, good quality of governance, low state capture index).

It is precisely this strong institutional framework that should be held responsible for both – for the success of gradual reforms in China and shock therapy in Vietnam, where strong authoritarian regimes were preserved and CPE institutions were not dismantled before new market institutions were created; and for the relative success of radical reforms in Eastern European, and especially in Central European countries, where strong democratic regimes and new market institutions emerged quickly. And it is precisely the collapse of a strong state and institutions, which started in the USSR in the late 1980s and continued in the successor states in the 1990s, that explains the extreme length, if not the extreme depth, of the transformational recession in the former Soviet Union.

To put it differently, the Gorbachev reforms of 1985–91 failed not because they were gradual, but due to the weakening of the state-institutional capacity, leading to the inability of the government to control the flow of events. Similarly,

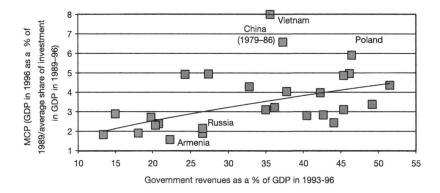

Figure 3.7 Contribution of government revenues to GDP and MCP in 1989–96
Source: Popov (1998a)

Yeltsin's reforms in Russia, as well as economic reforms in most other former Soviet states, were so costly not because of the shock therapy, but due to the collapse of the institutions needed to enforce law-and-order and carry out manageable transition.

To sum up, there is enough evidence that differing performance during transition, after factoring in initial conditions and external environment, depends mostly on the strength of institutions and not so much on the progress in liberalization *per se*. The institutional capacity, as measured by the contribution of state revenues to GDP, is strongly correlated not only with performance (GDP change), but also with capital productivity (Figure 3.7).

Institutional capacity, rule of law and democracy

Using the terminology of political science, it is appropriate to distinguish between strong authoritarian regimes (China, Vietnam and Uzbekistan), strong democratic regimes (Central European countries) and weak democratic regimes (most former Soviet and Balkan states). The former two are politically liberal or liberalizing, i.e. they protect individual rights, including those of property and contracts, and create a framework of law and administration, while the latter regimes, although democratic, are politically not so liberal, since they lack strong institutions and the ability to enforce law-and-order (Zakaria 1997). This gives rise to the phenomenon of 'illiberal democracies' – countries where competitive elections are introduced before the rule of law is established. While European countries in the nineteenth century, and East Asian countries recently, moved from first establishing the rule of law to gradually introducing democratic elections (Hong Kong is the most obvious example of the rule of law without democracy), in Latin America, Africa and now in CIS countries, democratic political systems were introduced in societies without a firm rule of law.

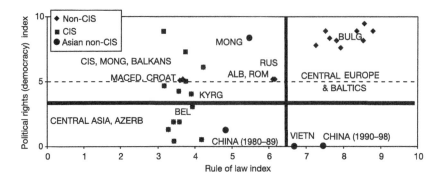

Figure 3.8 Indices of the rule of law and political rights (democracy), on a 1–10 scale, with higher values representing a stronger rule of law and democracy

Source: Popov (2000)

Authoritarian regimes (including Communist ones), while gradually building property rights and institutions, were filling the vacuum in the rule of law via authoritarian means. After democratization occurred and illiberal democracies emerged, they found themselves deprived of the old authoritarian instruments to ensure law-and-order, but without the newly developed democratic mechanisms needed to guarantee property rights, contracts and law-and-order in general (upper left quadrant in Figure 3.8). It is no surprise that this had a devastating impact on the investment climate and output.

As Figure 3.9 suggests, there is a clear relationship between the ratio of the rule of law index on the eve of transition, to the democratization index (on the one hand), and economic performance during transition (on the other hand), although the positive correlation for authoritarian countries is apparently different to that for democracies. Democratization without a strong rule of law, whether one likes it or not, usually leads to the collapse of output. There is a

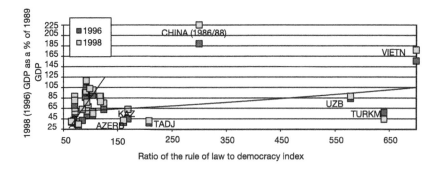

Figure 3.9 Ratio of the rule of law to democracy index and changes in output

Source: Popov (2000)

price to pay for early democratization, i.e. introduction of competitive elections of government under conditions when the major liberal rights (personal freedom and safety, property, contracts, fair trial in court, etc.) are not well established.

If the rule of law and democracy indices are included in the basic regression equation, they have the predicted signs (positive impact of the rule of law and negative impact of democracy) and are statistically significant (Popov 2000), which is consistent with the results obtained for a larger sample of countries (see the survey in Przeworski and Limongi 1993). However, the experience of transition economies seems to indicate that democratization has a marked negative impact on economic performance, especially in the absence of the rule of law. These conditions are captured by the ratio of the rule of law index to democracy index: the lower the rule of law and the higher the democratization, the lower is this ratio.

Including this ratio in the regression for output change yields impressive results: nearly 80 per cent of all variations in output can be explained by only three factors – pre-transition distortions, inflation and the rule-of-law-to-democracy index. If the liberalization variable is added, it turns out to be not statistically significant, and does not improve the goodness of fit. At the same time, the ratio of the rule-of-law-to-democracy index and the decline in government revenues are not substitutes, but rather complement each other in characterizing the process of institutional decay. These two variables are not correlated and improve the goodness of fit (when included together in the same regression), to 88 per cent – a better result than in regressions with either one of these variables. The liberalization index, when added to the same equation, only worsens the goodness of fit, is not statistically significant, and has the 'wrong' sign (Popov 2000).

In a sense, the overwhelming importance of preserving the strong institutional capacity of the state (as opposed to liberalization) for ensuring good performance may be considered as the main finding of this chapter, with strong policy implications. After allowing for differing initial conditions, it turns out that the fall in output in transition economies was associated mostly with a poor business environment, resulting from institutional collapse. Liberalization alone, when it is not complemented with strong institutions, cannot ensure good performance. The best performance during transition was exhibited by countries with low distortions and strong institutions (e.g. China, Vietnam), and the worst performance by countries with high distortions and weak institutions (e.g. the CIS) (Table 3.1). Moreover, the process of the collapse of output in transition economies is best described by the supply-side recession model, where the key determinants are initial conditions and the strength of institutions, while the impact of liberalization is hardly noticeable. It follows that the debate about the speed of liberalization (shock therapy versus gradualism) was to a large extent misfocused, whereas the crucial importance of strong institutions for good performance was overlooked.

Institutional capacities in turn depend to a large extent on the combination of the rule of law and democracy: the data seem to suggest that both authoritarian and democratic regimes with the strong rule of law can deliver efficient institutions, whereas under weak rule of law, authoritarian regimes do a better job in

Table 3.1 Main factors affecting performance

Institutions/ distortions	Weak	Strong
High	CIS	Central Europe
Low	Albania, Mongolia	China, Vietnam

Table 3.2 Patterns of institutional capacity

Rule of law/ democracy	Weak	Strong
More democratic	CIS, Mongolia, Balkans	Central Europe, Baltic states
Less democratic	Central Asia, Azerbaijan, Belarus	China, Vietnam

maintaining efficient institutions than do democracies. To put it in a shorter form, the record of illiberal democracies in ensuring institutional capacities is the worst, which, predictably, has a devastating impact on output. The most efficient institutions are in countries with a strong rule of law maintained either by democratic (Central Europe, Baltics) or authoritarian regimes (China, Vietnam). The least efficient institutions are in illiberal democracies combining poor rule of law with democracy (CIS, Balkans, Mongolia). Less democratic regimes with a weak rule of law (Central Asia, Azerbaijan, Belarus) appear to do better than illiberal democracies in maintaining institutional capacity and in economic performance (Figure 3.9 and Table 3.2).

How is it possible to increase the contribution of investment to GDP?

With low and barely improving capital productivity, growth prospects in the medium term will depend largely on the ability to ensure the flow of savings and investment, i.e. to compensate and perhaps even to counteract the poor quality of investment with a greater quantity of investment. However, regarding the availability of savings for financing investment, the future does not look encouraging either. Business profits and depreciation funds are low; personal savings, although high, are made mostly through accumulating hard currency (financing capital flight, not investment), whereas savings in roubles are decreasing; the government is running up a sizeable budget deficit; and the inflow of foreign direct investment is weak, so that a substantial trade surplus and international borrowing are barely enough to cover debt service payments and capital flight.

The prospects for increasing savings and investment and for achieving high growth rates thus seem to be bleak as well, unless something is done to reverse existing trends. Several measures discussed below seem to be especially promising in this respect. Most of these measures involve the redistribution of national income in favour of savings (which should then be transformed into investment), at the expense of consumption and hence are likely to face popular opposition. As in other areas, the feasibility of these measures depends largely on the ability to build consensus to carry out politically difficult decisions. The growth strategy should include at least four crucial policy changes.[5]

First, it would be necessary to keep the exchange rate considerably under-valued in order to encourage exports, restructuring and growth, while fighting inflation through tight fiscal and monetary policy (stemming increases in money supply caused by the growth of foreign-exchange reserves), not through a high-priced national currency. An undervalued currency is a necessary component of export-led growth. It used to be the strategy of Japan, Korea, Taiwan and Singapore some time ago, when those countries were still poor and were catching up with high-income states. This is currently the strategy of many new emerging market economies, especially that of China, which continues to keep the exchange rate at an extremely low level (five times lower than PPP rate) by accumulating foreign-exchange reserves at a record pace. It is by no means an accident that all very fast-growing economies are also famous for high and rapidly growing international reserves: China (including Hong Kong), Taiwan, Singapore, Malaysia and Thailand, account for a good 20 per cent of total world reserves, whereas the currency reserves to GDP ratio for these countries is normally above 20 per cent as compared with only 8 per cent for the world as a whole and only about 5 per cent for Russia. It was shown for developing coun-tries that overvaluation of the exchange rate is detrimental to economic growth (Dollar 1992, Easterly 1999). Unlike other measures to promote growth, it may be implemented relatively easily since it favours the interests of all of the powerful industrial groups (thus creating a stimulus for the export-oriented resource sector, as well as providing protection from import competition to secondary manufacturing and agriculture). Besides, the low exchange-rate policy, unlike import protection or direct subsidies, is a non-selective policy instrument, and as such creates fewer opportunities for corruption.

Industrial policy should favour strong, competitive, export-oriented industries, while subsidies to inefficient industries should be phased out and replaced by retraining and social programmes. In the past, industrial policy was largely a failure. It took the most inefficient form of price subsidies (supplemented by quotas and export tariffs for fuel, energy and raw materials), and supported the most energy-inefficient production in the world. It also did not succeed in supporting investment in competitive resource industries, or in allocating funds to those few high-tech industries (aerospace) that had good prospects of becoming competitive.

The industrialization process of the 1930s and beyond became a major isola-tionist import-substitution experiment: from that time on, the proportion of exports in Soviet GDP did not increase until large-scale fuel sales abroad started in the 1970s. The huge, perverted industrial structure, created without any regard for the costs and prices of the world market, proved to be stillborn and non-viable in 1992, when it finally faced foreign competition after half a century of artificial isolation.

Today, Russia is choosing once again between export-oriented growth and protection autarchy. On the one hand, there is the example of East Asian countries that managed to rely on exports as an engine of economic growth: in China, for instance, the proportion of GDP made up of exports increased from 5 per cent in the mid-1970s to over 20 per cent in the mid-1990s, while the GDP itself was growing at an average rate of about 10 per cent. On the other hand, there are much less appealing examples of, for example, 'the champion of isolationism' – North Korea and other socialist countries, and of many 'socialist' developing countries, which created their own heavy industries following advice and assistance from the Soviet Union, and also the example of India (where the share of GDP made up of exports remained frozen at a level of 6 per cent over the period from the 1950s to the 1980s), as well as many Latin American countries.

The option of promoting export-oriented growth requires massive and rapid industrial restructuring – mostly in favour of resource-based industries, but also in favour of some competitive high-tech sectors (such as aerospace), and, perhaps, particular capital and labour-intensive industries at the expense of agriculture and most secondary manufacturing industries. The other option – continuing support to major non-competitive industries – is a slower and more costly way of restructuring, implying the preservation of subsidies to and protection of weak producers. Paradoxically, this option, despite the intentions of those who propagate it to stop the de-industrialization of the country, may lead to exactly the opposite: poor performance of the resource sector will not generate enough revenues to support all non-competitive industries, with the result that even the few still competitive or potentially competitive secondary manufacturing industries will fail to obtain the necessary support and will slowly disintegrate.

Government commitments should be re-evaluated and government expenditure must be restructured, to make them financially sustainable and efficient. Withdrawal of agricultural and housing subsidies and pension-system reform seem to be most promising. Housing subsidies are even larger than agricultural subsidies: in 1996 they amounted to 4 per cent of GDP, since fees collected from residents were covering on average only 27 per cent of housing and related municipal services. A May 1997 presidential decree called for the withdrawal of all price subsidies (partly replacing them with direct income subsidies to needy citizens) by the year 2003. This measure, however, was extremely unpopular, was opposed by most regional authorities, including the powerful mayor of Moscow, and was not carried out.

Pension reform may produce even greater financial savings, although politically it may be more difficult to implement. Whether a transition from the current pay-as-you-go system to mandatory/voluntary fully funded pension plans can raise domestic savings or not is debatable (the evidence seems to be mixed). Irrespective of the debate, however, it is fairly obvious that the current Russian pay-as-you-go system is extremely inefficient and should be reformed. The existing system based on mandatory contributions to the off-budget Pension Fund by employers (28 per cent payroll tax) is apparently not working properly, yielding less than half of potential revenues, due to the unwillingness of employers to pay the very high social-security contributions. This is the fundamental reality of the

Russian economic situation: there is no short-term solution to the tax evasion problem and hence, it is the pension system (and government spending in general) which has to be adjusted to the financial abilities of the state, not vice versa.

Steps to reform the pension system have been modest so far. In 1997, the government planned to start transition (which would require three to five years) to the so-called 'individualized pension accounts', in which all contributions made by employers and employees will be personalized, but even these modest plans became enmeshed in bureaucratic red-tape. More radical plans, such as a transition to a Singapore-style mandatory fully funded pension system, were discussed, but not approved by the government in 1997. Given the limited ability of the government to collect taxes, it may well be that the pay-as-you-go system is an unaffordable luxury for Russia in the foreseeable future.

In a poor investment climate resulting from uncertainty caused by institutional collapse, it makes sense to increase government investment and to promote foreign direct investment into resource projects. In both areas, Russia did much worse than the emerging market economies, and its performance in recent years was actually worse than in most transition economies.

Overall in 1989–98, Russia received some US$9 billion of foreign direct investment, which on a per capita basis is 4 per cent of the Hungarian level, and only about 15 per cent of the level of Kazakhstan and Azerbaijan, where political stability and the business climate are not much better than in Russia. It means that Russia has obviously failed to use its 'resource advantages' to bring in foreign capital. On the contrary, Russia failed to prevent the reduction of investment and output even in competitive resource industries (oil and gas included) in recent years, which should be viewed as a major failure of government policy.

Another way to stimulate investment is to increase government investment in infrastructure – even at the expense of financing it through government borrowing. The available evidence suggests that public savings do not crowd out private savings one to one, but rather the private sector offsets each dollar of public savings by dissaving only US$0.25 to US$0.50. The very fast-growing economies of East Asia normally keep government investment high, despite relatively low ratios of total government expenditure to GDP, so that the share of capital expenditure in total government outlays is much higher than in other countries. To put it another way, even debt-financed government investment pays off by increasing the national savings and investment rates. Unfortunately, Russia has not been able to increase government investment in recent years – in fact, it has been falling at the same rate as private investment.

Finally, it is much easier to strengthen institutions in a growing economy rather than in a collapsing economy. In this sense, institution building and economic growth are mutually supportive and complementary. In transition economies, in recent years the contribution of investment to GDP has been positively correlated with the size of the government, i.e. the proportion of GDP made up by state revenues (Figure 3.10). It means that strengthening of the state would be good for investment, capital productivity and output, and vice versa.

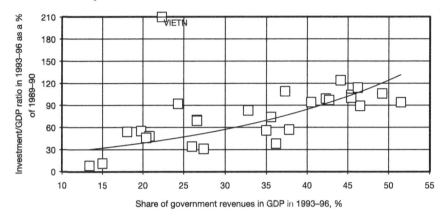

Figure 3.10 Investment and government revenues in 1989–96

Source: Popov (1998a)

The political economy of growth

Theoretically, the measures outlined here are technically feasible. Moreover, the political situation seems to be favourable – the best time for the 'unpopular measures' is of course the beginning of the presidential term. However, the logic of the political economy of reforms does not give much reason for hope. The unfortunate combination of a weak state and the need for massive redistribution resulting from large income inequalities between industrial sectors and social groups gives rise to the macro-economics of populism. Once there is a need, whether mythical or real, to redistribute income in favour of the poorest social groups and weakest enterprises, coupled with the inability of governments to raise enough taxes for this redistribution activity, the story unfolds pretty much in line with the Latin American experience and leaves a strong sense of *déjà-vu*. Constrained by the inability to raise tax receipts and by a simultaneous need to maintain redistribution in favour of particular social groups, the governments are basically left with only so many options for the indirect financing of subsidies.

The first option is to maintain control over particular prices. Controls over prices of non-resource goods do not solve the problem completely, since they require explicit subsidies from the budget in order to cover the losses of the companies producing those goods. In contrast, price controls on fuel, energy and other resource commodities effectively take away rent from the resource sector and redistribute it to consumers. The redistribution of rent does not require counter-subsidization of the resource sector in this case, especially if it is more efficient than the rest of the economy. This option is available to resource-rich countries, which may provide an additional explanation as to why the resource endowment is found to have a positive effect on the shadow economy and corruption, and a negative effect on growth.

The second way to maintain subsidies under budget constraints is to resort to trivial inflationary financing of the government budget. The government compensates for the shortfall in tax revenues by imposing an inflation tax on everyone, which is highly detrimental to growth.

The third way is debt financing – either domestic or external borrowing. Debt financing makes sense when it buys some time for maintaining subsidies while conflicting parties are negotiating a way to get rid of them. If it continues for too long, however, it only makes things worse, since debt-servicing payments impose an additional burden on the government budget.

Finally, the fourth way to continue redistribution with no funds in the budget is to maintain the overvalued exchange rate that favours consumers over producers, exporters over importers, and leads to increases in consumption at the expense of savings. Consumption increases, due to increases in imports financed through external borrowing or foreign exchange reserves, obviously provide only a temporary solution, leading to a balance of payments crisis in the longer term (Montes and Popov 1999).

Different countries at different periods resorted to one or more of the mechanisms of implicit redistribution. In Russia, the government initially (1992–4) relied on controlling resource prices and inflationary financing. Since 1995, when exchange-rate based stabilization was carried out and the rouble reached 70 per cent of its purchasing-power parity value (i.e. Russian prices, including resource prices, approached 70 per cent of US prices, which was an apparent overvaluation of the rouble), the government relied mostly on debt (domestic and foreign) financing and redistribution via the overvalued exchange rate. Since the 1998 financial crisis, leading to the collapse of the overvalued rate and to the cessation of international and domestic debt financing, the government has had to rely largely on price control (via export taxes and export restrictions) on major tradable goods (e.g. oil and gas).

At the time of writing (April 2000) there are no indications that the new Russian government will have the courage to break this vicious circle of populist policies and to embark on a new export-oriented growth strategy. Fast progress in adopting the measures outlined does not seem to be politically feasible, but some steps in this direction are more or less inevitable, especially in the longer term. One can be fairly certain, however, that rapid economic growth without major progress in most, if not all, of the above-mentioned policy areas is extremely unlikely.

Notes

1 In the neo-classical Solow model of economic growth, the increase in the investment (savings) rate does not lead to the acceleration of growth, since the positive impact of a higher proportion of investment in income is counteracted by the negative effect of the decreasing MCP. The Romer model, with endogenous technical progress, allows for the acceleration of growth due to a higher investment rate. However, this discussion is merely theoretical. Empirical evidence is quite unambiguous: a higher proportion of GDP made up of investment, as shown in the example of the 'Asian

tigers' is generally not counterbalanced completely by a decrease in capital productivity, so that growth rates increase with greater investment.

2 Data for China (World Bank 1996), Russia (Goskomstat) and Poland (Rocznik Statystyczny 1990, Warszawa; and data from Institut Finansow provided by G. Kolodko) do not include off-budget funds, which are very substantial in all three countries and are used mostly for social-security purposes. Defence expenditure is derived from official statistics, i.e. it is lower than Western estimates, which is likely to lead to an overstatement of spending for investment and subsidies at the expense of defence outlays. For USSR/Russia, the investment and subsidies are shown together.

3 In Russia, government revenues plummeted after the CPE was dismantled, falling below 30 per cent of GDP (including off-budget funds) in 1997. This is still more than in East Asian countries and other economies with similar GDP per capita, on average (Illarionov 1998; Mau 1998), but much less than in Central European countries, and much less than is needed to finance government commitments – the still very substantial agricultural and housing subsidies, the mostly free education and health care, and the universal pay-as-you-go system of social insurance.

4 To put it differently, apparently the Laffer curve is not applicable for macro-economic comparison with Western countries, because higher tax rates result in higher tax revenues despite the increase in the share represented by the shadow economy (e.g. tax avoidance). In transition economies, at least in those where institutions are weak, growth in the shadow economy (whether or not it is caused by higher tax rates) is so substantial that it more than counterbalances any possible increases in revenue collection.

5 For details, see Popov (1998b).

References

Dollar, D. (1992) 'Outward-oriented developing economies really do grow more rapidly: evidence from 95 LDCs, 1976–1985', *Economic Development and Cultural Change*, 40(3), April: 523–44.

Easterly, W. (1999) *The Lost Decades: Explaining Developing Countries Stagnation 1980–1998*, Washington D.C.: World Bank.

European Bank for Reconstruction and Development (EBRD) (1999) *Transition Report 1999*, London: EBRD.

Gardner, S. (1998) *Comparative Economic Systems*, 2nd edition, New York: Dryden Press.

Illarionov, A. (1998) 'How the Russian financial crisis was organized', *Voprosy Ekonomiky*, 11 (in Russian).

Mau, V. (1998) 'Political nature and lessons of financial crisis', *Voprosy Economiky*, No. 11 (in Russian).

Montes, M. and Popov, V. (1999) *The Asian Crisis Turns Global*, Singapore: Institute of Southeast Asian Studies.

Naughton, B. (1997) 'Economic reform in China: macroeconomic and overall performance', in D. Lee (ed.) *The System Transformation of the Transition Economies: Europe, Asia and North Korea*, Seoul: Yonsei University Press.

Popov, V. (1998a) 'Investment in transition economies: factors of change and implications for performance', *Journal of East–West Business*, 4(1–2): 47–98.

Popov, V. (1998b) 'Will Russia achieve fast economic growth?', *Communist Economies and Economic Transformation*, 4.

Popov, V. (2000) 'Shock therapy versus gradualism: the end of the debate (explaining the magnitude of the transformational recession)', *Comparative Economic Studies*, 42(1), Spring.

Przeworski, A. and Limongi, F. (1993) 'Political regimes and economic growth', *Journal of Economic Perspectives*, 7(3), Summer: 51–69.

Shmelev, N. and Popov, V. (1990) *The Turning Point: Revitalizing the Soviet Economy*, New York: Doubleday.

World Bank (1996) *The Chinese Economy. Fighting Inflation, Deepening Reforms: A World Bank Country Study*, Washington D.C.: World Bank.

World Bank (1997) *The State in a Changing World: World Development Report*, New York: Oxford University Press.

Zakharia, F. (1997) 'The rise of illiberal democracies', *Foreign Affairs*, 76(6), November–December: 22–43.

4 Institutionalizing capitalism

Changing labour market institutions in Hungary after state socialism

Maarten Keune

Introduction

The demise of state socialism in Central and Eastern Europe (CEE) has led to profound changes in the institutional context in which socio-economic action takes place. Indeed, in the past decade or so we have been witnessing one of the most far-reaching contemporary attempts at institutional innovation. Such innovation has been undertaken with a view to establishing democratic capitalist societies and has generally been conceived with explicit reference to the example of Western capitalist societies. Not surprisingly, we can see both institutional convergence and divergence between the former state-socialist countries. For example, while in all of them property has been increasingly privatised, mechanisms of privatization as well as their outcomes in terms of ownership structures have been quite diverse. On the one hand, this is because institutional change has occurred in one and the same global discursive context, which has by and large set the broad boundaries within which change has moved. On the other hand, institutional change has taken place in particular national socio-historical contexts and has been conceived and implemented by particular actors with particular visions and interests concerning the way that capitalism should be built (Blokker and Keune 2001). In this way, the CEE countries are constructing their own 'varieties of capitalism'.[1]

This chapter discusses one area of institutional innovation in one of the former state-socialist and new capitalist countries, Hungary, concentrating on labour market institutions and the way that they regulate labour market action. Since the 1980s, within the context of the (perceived) process of globalization, a major debate has been ongoing on the need to reform labour markets in Western capitalist countries (Boyer 1988, Buechtemann 1991, Pollert 1991, Schömann *et al.* 1998, Standing 1999, Esping-Andersen and Regini 2000). Much of this debate has centred around the issues of deregulation and flexibility. In essence, this deregulation/flexibility debate is a debate on institutions. It starts from the assumption that different institutional arrangements allow for higher or lower levels of flexibility and favour certain types of flexibility over others. The focus of the debate has mainly been on questions such as to what extent and/or in what way do economic organizations have to become more flexible in their use of labour to be able to respond to the 'new' exigencies of the global economy?; in what way should national institutional systems be (re)shaped to allow for or foster labour flexibility?; and what are the consequences for aggregate employment and the quality of employment?

The institutions, or modes of governance, at the heart of the debate are the market, the state (legislation, policy) and associations (unions and employers' organizations), and generally the virtues of market governance (read: deregulation) are contrasted with those of the state or associational governance. In the context of a strengthening drive towards neo-liberal views on the economy, there has been an increasing commitment to deregulation and the removal of 'rigidities', and thus to an increasing role of the market in regulating economic behaviour.[2] This strong and persistent insistence on the need for general deregulation reflects a rather crude version of a theory of convergence (Regini 1999). This claims that the modernization of advanced economies and societies must follow established paths, essentially dictated by exogenous factors, and takes 'successful' Anglo-American capitalism to be the example to follow for high-unemployment Europe. However, empirical work often does not support the conclusion that various types of state and associational governance necessarily affect economic performance, labour market adjustment or labour demand in a negative way (Bertola 1990, Buechtemann 1991, Morgan 1996, Bertola *et al.* 2000, Esping-Andersen and Regini 2000). Also, persistent empirical differences between countries and within countries – many countries do not make a clear, homogeneous choice between market governance or other types of governance and different types of governance affect different spheres of action – contradict convergence thinking (Regini 1999). There continues to be ample diversity, and there is no standard or best national model of capitalist societies or of labour market governance.

This, then, constitutes the starting point for the analysis of labour market institutions in Hungary in this chapter. It shows that such an analysis should not be constructed on the perception that institutional reform in the former state-socialist world moves towards a known or optimal outcome, the achievement of which depends on the direction and speed of reform. Rather, it points to the socio-historically constructed character of institutions and the open-endedness of change, as well as to the importance of the analysis of the particularities of the process of change, the actors and motives that drive it and the outcomes that result from it.

This chapter is divided into four parts. In the section after the introduction, I will first discuss the main actors who have shaped the project of building capitalism in Hungary, and their general orientations towards institutional reform. In the second section, I will discuss to what extent socio-economic policy-making in the 1990s has incorporated neo-corporatist elements. In the third section, I will discuss in more detail the changes in labour market institutions during the past decade. Here the focus is on the question of to what extent or in what way does 'really existing Hungarian capitalism' depart from an ideal-type (in the Weberian sense) neo-classical market economy (a social order in which economic processes are solely co-ordinated by market mechanisms)? I will do so by establishing the importance of other relevant modes of governance, in particular the state's employment and labour market policy, labour law and collective bargaining, the particular institutional form that they have taken and how they constrain or facilitate market regulation.[3]

Building capitalism: politics, neo-liberalism and the EU

In the early 1980s, most reform-minded Hungarian economists, sociologists and others did not so much oppose the socialist regime as strive for modification of the system from within. They could do so because the Kádár regime increasingly tolerated opposition. They discussed 'varieties of socialism', including a socialist 'mixed economy', socialist constitutionalism or democratic socialism, and debated the harmonization of the plan with the market, improving redistribution or achieving independent interest representation (Bozóki 1999; Eyal *et al.* 1998). Indeed, substantial reforms were implemented. Enterprise autonomy was increased, certain private entrepreneurial activities became possible, and an important so-called 'second economy' emerged. In addition, Hungary became increasingly integrated in the international capitalist system as exports to capitalist countries increased, and it borrowed heavily from the West, accumulating the largest per capita foreign debt in the entire former state-socialist region.

Among the central aims of these reforms and the approximation to the West was the adoption of some elements of capitalism, which were expected to increase economic efficiency and to raise the standard of living. Indeed, the reforms provided the economy and the labour market with much higher levels of flexibility. On the one hand, workers could combine the possibilities of the dual economy creatively in order to increase their income. On the other hand, enterprises obtained access to multiple solutions to production and productivity problems. Still, the economic crisis continued to deepen during the 1980s. Managers and technocrats, more and more frustrated with the difficulties of making the economy work, as well as intellectuals who increasingly rejected the political limits imposed by the regime, started to study liberal economic ideas, and distanced themselves more clearly from the Party. They were attracted by monetarism's strong rejection of Communism and Third Way alternatives and its promise of greater freedom coupled with greater control and predictability (Eyal *et al.* 1998: 90). Thus, by the end of the 1980s, the influence of neo-conservative and liberal discourses strengthened, calling for systemic instead of intra-systemic reform. This, they argued, would bring what socialism had failed to achieve. Political freedom would be increased and modern capitalism would bring prosperity for all, thus finally releasing Hungary from the peripheral position that it had had for centuries within Europe and opening the doors to the core of the continent.

The opposition, benefiting from the changing conditions in the socialist world, was successful. In 1989, the ruling party realized that its days were numbered and agreed to a negotiated regime change, culminating in the Round Table Talks that took place between June and September of the same year. The Round Table Talks above all turned out to be an occasion for the creation of a new political élite and of a political system dominated by political parties, at the expense of other organizations representing society (Stark and Bruszt 1998: 42–7). Other types of socio-political organizations (trade unions, corporatist organisations, mass movements) were weak and had only a marginal role in the Round Table talks. This is particularly true for trade unions who, although present in the Round Table discussions, practised severe self-restraint, leaving it to political parties to shape the future of the country (Tóth 2000; see also Bozóki 1993, Sajó 1996). This 'supremacy of political parties' (Stark and Bruszt 1998) has not been seriously challenged by any social grouping, and has survived until today. The main challenge to the various governing coalitions has come from the opposition parties, which have managed to oust the sitting governments in every election. This is, however, not so much because they presented a real programmatic alternative, but rather because the incumbent governments had been discredited by economic and social problems and corruption scandals.

There has been no doubt among the new political élite that Hungary's future is 'Western capitalism'. They were joined in this quest by many of the managers of state enterprises, some of whom, apart from the possibilities for a more productive economy, saw their chance to benefit personally from the systemic changes, clinging on to their position or forging profitable privatization deals. It was this coalition then which, instead of Weber's Protestant private entrepreneurs, became the bearer of the 'spirit of capitalism'.[4]

However, if, as argued by literature on capitalist diversity, there is a variety of Western capitalist systems with quite diverse institutional characteristics, what does 'Western capitalism' mean? In the CEE context, including Hungary, the interpretation of 'Western capitalism' has first of all been influenced by the globally dominant neo-liberal discourse, which had already attracted many in the late 1980s. Also, the majority of Western political and intellectual élites and the international financial institutions tried to push neo-liberal reforms in CEE, through political pressure or loan conditionality.[5] The neo-liberal influence was particularly strong in the early 1990s and was translated into a vision that the basic institutions of modern capitalism could be created through a very limited range of core reforms: macro-economic stabilization, liberalization of prices and trade, and privatization. Their main objective was the institutionalization of market governance, to be achieved through a programme of rapid reforms implemented by the state.

Added to this has been the ultimate priority given to accession to the European Union. Joining the EU has become so important to Hungary that 'the legitimacy of the transition itself depends on the success of EU accession' (Andor 2000: 2). EU membership is seen as the final step in breaking with the state-socialist past and in joining the modern democratic-capitalist world, and can thus be seen as the '*telos* of transition' (Orenstein 1998: 480). Additionally, accession is expected to bring direct economic benefits coming from increased trade and exchange of knowledge and technology with Western Europe or from the receipt of structural funds. Hence, since 1989, and in particular since the country's application for EU membership in 1994, Hungary has increasingly tried to adopt EU regulations and standards in order to prepare for membership. References to such regulations are regularly used to defend policy proposals and to justify choices. This has also broadened the outlook of reforms, as the scope of EU regulations and conditionality goes far beyond the narrow economistic approach towards reform of the international financial institutions.

Within the broad limits set by the neo-liberal philosophy and the requirements of the EU accession process, then, the reform programmes of the three post-1989 governments have all seen certain variations on – and sometimes also contradictions to – the main theme. To an important extent, these have been shaped by particular local circumstances, institutional constellations and interests, which have favoured certain development directions and restrained others. We will see some examples of this below.

The role of neo-corporatism

The above does not mean to imply that political parties have completely insulated decision-making from other socio-political organizations. Indeed, a number of national-level and decentralised institutions have been established since 1989, through which socio-economic governance was to be co-ordinated with other actors, primarily the social partners (ILO–CEET 1997, Tóth 1999, Héthy 1999 and 2001, Keune 2001). The most prominent of these was the Interest Reconciliation Council (IRC), a national-level tripartite organization and the country's key institution for social dialogue in the period 1990–8.[6] The impact of these bodies, and through them of the social partners, on policy-making has, however, been limited, as can be demonstrated through the example of the IRC.

First, the IRC was dominated largely by the government. Unions and employers have experienced serious problems, including internal fragmentation and conflict, low and declining membership, legitimacy problems, difficulties in organising small enterprises and foreign enterprises, etc. (Kollonay Lehoczky and Ladó 1996, Tóth 1999, Girndt 1996 and 2001, Cox and Mason 2000). These problems have seriously weakened their position and made it difficult for the social partners both to enforce IRC agreements internally and to put effective pressure on the government. They needed the IRC to *gain* legitimation, instead of having conquered their place on the Council because of their own strength. The issues for discussion, as well as the boundaries within which negotiations or consultations were to take place were defined primarily by the government, whose voice prevailed if no agreement was reached. As a result, the influence of the Council on economic and social policy formulation:

has been limited to a relatively narrow range of issues and has concentrated on short-term measures rather than strategic decision making. Council agreements were designed to help maintain 'social peace'. In this respect they have been relatively effective although their impact on the broader parameters of economic and social policy has been fairly marginal.

(Héthy 1995: 87)

Second, although both the Antall government (1990–4) and the Horn government (1994–8) claimed to promote tripartism, in several instances they simply ignored the other two parties, tried to undermine their positions, and reversed agreements. The Antall government actively attempted to weaken trade unions and neutralize them politically (Bruszt 1995). It particularly tried to weaken the MSZOSZ, the 'successor' union and the largest confederation in the country, which it regarded as an unwelcome relic from the previous system. Also, in many instances the Antall government acted in contradiction to agreements reached and prevented them from coming into force (Kollonay Lehoczky and Ladó 1996: 127; also Héthy 1995). The Horn government, led by the Socialist Party, practised a strong discourse of social partnership, and the Socialist Party had strong institutional links with the MSZOSZ. In line with this, during the first months of the governmental period, it set out to negotiate a four-year Social and Economic Agreement in the context of the IRC (Héthy 1999: 60). However, the proposals of the government met with serious objections, above all from the unions, and no agreement was reached. Subsequently, the government unilaterally imposed a draconian austerity package, which represented a serious blow for the trade unions. It did not mean the end of the IRC, however, and during 1996–8, apart from setting the minimum wage and issuing recommendations on wage increases, a series of agreements was reached on issues like the establishment of the Labour Mediation and Arbitration Service, the Labour Inspection Act, the establishment of the Labour Market Fund Steering Committee, and pension reform.

Summarizing, the IRC certainly played an important role in maintaining social peace, and provided both legitimacy and voice to the social partners in 1990–8. However, tripartism in Hungary in this period did not embody the institutionalization of trade-union and employers' organizations' influence on government policy in exchange for social peace. Rather, it was a mechanism in which the social partner organizations exchanged social peace for a certain amount of legitimacy and only to a limited extent for the possibility of influencing government policy, which was also restricted largely to narrowly defined labour issues.

However, while in the first two post-1989 government periods at least some corporatist elements could be found, these appeared to vanish rapidly under the Orbán government (1998–present), which aims to reject any corporatist attempts, to destroy the tripartite system and to further weaken the unions in particular (Tóth 1999, Boda and Neumann 2000, Héthy 2001). Also, considering the improvement of the national economy and the weakness of the social partners, the government deems it superfluous to (pretend to) seek the consent of the social partners to legitimise its economic and social policy. Thus, it has deprived workers and employers' organizations of their votes in the County Development Councils and has abolished the bipartite Self-Governments of Health and Pension Insurance. Moreover, in 1999, the Orbán government dissolved the IRC and replaced it by the National Labour Council (NLC), which has much more limited competencies. The government has also deprived the NLC of its exclusive right to set the minimum wage, assigning this to itself in case the NLC is not able to reach agreement, effectively eliminating the tripartite nature of minimum wage setting. The third post-socialist government thus seems to be bound to terminate any meaningful element of corporatism, and the tripartite experiment seems to be on the verge of being exhausted.

Changing labour market institutions: state policy, labour legislation and collective bargaining

This section discusses three main groups of labour market institutions and the shape that they have taken in the period 1990–2000, within the context of the processes discussed in the previous section. I will deal first with employment and labour market policies, then with the role of labour legislation in regulating collective and individual employment relationships, and finally with collective bargaining. As mentioned in the introduction, the focus here is on the question of to what extent or in what way the labour market in Hungary departs from an ideal-type neo-classical labour market in which economic processes are solely co-ordinated by market mechanisms.

The role of the state in the labour market: employment and labour market policy

One of the central questions in the analysis of labour market regulation concerns the role of the state. This has many dimensions. One is the state's involvement in the definition of the legal environment in which labour market action takes place, a subject that is discussed in the next paragraph. Another is the state as an employer. With privatization high on the agenda, obviously this role has become less and less important during the 1990s. However, in 1999, some 40 per cent of the employed had the state as their employer, and this figure had not changed much since 1996 (Laky 2000: 29). This includes employees in public administration and large parts of education and health care, but also railway, bus and air transport companies as well as companies owned by the State Privatization and Assets Management Holding (Laky 2000). Clearly, its status as employer makes the state a crucial player in the labour market.

The state also plays an active role in the economy through employment and labour market policies. Two questions are of interest here. One is the extent to which employment objectives play a role in the definition of state policy. The other is the way that it deals with the problem of unemployment.

The importance of these questions is underlined by the fact that one of the most characteristic features of socio-economic developments in Hungary has been the enormous contraction of employment. In the first four years of the 1990s, in the context of an 18.2 per cent fall in GDP, no less than 30 per cent of employment disappeared, and employment continued to decline until 1997, when it was 33.4 per cent below the level of 1990. Indeed, the fall in employment in Hungary was the largest in the entire CEE region in the 1990s (see, for example, Nesporova 1999; UN–ECE 2000). The main part of those losing their job have left the labour market to become inactive, particularly older workers, frequently through early retirement arrangements. A much smaller share has become unemployed.

Now how has the state approached the problems arising from this enormous decline in employment? Undoubtedly, in the early 1990s, employment objectives were doomed to a marginal place in economic policy as a whole (Frey 1997: 110). The objective of full employment, so characteristic of state socialism, was deemed unrealistic and it was argued that in a capitalist system the government has no role in stimulating labour demand. In this context, the government's employment strategy elaborated in March 1993 stated the following:

> Even though the state takes a significant role in lessening labour market tensions, we have to make the people realise that there is no such thing as full employment in a market economy, since it could only be achieved via a massive direct and administrative state intervention, which is in total contradiction to the basic principle of a market economy, thus irreconcilable with its functioning.
>
> (quoted in Frey 1997: 80)

There was a quite genuine belief in the 'power of the market' and expectations were that employment declines, anyway considered as inevitable, would be compensated for very quickly by large numbers of new jobs emerging in the private sector. Only towards the end of the Antall government, when the employment situation had already deteriorated dramatically, did employment objectives become slowly included in general economic policy-making. Still, direct employment creation measures remained largely outside the scope of policy. Rather, the state would aim to promote employment indirectly, through the promotion of economic activity and investment. Policy would then include, for example, tax incentives, financial incentives forming part of its regional policy, or the adjustment of the educational system to labour demand.

Little would change in this respect under the Horn government. Under its 1995 austerity package it downsized public expenditure, limited social benefits and drastically cut real public-sector wages. The austerity package reflected an economic philosophy which gave absolute priority to macro-economic stabilization, the balancing of the budget and privatization as the goals of economic policy, instead of the stimulation of economic growth, employment growth and income maintenance. Again, it was mainly the market that was charged with the creation of employment, while the state assigned itself the role of creating what it deemed the proper conditions for the market to do so.

The Orbán government, in its first two years in office, basically continued on the path set by previous governments. A change of discourse took place in early 2000, when in his annual state-of-the-nation address Prime Minister Viktor Orbán claimed that in 1999 Hungary had definitely left behind its state-socialist past and had created a Western-type market-oriented society with a viable, modern and competitive economy (*Budapest Sun*, 4 February 2000). He announced that, although the government wanted to maintain a balanced budget, it also wanted to raise government expenditure to stimulate economic growth and increase wages. The political State Secretary of Finance went as far as to claim that the current government was dominated by neo-Keynesian economists who supported an active role for the state (*ECONEWS*, 21 September 2000). It remains to be seen, however, to what extent this really represents a new approach to economic and social policy. While there do seem to be certain new elements in the policy of the Orbán government, in particular the increase of state subsidies to stimulate investment, it above all represents a continuity of the core policies of the two previous governments, and remains focused primarily on supply-side measures.

One of the more direct ways that the state has been influencing labour market processes is through its labour market policies. These have included a series of labour market services and job assistance activities – varying from training for the unemployed, to support to unemployed persons in becoming entrepreneurs, to subsidised employment. Many of these policies had already been in operation since the early 1980s and were originally designed to foster employment creation in a low-unemployment situation (Sziráczki 1993, Frey 1997). In the early 1990s, labour market policies were then redesigned to cope with rapidly growing unemployment, and have shifted away from employment creation measures towards income protection measures (Sziráczki 1993). In 1989, the first unemployment benefit scheme was introduced, financed from the state budget. In 1991, the Employment Act introduced the unemployment insurance scheme, with a benefit period of maximum two years and a benefit rate starting at 70 per cent of the previous wage. Unemployment benefit criteria were then adjusted on several occasions – generally to the detriment of the unemployed as they mostly tightened the level of benefits, the duration of benefits and the respective eligibility conditions. By early 2001, the maximum duration was 270 days and the rate of benefits amounted to 65 per cent of the average earnings in the previous four years.

The changes in benefit criteria reflect both budgetary considerations and a changing attitude to the phenomenon of unemployment as such. While in the late 1980s and early 1990s unemployment was largely considered to be a transitory problem that would soon be solved by the dynamism inherent to capitalism, it soon became clear that unemployment was there to stay. A clear sign of this was persistent long-term unemployment. This led to the introduction, in 1992, of unemployment assistance for those who had exhausted their unemployment benefits and who lived in households with a very low income per head. Moreover, in general, there seemed to be a move away from legally guaranteed rights to unemployment benefits, with these being replaced by an increasing emphasis on workfare and employability. It is indeed telling that between 1990 and 2000, the percentage of registered unemployed persons receiving unemployment benefits plummeted from 77.6 per cent to 32.9 per cent, while the number of registered unemployed has fallen every year since 1992. Thus, the role of unemployment benefits in income protection has been gradually eroded over the years. Unemployment assistance reached its highest coverage in 1996 – no less than 44.3 per cent of registered unemployed – to decline to 27.2 per cent in 2000.

Labour market policies have also included a range of so-called active programmes, which are designed by the tripartite Labour Market Fund Steering Committee. More than 300,000 persons participated in one of these programmes in 1999 for one or more days, up from some 150,000 in 1992 (Laky 2000). Labour market training is one important programme, involving around one-quarter of the participants in 1999. Most other programmes create or subsidise employment in one way or another, including public benefit employment (e.g. communal services), wage subsidies, and subsidies to job-creating investments and school-leaver programmes. On average, in 1999, around 80,000 persons were employed with the support of these programmes. While this is indeed only a fraction of the working population (some 2 per cent), the absolute number of jobs is not unimportant, and neither should the contribution of such programmes in employing certain vulnerable groups be underestimated.

Summarizing, the state has a pivotal role in the labour market as an employer. In the competitive sphere, however, it has increasingly limited itself to the definition of conditions within which employment creation and the matching between labour demand and supply are governed by market mechanisms. Through privatization, it has diminished its presence in the competitive sphere, even though in certain sectors it remains strong. The state stimulates employment creation mainly indirectly, through investment subsidies or tax benefits for investors, and through regional development programmes. For the unemployed it provides unemployment benefits, but only to a small and declining share of them. Finally, through labour market policies it contributes, in co-operation with the social partners, to the creation or continuity of a small but important fraction of employment, attending to the needs of certain vulnerable groups.

Labour legislation

In 1989, following the Round Table Talks, changes to the Constitution produced the first main changes in labour law, as they included the right to strike and the freedom of association. In spite of the strong anti-unionism and enthusiasm for liberal values prevailing at the time, the Constitution preserved certain provisions protecting workers' rights, mainly because of the significant role of international standards and the drive to harmonise legal norms with those of the European Union (Horváth 1991, Kollonay Lehoczky and Ladó 1996: 112–13). The changes to the Constitution triggered a real shake-up of labour legislation, starting in 1989–91 with a series of new laws concerning labour relations, several amendments to the Labour Code and the close involvement of the Constitutional Court in labour regulation (Kollonay Lehoczky 1991, Kollonay Lehoczky and Ladó 1996, Tóth 1999). One of the major modifications to the Labour Code was the extension of the right to collective bargaining to the public services, and the introduction of the modality of multi-employer collective agreements and national-level framework agreements. The intention of the modification was to promote collective bargaining as such and to extend the coverage of collective agreements (sectoral, national) to small enterprises where no unions were present. At the same time, the Constitutional Court produced a series of rulings concerning the rights and position of trade unions. Initially, and in line with the initial stance of the first post-socialist government outlined earlier, it seemed out to 'demolish' trade unions as undesirable leftovers from the past, and failed to 'distinguish between the general function of trade unions and the role they performed under Communism' (Kollonay Lehoczky and Ladó 1996: 115). Only after a year or two did the Court become involved in a more balanced and creative attempt to reorient trade unionism instead of only attacking it (Kollonay Lehoczky and Ladó 1996, Tóth 1999).

Obviously, these two tendencies in the early 1990s, one being the promotion of collective bargaining and the other the attempts by the government and the Constitutional Court to weaken trade unions, were in contradiction with each other. While the legal framework for collective bargaining was developed further, the position of what should be one of its main actors, the unions, was under fire. As we will see later on, this is one of the reasons that collective bargaining in Hungary has never developed into the strong institution that it was supposed to be.

The legal regulation of collective and individual employment relations finally became more consolidated with the adoption of a new Labour Code. The new Labour Code, adopted in 1992 and amended on many occasions since, served two main objectives: first to deal with the persistent industrial relations crisis, and second to establish a new system of labour regulation in line with the new economic and political system and with Hungary's aspirations in terms of international institutional integration.[7] It put in place a new legal framework governing individual and collective labour relations.[8] The main characteristic of the Labour Code is that it provides a legal framework which defines a series of minimum standards concerning the minimum wage, regulations on wage supplements, working-time arrangements, holidays, dismissals, etc. Placing clear limits on statutory employee protection and the influence of the state, it leaves it up to the individual or collective contractual partners to determine the actual working conditions, and it foresees an important role for institutions representing employee interests. The latter are modelled largely on the German industrial relations system and consist of three channels of representation (Tóth 1999, see also Prugberger 1998): the Works Council; work-place-level unions; and multi-employer collective bargaining combined with the possibility of extension of collective agreements to non-participating enterprises in the same industry. In addition, the Code provides for interest representation at the national level through the National Labour Council (the successor of the Interest Reconciliation Council).

Employee protection thus depends to a large extent on the strength and legal rights of the institutions representing employee interests. This is where the Hungarian system deviates from its German counterpart, becoming a hybrid rather than a copy. Hungarian Works Councils are only equipped with very limited co-decision rights, and are above all consultative bodies with a minor role in the enterprise. Also, as discussed before, the unions are weak and the IRC (later NLC) has quite limited legal competencies.

As far as collective bargaining is concerned, legislation provides ample opportunities to conclude work-place and multi-employer collective agreements. Clearly, the legislator envisaged an important role for collective agreements, at the work-place level but even more so at the industrial and sectoral level. Collective bargaining is actually explicitly promoted in the Labour Code. In general, the principle of the Code is that collective agreements can only deviate from its stipulations in favour of the employee. However, many exceptions to this general rule allow work-place collective agreements to specify working conditions less favourable to the employee than those stipulated in the Code. Multi-employer collective agreements have received even greater possibilities for such deviations. Nevertheless, as we will see in the next section, both the scale and scope of work-place and collective agreements are limited, multi-employer collective agreements have hardly developed, and the instrument of extending collective agreements has hardly been used. This leaves the definition of working conditions in the competitive sphere principally to the individual employment contract concluded between the individual employee and employer – two parties between which a structural asymmetry of power exists.

How is this individual employment relationship regulated in the Labour Code? The general philosophy laid down in the Code is indeed – with only few exceptions – one of a set of minimum standards, leaving the definition of the content of the employment relationship to the partners in the employment contract, i.e. to the market. It provides high possibilities for flexibility, mostly for the benefit of the employer, and provides only minimal security to the employee. Here are a few examples.

The law provides the employer with ample flexibility to employ the employee according to his/her needs, also outside his/her official duties or by another employer. In terms of time flexibility the employer can design extremely flexible working-time schedules in which the employee works between four and twelve hours a day, as long as the average working hours are equal to the normal working hours. In addition, work can be organised according to two-shift, three-shift, split-shift or non-stop schedules, and the employer can order up to 144 hours of overtime yearly (or 200 hours if by company collective agreement and

300 hours if by multi-employer collective agreement). Fixed-term contracts can be concluded for a period up to five years, while trial periods can be fixed for a period up to three months by agreement between the parties or by collective agreement.

Exit from employment is regulated more extensively. In the case of ordinary dismissals, a legal notice period of between thirty and ninety days applies, depending on the length of employment, and this notice period can be extended to a maximum of one year by agreement between the parties or by collective agreement. The employer must justify the dismissal and the employee has the opportunity to defend him/herself, introducing a substantive element into dismissal protection. The employee is also entitled to severance pay, which depends on the length of employment. Ordinary dismissal is not possible in certain cases related to sickness, nursing, maternity and army services. Particular protective regulations apply to pregnant women and women on maternity leave.

As far as wages are concerned, regulations are largely limited to two subjects. One is that they establish a minimum wage, to be specified regularly by the NLC or, alternatively, by the government. Certain exemptions apply, in particular concerning minors, partially disabled or part-time workers. The other is that they define a series of supplements for overtime, shift work or work during holidays.

Hence, there are only a few legal constraints on the definition of the content of the individual employment relationship. Obviously, because of the inherent power asymmetry between employer and employee, this leaves the latter in quite a disadvantaged position. In theory this could be softened by the conclusion of collective agreements at various levels of the economy, and indeed the legislator has to a certain extent aimed to promote such practices. However, this has met with little success, as we will see in the next section.

Collective bargaining

Apart from state policy and labour legislation, a third mode of governance which potentially can play an important role in the regulation of labour markets is collective bargaining, as formalised in collective agreements. As mentioned earlier, Hungarian labour law does not pose any real obstacles to collective bargaining, with the exception of civil servants, who are not entitled to conclude collective agreements. Indeed, collective bargaining was given an important place in labour law. However, it has also been pointed out above that the position of trade unions and employers' organizations was weak during the 1990s. Thus, while on the one hand collective bargaining has been assigned an important role in industrial relations and has been made possible (and to some extent promoted) by the law, on the other hand the main actors in the process of collective bargaining have seen their position weakened substantially ('old' trade unions) or have never managed to conquer a position of strength (employers' organizations, 'new' trade unions).

A recent summary of the coverage and content of collective bargaining in Hungary is presented in Nacsa and Neumann (2001). They show that in 1999, single-employer collective agreements covered just over one million employees, with a coverage rate of 39.3 per cent in the case of enterprises with more than five employees in the non-budgetary sector and of 34.5 per cent in the case of the central and local public employees. The coverage of multi-employer agreements, the authors show, is much lower, 17.9 per cent for the non-budgetary sector and 0.3 per cent for public employees. Hence, the Hungarian system of collective bargaining is a decentralised system in which the enterprise level is of prime importance, while sectoral and national-level bargaining are only of secondary importance (Neumann 2000, Nacsa and Neumann 2001) and complementary in nature (Tóth 1997). Because of overlap between the two, then, total coverage of collective agreements is some 42.4 per cent of all employees. And although detailed information on collective agreements has only been available since 1998, it seems that coverage has not varied dramatically during the 1992–9 period.

Information on the content of collective agreements is scarce. Nacsa and Neumann (2001) present an overview of the issues regulated by single-employer collective provide in the non-budgetary sector, and show that 63 per cent of them (covering 79 per cent of employees covered by such collective agreements) include wage/payment stipulations. Thus, a third of collective agreements do not have any effect on wages. Only 24 per cent of the collective agreements (covering 47 per cent of the employees falling under collective agreements) include agreements on the increase of basic wages/salary; only 2 per cent have agreements on the increase of average earnings; and 22 per cent (covering 34 per cent of employees) include more or less detailed tariff agreements according to the categories of employees. Apart from this, the effect of collective bargaining on individual wages of comparable categories of employees is only between 3–5 per cent in the non-budgetary sector (Neumann 2001). Thus, in terms of wages the regulative function of collective agreements is limited both in coverage and scope, leaving the definition of wages to a large extent to the individual negotiations between employer and employee.

As far as other areas of regulation are concerned (those touching upon procedural rules, industrial relations, the settlement of labour disputes and the regulation of the employment relationship), Nacsa and Neumann (2001) find that in many instances collective agreements simply repeat the stipulations of the law. A good example is that all collective agreements deal with the probation period at hiring, but only 45 per cent include regulations different from the law. Also, in many cases collective agreements stretch the issue of employee protection, using the exemptions offered by the law. For example, in 82 per cent of them the upper limit of the number of overtime hours that the employer can order is increased. Thus, the authors conclude:

> the analysis of the issues regulated by collective agreements shows that the majority of enterprise collective agreements cannot be considered a

workplace-level regulation strictly prescribing the conditions of individual employment.

Conclusions

Since 1989, a process of dramatic institutional change has been ongoing in Hungary under the flag of the construction of capitalism. This project has been characterized by the superiority of political parties over other socio-political organizations, in particular the social partners. This originates in the dominance of the former in the Round Table talks and in their efforts to marginalize trade unions. It also follows from the latter's problem to deal with legitimacy problems, infighting and low membership. The new political élite started a programme of reform strongly influenced by the neo-liberal school of thought. In the early 1990s, its main mission became the state-led institutionalization of market governance of the economy. The various post-1989 governments have all produced their variations on the neo-liberal programme, and its narrow concept of reform has been gradually replaced by a more complex view. However, the main direction of reform has remained in place.

The main objective of this chapter has been to establish how, in this context, labour market institutions in general, and, in particular, state employment and labour market policy, labour legislation and collective bargaining, have developed, and to what extent they have constrained or facilitated market governance. As far as the direction of institutional change is concerned, in general terms we can conclude that market regulation is increasingly dominating the labour market, that the state is more and more shifting its activities towards the creation of the conditions to allow for market regulation, and that unions and employers' organizations have failed to achieve the prominence that they were expected to achieve in the early 1990s, and are increasingly marginalized from policy-making. Indeed, this is evidenced by a number of developments: employment creation is increasingly left to the market; the level, length and coverage of unemployment benefits have been scaled down; labour legislation only sets low minimum standards and allows for high levels of flexibility; and collective bargaining is very much decentralised, with collective agreements having only a small effect on wages and their content often not deviating from the minimum standards of the law or even stipulating regulations less beneficial to employees. Non-market institutions less and less constrain the definition of the content of the employment relationship and more and more leave it up to the individual employer and employee to establish employment conditions. This obviously leaves employers in a strongly advantageous position over employees, not least in terms of defining or imposing flexibility. Also, it is increasingly up to the individual to deal with problems related to unemployment. Thus, it seems that Hungarian labour market institutions are increasingly moving towards what is generally understood to be a deregulated and flexible model of labour market governance, including low levels of employee security.

As far as the direction of change is concerned, the above is indeed true. However, concluding that institutional change in Hungary has simply established market dominance would not do justice to the complex and multifaceted nature of Hungarian labour market institutions. This is because there are a number of elements that do constrain market regulation to some degree at the same time. This is first of all underlined by the simple fact that the state acts as employer for some 40 per cent of the working population. Also, through labour market policies, the state, together with the social partners, subsidises a small but important fraction of employment. In addition, labour legislation, minimal as it is, does put important constraints on dismissal and includes several regulations aimed at promoting collective bargaining. Finally, collective agreements cover some 42 per cent of employees. This is low in comparison with most Western countries (except for the US and the UK) but far from meaningless.

To conclude, then, if we conceive of labour market regulation as a mix of various types of regulation (the ones discussed in this paper being the market, the state and associations), institutional change in the 1990s has been mainly about the institutionalization of market regulation. However, the role of the state remains important, as a promoter and guarantor of market regulation, but also as an employer, legislator and policy-maker. The role of associations in policy-making has been diminishing steadily; however, trade unions and individual employers continue to play their part in decentralized collective bargaining.

Notes

1 See the extensive body of literature showing that (Western) capitalist systems have varied widely and persistently both in time and in space (Crouch and Streeck 1997, Hollingsworth and Boyer 1997, Regini 1999, Coates 2000, Hall and Soskice 2001).
2 The basic reference here would be the OECD's Jobs Study (1994), which has become one of the most influential advocates of market governance.
3 The contrasting of market governance with the other modes of co-ordination should not give the impression that somehow market governance is given preference or is understood to be the 'fundamental' or 'pure' mode of governance of capitalist systems. Rather, it constitutes both a methodological choice and an attempt to counter the often used (implicit) argument that capitalism equals market economy.
4 See Gil Eyal's analysis of the Czech Republic, where, as he argues, the historical agent bearing the 'spirit of capitalism' has been an unlikely coalition between dissident intellectuals and former Communist technocrats (Eyal 2000). The case of Hungary is similar, although not the same.
5 Indeed, there were diverse views on how to make capitalism in Hungary, both within the country and in the West. In Hungary in the early 1990s the term 'social market economy' was floated regularly, referring more to a Scandinavian or German type of capitalism than to the neo-liberal view based mainly on the US or the UK. Also, the ideas of Mitterand and Kohl on the best way to approach and manage change in CEE differed markedly from those of the international financial institutions and the neo-liberal community (e.g. de Boer-Ashworth 2000). However, both failed to have a decisive influence on policy-making.
6 Other institutions in which workers and employers participated in 1990–8 include: the tripartite Labour Market Fund Steering Committee established in 1997 to manage the Labour Market Fund, as well as county-level Labour Market Councils

concerned with the decentralised resources of the Fund; the County Development Councils managing decentralized regional development funds; the bipartite Self-Governments of Health and Pension Insurance; and the Interest Reconciliation Council for Budgetary Institutions.

7 When reference is made to specific passages of the Labour Code, this concerns the Code's text as it stood at 31 March 2001, unless otherwise indicated.

8 The Labour Code has general applicability to all spheres of activity. However, for the so-called competitive sphere it is the only law in this area, while two additional acts were adopted for the public sphere: the Public Servants Act, corresponding to public services (education, health services, etc.); and the Civil Servants Acts, concerning the state administration. These two Acts regulate labour relations in more detail than the Labour Code. Here the discussion focuses on the latter.

References

Andor, L. (2000) *Hungary on the Road to the European Union: Transition in Blue*, Westport, CT, and London: Praeger.

Bertola, G. (1990) 'Job security, employment and wages', *European Economic Review* 34(4): 851–86.

Bertola, G., Boeri, T. and Cazes, S. (2000) 'Employment protection in industrialised countries: the case for new indicators', *International Labour Review*, 139(1): 57–72.

Blokker, P. and Keune, M. (2001) *How the Global Discursive Context Influences Local Discursive and Policy Practices: a Comparative Analysis of Post-Socialist Hungary and Romania*, Paper presented at the Fourth Pan-European International Relations Conference, ECPR, 8–10 September, University of Kent at Canterbury.

Boda, D. and Neumann, L. (2000) 'Social dialogue in Hungary and its influence on accession', *Transfer, European Review of Labour and Research*, 6(3): 416–33.

Boer-Ashworth, E. de (2000) *The Global Political Economy and Post-1989 Change: the Place of the Central European Transition*, Basingstoke, Hampshire: Macmillan.

Boyer, R. (ed.) (1988) *The Search for Labour Market Flexibility: the European Economies in Transition*, Oxford: Clarendon Press.

Bozóki, A. (1993) 'Hungary's road to systemic change: the opposition round table', *East European Politics and Societies*, 7(2): 276–308.

Bruszt, L. (1995) 'Reforming alliances: labour, management and state bureaucracy in Hungary's economic transformation', in J. Hausner, B. Jessop and K. Nielsen (eds) *Strategic Choice and Path-dependency in Post-socialism: Institutional Dynamics in the Transformation Process*, Aldershot: Edward Elgar.

Buechtemann, C. (1991) *Employment Security and Labour Markets: Assumptions, International Evidence, and Theoretical Implications*, Discussion Paper, Berlin: WZB.

Coates, D. (2000) *Models of Capitalism: Growth and Stagnation in the Modern Era*, Cambridge: Polity Press.

Cox, T. and Mason, B. (2000) 'Trends and developments in East Central European industrial relations', *Industrial Relations Journal*, 31(2): 97–114.

Crouch, C. and Streeck, W. (eds) (1997) *Political Economy of Modern Capitalism: Mapping Convergence and Diversity*, London/Thousand Oaks/New Delhi: Sage.

Esping-Andersen, G. and Regini, M. (eds) (2000) *Why Deregulate Labour Markets?*, Oxford and New York: Oxford University Press.

Eyal, G. (2000) 'Anti-politics and the spirit of capitalism: dissidents, monetarists, and the Czech transition to capitalism', *Theory and Society*, 29: 49–92.

Eyal, G., Szelényi, I. and Townsley, E. (1998) *Making Capitalism without Capitalists: the New Ruling Elites in Eastern Europe*, Londen/New York: Verso.

Frey, M. (1997) 'Employment policies and programmes in Hungary', in M. Godfrey and P. Richards (eds) *Employment Policies and Programmes in Central and Eastern Europe*, Geneva: ILO.

Girndt, R. (1996) 'Hungary's trade unions: division and decline', *Labour Focus on Eastern Europe*, 55, Autumn: 47–58.

—— (2001) 'Ten years of trade union co-operation', *South-East Europe Review for Labour and Social Affairs, Special Issue Hungary*, pp. 9–31.

Hall, P. and Soskice, D. (eds) (2001) *Varieties of Capitalism: the Institutional Foundations of Comparative Advantage*, Oxford: Oxford University Press.

Hausner, J., Jessop, B. and Nielsen, K. (eds) (1995) *Strategic Choice and Path-dependency in Post-socialism: Institutional Dynamics in the Transformation Process*, Aldershot: Edward Elgar.

Héthy, L. (1995) 'Tripartism in public policy formulation in Hungary', in R. Kyloh (ed.) *Tripartism on Trial: Tripartite Consultations and Negotiations in Central and Eastern Europe*, Budapest: ILO–CEET.

—— (1999) 'Hungary's tripartism – its past ten years and its future prospects', *South-East Europe Review for Labour and Social Affairs, Special Issue: the 10th Anniversary of the Fall of the Berlin Wall*, pp. 51–68.

—— (2001) 'Social dialogue in Hungary: its rise and decline', *South-East Europe Review for Labour and Social Affairs, Special Issue: Hungary*, pp. 55–70.

Hollingsworth, J. R. and Boyer, R. (eds) (1997) *Contemporary Capitalism: the Embeddedness of Institutions*, Cambridge: Cambridge University Press.

Horváth, I. (1991) 'The First Strike Law in Hungary', *International Journal of Comparative Labour Law and Industrial Relations*, 7: 223–31.

ILO–CEET (1997) *Hungary: Employment and Sustainable Livelihoods*, Budapest: ILO–CEET.

Keune, M. (2001) 'Local development, institutions and conflicts in post-socialist Hungary: an overview', in M. Keune and J. Nemes Nagy (eds) *Local Development, Institutions and Conflicts in Post-Socialist Hungary*, Budapest: ILO.

Kollonay Lehoczky, C. (1991) 'The changing face of labour law in Hungary', *The International Journal of Comparative Labour Law and Industrial Relations*, 7: 57–70.

Kollonay Lehoczky, C. and Ladó, M. (1996) 'Hungary', in H. Carabelli and S. Sciarra (eds) *Nuovi Modelli di Diritto Sindacale Nell'Europa Centrale. Repubbliche Ceca e Slovacca, Ungheria, Polonia*, Milan: Giuffrè Editore.

Laky, T. (2000) *Labour Market Report 2000: Main Trends in Labour Market Demand and Supply*, Budapest: National Centre for Labour Research and Methodology.

Morgan, J. (1996) *Employment Protection and Labour Demand in Europe*, Discussion Paper No. 108, London: NIESR.

Nacsa, B. and Neumann, L. (2001) *The System of Collective Bargaining in Hungary*, Paper presented at the National ILO Council of Hungary and ILO–CEET Conference on Promotion of Collective Agreements and the Question of Representativeness in Hungary in the Light of the Experience of EU Countries, Budapest, 20–1 September 2001.

Nesporova, A. (1999) *Employment and Labour Market Policies in Transition Economies*, Geneva: ILO.

Neumann, L. (2000) 'Decentralised collective bargaining in Hungary', *International Journal of Comparative Labour Law and Industrial Relations*, 16(2): 113–28.

—— (2001) 'Does Decentralised Collective Bargaining Have Any Impact on the Labour Market in Hungary? (Some New Statistical Evidence)', Unpublished Paper.

OECD (1994) *The OECD Jobs Study*, Paris: OECD.

Orenstein, M. (1998) 'A genealogy of communist successor parties in East Central Europe and the determinants of their success', *East European Politics and Societies*, 12(3): 472–99.

Pollert, A. (ed.) (1991) *Farewell to Flexibility?*, Oxford: Basil Blackwell.

Prugberger, T. (1998) 'Major features of the development of Hungarian labour law after the political transition', *South-East Europe Review for Labour and Social Affairs*, 3: 103–15.

Regini, M. (1999) *Between De-Regulation and Social Pacts: the Responses of European Economies to Globalisation*, Working Paper 1999/133, Madrid: Juan March Institute.

Sajó, A. (1996) 'The Roundtable Talks in Hungary', in J. Elster (ed.) *The Roundtable Talks and the Breakdown of Communism*, Chicago and London: University of Chicago Press.

Schömann, K., Rogowski, R. and Kruppe, T. (1998) *Labour Market Efficiency in the European Union: Employment Protection and Fixed-Term Contracts*, London/New York: Routledge.

Standing, G. (1999) *Global Labour Flexibility: Seeking Distributive Justice*, Basingstoke, Hampshire: Macmillan.

Stark, D. and Bruszt, L. (1998) *Post-Socialist Pathways: Transforming Policy and Property in East Central Europe*, Cambridge: Cambridge University Press.

Sziracki, G. (1993) 'Hungary: labour market trends and policies', in G. Fischer and G. Standing (eds) *Structural Change in Central and Eastern Europe: Labour Market and Social Policy Implications*, Paris: OECD.

Tóth, A. (1997) 'The role of multi-employer collective agreements in regulating terms and conditions of employment in Hungary', *Transfer, European Review of Labour and Research*, 3(2): 329–56.

—— (1999) 'The state of trade unions in Hungary', *Emergo: Journal of Transforming Economies and Societies*, 6(3): 16–32.

—— (2000) 'Indecision Rules (Nothing Could Be Settled. Everything Was Decided by Default). Trade Unions at The Roundtable Talks', Unpublished Paper.

UN–ECE (2000) *Economic Survey of Europe 2000*, New York and Geneva: United Nations.

5 Continuity in change

Social consequences of economic reform in Romania

Paul Blokker

Introduction

The demise of the Communist systems in Eastern Europe and their integration into wider global structures has enabled analysis of these former Communist countries in the context of the experience of other, non-Communist countries. The former Communist countries have been widely expected to follow patterns already set out (mainly) by Western countries. However, whereas the incorporation of the countries in Central and Eastern Europe (CEE) in the global capitalist system seems to be inevitable, the assumption that social, political and economic change will directly follow past Western experiences is less plausible.

Dominant approaches towards social change in CEE largely assume the feasibility of the outright adoption of a particular version of modern capitalism by the former Communist countries. In this the theories take a normative and widely negative approach towards the Communist past, and promote strategies of economic reform that should rid these countries of Communist structures and attitudes. In the form of the so-called triptych of economic reform – privatization, liberalization, and stabilization – the post-Communist governments should implement a version of capitalism that is characterised by a loss of faith in the capacity of political institutions to shape social reality and that instead offers markets as solutions for social problems. Alternatives to such a vision of modern society are barely considered in the light of the failure of 'true socialism' in the East and the demise of the welfare state in the West.

Here, however, I will argue for a more interpretative approach in my case study of Romania. I will do this in two ways: first of all, I place the post-1989 experiences in a socio-political historical context, and second, I will focus on the discourse and practice of political élites. The historical context helps us to understand the socio-political structure and the outlook of important actors *after* 1989. The focus on the actions of élites and their justifications for these actions serves both to emphasize the importance of agency in social change in Eastern Europe and to pinpoint the national varieties of dealing with post-Communist reality. Thus, my point of departure is the *variety* of experiences with capitalism in post-Communist CEE. This means that I will analyse current transformations in concomitance with both (historical) national specificities and the present international environment, regarding the unwillingness of political élites to adopt neo-liberal policies not foremost as political obstructionism of 'reactionary' forces, but rather as the outcome of particular national visions and circumstances.

Élite strategies towards economic reform in Eastern Europe are to be analysed from a perspective which involves: first, the current global context, in which neo-liberal visions on economic reform dominate (which also means that local alternative perceptions of economic reform have to be formulated *in opposition to* mainstream neo-liberal visions); second, the (historically developed) domestic socio-political structure; and, third, social consequences and resulting protests to economic reforms as such. Élites, being the major political actors in the transformation processes in Eastern Europe, in their political strategies are thus circumscribed by both internal and external factors. However, they do have some room for manoeuvre.

Élites have two major ideal-typical options in economic policy-making: first, the option of adopting, rather straightforwardly, a neo-liberal discourse and policy in national policy-making (discourse and/or policy then remains within the limits set by international context), and second, the rejection of the internationally dominant visions of reform, for instance through populism, which could ultimately mean the rejection of the neo-liberal package and need for integration in world markets. The first 'option', the downright adoption of neo-liberal policies, would *grosso modo* mean the implementation of the triptych of privatization–stabilization–liberalization and integration into the international economy. In reality, the majority of policy measures of such an approach to reform are aimed at diminishing the role of the state in the economy. However, a reduction of the state's influence creates several socio-economic problems in a country such as Romania. Privatization of state-owned companies necessarily leads to a massive loss of jobs, at least in the short run. As these jobs are not always replaced in a new private sector or in restructured former state firms, this can lead to increasing claims on social security, or exit from the labour market. In addition, the social-security system in itself is under pressure, because of the perceived need for stabilization of the state budget.

The growing importance of foreign companies and capital, as a result of the opening up and liberalization of the domestic economy, can result in a situation in which certain professional workers, for instance those that are employed in international firms, have relatively high wages and fairly good job security, whereas others increasingly seek safety in 'non-economic' activities such as subsistence farming. In short, in the Eastern European societies in which the state has historically played a hugely important role, a severe and rigid trimming down of the state's role is not always the most obvious answer to the socio-economic problems at hand. This then is one of the reasons that local political élites might try to find an alternative to the internationally dominant view. This would then be the second option, i.e. the development of a national alternative to neo-liberal reforms, which might take several forms. It might be articulated in 'Third Way' approaches that seek to offer state support for the social consequences of reform, as for instance has happened in Romania. More extreme versions of alternatives to the globally dominant reform model might be neo-Communism, authoritarianism and populism. Analytically speaking, however, it is important to keep the options open for other, 'milder' and more hybrid forms of alternative economic reform models. In reality, we indeed find elements of both ideal-typical options in the different reform programmes adopted by Eastern European élites after 1989.

Some theoretical considerations

The swift demise of Communism as a real and viable alternative to the capitalist development model, resulting from the changes in the Soviet Union and Eastern Europe, meant the apparent victory of (a particular kind of) capitalism throughout the world. This is particularly visible in the way that policy-makers and the academic world analyse the changes as such and prescribe policies to be implemented in order to ensure a smooth transition process for the countries concerned. Debates are dominated by various strands of what we could call (neo-) modernization approaches (Altvater 1998), which partially fall back on the modernization approaches of the 1940s and 1950s. Such approaches see the answer to major social problems such as underdevelopment and poverty mainly in terms of transformation and adaptation of the former socialist societies to a Western type of capitalist economy. The countries concerned need to adopt Western political, economic, legal and financial institutions and have to rearrange their state structures and budgets according to Western norms. In short, they have to transform their Communist societies into the contemporary dominant representation of Western capitalist and democratic society.

Prior to 1989, Communism was perceived – almost without exception – as a viable and stable system, and its sudden collapse could not be accounted for in any theoretical way. Even the totalitarianism approach, which regarded Soviet societies as ultimately unsustainable, perceived the same societies as completely centralised and its masses as completely atomised and therefore incapable of action, as a result of which radical change was not deemed very likely (von Beyme 1994, Müller 1997).

Whereas the downfall of the Communist systems proved the – partially ideological – insistence on the stability of the Communist project as ultimately wrong, the post-1989 debate on change in Eastern Europe largely ignores the legacies of that same Communist system. Before 1989, the institutions of the Communist states were perceived as bastions of power, not least the extremely hierarchical Communist Party which in the end presided over every aspect of social life. After 1989, however, the same institutions have been brushed aside as mere rubble inhibiting the establishment of a true 'modern' society, namely the Western experience of a modern state. Thus, shock therapies – triple adjustment programmes of privatization, price liberalization and stabilization – are promoted that should do away with the remnants of the past order, and create as soon as possible a situation in which the new democratic market economies can arise with a clean slate.[1] Therefore the notion of Communism as an evil order, fed by totalitarianism, has re-emerged, and is now conveniently supplemented by neo-liberal ideas that promote the complete destruction of the old order, so that the markets can spontaneously create a new one. The triple package of a shock therapy can then be executed and will result in a Western type of society (Burawoy and Verdery 1999: 5). The meagre results of these shock therapies are then interpreted as either signs of success (if one promotes the idea that post-socialist countries first have to go through a 'valley of tears' to emerge as stable and prosperous societies); as the consequence of bad management by international agencies such as the IMF and the World Bank; or, alternatively, form the outcomes of obstructionist behaviour by members of the old Communist *nomenklatura* (Burawoy and Verdery 1999).

The almost complete ideological defeat of Communist or socialist ideas after 1989 did not only lead to an overwhelming ignorance of what these systems actually entailed and how past changes affect current attempts at constructing societies, but it also undermined the idea of different ways of reaching a modern society (von Beyme 1994). So Barrington Moore's classical thesis that fascism and Communism represented alternative roads to modern societies was easily forgotten with the collapse of true socialism. Even more thoroughly, the triumph of the Western model as the only and universal one was widely recognized, while denying the status of this modernization paradigm as a new 'grand narrative'.

From the partial revival of modernizationist, theoretical ideas, as well as ideas of totalitarianism, follow approaches that largely disclaim any 'modern' aspects to the socialist experiments and push research towards normative and policy-oriented approaches that analyse current developments in the light of the future, that is to say in the context of a Western model of society. Taking the larger debate about Eastern Europe, the theorization of the changes has been dominated by what has been termed 'transitology', including descriptive as well as prescriptive approaches, and which shares some basic premises:

> the Soviet model is seen as having failed in competition with the west, and its legacy is reducible to after-effects: dysfunctional patterns of development and mentalities unadapted to the market continue to obstruct the progress of transformation. The victorious western model has, by the same token, become a blueprint for the future, and the agenda of the transition can be defined in terms of measures and policies which would bring the countries in question closer to this really existing ideal ... The most fundamental – albeit often latent – premise of transitology is that the current western constellation of capitalism, democracy, and the nation-state (allowing for some differences of opinion on the relative weight of the last factor) represents a universal and definitive model on its way to global ascendancy.
>
> (Arnason 2000)

Not only in the theoretical debate are these premises to be found in different guises, but also in the policy-making world. Assessments of the transformation of the countries concerned are made by the European Union (EU), by the European Bank for Reconstruction and Development (EBRD), by the Economic Commission for Europe of the United Nations (ECE/UN), by major rating agencies who assess countries' credit-worthiness and investor-friendliness, by the academic world itself, etc.[2] All these analyses accrue from the idea that these countries are located on a specific point of a continuum which consists of a socialist centrally planned economy on the one hand and a capitalist democratic society on the other. Assessments are made of where these countries are situated now, and how much is to be done to arrive at that final point, the Western democratic and capitalist society.

> Jeffrey Sachs and other *simpliste* expositors of the 'big bang' approach to transition seem to be advocating a rerun of Rostow's earlier 'take-off' theory. Like that earlier species of modernization idea, this new monetarist modernism throws utterly to the winds concerns of social solidarity and citizenship, let alone any sense of historical specificity
>
> (Alexander 1995: 44).

In this kind of reasoning, social change begets the nature of a *process* in which action is largely absent or primarily negatively assessed. For instance, the negative results of applied shock therapies in CEE have often been interpreted as consequences of obstructionist behaviour by members of the old *nōmenklātūra*. Any form of change is viewed in the light of some vague ideal-type of Western society, and the failure by local élites to implement reform on the basis of the triptych of privatization, liberalization, stabilization and international integration is seen simply as obstruction to change.

As opposed to the overwhelmingly negative accounts of the Communist systems of the post-1989 period,[3] prior to the by now seemingly self-evident downfall of Communism in Eastern Europe many theorists regarded Communism as an alternative strategy for constructing a modern society. Barrington Moore's study is the most well-known analysis of 'three distinct paths to modernity', in which he identifies two alternatives to the Western path of modernization, the Communist and the fascist one. Apart from various criticisms of his approach – ranging from the inability of avoiding an evolutionary approach (ignoring inter-societal relationships), to disregarding the role of ideology – the notion of different possible routes to a modern society as well as the acknowledgement of the modern elements of the Communist projects is present in his work. Within the field of sociological theory there were many others who regarded the Soviet world as a competing alternative form of society to Western capitalism (Müller 1997).

Outside the academic world, the Communist model provided many countries searching for a model of modernization with an alternative to Western capitalism. After the collapse of the socialist world, visions of alternatives to Western ideas of societal arrangements were conveniently argued away in the light of neo-classical economics, neo-liberal ideas and triumphant Western democratic models. The demise of the socialist system is still largely attributed to contradictions within the system itself. Although internal contradictions should be taken into account – for instance, the slow demise of legitimization as a result of the poor performance of the Communist economies and the growing informal sectors – this should not lead us to a homogenization of the Communist system and the experiences of the various countries. The theoretical rejection of alternatives to the Western model, as well as the existence of modern features of the Communist societies, however, leads not only to the negation of essential differences within and between the Eastern European countries (Burawoy 1992), but at the same time to a homogenization and simplification of the Western capitalist experiences.

The 'transfer of institutions', and especially the creation of a 'civil society' in every single post-socialist country, is supposed to lead to both political and economic structures that closely resemble Western ones, i.e. it is presumed that:

> transition is a relatively unproblematic implementation of a set of policies involving economic liberalization and marketization alongside democratization, enabling the creation of a market economy and a liberal polity.
>
> (Pickles and Smith 1998: 1)

'The challenge then', however, 'is to negotiate ways in which we can understand the *diversity of forms* of transition'. The failure to provide an insightful account of the different experiences in Eastern Europe, both before and after 1989, leads to a rather 'restricted understanding of social change' (Burawoy 1992: 774). As Müller (1995: 272) notes:

> [w]ithout too much exaggeration, one may discern a convenient merger between economic theory, political science and sociology: neo-classical economists argue on the basis of functional requirements of effective markets; political scientists cite the imperatives of Western-style democracy; sociologists refer to the institutional requisites for functioning markets. All this makes sense in discussion of what East European societies do *not* have. The real question, however, is how rudimentary markets with fragile democracies can operate in times of lost orientation and in an environment of delegitimized institutions. And the kind of dynamics that this triggers.

Reintroducing history and agency

Despite a pervasive disregard for history in many analyses of post-1989 Eastern Europe, particular theories – growing in importance within the field – take as their direct starting point the historical nature of the current transformations. An important theory in this respect is the path-dependency approach, which does not regard the transformation as basically 'a one-way process of change from one hegemonic system to another' (Pickles and Smith 1998: 1). Rather, current social change is seen as directly bound up with old social relations and institutions and therefore can only be understood in a historical way. The presentation of social change as merely a process of 'catching up' by adopting the right institutions is rejected (Pickles and Smith 1998, Burawoy and Verdery 1999, Arnason 2000). Indeed, path-dependency theory sees 'political economic transformation' as an 'evolutionary and path-dependent process ... based upon institutionalised forms of learning and struggles over pathways that emerge out of the intersection of old and new' (Pickles and Smith 1998: 15). In other words, path-dependency theory claims that current and future developments can only be fully understood if the past is reflected on, so that the constraints and confinements as well as possibilities for current transitions become clear (see, for instance, Chavance and Magnin 1997, some of the chapters in Pickles and Smith 1998, Stark and Bruszt 1998).

An important criticism of path-dependency could be that it underestimates the role of agency and strategic choice (Blokker and Keune 2001). An approach that builds on path-dependency theory but at the same time introduces the element of agency and its relation to structure is élite theory. One of the continuities in Eastern Europe is that the current renewed attempts at modernization in Eastern Europe are to an important extent projects of élites, i.e. relatively small groups of individuals in society who are capable of initiating projects for social change (Higley *et al.* 1998: 1). Élite theory, such as that developed by Ivan Szelenyi and others, historicises the role of élites in introducing modernization in Eastern Europe. They contend that in particular moments in history, in different societal contexts, *different* constellations of actors play the role of pioneers of a new society. Following Szelenyi, while admitting that a certain form of a capitalist society is in the making (without *a priori* excluding other types of outcomes), it is possible to perceive the appearance of different kinds of capitalism, although not always initiated by the same kind of actors. Indeed, Szelenyi *et al.* try to 'contrast different types of capitalisms to explore the range of possible actors and institutions that can sustain a functioning capitalist system' (Eyal *et al.* 1998: 3). Whereas in Central Europe contemporary modernization might be mostly a project of political élites in concordance with managerial élites, in Russia and SE Europe different constellations might be at work. Such an analysis of the changes in Eastern Europe after 1989 is ultimately a rejection of modernization being merely a repetition of earlier changes in other societies, notably Western ones. This means that there are various pathways initiated by different sets of actors, leading to a modern society. Indeed, Eyal *et al.* (1998)

> observe that Central European intellectuals have been attracted to various ambitious historical projects to reshape their societies, and we argue that whatever else may be, the power bloc that rules contemporary post-communism is heir to these projects.
>
> (Eyal *et al.* 1998: 11)

Variety is then shaped by the historical context of an attempt at modernization, the actors involved, their capacities and bases of power, and the ideas that they use to justify their attempts.

One element is however still lacking in élite theory dealing with the making of post-socialist societies, i.e. the external context in which changes take place (Blokker and Keune 2001). If we acknowledge that current élite strategies are based on earlier local experiences with modernity, and that these earlier experiences were inspired and influenced by developments elsewhere, notably in Western Europe, we should incorporate the contemporary meaning of modernization in the analysis. As Müller (1995: 273) has rightly remarked, 'modernization' as a sociological concept, but also as a model for policy-makers, has undergone paradigmatic shifts in its short history. Whereas the classical modernizationists (and policy-makers) based their ideas of modernization and modern society on the models of the post-war Keynesian welfare states, since then the Western models (far from being homogeneous themselves) have changed enormously. In the 1980s, the idea emerged of a modernization that combines a faith in international integration with a loss of faith in the capacity of political institutions to construct social life. A conceptual shift from the level of the state to the level of 'civil society' took place, after 1989 regarded as particularly useful in countries in which the state seemed to be completely de-legitimized. To grasp the significance of a changed global paradigm for élites seeking to create new societies in Eastern Europe, we need to introduce the global context as an important factor in the analysis. Anyhow, the introduction of the global context not only entails the acknowledgement of the *direct* influence of international institutions and the European Union on national discourses and policies. It also means a consideration of the role of local élites themselves in using, diffusing and justifying their actions through the 'appropriation' of external models and ideas. On the 'receiving end', models and ideas are

> sought after and integrated because they meet the strategic needs of the importing actors, and thus result from individual choices guided by incentives and rewards, hopes and expectations.

> (Badie 2000: 93)

In the following account of Romania I will focus on the discourses and practices of political élites pursuing strategies of (economic) modernization. The primary importance of *political* élites in post-1989 Romania is a direct result of, first, the regime change, in which the former Communist bureaucracy took over power, and, second, the oppression of other social actors by Ceauşescu, leading to a rather 'empty' power arena at the beginning of the 1990s. On a discursive level, these political élites partly build on historical experiences with modernity, articulated through certain kinds of discourses, and partly on elements derived from the internationally dominant neo-liberal discourse. In addition, their strategies are circumscribed by the direct influence of international actors, domestic power struggles and social protests against reforms.

Reform discourse and policy in post-Communist Romania[4]

Absence of a reform debate

The embracing of Western political and economic ideas by intellectuals and politicians and to a certain extent by the population in many countries in CEE after 1989 could hardly be discerned in post-Communist Romania. The rather ambiguous relationship to Western ideas in Romania was an outcome of the extreme suppression of intellectuals and the peculiar kind of 'national Communism' during Communist times, but also the result of a long-standing tradition of critique on Western modernity.

In the 1960s Romania was touched, just as other countries in the region, by the wave of post-Stalinist liberalization of the cultural, political and economic spheres of society, and the increasing influence of intellectuals, especially technocrats, in political and economic life. However, this liberalising trend was quickly undone at the beginning of the 1970s. Intellectual life was firmly subordinated to the party ideology as a result of Ceauşescu's own 'cultural revolution'. After a period of 'liberalization from above' from 1965 to 1971 (Tismăneanu 1993), political expressions were only allowed when underwriting the official nationalist ideology, a vocation which was picked up by 'court poets' (for instance Adrian Păunescu, Corneliu Vadim Tudor), hailing Ceauşescu's glory. The opposition therefore found its only mode of expression in 'resistance through aesthetics' (Culic 1999), which in reality led to an escape of intellectuals from political life. Repression was not limited to intellectual life, however. Particularly after the late 1970s, political cadres were frequently moved from one political post to another in a so-called rotation policy. In this way, failures of the Ceauşescu regime were attributed to the bureaucracy, which was blamed for disastrous economic policies and whose members were concomitantly reassigned to other posts (Nelson 1995: 204). More importantly perhaps, in this way the development of any lasting coalition against the heavily centralised regime of Ceauşescu was prevented. This practice was particularly prevalent in the economic ministries (Nelson 1995: 204). Societal organizations were equally impotent in influencing or even protesting against Ceauşescu's policies. For instance, only a single trade union existed, the General Trade Union Confederation of Romania, which was under the aegis of the Romanian Communist Party, and functioned mainly as an instrument to keep industrial labour from any action against the regime, through a 'total penetration of labour organizations, denying to workers any autonomous voice for collective action' (Nelson 1988: 39).

The official ideology of the regime was a Stalinist fascination with huge industrial projects, in concordance with the cult of personality of Ceauşescu. Mass production in huge industrial sites (particularly machine building, the petrochemical and steel industries) was the focus of the transformation of the Romanian economy. In the 1960s and 1970s, this economic policy actually seemed to work as Romania achieved extraordinary growth rates and 'socio-economic indicators usually selected to gauge "development", and "modernization" showed that Romania was rapidly becoming industrialized, urbanized, better educated and healthier' (Nelson 1995: 199). Although the irrationality of Stalinist economics eventually led to an economic, social and environmental disaster and helped to build up a huge foreign debt, Ceauşescu did not interpret these enormous failures as the outcome of his policies. Rather he blamed the bureaucracy, and – eventually – the foreign debt, and thus the outside world, for the economic crisis (Nelson 1995). A direct and organized opposition to the rather distorted model of development did not come about because of the atomization and subordination of intellectuals and the rotation of political cadres. The idea that the declining performance of 'really existing socialism' could be saved by the injection of Western elements remained more than taboo in Romania (Gabanyi 2000: 422–7). In reality, the more the outside Communist world emphasised the need for reform, the more Ceauşescu clung to old-fashioned Stalinist ideas, culminating in forced industrialization and the drive for autarchy. Additionally, control over state and society was in the hands of a very small oligarchic élite around Ceauşescu, which made effective opposition even more difficult (Gabanyi 1998).

All this meant that, first of all, after the regime change, Romanian intellectual life as well as other actors in Romanian society were not ready to present an organised and decisive model of change for Romanian society. Second, a strong tradition of intellectual debate between Westernisers and traditionalists (or 'nationalists', in the sense that they promote a national development path), resulted in the continuing viability of strands of thought that rejected or at least criticised Western ideas. Instead of a renunciation of the Communist past and an unreserved embrace of the West, ephemeral alternatives based on the Romanian 'nation' continue to be influential. Although not necessarily posing an alternative to the current order, versions of such ideologies do influence the political discourses and programmes, even of the main political parties. Additionally, and more importantly, major political parties in the post-1989 political landscape make use of appeals to the Romanian nation and national solidarity for reasons of particularism and political legitimacy. Such was the case, for instance, with the National Salvation Front, the party that took over political power after the December revolution, courting the state-sector employees as their electoral base by referring to 'Third Way' approaches to economic change, social stability and national solidarity, in this way – at least rhetorically – rejecting models for change coming from the West.

Third, the élitist nature of the intellectuals, their lack of pragmatism and inexperience with political life (stemming from their role in Communist times), led to a quick withdrawal of intellectuals from politics in the early 1990s. Despite attempts by individual intellectuals to participate in politics, dizappointment with power politics resulted in the resignation of many of them, leading once again to their passivity in political matters (Culic 1999, Mungiu-Pippidi 1999).

Romania's ambiguous attitude towards the West

After the 'revolution' of December 1989, political power was concentrated in the hands of the former Communist élite, also known as the *nomenklatura*. The elimination of the Ceauşescus led to a shift of power from the closed circle around the 'conducator' to a second level of the state bureaucracy. The extremely centralised nature of the Communist regime and the subjection of both lower levels of the state bureaucracy and potentially autonomous actors – such as intellectuals – to the regime, left power literally in the hands of the former 'state class'. Many intellectuals initially participated in politics, some by becoming members of the ruling party and others by opposing the new political order. However, within a few years of the 'revolution' the former had turned their backs to the ruling party, disillusioned by power politics, whereas the latter were increasingly marginalized, unable to bridge the gap between élitist discussion and the population at large. Moreover, the post-Communists directly and effectively challenged their 'claims of the truth'.

Another set of actors that at least hypothetically represented power, and thus some kind of challenge to the new regime, was the trade unions. Although the unions, partly as a reaction to the strong centralization of the single trade union during Communist times, have proliferated in the post-Communist era, and labour demands have had considerable influence on short-term policy-making, unions have not posed a major challenge to the primacy of politics in social change. According to Kideckel, the combination of increased politicization of and competition between unions has rendered their collective power quite ineffective, even if the frequent and sometimes violent strikes have given labour the image of being powerful (Kideckel 1999: 113).

In this light, the claim of Communist *continuity* in the Romanian case is not wholly unjustified. Indeed, former Communists stayed in power, first, by using their political positions and networks and, second, through a policy aiming at the reproduction of that power. However, continuity in political power and policy-making in the early 1990s should not be interpreted purely as the lack of change and as the continuation of the Communist project. First of all, the regional and international context had changed completely, calling for some kind of reaction also from the Romanian political élites. Second, the post-Communist party that ruled Romania from 1990 until the end of 1996 was, in reality, an amalgamation of different interests, among which there was no consensus whatsoever on the reform path to take after 1989, although outwardly in some ways it seemed to be a homogeneous bloc of post-Communists.[5] Third, the former Communists did not act out of nostalgia for the Communist past and did not set out to restore the old order, but were much more interested in staying in power as such, making it doubtful to characterise the first years of the 1990s as 'post-communist communism' (Verdery and Kligman 1992).

Political strategies aiming at power preservation were, among other things, visible in the reform policies, which were designed to prevent rapid change and ultimately led to the rather dubious transfer of state property into private hands.

This was particularly clear in privatization policies that aimed mostly at the privatization of small and medium-sized companies, leaving the huge state enterprises (the main part of the economy) largely untouched. In the early 1990s, the chosen model of privatization, i.e. case-by-case privatization instead of mass privatization, led to a relatively slow privatization process (van Frausum *et al.* 1994). The relative slowness and mode of privatization facilitated the informal appropriation of state property by private interests (Brucan 1998, Gabanyi 1998). At the same time, however, political strategies were visible that seem to have originated from quite different intentions, such as the neo-liberal policies initiated by the first prime minister, Petre Roman.

In fact, throughout the 1990s, political discourse and policy-making reflected the conflictual nature of Romanian politics, both within the political arena and in the state–society relationship. Indeed, in spite of their dominant role in socio-political change, political élites have not been omnipotent and have been influenced and constrained in their modernising strategies by:

1   the domestic socio-political structure, reflected in the various intra- and inter-party conflicts;
2   the social consequences of reform policies and general economic change, evoking various forms of social protest, most importantly labour action; and
3   the international environment, expressed in the globally dominant economic discourse, roughly consisting of ideas found in neo-classical economics and the globalization narrative, and actively promoted by international institutions such as the IMF and the World Bank, and by the European Union (EU) as well as by a large part of the international academic community.

In the following account of post-1989 politics in Romania, I will outline the economic policies of the various governments in the light of the above-mentioned influences and constraints. It shows that the reform policies, as promoted by international institutions, gained increasing importance throughout the first half of the 1990s. This tendency was not so much the result of direct external pressure on Romanian political élites, but was the outcome of the complex interaction between divided political élites and their inability to formulate a coherent alternative to the global paradigm.

Political conflicts and social protests (1990–6)

The most important political actor in the early 1990s was the so-called National Salvation Front (NSF). Initially this successor to the Romanian Communist Party had the status of a provisional government, but, to the surprise of many, it turned itself into a political party and won the first elections in May 1990. The NSF basically consisted of forces very closely related to the de-legitimized regime of Ceauşescu. In fact, it was formed mainly by the old bureaucracy, which had been a mere extension of Ceauşescu's power, but which presented itself as the true leader of change (Tismăneanu 1993). The NSF tried to sustain its position by promising stability, improved social conditions and piecemeal economic reform, so that transition from a centrally planned to a capitalist economic system would entail minimal costs for the population (Shafir, *Radio Free Europe*, 3 January 1992). Specific groups in society were especially receptive to such a message, i.e. industrial workers, peasants and the state bureaucracy, who – all for their own reasons – feared the negative consequences of rapid transformation and the opening up of the country to the outside world (Baleanu 1998: 4).

The NSF thus – in its attempt to appeal to a particular social base – promoted a 'social market economy' as opposed to the 'shock therapy' proposed by opposition parties such as the National Liberal Party and the National Peasant Party (Adamson 2000). The appeal to particular social groups was backed up by the political support of certain trade unions over others, representing specific (historically powerful) economic sectors. The NSF had strong ties with the National Confederation of Free Trade Unions, which basically replaced the old Communist General Trade Union Confederation and mainly represents state-controlled autonomous firms, in sectors such as utilities and petroleum (Kideckel 1999: 113, 116). Other sectors, including the chemical industry or non-unionised sectors such as textiles and clothing, were not protected by the state and therefore were exposed to pressures of privatization, heavy taxation, and low wages (Kideckel 1999: 121, Pauna and Pauna 1999: 12–13).

Trade unions initially sought to influence government policies in order to change the despised labour policies of Ceauşescu. Nonetheless, their effectiveness in political influence declined rather rapidly in the first years after the 'revolution', as the number of trade-union confederations quickly proliferated, while having different political orientations and social bases. Partly a reaction to the heavily centralized labour situation under Ceauşescu, this multiplication of unions led to a diversified landscape of labour representation, finding its expression in competition among the unions, and numerous strikes and other forms of labour action over the years. Ultimately, competition among unions, and their politicization, rendered labour power in general quite ineffective, 'even as they encourage the illusion of labour power in society and the scepticism of many concerning labour goals and policies' (Kideckel 1999: 113). Two phenomena, however, point to the continuing influence of at least part of the labour movement: first of all, the continuing state protection of large state-owned enterprises, the so-called *regii autonome*, representing employment in 'traditional' industrial sectors;[6] second, the role of unions in the continuous social protests against reforms in the 1990s, often leading to concessions by governments.

In early 1990 the post-Communist government appealed to its social base by providing wage increases, maintaining price controls on essential goods, and generally relieving the position of workers by shortening the working week and allowing early retirement in order to decrease official unemployment levels (Daianu 1999: 10, Roper 2000: 89). However, within the ruling party, an opposition, headed by Prime Minister Petre Roman, arose against this so-called Third Way. Roman steered towards a policy aimed at privatization through a land law, a mass privatization programme, and price liberalization and stabilization from the beginning of 1991 onwards. Basically he introduced a reform programme rooted in the internationally dominant 'triple reform package'. The tensions within the ruling party about the pace of reform led to a split in the party. The faction around Petre Roman advocated the acceleration of economic reforms by increasing the speed of privatization, general price liberalization, and introducing convertibility of the Romanian currency, the leu. In general, it stood for a reform programme aimed at increasing integration in the Western European economy. Around President Ion Iliescu the more conservative elements were gathered, who opposed rapid reforms. Roman was identified with new economic forces, while Iliescu represented the former *nomenklatura*, which tried to preserve its old social networks and economic interests.[7] Eventually, this strife led to the splitting off of Iliescu's faction, which founded its own Democratic National Salvation Front (DNSF). Also outside of the governing party Roman's reforms were controversial. The introduction of the so-called second stage of price liberalization in April 1991 led to considerable social unrest, and ultimately to the downfall of the Roman government in September 1991, directly triggered by the march on Bucharest of the miners from the Jiu Valley. Neo-liberal reforms thus (temporarily) faltered as a result of both political and social rejection.

However, the resignation of Roman and the follow-up government of Theodor Stolojan did not lead to a complete return to economic conservatism.[8] At the installation of his government, Stolojan promised to go ahead with and even speed up the reforms initiated by Roman, thus continuing a policy of integration into the Western European and global economies. Stolojan aimed to stabilise the economy, curtail inflation and achieve 'zero growth'. Privatization was introduced at the beginning of the year, although only two state-owned enterprises were privatized during 1992. In addition, the Stolojan government tried to increase foreign capital inflow by initiating export concessions and decreasing the restrictions on exports. It explicitly favoured the goal of improving the trade deficit and stimulating exports, over curbing inflation (Roper 2000: 92). However, in the run-up to the September 1992 elections, policies partly inspired by neo-liberalism were terminated in order to enhance domestic popularity. For instance, a wage policy implemented in July provided additional benefits to workers, and an indexation of wages (Roper 2000: 93).

The peculiar mixture between policies inspired by the 'triple reform package' and populist measures came to the fore again in the period after Iliescu's party won the elections of September 1992.[9] As Iliescu's victory was marginal, he had to rely on extremist parties to be able to govern. An overt alliance with parties of the extreme right and left was impossible however, as it would have led to international repercussions for the EU and the IMF, and would have undermined aspirations to join the Council of Europe.[10] Instead, Iliescu established a single-party minority government, including DNSF ministers and many independent technocrats, the latter to show his commitment to Western-type reforms. Nicolae Văcăroiu, an independent economist, was chosen as prime minister. Văcăroiu announced that he would go ahead with reforms, although 'social costs' would be offset by governmental policy, and that Romania needed to develop into 'a market economy of a social type'. Although Văcăroiu was generally known for being against swift reforms, this only partially came to the fore in his policies during the period 1993–6. After the implementation of a short-term programme in the winter, which dealt with immediate problems of the population, Văcăroiu introduced a long-term economic strategy, in general committed to the continuance of economic reforms. At the same time, the new economic programme was intended to distance the Văcăroiu government from its predecessors – the Roman and Stolojan governments – whose policies had been based on 'classical liberalism' according to the new programme.

The four-year programme entailed accelerated privatization (limited to trade, tourism, services and small enterprises, leaving out the *regii autonome*), cutting inflation, continued price liberalization and the introduction of a value-added tax, the stimulation of private economic enterprise and the modernization of agriculture (Dan Ionescu, *RFE*, 16 April 1993). The strategy emphasized the need to increase public investments, especially in the public sector, in order to boost employment and improve social housing. This was then affiliated with the emphasis on social protection in the governmental programme. In reality, the programme was criticized by the opposition for abandoning the key promises of the election campaign, that is to say, the heavy emphasis on social protection and the pledge to create a million new jobs. Instead, harsh economic policies such as price liberalization and the introduction of a value-added tax were pursued. Indeed, in the period 1993–6, various policies inspired by the neo-liberal reform package were implemented, ranging from price and trade liberalization to cuts in subsidies to state enterprises and the introduction of the second Mass Privatization Programme in mid-1995 (Roper 2000).

The political opposition's criticism of the government's commitment to the actual implementation of election promises seemed to be justified, as increased public spending only came to the fore in the run-up to the 1996 elections (Ionescu, *RFE*, 16 April 1993). In the run-up to the November elections, the PDSR consciously sought to favourably influence the elections by increasing public spending. The government introduced populist measures, especially after the local elections in June 1996, in which the PDSR performed poorly and the centre and centre-right opposition won in almost all major cities, including Bucharest (*Financial Times*, 9 July 1996, *RFE*, 21 August 1996).

In general, in the period 1990–6, neo-liberal-type policies were implemented mainly in between elections in order to secure international legitimacy and credits. In election periods, however, policies inspired by neo-liberal models were offset by social and populist measures in order to sustain domestic popularity. Hence analysts of this period often use the term 'stop-and-go' policies. The various post-Communist governments used a discourse that hinged upon two main thoughts: first, inasmuch as its social base consisted of a combination of conservative interests stemming from the old *nomenklatura*, state employees and peasants, the post-Communist movement promoted a rather vague alternative to the neo-liberal model, expressed in notions such as 'social market economy' and 'Third Way'. Second, having to deal with the continuing and worsening economic situation, governments searched for international aid in order to reform the economy, making it vulnerable to pressures of international institutions and the EU.[11] As such, it had to walk a tightrope by promoting European and global integration while at the same time professing nationalist values and social measures to compensate for unpopular economic reforms (Verdery 1999: 328).

In terms of policy-making, the rather ambiguous set of policies often labelled as 'stop-and-go' was partly the outcome of strategic action by former Communist élites. In fact, it was one of the ways in which they tried to keep hold of political power. Apart from strategic considerations, policy-making was informed and shaped by: first, social opposition to reforms,[12] pressurising the governments to react by taking *ad hoc* measures; second, the lack of consensus and divergent opinions within the governing party on the speed and scope of reforms; and, third, awareness in the governing party that, in order to survive domestically, it had to improve the economic situation (it considered that it could not do so without international loans). The attempts of the post-Communist governments in the first half of the 1990s to cushion the effects of integration into the international economy and the restructuring of the Romanian economy did not, however, produce the desired results. Official unemployment rates rose considerably in the period concerned, from 3.0 per cent in 1991 to 8.9 per cent in 1995[13] (National Commission for Statistics 1996, Magyari *et al.* 2001), and in 1994 the economy had contracted by more than 20 per cent relative to 1989 (Pauna and Pauna 1999: 3); the workforce was reduced by around 20 per cent (*Ibid.*: 5); inflation rates remained high; and living standards continued to deteriorate. Reforms were accompanied by the

> sharp reduction in labour market participation and many workers have chosen to respond by leaving the labour force, in general via retirement and early retirement.
>
> (Pauna and Pauna 1999: 5)

In the end, the policies of the post-Communist governments did not create a coherent alternative model to neo-liberal policies, as echoed in the government's policy programmes, but rather contributed to a further deterioration of the socio-economic situation. This resulted in an increasing reliance of the post-Communists on elements of the 'triple reform package'. The increased references to the need for foreign investments, privatization and EU membership, in combination with the promotion of a 'state social market' (in reality rooted in internationally dominant conceptions of the market), and the sharp decrease in radical statements against internationalism, formed the discursive strategy of the post-Communists in the middle of the 1990s.[14] Despite the initial resistance of the post-Communists to adopting policies inspired by the international context – a reluctance stemming from power politics and electoral considerations, discursive traditions and the limited influence of other actors (opposition, trade unions) – the ruling party increasingly sought recourse to elements of the internationally dominant discourse of neo-liberalism. Nevertheless, the increasing 'normalization' of the post-Communists' discourse was to no avail, and, after the general elections at the end of 1996, the PDSR had to step down. In the following period (1997–2000), the centre-right opposition tried to implement a reform programme explicitly based on neo-liberal reforms.

The opposition in power (1997–2000)

The defeat of both the PDSR and President Iliescu in the November 1996 parliamentary and presidential elections came as a surprise for many observers, although the local elections in June of the same year had already indicated a shift in voters' behaviour. A variety of factors played a role in the victory of the opposition. The Democratic Convention for Romania (CDR) rallied various opposition parties, among them the Social Democratic Union, headed by former prime minister Petre Roman, and the Hungarian Democratic Federation of Romania (the political representative of the Hungarian minority). The most important reasons for the radical political change were, first of all, the fact that the PDSR had been discredited by several socio-economic problems, such as continuing inflationary pressures and falling living standards. In addition, corruption scandals and the decline in the popularity of President Iliescu played a role. The highly personalized political system around Iliescu was, in fact, more and more identified with the past (Tismăneanu 1997: 440). Second, the opposition was much better organized than in 1992. With its 'Contract With Romania', entailing a list of problems to be solved in 200 days, modelled on the 1994 US Republican Party campaign, it appealed to fears about the further decline in living standards (Michael Shafir, *Transitions Online*, 27 December 1996).

Victor Ciorbea, a former trade-union leader and, at the time, mayor of Bucharest, headed the government coalition. Emil Constantinescu, the candidate for the CDR, won the presidential elections. The new government was decisively in favour of Western-type reforms and immediately started with an anti-corruption, anti-crime campaign, which led to the replacement of high officials in the army, the Romanian National Television and the banking sector. On 30 January, Ciorbea made public the government's reform programme, drafted with the World Bank and the European Union, encompassing more than eighty reform laws and consisting of the complete removal of price controls, and the acceleration of privatization to 3,600 companies in 1997, including the banking sector, with major banks such as Bancorex and the Romanian Bank of Development (*RFE*, 10 April 1997). The agricultural sector was also targeted, through reforms of state farms and the elimination of state subsidies for energy and staple goods. The new government was eager to stimulate foreign investment because it regarded the reform of the Romanian economy as being directly linked to the inflow of foreign investments, as opposed to the view of predecessor governments. Also, early EU and NATO entry negotiations were made a major foreign policy objective, although eventually the diplomatic efforts were rewarded neither with NATO membership nor with inclusion of Romania in the first 'wave' of enlargement. Despite, or perhaps because of, the quick implementation of the neo-liberal reform policies, its consequences had quite negative social implications. Price liberalization, such as the complete removal of price controls on energy and food prices in February and March 1997, and privatization measures, leading to closures and cuts in subsidies, led to a severe drop in living standards (which in total had already dropped by some 20 per cent since 1989 (*Financial Times*, 25 June 1997)). The precarious social situation of large parts of the population was only partly compensated for by indexation of salaries and social protection. Furthermore, it led to serious social unrest in the form of a multitude of strikes and demonstrations. However, at an early stage, the international institutions and the EU were pleased with the radical reform programme, as confirmed by the authorization of a second instalment of a loan approved by the EU in 1994 and the funding of about 1 billion dollars over the next 12 months by the IMF and the World Bank[15] (Baleanu 1998: 8).

Nevertheless, at the end of the year the satisfaction of international institutions changed into criticism, as privatization and industrial restructuring had been proceeding more slowly than planned, and growth, inflation and budget targets were not met. Intra-coalition struggles, international criticism and social unrest paralyzed the government. After a few months of standstill, with no reform bill passing through parliament, the government reshuffle undertaken in December 1997 was a direct result of infighting in the government's coalition between the National Peasant and Christian Democratic Party (PNTCD) and the Democratic Party (PD), stemming from differences in opinion about the pace of reform (Baleanu 1998: 11).

In April 1998, after six months of political paralysis, Radu Vasile, an economic historian, replaced Prime Minister Ciorbea. Ciorbea resigned because of the combined pressures stemming from both domestic and international forces favouring the acceleration of reforms, and more directly as a result of the deep crisis in the coalition (Szabo Matyas, *Transitions Online*, 1998). Vasile promised to go ahead with the reforms, admitting the continuity between his and the former government. A new economic reform programme was prepared, containing the curbing of inflation, the assumption of 'zero growth' and the consolidation of the budget to 3.6 per cent of the GDP (Baleanu 1998: 23). Moreover, privatization of 1,600 companies was to go ahead, and industrial restructuring – especially of big utilities – would be accelerated. The continuity with the Ciorbea government was not only visible in the economic programme, but also in the persisting political problems within the governing coalition. In September 1998, Vasile dismissed the Minister of Finance, Daianu, and the Minister of Privatization, Dumitriu, in a response to the continuous attacks on both ministers for failing to meet the planned pace of reform and privatization.

Apart from coalition problems, forms of social protest against the reforms continuously plagued the post-1996 governments. One of the gravest uprisings took place in one of the historically most important industrial sectors and a major debtor to the state budget: the mining industry (Martin and Cristesco-

Martin 1999: 397). As a direct reaction to government intentions to thoroughly restructure the mining industry, miners from the Jiu Valley went on strike in January 1999, led by Miron Cozma, a trade-union leader. In order to protest against the closure of several mines and factories and to demand an increase in wages, the miners marched on Bucharest[16] (Martin and Cristesco-Martin 1999, Roper 2000: 105). After concessions granted by Vasile, the social unrest in the Jiu area was not completely calmed, as interpretations over the concessions differed. In addition, relations with international institutions such as the IMF were undermined by the concessions made, since they prompted concern that reform was threatened (Kideckel 1999: 108). Moreover, the severe problems of the government in dealing with the miners indicated that forms of negotiation between representatives of labour and the state were largely absent, leading to unorthodox means of protest against the social consequences of reforms. In that sense, it should be noted that trade unions in general perform a rather unorthodox role in Romanian society. On the one hand, they agree with structural reform policies and privatization on a discursive level, thereby supporting government policy. According to the unions, restructuring and fully fledged privatization should lead to higher wages and more social protection (Kideckel, 1999: 109). On the other hand, however, unions call for state protection from the most immediate consequences, especially unemployment, thus criticising unrestrained neo-liberal reforms. In reality the unions lack formal and direct influence on a governmental level and often resort to 'industrial action', thereby paralyzing the government. Ultimately, unions represent *employed* labour. Paradoxically, however, they support privatization, irrevocably leading to the loss of jobs, and simultaneously want to serve the interests of their members, i.e. to safeguard employment in large state-owned enterprises (Kideckel 1999: 109, 118).

The neo-liberal programmes attempted by the centre-right governments in the end met neither the expectations of the ruling coalition nor those of the population at large. At the end of 1999, Mugur Isarescu, former governor of the Romanian National Bank, replaced Prime Minister Vasile, an act which was primarily inspired by the rapidly falling popularity of the government, especially in view of the elections planned for the end of 2000 (*România Liberă*, 9 June 1999). Indeed, important parts of the reform programme had not materialized. For instance, Vasile had failed to privatize major national companies such as the aeroplane producer IAR Ghimbav or the tractor factory Tractorul Braşov. The only major privatization deal implemented in 1999 was the sale of the Dacia car company to Renault (Marius Dragomir, *Transitions Online*, 2001). The legitimacy of the coalition was further undermined by the collapse of the National Investment Fund in May 2000, leaving thousands of Romanians without savings. To make the situation worse, no relief was offered by the government (Marius Dragomir, *Transitions Online*, 2001).

Not surprisingly then, Iliescu's party emerged as the victor in the parliamentary and presidential elections at the end of 2000. Interestingly enough, and in line with the observed trend in the mid-1990s, the new government party shows a much stronger discursive adherence to the globally dominant discourse than ever before, without, however, shedding its 'social' image. In the most recent political programme of Iliescu's party (recently renamed the Social Democratic Party, PSD) several statements can be found that adhere to neo-liberal notions of reform, the need to follow Western European practices and integration in Western European structures:[17]

> The PSD campaigns for: ... accelerating the privatization in all fields, the restructuring and re-engineering of production activities, the stimulation of investments, including foreign ones ... a synthesis between the kind of social market economy, as it has prefigured in developed European states, and the particular characteristics of the Romanian society ... The on-going preparation of the country for its dignified integration into European structures.
>
> (PSD 2000a)

In the years between 1997 and 2000, the centre-right government was eager to promote and implement its national version of the triple reform programme derived from the international hegemonic discourse. In reality, the implementation of a Romanian 'shock therapy' proved to be a rather unrealizable undertaking. Two major obstacles were crucial in this:

1   the lack of a political consensus on reforms, illustrated by intra-coalition struggles and several cabinet reshuffles (in fact, the governing coalition itself consisted of several coalitions, which, after initial agreement on the need for the acceleration of reforms, all pursued their own particular version of reform policies);
2   forms of social protest against the reforms, most importantly in the form of labour action. In the first years of governance of the centre-right coalition, the socio-economic situation continued to deteriorate, as shown, for instance, in negative growth figures in 1997 and 1998 (a drop in GDP by 6.9 and 7.3 respectively (UN–ECE 1999)), a deterioration of living standards in the same period (UNDP 1999), and continuously high unemployment rates (8.8 per cent in 1997, 10.3 per cent in 1998 (UN–ECE 1999)).

It is a difficult and probably unnecessary exercise to directly relate the decline in socio-economic conditions in these years to attempts at neo-liberal reform by the governing coalition. Nevertheless, the position of the centre-right governments became increasingly weakened and untenable in the face of the continuing socio-economic crisis. Both internationally and domestically, the centre-right coalition was exposed to strong criticism. International institutions criticised the reform process for being too slow, whereas domestic actors, above all the various trade unions, protested heavily against the reforms, often paralyzing the government. Arguably the largest problem in the Romanian economy – the restructuring of large state-owned enterprises in traditional industrial sectors – continued to take its toll on everyday politics.

Conclusions

The ambiguity of economic reforms in Romania and its experience with capitalism in general in the 1990s can hardly be understood by a single emphasis on the continuity in power of the former Communists. Other factors were at work that made a clear policy line – ideally-typically a choice between the options of either a strong alternative to, or a straightforward adoption of, Western models of reform – rather unlikely. First of all, a modernization strategy based on dominant Western ideas proved to be virtually impossible in post-Communist Romania, where Westernizing forces have historically been countered by a variety of 'traditionalist', nationalist or orthodox forces, creating a discursive space in which Western ideas are easily criticised as undermining the Romanian 'nation'. In such a historical context, the downfall of the Communist system did not find its ideological expression in the unconditional embrace of Western ideas, as occurred in many other countries in the region. The tradition of opposition to Westernizing forces in Romanian society – a position further weakened by the extreme subordination of almost all social actors (including intellectuals, the state bureaucracy and trade unions) to the Communist regime – made a 'return to Europe' not the most obvious option for Romanian policy-makers. Furthermore, Westernizing intellectuals undermined their own position and that of Westernizing forces in general by their inability to communicate their ideas to the population at large. Phrasing their ideas mainly in élitist language (Mungiu-Pippidi 1999), and lacking the ability to formulate a coherent alternative programme to the vague notions of a 'market economy of a social type' of Iliescu, made their political position rather weak at the beginning of the 1990s.

In addition, the population at large did not support rigorous reform policies, not least because a crucial share of employment in the country is provided by the large industrial complexes created by Ceaușescu, a rapid restructuring of which would most surely have led to a huge loss of jobs. Many attempts to implement Western-type reforms have in reality met with social unrest, as experienced by all post-Communist governments, mainly in the form of labour action. In that sense, trade unions have played an important role in resisting neo-liberal reforms. Their dispersed and politicised nature, the fierce competition among them and their tendency towards radical action have destabilised post-1989 politics to a major extent. Second, an alternative in the form of a restoration of Communism in Romania in the early 1990s was just as unlikely as an uncritical embrace of Western ideas by the political élites. The former Communists were too divided amongst themselves to pose any strong alternative to Western capitalism; they were not even interested in restoring a Communist regime and, in reality, pursued a rather ambiguous and at times contradictory reform policy.

What we see then by looking at the initial years of economic reforms in post-Communist Romania is the lack of a social foundation, as well as the absence of a willing élite in favour of a neo-liberal-type of reform programme. At the same time, however, we cannot conclude that the globally dominant version of modernization has had no effect on domestic reforms in Romania in those years. Not only has the political debate been largely framed within the discursive space of this global paradigm, that is to say, if we disregard the radical statements by both the extreme right and left, but also the former Communists had eventually to seek recourse to important elements of a neo-liberal modernization strategy. Lacking strongly formulated alternatives to neo-liberal recipes, the post-Communist governments resorted to policies such as mass privatization programmes and price liberalization, in concomitance with international assistance and loans.

When the centre-right coalition came to power in November 1996 it sought to directly appropriate neo-liberal discourse and practice – something it had striven for since the early 1990s. In reality, a straightforward adoption proved to be impossible in the Romanian context. Although the centre-right coalition as a whole was initially enthusiastic about European and Atlantic integration and rapid reforms, it saw its consensus on reforms diminish quickly when such a programme proved hard to implement. All the same, crucial aspects of the neo-liberal reform programme, such as the mass privatization of large state-owned enterprises, budgetary stabilization and European and Atlantic integration have never been removed from the agenda. Even after the enormous political landslide caused by the elections of 2000, when the centre-right coalition was obliterated and Iliescu appeared once again on the political stage, the reform agenda has not changed very much. Blueprints offered by Western institutions and experts alike seem hard to avoid for Romanian political élites, but at the same time are difficult to implement.

Notes

1 Even in the other 'extreme' of policy options for post-Communist societies (i.e. gradualism), the notion of doing away with the old and starting anew is highly present.

2 Interestingly, Müller (quoting Giddens) argues that – although being heavily criticised – the original modernization theory has survived in the

> wide variety of comparative studies conducted under the auspices of the international organizations, such as the reports of the International Labour Office (ILO), numerous special investigations by the International Monetary Fund (IMF), and the World Bank's annual *Human Development Report*.
> (Müller 1995: 269)

3 Indeed, Müller suggests the term 'negative sociology' for approaches that use 'a kind of applied theory of totalitarianism which maintains that, since the system of real socialism has totally failed, it will shortly totally disappear – a process often labelled "creative destruction" ' (Müller 1995: 277).

4 An earlier version of this paragraph can be found in Blokker and Keune (2001).

5 The ruling party that won the first elections (no serious opposition providing an alternative was available at that time) was in fact made up largely of members of the old bureaucracy, which for a long time had been a mere extension of Ceauşescu's power (Tismăneanu 1993).

6 Throughout the 1990s, these *regii autonome* have been largely excluded from the privatization process. It has been estimated that they provide a relatively large part of overall employment (Earle and Telegdy 2001).

7 See Blokker (2000). Although there might be a general truth to this, a clear-cut distinction between forces for and against the status quo is in reality hard to find. Roman's opposition in later instances to radical reforms, as well as Iliescu's current pleading for integration into the West, indicate the complexity of their political roles. The departure of pro-democracy intellectuals from the Front in its very early stages and its eventual split ups do, however, indicate that a major struggle between 'old' and 'new' forces was taking place.

8 Interestingly enough, Stolojan resigned from Roman's government in March 1991 to protest against the slowness of the reforms and was generally seen as more 'reformist' than his predecessor.

9 In the run-up to the elections of September 1992, the differences between the original NSF (now Roman's party) and the seceded DNSF (Iliescu's party) became very apparent. The NSF promoted the maintenance of the pace of reforms, whereas the DNSF called for a slowing down of economic reform. But both parties stood for integration into Western structures. The centre-right opposition, gathered in the Democratic Convention, pushed for actual acceleration of reforms and speeding up of integration into Western structures, whereas the extreme right and left parties were openly against integration and reforms (Michael Shafir, *RFE*, 11 September 1992).

10 In reality however, it relied heavily on the support of these parties in parliament. Moreover, the discourse used by the DNSF often included themes that were clearly part of the domain of the extremist parties, such as nationalist statements against minorities.

11 Many instances of the governments' quest for international credits and legitimacy can be found: the attempt by the Stolojan government in 1991 to continue privatization and its incorporation of members of the oppositional National Liberal Party (NLP) in order to seek international legitimization, above all in the eyes of the EU and the IMF; in 1993, the signing of the Association Agreement with the European Union and the admittance to the Council of Europe; and moreover, in October 1993, the signing of a bilateral trade agreement with the United States, which involved the restoration of the most-favoured-nation status (Michael Shafir and Dan Ionescu, *RFE*, 7 January 1994). Other instances of international influence on domestic policy-making are the various agreements for loans concluded with the IMF, involving specific demands set by the Fund (see, for instance, de Nève 1998) and the negotiations over accession with the EU.

12 In this respect, the miners from the Jiu Valley constituted the most 'direct' form of social pressure.

13 Unemployment is in reality a larger problem than official figures tend to show, because of withdrawal from the labour market and the formal economy through early retirement, labour in the informal economy, or self-subsistence farming (Kideckel 1999).

14 Adamson (2000) identifies several phases in the PDSR's ideological transformation throughout the 1990s. Initially referring to values of the 'revolution', the party more and more stressed stability in opposition to radical reforms. More recently, according to him, the party underlines reforms of a 'social-democratic' type. Although I agree with these typifications as such, I wonder whether the PSDR since the early 1990s started creating 'Romanian social democracy'. I would prefer to say that the PDSR started incorporating neo-liberal elements into its discourse.

15 In fact, the IMF had been heavily involved in the drawing up of the election and governmental programmes of the CDR (de Nève 1998).

16 The miners had marched on the capital before – twice in 1990 and once in 1991 – leading to the resignation of Prime Minister Roman. Miners' protests have a fairly

long history in Romania, miners being the only social group that was able to bring Ceauşescu to negotiate after a strike of almost a week in 1977 (Chiaburu 1999: 115). The miners' privileged position actually stems from Communist times and has prevailed throughout the post-1989 period. Attempts by the centre-right government to restructure the industry have met with heavy resistance, especially from the Jiu Valley, where most of the coal-mining industry is based. The industry's strongly unionised and politicised nature facilitates support from Iliescu and nationalist parties (Chiaburu 1999: 116). This, combined with the traditionally privileged position of the miners, poses a strong threat to the centre-right governments.

17 Similar statements can be found in the strategy of the PSD for the period 2001–4.

Bibliography

Adamson, K. (2000) 'The construction of Romanian social democracy (1989–1996)', in D. Howarth, A.J. Noval and Y. Stavrakakis (eds) *Discourse Theory and Political Analysis. Identities, Hegemonies and Social Change*, Manchester/New York: Manchester University Press, pp. 119–33.

Alexander, J.C. (1995) 'Modern, Anti, Post and Neo: how intellectuals have coded, narrated, and explained the "New World of Our Time"', in *Fin de Siècle Social Theory. Relativism, Reduction and the Problem of Reason*, London/New York: Verso, pp. 6–64.

Altvater, E. (1998) 'Theoretical deliberations on time and space in post-socialist transformation', *Regional Studies*, 32.7: 591–605.

Arnason, J.P. (2000) 'Designs and destinies: making sense of post-Communism', *Thesis Eleven*, 63: 89–97.

Badie, B. (2000) *The Imported State. The Westernization of the Political Order*, Stanford, CA: Stanford University Press.

Baleanu, G. (1998) *Romania at Historic Crossroads*, Conflict Studies Research Center, No. G65, http://www.pims.org/csrc/g65.htm (accessed 4 April 2002).

Beyme, K. von (1994) *Systemwechsel in Osteuropa*, Frankfurt am Main: Suhrkamp.

Blokker, P. (2000) 'The external modernization of Romania. The socio-economic consequences of transformation', in S. Blackwell *et al.* (eds), *Selected Conference Papers, Bucharest: Civil Education Project*, pp. 76–96.

Blokker, P. and Keune, M. (2001) 'How the Global Discursive Context Influences Local Discursive and Policy Practices: a Comparative Analysis of Post-Socialist Hungary and Romania', Paper presented at the Fourth Pan-European International Relations Conference in Kent, pp. 8–10, September 2001.

Brucan, S. (1998) *Social Change in Russia and Eastern Europe. From Party Hacks to Nouveaux Riches*, Westport, CT and London: Praeger.

Burawoy, M. (1992) 'The end of Sovietology and the renaissance of modernization theory', *Contemporary Sociology*, 21(6), November: 774–85.

Burawoy, M. and Verdery, K. (eds) (1999) *Uncertain Transition. Ethnographies of Change in the Postsocialist World*, Oxford: Rowman and Littlefield.

Chavance, B. and Magnin, E. (1997) 'Emergence of path-dependent mixed economies in Central Europe', in A. Amin and J. Hausner (eds), *Beyond Market and Hierarchy. Interactive Governance and Social Complexity*, Cheltenham/Lyme: Edward Elgar, pp. 196–232.

Chiaburu, D. (1999) 'Romania: the coal mining industry from plan to market', *South-East Europe Review for Labour and Social Affairs (SEER)*, 2(3), October: 111–22.

Culic, I. (1999) 'The strategies of intellectuals: Romania under communist rule in comparative perspective', in A. Bozoki (ed.) *Intellectuals and Politics in Central Europe*, Budapest: CEU Press, pp. 43–72.

Daianu, D. (1999) 'Structure, strain and macroeconomic dynamic in Romania', Paper prepared for the World Bank Conference 'Romania, Ten Years of Transition', Bucharest, 21–2 October 1999.

Earle, J. and Telegdy, A. (2001) 'Privatization and productivity in Romanian industry: evidence from a comprehensive enterprise panel', *Discussion Paper No. 326*, Bonn: Institute for the Study of Labor (IZA).

Eyal, G., Szelenyi, I. and Townsley, E. (1998) *Making Capitalism without Capitalists: Class Formation and Elite Struggles in Post-Communist Central Europe*, London: Verso.

Frausum, Y.G. van, Gehmann, U. and Gross, J. (1999) 'Market economy and economic reform in Romania: macroeconomic and microeconomic perspectives', *Europe–Asia Studies*, 46(5): 735–56.

Gabanyi, A.U. (1998) 'Neue Wirtschaftseliten in Rumaenien: von der Nomenklatura zur Oligarchie', in W. Hoepken and H. Sundhaussen (eds) *Eliten in Suedosteuropa. Rolle, Kontinuitaeten, Brueche in Geschichte und Gegenwart*, Munich: Südosteuropa-Gesellschaft, pp. 289–320.

—— (2000) *The Ceauşescu Cult*, Bucharest: Romanian Cultural Foundation Publishing House.

Gallagher, T. (1997) 'To be or not to be Balkan: Romania's quest for self-definition', *Daedalus*, 126(3): 63–84.

Higley, J., Pakulski, J. and Wesolowski, W. (eds) (1998) *Postcommunist Elites and Democracy in Eastern Europe*, London: Macmillan.

Kideckel, D. (1999) 'Storm and stasis: the paradox of labour in post-socialist Romania', *South-East Europe Review, Special Issue*: 107–32.

Magyari, N.L., Magyari-Vincze, E., Popescu, L. and Rotariu, T. (2001) 'The social construction of Romanian poverty: the impact of ethnic and gender distinctions', in R.J. Emigh and I. Szelényi (eds) *Poverty, Ethnicity, and Gender in Eastern Europe During the Market Transition*, Westport/London: Praeger, pp. 123–56.

Martin, R. and Cristesco-Martin, A. (1999) 'Industrial relations in transformation: Central and Eastern Europe in 1998', *Industrial Relations Journal*, 30(4): 387–404.

Müller, K. (1995) 'From post-communism to post-modernity? Economy and society in Eastern European transformations', in B. Grancelli (ed.) *Social Change and Modernisation. Lessons from Eastern Europe*, Berlin/New York: Walter de Gruyter, pp. 265–94.

—— (1997) *East European Studies, Neo-Totalitarianism and Social Science Theory*, Working Paper No. 4, Wissenschaftszentrum Berlin für Sozialforschung (WZB).

Mungiu-Pippidi, A. (1999) 'Romanian intellectuals before and after the revolution', in A. Bozoki (ed.) *Intellectuals and Politics in Central Europe*, Budapest: CEU Press, pp. 73–100.

National Commission for Statistics (1996) *Social Situation and Economy of Romania in 1995*, Bucharest: National Commission for Statistics.

Nelson, D.N. (1988) *Romanian Politics in the Ceauşescu Era*, New York/London: Gordon and Breach, pp. 38–56.

—— (1995) 'Romania', in Z. Barany and I. Volgyes (eds) *The Legacies of Communism in Eastern Europe*, Baltimore/London: Johns Hopkins University Press, pp. 198–226.

Nève, D. de (1998) 'Wirtschaftspolitik in Rumänien. Das Reformprogrammem der Regierung Victor Ciorbeas', *Osteuropa*, 8/9: 938–53.

Partidul Social Democrat (PSD) (2000a) *Programul Politic al Partidului Social Democrat*, http://www.psd.ro/pgpol/004.htm (accessed 2 October 2001).

—— (2000b) *Strategia PDSR. Privind dezvoltarea economico-socială a României pe termen mediu*, http://www.psdr.ro/documente/Consiliu_National_feb2000/strategia_PDSR.htm (accessed 2 October 2001).

Pauna, C. and Pauna, B. (1999) 'Output decline and labour reallocation in transitional economies; where does Romania stand?', Paper prepared for the World Bank Conference 'Romania, Ten Years of Transition', Bucharest, 21–2 October 1999.

Pickles, J. and Smith, A. (1998) *Theorising Transition. The Political Economy of Post-Communist Transformations*, London: Routledge.

Radio Free Europe (RFE), various contributions.

România Liberă, various contributions.

Roper, S.D. (2000) *Romania. The Unfinished Revolution*, Amsterdam: Harwood Academic Publishers.

Stark, D. and Bruszt, L. (1998) *Postsocialist Pathways. Transforming Politics and Property in East Central Europe*, Cambridge: Cambridge University Press.

Tismăneanu, V. (1993) 'The quasi-revolution and its discontents: emerging political pluralism in post-Ceauşescu Romania', *East European Politics and Societies*, 309–48.

—— (1997) 'Romanian exceptionalism? Democracy, ethnocracy, and uncertain pluralism in post-Ceauşescu Romania', in K. Dawisha and B. Parrott (eds) *Politics, Power, and the Struggle for Democracy in South-East Europe*, Cambridge: Cambridge University Press, pp. 403–50.

Transitions Online, various contributions, http://www.tol.cz.

United Nations Development Programme (UNDP) (1999) *National Human Development Report Romania 1999*, Bucharest: UNDP.

United Nations–Economic Commission for Europe (UN–ECE) (1999) *Economic Survey of Europe, 1999, No. 2*, Geneva: UN–ECE.

Verdery, K. (1999) 'Civil society or nation? "Europe" in the symbolism of Romania's postsocialist politics', in R.G. Suny and M.D. Kennedy (eds), *Intellectuals and the Articulation of the Nation*, Ann Arbor: University of Michigan Press, pp. 301–40.

Verdery, K. and Kligman, G. (1992) 'Romania after Ceauşescu: post-Communist Communism?', in I. Banac (ed.) *Eastern Europe in Revolution*, Ithaca/London: Cornell University Press, pp. 117–47.

6   Ukraine

Changing work conditions in a neo-patrimonial society

Hans van Zon

Introduction

Ukraine is now one of the worst-performing transition economies in Eastern Europe. In 2001, real GNP was about one-third of what it was in 1991, when Ukraine became independent. In 2000, industrial production was only 28 per cent of its 1990 level (*Ukrainian Economic Trends*, December 2000). Ukraine's record is even substantially worse than that of Russia. It is no surprise that the condition of the Ukrainian working class has deteriorated dramatically. The average wage was US$46.6 per month in 2000, only 64 per cent of that in Russia. Moreover, wages are not always paid.

In this chapter, I will analyse the changing work conditions in the quasi-state sector of Ukrainian industry that still dominates Ukrainian industry. These changes are explained in the context of the prevailing socio-economic system and government policies. Special attention will be given to the impact of Western advice and assistance upon social policies. As little research has been done in this area, I will make extensive references to my own experiences during field research in Ukraine.

It is argued that the transformation of the socialist 'estate' company, involving the erosion of the social-service network, the increased powers of enterprise managers and the redistribution of resources within the enterprise at the expense of labour, can be explained in the framework of the concept of neo-patrimonialism. Social practices linked to neo-patrimonialism have allowed a kleptocracy to develop. Neo-patrimonialism also hampers the marketization of enterprises. Moreover, unfortunately, Western assistance did not hamper the development of neo-patrimonial crony capitalism in Ukraine.

First I will analyse the impact of economic collapse on the living conditions of the population and the change in industrial structure, as a background for the description of changing work conditions.

Emergence of a kleptocracy, and growing mass poverty

The steep economic decline of Ukraine should be seen in the context of the abolition of the centrally planned economy; the dissolution of the Soviet Union;

the concomitant disruption of supply chains and markets; and the emergence of a kleptocratic regime. Per capita GDP at current prices declined to US$601 in 2000, less than half of that in Russia (US$1,672) and less than that of China (US$854) (*World Economic Outlook* 2001). Ukraine is the only transition country to have known nine consecutive years of economic decline (1991–9).

The living conditions of the population as a whole have deteriorated enormously since Ukraine gained its independence in 1991, and the fall in living standards for the majority of the population is even steeper than the decreases in GDP (in PPP terms) and industrial production suggest, given growing inequality.

Between 1991 and 2000, the contribution of food costs to the average family budget rose from 33 to 64 per cent. Seventy-four per cent of the Ukrainian population spends more than 60 per cent of their income on food. The calorie content of the average diet decreased in this period from 3,597 to 2,505 kilocalories, and the protein content from 105 to 73 grams. In this respect, Ukraine is performing more badly than Russia and Central European countries like the Czech Republic, Poland, Hungary and Bulgaria (*Zerkalo Nedieli*, 31 March 2001). Thirty-one per cent of the population has a daily diet of less than 2,100 kilocalories, the World Health Organization's poverty threshold indicator. Partly due to worsening diet and health care, the incidence of many illnesses has increased.

Among the new poor are many who used to be part of the middle class: doctors, teachers, scientists and engineers. In the year 2000, 65 per cent of the population considered themselves poor, according to the 'Social Monitoring Center' (in 1994 this was 47 per cent) (*Zerkalo Nedieli*, 31 March 2001). A poll conducted in February 2001, in which 1,200 respondents were interviewed, showed that 93 per cent of Ukrainians have a monthly income of less than 300 hryvna (approximately US$55 according to the going exchange rate), that is slightly less than the Hr 311 monthly subsistence level established by government (*Zerkalo Nedieli*, 31 March 2001). Many respondents have indicated that they are doing much worse than that. Seventy per cent of those polled put their monthly income at lower than 150 hryvna. According to a Ukrainian State Statistics Committee-sponsored opinion poll of industrial workers, about Hr 400 is believed to be the minimal monthly average income per family member to guarantee a subsistence level bordering on the poverty line (*Kiev Post Daily Press Digest*, 1 June 2001). In 2000, when (official) GDP started to grow, real income continued to fall, although real wages increased in 2000, according to government statistics, at the same time admitting that household consumption as a whole did not increase in the year 2000 (*Zerkalo Nedieli*, 31 March 2001).

So far I have simply given a short description of the economic collapse in Ukraine and the extent to which it affects the life of the population. Below I will focus attention on the *modus operandi* of state-owned and privatized enterprises.

The transformation of socialist 'estate' companies

The functioning of present state-owned and previously state-owned enterprises is still very reminiscent of Soviet companies. Historically, Soviet companies performed a number of key functions that were typically fulfilled by the market, municipal governments, trade unions, voluntary societies and other civil-social institutions in capitalist societies. The Soviet factory served as the 'melting pot' and community organizer for the largely peasant workforce. The Soviet factory encompassed a system of paternalism in which the workers were completely dependent on the enterprise management. However, due to structural labour shortages, workers also had some leverage.

As Simon Clarke observed,

> the Soviet company was almost as different from the capitalist enterprise as was a feudal estate from a capitalist farm. Like the feudal estate, the Soviet company was not simply an economic institution but the primary unit of Soviet society, and the ultimate base of social and political power. … The task of the company administration was not to secure the expanded reproduction of capital, but the expanded reproduction of the labour collective.
>
> (Clarke 1992: 7)

State-owned companies resembled large estates that provided, first and foremost, employment and social security for their employees. These estates provided housing, sports facilities, health care and a number of other services.

The larger enterprises would manufacture some products as a sideline, often especially for its personnel. For example, Zaporozhstal, the big steel enterprise of Zaporizhzhya, still has a sausage factory on its premises and also owns some collective agricultural enterprises. Like other large factories, it managed a district of the town, including heating and streetlights, theatres, hotels and sports facilities. It also managed holiday resorts. All these facilities were free of charge for the employees of the enterprise. In addition, the enterprise helped with funerals, marriages and other family events, through the provision of buses and restaurants. Within this *estate company*, the Communist Party was a motive force, not just an instrument of oppression. People could go with their complaints to the local branch of the party, which had the leverage to get things moving.

A *troika* headed the socialist company, consisting of the director of an enterprise, the secretary of the party committee and a representative of the trade union. They were responsible for the solution of functional problems. Within the company, there was a minimal delegation of responsibilities to subordinates. The task of company directors was not to optimize and control the labour process but to manage the external relations of the enterprise, which meant negotiating with the ministries in order to ease plan goals and to secure deliveries. Informal wheeling and dealing constituted an essential part of this management.

Within the workforce there were basically two groups of workers: the cadre stratum and the peripheral workers. The first group – mainly engineers – enjoyed many privileges, and mobility between both groups was very limited. Trade unions managed social conflicts within the enterprise and tried to particularize them by adjusting the delivery of differentiated social services, such as lodgings, nursery schools, summer camps, holiday resorts and medical services, which came under their responsibility.

Due to the shortage of labour, the workers had a certain leverage and some autonomy in the work-place, despite the subordination of workers in the sphere of production. Particularly among the peripheral workers, there was often an atmosphere of malaise that was expressed in widespread alcoholism and absenteeism. There was also a high rate of labour turnover. Twenty-five to thirty per cent of workers changed job every year (Maroudas 2000: 174).

The economic reforms during the *perestroika* years (1986–90) gave the directors more power, despite the pseudo-democratic rights allotted to the workers' councils. The position of trade unions was weakened and less attention was paid to job security and sanitary conditions. The economic stagnation deepened and safety regulations were poorly implemented. In 1987, there were 690,000 industrial accidents, with 14,600 fatalities, an extremely high figure by international standards (Maroudas 2000: 176). Within the enterprises themselves there was a defensive adjustment to the changing economic environment. And, during the *perestroika* years, there was an increasingly hostile attitude towards reform.

On the eve of independence, virtually all Ukrainian workers were employed in state-owned companies. When the newly independent Ukraine started to introduce tentative market-oriented reforms, and the economic crisis began to affect the resources of companies, the estate-like character of most state-owned enterprises came under pressure. The whole socio-economic ecology surrounding the big state-owned enterprises gradually disintegrated as a result of the reforms and a steep economic decline, although many features of the old estate-like companies do continue to exist.

First of all, the role of the party within the enterprise fell away and the role of trade unions drastically diminished. This gave greater powers to the board of directors, also because the state (i.e. ministries) withdrew as an effective owner. Differences between the cadre group of workers and peripheral workers diminished and a process of workforce homogenization took place. The privileges of the cadre workers diminished and the number of peripheral workers decreased dramatically due to the steep decline in production during the 1990s.

Relations between enterprises became increasingly governed by informal relations of trust, with the falling away of the co-ordination mechanism of the central planners (ministries and party). Enterprises constituted financial–industrial groupings (monopolistic structures) in which outsiders were kept out. Usually, directors were not replaced, and enterprise management remained dominated by the old *nomenklatura*. Unlike, for example, Poland, the cadre stratum lacked an influx of new managers with a new world outlook.

Clarke points to the weaknesses of many Western analyses of Eastern European enterprises:

> they are based on the argument that the economic irrationality of managerial behavior can be understood as a rational response to an irrational system. While such analyses provide useful insights, the narrowly economistic

conception of rationality that they deploy limits their ability to understand the dynamics of the system in change, for it implies that the liberation of management from political constraint would immediately lead to the spontaneous emergence of capitalist rationality as the enterprise sheds all the impediments of Soviet life.

(Clarke 1992: 6)

With economic disintegration, the social infrastructure of enterprises became the first victim. In Zaporizhzhya, located in south-eastern Ukraine, the sports facilities of Zaporozhstal were transformed into a sauna for the new rich. Kindergartens were closed. The conference centre was neglected and abandoned. But Zaporozhstal still owns a network of retail outlets, part of the housing stock in Zaporizhzhya, a hotel and *kolchozes* (communal farms).

The transformation of the socialist 'estate' company into a commercial enterprise focusing on core business has proceeded very slowly. For example, the state-owned car producer Avtozaz from Zaporizhzhya, which formed a joint venture with Daewoo in 1998, has still not undergone basic restructuring in 2001, as it has failed to spin-off recreation centres, nature reserves and other facilities irrelevant to the plant's core operations. Mr Shcherbina, president of the Ukrainian division of Avtozaz–Daewoo, said that the plant still supports unproductive infrastructure and is overstaffed (*Kiev Post*, 30 March 2001). When Avtozaz negotiated with Daewoo, one of the demands of Avtozaz was that all 20,000 personnel of the plant, which has stood idle for most of the previous two years, should remain employed at a salary that was twice as much as the average salary in Ukraine. The deal was that the whole workforce did indeed remain employed, but with an average salary that was the same as the average in the sector.

In 2000, the workforce of Avtozaz comprised 18,000 people, but only 8,000 were actually working. The rest were at home and being paid two-thirds of the average salary, which was on average 149 hryvna. It is obvious that this situation is not sustainable in the long run, but firing of personnel is out of the question for the company leadership, although since 1998 the plant has produced on average only *c.*9,000 cars per year (*Zerkalo Nedieli*, 27 May 2001). The survival of the company depends on government support. As such, workers were not only faced with enormous wage reductions, but also with drastically reduced enterprise services.

The whole complex fabric of social relations in and around the enterprise gradually unravelled, without being replaced by an alternative system of social protection. Some social services were transferred to the municipality. However, the municipality was starved of money and usually not able to maintain adequately the newly acquired services. The example of mine closures shows how the socio-economic texture of society is dependent on the estate company. Many settlements in Donetsk and Luhansk, where coal mining in Ukraine is concentrated, depend on just one mine. The whole social and physical infrastructure of these settlements, including housing, water pipelines, heating, electricity and gas networks, cultural institutions, sport establishments, medical services and pre-school establishments such as kindergartens, is owned by the mine. Numerous government initiatives tried to transfer the social infrastructure of mines to other institutions, primarily municipalities, but this process was very slow. Usually, the buyer wanted the assets free of debts and in good condition, which meant that they should be repaired, and this often prevented the transfer. The result was that in most cases the social assets had to be closed.

The closure of mines in these one-company towns has created ghost towns, or 'dead zones' as Ukrainians call them, where the whole socio-economic structure has disintegrated. For the inhabitants it is difficult to find work elsewhere because usually the transport infrastructure has also collapsed. Moving is difficult due to a shortage of houses. Everywhere in Ukraine there are numerous one-company towns. Also in the case of non-closure, most of these towns are faced with a disintegrating social and physical infrastructure because the company cannot any more afford to pay adequately for this infrastructure.

State-owned and privatized companies usually have not transformed into marketized enterprises with strict budget constraints. Although direct state subsidies have drastically diminished and indirect state subsidies have also decreased, cross-subsidization between enterprises has continued.[1] Thus, although budget constraints have been tightened somewhat over the last decade in state-owned and above all privatized enterprises, this has not been sufficient to induce radical changes in the management of these enterprises. Change is also hampered by an inertia that is deeply rooted in society. Although property assets, especially the social ones, are a great burden for the enterprise, the directors cannot refrain from expressing their delight about their size. The directors present their company as a kind of cultural, educational and recreational combine, while the production functions are placed in the background. A report about Donetsk has noted that:

> It is difficult for the directors to get rid of this material evidence of their past power and influence. It is equally difficult for them to give up their illusions, among which is the hope for the return of good old days of mass production.
> (Lyakh and Pankow 1998: 80)

According to the report, only in some cases did the enterprises sell above-mentioned property. In rich enterprises, there was a tendency to accumulate more assets. This is the reflection of an 'imperialist complex'. The few relatively well-to-do firms also increased employment, although neither production level nor sales volume justified this. This was partly related to pressure from local authorities.

Transformation of Ukrainian industry

Reformers assumed that with privatization the *modus operandi* of enterprises would change and that they would function more efficiently. But, apart from the anecdotal evidence mentioned above, is there any empirical evidence about the impact of privatization on the functioning of enterprises? To answer this question, first I will provide some data about the privatization process in Ukraine.

The manufacturing sector in Ukraine is dominated by large firms that are still state owned or used to be state owned. In 1999, 89 per cent of large firms (with more than 250 employees) stated that they were formerly state owned.

Firms that were not privatized were those with strong links to the Commonwealth of Independent States; firms that were the least profitable, like coal mines; and the most profitable firms, such as natural monopolies and other protected sectors like alcoholic drinks. In 1998, of Ukraine's ten most profitable firms, nine were state owned, while the tenth, Ukrnaft, had only 39 per cent of shares in state hands in 1999 (*Kiev Post*, 29 July 1999). Estimates of the share of the private sector in the economy vary widely.

According to official figures, in 2000 75.7 per cent of output was produced by the non-state sector and 85.7 per cent of enterprises were non-state. However, 85.3 per cent of enterprises have 'mixed ownership'. In many cases, the state has a stake in these enterprises. In the case of medium-sized and large enterprises, in 30 per cent of privatized enterprises the state owns 30 per cent or more of the shares (Szyrmer and Snelbecker 2000: 130).

Estimates of progress in privatization may differ according to the eventual inclusion of shadow economy. Also, the distinction between private or privatized enterprises is not always clear. Some enterprises in which the state still keeps a majority share are considered to be privatized.

In Ukraine, the divide between private and public is blurred. An example is the privatized Ferroalloy enterprise in Zaporizhzhya. Although the state has a minority share in the enterprise and has handed over management rights for a very small sum to the Ukrainian Credit Bank, it has continued to have a blocking vote in the shareholders' meeting (*Kiev Post*, 28 March 1999).

More important than the question of formal ownership is that of *de facto* control over enterprises. The main concern for enterprise managers is not formal ownership but control combined with opportunities to squeeze the state. It is telling that President Kuchma's own party, the People's Democratic Party, asked Kuchma 'to substitute the practice of privatizing property through distributing state corporate rights to "clan business structures"' (*News Agency UNIAN*, 7 December 1998). These clans usually have excellent relations with state structures. A characteristic of Ukrainian-style voucher privatization is that it has created diffuse ownership, which makes control of enterprise activity more complicated. Often, it means that there are no effective owners. This makes transformation of the enterprise more complex. Employees are the main owners of most medium-sized and a considerable number of large enterprises.[2]

As far as state-owned enterprises have actually been privatized, this has had little effect on enterprise governance, as numerous studies have shown. Djankov and Murrell (2000) conducted a survey of all available literature about privatization and enterprise behaviour in the area of the former Soviet Union, and have found that there is no statistically significant correlation between privatization

and enterprise restructuring. Pryor and Blackman (1998) did not find any difference between public and private firms as regards enterprise behaviour in their
surveys of enterprises in Ukraine. They explain this by the fact that ownership in
privatized firms may be too diffuse to allow new owners to push for changes in
company operations. Moreover, both public and privatized firms face an extensive system of governmental regulations and licensing, which appears to interfere
with the ability of enterprises of any type of ownership to recognize and use the
signals that the market provides. The bulk (85 per cent) of the shares were given
to incumbent managers and workers, through preferential share allocations
during the closed subscription phase (Pivarovsky 2001: 23). As a result, relatively
little has changed in the operation of most privatized enterprises. There was no
impetus for enterprise managers to change their behaviour. Later studies reveal a
slightly better performance for privatized firms, but the effects of privatization on
enterprise performance are as yet unclear and differ according to sector, size of
privatized firms, and methods of privatization. Enterprises that were privatized
on the basis of competitive methods performed better than those purchased by
workers' collectives. Pivovarsky (2001) found a positive correlation between enterprise performance and ownership concentration in Ukraine, especially in the
case of foreign ownership. In the case of ownership by an investment company,
there was no discernible impact upon enterprise performance.

Despite the lack of restructuring on the micro level, the industrial structure
changed drastically during the 1990s, not as a result of deliberate choice but as
the result of a differentiated decline that favoured labour-intensive and heavy
industries. Whereas in 1990 the share of power utilities, gas, oil, coal and steel
production in total industrial output was 39 per cent, this share increased to 63
per cent in 2000 (*Ukrainian Economic Trends*, December 2000). The number of
industrial production personnel declined from 5.9 million in 1992 to 3.6 million
in 2000 – a decline of 39 per cent (*Ukrainian Economic Trends*, December 2000).

Workers' representation

In most medium-sized and large Ukrainian enterprises, the patrimonial character of the company, like that of society at large, has become more pronounced.
With the falling away of the Communist Party, the power of the company leadership has been unchallenged and in many companies a process of asset
stripping has begun, usually at the expense of the workforce as a whole. Within
the company, a process of income redistribution has been set in motion. In the
new economic circumstances, there is no place for traditional socially minded
directors, and many have been pushed aside.

The rent-seeking behaviour of most company directors and management has
not been challenged, least of all by the trade unions, which have functioned
more or less as the industrial-relations department of the ministries. As far as the
official unions disagreed with government, they sided with anti-reform forces
within parliament. Trade unions did not engage in politics and parliamentary
elections. The right of trade unions to initiate legislation was abolished shortly

after Ukraine became independent. Parliament is dominated by a corpus of enterprise directors. They use administrative means to assure parliamentary seats in the elections, based on the district scheme (election offices are often within the enterprise and controlled by the directors).

Few strikes have occurred. This is not only related to the weak negotiating position of the workforce (due to the low demand for labour), but also to its compliant nature. It seems that employees will accept everything that is imposed upon them. This is related to a long history of submission to authoritarian rule. In many ways, workers are still tied to the disintegrating structures of the past. This is furthered by the way that workers are dependent on their company: the company still provides housing and a number of essential services. This constitutes a material base for semi-feudal relations at the shop-floor level.

The only sector where strikes and industrial action regularly take place is coal mining. In 1999, according to official statistics, 94 per cent of all industrial strikes (counted in lost work hours), occurred in coal mining (*Ukraina u tsifrach u 1999 rotsi*). This is related to the fact that industrial relations in this sector are fundamentally different to other sectors of industry. For miners, wages in cash have always been the most important part of the remuneration package, and the range of services offered by mines was always much more meagre as compared with other sectors of industry. Therefore, the decline in wages hit miners much harder than other workers. Another factor is that the nature of the work in mines, being heavily dependent on the help of one's colleagues, furthered mutual solidarity.

The mining industry has several relatively small independent unions that are militant but not able to constitute an effective countervailing force to mine directors, as they are not able to unite, and expend a lot of energy quarrelling among themselves. Simon (2000) noticed that:

> workers can display great social cohesion and power when mobilised but lack independent leadership and are frequently vulnerable within the enterprise.

Mine directors profited most from the big miners' strikes in 1993, which almost brought the government to its knees. Their debts were eliminated and fines for overspending on wages were abolished (Simon 2000: 149).

Working conditions

As economic conditions worsened, salaries were reduced and often were not paid or just paid in kind. In 2000, 69 per cent of all firms reported that they had great difficulties paying their wages (Standing and Zsoldos 2001: 39). More than 50 per cent of large firms pay their workers at least partly in kind. In 2000, more firms paid their workers partly in kind than in 1995 (Standing and Zsoldos 2001: 5). Approximately 10 per cent of medium- and large-sized firms pay more than 70 per cent of their workers in kind. Almost 30 per cent of firms were at least four months in arrears with wage payments. In large businesses the percentage is more than 42 per cent (Gray and Whiston 1999: 34).[3]

According to official figures, in 1999 4.4 million people were employed in Ukrainian industry, 1,484,700 were on unpaid leave (33.75 per cent) and 1,037,200 (23.5 per cent) were working part time, which means in practice working on average 20 hours a week (*Ukraina u tsifrach u 1999 rotsi 2000*: 191, 199). Even those not classified as working part time were working short working weeks, i.e. 32 hours on average, compared with the national standard week of 39.5 hours (2000).

About 12 per cent of all women nominally employed in Ukrainian factories were on long-term 'maternity leave', even though the fertility rate is extremely low. It seems that such leave was a way of laying off women workers. The extent of maternity leave was higher in firms that were in greatest economic difficulty and in which employment had fallen most.

Taking account of all forms of visible surplus labour, about one-third of all workers are laid off at any time, although these are still counted as employed. The ILO reported in 2001 that the effective unemployment rate was more than 20 per cent, although survey respondents said that they believed the figure could be double that level.

Legislation is such that it is very unprofitable for an enterprise to fire personnel. The fired workers have to be paid a large redundancy fee. It is cheaper to send an employee on unpaid leave or not to pay them while working.

In 2000, workers in manufacturing were unoccupied for 29 per cent of their working time. This means that the number of people employed in industry falls immediately by 29 per cent when calculated using the terms of full-time employment (*Ukrainian Economic Trends*, December 2000: 27). This means that labour productivity in industry has declined sharply since 1991, when workers were occupied most of the time. In the third quarter of 2000, labour productivity in industry was 65 per cent of the level of the first quarter of 1992 (*Ukrainian Economic Trends*, December 2000: 27).

On top of numerous salary cuts, some services that were free of charge in Soviet times now have to be paid for. When calculating the purchasing power of salaries, the disappearance of free or very cheap services is usually not taken into account. Specialist schools and university education were attainable for workers in Soviet times, but nowadays they are the privilege of the well-to-do because student stipends are very low, and for many services, including good marks, one often has to pay. In schools, contributions are expected, in kind or in money, in order to keep school services at a minimum level.

The rate of fatal injuries in the work-place has always been extremely high in Ukraine. In 1991 there were 12.1 fatal injuries per 100,000 workers employed, while the number was 1.4 in the UK (ILO 2000: 1239). During the 1990s, this ratio gradually declined to 10.2 per 100,000 workers employed in 1999. However, many registered workers are on unpaid leave or are working part time in 1999, while they were working full time in 1991. If correlated to full-time working-week equivalents, the ratio of fatal injuries more than doubled during the 1990s. This is related to the increasing use of obsolete technologies and equipment, and increasing carelessness.

According to a report of the State Department for Labour Safety (2001), about one hundred Ukrainians are injured at work daily, with one-third being disabled for life, and five dying of their injuries. According to the Chairman of the Department, Serhiy Storchak, 80 per cent of accidents at the workplace are due to carelessness and flouting of elementary labour safety rules (*The Day*, 25 September 2001).

A staggering 59 per cent of all industrial injuries occurred in Donbas (1998 data), although only 15 per cent of industrial employees work there. This is related to the type of industries located in the region, such as mining and steel. The extremely high injury rate in the mining industry is not so much related to lack of funding, but to a configuration of interests that produces neglect. Most accidents are caused by neglect and are related to ignoring safety rules. For example, oxygen equipment is manufactured in such a way that if miners carry it in the prescribed manner, their movements are severely impaired. As a result, they often do not carry the equipment when going underground. However, the equipment could be easily redesigned to allow greater freedom of movement. Also, miners' families get generous allowances in cases of death or injury. Miners often smoke in areas where it is dangerous, and work often continues when the methane content in the mines exceeds critical levels. This is related to the fact that a miner's pay is related to the amount of coal produced. The result is a death rate of between 300 and 350 miners per year over the past five years. It is telling that also the Ukrainian mine with the most modern equipment (Setka) has on average one gas explosion every five years and six fatalities per year.

According to international standards, labour turnover is now very high in Ukraine, being even higher than in Soviet times. In industry, the annual rate of hiring in 2000 (in the third quarter) was 28.1 per cent (17.6 per cent in 1993), while the annual rate of quitting work was 32.1 per cent in 2000 (in the third quarter) (22.5 per cent in 1993) (*Ukrainian Economic Trends*, December 2000: 27). A 32.1 per cent rate of quitting work means that every third worker will not work at the same factory during the next year. This high rate is related to the poor working conditions.

An important phenomenon is the de-skilling of the workforce. As in Soviet times, a very small proportion of the labour force constitutes skilled labour, despite the relatively high educational levels in Ukraine.[4] Across all manufacturing sectors, the share of blue-collar workers, who are doing manual or semi-skilled jobs, accounted for 76 per cent of all workers (Standing and Zsoldos 2001: 27). Although the percentage of unskilled jobs increased slightly during the 1990s, the extent of de-skilling is substantial because of erosion in the provision for institutional training and retraining (Standing and Zsoldos 2001: 46). Also, those sectors where average skill levels are low have gained in prominence.

Path dependency

It appears that transformation in the quasi-state sector has affected the labour force in many ways. Labour intensity and productivity have declined, remuneration has decreased drastically and a homogenization of the workforce has occurred. The network of social services of the firm has been eroded and social protection has diminished. Work safety has declined, resulting in a higher occurrence of injuries. The patrimonial character of the average firm has become more pronounced and workers are less protected. However, there has been virtually no marketization of these companies, even after privatization. Moreover, asset stripping of enterprises has been widespread, at the expense of the labour force.

It appears that social relations within the enterprise are very resistant to change, and that *Homo economicus* cannot easily replace *Homo sovieticus*. The socially motivated directors have tended to be sidelined, or forced into early retirement, while many others have seen their status not linked to efficiency and profitability of the enterprise, but to the size of the enterprise in terms of the labour force and the extension of social services and product range. Still, many enterprise directors feel like estate owners rather than entrepreneurs. The patrimonial attitude towards the labour force is reflected in a reluctance to sack workers and a resistance to cuts in the social-service network. Many directors, and certainly the overwhelming majority of workers, see it as amoral to dismiss workers. The enterprise is often considered as a type of family. Workers see the enterprise directors as representatives of the firm in their negotiations with ministries for privileges and subsidies, rather than as entrepreneurs who are primarily interested in profits. These enterprise directors function in networks of enterprises that operate on the basis of mutual trust rather than commercial relations.

The patrimonial belief system has led many to believe that, although all authorities should be mistrusted, the enterprise director represents their interests. It is also the enterprise director who is supposed to deliver the votes of their workforce in case of elections. The obedient nature of the workforce is rooted in ages of authoritarian rule.

Social relations in present-day Ukrainian society can be characterized as neo-patrimonial. However a new factor, as compared with Tsarist patrimonial culture, is the general lack of trust in society and anomie. The social structure is not now sanctioned by religious beliefs, and the traditional value-generating institutions have disappeared or been weakened. It seems that the most negative elements of traditional society have come to the fore in Ukraine nowadays. In common with Tsarist patrimonialism are the aversion to a book-keeper's mentality and the dominance of political over economic rationality. There is hardly a distinction between the sphere of economics and politics. There is also an absence of procedural rationality, and social mores are more important than laws.

The company is a reflection of society at large. As in society and the economy, relations within the enterprise are non-transparent and not governed by contractual relations. The director and management demand unconditional loyalty of their subordinates. Labour law and numerous regulations with respect to safety are not implemented. Enterprise management has numerous types of leverage over employees through arbitrary remuneration in kind and the distribution of numerous services.

Directors and managers pursue their interests in the context of a social environment, generally accepted social practices and related belief systems that put certain constraints upon the way that they perceive the range of possible actions. This means that corporate change in Ukraine has been path dependent. According to North, path dependency is a way of narrowing the set of choices conceptually and of linking decision-making through time (North 1990: 112). Path dependency points to the nature of constraints from the past imposing limits on current choices and therefore making the current choice-set intelligible (North 1990: 135). Path dependency is the key to an analytical understanding of long-term economic change.

The free-marketeers among the Western advisers to Ukraine were naïve to expect that privatization and liberalization would lead immediately to competition and 'economically rational behaviour'. The typical Ukrainian enterprise is a complex social institution in which the director is by far the most important actor, but is faced with numerous social and economic constraints.

Government policies and the role of international donor organizations

In its presentation of policies, government tunes in to the dominant belief systems. It talks about preserving the social balance and avoiding social conflict. In this context, it legitimizes the subsidies to ailing industries which, by the way, often disappear into the pockets of corrupt managers. With a web of numerous tiny privileges, the government tries to preserve the image of a caring government, while with the other hand allowing billions of dollars to be siphoned off in foreign bank accounts.

Western donor institutions did not do anything to prevent a robber capitalism from developing. The issues of social protection, income distribution and capital flight were ignored by these institutions, or given scant attention. Western donors pushed Ukraine to adopt many new laws that were aimed at liberalization and deregulation, privatization and the establishment of an institutional infrastructure for a market economy. The interests of oligarchs in Ukraine and Western donors merged and only those measures that did not harm the interests of these oligarchs were implemented. Western assistance contributed to the development of a kleptocracy, despite the rhetoric to the contrary. The West sanctioned the massive redistribution of Ukraine's national wealth.

Western institutions pushed for the splitting up of socialist estate companies, with the result that part of social infrastructure was transferred to municipalities that lacked the financial resources to sustain these services.[5] The population paid a heavy price. Western donors also pushed for rising energy prices while the majority of the population was earning such low salaries that they could not afford to pay their energy bills. On the other hand, Western advice has not targeted the problem of massive theft in the energy sector. More generally, Western institutions have ignored the issue of protecting the population against predatory practices.

Conclusions

The patrimonial character of the socialist estate company has become more pronounced since the centrally planned economy and the party-state were abolished in independent Ukraine. Behavioural patterns have proved to be very persistent at the enterprise level, and the unchallenged power of management has allowed massive asset-stripping. The position of workers has deteriorated in many respects: decreased remuneration, poorer safety on the shop floor, and less social protection. Workers' interests are hardly represented at the enterprise level. Part of the social infrastructure has been excised, although most medium-sized and large companies still have a sizeable, albeit crumbling, social infrastructure. Government policies, not challenged by Western donors, have been geared towards protecting a kleptocratic élite, squeezing the productive assets of the country and resulting in a steep economic decline.

Since the end of 1999, Ukraine has seen some economic growth, but the population as a whole has hardly profited from it, and household consumption did not increase in 2000, according to official statistics. Given the weak bargaining position of the workers, and high unemployment, it is questionable whether the condition of workers will improve even if economic growth continues. Only in some sectors where demand for labour outstrips supply can significant wage increases be expected.

Notes

1 If all implicit subsidies are taken into account, i.e. tax deferral, privileges, low-interest bank loans to enterprises, and state purchases of goods at prices higher than market prices or purchases of illiquid goods, total subsidies amounted to 19.22 per cent of GDP in 1996, 20.73 per cent in 1997 and 19.37 per cent in 1998.

2 A survey of 200 enterprises, conducted by the Institute of Reforms, shows that employees and managers own, on average, about 55.2 per cent of the shares.

3 Since 1998, wage arrears gradually diminished.

4 These figures are not available for Ukraine. For Russia, where the economic situation is similar, it has been estimated that only 5 per cent of the industrial workforce can be considered as skilled (*Ekonomika i Zhizn*, 44, 2000).

5 Western institutions usually base their advice on an idealized version of the Anglo-Saxon model of capitalism. With respect to company restructuring, few parallels are made between typical Ukrainian enterprises and the estate-like nature of many Western companies until the early 1970s, or even with the Japanese situation. The Japanese experience shows that companies which ensure that their employees have high levels of social security and an extended network of services are not necessarily inefficient.

Bibliography

Clarke, S. (1992) 'Privatization and the development of capitalism in Russia', *New Left Review*, 196(6): 3–29.

Djankov, S. and Murrell, P. (2000) *Enterprise Restructuring in Transition: a Quantitative Survey*, Social Science Research Network Electronic Library, http//papers.ssrn.com/sol3/delivery.cfm/SSRN_ID238716_code001031600.pdf?abstractid=238716 (accessed 2 April 2002).

Gray, T.A. and Whiston, W.B. (1999) *A Survey of Business in Ukraine*, Washington D.C.: Management Systems International.

International Labour Organisation (2000) *Yearbook of Labour Statistics*, Geneva: ILO.

International Monetary Fund (2001) *World Economic Outlook*, Washington D.C.: IMF.

Lyakh, A. and Pankow, W. (eds) (1998) *The Future of Old Industrial Regions in Europe: The Case of Donetsk Region in Ukraine*, Warsaw: Foundation for Economic Education.

Maroudas, L. (2000) 'Stratégies managériales et relations de travail pendant la période de transition en Russie', *Revue d'études Est–Ouest*, 31(1): 169–91.

North, D.C. (1990) *Institutions, Institutional Change and Economic Performance*, Cambridge: Cambridge University Press.

Pivarovsky, A. (2001) *How Does Privatization Work? Ownership Concentration and Enterprise Performance in Ukraine*, Washington D.C.: IMF Working Paper.

Pryor, F.L. and Blackman, M. (1998) 'The Ukrainian industrial sector in 1996 and 1997; insights from the rapid enterprise survey', *Ukrainian Economic Review*, III(4–5), 1997–8.

Simon, R. (2000) *Labour and Political Transformation in Russia and Ukraine*, Aldershot: Ashgate.

Standing, G. and Zsoldos, L. (2000) *Worker Insecurities in Ukrainian Industry*, Geneva: ILO.

Standing, G. and Zsoldos, L. (2001) *Worker Insecurities in Ukrainian Industry: the 2000 ULFS*, Geneva: ILO.

Szyrmer, J.M. and Snelbecker, D. (2000) *Reforms for Ukraine: Ideas and Actions*, Kiev: Alterpres.

Ugolnii konsultingovii tsentr TACIS (2001) *Bezopasnost na ukrainskix shaxtax*, Donetsk, February.

Ukraina u tsifrach u 1999 rotsi (2000), Kiev: State Statistical Committee.

Zon, H. van (2000) *The Political Economy of Independent Ukraine*, London: Macmillan.

7 Russia's regional labour markets

Coping with the pressures of globalisation

Andrey S. Makarychev

Introduction

In Russia, acquaintance with market norms and principles first started at the theoretical level, unleashing a lot of initial enthusiasm and energy. However, as soon as it came to the practical implementation of market reforms, immense problems became evident. The example of Russian labour relations is a prime illustration of this.

Economic reform, which features strongly in President Vladimir Putin's programme, only has the chance to be implemented if the country has adequate human capital, with an effective labour market at its core.[1] That is why it is so important to have a better understanding of Russian economic perspectives, in order to keep up with changes in labour relations.

In this chapter, I will focus on several main issues:

1 I will illustrate the diversity of labour market conditions in the Russian provinces;
2 I will address the issue of labour mobility, seen from both domestic and international perspectives;
3 I will demonstrate the unique features of Russia's unemployment;
4 I will pay particular attention to new business practices, which have a large impact on labour market evolution.
5 I will briefly discuss the 'dark side of globalisation' – the issue of 'shadow' labour markets;
6 I will look at the political dimensions of labour market development within the context of Putin's reforms.

Regional labour markets

Stratification and differentiation

Due to a significant amount of *de facto* powers, regional governments have a major impact on labour market evolution. Here I am referring to the regional authorities that are in charge of social infrastructure, supervise the policies of economic actors, and control business regulation measures.

Japanese scholar Sadayoshi Ohtsu has examined the striking variations in regional labour markets:

The first type of regional labour market was created in two 'cities of federal significance' – Moscow and St Petersburg, which are the centres of capital flows, investments, banking and insurance services, etc. The largest of Russia's cities – very much like those in the West – have started to play the roles of command posts for the operations of multinational corporations, turning into the back-bones of advanced services and information-related activities. Simultaneously, they are deeply fragmented social spaces, marked by extremes of poverty and wealth. The formation of dense labour markets and the concomitant emergence of extended webs of residential activities are among the most essential character-istics of large cities. At the same time, they function more and more as poles of attraction for low-wage migrants.[2]

The second type of labour market exists in the 'former industrial cities' of the Volga and Central areas that were mostly dominated by light industry (Yaroslavl', Ivanovo, Kostroma and Vladimir oblasts). Due to the weak competi-tiveness of their industrial output, they face the threat of de-industrialisation and social anomie.

The third type can be seen in the heartland regions, with machine building, heavy industry and military enterprises (mostly exemplified by the Ural regions), and the fourth type might be found in the Far East, with such determining factors as geographical remoteness from the central areas, and the sense of isola-tion from Russia's economic mainstream.

The fifth type is represented by peripheral ethnic regions (best exemplified by the Northern Caucasus), heavily dependent on subsidies from the centre and facing huge migration pressures.[3] These regions are known for their stronger clientelist networks and authoritarian political practices.

These variations tell us much about the diversity of the regional labour markets that have emerged in Russia in the 1990s. Unemployment and numbers of job vacancies show substantial variations across regions. For example, in some regions there is one job vacancy for every four people seeking a job, while in others the same ratio is one to one hundred. In some regional labour markets, profitable firms report a shortage of qualified workers. At the same time, unprofitable companies in declining regions are hoarding workers with desirable qualifications.[4] In some regions (Krasnoyarsk and Stavropol' krais, Orenburg and Omsk oblasts), the immigrants have settled in the countryside, while in others (Sverdlovsk, Cheliabinsk and Kemerovo oblasts) they are chiefly concentrated in the cities.[5] Some regions have intro-duced the 'social minimum' (the so-called 'survival level'), but others have not.[6] One can elaborate further on these differences across the regions, which indi-cate huge interregional contrasts all across Russia in terms of labour market conditions.

Labour mobility

Since we have seen that the labour market conditions differ from one region to another, the question arises as to whether there are significant labour migrations within Russia and immigration inflows from other countries, and if so, how can this problem be tackled?

Factors impeding labour force mobility

It is generally assumed that the geographical immobility of a population is a strain on a country's adaptation to the challenges of modernisation. Russia is a good illustration of this world-wide tendency.

On the one hand, a number of factors hinder labour force mobility. First, there is an over-industrialised pattern of employment, inherited from Soviet times, with an overwhelming predominance of traditional workers. This complicates the switch to a post-industrial model of labour relations and weakens labour mobility. Among the most disadvantaged categories are those employed in metallurgical, automobile, textile and other light industries, who are not able to make an easy transition to new ways of production and quality standards.[7] The bulk of the employees in these sectors will be unable to become part of the new labour markets due to low professionalism and an old-style mentality based on paternalism, patronage and lack of initiative. Hence, the regions with a higher concentration of these industries will face the biggest problems in adapting to world standards. For example, in the words of Sergei Kirienko, the presidential representative in the Volga Federal District, it was difficult to explain to the directors of state-owned factories that it is they themselves – not the federal government – who are responsible for recruiting or training the kind of workers that they need.[8]

The industries located in these regions lose out domestically in competition with foreign imports and are unable to compete as exporters internationally.[9] Politically, the leaders of such regional 'foot-draggers' are lobbying for greater protectionism, usually in the form of higher import tariffs.[10] There is a need for a comprehensive state-sponsored programme to revive the so-called 'depressed' regions, but so far no adequate projects have been implemented.

At the same time, regions with predominance of sectors like trade and commerce, export-oriented industries (wood processing, oil and gas extraction and reprocessing), catering, construction, real-estate, banking and finances have a greater chance to plug into the international milieu, due to higher flexibility and mobility.

Second, Russia's huge size is a hindering factor. The underdeveloped (although rather expensive by Russian standards) transport infrastructure makes changing residence a major challenge for ordinary people.[11]

Third, the poor development of the housing market is a huge problem. Realtor's networks in Russia are overwhelmingly unprofessional, badly managed and corrupt, which prevents people from looking for and taking jobs in remote localities.

Labour migrations

Different regions have been adapting differently to the flow of migrants. Two areas – the North and the Far East – are systematically losing their population. For example, during the mid-1990s Chukotka lost about 30 per cent of its population, Magadan oblast – 25 per cent, Koriak autonomous okrug and Evenkia – 15 per cent each, Kamchatka – 13 per cent, Sakhalin – 11 per cent, Taimyr and Nenets autonomous okrugs – 10 per cent each, Murmansk oblast – 7 per cent, and the Komi Republic – 6 per cent.

The North-West, the south of the Urals, Western Siberia, and the central provinces, on the contrary, are major recipients of immigrants (with the city of Moscow and Moscow oblast, Khanty–Mansy and Yamal–Nenets autonomous okrugs, Belgorod and Rostov oblasts, Primorie and Krasnodar krais at the top of the list).[12] The majority of newcomers are young and rather well-qualified people – from 20 to 29 years old,[13] i.e. successful labour market actors. For example, construction workers from Ukraine are strong competitors in many of Russia's regional markets. This fact has led to protests in the regions.

There are different categories of immigrants: Russian and non-Russian citizens, officially registered forced migrants, legal refugees, illegal migrants and others. Among 'near-abroad' (CIS) countries, the most significant exporters of labour are Ukraine (about 70 per cent of the overall migrant labour force), Belarus (8.3 per cent), Georgia (5.2 per cent), Moldova (5 per cent) and Armenia (4.5 per cent).[14] Among the immigrants, several categories can be distinguished: immigrants who wish to take up long-term residence in Russia, 'pendulum' migrants (going back and forth for trade purposes) and seasonal workers.[15] All of them usually face multiple challenges in adapting to the local labour markets. Basically they prefer to concentrate in those sectors (like commerce or construction) that allow for quick and reasonable revenues. According to some appraisals, the Azeri diaspora living in Russia transfer sums exceeding their country's annual budget, back to Azerbaijan,[16] basically from trade and commercial operations.

Migration – a global challenge – directly affects Russian regional labour markets and raises a number of issues. The most important one is the legal regulation of foreign labour.

The general principle in this field is the priority given to the employment of the Russian citizens. Formally, if an employer wants to fill the vacancy using a foreign contractor, they have to prove the efficacy and necessity of employing the foreign citizen (very much the same procedure as in many Western countries). The contract has to be approved by local executive authorities and the Federal Migration Service, and is issued for one year, with the possibility of extension. Job permission is non-transferable and valid only for a specific subject of the Russian Federation, in a particular area. Exceptions to these rules are made for a number of categories, including official refugees, citizens granted asylum, official temporary residents of Russia, scientists and artists staying in Russia in accordance with intergovernmental agreements with foreign countries, religious activists affiliated with registered religious institutions, student interns affiliated with Russian institutions of higher education, and some others.

According to Russian legislation, foreigners cannot be employed in courts, the militia, customs and public administration, and cannot be members of the crew in naval boats and aircraft. However, apart from these general legal restrictions, some administrative measures are also widely applied.

In many regions (Dagestan, Kabardino–Balkaria, Krasnodar and Stavropol' krais, Kurgan and Belgorod oblasts, Moscow city, and some others), it is extremely hard to get official residence registration, which is indispensable when applying for Russian citizenship, for getting a job, and launching a business. According to the information released at the Second Forum of the Migrants' Organisation, 67 per cent of the immigrants have faced the refusal of the regional administrators to register them officially.[17] At some federation authorities, additional registration fees have been introduced, which contradicts federal legislation. Some federal authorities have cancelled some of these undue restrictions, but *de facto* they are still in action. Even more problematically, some regional authorities, in overt conflict with the federal legislation, deny employment rights to those immigrants (even those with Russian citizenship) who are not registered within their specific region.

Obtaining Russian citizenship is even harder. This requires proving that the applicant (say, the resident of one of the former USSR republics) has no other citizenship, which is an immensely time-consuming and lengthy procedure.

There are serious practical obstacles to receiving the status of official immigrant and refugee. These include lack of official information and the need to travel regularly to the regional offices of the Federal Migration Service. Among the negative consequences of regional anti-migration policies are the marginalisation of newcomers, their exclusion from social and public life, and vast possibilities for exploitation of their cheap labour – the fewer rights they have and the more that they are dependent on local bureaucrats, the less expensive their labour.[18]

As a result, it is estimated that there are from 1 to 1.5 million illegal immigrants in Russia. Since they do not pay taxes, their damage to the Russian fiscal system is assessed by President Putin's thinktank as 5–7 billion US dollars.[19]

A number of Russian NGOs are committed to defending the immigrants' rights. These are primarily the 'Memorial' Centre and regional human rights associations. For example, the Centre for Migrants Assistance, affiliated with the Nizhny Novgorod Human Rights Society, releases annual reports detailing the most blatant cases of violation of immigrants' rights in the region.[20]

The main paradox of the immigrants' treatment in Russia is that the country faces a labour shortage and this will increase in the years to come. The areas targeted by the immigrants suffer from depopulation, which might be compensated for at least partially by immigration. For many Russian enterprises and villages,[21] workers coming from the CIS have allowed them to survive the economic crisis.[22] Zhanna Zaionchkovskaya, the director of the Migration Laboratory at the Institute for Economic Forecasts in Moscow has warned that, starting from 2006, Russia will lose about one million of its workers per year. In her assessments, if Russia closes its borders to immigrants, the country's population will shrink by 70 million by the middle of this century.[23] This means that immigration is one of the few hopes for the Russian labour market.

The overwhelming majority of CIS immigrants are ethnically Russian (from 60 per cent to 80 per cent), which facilitates cultural adjustment.[24] Research done in Irkutsk oblast describes immigrants as predominantly responsible and disciplined workers.[25] In the Far East, for example, workers coming from China fill those labour gaps that remain vacant even at high rates of unemployment.[26] Vilia Gilbras, an expert on China, deems that Russia is lucky to have such an immense source of workers close to its borders.[27]

The potential to accommodate migrants is still significant. However, the regional authorities are not ready to effectively meet the challenge of immigration and to use its potential for the sake of the country's development. For example, Tiumen' oblast governor Leonid Roketsky has frankly admitted that 'we are not very glad to accommodate people coming to our place, since they bring problems'.[28] What is needed is the creation of a migrant-friendly infrastructure, basically in border territories and major cities. The intensive circulation of people across the border has to be a part of the mutually beneficial transborder co-operation agenda.

Labour market regulations and new approaches to regional economic security

The sub-national anti-migration policies could be partly explained by the fact that the regional governments have to tackle the immigration issues themselves, with insufficient assistance from the federal centre. Only a few of them lobby for less-restrictive border-crossing procedures, understanding that cross-border trade and tourism do create new jobs. Restrictive policies are more typical. Many of the regional administrations in Russia introduce quotas for foreign employees. The Legislative Council of the Republic of Karelia appealed to the Ministry of Justice of the Russian Federation, expressing concern about the lack of mechanisms to enforce the decisions of Russian courts against foreign tax evaders. Since 1995, more than forty decisions of the High Arbitrary Court of Karelia concerning foreign residents have not been implemented. According to the media, about 500 citizens of Finland work illegally in Karelia, paying no taxes.[29]

In the areas bordering Chechnya (mainly in Stavropol' krai and Dagestan), local authorities have had to monitor the passport regime. Dozens of regional computer networks were established recently in order to keep track of foreigners residing in specific areas. Similar measures were introduced in Belgorod and some other oblasts.

In many regions, fears about an 'invasion' of foreigners are highly publicised, as is the case in the Far East concerning Chinese immigration. The fear of Chinese 'guest workers' is so acute that authorities in the Altai Republic, for example, are reluctant to construct the highway to connect the Trans-Siberian railroad with one of China's provinces.[30]

On the one hand, it is true that authorities in border regions have to tackle the 'dark side' of internationalisation on a regular basis – crime, illegal fishing, hunting, border-crossing or smuggling (drugs, guns, undeclared cash, etc.). In the Far East, for example, numerous murders of Chinese entrepreneurs – the bulk of them are executed by Chinese gangs – are registered each year. According to the tax authorities of Primorsky krai, 263 joint ventures created by Chinese entrepreneurs in the region (out of 405) do not submit their financial accounts, while another thirty-eight joint ventures were closed by the court decisions due to legal violations.[31]

On the other hand, anti-immigrant phobia is usually very much exaggerated and the need to introduce more liberal approaches is becoming increasingly obvious. Mikhail Kasianov's government has pledged to prioritise co-operation with immigrant communities over immigration control. It has ruled that all forms of discrimination in immigrants' registration have to be lifted, first of all in larger cities with better job opportunities. The practice of creating isolated immigrant communities has to be given up as well.[32]

Ethnic dimensions of labour migrations

Ethnicity may also be an issue for understanding regional labour markets. Immigration can change the ethnic composition of a population. Thus, the total number of Chinese immigrants in Russia is believed to be 800,000, predicted to increase considerably by the middle of the century.[33] Taking into account that the world Adyg diaspora is believed to be from 1 to 3 million, the government of Adygeya has adopted a programme of repatriation.[34]

Professor Valerii Tishkov, Director of the Institute of Ethnology and Anthropology of the Russian Academy of Sciences, assumes that one of the strongest impediments to labour market development in Russia is widespread xenophobia (as he figuratively puts it, 'we want to have water melons in the markets, but we don't want Azeri vendors'[35]). However, it is known that ethnic diasporas usually possess strong business potential and have their own information channels that might be used for the sake of the labour market as a whole.

Features unique to Russia's regional unemployment

The first labour-exchange offices were opened in Russia in 1991. Ten years afterwards one can state that unemployment rates essentially vary from region to region – according to data from the mid-1990s, from 5.2 per cent to 24 per cent and even higher. Among the regions badly affected by unemployment are North Caucasus (due to refugees and the inflow of migrants, the unemployment rate in Dagestan, North Ossetia and Karachaevo-Cherkessia might be as high as one-quarter of the economically active population); Siberia; the European North of Russia, and some areas in the country's heartland (Yaroslavl', Ivanovo and Vladimir oblasts).

However, the average registered unemployment rate is still very low in Russia, in comparison with other transition countries. Regardless of the assessment methods, the scale of Russia's official unemployment (not exceeding 3 per cent on average) is inadequate to explain the fall in production. It is believed that the number of officially registered unemployed makes up only one-fifth of the real jobless total.[36]

The explanation of this phenomenon is that employers, political authorities and workers themselves apply different strategies for concealing unemployment. *Employers* usually resort to:

- unpaid (or partly paid) breaks ('forced vacations') initiated by the administration. Workers on unpaid leave retain their rights to the non-monetary benefits that the company provides: such as the medical clinic, child-care facilities, housing, and the like;[37]
- part-time employment;
- wage arrears;
- raising prices for production, which allows unnecessary jobs to be subsidised (often practised by monopolists).

The problems of the 'GAZ' automobile factory in Nizhny Novgorod illustrate what was said above. It was estimated that for the sake of efficiency from 20,000 to 30,000 out of 110,000 of its employees will have to be dismissed eventually.[38] GAZ is also financially in charge of huge housing areas and supporting facilities, which will have to be transferred to the municipal budget. Both problems have an obvious social background.

Policy-makers have a number of tools at their disposal: for example, the regional government can grant subsidies to weak enterprises.[39] The regional government can also increase the number of jobs in the sectors that they control. The study of Vladimir Gempelson and Galina Monusova found out that the practice of 'public employment' is mostly rooted in largely poor regions heavily subsidised but enjoying relatively autonomous powers (e.g. ethnic republics).[40]

Policy-makers have a number of reasons to contain unemployment by supporting inefficient enterprises:

- the political sensitivity of the labour issue, which has a clear electoral dimension (votes);
- traditions of social paternalism and patronage which are both a psychological and political phenomenon in Russia;
- as they are short of funds, insolvent enterprises, if they file for bankruptcy, will be unable to pay the compensation stipulated by the law to their workers.[41]

Facing the 'unemployment or inflation' dilemma, the political class of Russia usually favours the second.[42] Artificially increasing employment rates has its price – the devaluation of labour;[43] the preservation of inefficient industries; decreasing the incomes of workers; undermining the stimuli and motivation for high-efficiency work; and in the long run promoting irrationality in the Russian economy.[44] Most experts agree that the strategy of keeping unemployment low impedes the modernisation of the Russian economy and its integration into global economic networks.

As regards the *employees* themselves, they also have their own strategies to counter unemployment. The labour market has become more flexible and more accommodating to the new needs and potentials of the population. Phenomena such as self-employment and secondary employment – basically in the small-scale industrial sector – have become widespread among about 35–40 per cent of the population.[45] This explains why a large part of the unemployed (about 13 per cent, according to some studies) think that they are fairly satisfied with their lives. This also helps to explain why a high percentage of those officially unemployed favour fostering economic reforms (28.7 per cent).[46]

New business and labour practices in the Russian regions

One of the greatest challenges of globalisation is that in today's world financial flows choose regions with better management and business practices, not those with larger numbers of workers.

Traditionally, Russians used to look for a better job through their own, personal and many informal networks. New forms of business practices are a direct result of liberalisation of both supply and demand for the labour force. First, the demand for highly qualified specialists is rising. The Russian economy is gradually becoming more service-oriented, which requires more highly skilled jobs. The most marketable specialists are sales managers, financial experts, office administrators, public relations practitioners, advertising agents, and securities market analysts. Basically they are recruited by foreign companies and joint ventures operated in Russia. Russian companies are much less willing to invest funds into human capital, preferring to buy expensive equipment and offices.

The Internet has also opened up new opportunities. In the summer of 2001, the Ministry of Labour launched a new online project announcing job vacancies all across Russia. E-commerce is gradually becoming a part of Russia's business life.

Second, contemporary recruitment practices have been introduced. Foreigners were the first to establish recruitment agencies in Russia, as early as the end of the 1980s. Of course, Moscow and St Petersburg – due to the concentration of finances and services – took the lead in recruiting practices. However, in 1993–5 recruitment agencies were being opened in the 'second wave' regions like Ekaterinbourg, Novosibirsk, Vladivostok and Nizhny Novgorod. Later, Samara, Saratov, Rostov-on-Don and Krasnodar joined the list. After 1995, 'the third wave' of recruitment agencies proliferated across Russia, to include such cities as Voronezh, Perm', Lipetsk, Yaroslavl', Omsk, Irkutsk and Kemerovo.

A number of factors facilitate recruitment in the regions. First, of utmost importance is the development of the financial and industrial infrastructure. Second, geographical location is also essential: those regions adjacent to the sea usually have a better-developed network of recruitment agencies (Murmansk, Sochi and other border cities are examples).[47]

Third, the advent of new owners has changed the labour-relations milieu. The new owners of major regional enterprises, being newcomers in the regions, were forced to make 'social partnership agreements' with regional administrations, pledging to honour 'social guarantees'.[48] Yet, in practice, the advent of new owners brings labour conflicts like those that occurred in the Lomonosov porcelain factory (Leningrad oblast), a metallurgical plant in Novokuznetsk, and the Krasnoe Sormovo shipyards (Nizhny Novgorod oblast). Their roots can probably be found in uncertainties about the legal aspects of the property transfer, the lack of information available to the workers, and the new owners' lack of sensitivity to the views of the workforce.[49]

Jean Toshenko, the chief editor of 'Socis' journal in Moscow, has stated that, for an average Russian worker, democracy means, among other things, the chance to comment on management decisions.[50] Widespread labour conflicts show that the old management is usually associated with customary order and habitual labour requirements, while the new management is perceived as something less certain, conducive to job cuts and 'rampant capitalism'. The most serious labour conflict, in the Vyborg paper mills[51] (Leningrad oblast) shows that not all of the new owners are effective managers and workers' protests may well be justified.

Fourth, the importance of professional education is also rising. Russian universities – being rather conservative institutions – by themselves might not want or be able to introduce more sophisticated materials, active teaching methods, and other practice-oriented assignments, but they might come under pressure from outside. Business education plays an important role in nurturing corporatism in most advanced enterprises.[52]

The dark side of globalisation

Shadow relations in the labour market

In general, during the course of Russia's transformation, covert processes – in the economy as well as in society – tend to prevail over open ones. The proliferation of shadow relations in labour markets proves this tendency.

There are several factors fostering the spread of 'shadow' labour relations. The first one is the practice of hidden and/or 'unofficial' employment, which fuels a 'black labour market'.[53] These are basically those jobs that at best are not taxed, and at worst are associated with crime (drug trafficking, prostitution, extortion, etc.).

Second, the whole sphere of the state's labour policy is insufficiently transparent, which fosters criminal and corrupt practices. For example, there have been some reports from the regions indicating that regional administrations have distributed cheap credit, for creating new jobs, among those enterprises that had bribed the officials.[54] Needless to say, these funds were misused and had no positive effect on labour market development.

Third, illegal immigrants, having no chances to legalise their jobs, are forced to bribe public officials and business administrators.[55] A good illustration of the lack of proper rights and protection is Alexei Kuz'min's assessment of the amount of bribes that customs officers demand from seasonal workers at border-crossing checkpoints – they could be US$30 on the Russian side and about US$100 on the Ukrainian side.[56]

According to figures from the High Commission on Refugees, some 30,000 persons from 'far abroad' were living in Moscow during the mid-1990s, while the Federal Migration Service accepted only 4,841 applications from them, and 78 were officially recognised as refugees.[57] In 2001, the vice-mayor of Moscow gave another figure – 400,000 foreign immigrants in the capital city.[58] In Primorsky krai, only one-third out of approximately 30,000 foreign nationals (basically of Chinese, Korean and Vietnamese origin) have legal status, working in construction, agriculture and commerce.[59] All across Russia, the number of illegal immigrants is estimated to be as many as *c*.3 million. In Kuz'min's assessment, only 30 per cent of labour immigrants *de facto* employed all across Russia were granted formal job permissions.[60] Coupled with the lack of deportation mechanisms (both in financial and legal terms), this situation obviously boosts 'black' labour markets and encourages criminal activity.

The way out could be found in better management of all issues related to the use of foreign workers. Of course, there is a need to strengthen security on Russian borders with CIS countries – especially with countries such as Kazakhstan – which are still overwhelmingly unprotected. This is imperative in order to avoid further criminalisation of the Russian labour market. In parallel, better co-operation between agencies in charge of tackling immigration issues is required. Actually three of them – the Ministry of Foreign Affairs (issuing visas), the Ministry of Federation (implementing migration policy) and the Internal Ministry (controlling foreigners residing in Russia) – are in charge, which makes co-ordination between them a high-priority issue.

Fourth, there is a gender dimension to the problem of the black labour market. Seventy-four per cent of all registered unemployed in Russia are women.[61] This is the unemployment that pushes many young women and girls into prostitution, both within Russia and abroad.[62]

Political aspects of labour market reform under President Putin

Taking into account the fact that labour-relations issues in Russia are so bound up with multiple controversies, it is not surprising that they have led to heated political debates.

Labour reform is one of the Russian government's long-standing obligations to the international financial institutions. The drafting of the new Labour Code was funded by the World Bank in 1997, which was a part of a US$28.6 million Social Protection Implementation Loan. In 1998, the government of Sergei Kirienko, by signing a joint memorandum with the Central Bank on the policies of economic and financial stabilisation, has committed itself to ensure the passage of the new Labour Code through parliament. In particular, there is an obligation to simplify the procedure of dissolving individual labour agreements.

However, the blueprint of the Labour Code drafted by Evgeny Primakov's government was considered in the West as being too left-wing, leading to the World Bank's refusal to release more funds in its support. Later, due to the efforts of the Federation of Independent Unions of Russia (FNPR) – the successor of Soviet-era trade unions – the Labour Code became a high-profile issue in Russian politics. By summer 2001, there were five alternative drafts presented to the parliament, but in fact the real conflict was between the more liberal government-sponsored draft and a more conservative proposal presented by FNPR. The latter claimed that the federal government intended to dismantle the remains of eighty-year-old legislation protecting workers' interests. Yet the real issue is that the FNPR was unhappy with losing its right to intervene in both the firing process and decisions on the composition of company management.[63] As the Deputy Minister of Economic Development and Trade, Maxim Dmitriev, put it, for the trade unions backed by the Communists, the Labour Code was a political revenge issue.[64]

In fact, the 'trade-union' project is geared towards maintaining the status quo, while the federal government wishes to make it possible for employers to do away with the 'peripheral' labour force, the part that is of low quality and inadequate for business demands. Consequently, the employers are encouraged to invest more funds in human capital development. The adherents of the government's Labour Code argue that human capital is the best protection from unemployment.[65]

The problems with introducing the new Labour Code are that the government did not go public with this issue, preferring to concentrate on working with specific parliamentary factions. Their opponents, on the contrary, have launched a broad public-relations campaign against the governmental text. The employers have not really taken part in the discussions (except for the Russian Union of Industrialists and Entrepreneurs), which has made the government's work even harder.[66]

It seems that President Putin understands that market efficiency and labour-rights guarantees may contradict each other. Keeping 'hard' labour guarantees is economically inefficient. However, if Putin is eager to implement the 'new social contract' and build up corporatist structures in Russia, all changes have to be made in a consistent and mutually binding way.[67] What is good for Russian democracy is that the whole process labour reform was implemented through negotiations.[68]

Putin's 'social contract' with the corporate élite is geared towards strengthening the social commitments of Russian business. Interros Holding, Alexander Khloponin, Norilsk Nickel, KamAZ, LukOil and other major financial and industrial groups of Russia are known to invest heavily in personnel retraining, supporting the social infrastructure (schools, hospitals and child care for employees), developing mortgage schemes, subsidising retirees and pensioners, and launching charitable projects.[69]

Of course these efforts do not solve all the issues. What is needed to breathe new life into labour relations is robust reform of the judicial system. As Russian experts suggest, the mean time-span for dealing with labour disputes in the courts is from two to three years, which makes the whole system of defending workers' rights extremely ineffective. Only a small percentage of people fired from industry try to use legal mechanisms to get their jobs back.

Conclusions

Russia has to adjust to the new situation in its regional labour markets, which are very much influenced by globalisation processes. The employers are gradually giving up their social functions (most of them are not in charge, as they used to be, of maintenance of housing, recreation and health care). At the same time, trade unions have to redefine themselves, since most of the employers treat trade unions and other workers' associations as annoying and unnecessary institutions.[70]

The relative share of labour and raw material costs in the value added to final products will continue to decline. On the contrary, the value-added share of information and service inputs (the cost of marketing, distribution, transportation, financing, information and technology content) will continue to rise.[71] These are the issues that the regions will have to address to create new jobs and provide better services.

There are several problems that impede the creation of effective labour markets in Russian regions. The first is the existence of a substantial non-market sector, consisting of ineffective Soviet-style enterprises. Evgenii Yasin, the head of the Moscow-based High School of Economics, estimates that about 40 per cent of Russian plants and factories are potentially insolvent. The problem with these companies is that they have invented a special adaptation model of survival that includes lobbying for state subsidies, tax evasion, barter exchange schemes and wage arrears.[72] In these organisations, the quantity of employees is not related to the effectiveness of the enterprise.

Second, the social-security system in Russia is obsolete and inefficient. It fails to react swiftly to changing economic realities and address its target groups. The role of NGOs (voluntary associations, churches, etc.) in providing social services is still weak and rather impractical.[73]

Third, the middle class – potentially the cornerstone of country – is still weak and nascent. The roots of its underdevelopment can be found in slow adaptation of the country to the demands of globalisation, the non-competitiveness of its major industrial sectors, and poor labour management. The introduction of new patterns of personnel management, based on social capital concepts might be helpful in this regard.[74]

Fourth, Western and international institutions also have to reshape their policies in relation to labour market development in Russia. Previously designed projects need to be reassessed, and their effectiveness carefully measured. For example, the World Bank has launched a number of projects in the areas of social security, employment, pension reform and labour migration in Russia (SPAL, SPIL and SAL 3). However, both in Russia and the West there are reservations concerning their efficacy. The outcomes of the regional pilot projects will also have to be reconsidered.

Notes

All websites accessed 28 June 2001.

1 National News Service website, at *http://www.nns.ru/analytdoc/exindk1.html*

2 Scott, A.J., 'Globalization and the rise of city-regions', at *http://www.lboro.ac.uk/departments/gy/research/gawc/rb/rb26.html*

3 Ohtsu, S., 'Characteristics of the Russian regional labour market', at *http://src-home.slav.hokudai.ac.jp/sympo/99summer/99summer-contents.html*

4 Friebel, G. and Guriev, S. (1999) *Why Russian Workers Do Not Move: Attachment of Workers Through In-Kind Payments*. Working Paper No. 283, October: The William Davidson Institute at the University of Michigan Business School, p. 1.

5 Zlokazov, I., 'Problemy obshego rynka truda gosudarstv uchastnikov SNG' (The problems of common labour market in CIS countries), at *http://pubs.carnegie.ru/books/1998/10gv/toc.asp*

6 *Vremya MN*, 111(722), 30 June, 2001, p. 1.

7 Bogomolov, Y. and Kulagina, N., 'Upravlenie professional'nim sostavom ekonomicheski aktivnogo naselenia v period do 2000 goda' (Professional management of economically active personnel till 2000), at *http://www.ptpu.ru/issues/4_97/16_4_97.htm*

8 Volga Federal District official website, at *http://www.pfo.ru/main/news.phtml?id=2749*

9 Baranenkova, T., 'Sostoyanie regional'nikh rynkov truda i problemy ikh regulirovania' (The state of the regional labour markets and the problems of their regulation), at *http://www.ptpu.ru/issues/4_98/8_4_98.htm*

10 '*Problems of Theory and Practice of Management*', Online Journal, at *http://www.ptpu.ru/issues/3_98/15_3_98.htm*

11 'Spiritual Heritage' thinktank website, at *http://www.nasledie.ru/oboz/N08_97/8_06.htm*

12 Vitkovskaya, G. and Panarin, S. (2000) *Migratsia i bezopasnost' v Rossii (Migration and Security in Russia)*, Moscow: Interdialekt, p. 103.

13 Zaionchkovskaya, Z., 'Rynok trudakak reguliator migratsionnykh potokov' (Labour market as a regulator of migration flows), at *http://pubs.carnegie.ru/books/1998/10gv/toc.asp*

14 Garcia-Iser, M., 'Edyniy rynok truda SNG: realii i perspektivy' (Common labour market in CIS: realities and perspectives), at *http://pubs.carnegie.ru/books/1998/10gv/toc.asp*

15 Kuz'min, A., 'Trudovaya migratsia s Ukrainy v Rossiu: potoki, pravovaya situatsia, posledstvia' (Labour migration from Ukraine to Russia: flows, legal situation, and consequences), at *http://pubs.carnegie.ru/books/1998/10gv/toc.asp*

16 *Migratsia i bezopasnost*, p. 171.

17 Fillipova, E., 'Polozhenie migrantov v Rossii – pravo i real'nost' (Status of migrants in Russia: the law and the reality), at *http://www.golos.ru*

18 Vitkovskaya, G., 'Vynuzhdennie migranty iz novykh nezavisimykh gosudarstv na rossiiskom rynke truda' (Forced migrants from CIS countries in the Russian labour market), at *http://pubs.carnegie.ru/books/1998/10gv/toc.asp*

19 Centre for Strategic Research website, at *http://www.csr.ru/conferences/bagr.html*

20 Russia's Human Rights Association website, at *http://www.hro.org/docs/reps/nnovmig/index.htm*

21 '*Nezavisimaya gazeta*' website, at *http://regions.ng.ru/printed/club-89/2000–04–11/5_ecodemo.html*

22 Kirillova, E., 'Ukrainskie trudovie migranty v Rossii' (Ukrainian labour migrants in Russia), at *http://pubs.carnegie.ru/books/1998/10gv/toc.asp*

23 *Itogi*, 29 May 2001, p. 39.

24 '*Nezavisimaya gazeta*' website, at *http://regions.ng.ru/printed/club-89/2000–05–16/5_gates.html*

25 Carnegie Endowment for International Peace (Moscow office) website, at *http://pubs.carnegie.ru/workpapers/1999/02/10.asp*

26 Carnegie Endowment for International Peace (Moscow office) website, at *http://pubs.carnegie.ru/books/1996/02gv/02portyakov.asp*

27 *Itogi*, 29 May 2001, p. 39.

28 '*Nezavisimaya gazeta*' website, at *http://regions.ng.ru/printed/club-89/2000–12–19/4_rokecky.html*

29 *http://www.regions.ru/news*

30 '*Nezavisimaya gazeta*' website, at *http//regions.ng.ru/printed/far/2000–02–22/6_altai.html*

31 *http://www.regions.ru/news/248742.html*

32 Programma pravitel'stva Rossii na 10 let (The programme of the Russia's government for ten-year perspective), at *http://www.akm.ru/rus/gosinfo/progr_gov/1_10.stm*.

33 *Itogi*, 29 May 2001, p. 39.

34 'Migratsia i bezopasnost' … ', p. 173.

35 *Izvestiya*, 17 March 2001.

36 Doklad o razvitii cheloveskogo potentsiala v Rossiiskoi Federatsii za 2000 god (Report on human potential development in the Russian Federation in 2000), at *http://www.undp.ru/rus/Anonses/Anonses.htm*

37 Linz, S. (1998) *Ownership and Employment in Russian Industry: 1992–1995*, Working Paper No. 138, March. The William Davidson Institute at the University of Michigan Business School, p. 4.

38 *Nizhegorodskie tovary*, 3, 2000, p. 7.

39 Mysnik, V., 'Sotsial'naya kharakteristika regional'nogorynka truda' (Social characterisation of the regional labour market), at *http://pubs.carnegie.ru/workpapers/1999/02/08.asp*

40 Gimpelson, V. and Monusova, G., 'Public employment and redistributive politics in Russian regions' at *http://src-home.slav.hokudai.ac.jp/sympo/99summer-contents.html*

41 Maleva, T., 'Rossiiskiy rynok truda i politika zaniatosti: paradigmy i paradoksy' (Russian labour market and the policy of employment: paradigms and paradoxes), at *http://pubs.carnegie.ru/books/1998/10tm/toc.asp*

42 Carnegie Endowment for International Peace (Moscow office) website at *http://pubs.carnegie.ru/workpapers/1999/02/07.asp*

43 *Problems of Theory and Practice of Management*, Online Journal at *http://www.ptpu.ru/issues/5_99/11_5_99.htm*

44 Kapeliushnikov, R., 'Chto skryvaetsa za skritoy bezrabotitsey' (What hides 'hidden unemployment') at *http://pubs.carnegie.ru/books/1998/10tm/toc.asp*

45 Kuddo, A., 'Politika zaniatosti v Rossii v kontekste mezhdunarodnogo ekonomicheskogo opyta' (Russia's employment policy within the context of international economic experience) at *http://pubs.carnegie.ru/books/1998/10tm/toc.asp*

46 Naskol'ko bezrabotny bezrabotnie (To what extent the unemployed are jobless), Moscow: Bureau of Economic Analysis Bulletin, 1998.

47 Bordin, A. (1998) 'Rynok truda v sovremennoy Rossii: istoria i geografia' (Labour market in today's Russia: history and geography), *Novoe pokolenie*, 4(2): Moscow: summer.

48 'Nizhny Novgorod Online' at *http://www.nizhny.ru*, 10 January 2001.

49 Russia's Human Rights Association website at *http://www.hro.org/docs/reps/1999/soceco/4.htm*

50 '*Birzha*', Weekly Web page at *http://www.birzhaplus.sandy.ru/birzha/7.htm*

51 '*Nezavisimaya gazeta*' website, at *http://regions.ng.ru/printed/gubern/2000–01–11/3_vyborg.html*

52 Lapin, A., 'Formirovanie systemy upravlenia personalom: regional'niy i mikroekonomicheskiy aspekty' (Forming the personnel management system: regional and microeconomic aspects) at *http://www.ptpu.ru/issues/5_00/14_5_00.htm*

53 Belokrilov, O.S. and Vol'chik, V.V., 'Trudovoe zakonodatel'stvo i perspektivy razvitia rynka truda v Rossii' (Labour legislation and the perspectives of labour market development in Russia) at *http://economics.lgg.ru/essay/labor_economics.shtml*

54 *http://www.liberal.ru/sitan.asp?Num=5*

55 *Nezavisimaya gazeta* website at *http://regions.ng.ru/printed/time/2000–05–30/7_china_market.html*

56 Kuz'min, A., op. cit.

57 *Ibid*.

58 *Itogi* 29 May 2001, p. 39.

59 Carnegie Endowment for International Peace (Moscow office) website at *http://pubs.carnegie.ru/workpapers/1999/02/11asp*

60 Kuz'min, A., op. cit.

61 'Spiritual Heritage' thinktank website at *http://www.nasledie.ru/oboz/N03–4_94/3–4_02.htm*

62 *http://www.e-journal.ru/p_bzarub-st9–15.html*

63 Glinski-Vassiliev, D. (2001) 'The politics of labour code reform in Putin's Russia', in E. Powers (ed.) *Program on New Approaches to Russian Security (PONARS). Policy Memo Series*, Memo No. 197, May, pp. 1–3.

64 'Liberal Mission' Foundation website at *http://www.liberal.ru/sitan.asp?Num=103*

65 'Liberal Mission' Foundation website at *http://www.liberal.ru/sitan.asp?Num=105*

66 'Liberal Mission' Foundation website, at *http://www.liberal.ru/sitan.asp?Num=104*

67 Zudin, A., 'Biznes i gosudarstvo pri Putine: novyi sotsial'nyi kontrakt' (Business and the state under Putin: new social contract) at *http://www.politcom.ru/c_b.html*

68 National News Service website at *http://www.nns.ru/interv/int3938.html*

69 'Russia's new corporate citizens', *Business Week*, European edition, 25 June 2001.

70 Vazgenov, A., 'Upravlenie trudovymi otnosheniami v usloviakh obostrenia sotsial'noy napriazhonnosti' (Managing labour relations under sharpening social tensions), at *http://www.ptpu.ru/issues/4_99/15_4_99.html*

71 Larsen, M.R., 'Baltic Sea cooperation beyond 2000: Visions and strategies on the local and regional level', at *http://www.bsssc.com/pages/documents/documents_bal.htm*

72 'Democratic Choice of Russia' party website, at *http://www.dvr.ru/demvyb/042001.htm*

73 *Transformatsia*, The William Davidson Institute and the World Bank, June 1999, pp. 5–7.

74 'Perspektivnie napravlenia politiki preodolenia bezrabotitsy' (Perspective ways of overcoming unemployment), *Bureau of Economic Analysis Bulletin, Moscow*, 1998, p. 2.

8 Labour relations in transition

Labour-intensive industries in Macau

Inês Trigo de Sousa

Introduction

The implementation of reforms encompassing whole economic systems is the main feature of *economies in transition*. Transition, in this sense, is not seen as a historical process, but as a *policy* whose main purpose is the transformation of the economic system in the direction of a model named 'market economy'. This transition requires certain conditions to be successful, in particular the existence of fundamental actors that are able to perform the key roles of the transition, like the state and entrepreneurs. Dependency theorists have highlighted the relationship between the state, foreign and local firms in promoting growth. The state, while being a political institution upholding a given order, is also the locus of action of the bourgeois élite *and* an entrepreneur engaged in production through state-owned enterprises. The interesting contribution of this theory is therefore translated in the effort to conceptualize dependency relations, among and within states, on foreign firms and foreign capital, in both sociological and economic terms.

In East Asia, the deviation from the liberal set of criteria pertaining to economic growth and social development, consists of recognising a single, party-based bureaucratic élite capable of administering the system and functioning technocratically (Breslin 2000: 232).[1] Yet, to theorize on developmental types of state, or 'core-states capable of governing or commanding the market' (Evans 1995)[2], a careful analysis of international and regional contexts is crucial for the understanding of the formation of East Asian states' national interests.

South Korea, Taiwan, Singapore or even China all share versions of a type of state capable of generating sustained developmental momentum.[3] At the same time, they differ substantially from one another in the means used by the state to achieve these development objectives, without jeopardising the central role performed by the state and its agencies in this process. In spite of the degree of insulation that these states may acquire, their relationship with the international system and especially with its key players, which are not necessarily states, remain to be more thoroughly considered. This is because the emphasis given to the distorting effects of integration into the international capitalist system, which are based on rigid, state-centred assumptions about the structural nature of the global economic system, overlooks and excludes the potential of traditional economic peripheries – such as the Guangdong province in China – from becoming regional economic cores.

The People's Republic of China is going through a process of change, mainly by the transformation of its economic system, but also of its political system, by accepting the market-economy model as the basic normative reference for its economic transition. One of the implications – among many others – of this process of change is what we may call 'the emergent global labour economics', or a new form of labour insertion in the functioning of the world economy. For more than two decades, the Chinese state has undoubtedly played a major role in conducting or governing the economic transformation process. The difference nowadays is that the Chinese state is steering the economy towards the liberal market model for the first time in its history, while becoming a major key-player working to build a 'new' world trade and labour economy, notably through its accession to the World Trade Organization and through the competitive edge that its enormous labour force exerts in the region.

In the new world economy, two major shifts have occurred in the last two decades. Amidst the continued geographical fragmentation and dispersion of manufacturing processes at the global level, there is increasing concentration and integration of industrial and commercial activities at various regional scales. These two parallel processes have begun to reshape the international division of labour into more complex and tightly connected networks of sourcing, manufacturing and marketing that cut across geographical and political boundaries of nation-states. In this light, concepts like national development and industrialization are increasingly perceived as problematic in facilitating the understanding of emerging patterns of economic and social organization crystallized around all kinds of economic activity (Gereffi and Korzeniewicz 1994: 3).

It is therefore important, in the light of contemporary global trade and labour problems, to reconsider the notion of region, by trying to rethink this concept as operating above and below the state level and cutting across traditional boundaries, politically defined spaces and political cultures. The concept of region is transcending territoriality and spatiality by intertwining state and non-state actors and structures that are not necessarily bound to traditionally defined geographical spaces. However, the intertwining of state and non-state actors is achieved mainly in the economic realm of social life, where efforts at co-operation and co-ordination between differentiated economic and political units are setting the pace in the overall development of regions. The repercussions for labour, either at the national or regional levels, provide interesting material to be studied as the economic and social role of trade unions and non-unionized workers are renewed, with or without direct intervention or tutelage from the state.

Striking a balance between economic reform and social stability has always been a difficult task for policy-makers. Changing labour relations, in a changing economic environment, pose a threat to social stability and economic development programmes. This is an issue that needs to be more thoroughly assessed, taking into account regional disparities and growing inequalities within and between sectors.

In China, just as in many parts of the world, trade unions have tended to remain national in scope. However, transnational linkages among unions have emerged throughout the 1990s, as traditional international agencies such as the ILO show an inability to deal with and regulate increasing labour demands as global economic restructuring takes place. Although these transnational linkages are not dealt with here, it is important to mention the increasing awareness of local South-east Asian trade unions of their European counterparts, mainly because of non-governmental organizations' efforts in 'bringing workers' within a far-reaching labour movement, with a sector or industry base, rather than a national one.

Labour movements outside the Chinese Communist Party's sphere of influence have remained marginal and with a limited impact as a well-defined social movement. However, there is a widespread belief that labour relations, even in state-owned enterprises, are being released from administrative control and increasingly being subjected to market forces. As market forces are uneven throughout China, there is the need for an approach that focuses on labour issues from a regional or local perspective. Indeed, drawing from such an approach, we may be able to find significant evidence for the fragmentation of labour interests, which *a priori* assume different characteristics, depending on the region or province where they are located.

Labour relations in Macau are a vivid example, on a micro-scale, of clashing interests within a political framework of *transition*, which are not equally addressed on the institutional level. Institutions in Macau reflect the transition process more acutely, as they are *decolonized* by the Portuguese administration and *recolonized* by a Chinese one. If the change in administration brings an effective convergence of administration and society, a more structured labour regime may emerge. This possibility, so far, seems to be contingent upon trade-union restructuring in the mainland and upon more concerted labour and migration policies with the Hong Kong government and with the provincial and municipal authorities of the Special Economic Zones.

The chapter is composed of three sections. First, it briefly considers the need for a regional or more localized approach to the study of economic dynamics in the People's Republic of China. In the second and third sections, attention is paid to the economic and social restructuring of Macau as integrated within a wider region – the Pearl River Delta – without overlooking its unique stand in what concerns industrial and labour policies.

The notion of region and its importance in understanding contemporary China

The emergence of successful regional economic clusters suggests that restructuring *processes* evolve in response to increased liberalization and competitiveness of global production, labour and trade, and as a means of redefining social interests and political authority. These processes also happen 'somewhere' and, as Braudel once wrote: 'geographical space as a source of explanation affects all historical realities, all spatially defined phenomena; states, societies, cultures and economies' (Braudel 1985). In this sense, spatial integration generating economic growth is seen as contingent upon the interaction of several agents, directly and indirectly involved in production processes, and their own perceptions of the geographical space where they operate. As the locus where increasing economic activities are taking place, the Pearl River Delta constitutes a specific geographical space, within a specific regional context.

This specific regional context entails two distinct dimensions, from a perspective of systemic contradiction between centrally planned and market oriented processes: a spatial economic complementarity between Special Administrative Regions (SARs) and Special Economic Zones (SEZs), and a degree of decentralization among the PRC's structures of power. The PRC central government is still a key player, but its intervening role is fading in the face of increasing interactions at the regional level, between local and non-local business groups and local government officials. At the enterprise level, its role is fading away, which launches new challenges for the emergent labour relations within a socialist market economy. The main assumption is therefore that the Pearl River Delta is undergoing a process of economic restructuring, where the integration of SARs and SEZs is gradually established within broader *regional economic networks*, which are shaping the mechanisms or channels through which public and private actors interact, from the institutional to the plant level.

Many scholars and writers have argued persuasively for the importance of clusters of related factor endowments located close together (Porter 1990, Ohmae 1995, Dicken 1998). Production factors perform better and generate more output when they exist in close geographical proximity. It does not follow that such geographical clusters must coexist within the borders of the nation-state and thereby participate in the same national interest. These clusters may work equally well – and perhaps even better – when they lie across political borders and when they are free of the burdens of national interest (Ohmae 1995: 98). Thus, the territorial lines that do make sense belong to what Ohmae calls 'region-states' – geographical units like Northern Italy, San Diego/Tijuana, Hong Kong, Macau and Southern China, or the growth triangle in Singapore – that constitute 'natural economic zones', which may or may not fall within the borders of a particular nation. The meaningful units of economic life are urban aggregations and their respective hinterlands. Where prosperity exists it is region based, and when a region prospers, it has spillover effects into adjacent territories inside and outside the political structures of which it is part (Ohmae 1995: 98).

Diverse terminology has been used to delineate the regions composing modern China. Notwithstanding the official divisions in provinces and municipalities, due to the vastness of the territory, there are many possibilities for dividing China into 'natural', 'political', 'linguistic' or, more recently, economic regions.[4]

In recent times, the most striking division for many analysts is between coastal and interior regions. Coastal regions occupy only 15 per cent of China's total land area, but are clearly 'economic giants', despite their small size. The coastal region is also far more densely populated than the interior areas, with more than 40 per cent of the total population. The GNP of the coastal regions constitutes over 50 per cent of the total, with the value of industrial production being over 60 per cent, the export value around 80 per cent, and 85 per cent of foreign capital received (Yabuki 1995: 173).

An important consideration in this study concerns a regional division into *market economy zones*. Several of these zones can be distinguished within and outside the PRC's jurisdiction. The *Bohai Rim*, comprising the Beijing and Tianjin municipalities and Hebei, Shandong and Liaoning provinces, the *Yangtze Delta*, the Shanghai municipality and the provinces of Jiangsu and Zhejiang and *South China*, with Guangdong, Fujian and Hainan provinces and Guangxi autonomous region. The region of Southern China can be further divided into three micro segments: *Taiwan Strait*, comprising Fujian province and its intimate links with the island of Taiwan (although not part of the PRC's territory), the *Hainan Strait*, with Hainan province and Guangxi autonomous region and, finally, the *Pearl River Delta*, comprising Hong Kong, Macau, Shenzhen and Zhuhai municipalities, and Guangdong province.

The defining element in these market economy zones is the close relationship between export markets and direct investment. Foreign investment, for example, is a strong mechanism for integrating Southern China. In the period between 1985 and 1989, Hong Kong and Macau accounted for an average of 61 per cent of total FDI in China, whereas in Guangdong province, approximately 90 per cent of the FDI cases and 70 per cent of the FDI capital came from Hong Kong and Macau (Yabuki 1995: 177). In ranked order of direct investment, Hong Kong (with Macau) holds the first place, investing in almost every area in the coastal regions (Yabuki 1995: 185). Japan's investment activities are concentrated in the North-east area, Taiwan's in South China, especially in Fujian province, and the United States' along the Yangtze River. We can also find Singapore, which along with Taiwan has become an important new investment source in the 1990s. Whereas Taiwan's investment is expanding in all of the provinces and cities of the coastal region, South Korean investment focuses on the geographically closer provinces of Liaoning and Shandong.

These market areas form a transnational rather than a local regional market area. However, the social and political determinants of a certain locality are important dynamics to take into account. This is because the many times mentioned 'overseas Chinese business communities' (Cen 1996) cannot be regarded as a monolithic concept. Depending on their region of origin – Taiwan, Hong Kong or Singapore – Chinese investors tend to vary considerably, not only in terms of targeted sectors, but also in business and managerial practices. These are important elements to take into account when analysing the organization of domestic production and of domestic labour, and are key in understanding why the local region is apparently functioning so 'harmoniously'.

The Pearl River Delta region

The Pearl River Delta area is situated in Guangdong province. Guangdong's economic growth story goes back to the 1980s, when its economy became more oriented to light and processing industries, driven by a strong export surge in Hong Kong. During this period, Guangdong's percentage of agricultural labour declined sharply while its industrial labour force increased (Chen 1994: 169). At the same time, there has been growing economic integration between the former colonial cities of Macau and Hong Kong – now converted into Chinese Special Administrative Regions (SAR) – and the surrounding areas in Guangdong province, respectively the Special Economic Zones (SEZs) of Zhuhai and Shenzhen.

Proximity to China, through Guangdong province, has played a key role in the economic development of both Hong Kong and Macau. The rapid economic growth in the bordering cities of Shenzhen and Zhuhai reflects an increasing connectedness between SARs and SEZs, through the building of roads and motorways and the deregulation of cross-border activities. These tangible factors, together with legal and political features and mechanisms – both in SARs and SEZs – designed to maintain the economic status quo of these areas, constitute the dynamic process through which these economic shifts also redefine the Chinese political economy at a central level. On the level of the regional political economy, the integration of economic networks spread along the Southern coastal area is intensifying, but the pace of this integration depends less and less on the traditional centre and is increasingly dictated by regional or local centres of power, growing not only in institutional weight, but presumably also in social influence. Yet, expressing political loyalty to the PRC's regime is still a centrifugal force in channelling popular support.

Thus, in the Pearl River Delta region, a mix of a rigid centre of authority and a freewheeling spirit of market entrepreneurship seems to 'reconcile' two contradictory systems – market oriented vs. centrally planned. The areas that form this region still tend to differ sharply in terms of political or economic regimes, legal and business practices. Through increasing economic co-operation and interaction between politically distinct SEZs and SARs, the integration of markets – including labour – becomes the crucial dimension of economic growth in the Pearl River Delta. Market integration can have either a spontaneous or intentional nature, depending, respectively, on the presence or absence of co-operation mechanisms among local/provincial governments and market-integrating groups like firms, enterprises or industrial leaders.

In this mixed situation, the Pearl River Delta integration is anchored on several key nodes, or large urban centres, which send and absorb investment flows and serve as major production sites and service links in the region (Chen 1994: 171). The social relations and socio-cultural environment where the sequential stages of input acquisition are embedded, shape processes of manufacturing, distribution, marketing, and consumption. Parallel processes of firm competition, business government co-operation and intra-industrial innovation are also shaped by the relationship between private and public actors, or, in other words, by the role and action of governance structures towards private economic agents (including the migrant workforce) and its consequences in the economic restructuring process. The emergent new division of labour is no longer confined to typical labour-intensive industries, such as garments and textiles (Chen 1994: 169), and is expanding into other more capital-intensive sectors like electronics, software products, pharmaceuticals and services networks, in order to sustain the growth of these sectors. Thus, the differential roles of SEZs and SARs raise several questions about the distribution of the economic surplus among the participants in industrial and commercial activities stretching across political and geographical boundaries, which include the way that these economic actors perceive this division and act upon it.

In an interesting development, the Hong Kong Special Administrative Government has recently commissioned a task force to evaluate the feasibility of establishing a 'cosmopolitan area' in the Pearl River Delta,[5] comprising Hong Kong, Macau, Shenzhen and Zhuhai. These four cities linked together can potentially establish a 'Super Special Economic Zone', with a population of around 13 million, total GDP of 14,786 billion yuan,[6] and an average GDP per capita of 870,000 yuan.[7] The main purpose is therefore to increase the economic advantages of each city, by re-aligning the economic activity of the four cities, in order to attain a more rational division of labour resources.

The Pearl River Delta region emerges then as a segment of a wider economic region – Southern China – and as 'Special Administrative Regions and Economic Zones' of the PRC. This delta area has been fashioned by the Chinese government as an 'open district' to pioneer innovations, resulting not only from a general context where the PRC is striving for geo-economic advantages in the wider East Asian Region, but it is also a regional/subregional project, sustained by viable economic growth and development patterns.

The restructuring process in Macau

Introduction

Macau, a Portuguese enclave since the middle of the sixteenth century, is located at the west coast of the Pearl River, 61 kilometres from Hong Kong. Like Hong Kong or Singapore, Macau is classified as a mini-region within which there is a scarcity of natural resources (Ieong and Siu 1997: 6). What makes Macau unique in the world economy is its particularity of historical development, industrial structure and socio-cultural diversity. As a mini-sized economy, its development process is subject to a wide range of internal and external constraints. Due to divergent paths in its social, political and economic progress in the last century, Macau is still at the 'crossroads', searching for its future socio-economic direction (Ieong and Siu 1997: 8).

The restructuring path followed by Macau in the last three decades resembles the development model adopted successfully by the well-known Asian NICs to a certain extent. This model combines export promotion with an entrepôt dimension, based on light-industrial manufacturing and an evolving services sector. However, having taken into account the above-mentioned particularities, it is necessary to keep in mind that the factors contributing to the success of the four NICs (Hong Kong, Singapore, South Korea and Taiwan) may not be applicable to the case of Macau.

In broad terms, the territory's economy is characterized by liberal guiding principles and operations. It sustains a 'liberal economic system, with limited government intervention and very low tax burden' and it is an open port, where all goods, except those under bilateral or international trade restrictive measures, are traded freely (Cremer *et al.* 1991: 176).[8] The currency of Macau, the pataca (MOP) is fully convertible and there are no restrictions on the movement of capital into and out of Macau. The taxation system operates at lower rates than in Hong Kong. To Macau is also reserved the right of establishing independent and autonomous industrial, commercial and monetary policies, as stated in the Basic Law. Additionally, Macau forms an independent customs territory, fully autonomous from the PRC, and may conclude and implement agreements with countries, regions and international organizations in fields such as trade, finance, shipping and communications, and may establish economic and trade missions abroad. Macau is a full member of the WTO, under the name 'Macau, China' and in international conferences or organizations limited to states, representatives of the territory participate as members of the Chinese delegation.

Macau as a Special Administrative Region and the role of the local government

The arrangement of Macau as a Special Administrative Region within China constitutes an important institutional change in the current economic and political structure. Even though Macau is supposed to remain in a free-market, capitalist-like social and economic system, the respective contributions of the public sector and the private sector to economic decisions will be altered. A key issue in the present and future trajectory of Macau as an SAR is 'localization and its effects on the decision making level of the economy' (Ieong and Siu 1997: 137). Localization is having a direct impact on the mix between public sector and private sector in deciding such basic economic questions as what to produce, how to produce it and how to sell it. An example of this is that the chief of the executive, the head of the local government, Edmund Ho, meets regularly with academics as well as representatives of the main economic sectors in order to discuss a wide range of issues. The end of the gambling monopoly and the granting of gambling licences constitute a priority in the governmental agenda. Also, China's accession to the WTO has been followed closely in Macau, raising questions about how to co-ordinate the trading position of the territory with the mainland.

As a Special Administrative Region, Macau enjoys a number of benefits, which are not available in other regions in mainland China, but also faces a number of institutional constraints, which derive from this arrangement. These rules – economic policies and regulations – guide the operation of economic activities, but have been subject to accelerated change under the Chinese–Portuguese common administration during the 1990s. For example, during the 1980s, the Macau Government, still under Portuguese administration, adopted a package of policies designed to promote industrial development and diversification to suit changing market situations. These policies provided a range of economic incentives, but also regulation and control instruments, in order to meet the requirements of trade agreements, systems of factory registration and the protection of industrial properties. Among these regulations was the registration of the enterprises for safety, health and segregation of use, especially in sectors with intensive labour characteristics.[9] Also, specific incentives were geared towards a more significant implementation of the electronics sector, reflecting the interventionist role of the government,[10] which differed sharply from the absence of benefits for specific industries in Hong Kong.

However, changes in economic institutions from the mid-1980s to the beginning of the 1990s, propelled by the Portuguese administration, did not reflect the need for industrial restructuring, which, as we will see below, is a critical issue faced by the domestic economy and by the present Chinese administration.

Industrial restructuring in Macau

Macau has a long history of restructuring of economic activities.[11] However, in the past few decades, structural changes within Macau's economy have been affected greatly by innumerable external factors and public-sector decisions. But the critical issue faced by the domestic economy today concerns its industrial structure (Ieong and Siu 1997: 88). Before discussing constraints and opportunities surrounding the industrial restructuring engendered in the 1980s, I will give a brief description of the stages of industrialization in Macau.

Up until the 1930s the early industrialization phase was characterized by the production of matches, firecrackers and incense. From 1930 to 1958, there was a structural shift towards the production of light-industrial products, without an export-oriented focus. Fish and fish products, textiles and garments – produced mainly for local markets – made a reasonable contribution to the export basket (Cremer *et al.* 1991: 15), but it was only at the end of the 1960s when Hong Kong industrialists set up production sites in Macau, that Macau's industrialization really took off. The combination of Hong Kong's success in light-industrial exports and import trade restrictions on textiles and garments, which were not applied to Macau (Cremer *et al.* 1991: 14–16),[12] were decisive factors in the growth of this sector in Macau.

Between 1981 and 1991, the average annual growth of the territory's economy was 16 per cent, transforming Macau into one of the areas with the highest rates of economic growth.[13] Another growth wave, with transfer of industrial capacity coming from Hong Kong during this period enabled Macau to diversify its manufacturing to a large extent into other goods such as toys, electronics and artificial flowers. Examination of the composition of exports during this period also reveals a comeback for textiles and garments, a position that has been steadily maintained up to the present day.[14]

However, the industrial dilemma has persisted for two decades: should Macau develop a relatively high-technology, capital-intensive industry or maintain a low-techonology labour-intensive industry? Or should it try to achieve a structure in between? Similar concerns exist regarding the tertiary sector. Should Macau allocate more resources to expand gambling businesses, or should attention be more focused on developing facilities for tourism? Or should there be a combination of both? All these concerns that flood the economic literature on Macau reveal a great need for the domestic industrial structure to change. In addition, the role of the public sector and its spending efforts in this area fan the flames of the controversy among private firms and the general public (Ieong and Siu 1997: 89). The pressure to achieve competitiveness in world markets pushes industrial efforts towards high-technology, capital-intensive industry. The 2001 anthrax crisis in the United States, for example, has been a focus of attention for Macau's industrialists. Hovione is a company that produces chemicals and specializes in the development of antibiotics for the treatment of anthrax. One of its largest facilities is located in Macau and, throughout October 2001, the demand for its products rose abruptly.

This push towards capital-intensive sectors, however, places serious constraints on Macau's labour force. As the traditional forms of manufacturing decrease in Macau, and with the rapid expansion of the tertiary sector, the structure of the labour force is changing constantly to cope with new requirements in the labour market, where more opportunities are provided to higher-skilled labour.

Textile and garment industries

External and internal constraints on Macau's labour force

Economic shifts and global-scale changes in the textile and garment industry and markets have major repercussions for the workers in these industries, especially in Macau, due to the importance of these industries in Macau's economic system.

Firms in the textile and garment industries tend to engage in practices such as international subcontracting and licensing agreements. This is because these industries are the most geographically dispersed of all industries in the developed and developing countries (Dicken 1998: 233). They are very complex organizationally, and have both old and new organizational and processing practices. The capital investment required is relatively modest, especially in the production of garments, which has been subject to little or no technological change. It is therefore a labour-intensive industry, where large pools of unskilled or semi-skilled labour are used in combination with easy access to raw materials, and these conditions are needed for it to flourish.[15] In this sense, global corporations are indirectly involved in the operations by reverting to the use of local capital and entrepreneurship, for example, through joint ventures or simply local plant or factory management.

The crucial dimension is that these industries absorb large pools of labour.[16] Yet, the official statistics understate the number of unregistered and illegal workers, employed both in the factories and at home. However, the general trend for the textiles industry has been to become more technologically intensive, since the output of the textile industry goes to several types of end use, of which the clothing industry is by far the most important (Dicken 1998: 235). The clothing industry, on the other hand, is far more fragmented and less sophisticated. While design and cutting processes are increasingly mechanized, sewing processes still remain practically unchanged and are an attractive area for international subcontracting and outprocessing arrangements.

In China, since the late 1970s, foreign direct investment has been introduced on an ever-greater scale, especially in the Pearl River Delta, in the Special Economic Zones of Shenzhen and Zhuhai. The textile and garment workers' own experience with this inflow of capital furnishes a stark contrast to the frequent claim that foreign firms or joint ventures have a scrupulous view of workers' interests and welfare. In Guangdong province, for instance, firms with foreign capital present a sharp contrast between the responsibilities and liabilities of workers and the firm's own responsibilities. In the case of clothing industry enterprises, many firms set extraordinarily high task quotas for workers, usually contracted on a piece-rate. Overtime is always adopted as an effective way to extract profit from workers and meet the orders, and many of the firms set rules and disciplinary measures at will, without any consultation with workers.[17] Labour disputes are notoriously high in this area, which in turn shows an extremely low level of unionization. And, of course, foreign ownership in principle resists the formation of unions for fear that it might interfere with management and production and hence increase labour costs. Even Chinese management in foreign firms has the chief concern of not scaring away foreign investment, preferring not to stimulate the collective organization of workers.

Macau is an important trade hub for the kind of goods which are produced in the Special Economic Zones, since close to 100 per cent of the goods sold through the territory come from China. According to Macau's Trade Directory of 1998, there are 373 registered garment manufacturers and ninety-nine registered garment exporters. For example, one common role of Macau's manufacturers in this industry is in the 'label-sewing business'.[18] Garments are processed via Macau as 'semi-products': if one button is missing, it is sewn there and the label will say 'made in Macau'. This role is enhanced through the above-mentioned existence of small-scale factories, buying houses or offices[19] and export companies.

One particular phenomenon are the 'work-gangs', usually small teams specialized in certain manufacturing processes such as ironing, button sewing, packing and so forth. The leader of the work gang has contacts with factory owners and managers, and will be informed when jobs are available in the factory.

In 1984, garments accounted for 48.6 per cent of manufacturing employ-ment, 48.1 per cent of gross output and contributed 44.9 per cent of value added in manufacturing. Textiles formed a much smaller share of manufacturing, with 15 per cent of employment, 21.6 per cent of gross output and 18.8 per cent of value added in manufacturing. In the same year the electrical components and electronics sector accounted for a small proportion – 3.8 per cent employment, 2.7 per cent gross output and 2 per cent of value added. In 1986, textiles and garments accounted for 69.7 per cent of total exports of Macau. Electronic goods had a share of 4.1 per cent. According to data collected in 1999, textiles and garments accounted for 83 per cent of the product export basket of Macau, signalling an increase of 2 per cent in relation to the previous year, a tendency that has persisted in the last decade. In the remaining 17 per cent of other export goods, electronic goods and equipment had a share of 3.7 per cent, a decrease in relation to 1986, but an increase in relation to the previous year.[20]

It is difficult to find data on the composition of labour in Macau, especially employed labour. This is mainly due to the fact that this economy is character-ized by large numbers of migrant and cross-border workers. Macau has a population of around 438,000, but these numbers exclude the 'floating workers', which reached 50,000 around 1996 (Sousa Santos 1998: 232).

In addition to this, the territory's administration has never determined an offi-cial poverty line and does not publish data on average income, household income, or the percentage of household workers that fall under the various income categories. Also, Macau has no minimum wage. According to a senior economic official, the Legislative Council considered a minimum-wage bill in 1998, but postponed final action pending an improvement in the economic situa-tion (Sousa Santos 1998: 301).

Labour legislation provides for a 48-hour week, an 8-hour work day and over-time and the law also requires a 24-hour rest period for every 7 days of work. The employer can change the work schedule if the company is facing losses or if employers have to increase productivity without hiring extra labour. In these cases, workers may have their working day increased to 11 hours. Law does not prescribe wages for overtime work and its calculation is left to the employing entity.

The repercussions for labour in Macau in the garments and textiles sector are considerable. From the official statistics of 1991, 32 per cent of employed or contracted labour worked on textiles and garments (Sousa Santos 1998: 226). Factories in this sector usually receive orders twice a year, which leads to a large supply of labour before orders. This fuels an underemployment situation, although most of this labour is non-resident.

The average monthly wage for workers in the garment industry in 1995 was 4,036 patacas (MOP) – around 520 US dollars – MOP 3,900 in 1996, MOP 4,177 in 1997, and MOP 4,096 in 1998.[21] In many sectors, workers are paid daily, as in the construction sector, or by piece rate, as in garments and other apparel. The payment in textiles and garments industries is still per piece rather than through a monthly salary, and about half of the employed labour is non-resident. The wage level of imported, temporary, migrant labour is said to be much lower than the real average wage, sometimes even only 50 per cent of the official estimates (Sousa Santos 1998: 213). The vast majority of migrant labour is still concentrated in industrial jobs. Eighty per cent of these migrant workers come from the PRC, while the remaining 20 per cent come from Thailand and the Philippines. These immigrants are usually women, employed in low-skilled services like housekeeping, entertainment or hairdressing. Temporary contracts seem to be the common practice in these kinds of jobs.

The workers in the apparel and footwear industry – as in other sectors of the Macau economy – receive only severance pay, if laid off, and paid annual holidays. In the absence of any statutory minimum wage or publicly administered social-security programmes, some larger companies provide private welfare and security packages (Somet 1999).

One final aspect is that, as the tertiary sector expands in Macau, the number of people working in restaurants, hotels and various kinds of services also expands, including the illegal migrants that work in prostitution, in areas close to the casinos, or even as domestic housekeepers. But the workforce released by the manufacturing and construction industries can hardly transfer to the services' sector, since it is mostly semi-skilled or unskilled. Therefore, the majority of the vacancies available in the services' sector are filled by new employees, either local graduates from high schools or university, new immigrants from China or overseas contracted employees (e.g. the Filipino maids). What this information may indicate is that real unemployment is rising as the domestic economy restructures and a large part of the workforce is expected to remain underpaid from time to time, especially those in the manufacturing industries.

Social progress in Macau

Economic and social development is a complex and dynamic process. Its structural features are in constant flux and the social and environmental consequences of this process are inevitable. In Macau, as well as in Hong Kong and Southern China, rapid economic growth has also had a negative impact. The degradation of environment and the loss of quality of life are reflected in the chaotic urbanization, the increasing population, speculation on real-estate and growing suburbanization and social exclusion. Issues of personal safety are constantly being raised, due to lack of legislation and specific policies on property issues, the legal status of people and goods and the rise of criminality and organized crime.

The structural factors of social reality no doubt influence the way that people and social groups live, experience and build reality, and react to it. Throughout the 1990s, with increasing economic growth and activity, Macau's society has also become more complex. As economic activity has become more diversified so have social and cultural activities. Although there seems to be an apparent change in the 'social structure' of Macau, the relationship between public and private agents apparently does not reflect this change (Sousa Santos 1998: 216).

Yet, as mentioned in an earlier section, the phenomenon or arrangement of 'localization' (Ieong and Siu 1997: 109) as a form of institutional change, has expanded the public sector. The changing proportions of civil servants between Portuguese, Macanese and domestic Chinese are a direct result of changes in policies for recruiting and promoting civil servants, not only through 'replacement', but also through the expansion of existing positions. It should be noted that in Macau, jobs in the public sector have much higher salaries than the private sector.[22]

Labour relations under the transition process

Macau's overall labour-relations framework is based on a 'consultation' pattern, through informal dialogue, and is characterized by a consensus policy, implying a good relationship between employer and employee (Sousa Santos 1998: 452). Yet, this 'striking a balance' attitude does not exclude the use of labour which is formally outside Macau's jurisdiction.

Migrant or temporary labour is a great cause of concern for Macau's authorities. There are three main areas of concern: the suspension of contracts (concealing illegal firing practices); the position of women, who despite existing legislation on equal rights to employment opportunities, still lack adequate legislation concerning pregnancy and parental leave; and finally, access to social security and benefits, which traditionally falls outside the administration's scope of action. Social security is organized by the companies for their own employers and the administration is no exception. The result is that there is less job security in Macau, because it faces wage competition from neighbouring municipalities located throughout Guangdong province.

Administrative intervention will largely depend on the degree to which workers' interests and employers' interests clash. Or, in other words, it is not through the territory's administration that labour relations are defined and constituted, but it serves as a last-resort mechanism to be used when the divergences between employers and workers cannot be solved through a dialogue policy. Either because of pressure from employers or because of Macau's small population, the demands from workers have been moderate and have not threatened social and political stability during the transition period.

Legislation on contractual relations between the employer and the employees is a relatively recent thing. Laws regulating these issues were first enacted in 1984, but these had a very modest impact, since labour relations in Macau had been freely established between employer and employee at that time, according to traditional ways of dealing in these areas, which, by the way, imply very little or no government intervention. Nevertheless, from 1984 onwards, Macau's administration has discreetly but persistently set up an institutional framework to deal with labour issues within the territory. The Labour Issues Office (Gabinete de Assuntos de Trabalho) and the Labour Inspectorates were established under the administration's Labour and Employment Head Office – Direcção de Serviços de Trabalho e Emprego (DSTE) – under the responsibility of Macau's

Economic Services. As an example of administrative intervention, in 1987 the Consultative Committee for Social Issues (Conselho Permanente de Concertação Social), under the DSTE, proposed the regulation of labour practices on health and safety issues, working hours and equal job opportunities for both sexes (Sousa Santos 1998: 455).

The administration is also responsive to the needs of the main industrial and commercial leaders, sometimes with a negative impact on the overall labour position. For example, concerning the 48-hour weekend, Macau's law stipulates that if the worker voluntarily works during the weekend, he or she receives double pay.[23] A new law enacted in 1990 was designed to circumvent this issue by distinguishing 'monthly workers' – to whom the double-income rule is applicable – from 'weekly workers' (usually migrants with temporary-contract jobs) who will receive the salary depending on the quality of the product produced. Within the group of weekly workers, there is also a distinction between the worker on 'piece rate' (usually found in the garments industry) and the worker on a 'daily rate' (found in the construction sector). Thus, having said that 'piece-rate' and 'daily-rate' workers have considerable weight in Macau's economy, legislation concerning weekly rests and double time in these industries has virtually ceased to have any practical results (Sousa Santos 1998: 456).

Associativism in Macau

Throughout the transition period the People's Republic has increased its influence in virtually all workers' and employers' associations. In a general way, most of Macau's entrepreneurs express loyalty to the PRC, through multiple associations, some of them with explicit links to the Chinese administration or even to the PRC's central power structures. This form of 'patriotic capitalism' serves mainly the interests of the entrepreneurs (Sousa Santos 1998: 212), a situation where it is not that clear what constitutes the workers' interests.

In Macau, as in other Chinese communities, there is a wide variety of voluntary associations. Occupational or professional associations such as the Chinese General Chamber of Commerce and the Manufacturer's Association are represented on the Consultative Committee of the Government's Economic Services. Macau's entrepreneurs in general are quite active in participating in all kinds of voluntary associations (Cremer *et al.* 1991: 92). There are close to 800 registered associations in Macau, although some may now have ceased to exist (Cremer *et al.* 1991: 92).

The most influential associations are overwhelmingly Chinese. Curiously, the leaders and presidents of charity and social assistance associations are usually the same as the main economic associations. For example, the president of the social assistance association Tong Sin Tong (Associação de Beneficiência Tong Sin Tong), also heads the Association of Construction Workers and Construction Enterprises (Associação de Construtores Civis e Empresas de Fomento Predial) (Sousa Santos 1998: 416). The same applies to Edmund Ho and Roque Choi, directors of Tong Sin Tong Associations and vice-presidents of the Macau Commerce Association (Sousa Santos 1998: 509). Since there are no systems of social security, except for government workers or civil servants, there are also voluntary associations related to social services – like Tong Sin Tong, but there are others – which provide, among other things, medical care, free primary education and material assistance to the poor.

As regards the political profile of Macau's associations, the 'politically independent' organizations are usually sports, recreation, gambling and related activity associations, which have considerable weight in Macau's society. However, 'politically influential' associations, expressing loyalty to the People's Republic, are spreading throughout all the associations, including sports organizations (Sousa Santos 1998: 509). However, due to the recent shifts towards a more service-oriented economy, these 'politically independent' associations are reflecting a convergence of interests within the workers in the services industry. Services are growing quickly, with an overwhelming number of gambling and tourism-related services, which are still the sectors that generate more income in terms of value-adding activities. These associations are exerting a growing influence in Macau's society, but again they do not seem to reflect any explicit or implicit political orientation.

Despite the tendency towards growing intervention from the administration in labour issues, customary resistance to upgrading labour standards seems to exist on the employer's side and, from the workers' side, to unionization. Notwithstanding the climate of change stemming from the transition, unionism in Macau does not seem to have any concrete or defined social and political base. In its place, there is a situation of 'professional associativism' (Sousa Santos 1998: 225).

With regard to the secondary sector workers, a 'negotiable unionism' situation seems to be happening in Macau. Macau's Association of Industrial Workers (Associação Geral dos Operários de Macau – AGOM) constitutes an interesting case, in the sense that, more than simply articulating workers' demands, it tries to strike a balance between capital and labour interests. Because of its small population and because of the tendency to employ migrant labour, there is a growing social imbalance between workers' and employers' interests. The AGOM has reflected this imbalance ever since the transition process started to come into full force. For instance, during the 1980s, the AGOM headed the protests against the shutting down of factories and transfer of production sites to the PRC. Small- and medium-scale enterprises with no access to export quotas – unlike the trading and buying offices – were severely affected, and local entrepreneurs were accused of illegally exporting products 'made in China' using certificates of origin from Macau in order to gain access to European markets. By the same token, Macau's government was also accused of consenting and allowing growing 'cross-border' labour, which in AGOM's view was connected with a slump in Macau's wages, pushed down by direct competition from the Chinese producers across the border in the SEZs. However, with the change of government,

AGOM's representatives have recently alerted public opinion to the negative influence on the population of Macau of the right to strike (Sousa Santos 1998: 212). Migrant labour seems not to feature on the agenda of AGOM's representatives, this issue normally being regarded as an exclusive concern of the employer, who, in many cases – especially in the hiring of Filipino domestic workers – is responsible for their work permits and residence documents.

Chinese economic reform and labour relations

Repercussions for Macau's labour force

As regards labour relations, the situation in China is complex to say the least. Traditionally, labour relations worked through a 'bipartite' structure, as opposed to the most common tripartite structure with management and capital holders, workers represented through unions and the state. Actually, in China, the union only dealt with the state, which at once owned and managed the enterprise. Now, the withdrawal of state power from enterprises leaves workers dealing with management or other representatives of foreign capital face to face. While workers' interactions with the state are, in principle, diluted, the interactions with enterprise management are intensified due to the fact that managers have stronger and more comprehensive control of labour in production. Conflicts between workers and management are therefore expected to increase.

Chinese labour relations seem to be under a process of 'reconstruction', within industrial enterprises. This reconstruction is unavoidable in the face of increasing differentiation among the Chinese working class, the impact of enterprise reform on workers and unions in the state sector and growing interregional income differences.

Chinese authorities are trying to counteract these trends by appealing for the introduction of traditional Chinese values in foreign and joint ventures in order to help improve labour relations. To this end, new laws, such as the Corporation Law, the Trade Union Law and the Labour Law, have been passed and implemented by the PRC. All laws are designed to eliminate the boundaries of ownership-type and to bring all the enterprises in the country under the same legal umbrella. This legal framework is intended to clarify the rights and responsibilities and to regulate the behaviour of all parties involved in the enterprise: management, workers and trade unions. There is still a big gap between the law and its practical application. A few problems remain, in particular the status of enterprises and workers, depending on the ownership type, which is still unclear. It is through the existence of collective or individual labour contracts that enterprises and workers are building and managing their own relations, independently of governmental, administrative or political interference. This, in turn, places constraints on both workers and enterprises: firms complain about the lack of freedom to hire or fire workers, and workers are frustrated with increasing pressures and growing workload, deteriorating working conditions, unemployment and poverty. With economic reforms, the worker was also gradually stripped of his/her right to ownership of the means of production, which is aggravated by the slow implementation of labour laws and by the lack of an effective disciplining mechanism to regulate the behaviour of the enterprises' legal personnel, especially the managers.

The transformation of labour relations is among the most significant changes brought about during the economic reforms. These changes are manifest in three main aspects. In the first place, the nature of labour relations is no longer the same. The relationship between workers and enterprises is now primarily based on an exchange of economic interests rather than on co-operative comradeship or collectivity. Contract and temporary labour contract are the prevailing practices in the emerging new system. Second, a co-ordinating mechanism of labour relations, founded on the new areas of conflict, is lacking. Traditionally, labour relations were controlled by the state via government departments. Issues of employment, wages, labour administration and protection were all spelled out in state codes and regulations. The tendency now is that the market replaces the state in labour control. For example, depending on the ownership type, a firm can now determine the size of the workforce, depending on its own assessment. Finally, a more tangible aspect concerns the growing income differential between workers and managers.

As the roles and functions of workers and managers become increasingly differentiated in production, the legal distinction between labour and management deserves to be clarified. However, this is not a problem that is exclusive to the mainland. Areas like Macau and Hong Kong, which do not have a tradition of state-level unionism, face the same pressures, but for different motives, in defining the position of labour and of management under an already increasingly open economy.

Although in Hong Kong there is a widespread concern about labour issues, the official approach in mainland China is that unions are bound by the Party's paramount concern to maintain social stability. For the Central Party Committee (CCP), social stability is an inescapable prerequisite for any reform project, and the Special Administrative Regions are key in the reform. The Party's gradualist approach to economic reforms implies that the redefinition of the status and role of trade unions will be a gradual and moderate process. Yet, there is no doubt that there will be a decisive impact on the labour force of SARs and SEZs. Chinese trade unions, including the ones in Hong Kong, are also affected by the sharply differentiated economic relations between management and labour, most evident in the growing income differentiation among industry jobs. The All-China Federation of Trade Unions (ACFTU) has been stressing the importance of unions in representing workers and has urged enterprise leaders to assert their legal position in the enterprise.

Another controversial issue is the adoption of the practice of collective bargaining, which would probably help to create a new path for Chinese trade unions in the 'socialist market economy'. This may indicate that some kind of new Chinese labour movement might be on the horizon, as traditional unions search for new identities in China's new socio-economic environment. How

Macau's pattern of professional associativism will relate to emergent changes on the mainland is a question that remains to be addressed. For the time being, in terms of labour and social policies, there is a distinct barrier between Macau and 'around-the-corner' Zhuhai. The differences in income levels, in social policies fighting poverty, or even in basic sanitation, are tremendous as one crosses the border into Zhuhai. However, the daily influx of labourers coming from Zhuhai, the border checks and the increase in smuggling practices and widespread corruption is a situation which cannot be sustained for long. According to the perception of locals, under the current government the overall security of the territory has improved in comparison with the Portuguese administration. Even with real unemployment rising, the attraction of Macau as a city of money-making opportunities is still strong, and a viable option for employment in comparison to Hong Kong. However, it is evident that Macau does not have the geographical capacity for a sustained influx of migrants. If rising unemployment persists and if the wage level slumps, labour associations will have to re-align their position according to the needs of the workers and according to the official approach of maintaining social stability. If the situation escalates, striking a balance will not be an easy task.

Conclusions

While discussing some of the implications stemming from the phenomenon of economic restructuring in Macau, it is impossible to ignore the background debates on Chinese economic reforms. It can therefore be argued that the growing economic integration of Southern China, Hong Kong and Macau is a regional response to global economic transformation (Chen 1994: 179), where the international division of labour is constantly affected and restructured, as countries and regions experience mobility within the global and regional economic systems. However, this approach fails to explain why Hong Kong, for example, did not make a labour-intensive manufacturing investment in China in the 1970s, when it was already moving towards a service-oriented economy. This is because the timing and pace of economic integration in the Pearl River Delta region, to a large extent, still warrants a state-centred explanation. One should note, however, that the notion of 'the state' in China is becoming increasingly fragmented into regional, provincial and local power structures. The frequency of intervention from the Chinese centre is reshaping the already differentiated regional interests in ways that will probably generate more regional competition. Therefore, to explain the spatial concentration of investment and production activities in the Pearl River Delta, there is a need not only to consider the broad political–ideological shifts, but also to identify the effect of location-specific policies on the activities engaged in by the societies within the Pearl River Delta.

In Macau, industrial and commercial policies, or rather policies and strategies designed to promote and strengthen various sectors of economic activity, must also relate to the political and economic realities surrounding the territory. With the incorporation of Macau into China as a Special Administrative Region, policy-level co-operation is becoming even more pronounced, where both public and private agents will have to show a higher degree of co-ordination, to sustain a form of integration and co-operation among areas with sharply different socio-economic systems.

In the light of contemporary labour issues, many questions remain to be answered, in particular, the function of Macau's medium- and small-scale businesses in local and regional markets: their export capability and their integration within wider international/regional and national industrial systems. Their relationship to foreign capital, or to larger economic agents such as multinational corporations and joint-venture operations will bring a new understanding of their impact on the local and regional division of labour.

Notes

1 One-party rule does not mean that political conflict and popular pressures are irrelevant in policy-making – they just take on a different form. This is perhaps why 'understanding the nature of inter-élite conflict remains the key to understanding Chinese leaders' perceptions of China's position in the global economy' (Breslin, 2000: 392).

2 Peter Evans (1995) argues that this capacity to govern the market is explained by the notion of 'embedded autonomy'. This view entails that the autonomy of well-developed bureaucracies has been embedded in a dense web of ties with both non-state and other state actors (internal and external) who collectively help to define, re-define and implement economic objectives.

3 The paradigm as applied to East Asia relates economic performance to institutional arrangements centred on the state. Priority is placed on economic development, operationalized in terms of growth productivity and competitiveness, with active state intervention in the market to guide, discipline and co-ordinate the private sector through strategic allocation of resources and the use of diverse policy instruments. For more on this, see Moon and Prasad, 'Networks, Politics and Institutions', 1998.

4 Besides the standard provincial division, the People's Republic has identified 'seven great joint industrial regions', 'ten great economic regions' and 'six central regions'. Behind these divisions, there are several imperatives of political control and complex systems for the mobilization of the economic and military resources. Obviously, these disparities have engendered a variety of economic and political contradictions. However, the policy entails that the coastal regions should be allowed to pursue economic development more freely and efforts to rein in development in the name of correcting the imbalance should not be pursued (Yabuki 1995: 36–179).

5 *Xindao Daily* (2001, 10–4 A5 Tuesday) 'Hong Kong plans big cosmopolitan area in the Pearl River Delta', copy in Chinese, translated by Xiaoke Zhang.

6 According to figures from *Xindao Daily* (2001–10–04), Hong Kong scores higher with a 12,314 billion yuan GDP, followed by Shenzhen (1,437 billion yuan GDP), then Macau (492 billion yuan GDP), and finally Zhuhai (253 billion yuan GDP).

7 Hong Kong again scores higher (183,000 yuan) but followed this time by Macau (110,000 yuan), then Shenzhen (36,000 yuan) and finally Zhuhai with 22,000 yuan. Source: *Xindao Daily* (2001–10–04).

8 Re-export goods, if they stay in Macau for less than fifteen days, are also tax free.

9 Investment Plan of 1984, as quoted in Sit *et al.* 1991, p. 397.

10 The Portuguese administration chose to provide packages of sectoral policies, including investment plans, to accelerate and promote Macau's growth before the transition (Cremer *et al.* 1991: 397). This prerogative, according with the Basic Law remains, in principle, unchanged.

11 After the Portuguese settled in 1557, it prospered as a trading port, between China and Japan. As Portuguese influence declined in South-east Asia and with the founding of Hong Kong by the British in 1842, Macau lost its traditional entrepôt role. Macau's activities were then reduced to gambling, the opium trade and gold smuggling, until World War II.

12 Under the pressure of increasing restrictions by foreign countries on their textile and garment imports, Hong Kong industrialists set up production sites in Macau, which were not under such restrictions then. In the early 1970s more countries took similar measures to restrict imports from Hong Kong. Under the General Preferences System (1976) granting preferential tariffs for selected developing countries, Hong Kong was excluded from preferential tariffs on products such as garments and electronic goods (Gunn 1996: 232).

13 These high rates are closely related to Macau's small population (less than 500,000 inhabitants). See *Macau em Numeros 1997*.

14 In 1999, it was observed that textile and garments make up 83 per cent of exports, although non-textile items like electronic goods now make up an increasing share (*Estatísticas do Comércio Externo de Macau* 2000).

15 Material availability is not a prerequisite, since cotton or similar materials are not difficult to transport.

16 The garment and footwear industry constitutes an illustrative example, in the sense that it is a labour-intensive sector, employing around 20 million workers in China, in 1999 (Kwan 2000).

17 There are flagrant examples of these issues found within reports about the working conditions in the factories producing for major-label Western sportswear brands. Although some of the companies display codes of conduct on labour relations, these are not properly implemented, since issues of profit-maximization in these industries take precedence in the dealings of the management with the workers (Kernaghan 2000).

18 Internal Report from the Clean Clothes Campaign, based on field research conducted in Macau and Hong Kong, February–June 1997.

19 Buying houses/offices are not agents or traders, but the 'company that brings the buyer to the supplier'. They charge 0 per cent, but occasionally they can work with traders, or trading companies, who buy stock and sell to various retailers. The advantage of working with a buying office is that the factories deal directly with the buyer, giving 'stability and easier communication'. Conversely, the advantage of working with a trading company is that the supplier doesn't need to wait for the approval of the buyer. The trading companies therefore buy stock according to what they think they can sell, and according to what the market wants. There are no strict delivery times, and they can buy in advance. *Ibid.*

20 *Estatísticas do Comercio Externo*, 1999, p. 18.

21 Statistics from A. Somet, 'Country reports on human rights practices', in *Wages, Benefits, Poverty Line and Meeting Workers' Needs in the Apparel and Footwear Industries of Selected Countries*, US Department of Labour, Bureau of International Affairs, Washington D.C., April 1999.

22 See Ieong and Siu (1997), p. 110, figure 5–2.

23 Macau's Basic Law, 1993.

Bibliography

Appelbaum, R., Smith, D. and Christerson, B. (1994) 'Commodity chains and industrial restructuring in the Pacific Rim: garment trade and manufacturing', in G. Gereffi and M. Korzeniewicz (eds) *Commodity Chains and Global Capitalism*, London: Praeger.

Braudel, F. (1985) *Civilisation and Capitalism 15th–18th Century*, Vol. III of *The Perspective of the World*, London: William Collins.

Breslin, S. (1996) *China in the 1980s: Centre–Province Relations in a Reforming State*, London: Macmillan; New York: St Martin's Press.

Breslin, S. (2000) 'China: geopolitics and the political economy of hesitant integration', in R. Stubbs and G.R.D. Underhill (eds) *Political Economy and the Changing Global Order*, Oxford: Oxford University Press.

Burkett, P. and Landsberg, M.H. (1998) 'East Asia and the crisis of development theory', *Journal of Contemporary Asia*, 28(4).

Cen Huang (1997) 'Chinese transnational enterprises in South China', *IIAS Newsletter*, 14.

César, G. (1993) 'Macau e o processo de integração económica no Delta do Rio das Pérolas', *Revista de Administração de Macau*, 21(VI).

Chamberlain, H.B. (1989) 'Party–management relations in Chinese industries: some political dimensions of economic reform', *China Quarterly*, 118, June.

Chen, X. (1994) 'The new spatial division of labour and commodity chains in the Greater South China Economic Region', in G. Gereffi and M. Korzeniewicz (eds) *Commodity Chains and Global Capitalism*, Westport: Praeger.

Cheng, C. (1990) 'A coordenação da construção de infraestruturas entre Macau e Zhuhai', *Revista de Administração de Macau*, 10(III).

Cremer, R.D., Sit, V.F.S. and Wong, S.L. (1991) *Entrepreneurs and Enterprises in Macau*, Hong Kong: Hong Kong University Press.

Dicken, P. (1998) *Global Shift: Transforming the World Economy*, London: Chapman.

Direcção dos Serviços de Estatística e Censos do Governo da RAE Macau (1999), *Estatísticas do Comércio Externo*, 4th Trimester.

Dittmer, L. (1994) *China Under Reform*, Oxford: Westview Press.

Evans, P. (1995) *Embedded Autonomy: States and Industrial Transformation*, Princeton: Princeton University Press.

Ferreira, N. (1995) 'A economia de Macau nos primeiros anos da década de 90: evolução e perspectivas', *Revista de Administração de Macau*, 27(VIII).

Findley, C. and Shun, J. (1992) 'Interest groups conflicts in a reforming economy', in A. Watson (ed.) *Economic Reform and Social Change in China*, London: Routledge.

Foot, R. (2001) 'Chinese power and the idea of a responsible state', *The China Journal*, 45, January.

GATT (1994) *Trade Policy Review: Macau*, Vols I and II, Geneva: GATT.

Gereffi, G. (1994) 'The organisation of buyer-driven global commodity chains: how U.S. retailers shape overseas production networks', in G. Gereffi and M. Korzeniewicz (eds) *Commodity Chains and Global Capitalism*, London: Praeger.

Gereffi, G. and Korzeniewicz, M. (1994) *Commodity Chains and Global Capitalism*, London: Praeger.

Gunn, G. (1996) *Encountering Macau: a Portuguese City-State on the Periphery of China*, Oxford: Westview Press.

Haggard, S. and Tun-jen Cheng (1987) 'State and foreign capital in the East Asian NICs', in F. Deyo (ed.), *The Political Economy of the New Asian Industrialism*, London and Ithaca: Cornell University Press.

Hong Liu (2000) *Sino-Southeast Asian Studies: Toward an Alternative Paradigm*, Paper presented at IIAS/NIOD Seminar Series 2000–2001 'Southeast Asia Across Borders', Amsterdam, 12 October.

Hopkins, T. and Wallerstein, I. (1994) 'Commodity chains: construct and research', in G. Gereffi and M. Korzeniewicz (eds) *Commodity Chains and Global Capitalism*, London: Praeger.

Ieong Wan Chong and Chi Sen Siu (1997) *Macau: a Model of a Mini-Economy*, Macau: University of Macau Publication Center.

Joint Declaration of the Government of the People's Republic of China and the Government of the Republic of Portugal on the Question of Macau (1987), Lisbon: Ministério de Relacções Exteriores.

Keijzer, A. (2000) *China: Business Strategies for the 90's*, Berkeley, CA: Pacific View Press.

Kernaghan, C. (2000) *Made in China: the Role of US Companies in Denying Human and Workers Rights*, New York: National Labour Committee.

Korzeniewicz, M. (1994) 'Commodity chains and marketing strategies: Nike and the global athletic footwear industry', in G. Gereffi and M. Korzeniewicz (eds) *Commodity Chains and Global Capitalism*, London: Praeger.

Kwan, A. (2000) 'Report from China: Producing for Adidas and Nike', Hong Kong Christian Industrial Committee, April 25.

Lei Básica da Região Administrativa Especial de Macau da República da China, April 1993.

Ling, L. (1996) 'Hegemony and the internationalising state: a postcolonial analysis of China's integration into Asian corporatism', *Review of International Political Economy*, 3(1).

Lok Wai Chong (1998) 'Lei básica de Macau pós 1999 – sua influência na concertação social', *Revista de Administração de Macau*, 39(XI).

Macau Economic Bulletin (1997) (4 issues), Research Department, Macau's Economic Services.

Macau Economic Bulletin (1998) (4 issues), Research Department, Macau's Economic Services.

Macau em Números (1997) Serviços de estatísticas e censos, Lisbon: INE.

Macau's Trade Directory (1998) IPIM, Macau Trade and Investment Promotion Institute.

Maruya, T. (1991–1992) 'The development of the Guangdong economy and its ties with Beijing', in T. Maruya, *Estatísticas Provinciais de Guangdong*, Lisbon: INE.

Miners, N. (1995) *The Government and Politics of Hong Kong*, Hong Kong: Oxford University Press.

Moon, Chung-in and Prasad, R. (1998) 'Networks, politics and institutions', in C. Chan, H. Clark and P. Lam (eds) *Beyond the Developmental State: East Asia's Political Economies Reconsidered*, London: Macmillan.

Morbey, J. (1990) *Macau 1999: o desafio da transição*, Macau: University of Macau Publication Center.

Nogueira, P. (1991) 'Zhuhai and Canton: a delta for the future', *Revista de Administração de Macau*, 12(IV).

Ohmae, K. (1995) *The End of the Nation State and the Rise of Regional Economies*, London: HarperCollins.

Oksenberg, M. (2001) 'China's political system: challenges of the twenty-first century', *The China Journal*, 45, January.

Overholt, W. (1993) *China: a próxima superpotência*, Lisbon: Difusão Cultural.

Porter, M.E. (1990) *The Competitive Advantage of Nations*, London, Macmillan.

Rabach, E. and Kim, Eun Mee (1994) 'Where is the chain in commodity chains? the service sector nexus', in G. Gereffi and M. Korzeniewicz (eds) *Commodity Chains and Global Capitalism*, London: Praeger.

Rosenau, J. (1995) 'Distant proximities: the dynamics and dialectics of globalisation', in B. Hettne (ed.), *International Political Economy*, London: Zed.

Rosenau, J. (1997) *Along the Domestic–Foreign Frontier: Exploring Governance in a Turbulent World*, Cambridge: Cambridge University Press.

SAR Macau Government (1998a) *Inquérito ao Comércio por Grosso e Retalho*, Direcção dos Serviços de Estatística e Censos.

SAR Macau Government (1998b) *Inquérito Industrial*, Direcção dos Serviços de Estatística e Censos.

SAR Macau Government (1999) *Estatísticas do comércio externo*, Direcção dos Serviços de Estatística e Censos, 4th Trimester.

SAR Macau Government (2000a) *Estatísticas do Comércio Externo*, Macau: Direcção dos Serviços de Estatística e Censos, 2nd Trimester.

SAR Macau Government (2000b) *Inquérito à Oferta de Formação Profissional*, Macau: Direcção dos Serviços de Estatística e Censos.

SAR Macau Government (2000c) *Inquérito ao Emprego*, Macau: Direcção dos Serviços de Estatística e Censos, 2nd Trimester.

Solinger, D. (1992) 'Urban entrepreneurs and the state: the merger of state and society', in A.L. Rosenbaum (ed.) *State and Society in China: the Consequences of Reform*, Boulder, CO: Westview.

Somet, A. (1999) 'Country reports on human rights practices for 1998', in A Somet, *Wages, Benefits, Poverty Line and Meeting Workers Need on the Apparel and Footwear Industries of Selected Countries*, Washington D.C.: US Department of Labor, Bureau of International Labour Affairs, April.

Sousa Santos, B. (1998) *Macau, o Pequeníssimo Dragão*, Edições Afrontamento, Instituto Português do Oriente.

Sum, Ngai-Ling (1996) 'The NICs and competing strategies of East Asian regionalism', in A. Gamble and A. Payne (eds) *Regionalism and World Order*, London: Macmillan.

Taplin, I. (1994) 'Strategic reorientations of U.S. apparel firms', in G. Gereffi and M. Korzeniewicz (eds) *Commodity Chains and Global Capitalism*, London: Praeger.

Teixeira, A. (1996) *Quality Management and Chinese Companies in Macau*, Macau Studies in Management Series, No. 5, Macau Foundation.

Van Kemenade, W. (1997) *China, Hong Kong, Taiwan, Inc.: the Dynamics of a New Empire*, Amsterdam: Alfred Knopf.

Wang Gungwu (2000) 'Southeast Asian studies in Singapore and China', Paper presented at 'Locating Southeast Asia: Genealogies, Concepts, Comparisons and Prospects', Amsterdam, March 2000.

Wang, X. (1997) *Reform of Large-or-Medium Scale Enterprises: Key of Transition from Central Planning to Socialist Market Economy*, Macau Studies in Management Series, No. 8, Macau Foundation.

Woo-Cumings, M. (1997) 'The political economy of growth in East Asia: a perspective on the state, market and ideology', in M. Aoki, Hyung Kim and M. Okuno-Fujiwara (eds) *The Role of Government in East Asian Economic Development: Comparative Institutional Analysis*, Oxford: Oxford University Press.

Wu Yongping (2000) *State, Social and Economic Organizations, International Context, and the Prosperity of Small and Medium Sized Enterprises in Taiwan*, Working Paper, University of Leiden.

Yabuki, S. (1995) *China's New Political Economy: the Giant Awakes*, Boulder, CO: Westview Press.

You Ji (1998) *China's Enterprise Reform: Changing State/Society Relations after Mao*, London: Routledge.

Young, S. (1992) 'Wealth but not security: Attitudes towards private business in the 80s', in A. Watson (ed.) *Economic Reform and Social Change in China*, London: Routledge.

9 Indonesian labour and the challenges of globalization (1966–2001)

J. Thomas Lindblad

Introduction

In the middle of the night, between Wednesday 28 and Thursday 29 March 2001, a group of 400 Indonesian strikers was attacked by an even larger group of unidentified persons armed with swords and home-made bombs. The workers were camping inside a Japanese-owned factory in the Pulogadung Industrial Estate in the outskirts of Jakarta. The confrontation on the factory premises left one dead and eleven injured, of whom one later died. The police arrived only after a considerable time when the thugs were already getting back in their buses. The suspicion was voiced that the criminals had been paid by the factory management to bring the strike to a halt. The strike had been going on for ten days, with the employer consistently refusing to acquiesce to the workers' demands, including a wage hike of 100 per cent and the dismissal of two unpopular supervisors. It transpired that the strike had been preceded by clashes between the several trade unions representing the workers at the factory. Later investigations also revealed that a former student activist, believed to act on behalf of the management, had urged one of the newly established militant trade unions in the Jakarta region to call off the strike as all requests had been granted, which was obviously not true (*Jakarta Post*, 30 March 2001, *Media Indonesia*, 5 May 2001).

The incident at the Pulogadung Industrial Estate highlights several interrelated themes that are highly relevant to an understanding of the labour market and labour relations in Indonesia today. One theme concerns the rise of export manufacturing, which has resulted in a proliferation of large-scale factories in special, protected zones of the type where this incident took place. Another theme is suggested by the foreign ownership of this factory: a massive influx of foreign investment has accompanied the drive towards industrialization. A third one refers to the extreme wage demands put forward by the workers, which suggests a backlog in wage claims that became an acute problem because of the economic crisis from 1997 onwards. A final theme points to the complicated and strained labour relations in today's Indonesia, with confrontations often taking precedence above negotiations. This contribution touches on all four themes in its discussion of the functioning of the Indonesian labour market in response to the challenges of globalization in the last three decades of the twentieth century. Our point of departure is the establishment of the New Order government under Suharto in 1966, and the lines of continuity are followed through up to the present day.

Three periods are distinguished, each with characteristics of its own. The first runs from 1966 up to about 1990. This was a time of rapid, albeit uneven, economic growth and strikingly little labour unrest. Growth was largely driven by exports of primary products, notably oil, whereas advancements in agricultural productivity created a vast rural reservoir of excess labour. The second period covers the 1990s up to the economic crisis in 1997. It was at this time that industrialization in Indonesia gained momentum, but labour unrest and activism increased. The final section is devoted to the years of economic crisis, from 1997 onwards, in which the Suharto government was brought down and political reform became a top priority for his successors. This was, and still is, a time of rapidly rising unemployment, democratization and labour activism. This chapter thus offers a historical perspective on some of today's important and complex issues with regard to the labour market and labour relations in Indonesia. It should be stressed, however, that an exhaustive survey of labour in Indonesia since the 1960s remains beyond the scope of this account. The international literature contains several excellent surveys that may serve that purpose (Manning and Hardjono 1993, Hadiz 1997, Manning 1998).

Rapid growth with quiet labour

Between the 1960s and the 1990s, Indonesia changed from being the 'chronic dropout' or 'underachiever' among the major developing countries, into what the World Bank classified, first as a 'medium-income country' by the early 1980s, and then into a so-called 'Highly Performing Asian Economy' (HPAE) by the early 1990s. The annual rate of economic growth averaged 7 per cent over the entire period 1965–97, which implies that the gross national product doubled every ten years, even after allowing for inflation. In the meantime, the rate of population growth slowed down, from nearly 3 per cent in the 1960s to about 2.5 per cent in the 1970s and 2 per cent during the 1980s. This means that real per capita income grew by 4.5–5 per cent each year over a very protracted period of time. This is an impressive performance by any measurement. After touching briefly on some characteristics of the pattern of economic growth, this section will discuss the consequences for employment and conditions in the labour market.

The re-integration of Indonesia into the world economy after the relative isolation during the Sukarno era was instrumental in speeding up economic growth. Foreign investment capital was explicitly invited from 1967 onwards, and contributed substantially to the enlargement of production capacity, especially in export production. Foreign exports did increase continuously, albeit at a slightly slower rate than the gross national product. Just as in the colonial period, foreign exports remained strongly geared towards primary unprocessed products, in particular oil and liquid natural gas. This resulted in massive windfall profits during the years of the oil boom between 1974 and 1981, which in turn retarded the further development of non-oil industrial production. Only falling oil prices and a temporary slowdown in economic growth in the early 1980s prompted a shift towards accelerated industrialization. Manufacturing production for exports was favoured in order to reduce Indonesia's dependence on oil revenues. Gaining a competitive edge in the world market for finished industrial goods, however, proved far more difficult than had been the case in the oil industry. Manufacturing exports started to climb in the second half of the 1980s, but at a rather modest pace. The influx of foreign capital, the dependence on oil revenues and industrialization for the benefit of exports all underscore the important link between globalization and economic growth in Indonesia during the New Order period. Globalization and rapid economic growth became two sides of the same coin.

The structure of the economy changed dramatically as a result of sustained economic growth. The contribution of agriculture to the country's GNP fell, whereas that of industry and services rose. Indonesia was thus transformed from a largely agrarian economy into an industrializing country in which manufacturing accounted for a larger part of national income than agriculture. The contribution of agriculture to GDP had already fallen to 23 per cent by 1980, and declined further to 20 per cent in 1990, whereas the contribution of manufacturing towards national income increased from 9 per cent to 15 per cent in 1980 and 1990 respectively (World Bank 1994: 13).

Both the pace and the pattern of economic growth had far-reaching consequences for the labour market. Demand for jobs increased especially quickly during the 1980s, when about two million people joined the country's labour force every year. This reflected the rapid growth of population during the 1960s, when fertility was still very high. The supply of jobs also increased rapidly, since a considerable proportion of the economic expansion occurred through larger inputs into the production process rather than through gains in labour productivity. Total employment increased by an average of 3.0 per cent in the 1970s and 3.4 per cent per year during the 1980s (Manning 1993: 64). In fact, more new jobs were generated than were needed to absorb part of the increase in the labour force that was caused by the growth of population alone. This facilitated an increasing female participation in the labour force. The percentage of women in the (urban) labour force rose from 37 per cent in 1971 to 43 per cent in 1985 (Manning 1998: 234). Meanwhile, the share of open employment in the labour force remained low at 2–3 per cent, whereas the evidence suggests that rates of underemployment, i.e. the numbers of people working shorter hours than they would like to, remained rather stable (Manning 1993: 65–7). The main quantitative effect of economic growth on employment consisted of many more jobs and more female employees.

There was also a qualitative side to the process of employment generation. The distribution of employment across sectors changed dramatically in the 1970s and 1980s, mirroring structural change in the economy. The percentage

Table 9.1 Indonesia: employment challenges

	1971	*1990*
Agriculture	66[a]	50
Industry	10	17
Services	24	33

Note:

[a] figures represent percentage contributions to total employment

contributions of each sector to total employment (Manning 1993: 69) convey the changes (Table 9.1).

Within the secondary sector, manufacturing accounted for two-thirds or more of total employment. A major component of the service sector is government employment. Public services increased especially quickly during the 1970s, but far less so in the 1980s.

The increase in employment was especially rapid in the secondary sector, at an average of 5.6 per cent per year and far lower in agriculture (1.7 per cent per year). Rapid growth in industrial employment obviously mirrored the substantial enlargement of manufacturing output, but, interestingly, the far slower growth in agricultural employment was also associated with a rapid enlargement of output as productivity rose quickly in the course of the so-called Green Revolution. For instance, by the mid-1980s Indonesia had, for the first time in its history, become self-sufficient in rice. The Green Revolution formed a precondition for the structural effect of economic growth on employment, i.e. the shift of workers away from agriculture to industry and services.

The shift from agriculture to manufacturing and services also had a geographical dimension. The urban labour force tripled in the 1970s and 1980s, reaching a total of nearly 20 million people by 1990 (Manning 1993: 65). The transfer of workers from the countryside to the cities was also linked to the increasing feminization of labour. During the 1980s, for example, the proportion of women employed in urban industrial activities rose from 23 per cent to 29 per cent and from 26 per cent to 34 per cent in urban services (Oey-Gardiner 1993: 208). The new jobs in the modern formal economy in the cities catered especially to women. In the countryside, on the other hand, formal employment remained dominated by men, whereas the proportion of women in non-formal employment increased. However, far from all jobs in rural areas are in agriculture. In fact, agricultural occupations as a percentage of rural employment fell from 75 per cent in 1971 to 68 per cent by 1985, which testifies to the high and increasing degree of diversification of the rural economy (Jones and Manning 1992: table 11.2). In this context, we must also note that data contrasting urban and rural employment need to be treated with caution as the distinction between urban and rural areas is becoming increasingly blurred in today's Indonesia. In Java in particular, there is a high degree of interaction between the cities and the countryside, so that inhabitants of rural areas may in fact work in urban centres.

An important qualitative aspect of the process of employment generation refers to the educational level of employees. The percentage of people who had at least completed primary school climbed from 30 per cent in 1971 to 50 per cent by 1985; the proportion was higher for men (40 per cent in 1971 and 55 per cent in 1985), but rose faster for women (from 22 per cent to 40 per cent). Secondary-school graduates remained a minority within the total labour force, rising from less than 10 per cent in 1971 to 20 per cent in 1985 (Jones and Manning 1992: table 11.8). These percentages look very different when we only consider the young Indonesians entering the labour force during the 1980s. As many as 37 per cent of the entrants then had completed secondary school, and, of those, one-third was female (Oey-Gardiner 1993: 205). The rising level of formal education in the labour force forms an essential precondition for the technological upgrading of economic activities, which is inherent in the shift from agriculture and a concentration on primary production towards industrialization and a focus on manufacturing for exports. It also carries the potential for productivity gains and higher wages, a matter to which I will return in due course. It is also worth noting that the higher educational level of the labour force in the 1980s coincided with a slower growth in government employment. The public sector, with its rigid wage structure, had then become less attractive to the more skilled workers, compared with opportunities opening up in manufacturing and private services.

The most positive effect of rapid economic growth on the labour market clearly was the massive generation of new jobs, a process from which female workers profited in particular. At the same time, it must not be forgotten that the large-scale transition of labour from agriculture to industry and services necessitated an adjustment, which was not always to accommodate. Hardship caused by displacement of workers has been noted, especially in agriculture in Java during the 1970s, as new techniques were introduced in rice farming and traditional home industries (Manning 1998: 73–6, Manning 1998: 247–8). Men have displaced women and as yet there are fewer opportunities to seek compensation in manufacturing in the cities. Such opportunities only arose in the 1980s. The time lag between the modernization in agriculture in the 1970s and the rise of manufacturing in the 1980s caused difficulties in terms of adjustment to structural change.

A key question with regard to the impact of economic growth on labour market conditions obviously concerns the development of wages. Did workers reap the benefits from growth or not? This question has been addressed in particular by Manning, the most authoritative writer on Indonesian labour today. The evidence appears quite conclusive, to the effect that the real wage rates of Indonesian workers have not risen in line with economic growth. Rates have stayed below regional standards and increases have been erratic. The minister responsible for economic planning, Ginanjar Kartasasmita, once provocatively exclaimed that real wage rates in manufacturing and rice farming actually declined during the 1980s (cited in Manning 1998: 115). In 1990, after more than two decades of sustained economic growth, wage rates for unskilled labour were still pitifully low, for instance in Jakarta where daily rates equal to $1.50 at the most were paid, far less than in Bangkok, Manila or Kuala Lumpur (Manning 1993: 81). Again, a word of caution is required. Daily wage rates may not fully represent actual earnings, as supplementary forms of remuneration such as overtime or piece-work payments as well as additional sources of income may also play a part.

A careful statistical analysis carried out by Manning shows the link between economic growth and wage increases to be quite weak. No statistically significant correlation could be found between the increase of GDP (outside the oil sector), on the one hand, and various measures of increases in wage earnings on the other. The logical explanation would seem to be found in a neo-classical frame-work of analysis, in which wage rates stay low because of an excess supply of workers above demand. However, such an explanation does not bring us much further. Wage rates in industry and services increased the most, albeit from a very low starting-point, in the 1970s, precisely when modernization in agricul-ture caused a large-scale displacement of labour in rural areas. In the 1980s, on the other hand, when demand for workers was increasing relatively fast due to the rise of manufacturing, wage rates remained rather stagnant, again contrary to expectation. The sole statistically significant result of Manning's analysis concerns the relationship between wage-rate developments across sectors of the economy. It appears that wage rates in the textile industry rose in a similar fashion as salaries in public services, indeed as if the government with its rigid remuneration policies served as a wage leader in the Indonesian labour market (Manning 1998: 119–26).

One explanation for the deviation of wage-rate developments from the growth pattern may be found in the degree to which regional labour markets were integrated into one cohesive market. During the 1970s, the oil boom failed to push wage rates in agriculture upwards, so that earnings in rural Java remained very modest in the midst of windfall profits. Large regional variations throughout the archipelago also suggest a lack of integration of labour markets (Manning 1998: 122–3). One case study about the Subang area in rural West Java demonstrates that the distribution of wage gains was very uneven between various groups of society, depending on their political capacity to negotiate wage increases. To put it in simple terms: some groups had access to political power and could gain more, whereas others remained behind (Pincus 1996: 190–1). This brings us to the institutional arrangements in the labour market.

The New Order government reaffirmed its grip on power in 1965–1966 by the destruction of Communist-affiliated organizations, involving mass killings on a scale unprecedented in Indonesian history. One obvious victim was the large left-wing labour federation, SOBSI (Sentral Organisasi Buruh Seluruh Indonesia, the All-Indonesian Central Organization of Labour). This not only eliminated the best-organized representative of labour's interests, but also legit-imized the repression of all trade-union activity that could, however vaguely, be associated with socialism, let alone Communism. The representation of labour was brought under the umbrella of the state ideology, *pancasila*, named after the five principles defining the Indonesian nation and stressing the corporate character of Indonesian society. Under a doctrine labelled *pancasila*, industrial relations, capital, labour and the state were all considered members of one big family. As a result, labour activism could easily be branded as being 'un-*pancasila*' or 'un-Indonesian', which in turn offered a legitimization for state repression. There was hardly any labour unrest at all in Indonesia during the late 1960s and early 1970s (Hadiz 1998: 113, Manning 1998: 204–5).

In 1973, the government formed a national labour organization by amalgamating various former rivals of the SOBSI. This was the FBSI (Federasi Buruh Seluruh Indonesia, the all-Indonesian Federation of Labour). Activities were strictly confined to the 'social and economic' sphere, and no involvement with politics was permitted. State control of labour relations was institutionalized, with an increasing participation by intelligence and security agencies. Labour unrest did erupt in the early 1980s, when the average number of strikes rose to 112 per year, a figure which should be compared with an average of sixty-six strikes per year in the late 1970s. Increasing unrest prompted a restructuring of the mechanisms for control of labour relations. In 1985, under the Minister of Manpower, Sudomo (a former security chief), the FBSI was transformed into the SPSI (Serikat Pekerja Seluruh Indonesia, the All-Indonesian Association of Workers), which was more centralized and more easily controlled by the authorities (Hadiz 1998: 114).

Labour unrest declined after 1985, as the annual number of strikes fell to forty-six and military involvement in the settlement of disputes became ever more widespread. By 1990, the SPSI counted about one million members, but still no more than 3–5 per cent of all employees or 5–10 per cent of employees in manufacturing chose to join (Manning 1998: 210–12). The degree of unionization in Indonesia was exceptionally low and, perhaps more importantly, the representation of labour's interests was highly ineffective in terms of negotiating wage increases in particular. This represented an institutional disruption of the functioning of the labour market that severely reduced the extent to which workers could profit from the sustained economic growth at the time.

Breakthrough in industrialization, and more labour unrest

The shift to non-oil manufacturing in Indonesian exports began in the 1980s and was accompanied by policies of economic deregulation and a more liberal investment climate, especially for foreign capital. There was a strong emphasis on large-scale labour-intensive production, using technologies at an intermediate level in order to make maximum use of Indonesia's comparative advantage as a low-wage producer. The breakthrough in terms of industrialization may be dated to the late 1980s and early 1990s. In 1990, oil and liquid natural gas accounted for 18 per cent of GDP, whereas manufacturing contributed 15 per cent. The expectation was, however, that in ten years' time the latter would supersede the former, climbing to a level of 23 per cent of GDP against only 12 per cent for the oil sector (World Bank 1994: 13). During the 1990s, Indonesia was to become not only an industrializing country but also one specializing in products other than oil.

The contribution of non-oil manufactured exports to total exports climbed from only 2 per cent in 1980 to 42 per cent in 1990, and almost 60 per cent in 1995. The fastest-growing export industries were textiles and footwear (14 per cent of total exports in 1995), wood products (12 per cent) and electrical machinery (7 per cent). The early 1990s also witnessed a slight shift in favour of heavy and chemical industry as opposed to light manufacturing (James and Fujita 2000: table 1, Thee 2000: 421). In 1996, manufacturing accounted for one-quarter of the total value added in the entire economy, an increase from only 8 per cent in 1965. During the New Order period, Indonesia ceased to be mainly a supplier of primary products and developed into a fully fledged industrializing country (Thee 2000: 421, Manning 2001: 25). This had profound consequences for the functioning of the labour market. The dynamics of the labour market are discussed here in conjunction with wage-rate developments and the increasing confrontation between labour and state within the institutional framework of the New Order government.

In 1988, the architects of the Fifth Five-Year Development Plan (*Repelita* or *Rencana penembangan lima tahu*) targeted the rate of employment growth in manufacturing at 6.7 per cent per year, faster than ever recorded in Indonesian history. Employment in this sector of the economy did increase by an average of 5.6 per cent per year between 1990 and 1996, which raised the contribution of manufacturing to total employment from 10 per cent to 13 per cent. At the same time, employment in agriculture actually declined, in both absolute and relative terms. By 1996, only two out of every five employees were engaged in agriculture. However, the displacement of labour in agriculture was not fully compensated for by the generation of new jobs in manufacturing, so that by 1996 more people were officially registered as unemployed than in 1990 (Manning 2001: 23, 27). Even in terms of employment, as opposed to GNP or value added, Indonesia ceased to be a country in which the rural economy and the primary sector played a dominant part. The increase in open unemployment, towards 5 per cent of the labour force in 1996, indicates the rise of an urban proletariat of formerly rural dwellers who were seeking employment in manufacturing or services in the cities. The simultaneous rise of employment in manufacturing and open unemployment suggests that the Indonesian labour market had become more 'modern' in the sense of being more akin to the situation prevailing in industrialized countries.

The immediate effect of globalization on the Indonesian labour market was the increase in the demand for labour in manufacturing in general. In order to understand what kinds of jobs the rising non-oil exports generated, we need to break down the employment effects sector by sector. A statistical reconstruction of job generation shows that manufactured exports generated 1.7 million jobs in 1985, 4.8 million jobs in 1990 and 5.8 million jobs in 1995. Most of the new jobs were in light industries, such as textiles, footwear, wood and paper products, although the contribution of light industries to the total dropped from approximately 50 per cent in 1985 or 1990, to 43 per cent in 1995 (James and Fujita 2000: table 2). The slowdown in the generation of manufacturing employment in the early 1990s as compared with the late 1980s reflects the beginning of a technological upgrading of industrial production in Indonesia. There was a shift towards more capital-intensive lines of production, as in heavy industry and the manufacturing of electrical machinery, especially electronics. The important point here is that the explosive increase in demand for workers in manufacturing was short lived, giving a stronger emphasis on skills than numbers. However, the supply of skilled workers increased as well, due to the higher levels of educational achievement. It has been demonstrated that the wages of skilled workers in manufacturing by and large increased more slowly than those of unskilled workers between 1977 and 1994, so the relative inequality between unskilled and skilled labour earnings in fact declined over time (Suryahadi 1999). This represents a more indirect effect of globalization on Indonesian labour at the time of industrialization.

The Indonesian economy was strongly export driven during the early 1990s. Foreign exports rose by an annual average of 12 per cent over the years 1990–5, which resulted in an income growth of 7.6 per cent per year or, when corrected for population growth (2 per cent), about 5.6 per cent per capita. Wage rates in manufacturing increased by on average 6.9 per cent over the same period, just as fast as in South Korea, but slower than in Thailand (Manning 2001: 21, 24). This suggests that workers in Indonesian manufacturing benefited slightly more than other Indonesians from economic growth in the early 1990s. There seems to have been a certain catch-up growth in average earnings as compared with the earlier period. Yet the benefits should not be exaggerated, considering the far faster growth in manufacturing output and exports and levels of skills in both supply and demand of labour had also risen. Wage gains during the industrialization drive of the early 1990s may simply reflect the fact that workers were moving into better jobs.

A major change in labour relations during the early 1990s was the introduction of nation-wide minimum wage legislation. Different regulations in this vein had become effective in various provinces during the 1970s and 1980s, but only in 1989–90 did the Minister of Manpower, Cosmas Batubara, impose specific standards that applied to all firms with more than twenty-five employees throughout the country. The wage rates were to be revised annually, and guidelines were issued for implementation and legal sanctions. The whole matter was highly publicized and received public backing by President Suharto. However, it must not be overlooked that the minimum wage rates were very conservative and often far too low to cover even the minimum physical needs of young workers without families. Compliance left much to be desired, and the refusal of employers to adhere to these standards became a frequent source of conflict during the 1990s. Real minimum wages increased on average by 15 per cent per year up to 1994, but then still amounted to no more than 50–60 per cent of average earnings of all waged workers (Manning 1993: 72–3, Manning 1998: 216–18).

The institutionalization of minimum wage rates represented an intervention by the government in the functioning of the labour market that may at first sight appear rather surprising, considering the general mode of deregulation in government economic policies as pursued since the mid-1980s. In addition, such legislation would clearly foster rising expectations among workers that a return to the previous situation would prove impossible for all intents and purposes. Several explanations may be advanced to explain the Indonesian government's action in this regard, including its apparently serious efforts to enforce compliance. One of these involved external pressures: complaints to the International Labour Organization (ILO) in Geneva about the poor labour conditions in Indonesia had been mounting since the late 1980s. Another explanation is connected with the government's push for human-resource development and rapid technological progress at the time: for example, the minimum wage rates could possibly induce productivity gains. There is little evidence that rising minimum wage rates constrained the generation of new jobs, even if there were complaints from highly labour-intensive export industries in the mid-1990s about stiffer competition from other low-wage producers such as Vietnam and China (Manning 1998: 225–6). In the final analysis, the minimum wage policy was probably too conservative either to convince foreign critics or to cause a sudden upward jump in productivity.

Aspects of labour conditions other than wage rates increasingly attracted attention. Case studies in manufacturing in West Java in the early 1990s revealed that labour conditions were lagging behind in qualitative terms, even if it would be an exaggeration to depict unskilled factory labour in Indonesia as a new form of slavery (White 1993). A separate problem was that of child labour, especially since this was not recognized as a problem by the authorities. According to the Department of Manpower, child labour simply did not exist in Indonesia. On the other hand, a regulation dating from 1987 intended to offer some protection to children below the age of fourteen who 'were forced to work to earn income because of socio-economic reasons'. However, this measure seems to have been largely ineffective. The problem with child labour therefore does not only concern the extremely meagre wages obtained, but above all the lack of protection enjoyed by these children (Tjandraningsih 1993: 235).

The institutional framework of labour relations remained by and large the same throughout the years 1990–7. In 1995, the government-controlled SPSI was converted into the FSPSI (Federasi Serikat Pekerja Seluruh Indonesia, the Federation of All-Indonesian Associations of Workers). The Minister of Manpower at the time, Abdul Latief, above all continued the policy to constrain the development of an independent labour movement in Indonesia. For the first time in two decades, the monopoly of the government-controlled labour organization was being challenged. The legal basis for this challenge dated from a regulation in 1987 stipulating that the establishment of a new trade union was indeed permitted, but only if it had a representation in twenty of Indonesia's twenty-seven provinces as well as in at least 100 districts and 1,000 enterprises (Hadiz 1993: 196). Full union activity was thus allowed in principle, but the obstacles in terms of its realization were almost insurmountable.

Two independent trade unions were established in the early 1990s, the SBM (Serikat Buruh Merdeka Setiakawan, the Solidarity Independent Workers Union), which was rather short lived, and the SBSI (Serikat Buruh Sejahtera Indonesia, the Indonesian Workers Union for Welfare), founded in 1992 by the energetic activist Muchtar Pakpahan. Both immediately entered into violent clashes with both the government and the SPSI (later FSPSI). The numbers of strikes rose rapidly, from the extremely low level of nineteen cases in 1989 to 114 in 1991 and further to 250 in 1992 and 300 by 1994 (Hadiz 1993: 187, Manning 1998: 214). Labour unrest, in Indonesian labelled *unjuk rasa* (literally: to show feeling), was strongly related to wage demands. Action often erupted when enterprises sought to circumvent the newly announced minimum wage requirements. The rise of labour activism in the early 1990s reflected an increasing consciousness among workers of their rights, which in turn may be related to the change in social environment as workers moved from agriculture and rural areas into manufacturing in cities. In that sense, more labour activism may be viewed as an indirect consequence of the globalization of the Indonesian economy.

In May 1993 a young woman, Marsinah, was sexually assaulted and brutally murdered, after having emerged as the informal leader of a strike in a watch factory in the Surabaya region in East Java. Interrogation coupled with torture and subsequent imprisonment of company officials was widely believed to serve as a cover-up for military involvement. There was an international outcry, and in June 1993 a delegation of the United States government threatened to withdraw preferential treatment from Indonesian–American trade should Indonesia's record in labour relations fail to improve (Hadiz 1998: 116, Manning 1998: 221–2). This was the most obvious example of external pressure on labour policies in Indonesia. Marsinah became a symbol for the struggle of Indonesian workers to improve their conditions.

In April 1994, massive riots erupted in Medan in North Sumatra in the wake of labour conflicts. A prominent local businessman was killed, and Muchtar Pakpahan was accused of masterminding the unrest. He was imprisoned and the government became ever more determined to crush the SBSI, especially since it maintained links with an outlawed left-wing political party, the PRD (Partai Rakyat Demokratik, the People's Democratic Party). The last couple of years before the economic crisis, i.e. between 1995 and 1997, witnessed a hardening government attitude towards all opposition, both in politics and labour relations. The independent trade union lost momentum, primarily because it was blocked from activities in workplaces. Contacts with workers had to be maintained outside the factories, which was far less effective (Hadiz 1997: 136). Spontaneous labour unrest continued to take place. In 1995, there were 276 strikes involving 127,000 workers, and by 1996 these numbers had risen to 350 and more than 220,000 employees respectively (*Kontan*, 16 October 2000). Such was the situation on the eve of the economic crisis in 1997: sharpened conflicts of interests in the wake of accelerated industrialization and an awakening labour movement.

Crisis and reform

The Asian crisis of 1997 hit Indonesia with exceptional severity. Just as in Thailand and South Korea, the collapse of the national currency and the financial system was the direct consequence of reckless lending and a virtual lack of supervision of the banking system. However, unlike elsewhere, the financial crisis in Indonesia deepened into a major economic, social and political crisis, culminating with the resignation of Suharto as president in late May 1998. This reflected the fundamental weaknesses in the political economy of Indonesia that already hid beneath the surface before the crisis and also the failure of the New Order government to handle the crisis once it had broken out. As such the economic crisis was, just as elsewhere, clearly a consequence, albeit not an inevitable one, of globalization, in particular the liberalization of international capital movements, but the severity and duration of the crisis in the case of Indonesia had internal causes. This section considers the effects of the crisis on the labour market and how it functioned.

In 1998, the worst year of the crisis, the national income of Indonesia fell by as much as 14.8 per cent, a decline of the same magnitude as the one that took place during the entire economic depression in the 1930s. Unemployment increased rapidly as scores of factories closed down. Numbers of workers in medium-sized and large manufacturing enterprises declined from 4.2 million in 1997 to 3.5 million in 1998, a decrease of 15 per cent in only one year. Unemployment rose even faster in smaller manufacturing firms (with less than twenty-five employees each) and cottage industries. Here numbers of employees dropped by 20 per cent, from 6.6 million in 1997 to 5.3 million in 1998. Labour-intensive industries such as food processing, textiles and transport equipment or machinery were hit the hardest (Thee 2000: 436, 439). Already, by March 1998, even before the collapse of the New Order government, some 300,000 workers in the textile and garments industry alone had lost their jobs (Hadiz 1998: 110). A study by the ILO predicted 7 per cent unemployment at the end of 1998, corresponding to 6.7 million people (ILO/UNDP 1998: 2, 26–7). Other estimates were even higher, and simultaneous projections of impoverishment cited figures of 80 million people living under the official poverty line.

Both unemployment and poverty did increase substantially, but by far less than the gloomy initial predictions. The actual rate of unemployment rose from 4.7 per cent in 1997 to 5.5 per cent in 1998 and 6.4 per cent in 1999 (Manning 2001: 26–8). In August 2000, the Indonesian authorities counted 5.8 million persons who were looking for a job. This corresponds to 6.1 per cent of the total labour force in Indonesia, i.e. the economically active part of the population above 15 years of age (totalling 95.6 million individuals). By implication, almost 90 million people worked in 2000, which explains why current estimates of the incidence of poverty are also considerably lower than the gloomy predictions in 1998. Yet, it must not be overlooked that only 60 per cent of the working population (58 million persons) have employment for more than 35 hours a week, whereas as many as 12 per cent (11.3 million) work less than 20 hours (BPS

2001a: 30, 55). Even if we take into account the large number of women deliberately choosing to work part-time, it is clear that the relatively moderate unemployment rate is accompanied by a substantial degree of underemployment. Many Indonesians today would probably need to work longer hours in order to support their families.

Signs of a cautious recovery became visible in 1999, conditioned by the optimism surrounding the democratic elections under President B.J. Habibie in June 1999, and his replacement in October 1999 by Abdurrahman Wahid, a president without links with the New Order government. The steep decline in national income in 1998 turned into a zero growth rate in 1999 and a modest positive growth in 2000. Projections for 2001 were initially rather optimistic, with a rate of economic growth at 4.5–5.5 per cent, but this figure was adjusted downwards to 3 per cent or less due to the lack of political stability during the final months of Abdurrahman Wahid's term as president (Pangestu and Goeltom 1991: 151, Thee 2000: 427). The resumption of economic growth, albeit it at a far slower rate than before the crisis, obviously explains why the situation in the labour market has not become catastrophic but in fact has improved somewhat. A supplementary explanation has been put forward by Manning, arguing that the Indonesian labour market has been remarkably flexible in adjusting to deteriorating conditions, so that the adverse effects were not fully felt (Manning 2000: 119–28). It also appears that the explosion in the incidence of poverty in 1998 was caused by a temporary acceleration of inflation, which drove costs of living up without wages being adjusted. Since then, inflation has slowed down, reaching a level of 11 per cent by 2000–2001 (Pangestu and Goeltom 2001: 152). In addition, there has been a dramatic increase in the export of labour from Indonesia. The numbers of Indonesians working abroad, often remitting considerable amounts of money to their families, rose from 380,000 to more than 500,000 between 1998 and 2000 alone (*Media Indonesia*, 21 September 2000). Whether or not the Indonesian labour market has proved exceptionally flexible in coping with the crisis, it has certainly been under greater strain in the last couple of years than ever before.

An important change took place in the institutional framework only six days after President Suharto had resigned and President Habibie allowed the restrictions on the formation of independent trade unions to be relaxed. Since then there has been a proliferation of trade unions at all levels and in all industries. In 2001, thirty-six trade unions operated nation-wide and many more are confined to a regional or even local scale. Several of the new unions are in fact reincarnations of organizations that already functioned in the Sukarno era but vanished under Suharto. Others have developed a strong Muslim identity. Unlike before, many unions now have close connections with party politics, for instance Pakpahan's SBSI and, surprisingly, also the FSPSI. A common ideological element is the reformist zeal, which since the campaigns against Suharto in early 1998 has come to characterize virtually any public organization in Indonesia today. On the part of the trade unions, this represents a belated ideological awakening considering that organized labour played scarcely any role at all in bringing down the New Order government in 1998. One consequence of the revival of trade unionism is a lack of cohesion within the individual enterprises when workers belong to different trade unions. This necessitates lengthy negotiations among trade unions before a common stand can be established *vis-à-vis* the employer.

The minimum wage policy has been continued during the Habibie and Wahid administrations. In July 1998, the first post-Suharto Minister of Manpower, Fahmi Idris, announced an unprecedented 15 per cent increase in the minimum wage rate. The rate for full-time employment then became Rp. 198,500 per month in the Jakarta region, which at the prevailing very low currency rate came down to only US$14.10 (Hadiz 1998: 122). The rate has since then been adjusted several times and by 2001 it amounted to Rp. 426,250 or US$40.60, which of course also reflects the appreciation of the rupiah since 1998. However, statistics for August 2000 show that only 43 per cent of employees surveyed in fact received more than the current minimum wage rate, and that a mere 12 per cent pocketed twice the minimum wage or more. Important gender differences hide behind such global averages. As many as 72 per cent of female workers earned less than the minimum wage, whereas this was the case for only about one-half of male workers. A similar discrepancy also applied to the urban *vis-à-vis* rural wages with respectively 51 per cent and 32 per cent earning more than the minimum. The wage statistics also make clear that manufacturing wages are lagging behind those in services (BPS 2001b: 11, 61). The disappointing figures on actual wage earnings reflect above all that a large proportion of the working population is not working full time. Underemployment in today's Indonesia means meagre earnings. It is a major challenge to the Indonesian economy today to create opportunities for work, not only to absorb those unemployed but also to increase the hours and earnings of those already working.

Waves of violent strikes surrounded the first year of crisis and the downfall of the Suharto regime. Numbers of strikes amounted to 234 in 1997 and 278 in 1998, with about 150,000 workers involved in each year. Labour unrest subsided in 1999, when there were 'only' 125 strikes involving less than 50,000 workers, but the year 2000 saw another increase, to 173 strikes, with more than 60,000 persons participating. Wage increases were counted as the foremost reason for labour action, but other grounds were frequently mentioned, including protests against dismissals, too meagre food provisions, violations of social-security rights and too little money given for transport (*Media Indonesia*, 22 January 2000). Large-scale attacks on factories, with civilians joining forces with striking workers, occurred frequently, but a massive national strike to demand 100 per cent wage increases announced by Pakpahan in October 2000 failed to draw a large crowd. There was much concern among employers about the adverse effects on the business climate due to violent labour unrest and the lack of security.

The situation by mid-2001 was rather indecisive. Labour unrest had been rising during the first half of the year. In February, 5,000 workers went on strike in a textile factory near Jakarta; in March the SBSI organized large-scale actions at the coal mines in East Kalimantan; in May the roads to Jakarta harbour, Tanjung Priok, were blockaded by striking workers; and in June the police clashed with protesting workers in Surabaya. Meanwhile, the economy, as it were, held its breath, in anticipation of the impeachment and removal of President Abdurrahman Wahid, which eventually did take place in late July 2001. Peace will not easily be restored in the turbulent labour market in Indonesia, but an acceleration of economic recovery would surely help.

Conclusions

A new cabinet was installed in Jakarta in early August 2001 shortly after Megawati Sukarnoputri had replaced Abdurrahman Wahid as president of Indonesia. The creation of new jobs was labelled a top priority in the first public statement made by the newly appointed Co-ordinating Minister for Economic Affairs, Dorodjatun Kuntjoro-Yakti (*Jakarta Post*, 13 August 2001). This was an overt recognition that crisis management in Indonesia has so far fallen short of alleviating the extreme pressures in a labour market haunted by high unemployment accompanied by underemployment, persistently low wages, and much labour unrest, often resulting in violent confrontations. By adopting a historical perspective, reaching back to the initiation of Suharto's New Order government in 1966, this contribution reaffirms that globalization in economic relations has had profound and irrevocable effects on the functioning of the labour market in Indonesia.

We may distinguish between five different effects of globalization in economic relations on the Indonesian labour market during the years 1966–2001. The first one is of a general nature and refers to the macro-economic conditions fostered by export-oriented industrialization aided by a massive influx of foreign capital. The result was sustained economic growth and structural change over more than thirty years, but, by the same token, Indonesia also became more vulnerable than ever before to adverse economic developments in the wider region of South-east Asia. In that sense, rapid growth and sudden crisis were two sides of the same coin. This first general effect provided the basic premises for change in the labour market.

The second effect refers specifically to the quantitative and qualitative changes that did take place in the labour market. There was a very considerable generation of new jobs, especially in manufacturing and especially for women. Yet the job creation process slowed down as the emphasis in industrialization began to switch in the 1990s from highly labour-intensive to more capital-intensive lines of production. Finally, of course, job creation turned into its opposite as the crisis of 1997 hit Indonesia, and both unemployment and underemployment rose rapidly. The qualitative side of the direct effects on the labour market included enhanced levels of education achievement in the labour force. All these changes were substantial and irrevocable. The Indonesian labour market today looks very different from one generation ago.

The third effect was indirect and has to do with the changing social environment of labour. The urbanization and in a sense 'modernization' of labour market conditions through industrialization gradually gave rise among workers to an enhanced consciousness of their rights. This may explain the rise of labour unrest in the early 1990s and the explosion of labour mobilization and activism after the collapse of the New Order government in May 1998. Confrontations between organized labour and the state have a short history in Indonesia, but are not likely to vanish in the short or medium term.

The fourth effect was unexpected, at least by the authorities, involving external pressures to improve labour conditions in Indonesia. This fuelled rising labour activism during the 1990s but might have become less important during the crisis as the emphasis shifted to the even more urgent matters of generating employment in the first place.

The fifth and final effect is of a slightly different nature, as it was expected but did not fully materialize. Here we are concerned with wage developments over time. Wage rates lagged behind growth rates throughout most of the New Order period, i.e. of the expected gains from growth, far less were actually passed on to the workers. The prime reason was the weak representation of labour's interests under the Suharto government. The introduction of minimum wage-rate legislation marked at least the beginning of a catch-up increase in the 1990s, albeit from a very low starting-point. The scope for an acceleration of this process was obviously limited by the economic crisis from 1997 onwards. The trade-off between economic recovery and long overdue wage increases will be a very important issue for the Indonesian government in the near future.

References

BPS (2001a) *Keadaan angkatan kerja di Indonesia/Labor force situation in Indonesia: August 2000*, Jakarta: Badan Pusat Statistik.

BPS (2001b) *Keadaan pekerja/buruh/karyawan di Indonesia/Laborers/employees situation in Indonesia: August 2000*, Jakarta: Badan Pusat Statistik.

Hadiz, V. (1993) 'Workers and working class politics in the 1990s', in C. Manning and J. Hardjono (eds) *Indonesia Assessment 1993: Labour: Sharing in the Benefits of Growth?*, Canberra: Australian National University, pp. 186–200.

Hadiz, V. (1997) *Workers and the State in New Order Indonesia*, London: Routledge.

Hadiz, V. (1998) '*Reformasi total?* Labour after Suharto', *Indonesia*, 66: 109–24.

ILO/UNDP (1998) *Employment Challenges of the Indonesian Crisis*, Jakarta: International Labour Organization and United Nations Development Programme.

James, W.E. and Fujita, N. (2000) 'Employment and manufacturing exports in Indonesia: an input–output analysis', *ICSEAD Working Paper Series*, 6, Kitakyushu: International Centre for the Study of East Asian Development.

Jones, G.W. and Manning, C. (1992) 'Labour force and employment during the 1980s', in A. Booth (ed.) *The Oil Boom and After: Indonesian Economic Policy and Performance in the Soeharto Era*, Singapore: Oxford University Press, pp. 363–410.

Manning, C. (1993) 'Examining both sides of the ledger: Employment and wages during the New Order', in C. Manning and J. Hardjono (eds) *Indonesia Assessment 1993: Labour: Sharing in the Benefits of Growth?*, Canberra: Australian National University, pp. 61–87.

Manning, C. (1998) *Indonesian Labour in Transition: an East Asian Success Story?*, Cambridge: Cambridge University Press.

Manning, C. (2000) 'Labour market adjustment to Indonesia's economic crisis: context, trends and implications', *Bulletin of Indonesian Economic Studies*, 36 (1), 105–36.

Manning, C. (2001) 'Labour markets and the East Asian economic crisis: lessons from Indonesia, Thailand and Korea', Paper presented at the 3rd IRSA International Conference on 'Indonesia's Sustainable Development in a Decentralization Era', Jakarta, 20–1 March.

Manning, C. and Hardjono, J. (eds) (1993) *Indonesia Assessment 1993: Labour: Sharing in the Benefits of Growth?*, Canberra: Australian National University.

Oey-Gardiner, M. (1993) 'A gender perspective on Indonesia's labour market transformation', in C. Manning and J. Hardjono (eds) *Indonesia Assessment 1993: Labour: Sharing in the Benefits of Growth?*, Canberra: Australian National University, 203–13.

Pangestu, M. and Goeltom, M.S. (2001) 'Survey of recent developments', *Bulletin of Indonesian Economic Studies*, 37(2): 141–71.

Pincus, J. (1996) *Class Power and Agrarian Change: Land and Labour in Rural West Java*, New York: St Martin's Press.

Suryahadi, A. (1999) 'Wage inequality between skilled and unskilled labour in Indonesian manufacturing', *Ekonomi dan Keuangan Indonesia*, 47: 271–88.

Thee Kian Wie (2000) 'The impact of the economic crisis on Indonesia's manufacturing sector', *The Developing Economies*, 38: 420–53.

Tjandraningsih, I. (1993) 'The dilemma of child labour in factories', in C. Manning and J. Hardjono (eds) *Indonesia Assessment 1993: Labour: Sharing in the Benefits of Growth?*, Canberra: Australian National University, pp. 229–39.

White, B. (1993) 'Industrial workers on West Java's urban fringe', in C. Manning and J. Hardjono (eds) *Indonesia Assessment 1993: Labour: Sharing in the Benefits of Growth?*, Canberra: Australian National University, pp. 127–38.

World Bank (1994) *Indonesia: Sustaining Development*, Washington, DC: World Bank.

10 Institutionalizing labour throughout Argentina's 'second great transformation'

Claudia Sanchez Bajo

Introduction

During the 1990s, the Argentinian labour force experienced dramatic changes at the national level, under the uninterrupted government of one man and one political party that appeared to be its foremost supporters, seemingly managing to articulate a viable type of capitalism combined with a democratic regime. As Novaro (1999: 14) affirms, 'there has been little recognition of any novelty produced by the politics of those years … either good or bad', and there is a need to construct a historical vision of the 1990s. It is important to focus on labour, given that it has not received as much attention as other areas of study (such as government, business or civil society). In this chapter I intend to explore two complementary hypotheses regarding the prospects for the institutionalization of a new regulatory framework for labour at the beginning of the twenty-first century.

The first hypothesis is that institutionalized labour (i.e. trade unions and labour organizations) was constrained in both its actions and discourse by three main contradictions during the 1990s, outlined here below:

1   The paradox of a conservative restoration portrayed as necessary to a recovery economic growth, by removing former obstacles to capitalism (including the alleged excessive political influence of the state and trade unions), with an additional promise of social cohesion and integration for all. Although some within the labour movement were conscious of the changes and challenges posed by both global economic restructuring and national structural reforms, as well as by the ideology that sustained both (Pries-Conosur, 1991), it appears that they could not properly articulate such knowledge in order to communicate it to a broader audience, or as if the latter was not capable of processing it further.

2   It was Perónism itself, with which the labour movement had been affiliated since the 1940s, that engineered this dramatic reversal. Labour organizations had found their most powerful expression through state-led growth under Perónism and, since the mid-1970s, had undergone a period of de-industrialization and repression by the military government, so how could they reject the call to renew national growth by those who identified them-

selves as Perónists? Moreover, Menem's leadership built upon a new type of populism that sneered at republican institutions and the scope and nature of rights and law. Traditional populism had appealed to workers and internal migrants, with the promise of incorporation into the political and economic system, mobilizing them and leading to the emergence of various socio-political organizations. Conversely, Menem's neo-populism attempted to demobilize them while appealing to the masses as such, without any mention of class discourse – indeed, it actually weakened trade unions and actors (Novaro, 1999: 34, in agreement with O'Donnell, 1994). This contra-diction blocked their action and undermined their *raison d'être*. Those who had embodied the very history and origins of organized labour and its insti-tutions were now depicting the latter as a backward force.

3   The devastating effect of pegging the currency to the dollar in a fixed rate of 1 to 1, orchestrated by Domingo Cavallo. Moreover, at least until 1995 and then again between 1996 and 1997, economic statistics reflected economic growth after Cavallo's policies, even though such growth never brought the expected increases in employment. Indeed, the most serious strike since 1991 took place in August 1996 (*Gazeta Mercantil Latinoamericana*, 1996: 11). Devaluing the peso has been unpopular in Argentina, but not to devalue it after the Mexican–Asian–Russian–Brazilian–Chilean–Turkish string of devaluations has proved to be a recipe for endless recession.

In the search to overcome the three above-mentioned contradictions, the labour movement has elaborated new types of actions and discourses. Its increasing resistance to the existing politico-economic model has so far shown a limited ability to create an alternative to the implemented model, in spite of an ongoing search to master weaknesses and shortcomings (e.g. the forum for new thinking – *Encuentro por un Nuevo Pensamiento*, see Lozano, 1999). Labour organizations, particularly union leaders, have hypothetically played a role in the building of the new labour regulatory framework. The question is: what role?

The second hypothesis, based on Weller's statement, is that:

> The institutionalization of labour played an important role in the develop-ment model of post-war … Latin America … With the crisis of this model many of its schemes of regulation of production and distribution lost strength, among which were those of the labour market … The current discussion on reforms of Latin American labour institutions must be under-taken within the framework of the present transformation of the development model … It may be affirmed that countries in the region, as other countries in the world, are in a searching process in which many and varied actors partici-pate. This process takes place at different levels from the enterprise to national legislation and even at international level, and has not yet found answers to some key questions with respect to a new regulation of the labour market.
>
> (Weller 1998, original in endnote, in Spanish)

Considering the transformation of the 1990s and its most visible effects, the new regulatory framework in Argentina seems to be enduring, and continues to be built step by step. The question is: has it reached a mature stage of legitimacy and sustainability?

The overall objective of this chapter is to better apprehend the role that labour may have played in the national restructuring of the 1990s, which in turn has been part and parcel of an overall world politico-economic restructuring. The two complementary hypotheses summarised above will now be discussed in two separate sections, after which conclusions and paths for further discussion will be presented.

Three contradictions and the role of labour

Contradiction 1: the similarity to Argentina's first 'great transformation'

> The worst is vertigo.
> Vertigo has neither fruits nor flourishing.
> The main feature of vertigo is fear, man
> acquires the behaviour of an automate,
> he is no longer responsible,
> is no longer free, neither does he recognise
> the others.
>   E. Sabato (*The Resistance*)

In 1989, in the vertigo of hyperinflation, Carlos Menem became President of Argentina, six months before the end of Raul Alfonsín's constitutional mandate. Menem, having reached presidential power on the basis of populist promises and evangelical messages, retained power for a whole decade, sustained by a coalition of neo-liberal and conservative economists, ideologues, and large economic and financial interests, as well as the clientelistic networks belonging to Perónism. After a few months of uncertainty, the Minister of Foreign Affairs, Domingo Cavallo, became Minister of Economics and opened the door to swift and radical reforms. The author still remembers the words of a work colleague in the mid-1980s, when democracy had been recently re-instated: 'We, the conservatives, will definitely obtain power through the Perónist party in the next presidential election. We are working for that.'

As Stephen Gill explained,

> the conception of the instrumental state presiding over a liberal economy that supplants an older moral economy can be traced back to the ideas of Ricardo, Bentham and Polanyi's account of the Great Transformation.
>
> (Gill 1997: 21)

The policies of the 1990s have commonly been termed the 'Washington consensus', and their contents postulated a monetarist discipline at the macro level through state enforcement of a stable exchange rate, a reduced public budget, and effective, widespread tax collection. They also rested on the independence of the micro-economic players, through financial, trade and investment liberalization, deregulation and privatization.

Turning back to history, the first Great Transformation (in Polanyi's terms) in Argentina occurred between 1880 and 1910. At the beginning of the twentieth century, a transition occurred in the Argentine political system, described as an 'oligarchic–conservative republic' by Natalio Botana (1978), aimed at a political pluralism that nevertheless failed to modify the basis of a highly concentrated economic power. Afterwards, between the 1930s and the 1980s, a system was constructed in which the state was embedded in both the economy and society, directly as a producer and indirectly by articulating and stimulating private groups. Argentina entered into mass-production for the first time, through which labour eventually experienced a change in its socio-political and economic role. Industrialization was led by national public enterprises, while the protection and growth of the domestic market was the engine of development, ensured by the active participation of private firms, workers and the urban population. The fast rate of industrialization under the modality of macro-Fordism (according to the definition in Ruigrok and van Tulder 1995), although not generalized to the whole of the economy, led to an explosive growth in the organization and power of the trade unions, politically linked to the 'nationalist popular' movement led by one charismatic leader, Juan Domingo Perón.

As expressed by Arturo Fernández, during the first half of the twentieth century, the labour movement experienced

> an increasing loss of internationalism … A growing disengagement from workers' political parties … the predominance of reformist positions … that made possible the development of 'social and political pacts'.
>
> (1998: 31)

This was, in the case of Argentina, most evident in the Perónist movement and political party. Expectations of economic growth remained optimistic until the 1980s, although Argentina could not manage to overcome a pendulum in economics as well as in politics, between expansive Perónist governments and conservative or monetarist dictatorships, with its breaking point each time a crisis in the balance of payments occurred. After the fall of Perón's government in 1955, however, a rather linear trend in the relationship between 'capital and labour' weakened both trade unionism and labour rights, through disciplinarian treatment and anti-trade-union measures by the state, in particular during the military and Menem governments (A. Fernandez, 1998: 53-ss, 128).

The previous development cycle had been ended by resorting to state policies of control, repression and de-industrialization, exerted by the military government and their political allies since 1976. Many dreamt of carrying Argentina back to its past glory of agricultural producer, while getting rid of anything linked to old-style Perónism. Industrial workers and their organizations were obviously a main target. Labour commissions were systematically harassed within each enterprise, and labour leaders were eliminated (half of the 'disappeared' belong to this category), while the country experienced a process of de-industrialization, with the loss of tens of thousands of jobs. As a result, by the 1990s, trade unions from industrial sectors had lost power in comparison to those representing state companies and services.

In the early 1980s, following the second oil shock of 1979, circumstances changed both at the national and world levels, leading to the debt crisis and to the state fiscal crisis. During the 1980s, internal recession, a slower growth in GDP, even compared to the 1930s, high inflation, capital flight and a public deficit defeated all attempts to stabilize the national economy. In 1982, the military junta risked everything by invading the Falkland/Malvinas Islands, trying to unite the population behind them. Just before, in March 1982, the first workers' demonstrations and the first large public meeting had taken place after many years of repression. Most noticeably, during those same months, Domingo Cavallo, then President of the Central Bank, converted the foreign debt, which had been mostly shouldered by the private sector, into a public debt.

As a consequence of the process that had commenced under the military dictatorship, the former modality of politico-economic development of industrialization, based on import substitution and Fordist production, was exhausted, which in turn entailed a 'passage from state regulation to a private one' (ECLAC/CIID 1994: 24). Industrialization based on import substitution and macro-Fordism, in which social relations were mediated by the state, increasingly gave way to a new system of production and distribution (closer to micro-Fordism), where financial, services and agricultural interests achieved the greatest prominence. Micro-Fordism meant that the state was no longer the mediator of social and economic relations, which were now centred on private strategies at the micro-level and regulated mainly by the core firm/s of a holding and/or chains of production and distribution. In addition to this, some Toyotist elements have been included in the emerging system, such as lean and just-in-time production, outsourcing, subcontracting, and quality control methods (Neffa 1999: 69–115).

The transition to democratic government in Argentina took place in 1983 (O'Donnell *et al.* 1986: 37–9), accompanied by a movement towards liberal values, in both the political and economic spheres. By the mid-1980s, there was a growing consensus about the inability to cope with the crisis and the need for a new national agenda, alongside a process of élite convergence.[1] The previously disunited élites converged on elementary democratic procedures, achieving a basic consensus on how to reach two main objectives: stability for the democratic regime and economic growth. The new consensus was basically worked out between business, government and international financial organisms, without the participation of trade-union leaderships. Hegemony was then gradually constructed through a myriad of institutions and intellectuals, from which labour scholars as well as a minority of politicians and civil-society leaders (from the Catholic Church, trade unions, women's groups, and NGOs) were excluded.

This process was generally perceived as a public good in itself – an achievement to be protected above all. However, uncertainty over the external debt, the fall in GDP and industrial production, apart from the recurrent high levels of inflation, provided other ingredients to the national crisis. Various social groups, including business as well as trade unions, competed for tax privileges from the state, and their conflicts were later used to justify the crisis in itself and to reduce their political legitimacy and appeal in society.

Then the 1990s arrived, after the so-called 'lost decade' of the 1980s. The consolidation of a national value consensus enabled the new 'national' project to be carried out, coalescing around 1991 after hyperinflation shocks. About a year after the fall of the Berlin Wall and the Soviet Union, no one thought that there was any alternative to Cavallo's policies or to Argentina's acquiescence to the influence of the United States. The discrediting of alternatives and the higher political cost that they implied at the time, made it difficult for labour leaders to oppose Cavallo's structural reform policies. Cavallo's economic team came to enjoy a high degree of autonomy in formulating and implementing policies (Dahlberg 1993), which were seen as long-term and unchallenged.

The first priority for both state and private sectors had become stability, in order to attract capital investment. Business representatives publicly and strongly supported the Ministry of Economy in implementing stability plans, as well as the election and re-election of a president that would sustain them. The passage of two laws at the very start of Menem's administration: the 'Law of State Reform' and the 'Law of Economic and Social Emergency' established that 'all legal norms, even labour ones, must accompany the measures taken to stabilise the economy and to impede a return to "hyper[inflation]"' (Battistini 1999: 274).

The 1990s policies were in line with the dominant scale of values, embedded within the Washington Consensus. The latter postulates a monetarist discipline at the macro level through state enforcement of a stable exchange rate, a reduced public budget, and an effective, widespread tax-collection system. Furthermore, the state is expected to withdraw its presence through deregulation and privatization. Such measures, together with the build-up of major independent players at the micro-economic level through financial, trade and investment liberalization, were to deliver economic growth.

In order to ensure such consensus, the national president needed to appear as 'strong, courageous, above parties and interests, macho – [someone who] will save the country' (*Ibid.*, 1994: 65) from economic chaos. That is, 'from suffering vertigo', in Sabato's words. Menem could thus govern in a highly arbitrary manner (i.e. 'he was given a blank cheque'), constrained only by business power groups, through decrees 'of need and urgency',[2] and with little or no horizontal accountability to other democratic institutions. In addition, the executive delegated legal competence to other actors for setting policy priorities and drafting bills. Also, the general perception of parliament was negative, due to predatory competition amid a fluid institutional representation of interests and identities. Finally, the other main political party, which had governed between 1983 and 1989, was in complete discredit and disarray. In brief, until the mid-1990s, the relationship between the executive and the legislative branches was rather irrelevant, and the one between the executive and civil society hardly controversial.

Guillermo O'Donnell (1994) argues that a new species of democracy evolved in the 1990s: 'delegative democracy', a type of polyarchy, which is less liberal and republican. Delegative democracy reflects a policy-making style that combines neo-liberal policies with neo-corporatist practices and the use of a neo-populist discourse, which assures a high degree of compliance and a low degree of protest, or at least it did until the first major world financial crisis in 1994–5. In cases where the judiciary system declared certain rules to be unconstitutional, the Supreme Court, which Menem had tailored to his needs, was always ready to act on the side of the executive.

This process has been analysed by K. Weyland (1996) and by J. Demmers, A.E. Fernáendez Jilberto and B. Hogenboom (2001), where further evidence and explanation is provided. Many of those highly generalized practices were later circumscribed as corruption, backed by an abundant literature of research publications and newspaper articles on Menem and his family, friends and networks, and their judiciary cases.[3] At the very least, the widespread, even public, recourse to all kinds of illegal payments and compensation made it unlikely that the public policies of the 1990s could have been implemented without these and their co-opting effects.

To summarise the process of reform, the most important changes in the regulation of labour are presented in Table 10.1. We can observe a process of change in norms and rules – rapid and confusing – with a very clear trend towards so-called 'labour flexibility', which may be seen as the central concept for the restructuring of labour relations, rights and obligations of workers, business and the nation-state in Argentina.[4]

What did this process of structural reform mean for labour organizations and unions? The ability of Perónism to internalise the contradictions of the political system, behaving at the same time as government and opposition, enabled 'Menemism' to prevent an effective autonomous opposition. This paradox also affected organized labour, the vast majority of which was Perónist. Perónist labour leaders, through negotiations with the Ministry of Labour as well as with deputies in parliament, representing the political party of Perónism, called 'Justicialista', granted decisive support for the structural reforms that were being generalized in Latin America, and what Smith and Korzeniewicz (1997) have labelled as the 'Second Great Transformation' in Polanyi's terms (Gill 1997: 21).

Almost everything was privatized: the national airline, trains, telephones, oil, gas, water, the postal system, social security, banks, etc. Privatization entailed high social costs: enterprises downsized, reduced salaries and work contracts, or gave incentives for retirement, supported by World Bank Programmes but also by illegal methods of harassment, threats and sanctions for those who did not want to retire (Ramirez 1999: 349–61).

Table 10.1 Labour reform in Argentina in the 1990s

Year	Legal norms	Rights	Others
1989	D1477/89: The use of *vales* (food vouchers) instead of money is accepted by the state, but is not considered part of the salary	The decrees, modifying article 105 of the law concerning labour contracts, were hence illegal. This was the beginning of a contradictory series of norms for and against the recognition of vales as legal salary remuneration (Against: D333/93, 433/94. D849/96, L24700 of 1996. For: L24241 of 1994, D773/96.) The last in the series states that this is not remuneration	The ILO Convention No. 95 establishes that such vales are remuneration
	L23696 (Law of State Reform) L23697 (Law of Economic Emergency)	Both laws 23696 and 23697 established the priorities for the 1990s	
1990			
1991	L24013 (National Law for Employment)	Collective work conventions in public enterprises are annulled. To formally register workers, the state would pardon employers if they disclosed data on employees. Women's work at night is permitted. Work time is deregulated by considering a collective average of hours at the end of the month	
	D1994/91 on strikes Modification to law on accidents in the workplace	The right to strike is strictly regulated by D1994/91	
	L. on Employment 24013, introduces the first four types of temporary work contracts Decree on Productivity D2284/91, ratified by L24307	Reduced workers' rights: establishes specific and reduced sums for the worker in case of accidents	
	More than 50 collective work conventions concerning sea and port workers are rescinded	Deregulated working hours, permitting more than 9 hours per day, for example	
1992	D340/92: Introduction of system of internships	Interns work for 8 hours without labour rights, either individual or collective, for up to 4 years	
1993	A government bill of 19 articles, proposing a thorough labour reform, fails in parliament	Imposes negotiations at enterprise level 'between the free worker and the free entrepreneur' (article 2)	
1994	A new government bill on labour reform is sent to the parliament in February 1994		Reform of the National Constitution

Year	Legal norms	Rights	Others
	L24347 concerning the new pension system based on private-pension funds		Tripartite Accord on 25 July among government, trade unions and business organisations. Pre-electoral time: a Framework Accord among CGT, business chambers and government is signed that opens the door to the 1995 laws
995	D290/95 (reduction of public expenditure)	On 27 February, after the Mexican crisis, reduction of salaries and massive lay-offs in a 10-day period	July: the government implemented pay-cuts of 5 –15% for all federal employees earning more than $2,000 per month
	L24465 (Law of Labour Flexibilisation): training contracts shall not be considered labour contracts and could be of up to 6 months. In 1998, L25013 stated the opposite, thus entailing labour rights and contributions	Deregulated work time and contracts and reduced labour rights for full-time jobs	San Juan province cut between 20 and 30% of the salaries of all provincial workers
	L24467 on Special framework for Small and Medium Enterprises (SMEs), regulated by D146/99	L25013 annulled some options concerning temporary labour contracts	
		SMEs of less than 80 workers are not covered by any labour-union convention. For small enterprises, if labour does not agree on new work conventions within the enterprise within 3 months, the existing ones cease to apply. New collective conventions should revoke the right to compensation in case of lay-off, with a one month's notice. The 13th month's salary, which used to be paid in one instalment, can now be given in three. Work holidays in SMEs can be spaced	
	L24522 Creditors of bankrupt firms can buy the firm without any obligation toward the workers	All bankrupt enterprises can suspend workers' recourse to their collective work convention	

	Law/Decree	Description	Context
	L24557: obliges workers to contribute to part of a private system of labour risk insurance, creating a secure market.	Article 39 of L24557 has been declared unconstitutional by the judicial system (see P.A. Prado at http://www.legislaw.com.ar/legislaw; accessed 26 January 2000)	
	L24635: sets an obligatory phase of mediation for workers in case of conflict		A 'Second State Reform' is proposed
96	L24700: sets out a list of benefits that shall not be considered work remuneration	Social benefits such as vales and food boxes are independent of the remuneration and thus should not contribute to the social system	
	New reduction of the minimum legal payment in case of lay-off.		Between May 1994 and May 1996, 976,400 jobs had been lost. Poverty levels reached 18.7%. Out of 10 workers, 4 were in the so-called informal job market. The work inspectors policing working conditions amounted to only 50 for 185,000 enterprises
	D770 and 771/96: Reduction of family subsidies D773/96 D849/96		
97	D137/97 (Health costs)	Health costs are not work remuneration; employers' contributions are considered to be social benefits	Protests and picketing increase
	D638/97 (Health services for managers and professional associations)	Sets options on the basis of L23660 (National Health Services)	
98	L25013, sanctioned on 2 September, and published in the National Official Bulletin on 24 September 1998	Nullification of various types of temporary labour contracts. Re-establishment of labour rights in many cases	In September, 4 weeks of protests by civil-society (MTA, CTA, CCC, the '62' labour unions, the Radical and the FREPASO political parties) to prevent the approval of labour laws brought in by Menem's government

Year	Legal norms	Rights	Others
1999	L25165 modifies the system of internships by reducing working hours and years. Revoked by D428/00 (which is illegal, since a decree cannot revoke a law) Menem leaves office, succeeded by De la Rua		Repression of workers' protest in front of the parliament on 19 April According to INDEC, the national statistics office, unemployment among the young active population reached 45% (Clarín, 28 July 2000)
2000	D487/2000 modifies an article of L25165 (this should have been done using another law, and not using a decree) D1096/2000: creates a Tripartite Commission to review OIT observations on Argentina.		
	L25250 (Law of Labour Reform): article 33 includes the word *intimatoriamente* (i.e. without protest or delay) after 'to dispose', which did not exist in the parliamentary transcripts concerning the law. This law, suspected of being approved by resorting to corruption, leads the vice-president to resign and D. Cavallo to return to power	L25250 raised the period for internships to several years and 6 hours work. The university, as intermediary for the placements of interns, can retain up to 20% of the intern's wages	
2001	L25445 (Law on Convertibility of Peso) L25453 (Law on Public Deficit) D761/01 (Accords for Competitiveness)	Introduced the Euro for certain cases (e.g. exports) New reductions to all salaries and benefits Tripartite accords (governments–business–labour) by sector. At the end of July, four sectors had signed an accord (wine, citrus fruit, bananas and yerba mate – a type of tea produced in Argentina)	

Contradiction 2

1990s Labour and Peronism: Raison d'être *or abiding memory?*

> Times were hard and Dr. Menem made no promise that they would get better soon. He referred to his government's stringent economic measures as 'surgery without anaesthetic'.
>
> (M. France 1999, *Bad Times in Buenos Aires*: 32)

The government's adoption of Perónism, and Menem's election as president, gave the population strong hopes of better salaries and working conditions, as well as the return of political power to the trade unions. However, the reversal of Menem's electoral promises and his alliance with neo-liberalism paralyzed labour leaders. As mentioned in the introduction, the first serious strike took place as late as August 1996 (*Gazeta Mercantil Latinoamericana*, 1996: 11). In order to understand this phenomenon better, one must look back at the history and political role of trade unions since 1955.

During the many years in which Perónism and its leaders were forbidden in Argentina, Perónist trade unions were prominent in organizing the resistance to several military governments, and the political representation of Perónism. Thus they acquired a central role within Perónism and eventually gained a strong bargaining position with the government. Since the 1960s, certain trade-union leaders have also acquired the traits of corporatism (e.g. the leader Vandor and his faction). During the 1980s, trade-union leaders constituted the main political opposition to the first democratic government.

For example, in 1984, those who were members of parliament blocked the government's attempt to replace Law 22.105 on professional associations, which regulated trade unions, with a new law. Through this struggle the two factions of CGT (the Perónist trade union – at that time the sole legal representative of all Argentinian workers), a pro-democracy faction and a quasi-military faction, became reunited. In 1984–5, after the defeat of the parliamentary bill, the government initiated a policy of social dialogue with, and incorporation of, the Perónist labour leaders. Several times it attempted a 'socio-political pact' with both trade unions and national business organizations. Between 1985 and 1988, several instruments became institutionalized: mechanisms for monthly consultative meetings with trade unions on salaries and prices, tripartite commissions (government–labour–business) to agree on economic policies, and the nomination of a leader from the labour faction called 'The 15' as Minister of Labour in 1987. Trade unions appeared to present an all-powerful opposition against any economic stabilization policies, using traditional instruments and tactics, such as general strikes, public discourses rejecting government proposals, or breaking up negotiations before joining in again. The much sought-after pact never materialized, while the government slowly began to privatize and liberalize trade. Inflation in the economic sphere, and military demands in the political sphere became sources of concern. The external debt reached approximately 45 billion dollars at the end of the first democratic government.

Meanwhile, Perónism digested its 1983 electoral defeat with its first ever internal elections, in which two groups (orthodox and renovation) competed against each other. The orthodox group won and Carlos Menem became the presidential candidate. A final '*coup d'état*' by business interests pushed Raul Alfonsín to resign from the presidency six months before his term ended. Amid a sense of chaos, Menem came to power. For the first time in sixty years, there was a peaceful and democratic transfer of power from one political party to another. At the same time, such a transfer was a lesson in economic discipline.

> We can say that the 1989 hyperinflation crisis defined a new characteristic in the orientation of the political system. This is the recognition by the political system itself, as the main base for legitimacy, of the need to build and to demonstrate a harmonious relationship with the dominant sectors.
>
> (Basualdo *et al.* 1999: 324)

Perónism was built on an ambiguous ideology around a charismatic leader who allowed no strong institutionalization of other actors or norms. Perónist discourse has always been vague and reluctant to discuss economic policies, thus allowing it to permeate contrasting social interests and sustain its political appeal. These characteristics made it politically feasible for Menem's government and conservative thinktanks to formulate neo-liberal economic policies and implement political centralization in the national executive. In addition, Menem's discourses and declarations were contradictory and even illogical, reinforcing anomie and disbelief (for example, he used traditional Perónist expressions and terms when denigrating trade-union leaders and actions). In the 1990s, Menem denounced the trade unions as supporting workers with stable and secure jobs, while neglecting the needs of the rest of the population searching for work. Perónism effectively incorporated workers into the political system – workers who expected reform from within capitalism and an alliance between capital and labour at the national level. At the time, capitalism was thought to bring about mass consumption throughout the country, while Communism was still viewed as a frightening rival ideology. The ratio of unionization of Argentinian workers was (and still is) particularly high (approximately 40 per cent to date), and the majority of workers have remained faithful Perónists. To belong to a trade union was the normal thing to do, and was highly respected.

Unexpectedly for the labour force, from the very beginning Menem's government took different simultaneous measures to limit the right to strike, including a parliamentary bill as well as judicial requests to declare some trade unions illegal and impose five- to six-year prison terms on workers who protested against privatization in the transport and communication sectors. Some labour leaders, for the first time in any Perónist government, sought autonomy and the possibility of criticizing the government, but others sustained Menem's decisions uncritically. Some trade unions opposed privatization, but others in the same sector were in favour of it (Battistini 1999: 276). As a result, labour lost its influence. After 1991, the Minister of Labour was no longer required to be a trade-union leader, and the government began to bypass trade unions in order to remove their powers from the workers' social-security system.

Ordinary people used to say: 'How odd it is to observe the acquiescence of labour leaders, in the face of the many drastic and undemocratic measures taken by Menem and his government, when the same labour leaders brought chaos to the previous government for much less!' It is obvious that labour leaders had gradually lost popularity, partly because of memories of their actions in the mid-1970s, which had helped pave the way for the military coup in 1976, and partly because of their antagonism to the first democratic government in the 1980s. Ordinary people were critical of Menem and Cavallo's policies, but they had a hard time finding Perónist trade unions ready to lead major public protests. Furthermore, any public dissent within the ranks of Perónism could be perceived by the financial markets as political destabilization, on which structural adjustment (the pegging of the peso to the dollar) and the legitimacy of the government were dependent.

The cohesion within the CGT suffered first. Menem's vision of neo-liberalism led to a divided CGT. In addition, some unions began to break away altogether, establishing the left-wing CCC (Combative Classist Faction). In 1990, the CGT San Martin (including workers in plastics, meat, catering, and construction, as well as taxi-drivers) backed Menem, while the CGT Azopardo (representing state workers, truck drivers, commerce, customs, train and postal trade unions) was critical of the president and his programme. A few small trade unions (e.g. banking and trade employees) continued to support Menem. The faction that backed the president triggered the division within the CGT. As Arturo Fernandez (1998) explains, this faction was led by the older generation. Moreover, from 1989 to 1994, there were only a few minor elections within the trade unions, and hence little open protest or renewal of the leadership. However, the old axis of the CGT, comprising those unions traditionally amenable to negotiation, still remained – 'the 62' and their leader Lorenzo Miguel (including oil and metallurgical workers). This nucleus was made up of trade unions that had grown at the pace of national industrialization and expected the state to perform a role of mediator in socio-economic relations. In 1994, it finally broke apart into groups with opposing views on government policies.

In 1994 – the year that can be seen as pivotal between the ascending and descending slopes of the government's economic programme – factions critical of the government created new organizations called the MTA (the Argentinian Workers' Movement) and the CTA (Congress of Argentinian Workers). However, the so-called 'official CGT', led by Rodolfo Daer, still remained the only organization recognized by the government, based on the tradition of having only one labour organization, and because it represented the largest number of unions. Closer to De la Rua's government as well as to the Perónist provincial government of Cordoba, this faction has recently been co-ordinating dialogue and negotiations between labour and government. An example is the 2001 Aerolineas Argentinas Airline conflict. This faction has also expressed the need for a coalition within the government (with elections due in October 2001), and between national business and labour. Its leaders negotiate directly with a handful of state representatives such as the Cabinet Chief Chrystian Colombo and the Minister of Labour Patricia Bullrich.

The dissident faction, the MTA – Argentinian Workers' Movement – has been led by Hugo Moyano of the truck-drivers' union. In conflict with the national government and closer to the Perónist governor of the Buenos Aires Province, Carlos Ruckauf, it also includes part of the old moderate nucleus mentioned above, and in fact never really aspired to break away completely from the CGT structure and name. In 2001, its leader was at a loss when two major unions – the SMATA and UOM (linked to the production of cars and metallurgy) – reached sectoral accords with the Minister of Economy, D. Cavallo. Moreover, during the 2001 elections, an alliance between his antagonist, Minister Cavallo, and his friend, Governor Ruckauf, seemed likely.

The CTA – Congress of Argentinian Workers – went further and consolidated its independence in 1994, holding its first congress in 1996 and obtaining legal recognition in 1997. Consequently, the CGT's labour monopoly, which had started in the 1940s, finally came to an end.

Table 10.2 shows the unions' strategies. Arturo Fernández distinguishes between the different types of political relations that labour undertakes with national governments:

1   participative – close to the government;
2   negotiating – in favour of dialogue but autonomous;
3   combative – critical; and
4   classist – supporting class struggle.

Table 10.2 shows that, with the exception of a short period in 1990, there were no negotiating types of trade unions, possibly because there was no political space or centre for negotiations during the 1990s (Fernández, 1998: 172–5).

After 1994, a period of protest and mobilization began, limiting government policies without really overwhelming the consensus of those in power. Yet, in 1994, the Federal March was the first event to overcome the isolation and atomization of previous protests, and opened the search for a new political consensus within civil society.

Table 10.2 Argentina: organized labour and types of relationship with the government (numbers in parentheses refer to trade unions)

Years	Participative	Negotiating	Combative
1987	'The 15' (30 trade unions)		CGT (50)
1990	CGT San Martin (50)	'The 62' (25)	CGT Azopardo (50)
1994	Official CGT (100+)		MTA–dissident CGT (15)
			CTA (2)

The internal disagreements within the CGT produced by the MTA; the non-ascription of the CCC (Combative Classist Faction) to any of these alternatives; the mass mobilization in memory of and in rejection of the military dictatorship on its twentieth anniversary; the five national strikes; the *Apagon* – (switch-off);[5] the continuing Wednesday pensioners' protests in front of the parliament building; the Teachers' Tent;[6] the succession of *puebladas*[7] from which the 'piqueteros' (i.e. pickets) emerged; and the long and successful conflict at the Malbran Institute[8] – all of these events, whose protagonists were popular organizations and workers, gave credence to the electoral results of October 1997 that, eventually, marked the breakup of monolithic Menemism.

Labour provided the first evidence of more autonomous mobilization, but other sectors in civil society were also moving. A new political party was emerging – the Frepaso (Front for a Solidarity-Inspired Country) – and many enjoyed democratic discussions during the constitutional convention. Since the Radical Party (a moderate centrist political party) had lost prestige after forming a government in the 1980s, a few of its leaders began to build an alliance with the centre-left Frepaso. Some ex-Perónist deputies, critics of Menem, also helped to cement the alliance.

Taking a look at the business side, it is possible to see some parallels. From 1990 until 1997, businesses unequivocably supported Menem. But when, in January 1997, Menem met the 'Group of Eight' to solicit business support for a third presidential term, business leaders told the press that they opposed the UIA's (the Argentina Industry Union – an umbrella business organization) call for the president to 'consider' a third term in office, which would have required additional constitutional reform. Two of the group affirmed that they were opposed to a third term. Instead, they supported further flexibility and labour reform (*Internet Headline News*, 731, 30 January 1997).

Contradiction 3

Stalling Argentina's capitalism and democracy

> For some time I have longed to
> tell this many people:
> Know that I hush in certainty
> and that I faint of obedience,
> and that I have not the least idea
> and that I despair forever.
>
> (M.E. Walsh, *Arte Poetica*, extract)

Countless Argentinians may recognise themselves in Maria Elena Walsh's verses. In 2001, they have been discussing whether capitalism can exist in a given area without either entrepreneurs or workers who are natives from the same area. They are not the only ones: well-known academics like Guillermo

O'Donnell, Professor of Political Science at the Notre Dame University in the USA, and Manuel Pastor, Professor of Latin American Studies at the University of California at Santa Cruz, have both harshly denounced the situation.

Manuel Pastor wrote with Carol Wise:

> The good life seems to be eluding Argentina once again. Unable to shake a deep recession triggered by Brazil's devaluation in 1999, a country that appeared to have achieved bona fide emerging-market status is looking more like the same old underachiever. The $128-billion external debt is looming, the Argentine stock market has lost 20 per cent over the year, and interest rates on government bonds have trebled since early June, rising to levels usually associated with a nearly 20 per cent probability of default. What's gone wrong? ... With devaluation ruled out, partly because this would implode a financial system in which 70 per cent of domestic liabilities are dollar-denominated, exports have stagnated and unemployment is endemic ... of the top 10 products accounting for nearly 70 per cent of total exports, all but 12 per cent are basic commodities like grain and meat.[9]

Pastor and Wise also point implicate the parliament: 'key legislation around tax reform, labor market deregulation and export promotion policies have continually bogged down in Congress.' O'Donnell draws attention to the way that financial capitalism in Argentina fails to deliver any public good. In other countries,

> financial capital has continued to play its due role in an economy oriented towards growth. That is, to smooth the relations among the other sectors of capital in order to facilitate, above all through credit and the functioning of the stock exchange, their capacity to operate and invest ... [An important part of financial capital] continues to be married to the development of productive structures – industrial, agricultural and commercial – ... These countries have achieved a few fundamental things. I refer, among others, to the maintenance of structures that are dynamic even though partly transformed, to the internalization and social dissemination (through education and work) of scientific and technological innovations, and to the reconstitution of a state that, by expressing and reinforcing those tendencies, has continued to be a basically credible agent of public good ... Unfortunately, almost nothing of this has occurred in [Argentina].[10]

Others, like Max Bergmann,[11] from Washington's Council for Hemispheric Affairs, and Morris Goldstein,[12] Senior Fellow at the Institute for International Economics and former Deputy Director of Research at the IMF, add to the portrayal of Argentina's woes. The latter also criticizes the IMF:

> Nothing illustrates the futility of the current [IMF] approach better than the situation in Argentina. It is in crisis because it has an unsustainable debt

burden – equal to about 450 per cent of exports – and an overvalued exchange rate. This is the third consecutive year of recession. The country has no effective policy instruments to solve its problems. Insistence on maintaining the convertibility regime means that it can neither loosen monetary policy nor devalue ... The recent initiative to go to a zero fiscal deficit has been forced on the authorities by double-digit real interest rate spreads and increasing difficulties in rolling over domestic debt obligations.

Argentinians ask themselves: how could all this have happened?

Our purpose here is not to forget the many signs of economic recovery during the first years of 'Convertibility', and the conditions under which the policy was conceived. Uncertainty over external debt, the fall in GDP and industrial production, and recurrent high levels of inflation, provided the other elements of the national crisis. Hence, the need for substantive consensus centred on macro-economic stability in order to guarantee capital accumulation. Stability has become the first priority for both the state and the private sector. Business coalitions have publicly and strongly supported the successive economic ministers in implementing stability plans, as well as the election and re-election of a president who would sustain their priorities. The shifting of boundaries between state and market has been conceptually articulated around neo-liberal values, which have enhanced the visibility of business people, but have brushed aside other socio-economic actors.

With the pegging of the peso to the dollar, and the feeling of stability that it created, the instrument became an end in itself, concocted through fear, and blocking Argentina's capacity to develop autonomous state policies. Cavallo's Convertibility Law, supported by the US government, the international financial organizations, national business and politicians in the parliament, pegged the peso to the dollar, establishing a 'dollar standard'. For every peso in circulation, there had to be a dollar in hard currency in the country, and vice versa. Stephen Hanke,[13] adviser to Cavallo, explained that 'President Menem and Minister Cavallo know their history. They were determined not to repeat Argentina's mistakes [of swiftly abandoning standards in the face of public criticism]'.[14] Protests were belittled as a nuisance.

The new political consensus covered three important points. First, the option for an automatic alignment with the USA, uncritically accepting demands for deregulation. Second, the issue of endogenous growth. Even though industry has become the main productive mode, it has never managed to consolidate its power through a co-ordinated decision-making system. New actors, mainly financial ones, have appeared since the 1970s (Barbero 1997). Even the newly privatized enterprises reflect an ambiguity concerning the endogenous development of industry. Concepts such as industrial co-operation and industrial networks have never been very significant. Third, the regulatory role of the state was to be reduced to the minimum, and thus current-account and trade deficits as well as national industrial development had to be accepted as givens. Instead, any new actor would be portrayed as dynamic and positive: someone advancing 'globalization' in business, government, finance or communication.

Inflation fell to 0.5 per cent in August 1991. There was an agreement with the IMF that signalled access to external credit and the start of privatization. The stock-market index rose by 100 per cent in September 1991, and credit was re-established, increasing the consumption of durable goods. Following import liberalization, the internal prices of tradable goods decreased, while non-tradables (services and labour costs) increased. From 1991 to 1994, the economy grew by 7.7 per cent per year. There was a consumption boom after so many years of starved investment and low household spending. This policy was extremely successful from a political point of view. Some people did dare to doubt, but few were ready to listen to them.

For trade unions critical of the government, it was very difficult to engage workers in demonstrations during Menem's first term. On the one hand, the changes introduced by Menem were daring and surprising, and the first economic results were quite impressive. On the other hand, thousands of workers realized that their jobs were at risk and reacted apprehensively.

At the end of 1994, the Mexican crisis plunged the Argentinian economy into recession, while its currency continued to be overvalued. Fortunately for Argentinian firms, Brazil began its economic recovery in the second half of 1993. With ups and downs, the Brazilian market and the attempt at regionalism with MERCOSUR (the common-market project of Argentina, Brazil, Paraguay and Uruguay) saved Argentina's neo-liberal consensus.

The appreciation of the currency brought about a trade-off between stability and competitiveness (ECLAC 1995a: 11). Easily reversible capital flows were attracted by privatization and high interest rates, as well as by debt–equity swaps, while Argentina's trade deficit grew, accompanied by large current account deficits, financed by those same inflows of foreign capital. When these capital inflows drastically slowed down, as with the Mexican financial crisis of 1994 and then again after the Asian financial crisis in 1997, while the supply of money remained fixed to the level of foreign reserves, the reversal of flows upset the chain of payments, leading to the contraction of domestic credit and economic activity, as well as bank insolvency. Furthermore, IMF financial packages arrived to prevent a financial crisis or default in Argentina itself, gradually building up external debt.

Therefore, adjustment through monetary policy has two main consequences. First, the defence of such stability provokes internal recession, with high social costs (ECLAC 1999: 20–1, 26–7). The picture is of a depressed aggregate demand and increasing unemployment and underemployment. Second,

> [t]he regulation through monetary policy is at the root of the transformations of the ensemble of labour relations (flexibility, precariousness, lower averages of real salary); technological changes are most of the time no more than an additional instrument to impose such transformations.
>
> (Chesnais 1996a: 262)

For Argentinian business people, the debate on regulation shifted to systemic costs, and the reduction of labour, fiscal, infrastructure and financial costs came high on the national agenda. Each time there have been capital outflows and recession, the state has cut social programmes, investment in education and research, justice and services, as well as salaries and pensions. The provinces have followed the same policies, since they depend heavily on funding from the central government. For example, in 1995, the province of San Juan reduced the salaries of all provincial workers by 20 to 30 per cent, while the central government cut 5 to 15 per cent of all federal employees' payments that had been more than US$2,000 per month.[15] These cuts have been recurrent and, although most of the time the courts have rejected them as being unconstitutional, they have always been implemented.

If exports are to sustain the 'dollar standard', with the shift of prices after the overvaluation of the currency, there will be fewer incentives to invest in tradable goods (Azpiazu and Nochteff 1994). The shift of interests within the private sector has focused on raw materials, such as the oil and gas industry, which have increased their dominance over other sectors with more value added. New investment has mainly focused on the food industry, oil and gas, and the automotive and mining sectors.[16] The automotive sector, a success story, was promoted and protected under a special national regime as well as under an Argentinian–Brazilian system embedded in MERCOSUR (Chudnovsky and López 1997).

In the rapidly opened-up economies, many Argentinian firms faced two crucial limitations: the traditional family management style and their ability to obtain capital from sources other than the state. Foreign direct investment evidently financed privatization but also went into the purchasing of some family businesses. Firms were also confronted with constraints such as inadequate infrastructure and reduced technological capacity. Their poor knowledge of foreign markets and the currency overvaluation hampered their progress. Indebtedness in both urban and rural areas, this time in dollars, with no exports or internal consumption, convinced many to close down their businesses – taking their money out of the country – or to move to Brazil. Meanwhile, the internal migration of the newly marginalized from small towns to the medium-sized cities intensified, bringing about urban poverty and increased crime.

After several financial crises, some within the World Bank and the IMF began to decry the Washington Consensus.[17] Within Argentina, however, those in power would not readily accept reforms. The only revision discussed has been the issue of transparency and institutional surveillance of the banking and judicial systems (Javed Burki and Perry 1998). Nevertheless, every time an effort is made to trap corrupt officials, the 'financial markets' penalize the country by threatening the exchange rate (as recently happened in the case of the Central Bank's president and the Parliamentary Commission on Corruption, between the end of 2000 and the beginning of 2001).

The conviction has been dashed that the policies of the 1990s would install a successful period of coexistence between capitalism, the Argentinian state and society. Hesitant to envisage alternatives within the politico-economic system, the politicians still hope to achieve governance of the complex situation. Labour organizations and leaders are now under pressure from both workers and the jobless to build a feasible political alternative in alliance with other social sectors. They seem, however, to be wavering between leading social protests, controlling social conflicts, and promoting a concrete political solution. Faced with the possibilities of devaluation and default, labour leaders also fear being accused of provoking either of these outcomes.

Mid 2001

Argentina's struggle for governance

> The rights of the workers
> A topic for the archaeologists?
>
> Eduardo Galeano, 15 April 2001

Concerning the institutionalization of the new labour-regulation framework, the tendency towards temporary work contracts; fewer obligations for entrepreneurs; and job contracts drawn up by enterprises and not by industrial branches, looks set to continue for the time being, and may intensify, if only step by step. Accompanying this trend, trade unions tend to divide further along multiple fault lines based on the articulation of different needs and agendas as well as ideologies, creating new methods of opposition and negotiation with other parties (state and civil society). Relations among them appear further estranged due to power struggles inside the enterprises. But is the new model self-sustaining, with fewer entrepreneurs and companies, reduced credit, poor circulation of capital and low consumption (for example, food choice has been reduced to very basic levels in small towns)?

On 26 June 2001, the Minister of Labour, Patricia Bullrich, officially called on the trade unions to renew the 1975 labour conventions, through negotiations with chambers of commerce, while a month earlier, the Labour Ministry had announced the formation of a tripartite commission (government, trade unions and business representatives) to discuss the International Labour Organization's request for governmental recognition of the various trade unions representing workers. Clearly, the two factions of the CGT reject the ILO request, while the CTA supports it.

The call for renewal of the 1975 legislation was predictable after the 2000 vote on the 'labour law'. This was the famous law that, due to the doubts about the methods used for its approval, finally provoked the resignation of the vice-president, the breakup of the political coalition between the centre-left Frepaso and centre-right Radicals, and the re-appearance of Domingo Cavallo. The latter came back as Minister of Economy and broker of a new centre-right alliance to sustain the rather isolated President Fernando de la Rua, who perceives the social conflict as unjust and rejects all protests against the latest Cavallo plan.

The 2000 labour law invalidated all of the labour conventions signed in 1975. The government set a legal limit of two years for the new negotiations. This infuriated the main trade unions: both fractions of the CGT – the participationist fraction under Daer and the confrontational one under Moyano – as well as the CTA of Víctor De Gennaro. Fearing lower salaries and more 'flexible' labour conditions, after three years of nation-wide recession and ever-increasing unemployment, they asked for a decree augmenting the minimum salary, which has remained at US$200 for several years (*Clarín*, 23 June 2001).

Meanwhile, beyond the trade unions, the social conflict in General Mosconi, Salta, northern Argentina, has emerged as the emblematic symbol of a marginalized fraction of the population organized in *piquets*. The *piquets* are groups of the unemployed and the poor, made up of men, women and children, who block the streets to protest against economic policies and social conditions. This new method of protest has gained strength since the mid-1990s, and its main goal is to obstruct vehicular traffic and trade. There is a perception that protesters remain on the streets for days not only to attract attention and obtain governmental aid, food and short-term work contracts, but also as a symbolic way of expressing that there is nowhere to go – that the present path leads nowhere.

In 2001, the national intelligence service counted 110 similar social conflicts to the one in General Mosconi, all with a common denominator: regional economies in crisis, unemployment, low salaries and massive lay-offs. Using the intelligence information, national deputies presented parliamentary bills calling for the creation of a commission to foster negotiated solutions instead of violent repression. One particular bill led by Alicia Castro and Elisa Carrio, who are among the most critical voices of the politico-economic model, was publicly supported by the trade unions, together with other social and human rights organizations (*Clarín*, 24 June 2001).[18]

On 1 August 2001, the *piqueteros* staged their first nation-wide protest, blocking routes and streets, supported by some trade unions, social and students' organizations, and more passively by the population in general (*La Nación*, 1 August 2001). Their capacity for and methods of communication and co-ordination have not yet been well studied. Contradictory hypotheses have been put forward concerning their autonomy, their alliances with other social and labour organizations and their alleged manipulation by trade unions. What is certain is that this first nation-wide protest was channelled completely outside the structures of the main trade unions and political parties – sceptically perceived as organizations with waning powers. During the protest, the *piquets* denounced the latest cut in salaries and pensions and the increasing repression, and requested the continuity of the 'Trabajar Plan' – the Governmental Work Plan ensuring short-term labour contracts.

'We want to go in a peaceful manner' answered the piqueteer ... 'What do you want us to do if we do not have enough to eat?' ... 'Yes – they have lowered our salary as well', the policeman said, shrugging his shoulders.

(*La Nación*, 1 August 2001)

A politician supporting the protest stated that a new social movement was emerging in the country, against the neo-liberal model and the methodology of repression, calling it a movement of civil resistance (L. D'Elia *Clarín*, 1 January 2001).

On the very same day of the national protest by *piqueteros*, two main labour organizations (the 'official CGT' and the MTA, also called 'dissident CGT') decided to join forces for the first time after ten years of division under Menem. It seems that some of the trade unions are capitalising on the *piqueteros'* unrest, developing a brand-new form of labour struggle in which the labour union plays a legitimizing role that unites the struggles of the poor and unemployed with those employed in poor and informal conditions. At the same time, the trade unions' own survival, another question mark, is strengthened.

Another new type of protest within both trade unions, most evidently epitomized by the teachers' union, as well as by supporters and leaders of the *piquets*, is fasting. An ultimate rejection of the policies of the 1990s, fasting is another symbolic novelty in a society that has historically claimed to be the 'grain haven of the world'. Meanwhile, within the political system, parties continue to break up on the basis of personal values – which at least clarifies who is who – and there is a discussion on whether to postpone general elections in such a volatile national context.

During the first half of the 1990s, Argentina for once appeared to be an astonishing neo-liberal story (similar to the countries of South-east Asia), where the state and trade unions were being dutifully carved out within the prevailing consensus. Ten years later, in the one and a half years from the end of 1999 to the middle of 2001, there has been a succession of seven adjustment programmes and six national strikes, the last one being carried out by the three main labour organizations on 19 July 2001. All those who wish not to experience similar unrest should carefully examine the Argentinian situation.

Conclusions and avenues for further discussion

What can we conclude from the two complementary hypotheses discussed above – about the role of Argentinian organized labour within the restructuring of the labour regulatory framework during the last decade and about the sustainability of the new model at the start of the twenty-first century? The role of Argentinian labour organizations in the 1990s was ambiguous, to say the least. Trade unions provided the much-needed support to make structural policy reforms politically feasible. In general, they seemed to accept the retreat of the state from both the economy and society. With each major agreement with the government, they accepted further reforms on labour regulation. But, for the same reason, they also limited the government by refusing to reform the labour laws (they always blocked parliamentary bills such as the 1993 'Labour Reform Bill' sent to the Deputies' Chamber, or further modifications to the 'Law of Labour Contracts' and the 'Law of Labour Collective Conventions') that affected their own organizations. Finally, they also outlined what would or would not be tolerated as regards the visible effects stemming from the new politico-economic model.

Thus, a number of their leaders and unions ensured a low degree of protest and uncritically accepted discourses, actions and even the corrupt behaviour of Menem and his government officials. However, another group of labour leaders and unions has been highly critical of the model as such, and not only of its effects. These have been the first organizations to oppose the 'delegative democracy' of the 1990s.

Within the politico-economic model of the 1990s, the working class as such has lost its alleged role as the main historical subject for the transformation of the capitalist society, and although labour organizations have appeared to remain strong, there has been a growth of the so-called informal sector and of an emergent social movement of unemployed. It is improbable that CGT will return to a vertical command structure and that it will devote itself simply to the representation of Argentinian workers. The role of trade unions will both affect and depend on the outcome of the deepening national crisis, both politically and economically. Labour will probably look for new alliances, and may accept a more humble position within each alliance. However, at least the trade unions may become more open to the suggestions of others.

The economic path seems uncertain and even a dangerous trap. Continuing with the 1990s model appears to be unsustainable. Reforming it would incur a high social cost, with a likely default on the interests of the accumulated debt. Some further options are also open, such as dollarizing the system, which is supported by some Perónist deputies, including Menem and Cavallo. Another may include the establishment of US military bases, suggested on the basis that only with strategic interests will the US government continue to sustain Argentina's 'development model'. Indeed, after the last financial package given to the country by the IMF, with US support, a provincial decree 3169/01 has accepted the setting up of a US base for nuclear research in Tierra del Fuego.

Besides, what about the political sustainability of the new labour regulatory framework? More unrest is possible. Perhaps there will be a return to old-style populism? Or will a new socio-economic coalition be strong enough to confront the perils and to put the country back on course for industrial and technological development? It appears that the major antagonism is defined by Argentine political and economic actors as 'productive versus financial capitalism'.[19] Could this antagonism finally be resolved? Or should we simply wait for a major change at the international level?

Argentina's case is by no means unique and is embedded in a larger process of global economic restructuring. It is, perhaps, an extreme case in the illustration of how public discourses and policies can produce glowing but ephemeral results, which fall short of sustaining local capitalist development and thus of legitimising those with economic and/or political power. Many guessed in advance that this would be the case, given the rate of technological changes and the increase in international economic competition.

Perhaps the uniqueness of Argentina's case resides in the stubbornness of its élites in following a path from which others have deviated. In every sense, it is a sad case. Díaz Dionis, in an excellent article dating back from 1988, expressed well how much Argentina needed new, intelligent, ethical and pragmatic élites to extricate the country from its moral, social and economic morass.

> The resurgence of social and ideological irrationality, of what the media calls 'the magical Argentina' ... is the least adequate for [solving the crisis], since international relations are fundamental to face the structural crisis affecting the country. Even more so with the foreseeable changes in the American executive and the European single market. Once more, presidential candidates of the majority forces are far from the real world in which they have to live, and, yet, they are representative of the dominant thought within their political organizations ... The old leading classes refuse to understand that their model of society has withered away, and that the world that has come forth after the second world war bears no similarity with the one existing in the XIX century, of which they are the direct heirs.
>
> (Díaz Dionis, 1988)

Indeed, the nineteenth-century type of liberalism seems to have little to do with globalization in the 1990s, which has given us a new model of industrial organization, with horizontal and vertical co-ordinated networks, and the integration of new technological and organizational production strategies. Thus,

> globalization of the world economy passes through the reorganization of production processes on a rather regional, even global basis ... The importance of economies of scale, which imposes the reduction in the number of units of production, and the need to standardize the processes of production ... combine in order to determine the new modes of articulation of products and processes of production.
>
> (Fontagné *et al.* 1996: 11)

Additionally, emergent and increasingly extensive governance structures now reach beyond states (Helleiner 1997: 97, Strange 1997, and Castells 1998). Hence, globalization may be leading to 'net-trade' and a 'net-economy' based on more or less co-operative strategies.

Without an easy way out, and no political coalition or consensus yet to stand up for an alternative, labour has found itself, like the rest of society, caught on the horns of dilemma. In the end, the solution may only be found through the construction of a different consensus that may better promote the capabilities of all Argentinians through a positive synergy. Hegemony is based on a socially constructed consensus, secured by belief and expectation, socialized through diverse institutions and finally sanctioned through regulation and enforcement. Hegemonic discourse has replaced the ideas of social norms, social class, society, distribution, solidarity, co-operation and cohesion, justice and human rights, with those of spontaneous co-ordination of the market, natural equilibrium, the individual, and efficiency. Hegemonic consensus is political power, as it builds a certain common sense and rationality, and then limits the options and the future of society. In this sense, both the CTA and the MTA seem to be aware of the need for constructing a new dialogue and rationality, as well as for new strategies beyond the nation-state (MTA 1998, Lozano 1999, Rigane 2000). For trade unions, the main challenges refer to democratic representation and organizational power, as well as their ability to cope with the international politico-economic restructuring using new strategies (i.e. within regionalism, world coalitions and inside transnational corporations and commodity chains). Their primary duty must not be to the unemployed, but rather to the search for employment through a model of development based on systemic competitiveness, enhancing respect for all and, in particular, for workers' rights. As for labour in general, the answer may be to construct democratic social power. For labour has a systemic power and cannot be taken as mere merchandise. Labour is an aspect of humanity, embodied in each product and service, which sustains the wealth creation of a region, together with its general level of consumption and of savings. Labour has the power of civilizing human relations, and disregarding the fact that it is part and parcel of humanity may bring about unfortunate consequences.

Notes

Websites last accessed on 6 August 2001.

1 Élites are decision-makers in political, economic, professional, communications and cultural organizations and movements in a society (Putnam 1976), who play a major role in securing procedural democracy (Gunther and Higley 1992) by taking 'politics-as-bargaining' and not 'politics-as-war' (O'Donnell *et al.* 1986: 9, Sartori 1987: 224–6).

2 From July 1989 to December 1992, in the first forty-two months, Menem used decrees 244 times – eight times more than all other constitutional presidents in the past 136 years. Before Alfonsín, there had been no more than twenty such decrees in Argentinian history. Alfonsín used decrees ten times while in office. Among Menem's decrees, 20 per cent concerned taxes, 12 per cent salaries, 11 per cent public debt, 9 per cent public organizations, and another 9 per cent a raft of issues including deregulation of the economy, downsizing of public administration, and donation of cement to Bolivia to build a road. In most cases, they modified or overruled laws or legislation reserved to parliament, without having been granted the facility to do so. Having the majority in the Senate and first minority in the Chamber of Deputies, parliamentarians' protests were subdued (*Clarín*, 6 June 1993).

3 A recent and spectacular step in this regard has been the public disclosure of the investigation undertaken by a special parliamentary committee led by E. Carrio. For the Report of the Parliamentary Investigative Commission in Spanish see *http://www.lanacion.com.ar/01/08/10/dp_326645.asp*, containing 16 files.

4 Table 10.1 was based on the work of L.E. Ramirez (1999), the information provided by P.A. Prado at *http://www.legislaw.com.ar/legislaw/*, and the National Parliament databases at *http://www.diputados.gov.ar*.

5 A type of public protest by which all citizens should turn off lights for an agreed number of minutes on a specific day at a specific hour. This protest was highly successful.

6 A large white tent placed in front of the parliament's square, in which successive groups of teachers were engaged in fasting, in protest against low salaries and cuts in the education budget. Citizens showed support by signing the teachers' petition, and public figures and the media visited the tent regularly.

7 Entire towns in spontaneous rebellion against local authorities, sometimes burning municipal buildings, in protest at the lack of local development policies, and against poverty and unemployment.

8 In December 1996, through Resolution No. 658, the government sacked 101 workers of seven major national health institutes, arguing a lack of funds. Yet, some institutes had fund reserves that could cover the needs of the others. But the government rejected this solution, even though it was requested by the institutes. Not only did the decision lead to the closure of the institutes, it also directly weakened the state's capacity to combat public-health epidemics such as cholera in the north of the country, against which the Malbran Institute was producing a serum (*Servicio Paz y Justicia, Buenos Aires*, 10 January 1997; see also *http://www.derechos.org/serpaj/*).

9 Pastor, M. and Wise, C. (16 July 2001) 'The good life jilts Argentina once again', *Los Angeles Times*, 16 July 2001, see *http://www.latimes.com/news/local/la-000058273jul16.story*.

10 O'Donnell, G., 1 March 2001, 'Una mirada y una propuesta sobre la crisis que sacude al pais', Pagina 12, see *http://www.pagina12.com.ar/2001/01–03/01–03–21/pag17.htm*

11 'Argentina's Future', *Washington Times*, at *http://www.washtimes.com/op-ed/20010816–81027164.htm*

12 'No more for Argentina', 17 August 2001, *Financial Times*, see *http://news.ft.com/ft/gx.cgi/ftc?pagename=View&c=Article&cid=FT3Y200WGQC&live=true*

13 Professor of Applied Economics at Johns Hopkins University, and Director of the Democratic Century Fund, an investment fund that belongs to the *Emerging Markets Group*.

14 See *http://www.umich.edu/~mjps/21/arg.htm*

15 See *http://www.umich.edu/~mjps/21/arg.htm*

16 From the beginning, those sectors led exports in the 1990s, doubling them from 'about US$12 billion in 1994 to almost US$24 billion in 1996' (*http://www.tradeport.org*).

17 Joseph Stiglitz made his speech in Helsinki, Finland, on 7 January 1998. The speech was reported in Joseph Hanlon's article, published in March 1998 in the quarterly newsletter of the Jubilee 2000 Coalition, a group of more than sixty European and African organizations calling for the cancellation of all debts owed by the world's poorest countries. Stiglitz has so far been the World Bank's most critical voice on the tenets of the Washington Consensus. He has declared that 'macro-economic stability is the wrong target', 'markets are not automatically better', and that 'competition, not ownership, is the key', among other concepts.

18 This article appeared in *Correio Sindical Mercosul*, No. 75, 25 July 2001, a project of the Southern Cone Trade Unions and the Friedrich Ebert Foundation, at *http://www.sindicatomercosul.com.br*

19 *Clarín Supplement*, see Bibliography.

Bibliography

All websites last accessed on 6 August 2001.

Azpiazu, D. and Nochteff, H. (1994) *El Desarrollo Ausente*, Buenos Aires: Tesis Grupo Editorial Norma.

Basualdo, E.M. (2000) *Concentracion y Centralizacion del Capital en la Argentina durante la Decada del Noventa*, Buenos Aires: Universidad Nacional de Quilmes.

Basualdo, E.M., Hourest, M., Lozano, C. and Fontana, B. (1999) 'Trabajo y civilización, los datos de la experiencia Argentina reciente', in C. Lozano (ed.) *El Trabajo y la Política en la Argentina de Fin de Siglo*, Buenos Aires: EUDEBA, pp. 323–47.

Battistini, O.R. (1999) 'Los sindicatos en Argentina: El peso de la cultura en el Estado', in C. Lozano (ed.) *El Trabajo y la Política en la Argentina de Fin de Siglo*, Eudeba, Universidad de Buenos Aires, Buenos Aires.

Botana, N. (1978) *El Orden Conservador: la Política Argentina entre 1880 y 1916*, Buenos Aires: Editorial Sudamericana.

Calvo, P. (2000) 'Menem se despidió con 104 decretos en un dia', *Clarín Digital*, 16 January 2000.

Castells, M. (1998) *End of Millennium*, Vol. III of *The Information Age*, Malden, MA: Blackwell.

Castillo, G., Godio, J. and Orsatti, A. (1996) *Los Trabajadores y el Mercosur*, Buenos Aires: Ediciones Corregidor.

Chesnais, F. (1996a) 'Mondialisation financière et vulnérabilité systémique', in F. Chesnais (ed.) *La Mondialization Financière, Génèse, Cout et Enjeux*, Paris: Syros: pp. 251–95.

Chesnais, F. (ed.) (1996b) *La Mondialization Financière, Génèse, Coût et Enjeux*, Paris: Syros.

Chudnovsky, D. and López, A. (eds) (1997) *Auge y Ocaso del Capitalismo Asistido: la Indústria Petroquímica Latinoamericana*, Buenos Aires: CEPAL/Alianza Editorial.

Clarín Supplement (2001) 'Que país queremos?', a synthesis of the diverse and opposing proposals by the main political actors in 2001, at http://www.Clarín.com/suplementos/zona/2001–08–12/z-00658.htm.

Courrier International (2001) 'Un peuple au bord de la déprime', Collection of Argentinian newspaper articles (in French), *Courrier International*, 566, 6–12 September: 30–5.

Cox, R.W. (1987) *Production, Power, and World Order: Social Forces in the Making of History*, New York: Columbia University Press.

Dahlberg, A. (1993) *The Argentine Miracle: How Orthodox Reforms Were Introduced in a Divided Society, 1989–1992*, University of Lund, Minor Field Study Series No. 35, Sweden: University of Lund.

De la Garza, E. (1999) *Los Retos Teóricos de los Estudios del Trabajo Hacia el Siglo XX*, Buenos Aires: CLACSO.

Demmers, J., Fernández Jilberto, A.E. and Hogenboom, B. (2001) *Miraculous Metamorphoses: the Neoliberalization of Latin American Populism*, London: Zed Books.

Diamand, M. (1989) 'Overcoming Argentina's stop-and-go economic cycles', in J. Hartlyn *et al.* (ed.) *Latin American Political Economy: Financial Crisis and Political Change*, Boulder, CO: Westview Press, pp. 129–65.

Díaz Dionis, G. and Coordinador Equipo Nizkor (1988) 'La crisis social e histórica Argentina', *Revista Española de Ciencias Sociales Razón y Fe*, Madrid, and KO'AGA ROÑE'ETA se.vii (2000) – http://www.derechos.org/vii/dionis2.html, 20 August.

ECLAC (1995) *Balance Preliminar de la Economia de América Latina y el Caribe 1995*, Santiago de Chile: ECLAC.

ECLAC (1999) *1998–1999 – Economic Study of Latin America and the Caribbean. Synthesis*, Santiago de Chile: ECLAC.

ECLAC/CIID (1994) CAN/93/S41. Cepal/Centro Internacional de Investigaciones para el Desarrollo (CIID) (1994) *Del Capitalismo Asistido al Capitalismo Incierto: El Caso de la Industria Petroquimica Argentina*, Joint Project ECLAC/CIID 'Reestructuracion productiva, organizacion industrial, y competitividad internacional en America Latina y el Caribe': Santiago de Chile: ECLAC: 24.

Fernández, A. (1995) *Empresas y Sindicatos Frente a la Flexibilizacion Laboral*, Buenos Aires: Centro Editor de América Latina.

Fernández, A. (1998) *Crisis y Decadencia del Sindicalismo Argentino*, Buenos Aires: Editores de América Latina.

Fontagné, L., Freudenberg, M. and Ünal-Kesenci, D. (1996) *Analyse Statistique des Echanges de Produits Intermédiaires*, Thème Commerce Extérieur, Série Études et Recherche, Luxemburg: Document Statistique, Eurostat.

France, M. (1999) *Bad Times in Buenos Aires*, London: Phoenix.

Gazeta Mercantil Latinoamericana (1996) several articles on page 11, Seminario del Mercosur, 11 to 17 August 1996: Buenos Aires.

Gill, S. (1997) 'Transformation and innovation in the study of world order', in S. Gill and J.H. Mittelman (eds) *Innovation and Transformation in International Studies*, Cambridge: Cambridge University Press, pp. 5–24.

Gunther, R. and Higley, J. (1992) *Elites and Democratic Consolidation in Latin America and Southern Europe*, Cambridge: Cambridge University Press.

Hanke, S. (1995) ' "Why Argentina is Solid", Forbes (May 8, 1995): 92', in G J. Michael (ed.) *The Effects of Economic Reforms on a Delegative Democracy: a Study of Recent Trends in Argentina*, http://www.umich.edu/^mjps/21/arg.htm.

Helleiner, E. (1997) 'Braudelian reflections on economic globalisation: the historian as a pioneer', in S. Gill and J.H. Mittelman (eds) *Innovation and Transformation in International Studies*, Cambridge: Cambridge University Press.

Lozano, C. (1999) *El Trabajo y la política en la Argentina de fin de siglo*, Buenos Aires: EUDEBA.

Michael, G.J. (1995) *The Effects of Economic Reforms on a Delegative Democracy: a Study of Recent Trends in Argentina*, http://www.umich.edu/~mjps/21/arg.htm.

MTA (1998) 'Un modelo con justicia social y desarrollo economico, Propuesta', in: http://www.cess.org.ar/macro/35-Oct.

Neffa, J.C. (1999) 'Crisis y emergencia de nuevos modelos productivos', in E. De la Garza (ed.) *Los retos Teóricos de los Estudios del Trabajo Hacia el Siglo XX*, Buenos Aires: CLACSO, pp. 69–115.

Novaro, M (ed.) (1999) *Entre el Abismo y la Ilusión: Perónismo, democracia y mercado*, Buenos Aires: Grupo Editorial Norma.

O'Donnell, G. (1994) 'Delegative democracy', *Journal of Democracy*, February: 59–61.

O'Donnell, G. (2001) 'Una mirada y una propuesta sobre la crisis que sacude al país', Professor of Political Science, Notre Dame University, USA, http://www.pagina12.com.ar/2001/01–03/01–03–21/pag17.htm

O'Donnell, G.A., Schmitter, P.C. and Whitehead, L. (1986) *Transiciones desde un Gobierno Autoritário*, Vol. III, *Perspectivas Comparadas*, Buenos Aires: Paidos.

Pastor, M. and Wise, C. (2001) 'The good life jilts Argentina once again', *Los Angeles Times*, 16 July 2001, see http://www.latimes.com/news/local/la-000058273jul16.story

Pries-Conosur (1991) 'Mercosur o la integración de los pueblos del Cono Sur, Analisis y Propuestas Alternativas', Material for seminar in Porto Alegre, Brazil, December 1991.

Putnam, R.D. (1976) *The Comparative Study of Political Elites*, Englewood Cliffs, New Jersey: Prentice Hall.

Ramirez, L.E. (1999) 'Terrorismo Laboral, el retiro (in)voluntario en las empresas privatizadas', in C. Lozano (ed.) *El Trabajo y la Política en la Argentina de Fin de Siglo*, Buenos Aires: EUDEBA, pp. 349–61.

Ranis, P. (1995) *Class, Democracy and Labour in Contemporary Argentina*, Transaction Publishers: New Brunswick and London.

Recalde, H.P. (2001) *Política Laboral Ilustrada, Drama y Humor*, Buenos Aires: Ediciones Colihue.

Rigane, J., General Secretary of FETERA–Energy Workers Federation (2000) 'La CTA y las Federaciones son parte del Cambio', in http://www.sindluzyfuerzamdp.org.ar/fetera_revista_/cta_federac.html.

Ruigrok, W. and Van Tulder, R. (1995) *The Logic of International Restructuring*, London and New York: Routledge.

Sabato, E. (2000) *La Resistencia*, Buenos Aires: Seix Barral.

Smith, W.C. and Korzeniewics, R.P. (eds) (1997) *Politics, Social Change and Economic Restructuring in Latin America*, Colorado: Lynne Rienner Publishers.

Strange, S. (1997) 'The problem or the solution? Capitalism and the state system', in S. Gill and J.H. Mittelman (eds) *Innovation and Transformation in International Studies*, Cambridge: Cambridge University Press.

Walsh, M.E. (1994) *Los Poemas*, Buenos Aires: Seix Barral.

Weller, J. (1998, November) *Los Retos de la Institucionalidad Laboral en el Marco de la Transformación de la Modalidad de Desarrollo en América Latina*, Serie Reformas Económicas No. 10, División de Desarrollo Económico, CEPAL/ECLAC: LC/L.1158.

Weyland, K. (1996) 'Neopopulism and neoliberalism in Latin America: unexpected affinities', *Studies in Comparative International Development*, 31(3): 32–44.

11 Responses of the Brazilian labour movement to privatization

Marieke Riethof

Introduction

The process of privatization represents one of the central pillars of Brazilian economic reform during the 1990s. The significance of the privatization process lies in its broader connection with the reform of the Brazilian state. This constitutes a fundamental shift from the previously dominant development strategy in Brazil: import-substitution characterized by a substantial and extensive role of the state in the economy, through state-owned enterprises, large public infrastructure projects, the promotion of particular economic activities, and protectionism. This chapter focuses on the political conflict surrounding the decision to privatize state-owned companies. Because there is no consensus on the nature of the effects of privatization, arguments related to the effects of privatization provide insight into the broader reform objectives of the government and the position of the opposition. The appropriate role of the state, the relationship between the state and market forces and the democratic content of reform processes become central themes in more specific struggles.

The topic of the first two sections of the chapter is the context and content of privatization policies. The following section discusses the possible effects of privatization on labour and employment.[1] The last section of the chapter analyses the different types of responses and alternatives to privatization, focusing on Brazil's largest central union organization, and several unions in specific cases of privatization. The conclusions address the question of why the trade unions have not been able to wage an effective opposition against privatization. The answer can be found in the ambiguity of trade-union strategies towards economic reforms in Brazil, and in the constraints that political and economic reforms pose to union action.

Privatization in context

Privatization can be defined as the transfer of assets, economic and social functions, and state tasks to the private sector. Privatization generally occurs in three forms: the sale of state property, deregulation and outsourcing. This chapter is mainly concerned with the sale of state-owned enterprises, but the other forms are connected in the following ways. Deregulation implies that the state flexibilizes rules and regulations in a particular area, or that it decides not to regulate an area that was formerly seen as the responsibility of the state. Examples of deregulation relevant to privatization are the flexibilization of state monopolies, leaving price levels to market forces, and the elimination or redirection of state subsidies. The examples show that deregulation is very close to 'reregulation', the establishment of new autonomous regulatory agencies dealing with areas from which the state has withdrawn. Deregulation means that there is more room for manoeuvre for the private sector, but a 'regulatory gap' might also emerge after the state has left. Regulation is usually strengthened as a result of the realization that market forces can affect the price levels of public utilities, quality guarantees and future investment plans in a way that does not correspond to expectations. A common form of deregulation in Brazil is decentralization of social and education policies to subnational (state and municipal) governments (Carneiro and Rocha 1999: 47).

Outsourcing entails the performance of some state tasks by private-sector actors. Some aspects of these tasks can still be performed by the state, and the state often retains the overall responsibility. In the Brazilian case, these tasks are defined as public services in general, but also consist of public utilities, sanitation, infrastructure, transport and communications. Other important examples are social security and pensions.

Privatization is not only about the extent of state intervention in the economy, it also affects patterns of power and coalitions in societies:

> Th[e] public sphere largely depends on the conviction, shared by both business and labor, that market imperfections are legitimately susceptible [to] political regulation. The contraction of the public sphere, as a result of the expansion of the market, tends to favor those actors that retain relative advantages for market exchanges.
>
> (Schamis 1992: 61)

This indicates that privatization changes the balance of key aspects of development strategies. In general terms, it entails the redefinition of the public and the private economic sphere. Property is transferred from public to private ownership, and economic functions and the provision of public services are increasingly performed in the private sector. Privatization affects workers directly through the dismissals that accompany restructuring of state-owned enterprises. The changing role of the state in the economy also affects workers and the labour movement indirectly, as corporatist structures are weakened (but not abolished). Furthermore, decentralized wage bargaining replaces wage indexation by the government, which means that trade unions have to shift the focus of their activities from the state to employers (cf. Schneider 1999: 302).

Debates on privatization are usually focused on the balance between public and private and the preferred role of the public sector in the economy and society. While trade unions argue for a further democratization of the private and public economic sphere, proponents of economic reforms argue that a reduction of the public sphere and its adaptation to the logic of market forces is the only recipe for solving economic and social problems. The following section further discusses Brazilian privatization policies, their origin and connection with other economic and political reforms.

Privatization policies and economic reforms

At the end of the 1970s, the military government initiated the first privatization policies. Within the framework of debates on the possible role of the Brazilian state in the economy and on the sustainability of the model of import substitution, other more specific factors led to the erosion of the consensus on the centrality of state-owned enterprises (SOEs) and state investment for the achievement of economic development. After the oil shocks in 1973 and the subsequent end of a period of high economic growth (also known as the Brazilian miracle, 1968–73), losses at state-owned enterprises increased. Government resources for investment in SOEs were reduced in response to the debt crisis of 1982–3, and continued to be restricted in the following years (Castelar Pinheiro 2000b: 16–19).

Before the 1990s, state-owned companies had a complex role in the Brazilian economy. On the basis of theories of import-substitution, the state was seen as the only actor that was capable of promoting economic growth and breaking the economy's dependence on core countries. In this view, the state-owned enterprise was the main pillar of economic policy. It was not only seen as a way to stimulate domestic industrialization in Brazil, but also as an instrument to influence price levels. The role of state-owned enterprises was highly political and central to Brazil's industrialization strategy, as:

> [s]tate enterprises fulfill a central function in this system of the bureaucratic political economy. They politicize capitalism in their input and output markets. Many private firms depend on state-firm contracts, pricing, and lending. State enterprises often are pioneers in development and stalwarts of national control.
>
> (Schneider 1989: 92)

SOEs could provide cheap subsidized supplies for companies, both domestic and under foreign ownership, and were guaranteed customers for products produced in other sectors. These subsidies also affected the price level for ordinary citizens. This promoted the double goal of expanding the domestic market for Brazilian products and the fight against inflation. Ideally, it would also reduce the social unrest resulting from high inflation. SOEs also provided substantial employment opportunities in the formal sector. Public-sector employment was more stable and provided more benefits than in the private formal sector.

The economic crisis of the 1980s, and the failure to find an effective response to hyperinflation, combined with social problems, reinforced the idea that the role of the state in the economy should be changed. In combination with a global environment that favoured a roll-back of the state and economic liberalization, this contributed to the introduction of a renewed privatization programme. The results of privatization in the 1980s were small, partly because the government was not strongly committed to privatization as a priority of reform. A lack of liberalization on the part of the government also contributed to the reduced attractiveness of state-owned companies. Furthermore, restrictions on foreign participation[2] and the effects of the recession after the debt crisis meant that there were few potential buyers (Baer 1995: 261, Carneiro 1998: 7). Castelar Pinheiro and Giambagi noted that state-owned companies were still used as an instrument of price policy under the government of the first civilian president José Sarney (1985–1999) (1999: 9).

Whereas Sarney was ambiguous in his commitment to full-scale economic reforms, the first directly elected president, Fernando Collor de Melo (1990–1992), based his electoral campaign on a thorough reform programme. The reform plan included measures to rationalize the public sector, and fiscal reform, as well as the introduction of measures to facilitate imports and expand exports, and a reduction of levels of protection (Chaffee 1998: 162–3). His contribution to privatization was the introduction of the Programa Nacional de Desestatização (PND – National Privatization Programme), on 12 April 1990.[3] Privatization and state reform were central pillars of his reform programme. Although Collor de Melo was firmly committed to privatization, he did not have sufficient political support in Congress and in the wider society. There was a lot of resistance against his plans to reform the public sector, and the failure of his financial stabilization plans meant that his initial basis of support was quickly eroded.[4] The successor of Collor de Melo, Itamar Franco, had a much more ambiguous stand on privatization. Even though the privatization process slowed down in the eyes of the proponents of privatization, several important companies, like the steel mill CSN and the aerospace company EMBRAER, were privatized.

In the early stages of privatization, under José Sarney and Fernando Collor, foreign pressure related to the renegotiation of external debt did not have much impact on the privatization programme (Velasco 1999: 186–8). The IMF and the World Bank generally promoted privatization as part of structural adjustment in Brazil, but the relationship between the Brazilian government and the international financial institutions was complicated until 1994, when Brazil signed the Brady Plan. According to Manzetti, a reason to limit financial support from international financial institutions was to pre-empt criticisms of left-wing and nationalist opponents of privatization and reforms. The role of international loans and technical assistance started to become more important under Cardoso's government, especially affecting the electricity and railway sectors (Manzetti 1999: 183–4).[5]

The first round of privatizations in the 1990s focused on industrial companies in the steel, petrochemical and fertilizer production sectors. One of the changes compared to the 1980s was that not only inefficient companies were privatized.

The government decided to extend the privatization programme to productive and successful companies as well. The most important companies in this round are USIMINAS (a steel-producing company), Companhia Siderúrgica Nacional (National Steel Company – CSN) and Embraer (Empresa Brasiliera de Aeronautica, a producer of small aeroplanes) between 1991 and 1994. The privatization of the steel sector was completed in 1994.

From 1995 onwards, the privatization programme was intensified under the presidency of Fernando Henrique Cardoso. A rather controversial decision was to add companies that were expected to remain in the public sector, like the Companhia Vale do Rio Doce (CVRD) – the largest Brazilian exporter (minerals and mining products) – to the privatization programme. Cardoso further centralized the decision-making structure of the privatization programme, making it answerable directly to the presidency (Manzetti 1999: 184–7). The institutional framework of the privatization programme shows that the possible influence of the legislature (Congress and Senate) is limited. The effect of this framework can also be seen in the focus of protest. Although political lobbying is undertaken, it has not been effective in halting the privatization process. Another important way to protest is to question the legality and constitutionality of privatization, which means that the judicial system also becomes involved.

The government of Cardoso signalled a new phase of privatization: of the infrastructure (railways, telecommunications, energy, ports, roads, sanitation and banks). In a controversial constitutional change in 1995, the public monopoly on telecommunications was removed, enabling the privatization of TELEBRÁS (Brazilian Telecommunications) in July 1998. The constitutional change marked a widening of possibilities for the transfer of public services to the private sector. This opened the door for the privatization of electricity distribution companies and several electricity generation companies, which is continuing. Water and sanitation companies are another candidate for privatization and concession. The only public monopoly remaining is that on petroleum exploration and refinery, although non-core sections of the Brazilian oil company Petrobrás can now be transferred to the private sector.[6] From 1996 onwards, privatization at the state level increased. The last major state-owned companies that remain are the federal banks Banco do Brasil and Caixa Econômica Federal, and the oil company Petrobrás. The privatization of the remaining state banks is one of the requirements of the aid package from the IMF negotiated in 2001 (Brazil, Federal Government 1998, Ministerio de Fazenda 1999, BNDES 2000a, 2001b, 2001c).

Privatization is an essential aspect of the structural reforms that accompany and sustain the Plano Real. The introduction of the Plano Real in 1994 was the result of a severe economic crisis and hyperinflation. After years of failed stabilization plans, always followed by a hyperinflation spiral, the Plano Real was the first plan that managed to bring down inflation. The initial purpose was that structural reforms would accompany the short-term heterodox stabilization measures. The reforms include privatization and restructuring of the public sector, fiscal reform, social-security reform (including pensions) and labour market and wage policy reform. Even though the reform package seems to be quite coherent, responding to the principles of the Washington consensus, its implementation is slow, incoherent and subject to a lot of protest. Reduction of inflation is appreciated by all, but the adjustment measures following the Mexican crisis in 1994 and the Asian/Brazilian crisis in 1997–8 have led to very high interest rates, which hamper the economy. Furthermore, issues like industrial policy, external and domestic debt, the future course of the economy and unemployment are not addressed, or they are left to chance. Because of tensions within the labour movement and a lack of willingness on the side of the government, a full transformation of the corporatist labour-relations system has not yet been implemented.

Cardoso characterizes the new phase of privatization as a search

for private sector partners to overcome major infrastructure bottlenecks, notably in the electric energy, transportation and communications sectors. Opening these areas to new entrepreneurs will enable the State to dedicate itself more effectively to its regulatory functions. The government will be able to provide investors with clear regulations and greater security, guaranteeing the quality and continuity of public services.

(Presidência da República 1995)

It is interesting to note that this quotation mentions the search for partners in the private sector, which will lead to concessions instead of privatization. The objectives of privatization are to correct the fiscal balance; to focus the government's activities on the social area; to transfer activities that were seen as strategic in the previous development model to private management; to stimulate the modernization and restructuring of the country's industrial sector; and to strengthen the capital market by broadening its basis (*Ibid.*).

The popularity of the Plano Real, especially the end of hyperinflation, certainly strengthened the support for economic reforms and privatization (Castelar Pinheiro 2000b: 20–2). However, the political climate changed at the end of the 1990s, when the emergency measures dealing with the financial crisis of 1997–8 had severe effects on employment and economic activity levels. Another blow to support for the privatization project is the energy crisis that started in summer 2001.[7] Customers (both corporate and individual) are required to reduce their electricity use by 20 per cent. The energy crisis is usually blamed on mismanagement on the part of the government.

The government argues that the total proceeds of privatization, the debts that are transferred to the new owners and the relief from public investment, are crucial in the reform of public spending and the state (Table 11.1). Critics of the privatization process argue that the results should be reduced, as the government has invested a lot in the restructuring of companies to be privatized, and as it provides cheaper loans, tax breaks and other concessions to the new owners. Another point of criticism is the expected denationalization of the economy.

Table 11.1 Brazil: proceeds of privatization, 1991–2000 (in millions of US$)

	Number of companies	*Proceeds of sale*	*Transferred debts*	*Total*
1991	4	1,614	374	1,988
1992	14	2,401	982	3,383
1993	6	2,627	1,561	4,188
1994	9	1,966	349	2,315
1995	8	1,003	625	1,628
1996	11	4,080	669	4,749
1997	4	4,265	3,559	7,824
1998	7	1,655	1,082	2,737
1999	2	133	–	133
2000	1	7,670	–	7,670
Total	66	27,414	9,201	36,615

Source: BNDES (2001) *Resultados de PND* http://www.bndes.gov.br/pndnew/period.htm (updated on 31 July 2001)

Participation of foreign investors has increased throughout the 1990s and is most substantial in the case of telecommunications (60 per cent), with a variety of participants, dominated by the United States, Spain and Portugal. The United States and Spain are also the main investors in federal and state privatizations, although participation is 35.9 per cent and 48.9 per cent respectively. The participation of foreign investors has increased from 4 per cent in 1995 to 46 per cent in 2000. The most important sectors in terms of proceeds are telecommunications (31 per cent) and electricity (30 per cent), followed by steel (8 per cent), mining (7 per cent), petroleum and gas (7 per cent) and finance (6 per cent) (BNDES 2000b, 2001a).

The effects of privatization on labour

One of the main effects of privatization is the reduction of employment. Although this is considered to be an understandable concern in the case of privatization, it is expected that the broader gains in efficiency, competitiveness and the reduction of public expenditure will cancel these negative effects. Proponents of privatization see this as one of the reasons why governments are reluctant to privatize, because public-sector workers and managers represent an important pressure group (Kikeri 1998: 1). This paragraph discusses the (potential) effects of privatization on labour and social issues. It is necessary to emphasize that the effects of privatization cannot be separated from the effects of economic reform and productive restructuring in Brazil in general.

Privatization usually entails a reduction of the workforce as part of a restructuring programme to make the company more attractive for potential investors. This means that the immediate impact of privatization is usually negative. To give an example, in the steel company CSN (Companhia Siderúrgica Nacional) the workforce was reduced by 30 per cent between 1989 and 1993 (Carneiro 1998: 8, Graciolli 1999: 221–2, 224). According to Castelar Pinheiro (1996), the average reduction of the workforce in state-owned and privatized companies between 1991 and 1994 was 49 per cent, and 75 per cent of this reduction happened in the process of preparing companies for privatization. Excluding dismissals in the process of restructuring before privatization, 39,631 workers have been dismissed from twenty-two former state-owned companies since 1991. This represents a reduction of 32.67 per cent.[8] Privatization of the Brazilian telecommunications system (TELEBRÁS is the holding) led to a fall in employment of 6.7 per cent, but the difference in employment in some telecommunications companies is more than 20 per cent between 1998 and 1999. The total number of dismissals is suppressed by an increase of employment in EMBRATEL (long-distance telecommunications company) and in call-centres and sales. Furthermore, telecommunications companies have outsourced sections of their activities, and this is expected to lead to a loss of job security and sometimes more precarious working conditions (DIEESE/Subseção FITTEL 2000, IMF 1998: 14, Castelar Pinheiro 2000a).

Proponents of privatization argue that increasing the efficiency and competitiveness of former state-owned companies will also create (industrial) employment, as companies grow. It is also expected that this will lead to jobs for highly skilled workers. This idea is based on the assumption that competitiveness of the national economy will lead to more employment, after the initial negative effects of reforms. The possible effect of employment creation after privatization is negated in the short run by dismissals to make companies more efficient and competitive. It is not clear or obvious that this will be balanced in the long run. In a developing country like Brazil, where underemployment and unemployment are major problems and where most employment creation occurs in the services sector and the informal sector, it is unlikely that the privatization of industrial companies will necessarily lead to absorption of the labour surplus (Baer 1995: 267). According to ILO figures for Latin America, between 1990 and 1998, 61 per cent of new employment was created in the informal sector (66 per cent in the traditional informal sector, self-employment and domestic work, and 34 per cent in micro-enterprises) and the modern private sector represents the remaining employment creation (ILO 1999: 41). Furthermore, people who are employed by privatized companies are likely to be highly skilled workers, and this level of skills is not attainable for a majority of workers.

There are several reasons why state-owned enterprises are seen as being less competitive and having less efficient use of labour, and these reasons are usually related to the social and political role that SOEs play in societies and to the subsidies that the companies receive. SOEs often employ a higher number of workers for political and social reasons. Because SOE employees work in the public sector, they often have more job security, higher wages and benefits than workers in the private sector (Kikeri 1998: 4). According to Hoeven and Sziraczki, privatization is likely to have limited effects on general employment levels, as employment in state-owned enterprises represents a small proportion of work in the formal sector in developing countries. The bargaining power of a union, and public pressure and protests against privatization make a difference for the position of workers in state-owned companies. Nevertheless, fragmentation of the workforce (dismissal and outsourcing), flexibilization of labour relations and transfer of workers to the private sector tend to weaken trade unions. Because of the centrality of privatization for state reform and the appeal to nationalism, representatives of trade unions feel disillusioned when they fail to prevent privatization or negotiate a better deal.[9]

Another issue is where dismissed workers from the public sector find new employment or sources of income. It is difficult to sketch a general picture of the effects of privatization on the employment trajectory of dismissed workers. According to representatives of the labour movement, many dismissed workers become micro-entrepreneurs (around 60 per cent). Although this could be an alternative to public-sector employment, a lot of micro-enterprises do not survive, workers lack job security and sometimes work under precarious circumstances (Carneiro 1998: 9). Privatization can also lead to outsourcing of certain activities to former employees. This can have positive effects in the case of highly skilled workers whose expertise and skills are in demand, but it can also lead to the creation of precarious working conditions and promotion of the informal sector.[10] Workers who are dismissed tend to be older and often more specialized. This makes re-integration more difficult, especially when industrial firms stress flexibility in skills and adaptability to new technologies (Carneiro 1998: 9).[11]

A related issue is that some state-owned companies dominate a particular town or region. This means that a large percentage of the population is directly or indirectly dependent on the company. Two of the clearest cases of this situation are the Companhia Vale do Rio Doce (CVRD) and the Companhia Siderúrgica Nacional (National Steel Company – CSN) in Volta Redonda (state of Rio de Janeiro), where around 20 per cent of the economically active population was dismissed from CSN before and during the process of privatization (Graciolli 1999: 224). In addition state-owned companies were obliged to spend a percentage of their annual turnover on local development projects.[12] These social projects represent an important form of public social policy. An important portion of the social projects financed by state-owned companies is now transferred to local governments. Local governments do not always have sufficient financial means to maintain the projects. The 'social responsibility' of state-owned enterprises has generally led to more generous secondary working conditions, such as pension funds, disability funds and schooling and training for workers and their children.

Responses of labour

The labour movement that emerged from opposition against the military regime (known as *new unionism*) criticized state intervention in labour relations. New unionism stressed the democratization of the work-place and the internal organization of unions, and the link between work, democracy and citizenship. New unionism is strongest in multinational companies, especially in São Paulo, but its importance has also begun to grow among rural workers and public-sector workers. Mobilization of unions belonging to the new unionism movement played an important part in the democratization process of the 1980s. This illustrates the innovative dimensions of new unionism and distinguishes it from other examples of labour movements in Latin America, especially in Argentina. It brings the Brazilian labour movement closer to social movements that are less attached to and focused on the state. New unionism represents the dominant group in both the largest central union organization CUT and the Workers' Party (PT) (Keck 1992, Rodrigues 1997).

Even though the newer currents among Brazilian trade unions try to distance themselves from their focus on the state, one can still speak of an ambiguity, related to the corporatist legacy and the importance of the state in wage settlements. Unions tend to view the state both as an instrument of the dominant classes and as a source of social and economic improvement or as the guardian of the common good. One could argue that the unions realize the potential positive role that the state can play in economic and social development and that they question the role of market forces. This often translates into the hope that a future (Workers' Party) president will change many things in the country.

This paradoxical view becomes especially clear when looking at the responses of the Brazilian labour movement to privatization. The first criticism is that the Brazilian state within current constraints and due to a preference for neo-liberal policy-making is not able to perform some basic tasks that are necessary for social improvement, especially in comparison with the 'welfare state' in Europe. Academics and the left alike accuse the Brazilian state of combining democratic and authoritarian decision-making processes and political processes. An example is the centralized and technocratic nature of the privatization process. In the view of the critics, this leads to a lack of commitment to social improvement and to a concern about the willingness and ability to further democratize Brazil. These authoritarian structures and 'leftovers' mean that there is little space for political participation or even influence on the political process by workers (Nogueira 1999: 57).

The labour movement's ambivalent view of the state can be partly explained by looking at the analysis that is made in documents of the CUT of the historical relationship between the Brazilian state and development strategies (mediated by corporatism), and the crisis of this relationship in the 1980s. The left criticizes Latin American states for being instruments of capital accumulation in the hands of the dominant classes after 1930 and as a result of this

> [t]he state ended up assuming very diversified functions, including the centralization of decision, the articulation and financing of private capital and also direct investment and management of enterprises.
>
> (CUT 1994: 4)

This type of development strategy and the particular role of the state has led to concentration of wealth, industry and finance, and one of the most unequal distributions of income in the world. The debt crisis reinforced the reduction of the public budget for essential social policy, and the cutbacks continued during the recessions of the 1980s and due to the problems related to the transition. With the presidency of Fernando Collor de Melo, this turned into the introduction of neo-liberal policies, the reduction of the role of the state, privatization and economic liberalization. The criticism of the CUT implies that this has been done without regard for areas where the state and state policies were working efficiently and effectively and without considering the need to improve social rights (CUT 1994: 4).

An important factor in the behaviour and responses of Brazilian unions towards privatization is the presence of public-sector workers in the labour movement. A factor reinforcing the differences between workers in the public and the private sector is the different nature of employment and unionism in the public sector as compared with the private sector. The rise of public-sector workers in the union movement stimulated a confrontational strategy for several reasons. On the one hand, public-sector workers did not have the same unionization and collective bargaining rights as in the private sector, so workers had to struggle to achieve this outside the means that were available to workers in the private sector. On the other hand, public-sector workers did not have to fear dismissals to the same extent as those in the private sector. Cutting wages was the most common way to reform the public sector in the framework of financial plans and structural adjustment programmes. This provoked strikes that demanded wage increases, while there was less risk of dismissal. Noronha argues that negotiation between employers and public-sector workers did not work as smoothly as in the private sector, with the result that strikes were longer (Noronha 1991: 120, 124). This illustrates the ambiguous role of the state as employer, investor and guardian of the labour-relations system at the same time.

The CUT's concern with the public sector and the state productive sector has grown with the increasing importance of public-sector workers in the labour movement. For example, at the sixth National Congress of the CUT (1997), 35.7 per cent of the delegates were civil servants and 19.3 per cent of the delegates were employed by state-owned companies. A large number of the members of the National Executive are originally from the public sector (Jard da Silva 1999: 65–6, 70–2). Budget reductions, the effects of structural adjustment on the public sector, the loss of job security and major strikes in the public sector all contributed to the CUT's targeting of public-sector workers. In the resolutions of the third National Congress of the CUT (1988), still before the main structural reforms of Fernando Collor, the CUT puts its position as follows:

> The CUT will struggle against the privatization of state enterprises, in the perspective of defending better living conditions for the population, who should have control over these enterprises. At the same time, the CUT will develop a campaign for the improvement of public services, including the immediate statization [*estatização*] of public services under the control of private capital, because we understand that these services are a right for all and a central element for the improvement of the living conditions of the

Brazilian population.

(CUT 1988: 36)

This quotation shows that the CUT interprets the public nature of services as crucial for social development. This notion would later also extend to the importance of the state productive sector for economic development in general.

The position of the labour movement: strategies and alternatives

The CUT's criticisms of the privatization programme are focused on the following issues: the effects on workers and on the position of the labour movement; the question whether privatization is necessary in Brazil; and the role of the state and the public sector in the economy. These issues are presented here through an analysis of trade-union strategies and alternatives to privatization. The reaction of the labour movement, even though it is critical of the role of state intervention and state-owned companies, is seen by proponents as old-fashioned and against the necessary modernization of the Brazilian economy.

The following strategies against privatization are used. One of the most common strategies is to strike. In the late 1980s, protests against privatization were connected with broader issues that ignited general strikes, such as the effects of financial stabilization and fair wages (Roxborough 1989: 93–5). For example, in one section of the Companhia Vale do Rio Doce (CVRD), privatized in 1997, workers went on strike for sixty-seven days. Other conflicts, sometimes violent, were related to people who lived or worked on land owned by state-owned companies. One of the violent protests against the effects of privatization of CVRD – against a new employment policy – was the destruction of a port in the state of Espírito Santo in December 1998. Four CVRD union leaders organized a hunger strike in protest against privatization. Other forms of protest included demonstrations during the auction of companies, for example at the auction of the company USIMINAS in 1994, or demonstrating at federal and state government buildings.[13] Other strategies include the formulation of alternatives for privatization on the basis of the views of organized labour regarding the state and state-owned companies (CUT undated/a, 1995a, 1995b, 1995c, DESEP/CUT 1993; Graciolli 1999: 146–8). Another strategy is to file lawsuits against aspects of the privatization of particular companies, or to try to prove that privatization is illegal or unconstitutional in a particular case.[14] This is combined with efforts to lobby politicians at the national level in order to initiate parliamentary investigations into privatization.[15]

The 1995 strike of the Petrobrás workers was a crucial point in the opposition to privatization. Both critics of opposition to privatization and critics within the labour movement itself argued that this strike was a losing battle. It meant that '[t]he tide began to turn clearly against this type of labor tactic', in the eyes of proponents of privatization (Manzetti 1999: 199). According to representatives of the labour movement, linking the original purposes of the strike to privatization was a tactical mistake, which provoked a strong reaction from the government and did not fulfil the workers' demands.[16]

The strike started as an attempt to force the management of Petrobrás to comply with the decision of the Superior Labour Court (TST – Tribunal Superior de Trabalho) to increase wages by 12 per cent instead of 10 per cent, the reintegration of those workers who were dismissed during the Collor government, and maintenance of the retirement programme. Because the strike coincided with the debate on a constitutional amendment that would flexibilize the state monopoly in the oil sector, the strike soon acquired broader political dimensions, rejecting the constitutional amendment and privatization in general.[17] The TST ordered the strikers to go back to work, and allowed dismissal of those who remained on strike. The continuation of the strike led to sixty-four dismissals and the occupation of several refineries by the army and the military police. Despite this situation, the majority of the petroleum workers' unions decided to maintain the strike until the government started negotiations on their demands. But the government did not want to accept the negotiations and as Petrobrás continued to replace strikers by new workers, the strike ended with none of its demands met (DIEESE 1995: 53–4).

Because of the political dimensions of the strike, the strikers felt the need to defend their position to the Brazilian population. Besides the general arguments against liberalization (or breaking) of the state monopoly, various pamphlets argued against the idea that employees of Petrobrás are privileged workers (*marajás*, or maharajas), benefiting from generous wages. A pamphlet by the Federação Única dos Petroleiros (Unitary Federation of Oil Workers – FUP) argues that workers are responsible for economic growth in general and the success of Petrobrás in particular. According to the FUP, the Brazilian government wants to destroy the company from within, starting with those who built it – the workers. Another point that is presented is that workers in SOEs are not necessarily privileged. They enter the company through public application procedures and are just as much victims of wage reductions as workers in other sectors.[18]

The Petrobrás strike, the liberalization of the state monopoly and the possibility that Petrobrás might be privatized has provoked a lot of protest by the petroleum trade unions and broader protest groups. These groups include the unions themselves, nationalist groups, left-wing political parties and groups, and even sections of the military. The pamphlets published throughout this protest presented the many arguments that are used to defend the state monopoly in the oil sector and the importance of the state productive sector for Brazil.

The arguments can be divided into the following types: geo-political/strategic; technological; consequences for economic and social development; and consequences for employment. For the first, it is argued that oil is one of the most strategic goods in the global economy, and it plays a crucial role in many wars. Oil reserves are usually not located in developed countries and this means that developing countries are in a strategic position. Therefore, oil is under strict state control in most countries. According to the opponents of privatization, selling Petrobrás to foreign companies would entail a loss of sovereignty. Moreover, while Brazil is already very dependent on oil imports, it would be even more vulnerable after privatization of Petrobrás.

The second type of argument touches on the important role of Petrobrás in technological development (especially deep-sea exploration), which is expected to have trickle-down effects for the rest of the economy. The third argument is similar to the arguments of those who emphasize the importance of state-owned companies in developing countries. Petrobrás, as a state-owned company, is present in all parts of the country and fuel prices are subsidized and low. It is expected that private capital will not be concerned with regional development. High fuel prices can hamper industries and the transport sector, and can also affect the poor, who have to pay higher rates for public transport or fuel for their own transport. The last argument focuses on the consequences for employment, as many are directly employed by the company or dependent on it. Privatization is usually accompanied by a restructuring of the workforce and it is also feared that foreign companies would prefer to employ their own nationals.[19]

As has been said before, one of the CUT's concerns is the effect of privatization on employment and on the position of workers after privatization. The CUT accuses the government of not providing adequate compensation and alternatives for dismissed workers. In general, the CUT expects privatization to lead to a further concentration of wealth, and doubts whether companies in strategic economic sectors will contribute to economic and social development when they are privatized. The assumption that privatization will lead to increasing employment and an improvement of working conditions is also questioned. The CUT therefore proposes that employment and wage policy should be firmly included in privatization and restructuring (DESEP/CUT 1993: 14). Nevertheless, the CUT considers workers in the public sector and in state-owned companies to be privileged. Public-sector workers 'were certainly not among those who were excluded by the development model that is now outdated' (CUT 1995c: 6). Furthermore, the CUT argues that these workers should realize their responsibility for building a more transparent state sector, geared towards social development. SOE workers should not be tempted to be co-opted by the state in the privatization process, as the labour movement is already weakened substantially and this would further undermine the position of public-sector unions (DESEP/CUT 1993: 14).

There are some attempts to involve trade unions in the privatization process. All workers have to contribute to the Fundo de Garantia por Tempo de Serviço (Guarantee Fund for Time Worked – FGTS)[20] for unemployment compensation. In 1992, the president of the BNDES proposed using part of the capital in this fund to facilitate acquisition of shares at a discounted price. The argument was that this would allow broader popular participation in the privatization process. The representatives of trade unions in the FGTS did not accept that this money could be used without participation of workers in the decision-making process of privatization. The conflict about the use of FGTS money resulted in a split between the leadership of the CUT and rank-and-file members. Workers in state companies could buy FGTS shares in privatized companies, at a discount. Because this would imply a fairly high revenue for workers, many of them decided to stop opposing privatization.[21] The CUT criticized the use of FGTS and FAT[22] funds for issues like privatization. It argued that because both funds contain money deposited by workers, workers should have a bigger say in the way that it is spent and that this money should be used for social development instead of privatization (Neto 1996).

Alternatives to privatization

In relation to the question of whether privatization is unavoidable and whether it will solve Brazil's economic and social problems, a common reaction is that there are better solutions. Vicente Paulo da Silva and Marcelo Sereno of the CUT compare one of the purposes of privatization, the reduction of public debt, to a person who starts 'to sell the fridge, the car and in the end his own house in order to pay interest on his debts' (undated/a). This refers to the argument that privatization implies losing national control over natural resources and the national heritage and selling companies that are profitable. The importance of state-owned companies for the development of infrastructure and industrialization should also not be forgotten, according to the opponents of privatization (CUT 1995c: 4).

This does not mean that the CUT argues that state-owned companies are perfect. The CUT accuses state-owned companies of backlogs in investment, modernization and customer services. Moreover, the privatization programme is not a reflection of democratic domestic policy considerations, but of the powerful position of international creditors and international financial institutions. In this sense, economic restructuring is an issue of liberalization and deregulation, which is not the best solution for Brazil's social and economic problems (DESEP/CUT 1993: 8–9). Reflecting the ambivalent view of the state, the labour movement criticizes SOEs as a pillar of the development strategy of the military regime, it criticizes the way that SOEs were used as instruments of price-setting – a mechanism which subsidized the private sector – and the way that they were a source of political patronage.

According to the CUT, the parameters of the public sector should be public control in the case of natural monopolies; preserving public control over industrial and technological policies; and the question of how development can be promoted and which sector should be the 'engine of growth' (DESEP/CUT 1993: 12). The CUT is not against privatization, or as Jair Meneguelli, the then president of the CUT, said in relation to the privatization of the steel mill USIMINAS in 1991: 'Real existing socialism has already proved that statism is not always the best solution.'[23] The labour movement questions the assumption that the private sector is capable of making strategic investment decisions and of being an engine of development, including the provision of adequate employment and social development:

Besides not solving the fiscal, financial and heritage [*patrimoniais*] problems of the State, neither in the short nor the long term, the privatization programme was not capable of promoting economic growth through the increase of investment in enterprises that now pertain to the private sector.

(CUT undated/a)

It is argued that the role of public enterprises should be the following:

- to contribute to universal and non-discriminatory access to the infrastructure, adequate for the situation in Brazil;
- to contribute to the redistribution of the wealth and resources of the country (including land) in order to reduce social and regional inequalities;
- to contribute to the autonomous and sovereign integration of Brazil in the world economy, promoting international trade, the reduction of external vulnerability, competitiveness and technological development (CUT 1995c: 13).

The alternative proposed by the CUT during the mid-1990s was to democratize state-owned companies and to promote public management under democratic control – the 'moralization' and democratization of state-owned companies. The state-owned company system that developed during the twentieth century cannot be equated with public or democratic companies. As Ben Ross Schneider argues,

[i]t is the executive's control over resources that moves politics into the bureaucracy, and the executive bureaucracy dominates both politics and economics. The various entities of this bureaucracy run state enterprises and banks, fix tariffs, subsidize credit, and otherwise budget and plan government intervention into the economy.

(Ross Schneider 1999: 296)

State-owned enterprises were subject to corruption and were often used for political purposes and clientelism. Although this is not the type of SOE that the opponents of privatization promote, they are often pushed into the corner of defending the old system. Proponents of privatization use this to accuse their opposition of being 'anti-modern', defending economic policies that led to disaster.

The CUT argues against the belief that the public sale of companies, and the possibility of the wider population participating in the process, represent a form of societal control. The importance of the autonomy of the management of companies is acknowledged and therefore a 'management contract' is proposed, which sets goals and objectives of investment and production. The negotiation and implementation of the management contract should involve civil society, the government, management and trade unions of the companies involved. The National Congress and employees of state-owned companies should have a large role in the control of public companies. There should be transparent and accountable forms of management, and all parties involved should be autonomous and free from narrow political considerations.

The unions of the Companhia Vale do Rio Doce proposed a Social Agreement (*Acordo Social*), the result of a visit to privatized companies in several European countries. The document stresses the importance of the Agreement for an increase of productivity through the implementation of a system of Total Quality Management, with the participation and consultation of employees (a partnership between labour and capital). The resulting productivity increases are expected to result in higher wages, as wages are not 'a problem of costs for entrepreneurs anymore, but a factor in the increase of competitivity of the enterprise ... ' (SINDIMINA 1996: 5). The document supports the acquisition of shares by employees of CVRD, also with the note that Total Quality Management does not exclude the participation of workers in the administrative council of a company (SINDIMINA 1996). This alternative strategy, aimed at the inclusion of workers in the newly privatized company, was only successful in achieving a 10 per cent offer of preferred shares to the employees. It was not possible to negotiate the other aspects of the proposal. The experiences of the unions of CVRD with participation through shareholding are not wholly positive, as the Clube de Investidores, which was established in order to take full advantage of the employee offer, does not want to have much to do with the representation of workers, except for the position of workers as shareholders.[24]

A document of the Sindicato dos Engenheiros of the Companhia Siderúrgica Nacional stresses that the work-place in state-owned companies should be democratized, which includes the right to information for trade unions, work-place organization (factory commissions), participation of unions in the formulation of new company policies, and fair admission procedures for new workers (SENGE/VR 1990: 35–6). It has been emphasized many times that there should be clear rules, regulations and agreements between the government, the companies and society (CUT 1995c: 15–18).

The effects of the ambivalent strategies of local unions and the CUT became especially clear in the case of the privatization of the Companhia Siderúrgica Nacional (National Steel Company – CSN) in Volta Redonda. An important factor was that the CUT itself was split between political groupings at the national and at the local level. This was further complicated by the establishment of a new central union organization, Força Sindical, in 1991. Força Sindical claimed that it represented a non-ideological type of unionism, a 'unionism of results'. This entailed entering into a dialogue with the government, and supporting Collor de Melo's economic reforms, including privatization (Força Sindical 1993: 46–53, Barros 1999: 38–42). This posed a problem for the CUT, as it had to redefine its own position on negotiation with the government or confrontation. Before the privatization of CSN, the CUT lost the leadership of the local metal-workers' union to Força Sindical. Conflicts between the CUT and Força Sindical about wage negotiations and co-operation or confrontation with the managers of CSN about privatization and restructuring of the company (especially dismissals), eventually led to a victory for Força Sindical in union elections in 1992.

The aim of the more moderate groups in the CUT in Volta Redonda was to increase workers' influence on the privatization process. The more radical groups were against privatization and saw a strategy of influencing the process as a way to legitimize privatization.[25] The new Força Sindical leadership supported the privatization of CSN and attempted to negotiate a higher percentage of shares that could be bought by workers. For this reason, it established a Clube de Investidores (Investors' Club), as this would 'democratize' the sale of CSN. In a reaction to this the CUT opposition in Volta Redonda launched an independent investors' club in order to profit from the privatization of CSN and to mobilize workers. This split and the subsequent agreement on workers' participation did not just correspond to the objective of the government to 'tie' workers to privatized companies, or to incorporate them into the process, but also meant that possible union opposition was severely weakened. Although the national CUT opposed privatization, it could not formulate an effective answer to the participation of its members in the investors' clubs. The CUT expected participation in privatization to lead to marginalization and an absence of influence on the management of privatized companies, but this did not stop local unions and their members from buying shares (CUT 1995c: 10). According to Graciolli, this is an indication of the shift of the CUT to negotiation and participation in reforms (Graciolli 1999: 125, 186–8, 200, 207–8).[26] Job security for workers after privatization (which was negotiated in the case of some electricity companies in the state of São Paulo) and share preferences for workers can be considered as positive gains for unions in the privatization process. Nevertheless, the national CUT still interprets this as giving in to privatization, if not in the practice of its affiliated unions, then at least in its political statements.

Conclusions

Although the Brazilian socio-economic environment has given rise to severe conflicts about socio-economic inequalities and the distribution of economic gains, the labour movement has difficulties in formulating and implementing an effective opposition strategy. The cause of these problems can be found in the restriction that recent democracies pose on popular participation and in the labour movement's own difficulties in designing a political strategy that goes beyond its focus on the state. This is not to say that trade unions are able to change a whole system or halt neo-liberal reforms. A strategy of participation leads to conflicts within the labour movement: between sections that see mobilization and confrontation as the only viable strategy and those who are willing to negotiate with the government and employers.

The points of view of the Brazilian government and of the labour movement clash fundamentally, even though the CUT's point of view is not so radical as to reject privatization completely. This precludes possibilities of negotiation with the government, while company-level unions are willing to participate and negotiate in the privatization process. The attempts of the BNDES to involve workers in the privatization process have led to splits between central union organizations and within the CUT itself between the national leadership and rank-and-file members.

The analysis of the responses of the labour movement to privatization shows that the difficulties in influencing the privatization process have to do with a political environment that does not enable the participation of social actors and that is not open to alternatives to reform. The decision-making process is highly centralized and technocratic, and reforms such as privatization are presented as inevitable. This leads to a situation in which opponents turn into defenders of the old system, a situation to which no one wants to return. The constraints of recent democracies also lie at the root of these problems (cf. Roberts 1998: 30). After the democratic reforms in the 1980s, unions find it difficult to extend democracy to the work-place of the state-owned or privatized company. The market mechanism, competitiveness and labour relations as a partnership are the new rule. Initial high expectations of the social effects of democracy are not met, as social problems are not yet solved and current economic problems require neo-liberal reforms and a firm commitment to change, according to the government. Paradoxically, the possibilities for opposition and alternatives are limited, because socio-economic inequalities put pressure on democracy.

Notes

1 Studies on the effects of privatization on labour generally suffer from a lack of statistical evidence on employment and labour effects. The same is true for studies of privatization in Brazil. Furthermore, the effects of privatization on the wider economy can only become clear in the long run, as it is not yet always possible to say whether privatized companies are more efficient or whether they create employment. See Hoeven and Sziraczki (1997: 8–9). The same is true of the general effects of privatization. For an overview of the arguments in favour of privatization, see Guislain (1997: 6–10), and on the reason why there is no consensus about the effects of privatization, see Hoeven and Sziraczki (1999: 2–3, 7–11).
2 These include an obligation to keep capital in Brazil for at least twelve months, and it was forbidden to sell shares within two years (Carneiro 1998: 7–8).
3 In 1995, the National Privatization Council (Conselho Nacional de Desestatização) was established as the institutional framework for privatization. The CND is the highest body dealing with privatization, and reports directly to the president. The Council consists of the Ministers of Development, Industry and Trade, the Minister of Finance, and the Minister of Management. In the case of bank privatization, the President of the Central Bank is also involved. The decision to privatize a company is the exclusive prerogative of the president of Brazil (BNDES 2001d).
4 See Sarles (1995: 175–6) and Manzetti (1999: 152–3) on the mechanisms that Collor used to broaden support for privatization.
5 See Kikeri (1998) for an overview of technical assistance to privatization projects in Brazil and the rationale of the World Bank in this respect.

6 The constitution was changed in order to make this possible.

7 The energy crisis is commonly known as the *Apagão*, the big switch-off.

8 See Castelar Pinheiro (2000a) and Santos, Chico, '"Privatizados" cortam 39,6 mil empregos', Folha de São Paulo, 3 March 1997.

9 Interview with Marcelo Sereno, Member of Executive Board CUT for Union Affairs (1995–9), Director of Union Affairs, Partido dos Trabalhadores, São Paulo, 17 December 1999; Interview with board of SINTTEL, Sindicato dos Trabalhadores em Telecomunicações, Brasília, 9 November 1999.

10 Interview with Walter Tesch, president of (Fetrabalho), Federação das Cooperativas de Trabalho do Estado de São Paulo, São Paulo, 27 October 1999; 'Como manter uma cooperativa de pé, mesmo quando o pior ainda está por vir', *Cooperativa e Trabalho*, 2.

11 See also the article 'Muito alem da Vale' in *CVRD: Privatização da Vale do Rio Doce*, ed. by Centro de Pesquisa Vergueiro, São Paulo (1997).

12 The Companhia Vale do Rio Doce (CVRD) had to put 8 per cent of its annual profits into a social fund. The fund provided funds for schools, environmental projects and services for trade unions. After privatization, the new owners would only have to pay for projects that had already been approved. Interview with Marcelo Sereno, 17 December 1999; 'Muito além da Vale' (1997).

13 The CVRD operates in the Amazon states and owns large amounts of land there. This has provoked, among others, protests from rubber-tappers' and landless farmers' organizations, such as the Movement of Rural Landless Workers (Movimento dos Trabalhadores Rurais Sem Terra – MST). See Folha de São Paulo 'Bloqueio causa prejuízo de R$5 mil à Vale', 10 July 1996; FSP 'Exército pode retirar garimpeiros no PA', 21 October 1996. FSP 'Termina greve de fome na Vale', 2 December 1997. FSP 'Protesto destrói porto no Espírito Santo', 3 December 1998; FSP 'Meneguelli defende ocupação da Usiminas', 20 September 1991.

14 See Gazeta Mercantil, 'Urucum não impede venda da Vale', 16 August 1997; Folha de São Paulo, 'Leia a principal ação contra a venda da Vale', 2 May 1997.

15 Folha de São Paulo, 'Projeto de PT sofre investida', 26 November 1996.

16 Interview with Argemiro Pertence Neto, Secretario de Comunicação, Associação de Engenheiros da Petrobrás (AEPET), Rio de Janeiro, 6 September 2001; Interview with Julio Turra, Diretor Executivo (Secretaria de Relações Internacionais), CUT, São Paulo, 21 August 2001.

17 Privatization and the employment situation in the public sector (after dismissals in the early 1990s) triggered many public-sector strikes in 1995, including those in the electricity sector, education and telecommunications (DIEESE 1995: 53).

18 The analysis is based on the following pamphlets: Federação Única dos Petroleiros (FUP) (1995) *Carta Aberta á População Brasileira*, September; Assessorias de Imprensa dos Sindicatos de Petroleiros do Estado de São Paulo (1994) *Defender o monopólio do petróleo: Um desafio para a imprensa sindical*.

19 The paragraphs on the arguments against the privatization of Petrobrás are based on an analysis of the following pamphlets: Movimento Defesa do Monopólio Estatal do Petróleo (1995) *Petróleo sempre Monopólio*, May; *A Corrida do Ouro Negro: a disputa pela riqueza que movimenta meio mundo* (1995) Série O Petróleo Brasileiro, No. 1; Federação Única dos Petroleiros (FUP) (1995), see Note 18; Diretoria dos Sindipetros Campinas, Cubatão, Mauá, São José dos Campos e São Paulo (undated) *Petróleo sempre Monopólio*; Movimento em Defesa do Sistema Petrobrás (undated) *Manifesto á População: 'Monopólio Estatal do Petróleo e Moralização das Empresas Públicas: Essa Luta é de Todos'*; Movimento Petrobrás [1991] *Brasil, longe da guerra mas perto das multinacionais do petróleo*.

20 The military regime introduced the FGTS in 1966 in order to reduce the costs of dismissal.

21 Montero (1998: 47–9); Interview with Marcelo Sereno, 17 December 1999.

22 Fundo de Amparo ao Trabalhador (Fund for Worker Support): fund for unemployment benefits established in 1986.
23 Folha de São Paulo, 'Meneguelli defende ocupação da Usiminas', 20 September 1991.
24 Interview with Luiz Vieira and Celso Vianna de Fonseca, respectively, President, and Communications Officer, of SINDIMINA. Rio de Janeiro, 15 August 2001.
25 The national CUT is divided between moderate groups who support a combination of negotiation and confrontation. The main group is called Articulação Sindical. Unionists in this group played an important role in the re-emergence of union action at the end of the 1970s and in the founding of the Workers' Party (PT). The socialist groups are based on union groups with a more radical, socialist view of politics and the labour relations system (I.J. Rodrigues 1997: 43–4).
26 A similar conflict happened in the case of privatization of Usiminas. Folha de São Paulo, 'Presidente do Sindicato defende privatização: Sindicalistas divergem sobre destino da Usiminas', 3 October 1991; 'A praça da bagunça: O leilão da Usiminas é derrubado em meio a um festival de selvageria', *Veja*, 2 October 1991.

Bibliography

Baer, W. (1995) *The Brazilian Economy: Growth and Development*, Westport: Praeger.
Banco Nacional de Desenvolvimento Econômico e Social (BNDES) (2000a) *Privatizações em andamento: Agenda de Privatização 2000–2001*, http://www.bndes.gov.br/pndnew/cronus.htm (accessed 31 July 2001).
—— (2000b) *Privatization in Brazil: Results and Agenda*, Rio de Janeiro: BNDES September.
—— (2001a) *Resultados Gerais*, http://www.bndes.gov.br/pndnew/already.htm (accessed 31 July 2001).
—— (2001b) *Histórico*, http://www.bndes.gov.br/pndnew/history.htm. (accessed 31 July 2001).
—— (2001c) *Resultados por Empresa – PND*, http://www.bndes.gov.br/pndnew/compriv.htm (accessed 31 July 2001).
—— (2001d) *Estrutura Institucional*, http://www.bndes.gov.br/pndnew/struct.htm (accessed 7 November 2001).
Barros, M. Rands (1999) *Labour Relations and the New Unionism in Contemporary Brazil*, New York: St Martin's Press; London: Macmillan.
Brazil, Federal Government (1998) *Letter of Intent* to the International Monetary Fund, Brasília: 13 November. http://www.imf.org/external/np/loi/111398.htm (accessed 10 April 2002).
Carneiro, F. Galrão (1998) 'Privatizações na América Latina: Seus Efeitos e Impactos sobre o Mercado de Trabalho', *Estudos Empresariais*, 3(2): May–August: 3–13.
Carneiro, F. Galrão and Rocha, C.H. (1999) 'Reforming the public sector in Latin America: a cross-country perspective', in A. Castelar Pinheiro and K. Fukasaku (eds) *Privatization in Brazil: the Case of Public Utilities*, Ensaios BNDES 10, Rio de Janeiro: Banco Nacional de Desenvolvimento Econômico e Social, pp. 31–52.
Castelar Pinheiro, A. (1996) *No que deu afinal a privatização?*, Texto para Discussão no. 40, Rio de Janeiro: Banco Nacional de Desenvolvimento Econômico e Social, May.
—— (2000a) *Após a Privatização*, Departamento Econômico, Área de Planejamento, Rio de Janeiro: BNDES, 4 December.
—— (2000b) *A Experiência Brasileira de Privatização: o Que Vem a Seguir?*, Texto para Discussão 87, Rio de Janeiro: BNDES, November.
Castelar Pinheiro, A. and Giambagi, F. (1999) 'The macroeconomic background and institutional framework of Brazilian privatization', in A. Castelar Pinheiro and K.

Fukasaku (eds) *Privatization in Brazil: the Case of Public Utilities*, Ensaios BNDES 10, Rio de Janeiro: Banco Nacional de Desenvolvimento Econômico e Social, pp. 5–29.

Central Única dos Trabalhadores (undated/a) *A CUT e as Privatizações*, Mimeo, http://www.cut.org.br/a20212.htm (10 April 2002).

—— (1988) *Resoluções do III CONCUT*, São Paulo: CUT.

—— (1994) *Modelo de desenvolvimento, política industrial, e reestruturação produtiva: As propostas da CUT*, Propostas para Debate, São Paulo: CUT.

—— (1995a) *Relatório do Seminário 'A Empresa Pública e seu controle social'*, Brasília: 16–17 March.

—— (1995b) *Análise da Lei de Concessões*, Preparatory document for seminar 'A Empresa Pública e seu controle social', Mimeo, São Paulo: CUT.

—— (1995c) *O Papel das Empresas Públicas e seu Controle Social*, Discussion document and preparatory document for seminar 'A Empresa Pública e seu controle social', Mimeo, São Paulo.

Chaffee, W.A. (1998) *Desenvolvimento: Politics and Economics in Brazil*, Boulder, CO, and London: Lynne Rienner.

Departamento de Estudos Sócio-Econômicos e Políticos (DESEP)/CUT (1993) *A Crise Brasileira e os Trabalhadores*, Relatório-Síntese, São Paulo: DESEP/CUT, August.

Departamento Intersindical de Estatísticas e Estudos Socio-Econômicos (DIEESE) (1995) 'As greves de junho de 1995', *Boletim DIEESE*, No. 172, July.

DIEESE/Subseção FITTEL (2000) *Evolução do Emprego no Setor de Telecomunicações*, DIEESE/Subseção FITTEL, May.

Força Sindical (1993) *Um projeto para o Brasil: a proposta da Força Sindical*, São Paulo: Geração Editora.

Graciolli, E.J. (1999) 'Um Laboratorio Chamada CSN: Greves, Privatização e Sindicalismo (A Trajetoria do Sindicato dos Metalúrgicos de Volta Redonda – 1989/1993)', Unpublished Ph.D. thesis, Universidade Estadual de Campinas.

Guislain, P. (1997) *The Privatization Challenge: a Strategic, Legal, and Institutional Analysis of International Experience*, Washington D.C.: World Bank.

Hoeven, R. van der and Sziraczki, G. (1997) 'Privatization and labour issues', in R. van der Hoeven and G. Sziraczki (eds) *Lessons from Privatization: Labour Issues in Developing and Transitional Countries*, Geneva: International Labour Organization, pp. 1–19.

International Labour Organization (ILO) (1999) *Panorama Laboral 1999*, Informa 6, América Latina y el Caribe, Lima: ILO.

International Monetary Fund (1998) *Brazil: Recent Economic Developments*, IMF Staff Country Reports No. 98/24, Washington D.C.: IMF, April.

Jard da Silva, S. (1999) *'Companheiros Servidores': Poder político e interesses econômicos do sindicalismo do setor publico na CUT*, MA Thesis, Department of Political Science, Universidade de São Paulo.

Keck, M.E. (1992) *The Workers' Party and Democratization in Brazil*, New Haven and London: Yale University Press.

Kikeri, S. (1998) *Privatization and Labor: What Happens to Workers When Governments Divest?*, World Bank Technical Paper No. 396, Washington D.C.: World Bank.

Manzetti, L. (1999) *Privatization South American Style*, Oxford: Oxford University Press.

Ministerio de Fazenda (1999) *Memorandum of Economic Policies, July 05, 1999*, Brasília: Ministerio de Fazenda, http://www.fazenda.gov.br/ingles/ajuste/ifmimte01.htm (accessed 12 June 2001).

Montero, A.P. (1998) 'State interests and the new industrial policy in Brazil: the privatization of steel, 1990–1994', *Journal of Interamerican Studies and World Affairs*, 40(3): 27–62.

Neto, J. Vaccari (1996) 'E a função social?', *O Globo*, 12 September 1996, http://www.cut.org.br/a20202.htm (accessed 10 April 2002).

Nogueira, A.J.F.M. (1999) 'Emergência e Crise do Novo Sindicalismo no Setor Público Brasileiro', in I.J. Rodrigues (ed.) *O Novo Sindicalismo: Vinte Anos Depois*, São Paulo: Vozes, pp. 51–72.

Noronha, E. (1991) 'A explosão das greves na decada de 80', in A. Boito, Jr (ed.) *O Sindicalismo Brasileiro nos Anos 80*, Rio de Janeiro: Paz e Terra, pp. 93–135.

Presidência da República, Governo Fernando Henrique Cardoso (1995) *Privatization Enters a New Phase*, Brasília: Presidência da República, August.

Roberts, K.M. (1998) *Deepening Democracy? The Modern Left and Social Movements in Chile and Peru*, Stanford, CA: Stanford University Press.

Rodrigues, I.J. (1997) *Sindicalismo e Política: a Trajetória da CUT*, São Paulo: Edições Sociais.

Roxborough, I. (1989) 'Organized labor: a major victim of the debt crisis', in B. Stallings and R. Kaufman (eds) *Debt and Democracy in Latin America*, Boulder, CO: Westview Press, pp. 91–108.

Sarles, M. (1995) 'Political and economic reform in Argentina and Brazil: contrasting priorities, contrasting success', in J.A. Lawton (ed.) *Privatization Amidst Poverty: Contemporary Challenges in Latin American Political Economy*, Miami: North–South Center Press, pp. 163–78.

Schamis, H.E. (1992) 'Conservative political economy in Latin America and Western Europe: the political sources of privatization', in D.A. Chalmers, M.C. Campello de Souza and A.A. Borón (eds) *The Right and Democracy in Latin America*, Westport: Praeger, pp. 48–67.

Schneider, B.R. (1989) 'Partly for sale: privatization and state strength in Brazil and Mexico', *Journal of Interamerican and World Affairs*, 30(4).

—— (1999) 'The *Desarrollista* state in Brazil and Mexico', in M. Woo-Cumings (ed.) *The Developmental State*, Ithaca and London: Cornell University Press, pp. 276–305.

Sindicato dos Engenheiros de Volta Redonda (SENGE/VR) (1990) *Privatização? Não Obrigado!*, May, Volta Redonda: SENGE/VR.

SINDIMINA (1996) *Proposta: 'Os trabalhadores da CVRD diante da privatização'*, Aracaju, Brazil: SINDIMINA.

Velasco, L. (1999) 'Privatização: mitos e falsas percepções', in F. Giambiagi and M. Mesquita Moreira (eds) *A Economia Brasileira nos Anos 90*, Rio de Janeiro: BNDES, pp. 183–215.

12 Neo-liberalization of industrial relations

The case of Chile

Alex E. Fernández Jilberto

Introduction

Chile is still undergoing a long-term transition to democracy. The installation of a democratic regime took a whole decade, but democracy now co-exists with the neo-liberal restructuring project implemented by the dictatorship (1973–89). The triumph of democracy signified a change of political regime while preserving the neo-liberal state created by the dictatorship; adopting neo-liberal economic policies; and irreversibly accepting the economic transformations generated by the neo-liberal restructuring of the state sector. Just like other sections of the democratic opposition, the labour movement, here especially the Central Workers' Union (CUT – *Central Unica de Trabajadores*), played an important role in resisting the dictatorship. The CUT hoped that the democratization process would be accompanied by a restructuring of the relations between capital, labour and state that were characteristic of the *Compromise State* (1930–70). The political alliance that facilitated the democratic transition, the 'Concertación' of the Parties for Democracy (the Socialist Party, the Christian Democratic Party, the Party for Democracy and the Radical Party) recognized the role of entrepreneurs and other economic groups. These actors had benefited from the privatization of public enterprises, as privileged actors of economic development during the first Concertación government in 1990.

The globalization process confirmed the perception of the irreversibility of neo-liberal transformations. In Chile, globalization is understood as a model for maintaining competitiveness between open economies, based on substantial differences in (low) labour standards. It was impossible to eradicate the heritage of the dictatorship in an only partially reformed economy (flexible labour, precarious jobs, 'informalization' of the formal sector and low salaries). Later on, the negative effects of the Asian crisis (1997–8) confirmed the opinion of the government about labour flexibilization as a virtuous strategy leading to the intensification of Chile's global economic competitiveness. After the transition, the permanent weakening of the political capacity of the Chilean labour movement, the low level of its representativeness and its weak bargaining power (the topic of this chapter) were not only the results of the effects of the international financial crisis, but also of the policies and efforts of the democratic regime to manage the effects of the globalization drive and the results of previous neo-liberal restructuring.

Because of the political consequences of the neo-liberal economic transfor-mations, Chilean trade unions failed to restore their previous opposition strategy. In 1973 the main purpose of the military was to restore the market mechanism in the Chilean economy, as a reaction to the policies of the previous government. The economic policies (nationalization of the industrial, banking and financial sectors, and the thoroughgoing agrarian reforms) implemented by the previous *Unidad Popular* (Popular Unity) government (1970–3) disarticulated the operation of market forces. Repressive policies based on the anti-Communist National Security Doctrine persisted together with the anti-industrialist tendencies of Chilean neo-liberalism. The objective of repression was to eradicate the political and economic protagonists of the labour movement, which had been strength-ened during the period of import-substituting industrialization policies. As a reaction, the military government initiated a model of 'capitalist reform'. This signified a reduction of the size of the public sector, a concentration of power in the private sector, economic liberalization and an emphasis on the comparative advantages of the Chilean economy. Pressures from trade unions and political parties for a policy of income redistribution had to be prevented.

Latin America

Labour relations and financial crises

The Mexican peso crisis of 1994 (the Tequila crisis) provided three lessons which invalidated the Latin American neo-liberal paradigm of 'productive transforma-tion with equity' inspired by the Economic Commission on Latin America and the Caribbean (ECLAC). First, this approach emphasized the need to fortify domestic savings in order to diminish dependency on the economic fluctuations of the global economy. Second, macro-economic stability of neo-liberal economies is not permanent and can always be altered by negative external factors engen-dered by the global economy. Third, the creation of employment and the introduction of policies to reduce poverty do not only depend on national macro-economic stability, but also largely on a stable world economy (ECLAC 1990).

The crisis of 1994 (Figure 12.1) put an end to Latin American neo-liberal optimism that considered globalization as a new opportunity for re-establishing sustained economic development after the debt crisis of 1982. Moreover, it revealed how economies were very vulnerable to unstable capital flows. In 1994, the Mexican trade deficit equalled US$29.9 billion (current account deficit), which was one of the most important causes of the crisis. The Mexican economy's openness to the world market and its integration into NAFTA stimu-lated short-term capital flows looking for fast and high profits. Only the contribution of some US$50 billion provided by the IMF, the World Bank and the US, and guaranteed by Mexican earnings from oil exports, succeeded in stabilizing the Mexican economy.

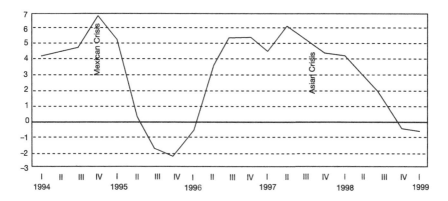

Figure 12.1 Latin America: GDP and financial crises (roman numerals represent quarters)

Source: ECLAC (2000) (based on official statistics of Argentina, Brazil, Chile, Colombia, Mexico, Peru and Venezuela)

This situation affected the Latin American economies in different ways. In the case of Chile, it temporarily affected the stability of the country's financial system. The Asian crisis also had profound repercussions on the Latin American economies. GDP growth decreased from 5.4 per cent in 1997 to 2.3 per cent in 1998, and a cyclical recession was initiated, which would cause a fall of total export values and a deceleration of import growth for the first time in ten years. Foreign capital flows and FDI amounting to US$60 billion contributed to the stabilization of the foreign account balance. The fact that the deficit had obliged the countries to utilize their reserves for the stabilization of the foreign account balance did not affect capital flows. This led to the reduction of the deficit with US$85 billion in 1997 and with US$68 billion in 1998.

International speculative movements against the Brazilian Real in October 1997 strongly resembled the Mexican peso crisis of 1994. The reaction of the Brazilian and Argentinian governments to the Brazilian crisis of 1997 was to raise interest rates in 1998, and the Brazilian government devaluated the Real in 1999. This ultimate remedy negatively affected economic relations and the competitiveness of the MERCOSUR countries. Chile, with its overvalued peso, had to face a contraction of its non-traditional exports, but also of its GDP (Figure 12.2). An additional effect was the Russian debt crisis of August 1998, which increased the costs of external financing for Latin American countries and reduced the inflows of foreign capital.

As a result of the Asian crisis, Chile experienced a recession starting at the end of 1998 and lasting for more than one year. This crisis terminated a period of fifteen years of sustained economic growth and stability that had permitted a consolidation of the political transition process from dictatorship to democracy. For the first time since 1990, the third Concertacíon government had to face an economic crisis with rising unemployment from 6.8 per cent in August 1998 to 9.8 per cent in 1999, and stabilizing at 9.4 per cent during the first month of

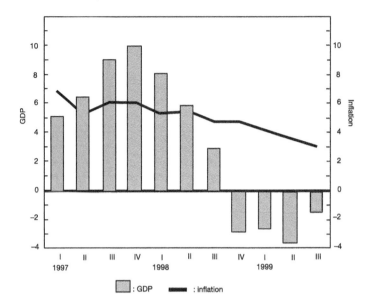

Figure 12.2 Chile: GDP and inflation (annual variations in percentages; roman numerals
        represent quarters)

Source: ECLAC (2000)

President Lagos' incumbency (Table 12.1). This posed a threat to the viability of
the Social Pact between entrepreneurs, workers and the state, signed during the
first democratic government of President Aylwin (1990–4). The effects of the
Asian crisis and the recession once again revealed the vulnerability of neo-liberal
economic policies.

Since 1979, workers and labour organizations have been regulated by the so-
called *Plan Laboral* (Labour Plan). The Plan introduced an extreme form of
labour flexibility within the context of a thorough neo-liberal restructuring of
the economy and a radical change in the typical Keynesian relations between
capital, labour, and the state which had been so characteristic in Chile.
Economic restructuring reinforced labour flexibility, and so a new form of
labour relations within the firm emerged. This meant, on the one hand, that
some well-defined production processes used external labour. On the other
hand, forms of subcontracting caused a loss of job security, precarious employment, characterized by temporary short-term contracts and working hours, a
high degree of job instability, and labour contracts stripped of any social protection and security (Escobar 1999: 99). The effects of the Asian crisis and the
generalization of the recession accentuated the phenomena mentioned above,
hindered the collective actions of workers and trade unions, and boosted the
process of labour fragmentation.

Table 12.1 Chile: main economic indicators

	1997	1998	1999	2000
	Annual variations in percentages			
GDP	7.0	3.9	-1.1	5.5
Consumer prices	6.0	4.7	2.3	4.7
Real wages	2.4	2.7	2.4	1.5
Exchange rate	3.8	-11.6	0.4	1.8
	Percentages			
Unemployment rate	6.1	6.4	9.8	9.4
	Million US$			
Export of services	20,772	18,949	19,406	22,150
Import of services	22,281	21,580	18,056	21,180
Current account balance	-3728	-4143	-78	-865
Capital and financial account	6,913	2,004	-670	365
Total balance	3,185	-2,139	-748	-500

Source: ECLAC (2000)

The heritage of the dictatorship and the transition to democracy

At the end of the dictatorship, in 1989, workers and labour organizations hoped that the transition government would substantially reform labour relations, legislation on trade unions and legislation regulating labour contracts. The need for a new *Institucionalidad Laboral* (labour institutionality) led to an explicit agreement in the governmental programme of the Concertación of the Parties for Democracy. The current system of labour legislation originates in the *Plan Laboral*, promulgated by the dictatorship in 1979, which completed the deregulation of the labour market. The deregulation process was initiated *de facto* in 1973 by the repression and eradication of any form of autonomous representation of the labour movement. In addition, the *Plan Laboral* gave absolute power to the firm in matters of wages and factory rules, and permitted the existence of more than one trade union per enterprise and the emergence of independent workers' associations bargaining without the support of the regular unions.

The aim of these proposals was to produce an *atomization of the labour movement*. Collective bargaining was limited to the level of the enterprise, and collective agreements covered a minimum period of two years, with bargaining procedures described in rigorous detail. Moreover, entrepreneurial lock-outs were authorized, and workers on strike could be replaced if the number of strikers exceeded more than 50 per cent of the firms' total workforce. In addition, legal provisions allowing the state to intervene in labour relations (in the settlement of wages and the setting of the minimum wage) were suppressed. Of course, the

Plan Laboral excluded any form of worker participation in matters of manage-ment, capital and profits made by the enterprise.

With the introduction of the *Plan Laboral*, the dictatorship put an end to a long period (1973–9) of repression of the trade-union movement and suspended any form of collective bargaining or labour conflicts. At the same time, the insti-tutional and legal provisions embodied by the Labour Code and the totality of the system of labour relations as designed by the *Compromise State* from the 1920s until 1973, was suspended. The *Compromise State* was shaped by three coexisting processes within Chilean society:

1   a process of import-substituting industrialization (ISI) supported by the state and oriented towards the internal market;
2   a continuing process of incorporation of marginal social groups into society; and
3   the existence of a democratic political regime that has constantly broadened civil rights and social improvements.

The Chilean political class shared, at least until 1970, the consensual view that maintaining the equilibrium between industrialization, participation and democracy was a necessary concept of control. Without any doubt, a policy of income redistribution and wage increases for urban workers was intended to fortify a consumption pattern sustained by a process of state-led industrialization in close connection with the development of the domestic market. This policy also created an insoluble contradiction, which explains the crisis of a political system based on an ISI policy: the dilemma between higher wages and faster accumulation of capital. The crisis of the *arreglo democrático chileno* (Chilean demo-cratic arrangement) and of a political regime supporting an ISI policy, occurred in a political context in which the state supported a policy of compromises between capital and labour, and played the role of interest mediator in labour relations.

New forms of labour relations

The *Plan Laboral* of the military regime required a political regime without any form of regulation of labour relations and without any room for interest media-tion, or alternatively a state system open to the social and economic demands and increased autonomy and political influence of the entrepreneurial sectors. Therefore, trade unions were considered as political obstacles to free-market forces. Political opposition was initially represented by the Democratic Alliance, and later on by the groups and parties that defended a 'no vote' in the refer-endum of 1988 and defeated Pinochet's plebiscite, and finally by the Concertación of the Parties for Democracy, that succeeded in having Patricio Aylwin elected president in 1989. Aylwin's coalition aimed at legitimizing and institutionalizing the heritage of the former dictatorship. The first transition government (1990–4) discussed the possibility of satisfying trade-union demands for a profound transformation of labour institutions. However, Chilean democracy, with its two-party presidential regime was suffering from limitations imposed by the former authoritarian regime, which appointed a number of senators. The latter could obstruct any majority required for a revision of the constitution inherited from the dictatorship.

After the electoral victory of the opposition in 1989, the Concertación government decided to radicalize its original political programme. The opposition had to admit that neo-liberal policies had led to high social costs during the 1980s, but also that the policies had generated positive results (high economic growth, falling unemployment and a long-term improvement of the terms of trade). Any changes to the guidelines of the economic policies implemented by the dictatorial regime could discourage the entrepreneurial interest groups that had been the driving forces of the neo-liberal economic order. This could give birth to the creation of a double anti-governmental development: the politicized military in combination with the outbreak of an economic crisis (Montero 1999: 43). In the end, neo-liberal policies were accepted and partially adapted to the democratic regime, although they were less favourable to trade-union demands than in the original opposition programme. Moreover, the first democratic government left the regulation of labour conflicts (which had belonged to the functions of the state), to the market. The dominant new economic groups that took advantage of the privatizations following the structural adjustments after the foreign debt crisis of 1982 consolidated their power during the first stage of the democratization process. As far as the government was concerned, this dismissed entrepreneurial fears that a return to democracy would initiate a period of political instability because of the Concertación's inability to contain the social demands that had accumulated during the dictatorship.

The transition to democracy emphasized the role of economic groups as key actors in the democratic regime, and they remained privileged actors, who defined the principal variables of economic change, growth and employment. These groups also defined themselves as modern entrepreneurs (Montero *et al.* 1997) and as ideological and political innovators. With their sense of profitability, ability to create markets and obtain market shares, they depended far less on political clientelism than their predecessors.

Labour politics and the transition governments

The government of Patricio Aylwin (1990–4) decided to continue neo-liberal policies in combination with the political principle of *development with equity* and the construction of a *democracia de los acuerdos* (democracy of accords). The government implemented the so-called second stage of export promotion, consisting of a planned shift from an economic growth strategy based on commodity exports to a strategy to export products with a higher added value. In order to attain the goal of a revision of the labour institutions inherited from the dictatorial regime, the government admitted that neither the state nor the market could become the exclusive base for the new model of labour relations. A dialogue between entrepreneurs and the Central Unica de los Trabajadores (CUT) led to the conclusion of the *Marco de Referencia para el Dialogo* (Reference Framework for Dialogue) and later on, when the government joined, the *Tripartite Agreement*. With the help of this tripartite system, the government hoped to obtain union support for a continuation of its economic policies, and that entrepreneurial organizations and trade unions could agree on the basic principles of a market economy with free entrepreneurship and openness to the world market from that moment on.

The framework agreement was based on the following principles. Trade unions and entrepreneurial organizations accepted the need for permanent education and human resources management. The state had to balance macroeconomic variables and had to intervene in favour of those people excluded from the benefits of the market economy (war on poverty, minimum wages). The Aylwin government implemented a series of labour reforms suitable for inclusion in collective agreements. They limited the legal dispositions of 1978, regulating the exclusion and reintegration of strikers and facilitating the establishment of intra-enterprise collective agreements. This reform eliminated the cooling-off period to be observed before going on strike and facilitated the reconstruction of trade unions, especially the CUT, which achieved legal status. It also cancelled the provision of a minimum union membership and it permitted the automatic transfer of union dues from entrepreneurs to trade unions. With respect to collective agreements, the entrepreneurial right to dismiss workers without an explicit cause and without advice from the Labour Inspection Office was limited, and dismissal reimbursements were extended from five to eleven weeks per year of service.

With this labour reform act, the first Concertación government demonstrated that the state would remain important and that democracy could impose limitations on the dogmatic neo-liberalism promoted by entrepreneurial and economic interest groups. These reforms also showed the limits of the reforms mentioned above, because they do not affect labour-market flexibility, as the government took into consideration the danger of external shocks and the loss of competitive advantages for an open economy such as Chile. For this reason, it was vital that trade unions changed their ideological attitude towards labour conflicts in enterprises. Workers could take advantage of the economic policies of the government, as the purpose of tax reforms was to optimize tax revenues and to finance governmental income-redistribution and social programmes for the poor.

With respect to the business community, the government's labour policy had gained the confidence of the Chilean entrepreneurs in a democratic regime. The business sector considered the democratic regime to be their worst enemy at the beginning of the 1970s, because of the nationalization of the industrial and banking sectors and the expropriation of the big estates (the agrarian reform). One has to remember that in 1988, when General Pinochet lost the plebiscite that had to prolong his rule until 1999, and in 1989, when the Right lost the presidential elections, the business leaders started to fear the restoration of an interventionist state. Confronted with this situation, entrepreneurial organizations quickly distanced themselves from the Right and concentrated on the defence of the neo-liberal market economy, which they now designated as the *newly institutionalized economy*.

The *Confederation of Production and Trade* (Confederación de Producción y Comercio), which was at that moment the major entrepreneurial organization, participated before the elections of 1989 in joint commissions with economists of the Concertación in order to discuss a continuation of the dictatorship's economic policies. This discussion was facilitated at that time by the fact that the leaders of the democratic opposition could agree on the necessity of preserving economic stability during the transition period from dictatorship to democracy. They thought that entrepreneurial support for the government's project would become indispensable (Muñoz and Celedón 1993: 129).

At the beginning of the second transition government, under President Eduard Frei Ruiz-Tagle (1994–9), the Chilean trade unions criticized the transitional labour policy of the period between 1990 and 1994 and the suitability of the so-called *vía concertacionista* ('Concertaciónist' procedure) for solving labour problems. The Concertación government thought that neither the state nor the market would be exclusively in a position to articulate its new labour policy. Therefore, another labour order had to be created, somewhere midway between the extreme neo-liberalism defended by the entrepreneurs and the regulated labour regime that a majority of the trade-union leadership was aspiring towards. Without any doubt, the concerted action had proved its efficiency by closing the era of confrontational trade unionism and strengthening the institutional dialogue between the CUT and the entrepreneurial organizations. Trade-union leaders admitted that the inherited economic model would not be challenged and they recognized the pre-eminence of private initiative, free competition, economic openness to the outside world and a flexible labour market. From a political point of view, the trade-union movement did not want to gain more room for manoeuvre within the decision-making system, while the entrepreneurs saw themselves as the privileged actors of economic policy and the new labour order of the transition government. The Frei government was aware of the need to broaden labour reforms implemented during the previous government in order to strengthen political stability. It was necessary, therefore, to re-establish some trade-union rights, such as the right to be informed about the situation of the enterprises, the right to collective bargaining at the national or sector level, and the right to indemnities paid to individual trade-union militants in case of anti-union actions by the entrepreneurs. The National Congress, which was dominated by the Right, indefinitely delayed a significant part of these reforms, and the reforms were also affected by senators appointed by the dictatorship.

The reforms implemented by the Frei government were presented as a supplement, not as a change of the labour regime inherited from the dictatorship and the initial reforms by the Aylwin government. The CUT and the entrepreneurial organizations subjected them to severe criticism. To the labour organizations, the reforms were clearly inadequate from the perspective of re-establishing full trade-union rights. The employers' organization *Society for Factory Promotion* (Sociedad de Fomento Fabril) argued that these reforms would destroy business confidence and increase unemployment. As a result, a permanent dialogue or concerted action between entrepreneurs and the CUT was organized independently from the state.

The deadlock between labour and capital had to be overcome. During the Frei presidency, many labour demands had to be satisfied, such as reforms of the system of professional education, the creation of a *National Tripartite Board*, the implementation of professional training schemes in companies, a strengthening of control mechanisms, and the enforcement of the *Dirección del Trabajo* (Labour Directorate) of the Ministry of Labour, and many other reforms, such as the project to improve job security and broaden the bargaining rights of trade unions, which had been delayed by extensive parleys and debates. Therefore, the Frei government consolidated a system of labour relations that did not alter radically the collective bargaining system instituted by the dictatorship, while at the same time proposing more political autonomy for the trade-union movement. In this way, the democratic system facilitated the creation of a trade-union movement. But one also has to consider the constraints of a regime of labour-market flexibility compatible with the exigencies of Chile's economic competitiveness and the need for labour discipline expected by entrepreneurs, who considered themselves as the driving force of economic growth.

The entrepreneurs rejected and hampered the implementation of the labour reforms, arguing that the reforms would restore the former labour system with its openly politicized trade unions wanting to exercise control over business and to limit managerial autonomy. They argued that productivity, quality and efficiency could not become subject to collective bargaining, and that collective bargaining at the national or sectoral level would have a negative effect on the growth in productivity. The major point of understanding and convergence was the rejection of an institutionalized form of *tripartismo* (tripartism) in labour relations. Both employers and unions agreed upon the fact that the state had to keep out of any participation in collective bargaining or conflicts between labour and capital.

The third Concertación government (from March 2000 to the present), under President Ricardo Lagos, inherited the labour-relations legislation proposal that was sent to parliament at the end of President Frei's term. Both the senators of the Right (including those appointed by Pinochet) and those on the left, had defeated the Frei project with the argument that these reforms would have a negative influence on productivity growth, and that they were inspired by electoral reasons. At the same time, entrepreneurial organizations like the *Confederation of Production and Trade* (Confederación de Producción y Comercio) accused presidential candidate Ricardo Lagos of creating entrepreneurial distrust when insisting on the need for labour reforms. Concomitantly, the same entrepreneurial organization appealed for the formation of a broader entrepreneurial organization called the *Labour Defence Front*, in order to co-ordinate the strategy of the several entrepreneurial organizations against the future projects for labour reforms (*Dirección del Trabajo* 1999: 21).

Confronted with the rejection of the labour-reform act in Parliament, the CUT decided to institute a protest campaign, and submitted a complaint against this transgression of trade-union rights and collective bargaining rules to the International Labour Organization. The ILO Conventions Number 87 (on freedom of association and on protection of the right to organize) and Number 98 (on the right of organization and on collective bargaining), signed by the government, had been broken. The trade unions hoped to compel the new government and the entrepreneurial groups to bring Chilean labour legislation into line with international labour conventions ratified by the government.

At the same time, the new government had to face the unemployment problem. The government hoped to solve it by increasing labour flexibility, by ameliorating workers' employability and promoting higher labour-market partic-ipation rates, especially of younger workers and women. According to many economists who support the government, the Asian crisis was the main cause for increases in unemployment, which rose to 11 per cent of the working popula-tion. The high level of unemployment was also due to structural causes inherent to the economic development patterns introduced by the dictatorship and continued by the Concertacíon governments. During the previous fifteen years, sustained economic growth was obtained due to a dynamic and capital-intensive export sector demanding a low labour input. This was the well-known structural cause of the decreasing impact of economic growth on employment, which resulted in a decreased degree of elasticity between production growth and employment. This elasticity was at its highest during the 1980s, when a growth in productivity of 1 per cent per year generated an increase of 0.7 per cent in employment. In the 1990s, this had fallen to a 0.3 per cent growth in employ-ment, and only 0.2 per cent in 1999. This also signified that during the past twenty years a 1 per cent growth in GDP had generated 37,600 new jobs per year. Today, this number has decreased to 10,800 additional jobs a year (*Dirección del Trabajo* 2000: 10–11).

At the end of the year 2000, the Lagos government introduced a new labour bill into parliament in order to satisfy trade-union demands and to observe the convention signed with the ILO. This time, the bill was supported by the *consensus strategy*. According to the government, the bill was supposed to exclude any matter of conflict between capital and labour. It would entail the right to collec-tive bargaining, sectoral trade-union representation, and an abolition of the entrepreneur's right to dismiss workers on strike. The government's new Labour Reform Bill recognized the need for a trade-union movement contributing to the future of the enterprise, increased productivity and better working conditions. The government tried to put an end to conflicts and polarization between the CUT and entrepreneurs. With respect to the CUT, the new government intended to draft a *proyecto light* ('light project') for its labour policy, but continued to ignore the ILO conventions. This signified that none of the three Concertación governments were willing to implement thorough labour reforms. This was due to the dominant position acquired by the neo-liberal technocracy in the three transition governments (*Dirección del Trabajo* 2000: 7).

Loss of representativeness and weak bargaining capacity

The political unwillingness of the Concertación governments to introduce real labour reforms; the refusal of the oppositional parliamentary Right to consider any form of collective bargaining; and the refusal to accept the labour reforms proposed by the trade unions, was not only based on a different perspective on a well-functioning labour market, but also on the argument that the representativeness of the trade-union movement was low, because of the low percentage of union membership.

After 1992, membership steadily declined from 15.4 per cent in 1991 to a mere 11.3 per cent in 1998 (Table 12.2), a tendency that has not yet been reversed. If only the trade-union membership involved in collective bargaining is considered, the percentage does not exceed 8.9 per cent. These figures prove that the labour movement has to improve its bargaining power and its degree of representativeness, which would require a re-establishment of collective bargaining rights and a broadening of trade-union rights. Moreover, this also explains why trade unions have difficulties explaining their failure to implement working-class demands to the rank-and-file membership, which leads to a loss of mobilization capacities and decreases the appeal of the trade union.

As a result of economic restructuring and labour flexibility, new types of labour contracts have appeared, as well as new forms of labour relations. Outsourcing of services and workers is a third phenomenon that influences the relations between labour and capital. Many surveys conducted by the Research Department of the *Dirección del Trabajo* point at the growing importance of the latter phenomenon. Between 1997 and 1998, for example, 51.4 per cent of enterprises employed external workers in their production facilities (Aravena 1999: 67). Temporary labour contracts, contracts with fixed terms, without fixed salaries or written labour contracts become the modalities of these forms of outsourcing (externalization). A complete loss of job stability and social security, and a generalized job uncertainty, are all elements of these precarious

Table 12.2 Chile: evolution of trade-union membership, 1983–98

Year	Workforce (millions)	Membership (thousands)	Membership (in percentages)
1983	3.2161	320.903	10.0
1985	3.5374	360.963	10.2
1987	4.0108	422.302	10.5
1989	4.4248	507.616	11.5
1991	4.5404	701.355	15.4
1993	4.9857	684.361	13.7
1995	5.0258	637.570	12.7
1996	5.2987	655.597	12.4
1998	5.4324	611.535	11.3

Source: Departamento de Relaciones Laborales, Dirección del Trabajo, República de Chile (2000)

Table 12.3 Latin America: precarious jobs in the 1990s

	Wage worker [a]		*Labour costs* [b]			
	Temporary contract	*No contract*	*Total contract*	*Temporary*	*No contract*	*Indefinite*
Argentina	12.7	33.0	35.7	3.5	2.8	6.1
Chile	14.7	15.6	30.3	1.4	1.0	2.1
Colombia	8.3	31.0	39.3	1.9	1.6	3.3
Peru	32.6	41.1	73.7	1.4	1.1	2.1

Source: Tokman and Martínez (1999); Klein and Tokman (2000)
Notes:
[a] percentage of total waged workers
[b] in US dollars

jobs (Table 12.3). This fragmentation process constitutes an obstacle and an impediment to any form of collective action of workers who have a precarious job, and eventually hampers attempts at unionization (Gonzales 1998: 68). Falling trade-union membership can be explained as the result of this outsourcing tendency, now that the subcontracting firms are employing a reduced number of workers with trade-union rights (Frias 1996: 216).

Like in other Latin American countries, the goal of the government's provisional labour legislation and its hesitation to restore collective bargaining procedures were motivated by the intention of reducing wage costs. One has to keep in mind that these costs constitute an important part of total production costs, and that a reduction in the wage costs substantially ameliorates competitiveness. Labour fragmentation, precarious jobs and outsourcing are functional elements of a policy aiming at preserving the competitiveness of firms. Entrepreneurs believe that flexible labour contracts and far-reaching flexibilization of the labour market are good instruments for improving Chile's international competitiveness. The currency devaluations in the South-east Asian countries after the crisis of 1997 (Malaysia with 38.4 per cent, Thailand with 24.8 per cent, Indonesia with 34.9 per cent, Korea with 33.1 per cent, and the Philippines with 28.1 per cent) makes these instruments necessary, because the currency devaluations of the Asian countries reduced their labour costs in dollars and forced the Latin American economies to preserve their pre-crisis competitiveness by reducing their overall production costs by 20 to 60 per cent (Tokman and Martínez 1999: 67).

Conclusions

In Chile, the trade-union movement has played a decisive role as a political actor resisting dictatorship, and as an important pillar of the democratic transition period. In 1990, trade-union organizations thought that a substitution of the authoritarian regime for a democratic one would succeed in restoring the labour-relations system from before 1970. This would require the abolition of the *Plan*

Laboral of 1979 and the complete and immediate application of ILO Conventions Number 87 (on freedom of labour organization and the right to organize) and Number 98 (on the right to organize and on collective bargaining). At the same time, the CUT had to assume the task of restructuring and reconstructing its seriously disrupted trade-union organizations. The CUT's internal organizational structures still reflect the composition of the influence of the associated political forces (socialists, Communists, Christian-democrats and radicals) that were present at the moment of its foundation in 1953.

None of the three transition governments realized the goals that the trade-union movement had been aiming for during the whole process of democratic restoration. This was not only due to the integral application of the neo-liberal policies already implemented during the dictatorship, but also to the prevailing opinion of the political class and the government – both sharing the view that competitiveness between national economies operating under different labour standards constituted a major factor for the attraction and mobility of transnational capital. Any radical change introduced to the flexible rules of the Chilean labour market or a possible restoration of *tripartismo* was considered to be potentially negative for the influx of foreign capital and Chile's international competitiveness. In addition, an anti-union discourse was pleading for the abolition of Chile's militant trade unionism (with its low level of union affiliation and its strongholds among the Chilean labour aristocracy), which was considered as an obstacle to economic growth and to the regionalization and globalization of the national economy.

The CUT reacted by launching unionization drive in order to increase its representativeness among workers, by acquiring more influence among the inhabitants of shanty towns, where workers are concentrated and whose mobilization possibilities could be utilized. The CUT took a more realistic stance in matters of collective bargaining and admitted that an ongoing economic modernization process had to be accompanied by a policy of labour-market flexibility in order to protect Chile's economic competitiveness in a globalizing world economy. The Asian crisis showed that Chile's economic openness made the country vulnerable to many challenges and uncertainties, which necessitated an augmentation of its productivity and required a substantial improvement of its human capital.

The CUT's restoration strategy launched during the transition period failed because of the CUT's incomprehension of the very nature of the democratic transformation process, which was not merely a regime change with regard to the state form (a neo-liberal state) shaped by the dictatorship, but also because of its inability to grasp the irreversible nature of the neo-liberal restructuring process that occurred at the level of the enterprise. It is worth mentioning the breakup of the vertically integrated conglomerates into smaller entities, and the disappearance of many of their subsidiaries. This process speeded up the outsourcing of many activities of the enterprises. Big business had grown in importance after the privatization of state-owned companies, and the conglomerates framed a strategy of breaking up their large subsidiaries into more specialized ones, all having their own financial autonomy and responsibility. From the point of view of labour, outsourcing was a Taylorist method that would lead to more intensive control of workers in the production process. The entrepreneurs took advantage of the existing openness of the economy and the repressive nature of the state in order to disarticulate the trade-union movement, to avoid collective agreements and to impose labour flexibility.

In the case of Chile, labour flexibility simultaneously acquired three different and complementary dimensions:

1 a functional labour flexibilization favoured a revision of job classifications, without respecting vested trade-union rights;
2 labour flexibility permitted a hiring-and-firing policy without any legal constraints; and
3 the possibility of wage reductions facilitated a major increase in precarious jobs in a period of economic slowdown.

Democracy did not just confront the Chilean labour movement with the political heritage of the repressive state, but also with a proliferation of authoritarian entrepreneurial regulations.

Bibliography

Agacino, R., Gonzáles, C. and Rojas, J. (1998) *Capital Transnacional y Trabajo: El Desarrollo Minero en Chile*, Santiago: PET/Lom.

Aravena, A. (1999) 'El sindicalismo en el sector comercio', *Revista Economía y Trabajo*, 9: Santiago de Chile: Programa de Economía del Trabajo (PET).

Cortázar, R. (1993) *Política Laboral en el Chile Democrático*, Santiago: Dolmen.

Cortázar, R. and Vial, J. (1998) *Construyendo opciones: Propuestas económicas y sociales para el cambio de siglo*, Santiago de Chile: Cieplan/Dolmen Ediciones.

Dirección del Trabajo (1999) *Informe de Prensa: Relaciones Laborales*, Santiago de Chile: Dirección del Trabajo, Ministerio del Trabajo.

—— (2000) *Informe de Prensa: Relaciones Laborales*, Santiago de Chile: Dirección del Trabajo, Ministerio del Trabajo.

Economic Commission for Latin America and the Caribbean (ECLAC) (1990) *Transformación Productiva con Equidad*, Santiago de Chile: ECLAC.

—— (2000) *Estudio Económico de América Latina y el Caribe 1998–1999*, Santiago de Chile: ECLAC.

Ensignia, J. and Castillo, G. (1998) *Libre Comercio, integración regional y dimensión social: Desafíos para el sindicalismo latinoamericano*, Santiago de Chile: Fundación Friedrich Ebert/International Labour Organization (ILO).

Escobar, P. (ed.) (1999) *Trabajadores y empleo en el Chile de los noventa*, Santiago de Chile: PET/Lom.

Fazio, H. (1997) *El Programa Abandonado: Balance Económico Social del Gobierno de Aylwin*, Santiago de Chile: Arcis/Lom/Cenda.

Frias, P. (1989) *El Movimiento Sindical Chileno en la Lucha por la Democracia*, Santiago de Chile: PET.

——— (1996) 'Desarrollo del Sindicalismo Chileno: 1995–1996', *Economía y Trabajo en Chile 1995–1996*, Informe No. 6. Santiago de Chile: Programa de Economía del Trabajo (PET).

Gonzales, C. (1998) 'Notas sobre empleo precario y precarización del empleo en Chile', *Revista Economía y Trabajo*, Informe No. 7 Santiago de Chile: PET.

International Labour Organization (1998) *Chile: Crecimiento, empleo y el desafío de la justicia social*, Santiago de Chile: ILO.

Klein, E. and Tokman, V. (2000) 'La estratificación social bajo tensión en la era de la globalización', *Revista de la Cepal*, 72: 7–30.

Meller, P. and Donoso, R. (1998) *La industria chilena y el MERCOSUR*, Santiago de Chile: Dolmen/Universidad de Chile.

Montero, C. (1997) *La Revolución Empresarial Chilena*, Santiago de Chile: Dolmen.

——— (1999) 'Las Relaciones Laborales: un asunto público?', in O. Muñoz (ed.) *El Estado y el Sector Privado: Construyendo una nueva economía en los años noventa*, Santiago de Chile: FLACSO.

Montero, C., Alburquerque, M. and Ensignia, J. (1999) *Trabajo y empresa entre dos siglos*, Caracas: Nueva Sociedad.

Morales, J. and McMahon, G. (1993) *La Política Económica en la Transición a la Democracia: Lecciones de Argentina, Bolivia, Chile y Uruguay*, Santiago de Chile: Cieplan.

Muñoz, O. (ed.) (1999) *El Estado y el Sector Privado: Construyendo una nueva economía en los años 90*, Santiago de Chile: FLACSO.

Muñoz, O. and Celedón, C. (1993) '*Chile en transición: estrategia económica y política*', *Revista de Ciena Politica*, 15: 87–122.

Peres, W. (ed.) *Políticas de Competitividad Industrial: América Latina y el Caribe en los Años Noventa*, Mexico City: Siglo XXI.

Pizarro, C., Raczynski, D. and Vial, J. (1995) *Políticas Económicas y Sociales en el Chile Democrático*, Santiago de Chile: Cieplan/Unicef.

Rozas, M. (1998) *Globalización y Concertación Social en Chile*, Santiago de Chile: International Labour Organization.

Tokman, V. and Martínez, D. (eds) (1999) *Flexibilización en el Margen: la Reforma del Contrato de Trabajo*, Santiago de Chile: International Labour Organization.

Weller, J. (2000) 'Tendencias del empleo en los años noventa en América Latina y el Caribe', *Revista de la Cepal*, 72: 31–50.

13 The condition of labour in the new Cuban economic model

Antonio Carmona Báez

Introduction

When it comes to fashionable trends in 'neo-liberal globalization', 'structural adjustment programmes', 'market orthodoxy', and 'transitional' or 'post-socialist' regimes, Cuba is often considered to be the exception to the rule. Despite the efforts of Washington's allies in Miami, the US economic embargo, the lack of access to international financial credit, and a turbulent economic crisis caused by the fall of the Socialist Bloc, Cuba remains firm in adhering to the Communist Party's (PCC) principle of state supremacy over the market. Ten years have passed since the end of the Cold War and, almost miraculously, Cuba's state-run market – which has undergone a series of autochthonous reforms – continues to experience real social and economic growth. However, the revolutionary leadership's success in surviving global pressures to privatize state corporations has not come to the fore without real structural changes in Cuba's line of production. Although Fidel Castro and the PCC leadership contend that the structural changes experienced in Cuba's political economy during the last decade have nothing to do with neo-liberalism, scant attention has been given to the striking similarities between the outcome of market-like reforms and the typical trends in the 'modes' of production found elsewhere (Castro 2000). Naturally, this study should concentrate on the condition of labour in Cuba and its transformation since the application of certain market reforms. By conditions of labour I mean here the various changes in working conditions and the wage framework, employment/unemployment, relations between workers and management, normative or legal standards in labour policy regarding flexibility and worker representation in public and governmental bodies.

The purpose of this chapter is to demonstrate how Cuba's state-run economic model has resisted global trends in state reductionism, while adjusting workers to new market conditions.[1] In essence, this is a survey of how labour relations have been affected by recent structural changes, and how labour has become more flexible. My principal argument is that when it comes to the specific issue of labour flexibility, Cuba's mode of production (with exceptions in certain areas of interest) does not differ that much from other countries in the present global political economy. My research reveals the government's eagerness to maintain supremacy over the market, and measures the elasticity of this socialist regime. The first task is to summarize Cuba's economic growth, the PCC's continuous commitment to social development and the normative (legal) parameters that have allowed for the same. Second, and as a contrast to the Communist euphoria, this article critically addresses two specific areas that reveal labour flexibility; these are the new *self-employment* and *the new Cuban enterprise system*.[2] To conclude, this chapter prepares the stage for future discussion on the theoretical consequences and considerations inspired by the Cuban experience.

The Special Period

The economic crisis that Cuba suffered during the first half of the 1990s can primarily be attributed to the gradual demise of the socialist market system (known as COMECON) and the eventual fall of the country's principal Cold War ally and economic sponsor, the Soviet Union. When the aforementioned entities fell, Cuba lost over 70 per cent of its trade and 40 per cent of the nation's purchasing power (Rodriguez Beruff *et al.* 1995). Additionally, anti-Castro forces in Miami and Washington, who were excited by the fall of socialist regimes in Europe, stepped up their efforts to destabilize the Cuban economy by enforcing the forty-year-old economic embargo.[3] Steadfast and loyal to the Revolution of 1959, the Cuban government sought measures for carrying the island through the drastic changes by implementing new laws and opening to market initiatives. This was called *el Periodo Especial en el Tiempo de Paz* (Special Period in the Time of Peace) (Eckstein 1994). Besides the austerity measures, whose burden was placed mostly on the people and not government leaders, the state employed a number of radical policies that changed the Cuban political economy for ever. Among the most important were the Constitutional Reforms of 1991, whereby the state no longer belonged to the 'proletariat', rather, it became the maximum expression of the 'people'. Also, the state went from being the proprietor of all of the means of production to owner of the most essential of the country's natural resources and economic structures (August 1999). Additionally, new laws came into being that were unheard of before the start of the economic crisis. For instance, in 1993, the government legalized the possession and use of hard currency (US dollars) by nationals (González Gutiérres 1998, Marquetti Nodarse 1998). Since most import commodities had to be paid for in hard currency, this created a gap between those with access to US dollars and those that did not. In the same year, the state officially recognized self-employment, which is dealt with throughout this chapter. Finally, in 1995, Cuban legislation allowed for foreign private entities to invest directly and up to 100 per cent in enterprises on the island (Carmona Báez 2000). As a result, the country started experiencing a slow recovery.

Demonstrable economic growth

Since 1996, the growth of Cuba's GNP growth rate has averaged 4.6 per cent per annum. In 2000, the GNP registered a growth of 5.6 per cent. This overall growth was fostered and accompanied by a 2.9 per cent reduction in energy use, a 3.5 per cent increase in labour productivity and a 16 per cent increase in domestic and foreign investment. The demonstrated growth in productivity in communal and social services was recorded at 3.4 per cent. Meanwhile, state workers' salaries have increased by 7.7 per cent, with a global increase targeted at schoolteachers and health-care workers. In terms of trade, Cuba remains a service-oriented economy, as 62 per cent of its exports are concentrated in services. Nevertheless, there was a 16 per cent increase in the export of goods and an 11 per cent increase in imports for domestic consumption.[4]

Towards the end of the 1990s, Cuba's unemployment rate dropped considerably. Whereas in 1998, the official unemployment rate was 7 per cent, this number dropped during the course of 2000 to 5.5 per cent.[5] This was especially due to the creation of jobs by gearing the country's economy towards tourism. Opening of new enterprises with foreign capital has also helped the economy. But, as is demonstrated in the section concerning self-employment, the reduction in unemployment is also dependent on the flexibility of labour that emanated from the reforms carried out during the last decade. Nevertheless, in 1999, 87,000 new permanent jobs were created in tourism in the eastern provinces of the country (Oriente). The average salary among Cuban state workers went from 211 pesos in 1998 to 223 pesos in 1999, indicating a 5.7 per cent increase. This is excluding bonuses that are given in dollars. Work-place bonuses increased by 18.9 per cent between 1999 and 2000, whereas in 2000, US$53.2 million was distributed throughout the work-place as bonus incentives (*Notimex*, 1 June 2001: 1).

It is this miracle that keeps global economists, friends and enemies of the Revolution in awe. How does a basic-level industrial and service-oriented Third World economy of socialist government and state supremacy, with an anti-neoliberal stance demonstrated in its discourse, produce such exceptional results while maintaining, for the majority of the population, a guaranteed access to health care and education? According to government propaganda, this economic growth is not yet satisfactory and still does not resemble that experienced during the 1980s, prior to the collapse of the former Socialist Bloc. Nevertheless, the country has just begun to recover and, according to government propaganda and the country's leading economists, is on its way to irreversible social and capital growth (Pages 2000). Things like power outages, abandoned cars on the sides of roads and a lack of variety in products – that were all prevalent up until 1996 – are not that common today (Rangel 2001).

The causes of economic growth

There are four principal factors that have contributed to the economic success story and, more specifically, those that have contributed to the acquisition of foreign capital. First, the growth can be attributed to having geared the economy to the service sector, especially in tourism. This sector experienced growth during 2000 with 1.8 million visitors primarily from Canada, Germany, Italy, Spain, France, the UK, Mexico and Argentina. This is five times more visitors than in 1990 (the start of Cuba's economic crisis) (*Granma Internacional*, 15 May 2001). Additionally, in 2000, foreign investors and Cuban state corporations poured US$21.6 million into the tourism industry. Tourism now employs 90,000 workers directly (in hotels, airports, and transportation and as guides). Indirectly, this service industry links a network of 300,000 workers in the service line (renting of automobiles and other popular services provided for tourists, such as massages, mineral baths, sports facilities and restaurants) (*Ibid.*).

The second area of improvement that contributed to Cuba's economic growth was the reduction in wasteful energy use through efficiency plans rather than austerity measures. The PCC pointed out that in agriculture, for example, a more efficient use of energy has been demonstrated. In 1989, the harvest of one metric tonne of tropical vegetables and tubers used up 95 kg of diesel and 19 kg of gasoline. In 2000, 37 kg of diesel and 3 kg of gasoline were used to produce the same amount. Efficient use of energy was also demonstrated in nickel production.[6] The third causal attribute to Cuba's new economy has been the increase in the extraction of local petroleum and its use to generate electricity, and in the production of cement and nickel. This has led to a greater independence for the country's energy sector. The prospects for more exploitation of local oil seem to be quite good, as recent geological reports have revealed large untapped petroleum wells on Cuba's west coast (Cuban territorial Gulf of Mexico). In 2000, 2.8 million tonnes of crude oil were discovered on Cuban territory. The increase in petroleum production saved the state US$400 million in 2000. Currently, the burning of petroleum produced by domestic oil reserves generates 70 per cent of the country's electricity (*Granma Internacional*, 15 January 2001).

Finally, foreign investment can be lauded as the most important contributor to Cuba's economic growth. Without it, the sectors of tourism, petroleum extraction and tobacco exports would not have experienced growth. Although most investors are still participating through partial ownership contracts with the Cuban government, direct investment up to 100 per cent has increased since the law on foreign direct investment (FDI) was passed in 1995. Between 1996 and 2000 approximately US$4 billion has been invested in the country by FDI. In total, there are currently 394 associations operating with foreign capital (MEP 2001: 3–4).

Social development

Cuban government discourse and propaganda often reiterate the importance of social development in parallel with economic growth.[7] In Cuba, the allocation of resources to the programmes that guarantee social development are not considered to be mere costs, as is the case in most countries that practice the neo-liberal reduction of the state. Rather, investment of capital and materials into social programmes are considered to be satisfying the PCC's priorities. This was demonstrated during the years of economic crisis (during the 1990s), when the government continued to pour money into education and health care. But the state's contribution to social development is not simply moralistic. The investment into maintaining social development is rewarded with the production of a highly educated and healthy cadre of workers that are ready to confront the current global political economy.

The largest source for social development reports has come out of the United Nations Human Development Report of the United Nations Development Programme (UNDP), which uses tools such as the Index on Human Poverty (IHP). According to this tool of measurement in 1997, Cuba has only 5.1 per cent of its population living below the poverty level. That places the country second out of the seventy-eight countries that have allowed the UNDP to measure their social development standards (UNDP 1997).[8] The same organization measures what is called the Index for Gender Development (IGD). The purpose of this tool is to measure equality between the sexes in terms of standard of living, education and employment (profession and salary). The UNDP includes 104 countries this report, including industrialized and economically advanced countries (the United States, The Netherlands and Japan). Cuba ranks 21st, with more than half of its technical managers and engineers being female (UNDP 1997).[9]

Cuba's social record has even caught the attention of international financial institutions which have promoted many of the neo-liberal policies that the revolutionary leadership rejected. According to World Bank indicators and statistics, Cuba, despite its slow and stable progress to economic recovery, has a record that demonstrates the enhancement of its social achievements. The health-care system has reduced the country's infant mortality rate from 11 per 1,000 in 1990 to 7 per 1,000 in 1999. This places Cuba firmly in the ranks of the most economically advanced nations. According to World Bank Vice-President for Development Policy, Jo Ritzen, the infant mortality rate for 2000 stood at 6 per 1,000. This can be attributed to the fact that the government dedicated 9.1 per cent of its GDP during the entire decade of the 1990s to health care; this is equivalent to Canada's rate for the same time period. In 2000, Cuba achieved the highest doctor/patient ratio in the world; the rate was 5.3 doctors per 1,000 people (Lobe 2001). It is therefore little wonder that Cuba does not have a problem sending medical experts to disaster areas in neighbouring Latin American countries, free of charge.[10]

In 2000, public spending on education amounted to approximately 6.7 per cent of Cuba's gross national income; this continues to be twice the proportion in other Latin American and Caribbean countries and even in places like Singapore. In 1997, there were twelve primary-school pupils for every Cuban teacher; this ratio ranked equally with Sweden (Lobe 2001). These statistics reflect a growing appreciation in the World Bank for Cuba's social record, despite the fact that Cuba's economic policies are virtually the antithesis of the 'Washington consensus' on neo-liberal economic orthodoxy, with its structural adjustment programmes. It is ironic that the same institutions that prescribed privatization and state reductionism now praise Cuba's anti-model. Productivity and increasing GNP were often considered to be the prerequisites for social development. Cuba's experience, even during the worst years of the Special Period, has proven this assumption to be wrong.

However, although social and economic indicators can be very telling of how the country's leadership successfully inserted the national economy into the world market, the condition of labour needs to be studied at a different level. Essentially, two structural changes affected labour relations in Cuba since the 1990s. These are the formalization and recognition of self-employment and the decentralization of state-owned enterprises.

Cuentapropismo

The new self-employment in Cuba

In 1993, the Council of State and Cuba's national parliament (the National Assembly of People's Power) passed Decree-Law 141, which formalized a system allowing individuals to create their small private businesses.[11] Maintaining the socialist theme of prohibiting 'the exploitation of man by man', the new system became a means for capable individuals to use their own time and resources for profit. As mentioned above, the law of self-employment is one of a series of legislative actions taken by the Cuban state leadership to cope with the economic crisis of the 1990s. Where the state was incapable of providing goods and services to the general population, the black or underground marketeers stepped in to meet the daily needs of the people. The Cuban government sought a cure for black-market activity, where goods and services were produced without the state benefiting from them and where the police force was used, albeit in a futile fashion, to stop a popular means of survival. This, together with the state's inability to provide the population with the most basic of daily needs, is what created the new system of self-employment known in Cuba as *trabajo por cuenta propia* or *cuentapropismo*.[12]

Initially, the opening up to self-employment was thought of as the precursor of small-scale private capitalism in Cuba (Espinosa 2000). With this in mind, some critics of the Revolution might have assumed that state supremacy over the market was at an end. The hopes of Cuba opening up to small-scale, private capitalism have been constantly expressed in Miami-based newsgroups like Cubanet Independiente (see *http://www.cubanet.org*, accessed 13 June 2001). In a growing economy, it was thought, self-employment should have become a more popular means of obtaining income. Curiously enough, as the national economy experienced relatively stable growth in almost all sectors, the number of regis-tered self-employed workers has steadily decreased since the implementation of the new tax regime in 1996. Until 1995 no revenue service for individual income had existed. Where in 1995 there were 208,346 registered *cuentapropistas*, by mid-2000 the number had fallen to 109,502 (Figure 13.1).

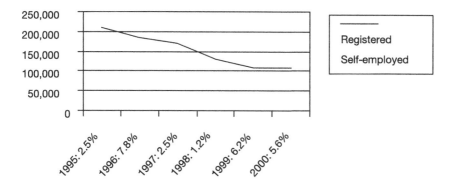

Figure 13.1 Cuba: number of registered self-employed in comparison with the rate of growth of GDP

Source: Cuban Ministry of Economic Planning and Ministry of Labour and Social Security (Ministerio de Economiía y Planificación and Ministerio de Trabajo y Seguridad Social) *Informe Económico, 1996–2000; Informe sobre el cuentapropismo, 1995–2000*

A sharp fall in the numbers of self-employed was experienced in 1996, when 19,668 *cuentapropistas* left self-employment for unemployment, the black market or back into the state sector. In 1997, when the rate of growth of GDP increased – but was not as high as the year before – only 14,417 *cuentapropistas* were registered. When economic growth slowed down in 1998, over 41,000 *cuentapropistas* revoked their licences. However, between 1999 and 2000 the number of self-employed individuals did not rise, as did GDP. Conversely, it fell slowly and then levelled off. According to government sources, the drop in self-employment can be attributed to the implementation of new tax regime and new employment possibilities.[13] But this is only partially true. From my own surveys and interviews, in combination with government reports and other documentation, I have found that the state leadership intends to reduce this sector or at least curb the number of its participants. By analysing this tendency of the state to control the self-employed sector (and doing so secretively or without a clear PCC statement), some important socio-political contradictions concerning the impact of Cuba's insertion into the global political economy can be revealed.[14]

The new self-employment system presents Cuban society with a number of problems. Five of these problems are dealt with here. The first three are problems that cannot be quantified, as the impact or damage produced by the contradictions have not been tested due to a lack (intentional or not) of government information. The last two are measurable, as they present a proven problem for the domestic political economy.

The first issue that concerns *cuentapropismo* is the question of recognizing private incentives for work. This was more of an ideological problem than a practical one, as self-employment relieved the issue of food distribution and other services during the Special Period. But when ideology is intended to be manifested in economic reality, then the maintenance of *state supremacy* over the means of production and services is put into question. Second, the monitoring of business practices put another cost on government spending, whereas new positions and committees for research in the self-employed sectors had to be set up. Additionally, a group of health inspectors are employed to control standards in the sale of food (MFP 1996). There is no way of measuring this phenomenon, as the amount of money spent on police control of the self-employment system and on research is currently not available from the Cuban government. The third problem is the unjust, quite rigid, and rudimentary means of collecting taxes. The state depends on a badly trained, inexperienced group of inspectors and tax collectors, often accompanied by the police, to handle the contribution that *cuentapropistas* produce for the national economy. It does not require much imagination to consider the possibilities for corruption, abuse against the self-employed and government losses.[15]

Among the real or proven problems that *cuentapropismo* presents in Cuba today, there is a fourth, the accelerating problem of varying levels of income. This presents not only an ideological problem, but also a concrete contradiction in the socialist project of maintaining economic equality for its citizens (González Gutiérrez 1998: 16). Since the new law on self-employment made *cuentapropismo* open to the dollar market, many individuals began making money in high dollar rates. An example based on my own 1999 enquiry,[16] demonstrated a grotesque difference between individuals actually earning a net income of US$500 per month versus those state employees earning the average and miserable US$10 per month (223 pesos). The difference is not only reflected in comparing *cuentapropistas* with state workers, but also by distinguishing those self-employed individuals earning in pesos and those earning in dollars. According to state sources, the government is prepared to acknowledge and tax self-employed dollar earners making over US$60,000 per year.[16] All of the dollar-earning self-employed that I have interviewed have family residing outside Cuba. This indicates that many of the new and successful businesses like *paladares* (home restaurants) and bed-and-breakfast hotels are generally funded by family abroad, who were able to send their Cuban relatives dollar remittances to start and maintain high-income earnings.

Income disparity has been somewhat curbed by the implementation of the tax system in 1996; prior to this (between 1993 and 1995) the difference in income levels must have been astronomical. But, according to one PCC representative, today there are millionaires in Cuba, who have worked both legally and illegally in order to accumulate wealth and property (Interviews 2001). Indeed, while state workers are receiving their miserable salaries, some *cuentapropistas* are making tens of thousands of US dollars.

The majority of those *cuentapropistas* interviewed in my survey stated that they did not consider themselves to comprise a social or economic class different from state workers. The reason being, the bulk of their earnings fall into the hands of the state in the form of taxes or monthly contributions.[17] Additionally, the *cuentapropistas* are forced to purchase all of their input from state businesses and wholesale. So even if some self-employed individuals and small business owners may have ideas about themselves that resemble a certain divergence from the reality of most Cuban workers, their position in production and providing services remains subordinate to the state. Nevertheless, income disparity provides Cuban society with a class-like structure that distinguishes between those with greater economic opportunities and comfort, and those without. Essentially, *cuentapropismo* and the income disparity that follows from this undermine the Revolution's mission to implement economic equality among Cubans.

The fifth problem is that of representation of self-employed interests in the party–state apparatus, whereas the *cuentapropista* has no collective voice in the national trade union (Central de Trabajadores Cubanos – CTC). Again, in 2000, there were over 109,502 people registered as officially self-employed, which is 3 per cent of the entire working population. The percentage may be small, but the number still represents a significant number of Cuban workers who do not participate in labour organizations.

To this day, few government reports on *cuentapropismo* have been made public, and few, if any, of the above-mentioned problems are dealt with within PCC discourse. The only interesting point of discussion presented by the government was the reduction in the number of participants in the self-employed sector. As mentioned earlier, the reduction in the number of officially registered *cuentapropistas* was – according to the government – related to overall national economic growth; however, this is not entirely the case. Although the PCC does not make its attitude towards the self-employed obvious in public discourse, the restrictions under which *cuentapropistas* must operate indicate a number of considerations that should be analysed. Among them: strict control over this sector, steep taxation, the use of police force for control, and the link between self-employment and unemployment.

State regulations concerning *cuentapropistas* are outlined in a document called *Orientaciones a Trabajadores por Cuenta Propia* (Orientations for Self-employed Workers), published by the Ministry of Labour and Social Security (MTSS 1995). This document makes clear who can and cannot participate in the new self-employment system: the rules concerning the conduct of business, the procedure for the paying of taxes and monthly contributions, the number of partners a *cuentapropista* may have, etc. The rules are strict and sometimes complicated. For instance, recent university graduates are barred from participating in *cuentapropismo*, whereas a retired or displaced worker with a university degree may set up his or her own business. At some points, the rules can be fastidiously detailed. For example, elaborate or processed food (pizza, cakes, sandwiches) in one's home cannot be served on a plate or with utensils. The popular *paladares*, or family-run restaurants, can only have twelve seats to service their customers. These examples demonstrate what the state wants to allow in the space that it provides for private business. Since the state is the proprietor of most of Cuba's restaurants, it would not want to have a domestic competitor. Whether or not this control is effective is another question (especially when *paladares* are known to serve better-quality food at a cheaper price), but the state's intentions are hence revealed (Martín Pérez 1999).

Eventually, *cuentapropismo* has proved to be a new state mechanism that recouped 'an excess of liquidity' that was running through the hands of the population, in addition to the losses that the state experienced via black-market activity. The new revenue (tax) system, run by the Office of Tributary Collections (ONAT), implemented in 1996, was the mechanism that assisted the state in reaping a considerable amount of money from this sector.[18] In 2001, the Ministry of Finance and Prices (MPF) published the amount of state income generated by taxes on the self-employed. During the whole of 1999, the state recouped 1.05 billion pesos from taxes imposed upon this sector. That is, state income generated from the official self-employed system amounted to approximately US$50 million.[19]

The *cuentapropista* must pay both an annual income tax and a monthly contribution. The amount of money to be paid to the ONAT is set according to the profession and to the area in which the self-employed are conducting their business (MTSS 1995). For instance, someone operating a guesthouse out of his or her home in Varadero (a popular tourist area with beaches and five-star hotels), will pay close to US$1,000 per month, as opposed to his or her counterpart in the centre of Santiago city who would pay US$300–500 per month (Interviews 1999). On top of the monthly contribution, the *cuentapropista* will pay an additional tax on the 'excess' amount of profits made throughout the year. The annual profit tax is scheduled by the provincial committee of the ONAT, which obliges every private establishment to carry a book of records indicating sales or services provided on a daily basis. The register book should be available to inspectors and police on demand (MTSS 1995).

Another form of control that is employed by the government is the use of the police force and the group of inspectors that are delegated to control *cuentapropismo*. As mentioned in the endnotes for this chapter, the police accompany provincial inspectors of the MTSS in order to implement state policy and execute controls like fines and taxes. This makes it more difficult for those who choose to participate in illegal or unregistered activity. As a tourist or dollar holder, it is not uncommon to be invited to illegal *paladares*, for instance, where a home-cooked meal can be served at a reasonable price. But if one goes to these illegal establishments, one will always sense the fear and secretiveness of those who are serving. At times, police raids are conducted upon the houses of *cuentapropistas*. The fear of police repression, as well as being turned in by 'neighbourhood spies', is real. Another example is the control over self-employed taxi drivers who use their own cars for transportation services. Tourists, once in Cuba, can travel freely throughout the island at their own expense, but Cuban self-employed taxi drivers are prohibited from serving tourists. Therefore, police blockades and control points are seen everywhere on the roads of the island. If a foreigner is 'caught' in a *cuentapropista* taxi, the taxi driver (and not the tourist) is fined up to US $100 (Interviews 1999).

But there is more to placing strict controls on the *cuentapropista* than just bureaucracy for bureaucracy's sake. Out of all the reforms that came out of the Special Period, this was the most backward and contradictory to the model of full employment by the state under a so-called socialist economy. The conditions under which the participants work might have been acceptable under the emergency circumstances that were experienced during the years of economic crisis. However, the present self-employment regime cannot last that much longer in its current form, as police oppression, theft and corruption occur on a daily basis, in a growing economy where the demands for goods are high. One could not expect that a highly educated *cuentapropista* would tolerate the volatile conditions which *cuentapropismo* has to offer. However, no PCC programme concerning the self-employed has been adopted.

From studying the experiences of the self-employed, one can conclude that the dip in the number of practising and registered *cuentapropistas* between 1995 and 2001 was not only attributable to improvements in the Cuban economy. Rather, the drop is also related to the realization that many self-employed individuals cannot handle the pressures imposed on them by the government (Interviews 1999). On the other hand, with the exception of recent university graduates, Cubans are free to choose their job occupation. Although some may have to enter the world of theft and prostitution in order to make ends meet in their household, no one is forced to apply for a licence for self-employment. Or are they?

According to figures provided by the Ministry of Labour and Social Security, 30.8 per cent of those officially registered as self-employed were previously considered to be unemployed or displaced workers. Another 24.9 per cent held regular state-sector jobs, 23 per cent of the registered *cuentapropistas* are retired state workers, and another 19.2 per cent were formally housewives. The remaining 1.9 per cent of those who are officially registered as self-employed are classified as having 'another' economic history (Núñez Moreno 1998). Whether or not Cuba's housewives exist justifiably apart from the unemployed is a question to be dealt with by economists. But that over 30 per cent of Cuba's *cuentapropistas* were previously and formally considered unemployed, is quite telling as regards the state's purpose for maintaining the small individual private market.

The significance of *cuentapropismo* is that the state has recognized that unemployment is a chronic problem in Cuba, meaning that it will never be solved under the restrictions that it is facing: the restrictions have been caused by global and domestic factors which dictate or define Cuba's new political economy, i.e. partly beyond the state's control. Even though the state in its discourse is bent on reducing the unemployment rate, there are no guarantees that unemployment will cease to exist.[20] One of the measures that the government has taken in order to control unemployment has been the reduction of class sizes in order to open the job market for more elementary school teachers (*Notimex*, 1 June 2001: 1). But this solves only the problem of unemployment among university and middle-level educated youth.

Cuentapropismo is also seen as a relief for retired citizens (many of whom are members of the PCC), by adding to their household income and offering an alternative activity to occupy their day (Núñez Moreno 1998: 3, Interviews

1999). But it is really the need to earn extra dollars that turns retirees to self-employment. The same is true for housewives; why would a housewife opt to work under the strict conditions imposed upon *cuentapropistas* instead of working for a government business, agency or organization? If the housewife is willing to use her home as a place of employment, or walk the streets to sell peanuts, this would mean that she is in search for an extra income. One may conclude that unemployment has come to stay for a while in Cuba and *cuentapropismo* is a small remedy that the government offers to the most vulnerable sectors of society. However, if the government finds a partial remedy to unemployment in *cuentapropismo*, then why all the control and harassment of self-employed individuals?

From the sample provided by my enquiry, I found that those who earn in dollars while receiving benefits from family abroad tended to rate the Cuban government less favourably than their peso-earning counterparts.[21] It appears that the state is intentionally avoiding the building of a *petit-bourgeoisie*. But, while it does this, the ones that suffer the most are those poorer sectors of society that have no alternative other than to turn to *cuentapropismo*. At the same time, while self-employment is a controlled and suppressed alternative to state employment, it can also offer a higher level of income than state salaries. Those who are earning hundreds and even thousands of dollars on a monthly basis can be expected to remain among those labelled *cuentapropistas*, because somehow they can afford to pay taxes and maintain friendly relations with inspectors. This problem can become dangerous for the PCC, as it groups a number of self-employed individuals into an anti-state or state's competitor category.

The Cuban state has reaped rewards from the self-employed, but this has not occurred by the government pulling out of the sphere of small production and services. On the contrary, by creating this animal – called *cuentapropismo* – the state has appropriated a portion of what was formally the black market. In short, the state has expanded its control over the economy while recognizing flexible labour. The future of self-employment will depend on how serious Castro's government is about reducing the level of unemployment in addition to creating new permanent jobs for the next generation of healthy and educated Cubans.

Cuba's most radical change

During the Fifth PCC Congress in 1997, the themes of decentralization, economic efficiency and competition became more pronounced in party discourse.[22] Cuba's political economy was said to have reached a new stage of development. In turn, Party discourse became officially a programme for furthering economic growth and national development. It called for a change in the line of production and a transformation in the mentality of entrepreneurial leadership, in order to behave and conduct business as if the Cuban economy was based upon private market capitalism. The purpose was to increase productivity, especially for exports such as nickel.[23] This was possible by giving more autonomy to the directors of enterprises, to act as they see fit, but within the confines of state or public ownership. Hence, production in socialist Cuba is no longer geared towards meeting the basic needs of its citizens, but clearly to the demands of consumers both inside and outside Cuba. Along with this change in the *raison d'être* came a decrease in the state's subsidization of inefficient or unprofitable production. This process became known as *el sistema de perfeccionamiento empresarial* (entrepreneurial perfection), hereafter, SPE.

The SPE has its roots in the reform processes experienced by the nation's military–industrial complex, headed by General Raul Castro (Fidel Castro's brother). Military–industrial complex refers here to the business line that the military created for its own purposes. During the Special Period, even the military cut expenditure, and conditions proved difficult for career soldiers. Troops were no longer sent to foreign countries, and had to concentrate on producing their own food for subsistence. Raul's famous words were that 'beans are more important than guns' (*Economic Intelligence Unit/Country Profile*, 1993: 7, *Granma Internacional*, 5 May 1993: 4). The military's main contribution to society during the years of economic crisis was the transport of produce to markets and government centres for redistribution, and sugar-field work. But when it did so, it was efficient. This meant that when the military took over a business or task that was usually done by civilians, it reduced the number of workers involved, and it completed the task in a timely fashion (Interviews 2001). The guiding principle was to produce more and better-quality results with a smaller workforce, less energy and no waste. After the worst years of the economic crisis (1996 and onwards), Raul Castro remained in control of the tasks that were taken over by the military. As the entire nation went in search of hard currency, the military likewise sought capital growth. Raul Castro became, then, a sort of President–CEO of the entrepreneurial FAR (Revolutionary Armed Forces).

Among the existing entities that produce for military consumption and sale are: *Uniones Agropecuaria Militar*, which deals with agricultural products produced by the army, mostly sugar; *Industria Militar*, which produces everything from military clothing to guns and tanks; *Construcciones Militares*, which produces cement and construction materials for public housing; defence centres, schools and hospitals, and *GEOCUBA* which is an excavation company that locates and exploits natural petroleum deposits. These four companies are under the direct leadership of Raul Castro (*Granma International*, 18 May 2001: 2).

The Council of State, together with a number of unnamed social and economic research centres in Havana, the FAR, and also a number of business leaders formed a working group that sought means to implement the military mode of production at all state enterprises.[24] Officially, this entity, known as the Executive's Commission for the SPE, came into being in 1998. Nevertheless, I would venture to say that the working group was started well before the Fifth PCC Congress, as the Party Congress' documents and Economic Resolution legitimized the SPE. The military's experience was to be applied to state corporations and to serve as a model for the future Cuban economy. Currently, the Executive Commission for the SPE continues to be monitored by the FAR.[25] Its current Director is the former military Colonel Armando Betancourt Perez. As of the year 2000, the FAR have five *Juntas de Gobierno* (government boards of direction), which monitor businesses in the SPE. According to General Raul Castro, 'the SPE has to be a journey without delay and no return'. The actual workings of the SPE have been documented by the MTSS and its SPE Executive Commission (*Granma Internacional*, 18 May 2001: 2).

While recognizing that production in an isolated socialist economy does not directly serve the needs of the workers, the language in the texts prepared for the SPE also demonstrates the changes in labour relations. The PCC-sponsored texts are embellished with socialist rhetoric, but their structure recalls those of the private corporations found in market economies (see Government of Cuba on *http://www.nuevaempresa.cu* (accessed 13 June 2001)). The ultimate goal of the SPE is to transform all national businesses into modern, efficient and globally competitive entities that produce commodities and provide services that are marketable and profitable. In order to do this, each company must conform to the standards and prerequisites that make national enterprises eligible to partici- pate in the new economy without major investments coming from public resources.

Application of the SPE entails subjecting each participating company or corporation to a series of four phases. The first phase involves organizing and computerizing all systems of accounting in order to make the companies nation- ally compatible with the standards that guide the SPE. The second phase is to achieve an accurate balance of expenditure and income in order to prepare for profit maximization. The third phase consists of implementing the new hierar- chical structure of production and management that is indicated in the documents that govern the SPE's activities. This phase includes reducing the number of overlapping positions within the company in order to reduce costs, i.e. downsizing. The final phase is to reach a substantial level of profit gain that is planned by a compromise between the Executive Commission for the SPE and the Directorship Committee (explained in detail below) of each enterprise within a two-year period. Additionally, this phase will include a demonstrable continual decrease in energy use and an annual reduction in waste. In order for a corpora- tion to be considered as a participant in the SPE, it must follow these phases. Again, the Executive Commission of the SPE, which is heavily influenced by the military leadership, strictly controls the approval of each phase (*Government of Cuba, Introducción*: 3–14).

Structural changes in production

The Executive Commission of the SPE appoints a director for each business, company or corporation; this guides the entity in every aspect of operations, personnel relations and financial planning. Under the director, there are three vice-directors who control specifically the areas of accounting, management and future planning. To assist the director of each entity, a directorship committee will serve as a board to deal specifically with personnel relations and to monitor planning and economic growth. The directorship committee consists of a group of economic experts appointed to oversee the changes being made during integration into the SPE. This committee of experts has no executive power, but rather serves as a witnessing group and base for input in ideas for discussion, suggestions and considerations. It is also considered to be an organ of conflict resolution, and a unit for studying problems arising between management and workers. This committee is the 'democratic' and 'socialist' face of the SPE. It is composed of five to seven members, which include one position reserved for the worker's union (CTC), one for the UJC (Union of Young Communists) and two or four workers elected from their colleagues. A member of the PCC may also be invited to participate in this committee. This Directorship Committee replaces many of the functions of the CTC representatives in each work-place, including planning, work scheduling and regulating personnel (*Government of Cuba, Política laboral y salarial* (hereafter PLS): 1).

In a company that is applying the SPE, a certain hierarchy exists that distinguishes between the various levels of production. Although the distinctions have always existed in Cuba, they have never been as pronounced and ordained by state authority as they are today. In a state-owned corporation, workers are divided up into categories that reflect the same kind of division of labour found in any capitalist economy or private company. The various levels involved in production are broken down into the following categories: Workers, Service and Dispensation Operators, Administration and Secretarial Workers, Technicians and Project Managers, and the Directors (PLS: 3).

The salaries are offered on a sliding scale and are graded according to experience and capacity. The grading system works on a scale from I to XXI. Workers, service operators and administrative staff start off with a grade I salary and can eventually attain a grade IX. Grade I workers start off earning 150 pesos per month and grade IX workers earn 345 pesos per month. Service operators can start off at 130 pesos per month and their grade IX is, at best, 285 pesos per month; the same scale is used for administration. Technicians can receive salaries from grades IV to XIII. Directors' grades range from III to XXI, depending on the size, productivity and capacity of the company. Technicians starting at grade IV–V earn 205 pesos per month and may eventually earn salaries up to 375 pesos per month. The starting salaries for directors are 205 pesos per month and their grade XXI is 700 pesos per month. These salaries represent the minimum wage and do not include added tips and profit sharing that are offered according to productivity. All in all, the minimum wage for all participants in the production process can range from 130 pesos per month to 700 pesos per month. In hard currency, that would be US$6.50 per month up to US$35 per month. The average salary earned in an SPE enterprise (in hard currency) is hence $20.75 per month. The salaries are dispensed directly by the company's administration and no longer by the MTSS or CTC representative, as was the case prior to the SPE (PLS: 3–5).

These salaries reflect only the minimum wages for workers, managers and directors. What is peculiar to the SPE is the possibility and/or need to earn more than the salaries indicated by law. Although the average minimum salary in an SPE enterprise amounts to US$20.75 per month, no one is expected to live off this small amount of money. Propaganda concerning workers' wages, specifically those clichés stating that salaries are low because other costs are covered or subsidized by the government (i.e. housing, health care and education), has fallen by the wayside during the Special Period explained at the beginning of this chapter. Since the economy has been dollarized, and most material goods of value related to the increase in standard of living are sold in hard currency only, Cubans continue to be limited in their purchasing power. Again, only those with access to US dollars can purchase materials that will improve their living conditions beyond the basic welfare measures maintained by the state. Hence, a supplementary system has been developed alongside the SPE, which allows the director, together with the directorship committee, to set standards in salary increases. The salary increments are not uniform and are to be related directly to the productivity and profits of each company individually, after the company makes its contribution to the national budget. This is where the old system of equal income for all workers is replaced by a market-like plan of worker compensation (PLS: 7–14, Interviews 2001).

Prior to the SPE, no worker (including the manager) of a company had his or her salary directly linked to the level of production or amount of services provided by the company. Under the new system, the salaries of all employees and directors depend directly on output. This implies a development of unstable salaries and a direct dependence upon global structures and financial fluctuations. For the first time, the Cuban government is exposing its workers directly to the oscillating trends of the domestic and world market, the difference here being that certain human rights considered by the PCC are guaranteed, such as housing, education, medicine and social security. But, for the first time in Cuban revolutionary history, managers are being rewarded according to the results of their subordinate's work. Not only managers, but also administrators and workers, have their monthly income adjusted on an irregular basis. Nevertheless, it is the top directorship that handles accounting and reports on profit increases to the MTSS and the Ministry of Finance and Prices. One does not have to be an expert to imagine the level of corruption that this new system of supplementary income might attract. But corrupt or not, the fact is that a central authority is no longer responsible for overseeing the redistribution of profits in the workplace. If the Directorship Committee does its job justly, then the results can imply an increase in the standard of living for Cuban workers. If not, the Cuban worker will fall victim to the same market forces as his/her counterpart in a market society. Despite the danger, the SPE's website publication, *Nueva Empresa Cubana*, states that the organization of salaries is specified to reflect the application of the socialist principle of distribution: 'from each according to his/her capacity and to each according to his work' (PLS: 1).

Together with the SPE's new structural scheme, there exists a policy that relates specifically to the position of contractual labour rules and personnel relations. A new contracting system was invented – or, rather, copied – from the market system of corporate employment. All workers, managers, technicians and other employees under the Director are currently obliged to sign a Work

Contract that guarantees employment and spells out position requirements and duties. The contract is based on a year's service including a three-month evaluation period where the worker can demonstrate his/her commitment to the enterprise. At any point, the Director may feel free to dismiss workers for their non-compliance with company regulations and work standards. Prior to the Special Period and the construction of the SPE, firing an employee was a much more difficult mission, and no evaluation period was ever required. Additionally, the Director, together with the Directorship Committee has absolute control over benefits like paid holidays. Again, what was once controlled centrally by the state is now rendered to the will and discretion of the decentralized administration (PLS: 2–3).

Since downsizing is an essential characteristic of the implementation of the structural reforms of self-management and decentralization, the SPE had to formulate a national policy of labour dismissal that was compatible with the PCC's concerns about reducing unemployment, which were mentioned in the documents prepared by the Fifth PCC Congress. Workers can be dismissed from their work-place on the basis of necessary downsizing, low levels of productivity or the expiry of a contract period. In order to keep a human or socialist face on labour relations, the termination of employment is phrased as 'worker relocation' or 'displacement' (PLS: 2–3). According to this policy, the SPE set for itself a responsibility with which the state no longer deals. That is, unemployment benefits and guaranteeing a new job for the displaced worker.

The central government via the MTSS continues to provide social security for these displaced workers, but only through the company's budget and up to six months (PLS: 10). Thereafter, if no other employment is found the salary will be reduced to 50 per cent. If after a full year no employment or contract is designated to the worker, then the worker will be sent to a temping agency and the company will be obligated to offer the ex-employee a three-option solution outside the sphere of influence in which the company usually operates. One of these options could be self-employment. But it suffices to say here that no engineer in his/her right mind will opt for self-employment and the rigid conditions that the system entails when one has his/her salary and tips linked to productivity in an efficient state enterprise, foreign company or joint venture. Therefore, the state-corporation really offers only two alternatives after the worker is dismissed from a job. Currently, the SPE is developing a relocation policy where a dislocated employee may have the right to find employment within the SPE system (Interviews 2001).

So far, only a few companies have been successful in the application of the SPE and have conformed to the rigidity of the programme. Again the guidelines include: a substantial profit gain within the period of two years; a small number of full-time employees; a continual decrease in the use of energy in relation to the production of services; and an annual reduction of waste. In 1998 300 companies attempted to enter into the new system. By the end of 1999, 295 enterprises were suspended from the programme for not having kept proper accounts. Nevertheless, the SPE spread rapidly within a two-year period. As of

March 2001, sixty-four state-owned businesses have conformed to the requirements of the SPE and have passed the four principal phases. By the end of 2001,
300 companies will have applied the SPE and will be working under its new
market system of initiatives. According to SPE publicity, by the end of 2001, all
of the nickel industry, a high portion of the petroleum industry, and a substantial
percentage of the mineral-processing industry – in short, practically all of the
Ministry of Basic Industry – will be under the SPE. The Institute of Hydraulic
Resources will be included as well. The nickel and electricity companies are the
most successful. The new companies, e.g. the new oil companies, are most likely
to succeed, as they are starting from scratch and do not have an accounting
history to clean up (*Granma Internacional*, 16 March 2001). In the sixty-four
companies that have undergone the managerial reforms, around 2.5 per cent of
the employees were laid off and gradually relocated to other companies (*Granma
Internacional*, 16 March 2001).

Conclusions

Cuba's experience throughout most of the 1990s, and the start of the new
millennium, has demonstrated new possibilities in state-run economies. The
government has proven to be flexible, and economic efficiency has overridden
the traditional PCC ideology, or at least adjusted it to accommodate for income
disparity and the disposal of workers at the management's behest. In a state-run
economy labour can also become flexible; it can even allow for small private
enterprises to exist in the form of self-employment. Decentralization plans,
which allow business leaders to become more autonomous in directing their lines
of production, can also exist without threatening the base of political power in
central government. This was demonstrated through the military's influence over
the new state corporation. The information provided on the Cuban mode of
production might be disheartening for left-wing romantics, as income disparity
and unemployment are presented as new contradictions. But it should not be as
disturbing as it is to orthodox economists who have insisted that state-run
economies are doomed to fail.

While during this era of neo-liberal globalization, where the state (especially
in developing countries) is often characterized as a declining actor in national
economies, the Communist Party of Cuba and its ageing leader Fidel Castro
proved that economic and social progress is possible while maintaining state
supremacy over the market. Whether state corporations in Cuba have competed
successfully and to their potential or not, is something to be dealt with in
comparative case studies. For now, the Cuban economy is a growing entity,
capable of acquiring new technologies and foreign investments.

Hence, the social scientist is left with a few points for future discussion. First
there are questions regarding Cuba's internal affairs. How long will the military
keep hegemony over the state corporations in Cuba? Would it be possible for a
future generation of business directors to break with their loyalty towards the
PCC? Finally, what conditions would be necessary to allow for a growth in the

number of self-employed individuals; or is this group doomed to extinction? The answers to these questions will determine the future of Cuba's economic model, and the link between a socially conscientious Communist Party that advocates high spending in education and health care, and those who directly control the means of production.

The second group of questions is composed of those that come to the fore when considering the global political economy as a whole. Are global economic forces and neo-liberal trends so powerful that they can penetrate even the most coherent state-run economy? Are the issues of unemployment and income disparity directly related to global structures? Lastly, when it comes to modes of production and labour flexibility, is there really a difference between private (capitalist) markets and state-run economies; or does the state simply substitute for the private capitalist in its role?

At the beginning of this chapter, I highlighted (in short) the significance of social spending for the Cuban government. The guaranteed access to health, housing and education are equally significant to the Cuban citizen. For these reasons, one can understand why the Cuban government continues to receive overwhelming support from the majority of Cuban people (August 1999: 253–377). If any difference between Cuba's state-run economy and private capitalism is to be emphasized, then the distinction should rest on the welfare programmes that the government provides for its people. Another possible difference might be considered when looking at the Directorship's Committee, which is composed of union representatives, PCC/UJC members and workers elected by their colleagues. In terms of corporate planning and discussing labour relations, the private market has never come this far. However, in both cases, general economic planning, management and the allocation of the country's resources remain in the hands of a few. In private capitalism, it is the individual entrepreneur who holds power over production. Currently, in Cuba, planning and the organization of production and labour relations are ultimately under the direction of the military leaders who are loyal to the PCC. Other than that, labour relations are basically the same. The threat of unemployment is the same, yearly contracts are the same, and the option of self-employment (whether legal or not) is practically the same.

Perhaps the condition of labour in Cuba or elsewhere does not rely so much upon whether or not the state intervenes and controls the market. For better or for worse, global trends that have been found in other countries are now replicated on this socialist island. In the future, any improvement in the line of production will most probably depend on how workers directly influence economic structures and modes of production.

Notes

1 This study is based on the author's doctoral research. The issue of state reductionism is dealt with by a number of political economists, for instance Strange (1996). See also Wallerstein and Hopkins (1996).

2 In Spanish these terms are translated accordingly into: *Trabajo por cuenta propia* and *Nueva empresa cubana*.

3 United States Department of State, Torricelli/Cuban Democracy Act of 1992; see also, Helms-Burton/Cuban Liberty and Democratic Solidarity Act of 1996.

4 The sector that experienced the largest growth, in 2000, was agriculture, which registered a 14.5 per cent increase in comparison to the previous year. This was followed by transport and communications with a 9.3 per cent increase for the same period. Industry, including small-arms production, mining/mineral-petroleum processing and manufacturing grew by 5 per cent. Cuba's historical and traditional primary export industry, sugar, likewise experienced a relative growth towards the end of the crisis decade. During the 1999–2000 harvests, the country produced 4,058 million tonnes of sugar within 114 days. This represents a 7.3 per cent increase in relation to the previous year. The gains from sugar export after the last harvest totalled US$2.2 million according to the Ministry of Sugar (MINAZ 2001; Ministerio de Economía y Planificación (MEP) 2001: 1–5).

5 Unemployment in Cuba was recognized publicly for the first time in 1997 by the Ministry of Labour and Social Security. See MEP (1999, 2000).

6 Pages (2000: 1–3). In Cuba's most important and productive nickel mining and refinery plant, Ernesto Che Guevara, located in the Municipality of Moa, half of the amount of combustible material used to produce a tonne of the mineral in 1989 was used in the year 2000. During this last year 72,000 tonnes of nickel were produced. This reflects a big step in nickel production, as the total amount of nickel produced in 1989 was only 45,591 tonnes. See *Granma Internaciona*, 21 April 2001.

7 Source, Government of Cuba web page on Social Development (*http://www.cubagob.cu/des-eco/mep/plan-econ200.html*) (accessed 13 June 2001) (2001: 1).

8 United Nations Development Programme (1997a) Index on Human Poverty.

9 United Nations Development Programme (1997b) Index on Gender Development.

10 In February 2001, Cuba's International Medical Brigade sent fifty-two health professionals to assist the government of El Salvador in caring for 51,000 victims of an earthquake that destroyed 163 municipalities. See *Granma Internacional*, 8 March 2001.

11 Source, Council of State Decree-Law No. 141, 8 September 1993; see also Ministerio de Finanzas y Precios (hereafter MFP) web page on *Legislación Tributaria* (*http://www1.cuba.cu:8084/economia/finanzas*) (accessed 13 June 2001). After the 1959 Revolution, self-employment did not actually cease to exist in Cuba. Mostly of rural origin, the self-employed were characterized as non-state or informal workers. This group of people suffered under many revolutionary state reforms, which led to a fall in their numbers. According to some official estimates, the self-employed sector represented only 4.2 per cent of the labour market by 1988, see Espina (1993). Today in Cuba, the term *trabajo por cuenta propia* (self-employed) refers only to those individuals registered with the Ministry of Labour and Social Security (MTSS) as self-employed workers who earn in either dollars or pesos and pay all the required taxes (MFP, 18 April 1996).

12 The parallel black market continues to flourish in Cuba, however, there are no available statistics for it. According to the norms of research found in documents prepared by the International Labour Organization and the Centre for Labour Studies of Cuba, for every registered self-employed worker, there are approximately 3.5 individuals conducting small informal businesses or involved in illicit activity. See Núñez Moreno (1998).

13 In 1995, the Cuban government passed the Ministry of Finance and Prices Resolution No. 24/95 (effective in 1996) based on Parliamentary Law No. 73 on Revenues (4 August 1994). The organ that controls the arrangement of tax payments is called the Office of Revenues Collections (ONAT) MFP, *http://www.cuba.cu:8084/economia/finanzas/leyes* (accessed 13 June 2001). Since this law

on tax payment was implemented, the number of registered self-employed individuals has fallen dramatically. See Núñez Moreno (1998).

14 I base my assumption of the state's tendency to reduce unemployment in the interviews that I conducted with former Cuban Ambassador to The Netherlands, Sonia Díaz Llera in April 2001, an interview with Abelardo Curbelo Padrón of the Department of International Relations of the Central Committee of the Communist Party of Cuba (PCC) in May 2001 (hereafter, *Interviews 2001*), in addition to my interviews with 179 *cuentapropistas* at random in Havana, Santiago, Varadero, Camaguey, Ciego de Avila and Trinidad during the month of January 1999, whereby a personal profile and survey on the opinions of those interviews were recorded in detail (hereafter Interviews 1999).

15 In my interviews with 179 *cuentapropistas* I found, and witnessed, police accompanying revenue inspectors who physically confiscated money in cash, cooking materials and food. Additionally, I witnessed family restaurants and street-vendor cars being shut down during operations. The actions were often carried out in a violent manner.

16 MFP, Resolution No. 24/95.

17 One hundred and fifty out of 179 *cuentapropistas* stated that they do not consider themselves to be of a different class to the general working population (Interviews 1999).

18 MFP Resolution 24/95.

19 MFP *Ley del Propuesta para 2000*, 1 December 1999.

20 Economic Resolution of the Fifth PCC Congress, 1997 (Part II), Havana, 1998.

21 Of those 179 interviewed, who on average earned more than $100 per month (fifty-three individuals), all rated their sympathy towards the Cuban government on a scale of 0–10 (whereby 10 signifies enthusiastic support towards the government and 0 equals absolute hatred towards the same), to be less than 5 (Interviews 1999).

22 Economic Resolution of the Fifth PCC Congress, 1997 (Part I and II), Havana, 1998.

23 *Ibid.*

24 No economic research centre is mentioned directly in the documents presented by the MFP.

25 Council of State/Parliament Decree-Law 187/98, *Sobre las Bases Generales del Perfeccionamiento Empresarial*, Havana, 1999.

Bibliography

All websites accessed 13 June 2001.

August, A. (1999) *Democracy in Cuba and the 1997–98 Elections*, Havana: Editorial José Martí.

Carmona Báez, A. (2000) 'Cuba: reforms and adjustments versus transition', *International Journal of Political Economy*, 30, Spring.

Castro, F. (2000) *Capitalismo Actual: Consideraciones y Contradicciones del Neo-Liberalismo y Globalización*, New York: Ocean Press.

Cubanet Independiente, http://www.cubanet.org.

Eckstein, S. (1994) *Back From the Future: Cuba under Castro*, Princeton, NJ: Princeton University Press.

Economic Intelligence Unit (1993) *Country Profile*, 1993: 7, Economic Intelligence Unit.

Espina, M. (1993) 'Reproducción Socioclasista en Cuba', Unpublished Doctoral Dissertation, Universidad de la Habana, Centro de Investigaciones Psicológicas y Sociológicas, Havana.

Espinosa, C. (2000) 'Cuentapropismo', in *Cubanet Independiente*, on http://www.cubanet.org, 22 December.

González Gutiérrez, A. (1998) 'Economia y sociedad: los retos del modelo económico', *Temas*, 11, Havana.

Government of Cuba, web page on Social Development http://www.cubagob.cu/des-eco/mep/plan-econ2000.html.

Government of Cuba, web page on economic restructuring in state enterprises http://www.nuevaempresa.cu.

Granma Internacional (digital) (GI) (various dates), Official Organ of the Communist Party of Cuba, http://www.granma.cu.

Lobe, J. (2001) 'Learn from Cuba, says World Bank', *International Policy Studies*, 5 May 2001.

Marquetti Nodarse, H. (1998) 'La economía del dollar: balance y perspectivas', *Temas*, 11.

Ministerio de Economía y Planificación (MEP) (2001) *Informe Económico 2000*, Havana: MEP.

—— (1999) *Informe Económico 1998*, Havana: MEP.

Ministerio de Finanzas y Precios (MFP) (1996) *Sobre Cuentapropismo*, 18 April 1996.

—— (MFP), web page on Legislación Tributaria http://www.cuba.cu:8084/economia/finanzas.

Ministerio de Trabajo y Seguridad Social (MTSS) (1995) *Orientaciones a Trabajadores de Cuenta Propia*, Havana: MTSS.

Ministry of Sugar (MINAZ) (2001) *Annual Report on Sugar Production*, Havana: MINAZ.

Notimex, 1 June 2001: 1; http://www.notimex.com.mx.

Núñez Moreno, L. (1998) 'Más allá del cuentapropismo', *Temas*, 11, Havana.

Pages, R. (2000) 'Estabilidad económica en los últimos cinco años', *Granma Internacional Digital*, 22 December 2000, http://www.granma.cu/espanol/di3/leconomia-e.html.

Pérez, M. (1999) 'Regulaciones estatales reprimen aún más a los cuentapropistas', *Cuba Free Press*, 15 December.

Rangel, D.A. (2001) 'Cómo superó Cuba una crisis', *Granma Internacional Prensa Latina*, 20 April 2001.

Rodriguez Beruff, J., Pérez, S., Domínguez, J., González Nuñez, G., Dilla Alfonso, H., Vicentelli, A.T., Valdés, N., Pérez Stable, M. and Pagán, N. (1995) *Cuba en crisis: perspectivas económicas y políticas*, San Juan: Editorial Universidad de Puerto Rico.

Strange, S. (1996) *The Retreat of the State: Diffusion of Power in the World Economy*, Cambridge: Cambridge University Press.

United Nations Development Programme (UNDP) (1997a, b) *Human Development Report Index on Human Poverty*, New York, http://www.undp.org./news/hdr97.

Wallerstein, I. and Hopkins, T.K. (1996) *The Age of Transition: Trajectory of the World System 1945–2025*, London: Zed Books.

14 Union responses to privatization: lessons from the Mexican case

Claudia Báez-Camargo

Introduction

This chapter analyses the responses of labour leaders to the privatization of state-owned enterprises in Mexico. It is argued that democratization has a substantial impact on the ability of trade unions to respond to the challenges posed by globalization. The degree of union democracy and the partisan links of union leaders provide additional insights that are necessary for a more complete understanding of the outcomes for organized labour in liberalizing economies.

The analysis focuses on the 1990 privatization of the monopolistic telephone company Teléfonos de México (Telmex), during the administration of President Carlos Salinas de Gortari (1988–94), and the 1999 attempt by the government of Ernesto Zedillo (1994–2000) to allow private investment in the electrical sector. The unions under consideration are the telephone workers' union (Sindicato de Telefonistas de la República Mexicana, STRM), and the two unions in the electricity sector (Sindicato Mexicano de Electricistas, SME and Sindicato Único de Trabajadores Electricistas de la República Mexicana, SUTERM).

These cases provide an interesting opportunity for studying the effect of regime change on the strategies pursued by union leaders when dealing with economic reforms, because the privatization of Telmex took place in a much more authoritarian context than the initiative to privatize the electrical sector. The effects of union democracy and of the partisan links of the leaders on their responses to privatization will also be addressed.

The chapter starts with a discussion of the economic and political changes that Mexico has experienced since the early 1980s, followed by a more specific account of privatization experiences. The case studies include a brief summary of the internal characteristics of the unions and of the party ties of the union leaders. These elements provide a basic background for understanding the actions of the union leaders when their respective firms faced privatization.

The debt crisis and economic reform

During the 1970s, state-owned enterprises, employment in the bureaucracy, and social spending all experienced rapid growth (Aspe 1993). In that decade,

Mexico's credit-worthiness had improved substantially after the discovery of large oil deposits. The increase in the country's expected oil revenues prompted the government to embark upon many ambitious investment projects, running up huge deficits that were financed through borrowing from the international markets. As a result, public foreign debt totalled almost 60 billion US dollars by 1982, fourteen times the amount in 1970 (Bruhn 1996: 153).

However, a dramatic fall in oil prices, followed by an increase in international interest rates, triggered a crisis of unexpected proportions in 1981. In August 1982, the Mexican government announced that it would be late in honouring its debt commitments. This was much more than a simple liquidity crisis, because economic growth had been lagging behind since the early 1970s, and it was widely perceived that drastic measures had to be taken if growth was to resume.

Initially, it was assumed that the economy would recover effectively after some short-term austerity measures. The government of President Miguel de la Madrid (1982–8) implemented a strict stabilization programme in 1983, which included substantial cuts in expenditure and the reduction of government subsidies, in order to reduce the public deficit. Furthermore, in order to minimize the risk of fuelling inflation, de la Madrid imposed wage restraint by setting the level of the minimum wage twice a year.[1] In spite of those measures, by 1985 it had become increasingly clear that the economic situation of the country was not improving and that deeper reforms would be needed.

In fact, 1985 was a cataclysmic year for the Mexican economy because of a pronounced fall in oil prices at a time when government finances still depended critically on oil revenue. The public deficit, as a percentage of the GDP, grew back to the same level that it had before the implementation of the 1983 stabilization programme. Consequently, the de la Madrid government expanded the scope of economic reforms by taking measures to open the Mexican markets and to limit the role of the state in the economy. In that context, Mexico joined the GATT, began lowering tariffs and started the privatization of state-owned enterprises.

Again, those measures in themselves were not enough to stabilize the economic situation of the country, because by the end of 1987 Mexico was on the brink of hyperinflation. The crisis was brought under control by means of a stabilization plan that rested upon the negotiation of an income policy among government, business and unions. This tripartite scheme was continued throughout the administration of Carlos Salinas and was successful in bringing inflation under control.

President Salinas adopted a neo-liberal model that was much more far-reaching than the liberalization initiatives of his predecessor. Salinas' programme may be characterized as 'an export-led industrial model driven by private investment and cheap labour inputs' (Pastor and Wise 1997: 429). It involved a strict application of neo-liberal prescriptions: the privatization of state enterprises, the liberalization of prices, and opening the trade and capital markets. In 1989, the financial market was liberalized, restrictions on foreign investment were relaxed, and new areas of the economy were opened to foreign capital (Clifton 2000). During those years, privatization of state-owned enterprises also continued.

The Salinas administration attained some economic stability. However, this would soon prove to be quite fragile. Although inflation was effectively brought under control, it was mainly achieved through the use of a fixed exchange rate. This caused the peso to become extremely overvalued. As a consequence, the trade balance turned from a surplus of 8.8 billion US dollars in 1987 to a deficit of 18.5 billion US dollars by 1994 (Pastor and Wise 1997: 422). The trade deficit led to high current account deficits, which in turn were financed through a substantial flow of highly volatile foreign capital.

The final year of the Salinas administration was bad news for the economy. Beginning with the Zapatista uprising in the state of Chiapas on New Year's Eve, followed by the assassination of the ruling party's presidential candidate, Luis Donaldo Colosio, political instability turned into financial unrest as confidence in the Mexican economy was eroded and capital began leaving the country in large quantities. By the time that Ernesto Zedillo took office as the new president on 1 December, the central bank's foreign currency reserves had gone from 29.6 billion pesos in February to 6.3 billion pesos. Finally, when later that month the new government announced a devaluation of the peso, confidence in the Mexican economy hit rock bottom.

By the end of 1994 the peso had lost 30 per cent of its value relative to the US dollar and in just a few days the country had lost between 7 and 8 billion US dollars in foreign-exchange reserves (Ramírez 1996: 129). Subsequently, the government announced a new austerity plan that would seek to bring the economy under control. The new emergency plan again involved spending cuts in many socially sensitive areas, as well as wage restraints to reduce the budget deficit and to curtail inflationary pressure. The result was that the economic downturn of 1995 was steeper for a single year than at any other time during the crisis of the 1980s. That year, domestic investment fell by 30 per cent and the unemployment rate nearly doubled. Social programmes were cut by 12 per cent and public investment fell by 17 per cent (Koechlin 1998).

The Salinas years had seen an exponential increase in available credit and booming consumer spending. However, after the balance of payments crisis occurred in December 1994, interest rates soared, reaching levels as high as 120 per cent. As a consequence, many families had to spend an average of 43 per cent of their income in credit-card debt, while many others (as many as six million) simply defaulted on their debts, leaving the country's financial institutions in danger of becoming insolvent (Ramírez 1996: 143).[2]

After the initial crisis was overcome, the government of Ernesto Zedillo continued to adhere to a strict orthodoxy in economic policy-making. Fiscal discipline was always observed, as was the case when a fall in oil prices during 1998 led to important expenditure cuts.

The stabilization and structural reform measures that were implemented throughout the 1980s and 1990s imposed a heavy burden on the population. This was particularly true in the case of the working classes, because of the deterioration in the purchasing power of wages. From 1982 to 1987, both the real minimum wage and the real average industrial wage fell by more than 30 per cent (Pastor and Wise 1997: 432). Just between 1983 and 1984, the real minimum wage index fell more than 20 per cent (Molinar 1991: 206).

Although the Salinas administration presided over a modest economic recovery, the pattern of growth proved to be regressive. Manuel Pastor and Carol Wise (1997: 426–7) analysed the annual rate of growth of real monetary income for household deciles between 1989 and 1992 and found that several deciles, including the two poorest, experienced a decline. During Salinas' term, the government continued to set the minimum wage through yearly deflationary agreements negotiated with business and labour organizations. The result was that the real minimum wage continued to fall, in 1994 reaching a value equal to only 40 per cent of its 1981 level (OECD 1997: 94).

Even though the real average wage did recover between 1988 and 1993, it failed to reach its pre-debt crisis level. These trends suggest an overall worsening of the income distribution where actual wage gains were concentrated in a few hands, while 49 per cent of the economically active population continued to earn between one and two times the minimum wage. Then again, during the crisis of 1995, the social costs were high, because real wages fell by 22 per cent in a single year (Koechlin 1998).

There were also important costs in terms of job losses. Manufacturing employment decreased by 9.5 and 1.1 per cent in 1983 and 1984 respectively, stabilized in 1985 and fell again by 4 per cent in 1986 and by 3.3 per cent in 1987 (Molinar 1991: 208). However, the exact costs in terms of unemployment are very hard to measure. Official statistics typically show very low rates of open unemployment (around 6 per cent during the worst years of the crisis). The main reason for this is that the way in which unemployment is measured excludes all of those who work in the informal sector.[3] An approximation of the extent to which this method of measurement minimized the problem can be reached by looking at the number of workers who do not receive formal wages, which for 1999 was, according to the National Employment Survey, 39 per cent of the EAP (economically active population).

Furthermore, as the work of Rendón and Salas (2000) suggests, given that paid jobs constitute the main source of income for most Mexican families; that savings rates are very low; and that there is no unemployment insurance, the employment problems of Mexico do not translate directly into an increase in the unemployment rate. Instead, job losses are reflected in the increased precariousness of paid work and in an increase in the number of income providers per family. Evidence that the quality of available jobs has decreased during the period from 1970 to 1999 include the proliferation of very small-scale activities, an increase in unpaid family work, and an increase in the proportion of the workforce that receives no benefits from its employers.

In sum, the 1980s and the 1990s were extremely hard for the Mexican economy. Declining wages, the precariousness of the job market, and the withdrawal of the state from many areas of public spending were all part of the difficult context that union leaders had to face at that time. Although the early 1990s brought an apparent economic recovery, this proved only transitory, as an economic crisis of grave proportions broke out again in late 1994.

The Mexican democratization experience

The political system that emerged after the Mexican Revolution of 1910 was characterized by the dominance of a hegemonic party, the *Partido Revolucionario Institucional* (PRI). A defining characteristic of the system was the absence of true electoral competition. Although elections had always been held regularly, the PRI would always win, mainly due to corruption. Political power was greatly centralized in the hands of the president, who was also the undisputed leader of the PRI. As such, the president would perform the transfer of power every six years by designating the next PRI presidential candidate, or in other words, his successor.

The democratization of the Mexican political system progressed in a piece-meal fashion over a long period of time (one may date it to as far back as the early 1970s). However, it was after the economic crisis of 1982 that the pressures for a greater political liberalization escalated. Still, political liberalization proceeded very gradually through negotiation among élites and the struggle from growing opposition parties to obtain concessions from the regime.

Needing an outlet for popular frustration in the context of a terrible economic crisis, Miguel de la Madrid's government initially signalled that it would tolerate real electoral competition at the local level. During the first year of his administration, the PRI recognized the victory of opposition parties in municipal-level elections in seven major cities. However, this trend did not continue into the 1985 mid-term congressional elections. That year, as Cornelius (1986: 130) describes, 'on the basis of very partial, unofficial results, the PRI immediately claimed victory in all 300 congressional races and all seven gubernatorial contests'.[4] From then on, the PRI returned to its tactics of electoral manipulation.

The final years of the de la Madrid administration were characterized by new tensions among traditional political actors. For the first time in many decades there were serious divisions inside the ruling party, which threatened the continuation of its monopoly of political power. One of the primary reasons for those fractures was a pronounced centralization of the major positions of the cabinet in the hands of the so-called *tecnócratas* (or technocrats) at the expense of the old-style *políticos*.[5] These technocrats, who virtually monopolized the highest offices in the executive cabinet, almost invariably lacked a career in partisan politics. From the perspective of some traditional *político* groups, the technocrats were breaking the unwritten rules of the game by monopolizing the most coveted posts in the cabinet.

Tension among those groups reached breaking point after Carlos Salinas de Gortari, a prominent technocrat, was nominated as the PRI's presidential candidate for the 1988 elections. A group of influential PRI militants formed the

Corriente Democrática to protest the lack of internal democratic procedures, and abandoned the party after Salinas' nomination. Headed by Cuauhtémoc Cárdenas and Porfirio Muñoz Ledo, this group went on to form a heterogeneous alliance with many groups from the Mexican left, and launched the candidacy of Cárdenas for president.

The 1988 elections were an important turning point in Mexican politics. Cárdenas campaigned strongly against the neo-liberal economic policy that Salinas would evidently continue to pursue.[6] He argued in favour of state involvement in the economy, and even proposed to roll back many of the economic reforms of the previous administration. After six years of severe economic crisis, which greatly affected the standard of living of most Mexicans, Cárdenas' discourse appealed to a substantial segment of society. As a result, the 1988 elections were probably the most disputed in Mexican history. In fact, many claim that in all likelihood the PRI managed to keep the presidency only by resorting to a huge electoral fraud that snatched victory from Cárdenas (see, for example, Krauze 1997).

Aside from the highly questionable results of the presidential race, the 1988 elections represented a serious blow to the PRI's hegemonic position. For the first time the PRI did not obtain sufficient seats in the chamber of deputies to pass constitutional amendments on its own.[7] Also, one-quarter of the PRI's candidates was defeated in those elections. These events effectively broke one of the golden rules of the Mexican political system: the almost absolute certainty that PRI candidates would win.

Salinas came to power amidst a serious questioning of the legitimacy of his presidency. A consequence of this was that the new president started out his term by setting a harsh tone towards his critics. Once in office, Salinas demanded from his party the strictest obedience to his mandates and reacted strongly to his opponents elsewhere. As Grindle (1996: 92) notes, Salinas used both rewards and punishments to send signals about the importance of being on the presidential bandwagon. The potential costs of dissidence were evident for union leaders as well. The arrest of the leader of the petroleum workers' union, Joaquín Hernández Galicia, 'La Quina', soon after Salinas took office, was interpreted as a warning of what may happen to other undisciplined leaders (Bizberg 1990: 102).[8]

A selective process of political liberalization characterized the Salinas sexenio (six year administration). On the one hand, Salinas engaged in negotiations with the *Partido Acción Nacional* (PAN), a centre-right opposition party, to pass legislation that required the vote of at least three-quarters of the legislators. These negotiations, which came to be known as *concertaciones*, typically involved the recognition of the PAN's electoral victories in exchange for support for some of Salinas' key reforms. Under these circumstances, the PAN slowly began gaining electoral seats. On the other hand, the Partido de la Revolución Democrática (PRD), the party that emerged from Cárdenas' movement, was never accorded any significant electoral victory outside the chamber of deputies. Furthermore, many PRD members were harassed during the Salinas administration.

Both the PRD and – to a lesser degree – the PAN denounced electoral irregularities throughout the Salinas administration. Faced with growing public manifestations of discontent from the opposition, the Salinas government enacted a series of electoral reforms. In July 1990, the federal congress approved a new federal electoral code that contained provisions for the compilation of a new electoral roll, for reforms to the Federal Electoral Institute (IFE), which is the institution in charge of organizing all federal elections, and the creation of a federal electoral tribunal. These reforms were nevertheless harshly criticized by various opposition groups, the most vocal of which was the PRD, mainly due to the fact that under the new scheme the IFE remained under the control of the president.

The PRI was able to make a substantial recovery in the 1991 mid-term congressional elections, obtaining 61.5 per cent of the vote, which translated into 320 seats out of 500 in the chamber of deputies. Accusations of electoral fraud continued to be common, and in July 1993 the government responded by presenting a proposal for a new electoral reform, which included provisions for greater access to the media to all parties, and restrictions on party funding.

The 1994 election was more open than any previous election held during the PRI's hold on power. Electoral observers from the UN and several NGOs were allowed into the country for the first time to witness the transparency of the process. Electoral intention surveys and exit polls were other monitoring tools that were introduced, and this contributed to the perception of a genuine victory for Zedillo in the presidential election. The declining trend in the PRI's electoral performance continued as Zedillo was elected president with 48.8 per cent of the votes, the lowest percentage ever obtained by a PRI presidential candidate.

From the beginning of his term, Zedillo announced that he would keep a 'healthy distance' from his party, suggesting that he would cease to act as the unquestionable party leader that the president had always been under PRI governments. This announcement estranged him from many groups of *políticos* who were already resented by voters. Zedillo also pledged that under his government the elections would be clean and all victories of the opposition would be recognized.

Zedillo's government proceeded with the political reform he had promised during his campaign. An important step towards expanding electoral competition took place in 1996, when the PRI, PAN, PRD and PT (Partido del Trabajo) agreed on a series of reforms that introduced direct elections for the government of the country's capital; increased and regulated public financing for political parties; introduced proportional representation to senatorial elections; and finally gave the IFE full autonomy from the executive power.

During Zedillo's administration, both the PAN and the PRD won various state governorships, but it was the 1997 election that was to become an important landmark for the democratization of the regime. In those elections the PRI lost its majority in the chamber of deputies, which meant that for the first time a *prísta* president would not have enough support in the legislature to have his initiatives passed automatically. The implications of this became more concrete when, in the aftermath of the congressional elections, the main opposition parties (PAN, PRD, PVEM and PT) agreed on an informal alliance, as a result of which they succeeded in taking control of the most important legislative committees. Another crucial outcome from the 1997 elections was the victory of the PRD candidate, Cuauhtémoc Cárdenas, in the race for the government of the Distrito Federal.

As the next presidential election approached, Zedillo's commitment not to choose his successor became an increasingly critical issue. However, the president appeared to honour his promise and distanced himself from the process of candidate selection. In May 1999 the PRI announced that, for the first time ever, nation-wide open primaries would take place to select its presidential candidate. Four candidates contended for and actively campaigned in these primaries which took place in November and in which Francisco Labastida secured the presidential nomination of the PRI.

The countdown to the 2000 elections was characterized by continuous assurances made by the president of the now independent IFE, José Woldenberg, that the electoral process would be clean. Huge quantities of money were invested in the infrastructure for the election, including a very sophisticated computer program for counting the votes, which was advertised as being basically fraudproof.

The elections of 2 July 2000 were truly unprecedented, because the winner of the presidential race was not Francisco Labastida but Vicente Fox, the PAN candidate, whose victory brought to an end more than seventy years of uninterrupted PRI presidencies.

During the eighteen years that comprised the administrations of Miguel de la Madrid, Carlos Salinas and Ernesto Zedillo, Mexico became a functional electoral democracy. Two basic phases can be identified. The first, during the governments of Miguel de la Madrid and Carlos Salinas, was still characterized by a significantly authoritarian context in which there was very limited tolerance towards the opposition, from either political parties or social movements. The second, during the Zedillo administration, in which new political opportunities were opened up, saw shifts in the balance of power, and the overall reconfiguration of the political system made for a very fluid environment, which provided social movements with greater scope for action.

The Mexican privatization experience

In post-revolutionary Mexico, the state assumed the role of a large-scale entrepreneur and employer (González Casanova 1990). The state acquired strategic, and not so strategic, enterprises as part of a nationalist policy, and those firms were created to serve not only economic, but also social and political goals. Employment in the public sector served as a means to provide patronage for political supporters. As Teichman (1996) describes, managers of public enterprises often acted on a political rather than economic rationale, working mostly to increase their political power. As a result, public-sector enterprises became terribly inefficient.

After the economic crisis of 1982 and the shift to market-oriented reform that ensued, those state-owned enterprises with artificially high employment levels and a protected domestic market increasingly came to be seen as a source of problems. Highly inefficient and unprofitable, public enterprises became a fiscal burden at a time when the state was already having problems with high deficits and debt payments.

Consequently, privatization of those firms became an important element in the overall economic strategy of stabilization and structural reform throughout the 1980s and the 1990s. The magnitude of the privatization effort was huge. Whereas in 1982 there were more than 1,000 state-owned enterprises, by mid 1991 there were only 269 (Lustig 1992: 105). In this process, the role of the state as an employer was curtailed significantly. According to the OECD (1997: 80), while during the period 1980–6 employment in public enterprises grew at an annual rate of 6 per cent, the same measure averaged –3.7 between 1986–90, and then reached –13.9 per cent in 1991, –30.2 per cent in 1992, and –17.7 in 1993.

Important revisions to union rights and collective contracts were executed in order to make the state-owned firms attractive to potential investors. As Lustig (1992: 105) has argued,

> the government did not want to sell the larger and potentially more profitable public enterprises before their financial situation was sound and the regulatory framework made their purchase attractive.

In those enterprises, as in many in the private sector that needed to modernize, the strikes that resulted from routine contract revisions were used as a justification to delete fringe benefits and union prerogatives from the collective contracts and to impose lay-offs (Zapata 1996). Sometimes the measures were even harsher.

The case of the state-owned airline is an example of the harsh tone set by the de la Madrid administration. In April 1988, the union of Aeroméxico called a strike in response to a move by the management that violated the collective contract to unilaterally restructure work conditions. This decision implied getting rid of thirteen aeroplanes and firing almost 4,000 workers. After three days on strike, the directors of Aeroméxico filed for bankruptcy at a tribunal. The support of the government for that move was strong, as is clear from some statements that the president made at about that time:

> Mexico cannot have uncompetitive enterprises anymore, therefore they must pursue their programs for efficiency and productivity and even radical restructuring, as is the case of the national aviation service.
>
> (quoted in Zapata 1996: 177)

During the bankruptcy procedures, the administrator in the case, the *Banco Nacional de Obras y Servicios Públicos*, formally requested the termination of contractual relations from the labour ministry and, as a consequence, the lay-off of all workers. The union sought an appeal and challenged the legality of the measure; however the appeal was revoked. Furthermore, fourteen days after the strike began it was declared invalid by the labour authorities. The government announced the creation of a new airline and the previously existing collective contracts disappeared.

As Clifton (2000: 70) argues,

> Privatization during the de la Madrid government had been associated with ruthless repressive tactics by the government. The fate of the Aeroméxico workers – all of whom had been sacked on the grounds that their strike in protest at threatened job cuts had rendered the company bankrupt – hung like a spectre over other unions facing a similar position.

In that context, President Salinas privatized several other key sectors, perhaps most visible of which were the monopolistic telephone company, Telmex, and the banks. As the Salinas administration continued with its privatization programme, so the limited tolerance towards combative unions persisted, sometimes even aided by co-opted union leaders. An example of this was the case of the miners' union at AHMSA (a firm in the iron and steel industry). On January 1989, the firm demanded various modifications to the collective contract and the dismissal of 4,500 workers. The intent was to make AHMSA attractive for privatization. The firm's manager threatened to shut down the plant unless the modernization measures were achieved. The union organized a strike for 2 April but, before the deadline came, the national leadership of the miners and metalworkers' union accepted the conditions set by the firm. The workers in the local union ignored this, demanded the removal of their section representative, and invoked the federal labour law to support their claims of their right to preserve their contract. Nevertheless, the national union vetoed their resolutions, and the workers had no choice but to accept the deal offered by AHMSA.

By the time that Ernesto Zedillo took office, most of the state-owned industries had been privatized. Although the most prominent exception was the oil industry, which carries a deep significance for Mexican nationalism, other sectors such as the electrical industry remained in the hands of the state. However, fewer privatizations took place during Zedillo's term, although the most notorious were the reform to transfer social-security pensions to private financial institutions and the attempt to allow private investment in the electrical sector.

In general terms, despite the fact that Zedillo's labour policy was not as harsh as that of his predecessors, it was not totally responsive to union combativeness either.[9] The administration was characterized by a much more tolerant attitude towards social movements, mainly because the democratization of the regime limited the powers of the presidency, and because greater freedom of expression in the media increased the political costs of any move by the administration to silence its critics.

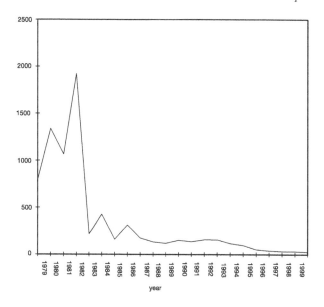

Figure 14.1 Mexico: number of strikes, 1970–2000

Source: International Labour Organization (various years) *Yearbook of Labour Statistics*, Geneva: ILO and Mexico's Labour Ministry, online at: *http://www.stps.gob.mx/stps1/stpsvp.htm*

It should be noted that the governments of de la Madrid and Salinas were characterized by their intransigence with combative unions, not just when dealing with candidates for privatization. Many strikes were terminated harshly throughout both administrations. For instance, in 1983, the unions of DINA and Uramex went on strike, demanding wage increases above those decreed by the government. In DINA the conflict ended after a month, the union was forced to accept an increase within the official guidelines, and one-third of the workforce was laid off. In the case of Uramex, the conflict ended when the firm closed down and all its workers were laid off. According to Zamora (1990: 128), government officials used these strikes as a warning about the consequences for unions that did not abide by the government's wage limits.

During the Salinas presidency, the approach to strikes was similarly stringent. Lowering inflation became one of the most urgent goals of the Salinas administration, and this was achieved by relying on price and wage controls through tripartite pacts with employer and labour organizations. Wage controls were widely criticized, but the labour ministry enforced them strictly, in some cases even rejecting collective contracts that had been approved previously by both employers and workers (Bizberg 1996: 104). Unions came to understand that a strike movement demanding higher wage increases would be declared invalid by the government. Throughout the period, this intolerance towards industrial conflict did result in a substantial decrease in the number of strikes, as shown in Figure 14.1.

The administration of Ernesto Zedillo saw a continuation of the decline in strike actions. Between January and March 1998 there were thirty-three strikes – 25 per cent of the number for 1995. According to official statistics, in the first semester of 1999 only eleven strikes occurred at the federal level, the lowest number in the last twenty-five years, and in the first semester of 2000 only fifteen strikes were registered (*Excélsior*, 6 July 2000).

In general terms, the administrative review of proposed strikes was tightened, strike coalitions were prohibited and the procedures covering wage negotiations were altered. Many changes were introduced by relying heavily on élite negotiations and corporate bargains to control unions and wages (Morris 1995: 57). As a consequence, it seems that strikes ceased to work as an effective instrument for union struggle, which may partly explain why we find the decreasing number of strikes reported in Figure 14.1.

STRM and the privatization of Telmex

Francisco Hernández Juárez became Secretary-General of the telephone workers' union after leading a movement that ousted PRI co-opted leader Salustio Salgado in 1976. After that, the STRM widely came to be recognized as a very democratic union, and Hernández Juárez enjoyed a high level of support among workers.

However, although its statutes describe it as a very democratic union, the actual democratic practices in the STRM have come to be somewhat less than flawless. The union's national executive committee does not permit the participation of groups hostile to Hernández Juárez, although it does open the door to the less aggressive opposition. Some degree of participation of the rank and file is allowed through assemblies and regular elections, but this limited democracy appears to be combined with authoritarian practices aimed at guaranteeing the dominance of the group in power and the implementation of their programme (Mondragón Pérez 1994).

Still, the participation of workers in local assemblies is substantial and, perhaps more importantly, the figure of Hernández Juárez seems to retain a great degree of legitimacy among most workers. Besides his role in the 1976 democratic movement, this popularity is due to the fact that he also cultivates a paternalistic image among workers.[10] Furthermore, workers for the most part acknowledge the tangible benefits that their leader has negotiated on their behalf. In fact, it appears that the legitimacy that Hernández Juárez commands among workers stems more from his ability to deliver benefits than from the democratic nature of his appointment.

The limited democracy in the union gives Hernández Juárez some autonomy from pressures from below when dealing with the economic policy of the regime. But he also has an incentive to respond to the demands of workers in order to preserve his legitimacy among them.

The statutes indicate that the union is completely apolitical and does not encourage its members to affiliate to any political party. But Francisco

Hernández Juárez has a proclivity to cultivate personal ties to political parties and politicians. The partisan ties of Hernández Juárez are most evident in his membership of the PRI's National Political Council, although he has always stressed the personal nature of this affiliation.

For many years Hernández Juárez held the conviction that working with the official union establishment could be made to further the union's interests, and during the Salinas government a close relationship developed between Francisco Hernández Juárez and the president (Méndez and Quiroz 1994, Samstad and Collier 1995).

During 1988, rumours began to circulate about the privatization of Telmex. In fact, on 19 May, the presidential candidate Carlos Salinas said during a speech that Mexico's telecommunications urgently needed to modernize, but that the state had no resources to provide adequate investment. Therefore, the opportunity to invest should be given to those who could afford it.

At first, Francisco Hernández Juárez publicly opposed the privatization and stated that the union would not allow it. Nevertheless, in spite of public opposition to the rumours of privatization, Hernández Juárez was not really contemplating a strategy of confrontation with the government. According to Rangel Pérez (1989: 95), at the same time he made public his opposition to privatization, Hernández Juárez started to spread the word among Telmex workers that if Salinas won the presidency, privatization would surely take place. In that case, he argued, and since it seemed that Salinas would indeed win, the best strategy would be to support the presidential candidate in order to avoid future reprisals.

Indeed, the STRM leader strongly pursued that plan. In his 1988 report to the union, Hernández Juárez made it clear what his strategy was, since he described the closely contested elections of that year in the following terms:

> The [electoral] process […] benefits everyone to the degree that we know how to understand it and take advantage of it. What is clear is that Mexico won, and the telephone workers, given that we permanently supported the winner, will be able to advance towards the goals we have set for ourselves. It has been said that we hurt the interest of workers by entering an alliance with the government. Fortunately, the facts speak for themselves and based upon them we may conclude that we were right in that the most convenient strategy was to unite with whom had the greatest probability of gaining the presidency.
>
> (Quoted in Rodríguez Castañeda 1995: 109)

The open statements of Hernández Juárez regarding the benefits of establishing close links with the winner show the strategic approach of this leader in seeking the best position possible from which to advance his interests and those of his union.

Nonetheless, Hernández Juárez still maintained a discourse against privatization, defending the idea that the expansion and modernization projects needed by the firm could be achieved with Telmex in the hands of the Mexican state. At the same time he also asserted the willingness and capability of telephone workers to participate in the restructuring needed to introduce new telecommunications services. However, neither political ties nor the disposition to negotiate sufficed, because after Salinas took power it became clear that the privatization of Telmex was one of the priorities of his administration.

The limits of the alliance between Hernández Juárez and Salinas became clear when, in April 1989 with the privatization imminent, the STRM was forced to admit that its collective contract had been unfavourably modified, as was the experience in other public enterprises. The government and Telmex pressed the union to accept a harsh modernization project and, when the union refused to alter the collective contract, Telmex threatened massive lay-offs if its project was not accepted (Mondragón Pérez 1994). The union ceded, and the Secretary of Communications and Transportation, Andrés Caso Lombardo, and the Secretary of Labour, Arsenio Farell, negotiated with Hernández Juárez modifications to labour conditions in Telmex. As a result, fifty-seven individual labour agreements were eliminated, and the number of job categories was reduced from one thousand to just one hundred and forty. Telmex also obtained the right to reassign workers to different areas according to the requirements for the expansion, modernization and increased quality of the telephone service (Rodríguez Castañeda 1995: 62).

The harsh response from the government implied that opposing the privatization would be very risky. Subsequently, with privatization becoming a seemingly unavoidable fact, Hernández Juárez changed his position. Instead of continuing his opposition to privatization and maybe resorting to mobilization, Hernández Juárez strengthened his links to the president even more and gave privatization his full support. A sign of the close relationship between the president and Hernández Juárez was that Salinas gave the first announcement of the privatization during an STRM assembly on 18 September 1989.

In fact, the shift in this leader's position regarding privatization was very dramatic. Hernández Juárez went from opposing privatization to promoting and supporting not only the particular case of the sale of Telmex, but the whole economic model of trade liberalization and privatization of state-owned industries. In his own words:

> In this modernization process, privatizations have shown that societies, their organizations and their initiatives are an alternative to the government, and also that in productive restructuring society itself can be an ally and not an enemy, a source of support and consensus and not the subject of tutelage and punishment. In Mexico, the processes of modernization and state reform have allowed the demystification of neoliberalism as dogma, phantom, even as enemy.
>
> (Hernández Juárez 1991)

In a book he co-authored at the request of President Salinas, Hernández Juárez described the position of the union:

> taking into account the strong need for increased resources that the modernization of Telmex required, the union understood privatization to be one of the options through which the modernization of Telmex could proceed.
>
> (Hernández Juárez and López 1993: 97)

It could be said that Hernández Juárez was trying to set the standard for a new kind of unionism that would befit the new economic model.

The privatization of Telmex was carried out in a manner that seemed to confirm that economic policy-making in the Salinas administration would not be subject to debate. It should be recalled that during the 1980s and early 1990s, the state used all its power to implement its new economic programme, and the political context in which that privatization took place was seriously hostile to combative unions.

The sale of the country's only telephone company did not need congressional approval, and most of the modifications to the regulations that were required for the privatization were done in a very low-profile manner, away from the public eye. The changes to the concession title of Telmex were prepared by members of the Ministries of Communications and Transportation, Finance, Budget, and Commerce, as well as by the management of Telmex. These modifications might have been challenged by political parties or at least discussed in the media, but the document was drafted in a secretive manner. The modifications came into effect on 10 August 1990, but they were not publicly available until the time that they were published in the official newspaper on 10 December, which was a day after the winners of the auction for the sale of Telmex were publicly announced.

After the privatization was completed, Hernández Juárez underscored that the union had obtained important gains from the process. The STRM acquired 187 million stocks, equivalent to 4.4 per cent of the firm's capital, through a credit from the federal government. The workers would receive the stocks as soon as the credit was paid and according to a distribution plan based upon seniority and responsibility levels. The financial value of this move was substantial, since the value of the shares more than doubled in the first two years. But possibly the most relevant outcome of privatization in terms of gains for the workers was that Telmex pledged to avoid lay-offs during its modernization process (Samstad 1998: 311–16). Given the massive dismissals that took place in other privatized firms, this was an important achievement for the workers of Telmex.

Other gains were of a more personal nature. After privatization, Hernández Juárez obtained the government's legal recognition for a new union federation that he co-founded. This federation, the Fesebs, claimed to represent workers in modernized sectors of the economy, and portrayed its members as the future of a new unionism that embraced the goals of increasing productivity and competitiveness.

SME and the SUTERM, and the attempt to privatize the electrical sector

The SME is one of the most democratic unions in Mexico and has a long tradition of autonomy and combativeness. There is a great degree of worker involvement in the internal affairs of the union, and leaders enjoy high legitimacy among the rank and file. The elections of union leaders and representatives are extremely competitive and there is a series of provisions in place that make electoral fraud virtually impossible to commit.

Rosendo Flores has been Secretary-General of the SME since 1997. Before him there was a consistently high turnover in that position. The legitimacy derived from the democratic process and the high participation rates of workers in elections and, more generally, in union affairs give the leadership of this union the ability to engage in a very effective mobilization of its workers. This is undoubtedly one of the great strengths of Rosendo Flores as leader of the SME.

Neither Flores personally nor the SME as an institution have formal links to any political party. Therefore, this leader's response to policy should not be affected by considerations of party discipline or partisan agendas.

By contrast, internal democratic procedures are basically non-existent in SUTERM. Leonardo Rodríguez Alcaine has been 're-elected' Secretary-General of the union since the mid-1970s through rather obscure mechanisms, and he centralizes all relevant decision-making in the union. The authoritarian practices that prevail in the union enable the leader to support unpopular measures without having to face the possibility of being ousted from their leadership position by the workers.

The lack of democratic procedures, of real factory-level penetration and of representativeness, make the leadership of the SUTERM appear illegitimate in the eyes of its workers. Under these conditions, the leader is likely to avoid the prospect of generalized worker mobilization, as he/she cannot be sure of the degree of control he/she could possibly exert over it. This adds to the authoritarian tendencies within the union, because the leader will fear dissidence and therefore will be willing to eliminate it.

However, it would be incorrect to suggest that only repressive measures have kept this leader in his position. Under PRI governments, authoritarian unions persisted largely because they were granted subsidies and resources to distribute among their rank and file.

The SUTERM has very clear structural links to the PRI, both as an individual union and as a member of the biggest labour confederation affiliated with the PRI, the Confederación de Trabajadores de México (CTM). As a member of the CTM, the SUTERM must follow the policy guidelines set by the confederation, which are typically those of the PRI. Also, as part of the union's strategy that is outlined in the statutes, the SUTERM advocates the use of political actions to support PRI governments. The pay-offs to this support are reflected by the fact that Rodríguez Alcaine and other members of the national executive committee of the union are also top party leaders and frequently receive nominations to elective office.

These partisan links entail, on the one hand, a restricted ability for the leader to set an autonomous position regarding economic policy. But, on the other hand, the leader can expect to receive rewards from the party in the form of appointments and nominations that promote a career in politics.

On 2 February 1999, in the unprecedented context of a president lacking majority support in congress, Ernesto Zedillo announced a proposal to allow private investment in the electricity sector. The proposal generated heated debate among political parties, the media and other groups in society, including the two unions in that sector.

Being a nationalized industry, the proposed reform of the electrical sector required a constitutional amendment. This meant that the opposition parties would play a determining role in the fate of the president's initiative. Both the PAN and the PRD refused repeatedly to include the reform of the electricity sector in the legislative agenda, and by 30 January 2000, almost a year after the initiative was first announced, President Zedillo recognized that the reform would not take place during his administration. Such an announcement was quite remarkable in terms of its significance for the Mexican political system. This was a proposal clearly of great interest to the president, and it ultimately failed to gain enough support to be approved.[11]

From the start, the SME's Secretary-General, Rosendo Flores, forcefully rejected Zedillo's proposal, arguing that privatization was unnecessary and would hurt the electrical workers. Flores argued that the financial problems of the electrical sector were due to a badly drafted scheme of subsidies and not to public ownership in itself.

Other arguments against privatization put forward by this leader referred to the previous examples of privatizations with very unsatisfactory results. Flores even argued that the approval of the initiative would mean a loss of sovereignty for the country.

A crucial issue for Flores was his concern with protecting the union's collective contract, which he considered would be damaged by the proposal. President Zedillo promised that the labour relations of the firms in the electrical sector would continue to be regulated by the federal labour law. Nevertheless, the collective contract of the SME includes clauses that go beyond what those laws specify, and those clauses could be eliminated during the transition of the SME's employer, Luz y Fuerza (LyF), to a scheme of private participation.

One of the immediate actions that Flores took in order to oppose Zedillo's reform was to urge other labour and social organizations to join the SME in a resistance front against the privatization of the electrical sector. In the months that followed, a substantial group of very diverse organizations and groups expressed their full backing of the SME's movement. Flores gathered support from unions belonging to the Federation of State Workers' Unions (FTSE),[12] the Coordinadora Intersindical Primero de Mayo (CIPM), a heterogeneous alliance of independent unions and civil society groups that reject neo-liberal economic policies, and the Unión Nacional de Trabajadores (UNT), a newly created union confederation that condemns state controls over organized labour and is headed by Hernández Juárez. These organizations signed a solidarity pact and pledged mutual support with the SME. The Fesebs and the FAT, which are two other autonomous union federations, also supported the SME, as well as El Barzón, an organization of debtors which was created after the financial crisis of December 1994, and the Asociación Nacional de Abogados Democráticos (ANAD).

Other allies included the Partido de la Revolución Democrática (PRD) and the Corriente Renovadora and the Corriente Crítica, both of which are groups within the ruling PRI, which publicly announced their support of the SME's movement. Also key to the anti-privatization campaign was the support of three other groups. First, the student movement of the national university (UNAM), which protested against an attempt to increase tuition fees and closed the country's largest university for almost a year. Both the SME and the student movement committed their mutual support, attending each other's demonstrations. Second, on 16 March the SME and the Ejército Zapatista de Liberación Nacional (EZLN) committed their mutual support to 'defend the country's sovereignty'. Finally, rank-and-file workers from the SUTERM also participated in the protests and demonstrations organized by the SME.

In sum, the SME was able to summon all the most prominent anti-neo-liberal voices in Mexican society and unite them around the rejection of President Zedillo's initiative to privatize the electrical industry.

The SME was also active in holding demonstrations and rallies to raise public awareness and to show their determination to fight the proposed reform. The union mobilized its workers to block important avenues in Mexico City, and staged demonstrations outside the federal congress and the senate. On 18 March, the anniversary of the nationalization of the oil industry, there was a massive demonstration at the Zócalo that brought together the SME workers with the striking students of the national university. Also attending were important members of the PRD, the leader of the UNAM union, Agustin Rodríguez, Francisco Hernández Juárez, and representatives of the EZLN. The main topic was the fight against neo-liberal policy in general, and the privatizations of electricity and public education in particular. They demanded a new economic policy and the end of neo-liberalism.

Other elements that Flores used to counter the privatization of the electrical sector included the use of the media to make the union's position known to the public. As early as 3 February, the SME placed a public manifesto in the newspapers, rejecting the government's proposal to reform Article 27 of the Constitution. Later, on 15 February, a letter to the president was published in the newspapers, in which the SME, via its Secretary-General, restated the idea about the right to the nation's ownership over its natural resources, which is linked to the concept of national sovereignty. The explicit purpose of that letter was to ask the president to withdraw the reform initiative.[13]

Finally, Flores' strategy included the establishment of a dialogue with all legislative fractions in the federal congress and in local legislatures. Also, in September 1999, the SME presented to the chamber of deputies its own proposal for reform, which argued for the participation of workers in the process of modernization and suggested means other than privatization to guarantee the viability of the firm.

In stark contrast, the most salient feature of the response of the SUTERM was the silence of its leader who, during the first couple of weeks after the announcement, refrained from making public declarations. Even when confronted by reporters, Rodríguez Alcaine refused to comment on whether the SUTERM would join the front for the defence of the electrical sector that the SME had formed.

After the initial silence, it eventually became clear that the position of the union leadership was to support totally the presidential initiative. On 16 February, Rodríguez Alcaine finally spoke out and said that the reform was a positive measure, and that he agreed with it because he considered it important to the country. Rodríguez Alcaine reaffirmed his union's stance by stating that the electrical workers were always committed to the best and highest interest of the country, and that 'we trust that the president will know how to adjust his acts, as he has done so far, to the national interest'.[14] On 9 March, Rodríguez Alcaine invited Rosendo Flores to pay a joint visit to President Zedillo to negotiate jointly both unions' wage increases. Flores rejected the offer saying that any agreement had to be reached in a union assembly.

Rodríguez Alcaine's position soon generated responses within the SUTERM. On 18 March, the leader met with heated protests from more than five hundred workers, who demanded that he openly reject the initiative or else resign from the position of Secretary-General of the SUTERM due to his failure to represent its members. The workers, from sections 123 and 186 of Tula, Hidalgo, also protested against the intimidation they were subjected to by union officials when they attempted to hold local assemblies to discuss the proposal and define their position.

By late March, the newspapers were still reporting an increase in SUTERM dissidence. According to the newspaper *Reforma*, more than half of the SUTERM representations in the country warned Rodríguez Alcaine that they would join the SME in their fight against privatization. One of the SUTERM leaders in Tula commented on the position of their national leader: 'either he hasn't noticed or he has obligations beyond the defence of electricity, but the truth is that Rodríguez Alcaine has not fully recognized the fractures in the union due to his support to privatization'.[15]

The bouts of internal dissidence and the increased visibility of the SME may have had an influence on the fact that the SUTERM leader moderated his position later on. While still approving of the reform in general terms, by 11 April, Rodríguez Alcaine announced that the initiative would not be discussed in the current session of congress. He said that the PRI labour faction in the chamber of deputies, including SUTERM deputies, was studying some modifications to the initiative. He also said that although the SUTERM's position was to accept private investment, it did want to make sure that the state would keep control of the sector.

Later on, SUTERM announced that it would try to reach an agreement with the SME regarding the reforms the electrical sector before the senate opened the discussion of the presidential initiative. This was the first and only formal proposal to try to work jointly with the SME. The SME responded to the proposition, stating that it remained open to dialogue as long as the goal was to improve the situation of the electrical industry. Rosendo Flores said that his union would evaluate the invitation and, if conditions were appropriate, would meet with Rodríguez Alcaine. An alliance between the two unions never took place.

Unrest continued to grow within the SUTERM. On 19 April, during an assembly with at least a hundred regional representatives, Rodríguez Alcaine was jeered at, and the delegates demanded that he firmly oppose the initiative of the president. They criticized the 'ambiguous position' of their leader. The session had to be terminated after thirty-five minutes because of disorder. On 22 May, thousands of SUTERM workers took the streets and protested against the privatization of the electrical industry and the support that their leader had given to it. The demonstration brought together more than three thousand workers from about forty sections of the union, from all over the country.

On 5 June, workers formed a 'national group of SUTERM workers against privatization', which claimed to have about 10,000 members. The group demanded that Rodríguez Alcaine promote a consultation, through direct and secret voting, among the six union members, so that the workers could define the position of the union regarding the presidential initiative. There were complaints about authoritarian practices within the union, according to one worker:

> twenty-three years of union domination by political bosses have taken their toll, whoever dares publicly denounce his disagreement or criticize Rodríguez Alcaine, can expect to be expelled from the union and consequently lose his job; there is fear of expressing one's thoughts.[16]

In spite of all this, Rodríguez Alcaine maintained his position of supporting the reform and the government. He even committed the vote of his union for the 2000 elections in order to:

> prevent that the power that the people have exercised through the governments emanated from the Mexican Revolution be taken away by the most reactionary groups or those who support intolerant positions which have no foundation for a real transformation because they are based upon utopias and promises that cannot be kept.[17]

Conclusions

The rationale given for privatization was strikingly similar in both the cases of Telmex and the electrical sector initiative. This was mainly that, given the lack of state resources and the urgency and importance of the social needs in the country, the indispensable expansion and modernization of state-owned enterprises would have to be carried out with private investment. However, one privatization succeeded and the other failed. Also, the responses of the trade unions that have been analysed vary significantly. What stands out between the two privatization experiences is that the political context was substantially different.

The privatization of Telmex took place in a similar way to that of previous privatizations and according to the way in which general economic policy was conducted in Mexico at that time. The president was the undisputed authority, with no counterbalancing powers to limit his power. In the context of an authoritarian regime, such as that which prevailed early in the Salinas administration, some form of repression would have been a likely outcome of mobilization. Thus, the most rational strategy for Hernández Juárez was to work in alliance with the government.

The combination of two elements made possible the success of Hernández Juárez's strategy. On the one hand, his personal links to President Salinas provided direct access to the man who had the ultimate power in decision-making and who could grant concessions to the leader and his union. On the other hand, Hernández Juárez's legitimacy among workers represented a crucial element that gave the leader credibility as a negotiator. Having enough legitimacy among the rank and file was essential for this leader to commit the involvement of workers in the modernization plans of Telmex and to gather consent among workers for the privatization without generating serious internal disruption.

Clearly an important goal for Salinas was to promote the image of an economy of efficient and competitive enterprises. The fact that Hernández Juárez was able to commit his union to the modernization and restructuring plans that Telmex needed was exactly what Salinas was looking for. By presenting himself as a modern leader, committed to the modernization of his firm, Hernández Juárez obtained important concessions from the process of privatization. In a context where most previous privatizations involved substantial job losses, Hernández Juárez obtained the guarantee from Telmex that no lay-offs would result from the change to a private management of the firm. This was indeed a positive gain in the interest of workers.

Thus, given the prevailing political climate, by accepting the fact that the privatization was going to be carried out, Hernández Juárez could still successfully negotiate an advantageous outcome for the workers in his union.

Almost ten years later, democratization made a big difference in terms of the opportunities available to unions. It was clear that the electrical sector initiative was of great importance to Zedillo's government. However, the president was unable to gather enough support in congress, and even had trouble obtaining support from his own party. This circumstance, in which the president could not implement his agenda due to lack of support from the legislature, is rather new in Mexico, and the case of the electrical sector shows how this new context can be used by the unions to advance their causes.

The Zedillo government was significantly more tolerant to opposition both from political parties and from diverse groups in society.[18] And even in the relationship with unions there were some signs that the president was willing to allow corporatist controls to subside.[19] Thus, the political context at the time of Zedillo's proposal for privatization of the electrical industry signalled that the costs of mobilization had decreased relative to previous governments.

The SME was able to exploit the weakness of the government due to its lack of allies in congress, which enabled the union to maintain the most extreme position of total rejection of the initiative. Additionally, even though it does not have any strong party links, a more democratic regime did open the opportunity for the SME to seek access to legislators and to push the demands of the union to congress.

Democratization also had the effect of opening the door to the creation of alliances with other groups that had emerged under a more tolerant regime and with other unions that previously may have found it too risky to engage in combative actions.[20] The SME made itself heard though demonstrations, newspaper reports and by joining forces with some of the most notorious, and radical, movements in the country. Although it is difficult to pinpoint exactly the degree of influence that the SME had upon the failure of the reform, it undoubtedly had an important role. From the beginning, and throughout the debate, the SME was able to command the attention of Mexican society. Thus, the ability of its leadership to mobilize a substantial number of workers and to stage massive demonstrations proved to be one of its most important sources of strength.

All this notoriety raised the political costs of ignoring the union's demands and gave the union public recognition as an important actor. In an electoral year, this probably proved to be decisive for the failure of the initiative. In this sense, it is important to point out that the timing of the reform, in terms of the electoral calendar, may also be an important element to consider. Zedillo introduced his proposal during the fifth year of his government, when the calculations for the next presidential elections were already gaining importance. In a way, Zedillo began to be labelled as a lame duck. Salinas, on the other hand, was only beginning his term in office, which is a time when presidents tend to have the most power.

In sum, the combative strategy of Flores was successful because he was able to exploit the opportunities brought about by a more democratic regime. Crucial in this sense were the lack of congressional support for the president and the more tolerant attitude of the government toward social movements, which permitted the formation of alliances with other groups, the staging of massive demonstrations, and other forms of combative activity.

But the importance of the democratic nature of the union and of its lack of partisan ties should also be noted. Without the legitimacy that democratic internal practices confer to the SME's leaders, it is very unlikely that massive mobilizations of workers could be feasible, and the lack of partisan commitments also provide more alternatives for the leader to channel the union's demands into the political system.

The fact that Rodríguez Alcaine remained supportive of the initiative, even at the expense of increasing internal dissidence, speaks volumes about the constraints that this kind of leader faces. The lack of union democracy and the loyalty to the ruling party are decisive determinants of his actions, given that his career is much more in the hands of the party than in those of the workers. What this suggests is that political links can be useful to negotiate benefits for workers, but are not enough. The case of Hernández Juárez would indicate that it is also necessary for a leader to command sufficient legitimacy among his/her workers in order to be able to commit to the goals of productivity and competition that a liberalized economy demands.

For union leaders such as Rodríguez Alcaine, who relied for years on his political links to an authoritarian regime to maintain his position, democratization was debilitating. The increase in the number of players in the system who were able to exercise a veto, coupled with the distancing of Zedillo from the PRI, curtailed the bargaining strength of top party leaders such as Rodríguez Alcaine. Also, with more open and competitive elections, the corporatist vote of official unions began to carry less weight. The party needs to appeal to a wider fraction of the electorate in order to gain access to elective posts, and this further reduces the relative bargaining power of the labour sector. Both considerations reduce the feasibility of corporatist union leaders having an active role in dealing with economic reform.

In fact, leaders such as Rodríguez Alcaine are now in a very uncomfortable position, without much room to manoeuvre. On the one hand, the leader lacks mobilizing power because of his/her lack of legitimacy among workers. On the other hand, his/her bargaining power inside the party has diminished as a result of the democratization of the regime.

In sum, Rodríguez Alcaine, in spite of having centralized decision-making within his union, is a weak leader. He lacks the ability both to mobilize workers and to influence top-level decision-makers in a more democratic regime. For these reasons, the only strategy available to him when dealing with economic reform is one of passive acceptance.

Thus, under a PRI government, it is to be expected that leaders of the traditional corporatist unions of that party continue to unconditionally support economic reforms. The question remains how these leaders will behave under a non-PRI government. However, the authoritarian nature of their leadership and their lack of mobilizing power make it very unlikely that they will become more militant.[21] Perhaps the real issue at stake is how long this kind of leader can endure increased bouts of dissidence among the rank and file.

Notes

1 The level of the minimum wage is a key economic variable because it is widely used as a reference during collective bargaining throughout the economy.
2 Many blamed the Salinas administration's dubious process of bank privatizations for the financial crisis, given that it was characterized by pervasive corruption and that banks had been sold to individuals with virtually no experience in the management of financial institutions. Between 1995 and 1997, a state agency, FOBAPROA, assumed around 65 billion US dollars in bank liabilities in order to save the financial system from bankruptcy. That measure prompted a great public outcry, especially from the

opposition parties, and became one of the most contested political issues of Zedillo's presidency.

3 A person is considered to be employed as long as he or she worked for one hour, whether paid or not, during the week of reference.

4 While eleven of the PRI's 300 claimed congressional seats were subsequently awarded to opposition party candidates as a result of successful challenges to the results in the electoral college, all of the PRI's gubernatorial victories were certified.

5 The term *tecnócrata* is commonly used to refer to young politicians with an extensive technical training (usually from prestigious universities in the United States or Europe). *Políticos* refers to politicians who identify themselves as representatives of the revolutionary heritage and whose careers are based on a partisan trajectory rather than on technical training.

6 Salinas had been Secretary of the Budget during the de la Madrid administration and was recognized as the main architect of the economic programme that was implemented during those years.

7 Constitutional amendments require the vote of at least two-thirds of the legislators in the chamber of deputies.

8 Early in 1988, La Quina publicly criticized de la Madrid's economic policy and the stabilization pact. He and other leaders of the oil workers' union made explicit their disapproval of Salinas' nomination and since late 1987 started supporting the candidacy of Cuauhtémoc Cárdenas. In the election results that year, most of the electoral districts controlled by the oil workers' union had voted against Salinas (Méndez and Quiroz 1994: 184).

9 For instance, his government did not hesitate to take control over striking firms in strategic sectors (*requisa*) whenever it was deemed necessary.

10 Every Monday, Hernández Juárez personally receives up to 150 workers to listen to their grievances and to promise solutions (Interview with Eduardo Torres, press secretary of the STRM, Mexico City, 28 July 1999).

11 That this was an important reform for Zedillo may be inferred from the repeated calls he made to urge its approval. Throughout 1999, both Zedillo and Secretary of Energy Luis Téllez pleaded continually to opposition legislators for them to approve the proposal. Téllez appeared before Congress on several occasions in order to defend the initiative.

12 Although the FTSE's leader Joel Ayala supported the privatization initiative, leaders of individual unions affiliated to the FTSE rejected it and promised their support to the SME's campaign. These unions were the Sindicato Nacional de Trabajadores de la Comisión Nacional Bancaria y de Valores (SNTCNBV), of the Instituto Mexicano del Petróleo (SNTIMP), of the Consejo Nacional de Ciencia y Tecnología, and of Conasupo (SNTC) (*La Jornada* 5 February 1999).

13 Other manifestos appeared in newspapers on 4 March, 18 March, 27 September and 2 February 2000.

14 Quoted in *La Jornada*, 27 February 1999.

15 Quoted in *Reforma*, 1 April 1999.

16 Quoted in *La Jornada*, 6 June 1999.

17 Quoted in *La Jornada*, 14 August 1999.

18 Examples of this were the restrained attitude of the regime towards such militant movements as the strike organized by students of the national university.

19 An example of this was the judicial decision eliminating the closed shop in the bureaucracy, which allowed workers to form and join alternative unions to those affiliated to the PRI.

20 Although we can only speculate what the response of Hernández Juárez might have been had the privatization of Telmex taken place under a more democratic context, the fact that during the Zedillo administration that leader changed his position from

supporting privatizations to totally rejecting them, may suggest that an authoritarian context did indeed preclude a more combative response from the STRM.
21 The passiveness of those unions during the time that Panista president Vicente Fox has been in office would seem to support that hypothesis.

References

Aspe, P. (1993) *El Camino Mexicano de la Transformacion Económica*, Mexico City: Fondo de Cultura Económica.

Bizberg, I. (1990) 'Corporativismo y modernización', in J. Woldenberg and C. García (coordinators), *Sindicalismo Mexicano de los 90's*, Mexico City: Instituto de Estudios para la Transición Democrática.

—— (1996) 'Restructuración Productiva y Transformación del Modelo de Relaciones Industriales: 1988–1994', *Foro Internacional*, 36(1–2): 80–106.

Bruhn, K. (1996) 'Social spending and political support: the "lessons" of the National Solidarity Program in Mexico', *Comparative Politics*, 28(2): 151–77.

Clifton, J. (2000) 'On the political consequences of privatization: the case of Teléfonos de México', *Bulletin of Latin American Research*, 19: 63–79.

Cornelius, W.A. (1986) 'Political liberalization and the 1985 elections in Mexico', in P.W. Drake and E. Silva (eds), *Elections and Democratization in Latin America 1980–1985*, San Diego: UCSD.

González Casanova, P. (1990) *La Democracia en México*, Mexico City: Ediciones Era.

Grindle, M.S. (1996) *Challenging the State: Crisis and Innovation in Latin America and Africa*, New York and Cambridge: Cambridge University Press.

Hernández Juárez, F. (1991) 'El nuevo sindicalismo', *Nexos*, 161. Online: http://www.nexos.com.mx/archivo_nexos/detalle.asp?id=2231 (accessed 10 April 2002).

Hernández Juárez, F. and López, M.X. (1993) *El sindicalismo en la Reforma del Estado*, Mexico City: Fondo de Cultura Económica.

Koechlin, T. (1998) 'Liberalization and Mexican labor markets', in P. Dabir-Alai and M. Odekon (eds), *Economic Liberalization and Labor Markets*, Westport, CT, and London: Greenwood Press.

Krauze, E. (1997) *La Presidencia Imperial*, Mexico City: Tusquets Editores.

Lustig, N. (1992) *Mexico: the Remaking of an Economy*, Washington D.C.: Brookings Institution.

Méndez, L.H. and Quiroz, J.O. (1994) *Modernización Estatal y Respuesta Obrera: Historia de una Derrota*, México City: Universidad Autónoma Metropolitana.

Molinar, J. (1991) *El Tiempo de la Legitimidad: Elecciones, Autoritarismo y Democracia en Mexico*, Mexico City: Cal y Arena.

Mondragón Pérez, Y. (1994) 'Cambio en la Relación Corporativa entre el Estado y los Sindicatos: El Caso del Sindicato de Telefonistas de la República Mexicana', Unpublished Master's Thesis, Instituto de Investigaciones Sociales Dr. José MA Luis Mora.

Morris, S.D. (1995) *Political Reformism in Mexico*, Boulder, CO, and London: Lynne Rienner Publishers.

OECD (1997) *Mexico Economic Surveys 1996–1997*, Paris: OECD.

Pastor, M. and Wise, C. (1997) 'State Policy, Distribution and Neoliberal Reform in Mexico', *Journal of Latin American Studies*, 29(2): 419–57.

Ramírez, M.D. (1996) 'The latest IMF-sponsored stabilization program: does it represent a long-term solution to Mexico's economy?', *Journal of Interamerican Studies and World Affairs*, 34(4): 129–56.

Rangel Pérez, M. (1989) *Los Telefonistas Frente a la Crisis y la Reconversión*, Mexico City: Editorial Nuestro Tiempo.

Rendón, T. and Salas, C. (2000) 'La evolución del empleo', in G. Bensusán, and T. Rendón (eds), *Trabajo y Trabajadores en el México Contemporáneo*, Mexico City: Grupo Editorial Miguel Angel Porrúa.

Rodríguez Castañeda, R. (1995) *Operación Telmex: Contacto en el Poder*, Mexico City: Grijalbo.

Samstad, J.G. (1998) *Union Legacies and the Politics of Productivity: Corporatism, Clientelism and Firm Reorganization during the Transition to Export-Led Development in Mexico*, Unpublished Ph.D. Dissertation, University of California, Berkeley.

Samstad, J.G. and Collier, R.B. (1995) 'Mexican labor and structural reform under Salinas: new unionism or old stalemate?', in R. Roett (ed.), *The Challenge of Institutional Reform in Mexico*, Boulder and London: Lynne Ricnner Publishers.

Teichman, J. (1996) *Privatization and Political Change in Mexico*, Pittsburgh: Pittsburgh University Press.

Zamora, G. (1990) 'La política laboral del estado Mexicano: 1982–1988', *Revista Mexicana de Sociología*, 52(3): 111–38.

Zapata, F. (1996) 'Mexican labor in the context of political and economic crisis', in L. Randall (ed), *Changing Structure of Mexico*, New York: M.E. Sharpe.

15 Structural adjustment and trade unions in Africa

The case of Ghana

Piet Konings

Introduction

Faced with a deep and prolonged economic crisis, virtually all African governments have been compelled since the 1980s by the International Monetary Funds (IMF), the World Bank and Western donors to implement a 'neo-liberal' reform package, in the form of Structural Adjustment Programmes (SAPs). The aim of SAPs has been to reduce the government's role in the economy, to establish free markets and a secure environment for private capital, and to enhance Africa's competitiveness in the global economic order. Their central demands include drastic cuts in public expenditure, such as the elimination of subsidies, dismantling of price controls, 'rationalization' of the public sector through privatization, lay-offs, wage cuts and company closures, liberalization of the economy guided by 'market forces' domestically and 'comparative advantage' internationally, promotion of commodity exports and foreign investment, and currency devaluation. In terms of macro-economic performance, structural adjustment has produced widely diverging results in Africa, but in terms of social consequences the outcome has been more uniformly negative. It is now generally recognized that employees have been among the most seriously affected by the economic crisis and structural adjustment. They are confronted with retrenchments and job insecurity, wage restraints and the suspension of benefits, soaring consumer prices and user charges for public services, 'flexible' management practices and subcontracting, and an intensification of managerial efforts to increase labour productivity.

World Bank reports have often attempted to justify these anti-labour measures, both in economic and political terms (Bangura and Beckman 1993, Adesina 1994, Gibbon 1995, World Bank 1995). The economic justification for structural adjustment is that workers are 'too many and too costly'. This is attributed to misconceived policies, including the development of an overprotected and oversized import-substituting industrial sector. Another problem is the growth of overstaffed state enterprises and public services, with wage bills out of proportion to their carrying capacity and deficits paid by state subsidies, due to a combination of budgetary laxity and the influence of corrupt and clientelistic modes of labour recruitment. Such policies have worked against the development of the private sector and increased competition in the global market. The political justification for structural adjustment is that workers are 'powerful and selfish'. The World Bank argues that organized labour has been a major beneficiary of pre-adjustment policies, stressing that the historical influence of African trade unions has led to excessive levels of wage employment, inflated wages and a pro-urban, pro-worker allocation of public funds. It is interesting to observe that this argument comes close to earlier populist positions, such as 'labour aristocracy', 'urban bias' and 'urban coalition', which tended to view workers as a privileged minority, pursuing narrow self-interests at the expense of the urban poor and peasantry, taking advantage of better organization, and being in coalition with the urban élite (Waterman 1975, Lipton 1977, Bates 1981, Ferguson 1999). Jamal and Weeks (1993) presented a detailed refutation of the argument, showing that the so-called rural–urban gap was largely illusory and had in any case been closed before the harsh SAP measures were applied to correct it. These views have nevertheless often been used by African leaders, like Rawlings in Ghana (Kraus 1991), to legitimize the implementation of SAP measures and to suppress any trade-union opposition.

Although SAPs pose a formidable challenge to trade unions in Africa, there is still a dearth of studies on trade-union responses to SAPs. Moreover, existing studies appear to differ on the actual role of trade unions in African post-colonial states, with some authors refuting the World Bank assumption that trade unions are occupying a powerful position in African societies (Konings 2000). The latter are inclined to take an extremely pessimistic view of the role of African trade unions. They argue that trade unions are usually not only small, organising only a tiny minority of the working population in the predominantly agrarian societies in Africa, but are also subordinated to state control in the aftermath of independence for the sake of national development. These views are contested by other Africanists, particularly those who have carried out intensive research on trade unions in Africa (cf. Sandbrook and Cohen 1975, Freund 1988). They are ready to admit that trade unions in Africa show a number of weaknesses, but they equally stress that trade unions are among the few organizations that have been able to survive the onslaught on civil society by authoritarian post-colonial regimes. They argue that African governments have found it hard to control trade unions. Even in countries where post-colonial governments did achieve a large measure of control at the national level by co-opting trade union leaders into the regime, they often failed to control unions at regional and local levels (Bates 1971, Konings 1993). Paradoxically, certain state-corporatist strategies, like the centralization of the trade-union movement, the allocation of substantial funds, the introduction of the check-off system, and assistance in trade-union education have tended instead to strengthen the organizational capacity of the unions, which, in turn, has been of great significance to future union struggles for autonomy (Akwetey 1994, Hashim 1994).

This latter group of authors tend to be more optimistic than the former about the role of trade unions in African post-colonial states. They usually refer to certain specific factors which guarantee trade unions an exceptional position among civil-society organizations. First, trade-union members may account for only a small proportion of the working population in Africa, but they are concentrated in the cities and active in strategically important sectors of the economy. As such, they may exercise considerable political power, being potentially capable of paralysing the economy and threatening the regime in power. Second, trade unions are among the oldest civil-society organizations, with a long history of struggles against oppressive and exploitative regimes (cf. Jeffries 1978, Sandbrook 1982, Freund 1988). Third, trade unions often enjoy a higher degree of international solidarity than other civil-society organizations. International trade-union organizations and the International Labour Organization (ILO) in Geneva have frequently requested authoritarian regimes to release trade-union leaders from prison and to ensure a minimum of trade-union liberties (Kester and Sidibé 1997).

Following the implementation of SAPs in African states, however, the optimistic authors appear to have come closer to the views of the pessimistic ones. Most now maintain that SAPs have weakened the position of trade unions in African post-colonial states (Isamah 1994, Mihyo and Schiphorst 1995, Simutanyi 1996). A number of recent studies have shown that trade unions have attempted to oppose structural adjustment, but that the effectiveness of their resistance has by and large been limited. Not only were they likely to operate in a hostile political environment, but also the logic of structural adjustment tended to constrain the ability of trade unions to defend their members' rights effectively. With mass retrenchments of labour in the public and private sectors leading to substantial losses in trade-union membership and trade-union revenues, government abolition of legislative provisions concerning job security, participatory rights or guaranteed collective bargaining rights, and outright government oppression to any oppositional trade-union action, trade unions had their backs to the wall. In these circumstances, there was little the trade unions could do for their members. Increasing job insecurity and a fall in real earnings have forced the rank and file to search for alternative sources of income, straddling between the formal and informal sectors and subsistence farming, as well as engaging in illicit income-generating activities. The 'fusion' of labour markets has ensured the survival of workers but, according to some authors (Jamal and Weeks 1993), it also signifies the virtual collapse of the wage-earning class as a distinct entity. As a result of these developments, trade unions are said to be facing a deep crisis of identity, having not yet devised any new strategies to deal with these dramatic changes.

To test such views, I shall focus in my study on the role of trade unions in structural adjustment in Ghana. Ghana provides an interesting case study, due to the spectacular adoption in 1983 of a 'neo-liberal' reform package by a radical populist military regime, the Provisional National Defence Council (PNDC), which had constantly proclaimed to be committed to popular democracy and anti-imperialism. And, even more significantly, the PNDC's rigorous execution of the SAP earned Ghana the reputation among Western donors of being 'one of the most impressive reform efforts in Africa, the lessons of which are being closely observed in other African countries' (Graham 1988: 42). Even after the transition from the military PNDC regime to the civilian National Democratic Congress (NDC) government in 1992, Rawlings, having been promoted in the meantime from PNDC chairman to elected president of Ghana's Fourth Republic, stressed the continuation of the SAP, with the declared intention of improving economic conditions and achieving sustained economic prosperity for all Ghanaians. And, above all, there is the firm belief among many scholars that Ghana has a relatively strong labour movement, with a substantial capacity for ensuring independence and a long tradition of militant struggles on behalf of workers' rights and interests (Konings 1977, Jeffries 1978, Kraus 1979, Crisp 1984). Freund (1988: 108), for instance, observed, 'A sensitive analysis of developments in a country such as Ghana also shows that the unions are conduits at times for shocks that can present difficulties for regimes'.

In this study, I will first assess the impact of structural adjustment on the labour markets in Ghana, and then describe the response of the Ghana Trades Union Congress (GTUC) under both the PNDC and NDC governments.

Structural adjustment and labour markets in Ghana

When the PNDC under the leadership of Flight-Lieutenant Jerry Rawlings seized power on 31 December 1981, the economy of Ghana was in a state of prolonged recession, disinvestment and virtual collapse.

Between 1970 and 1981 per capita GDP fell by over 30 per cent, mineral production decreased by 32 per cent and cocoa production, the largest foreign-exchange earner, dropped from 400,000 to 225,000 metric tonnes. Declines in exports led to severe foreign-exchange shortages, which strangled imports and created recessionary declines in other sectors because of shortages of inputs, spare parts and transportation. By the early 1980s, the inflation rate was in excess of 100 per cent and the nation was experiencing one of the worst droughts and famines in its history. The sudden expulsion and repatriation of well over 1 million Ghanaians from Nigeria added fuel to the already existing high unemployment and inflation rates (Kraus 1991, Konadu-Agyemang 1998).

No single explanation suffices to elucidate why a country like Ghana whose development potential appeared to be much brighter than most other African countries at the time of its independence in 1957 – being the world's leading exporter of cocoa and disposing of considerable foreign reserves (estimated at US$532m), substantial mineral deposits (gold, diamonds, bauxite, etc.), a comparatively good infrastructure and a relatively well-trained and educated labour force – should suffer such socio-economic ills. Neo-liberals are inclined to attribute these problems first and foremost to internal factors such as the post-colonial state's excessive intervention in the economy, mismanagement, corruption and patronage politics. They blame the Ghanaian post-colonial state in particular for expanding public services (such as 'over-subsidized' educational and health facilities) and establishing an oversized and overprotected public sector, both largely financed by heavy taxation of cocoa farmers and frequent resorts to foreign loans, over-regulation, productivity disincentives, the inability to control inflation and the tolerance of an over-valued currency. It is these so-called 'internal constraints' to development that the IMF and the World Bank seek to address and resolve through SAPs. What is often left out of the neo-liberal diagnosis of underdevelopment is the role of external forces in helping to create the situation in the first place (Hutchful 1989).

After an initial fifteen-month period of populist mobilization and experimenta-tion, during which Ghana's woes were attributed to 'imperialist' and 'neo-colonialist' forces, the PNDC was compelled to adopt a more pragmatic stance on economic issues. In the absence of a realistic alternative from the intel-lectual left and assistance from 'socialist' countries, the technocratic faction convinced Rawlings in 1983 that the best possible solution to the challenges posed by the desperate economic situation was to seek help from the Bretton Woods institutions (Rothchild 1991, Yeebo 1991). The persistent rhetoric of populism then became linked to a 'neo-liberal' reform package, in the form of an SAP which was designated in Ghana as the Economic Recovery Programme (ERP). The military-led populist regime had considerable leverage to manoeuvre, enabling it to impose a variety of harsh measures intended to rehabilitate the economy.

The PNDC formally launched the SAP in April 1983. It contained the conventional measures, including adjustment of the cedi (the Ghanaian currency) to market forces, import liberalization, tightening financial account-ability, reducing deficit financing, increasing prices for cocoa, cutting back on public services, marketing boards and parastatal bodies, and 'cost recovery' for much-needed social services.

By the end of the 1980s the IMF and the World Bank were in a state of euphoria about Ghana's performance. Compared with other African countries, Ghana appeared to have fared better from a macro-economic point of view. For example, the country had an average annual growth rate of 6.3 per cent in the period 1984–6 and of 5 per cent in the period 1986–92. There were noticeable improvements in infrastructure – roads, rail and seaports – in order to promote export production. Substantial improvements occurred in Ghana's balance of payments. Although the country did not regain its position as the number one producer of cocoa in the world, exports of cocoa and other products recovered appreciably. The recovery of exports such as gold, diamond and timber was facilitated largely by the heavy capitalization of mines previously starved of funds, and the provision of credit facilities to timber companies by the World Bank and other international financiers, with guarantees from donor nations (Panford 1997). Approximately US$9 billion was injected into the Ghanaian economy by the international community between 1983 and 1992.

Since the beginning of the 1990s, however, international praise of the 'Ghanaian model' has died down somewhat. International donors were shocked when the political liberalization process appeared to have caused a slackening of fiscal controls, leading to substantial budgetary deficits and (temporary) with-drawal of 'aid' (Sandbrook and Oelbaum 1997). Moreover, the structural weakness of the domestic economy has become more and more visible. Ghana's recovery remains vulnerable to international commodity price changes. Declines in export commodity prices and increases in import prices, most notably of oil, and Ghana's heavy external indebtedness continue to act as constraints on economic growth. In addition, the intensified focus on the export of primary products has not been accompanied by any significant industrial growth. Some authors even observe a pattern of 'de-industrialization' in Ghana (Panford 1994, Hutchful 1996). Manufacturing climbed 16.1 per cent in 1984–6, 7.6 per cent in 1987–8, and a mere 2.8 per cent in 1989–90. This suggests that early growth involved recovery from profound lows on the basis of improved access to imported raw materials and other inputs as well as price decontrols. Estimated capacity utilization still remained below 40 per cent in 1990. Industrial restructuring and competitive ability have been severely impeded by a number of factors. Devaluation sharply raised the cost of imported inputs and eroded liquidity, and while, in principle, price liberalization allowed price increases to be passed on to consumers, in practice many manufacturers could not do so because demand was constrained by stabilization measures and increased competition. Tight credit and high interest rates (over 30 per cent) have squeezed working capital, and lack of access to long-term finance has constituted an important constraint on restructuring. Excessively rapid liberalization has led to competition from a flood of imports even before domestic manufacturers have had an opportunity to adjust to the new economic environment. And, last but not least, the political climate has not been conducive to private investment. Rawlings and other state personnel have often displayed a hostile attitude towards local business people, perceiving them as corrupt and bent on quick returns as well as supporting the political opposition. As a result of these economic and political factors, a lot of domestic manufacturers found it hard to survive, and some even had to wind up their businesses. Rawlings' persistent populist rhetoric was also a prominent factor in explaining why Ghana failed to attract much foreign investment (Kraus 1991, Hutchful 1996, Tangri 1999).

Given Ghana's continuing dependence on primary commodity exports and lack of industrialization, structural adjustment appears to have failed to restructure an essentially colonial economy. It tends to encourage a world order in which Africa continues to export raw materials and import even basic goods that it had previously manufactured. Such a division of labour, which is often justified in terms of 'comparative advantage', constitutes one of the major obstacles to any meaningful form of regional co-operation in Africa at a time when other parts of the world are maximizing their economic competitiveness through the creation of powerful regional groupings (Konings and Meilink 1998).

While the aura of success surrounding Ghana's adjustment efforts is fading, the effects of structural adjustment on the urban labour markets have been devastating. Workers are now confronted with low real incomes, a drastic reduction in formal-sector employment and job insecurity, and a formidable expansion of informal-sector employment.

Low real wages

Rawlings and his lieutenants have always thought that trade unions were selfish and protected the privileged interests of costly workers who did little. Their views simply denied the socially destructive annual inflation rate, averaging over 50 per cent, which impoverished and demoralized workers in the years preceding the introduction of the SAP (1975–81). Rising allowances apart, the index of real minimum wages dropped from 75 in 1975 to 15 in 1981 or 80 per cent (Table 15.1). Even if a significant income gap between urban wage earners and the rural population ever existed in Ghana – a thesis which has been contested by earlier empirical studies in the 1960s and 1970s (Konings 1977) – the characterization of the mass of urban workers as an 'aristocracy of labour' clearly no longer applies. Strikingly, higher skilled and higher paid workers suffered a proportionally greater reduction in their real incomes, compressing the wage structure (Vandermoortele 1991: 86, Jamal and Weeks 1993). In 1981, the differential between the highest and lowest paid workers in the civil service had shrunk drastically to 2.5:1. As a result of these developments, all workers had lost the incentive to work hard. Most felt compelled either to engage in simultaneous informal-sector activities or to flee the country in search of greener pastures. During this period, Ghana suffered a severe brain drain.

Following the introduction of the SAP in 1983, the real minimum wage dropped to its lowest level, barely rising in 1984, when it was a mere 11.5 per cent of its 1963 value. There was a substantial increase in 1985, when real earnings almost doubled to 21.4 per cent of their 1963 value – a level that was more or less maintained in subsequent years (Table 15.1). The regime persistently attempted to control and restrain the minimum wage level. It soon introduced the notion of a 'minimum rationalization wage'. The state of the economy could accommodate a simple restoration of the existing value of wages (Table 15.2), but could not allow a real increase in the value of incomes, which could only be based on an increase in labour productivity (Adu-Amankwah 1990: 108). The regime was also quick to invoke the poverty and relative productivity of the rural population and the urban bias inherent in the existing patterns of resource allocation as a justification for demanding sacrifices of urban workers. Increases in producer prices for cocoa and other agricultural commodities were readily cited as the real cause of the government's inability to provide a living wage.

While the PNDC was initially inclined to offer higher wage increases to the lowest-paid workers in the public service, thus further compressing differentials between the highest and lowest wages to 1.8:1, it changed its wage policy in 1986 by increasing the differential between the highest and lowest paid to 4:1. Urged by the World Bank to be more sensitive to incentives than inequality, it widened pay ranges to 5.4:1 in 1988 and 10:1 in 1990 – a move opposed by the trade-union movement (Kraus 1991: 145–6).

What does the minimum wage mean in Ghana? In 1990, when a worker on the minimum wage received, including allowances, approximately 400 cedis per

Table 15.1 Real minimum wage index in Ghana, 1963–88

Year	Real minimum-wage index
1963	100.0
1965	66.4
1966	58.3
1967	68.6
1968	67.9
1969	63.5
1970	61.2
1971	56.0
1972	68.1
1973	57.1
1974	73.2
1975	75.2
1976	48.1
1977	33.4
1978	25.6
1979	16.7
1980	16.6
1981	15.4
1982	12.6
1983	10.2
1984	11.5
1985	21.4
1986	22.0
1987	19.7
1988	20.5

Source: Kraus 1991: 123

day, a ball of *kenkey* (one of the domestic staple foods) cost 50 cedis, one chicken roughly 2,500 cedis, one small fish 300 cedis, one loaf of bread 250 cedis, and one bottle of beer 350 cedis. Clearly, such a wage could scarcely support the workers' own food requirements, let alone those of their families or additional necessary expenditure on housing, clothing, health care and other costs. Even for better-paid skilled and clerical workers, it was difficult to make ends meet (Jeffries 1992: 211). Indeed, estimates show that the average low-income family in Accra spent the equivalent of more than eight times the minimum wage (ISSER 1994, 1995). As Table 15.2 clearly shows, the present daily minimum wage is still below the UNDP human poverty index of US$1 in spite of the so-called 'SAP miracle' in Ghana (UNDP 1997: 3).

Since the introduction of the SAP in 1983, workers have been burdened with the cost recovery scheme ('pay or perish', as it is called in Ghana), raising user charges for water, electricity, sewage, health and educational services to increasingly prohibitive levels. Occasional reports on social responses to such price hikes are gloomy. They reveal widespread withdrawal from medical and educational facilities. Parents can no longer afford to pay school fees for their children and a

Table 15.2 Daily minimum wage equivalent in US dollars for Ghana,
1980–98

Date	Minimum wage (in cedis)	Exchange rate (cedis/US$)	Minimum-wage equivalent (in US$)
October 1980	4.00	2.75	1.45
November 1980	12.00	2.75	4.36
March 1983	12.00	9.56	1.25
April 1983	25.00	9.56	2.61
January 1984	25.00	35.99	0.69
April 1984	35.00	35.99	0.97
December 1984	52.00	35.99	1.44
January 1985	70.00	54.37	1.28
January 1986	90.00	89.21	1.01
January 1987	112.00	162.37	0.68
January 1988	146.25	202.34	0.72
January 1989	170.00	270.01	0.63
January 1990	218.00	326.28	0.67
July 1991	460.00	367.73	1.25
January 1992	460.00	437.09	1.05
January 1993	460.00	648.98	0.71
January 1994	790.00	956.73	0.83
January 1995	1,200.00	1,200.40	1.00
January 1996	1,700.00	1,637.24	1.04
May 1997	2,000.00	2,050.28	0.98
January 1998	2,000.00	2,314.15	0.86

Source: Yanney 2000: 33

growing number of children have no choice but to join the informal-sector labour market (Ninsin 1996, Panford 1997).

Workers are now compelled to extend their outreach over the whole gamut of economic activities to survive, from wage labour to informal-sector activities and even to subsistence farming. According to Jamal and Weeks (1993), any previous formal–informal and rural–urban dichotomies no longer apply. Low real wages are also driving people to illicit activities such as theft, corruption, black-marketeering and prostitution (ISSER 1994, 1995).

Despite the unprecedented fall in urban real wages and the narrowing of the income gap between urban workers and peasants, rural–urban migration has continued unabated. Jamal and Weeks (1993) argue away this paradox by pointing out that rural–urban migration has become part of the survival strategy of the extended family. The rural population is also becoming increasingly impoverished. Only the larger cocoa farmers appear to have benefited from increased producer prices (Rothchild 1991). Green (1988) estimated that the number of urban dwellers living below the poverty line increased from an average of 30–35 per cent in the late 1970s to 45–50 per cent in the mid-1980s. For rural people, there was an increase in poverty from a range of 60–65 per cent in the late 1970s to 67–72 per cent in the mid-1980s. The Ghana Living Standard Survey partly supports this assertion (Ghana Statistical Service 1989).

With poverty, hunger and near hopelessness mounting on all fronts, workers tend to rely on the trade unions to defend their interests. In a situation of structural adjustment, however, trade-union leaders are bound to experience difficulties in delivering the desired result – an increase in wages.

Massive retrenchment, job insecurity and unemployment

The SAP in Ghana has caused unprecedented retrenchments in public and private-sector employment alike. Although Table 15.3 appears to underestimate the number of workers in both the public and private sectors, it nevertheless provides a clear indication of the extent of these retrenchments: formal-sector employment fell from 455,000 in 1975 to an all-time low of 186,000 in 1991.

As many as 71,500 workers in the civil service and field of education had been retrenched by the end of 1994 (Fokuoh 1996). Reorganization, divestiture and liquidation of state-owned enterprises contributed to massive lay-offs in the public sector. Approximately 75,600 jobs were lost in Cocobod (the former Ghana Cocoa Marketing Board) between 1985 and 1992, and over 50,000 jobs were cut in other state enterprises between 1987 and 1994 (Gyimah-Boadi 1991, Hutchful 1996, Konadu-Agyemang 1998). Since the costs involved in such retrenchments tended to be high, the government often attempted to postpone and reduce the fairly liberal end-of-service benefits won by workers through collective bargaining (Adu-Amankwah and Tutu 1997).

Several factors account for the severe job losses in the private sector. The problems faced by domestic manufacturers as a result of economic liberalization, leading to either closure of their enterprises or drastic retrenchments, have already been discussed. Another factor is the World Bank's continued insistence on government withdrawal of existing labour laws and collective agreements protecting workers' job security. One such legal provision is the requirement that

Table 15.3 Trends in formal employment in Ghana, 1960–91 (1,000s)

Year	Public sector	Private sector	Total
1960	184	149	333
1965	278	118	396
1970	288	110	398
1975	318	137	455
1980	291	46	337
1985	397	67	464
1986	347	66	413
1987	315	79	394
1988	252	55	307
1989	177	38	215
1990	189	40	229
1991	156	31	187

Source: ISSER 1995: 139

enterprises obtain the authorization of the Ministry of Labour for any lay-offs. Protective legislation and collective agreements are now commonly ignored, strengthening managerial control over the labour process manifest in the introduction of flexible employment contracts, working times, rules and wages. As a consequence of increased managerial flexibility in hiring and firing labour, even the employed are faced with permanent job insecurity. The latter is even being emphasized by the growing tendency among employers to recruit casual workers alongside a core of permanent workers, capitalizing on the existence of a swelling 'labour reserve army', and to introduce 'new' forms of employment such as subcontracting and a farming out of substantial parts of the production process (cf. Thomas 1995).

Redeployment schemes, like the Labour Redeployment Programme and the donor-supported Programme of Actions to Mitigate the Social Costs of Adjustment (Pamscad), which aim at assisting retrenched workers through job counselling, retraining and placement in the agricultural as well as formal and informal sectors of the economy, had little impact due to limited resources (Fokuoh 1996, Hutchful 1996, Panford 1997).

One of the consequences of the massive labour retrenchment has been a large drop in trade-union membership. Membership of the Ghana Trades Union Congress (GTUC) shrunk from 700,000 in the 1980s to 551,447 in August 1992 (Panford 1997). For the first time in post-colonial Ghana, the unions had to bargain with employers from a weak position.

Another consequence is the high rate of unemployment (see Table 15.4), particularly among the educated, including university graduates. No less than 14.3 per cent of those with post-secondary education were unemployed in 1987–8 compared with 5.2 per cent of those with primary education and 3.4 per cent of those with no education at all (ISSER 1995: 145). A symptom of the growing socio-economic malaise is the unemployed youths who roam the streets in urban areas, plotting their escape from Ghana to try their luck in Europe, North America and elsewhere. Most of the retrenched workers and the unemployed see no alternative but to look for gainful activities in the informal sector, whose capacity to absorb new entrants has slowed down.

Table 15.4 Average unemployment rates in Ghana, 1960–93

Period	Unemployment rate (%)
1960	6.0
1966–9	11.1
1969–79	6.0
1984	15.6
1990–3	19.0

Source: ISSER 1994: 143.

Major growth in informal-sector employment

Retrenchments, low real incomes and lack of domestic and foreign investment in the formal sector have precipitated a shift towards the informal sector (Ninsin 1991, Aryeetey 1996). The relative share of informal-sector employment in total non-agricultural employment increased from 25 to 44 per cent in the period 1970–90. At present, for every worker employed in the formal sector, there are 5.5 workers employed in the informal sector (Table 15.5). The informal sector is particularly important for the urban population. It is estimated that between 60 and 85 per cent of the urban population is currently operating in the informal sector (ISSER 1994: 142).

The informal labour market has not just been deregulated, it has also become increasingly segmented (Clark and Manuh 1991, Jamal and Weeks 1993, Mihyo and Schiphorst 1995). There are the small entrepreneurs who possess assets and skills. Earnings of heads of informal enterprises tend to be higher than the official minimum wage, even sometimes higher than the average wage in the formal sector. However, the wages of hired workers are usually lower than in the formal sector, while apprentices, who form up to three-quarters of informal-sector labour, often receive no wage at all. After completing their apprenticeship period, few apprentices continue as wage earners in the informal sector, since it is more remunerative to set up their own small workshops.

Alongside these small entrepreneurs and their workers, there are increasing numbers of new entrants without assets and relevant skills, competing for a stagnant or falling number of casual employment opportunities. Many are young people engaged in petty trade, retailing and hawking everything from dog-collars and apples to sunglasses (Panford 1994: 88). They often have no control over their markets but have to comply with the terms dictated by their creditors – subcontractors and large retailers. Like these young hawkers, the majority of women engaged in the informal sector in petty trade, tailoring and food preparation belong among the poorest section of informal-sector employees.

The shift of employment from the formal to the informal sector obviously poses a serious challenge to the unions. They have not yet made any significant inroads into organising workers in the informal sector, while daily losing members from the formal sector.

Table 15.5 Informal-sector employment in Ghana, 1970–90

Informal-sector employment	1970	1980	1985	
Total number (thousands)	356	683	946	1
As % of formal-sector employment	89	203	204	
As % of total employment	10	16	19	
As % of non-agricultural employment	25	35	41	
Number of women (thousands)	114	219	303	

Source: ILO/JASPA Africa Employment Report (1990)

The GTUC and structural adjustment under the PNDC (1981–92)

When the PNDC seized power on 31 December 1981, the labour movement was in a state of disarray. The leadership of the GTUC was severely compromised in the eyes of many of its members, who accused it of bureaucracy, opportunism, betrayal of workers' interests and self-perpetuation in office. In recognition of a series of measures favourable to the labour movement, the GTUC leadership had refused to support the protest actions of other civil-society organizations against the corrupt and oppressive Supreme Military Council regime (1972–9) which was eventually overthrown by Rawlings during his first coup in June 1979. Neither had it offered any effective leadership in the labour disputes that destroyed the subsequent Third Republic (1979–81) (Kraus 1979, Chazan 1983). Shortly after the 1981 coup, a group of militant trade unionists in the Accra–Tema area, organized in the so-called Association of Local Unions (ALU), launched a *putsch* of its own, taking over power from the compromized GTUC leadership.

The new leadership expressed its objectives in terms of building a dynamic, revolutionary and democratic trade-union movement (Adu-Amankwah 1990, Yeebo 1991). From the very start, the PNDC had supported the change of leadership, which, it thought, would bring the trade-union movement more in line with the regime's populist orientations. The new leaders were indeed more committed to the 'revolution' than their predecessors. Nevertheless, they continued to assert the independence of the labour movement and its right to represent the interests of workers. The latter claim became an immediate source of friction between the revamped trade-union movement and the PNDC, since new, and apparently competitive, labour organizations had been created in the early days of the 'revolution'.

After the coup, Rawlings called for the formation of People's and Workers' Defence Committees in local communities and work-places as an expression of the importance that the radical populist regime attached to 'people's power' and 'popular participation' (Konings 1986, Ray 1986, Hansen and Ninsin 1989). Subsequently, Workers' Defence Committees (WDCs) began to emerge in work-places even before full guidelines on their structure and functions had been issued and their relationship with the existing trade unions had been clarified.

The installation of these 'revolutionary' organizations undoubtedly formed the greatest challenge in Ghanaian labour history to the existing power relations within enterprises. The WDCs had wide-ranging responsibilities, including the propagation and defence of the revolution, the exposure of management malpractices and corruption, the distribution of essential commodities, supervision of promotions, demotions, transfers and dismissals, and – even though this was barely visible during the most radical phase of the populist regime – disciplining workers and raising productivity. Above all, the WDCs were supposed to secure an active role for workers in the decision-making process. The PNDC passed a decree which created interim management committees (IMCs) on

public boards and in corporations. These were to be composed of four representatives from management, two from the WDCs and only one from the trade
unions. WDC actions led to desertion by some management personnel, the
setting up of committees of enquiry and, in some of the boldest and most far-
reaching cases, culminated in the forced take-over of some companies by
workers (Graham 1989, Nugent 1995).

Understandably, the initial absence of clear guidelines for relations between
the newly formed WDCs and the trade unions also led to numerous power struggles within enterprises, between the WDC and trade-union leaders. Most union
leaders were inclined to perceive the WDCs as instruments of the PNDC's
hidden agenda to either replace or control the unions. The worst fears of union
officials seemed justified when PNDC guidelines in April 1982 specified that
WDCs were to be responsible for the supervision of local union affairs. Public
statements by PNDC officials did little to shed light on the matter. On 1 May
1982, for example, Rawlings declared that the WDCs were not intended to
replace trade unions, but he failed to elucidate the division of functions. Not
surprisingly, many newly formed WDCs interpreted government policy to mean
that they were the sole legitimate representatives of labour interests (Graham
1989, Yeebo 1991, Nugent 1995). Given this situation, the GTUC leadership
took the unprecedented step of calling on the ILO to help resolve the issue of
who legitimately represented the workers (Gyimah-Boadi and Essuman-Johnson
1993: 202). Although the ILO proved incapable of resolving the dispute, the
conflict between the two labour organizations was gradually more or less
'settled', albeit differently in each particular setting. In some cases, the WDCs
were decisively rebuffed, while in others they became the senior partners. In a
number of instances, especially where conflicts between management and
workers were most acute, the two sides co-operated closely.

With the abolition of the People's Defence Committees (PDCs) and the
WDCs in late 1984, and their replacement by Committees for the Defence of
the Revolution (CDRs), the unprecedented level of workers' participation in
management and policy-making contracted significantly. It is important to note
that the CDRs were placed under the strict control of the regime and that their
role in the system of industrial relations was no longer relevant, being restricted
to labour discipline and productivity. About the same time the IMCs were
dissolved and replaced by Joint Consultative Committees, which had only a
supervisory capacity. The management of public boards and corporations now
reverted to technocrats and professional managers. Hutchful (1989) convincingly
showed that the World Bank continuously insisted on the abolishment of the
WDCs as a major condition for the allocation of funds: 'the concentrated fire of
the World Bank was reserved for the WDCs' and their alleged 'propensity to
engage in disruptive tactics', in particular 'the harassment of private enterprise'.
Clamping down on these 'revolutionary' organs was therefore viewed by the
PNDC as a necessary prerequisite for reassuring the Bretton Woods institutions
of a peaceful environment – both industrially and politically – to permit the
'optimum utilization' of their global financial resources. The PNDC had an

additional interest in their abolition, having often accused the national coordina-
tion of the Defence Committees of 'revolutionary overzeal' and the
'establishment of a parallel government' (Konings 1986, Yeebo 1991). The
curbing of the WDCs' power, however, had the probably unintended consequence of reunifying the labour movement in its struggle against structural
adjustment.

A wider gulf between the PNDC and organized labour developed after the
presentation of the first SAP-inspired budget in April 1983. Its announcement of
severe curtailments in public subsidies and price rises came as a shock to the
workers who had been the main supporters of Rawlings' 'revolution'. This led to
a rapid loss of PNDC legitimacy among the majority of workers. The ALU
leaders of the GTUC had not been consulted in advance and refused to mobilize angry workers against the anti-labour budget. Still being strongly committed
to the revolution, they appealed to the workers to exercise utmost restraint in
order not to jeopardize the long-term goals of workers' struggles (Herbst 1991:
186). Nevertheless, they expressed reservations about the budget as a whole and
called for the suspension of some aspects, in particular the increased price of
petrol and the severe limits set on wage increases through collective bargaining.
Their criticism provoked a violent WDC assault on the GTUC headquarters –
no doubt, with the support of the PNDC.

An important event for future relations between state and organized labour
took place at the end of the same year. After successive postponements, the
GTUC delegates' conference was finally held. The ALU leadership was voted
out of office, being generally perceived as too subservient to the Rawlings regime
(Yeebo 1991), and was replaced by the 'old guard', led by A.K. Yankey. These
old-guard leaders were not concerned with safeguarding the ideals of the revolution, since they had been among the principal casualties in 1982. They were
more worried about preserving trade-union autonomy versus the state and
upholding what they considered the essential task of unions: the defence of
workers' interests, even if it meant jeopardizing the good relationship that had
been established.

At the congress, Rawlings addressed the assembled delegates in a speech
which was to foreshadow future conflicts. He warned them that the GTUC was
viewed by the 'people' as an organization which had 'attempted to hold the rest
of the community to ransom in order to extract benefits for its members'. This,
he asserted, was untenable in the 'revolutionary situation, in which we are all
working for the common good'. Yankey, in reply, said he hoped that the labour
movement would be consulted on all future economic measures, and ended by
asserting that the GTUC was fully behind the PNDC's efforts to rebuild the
country. This was immediately belied in the PNDC's eyes when the GTUC
called for a minimum wage of 300 cedis a day at a time when the lowest-paid
workers could expect only 21–5 cedis. Rawlings greeted the demand with deri-
sion and anger: it was 'absolute rubbish – the outcome of ignorant minds. Are
such people enemies?' (Adu-Amankwah 1990: 100). The distance between the
PNDC and the GTUC on what was a reasonable wage remained.

The new GTUC leadership, in fact, started attacking the various SAP measures for their nefarious effects on workers' living and working conditions, leading to the development of increasingly antagonistic relations between the unions and the regime. For example, a resolution adopted by the GTUC Executive Board in 1984 noted:

> As a result of these IMF and World Bank conditions, the working people of Ghana now face unbearable conditions of life expressed in poor nutrition, high prices of goods and services, inadequate housing, continuing deterioration of social services and growing unemployment above all ... . We caution government that the above conditions pose serious implications for the sharpening of class conflict in the society.
>
> (quoted in Herbst 1991: 184)

The GTUC repeatedly demanded the withdrawal of the SAP 'as being imposed by the Bretton Woods institutions on Ghana', the restoration of collective bargaining procedures and union participation in the economic decision-making process (Adu-Amankwah 1990). However, while they continued to agitate against the reforms, the new leaders clearly recognized that, given the autocratic nature of the PNDC, there were limits to the regime's patience in confronting actual protests. The new Secretary-General, Mr A.K. Yankey, therefore sought to operate cautiously, doubting the ability of the GTUC to survive a war of attrition. Consequently, he usually tried to make known the GTUC position by the presentation of memoranda to the government and press communications to the general public. This form of trade-union protest appeared to have little impact on the government, which mostly ignored union demands. Only on rare occasions did the regime feel compelled to make concessions (Adu-Amankwah and Tutu 1997).

The greatest victory ever won by the GTUC during this period occurred in 1986, when the government unilaterally cancelled leave allowances for public-sector workers. The GTUC leadership told the government that lack of communication between the regime and the unions left it with no other choice but to call a general strike. It exhorted workers to wave red flags and wear red armbands (the customary sign of mourning). The outrage expressed by ordinary workers suggested that the strike enjoyed the overwhelming support of its members. The PNDC realized that it had gone too far and swiftly reinstated the allowances. In addition, it soon reactivated the existing tripartite institutions and bilateral forms of consultation. Subsequent government attempts to convene these fora on an *ad hoc* basis and to use them as instruments for compromising the unions (by having them accept already predetermined wage levels), created new sources of conflict between the PNDC and GTUC.

Generally speaking, however, the PNDC effectively deployed a variety of strategies to contain trade-union opposition. First, the government and its leading spokespeople, using the state-controlled media, continued to accuse the trade-union movement of being 'selfish', making 'unrealistic' demands, misleading the workers, and being engaged in subversive activities aimed at destabilizing and derailing the revolution (Adu-Amankwah 1990, Gyimah-Boadi and Essuman-Johnson 1993). Second, the PNDC continued to use divide-and-rule tactics against organized labour, capitalizing on the fact that the SAP was having a differential impact on the various sectors of the economy. Thus, the Ghana Private Road Transport Union (GPRTU), which generally endorsed the liberalization measures (increased fares, imports of vehicles and spare parts), and the Railway Workers' Union, which had benefited from the rehabilitation of the railways, were easily pitted against the Industrial and Commercial Workers' Union (ICU), whose members were threatened by privatization and job losses (Nugent 1995). Third, while radical trade-union leaders were being hounded by the security agencies, the PNDC was careful to nurture its relationship with those it perceived as moderates. In 1988, for example, the PNDC effectively prevented the radical General Secretary of the ICU and Acting Secretary-General of the GTUC, Mr L.G.K. Ocloo, from being elected Secretary-General of the GTUC. Yankey, who was then re-elected with the support of the PNDC, subsequently became more or less co-opted into the regime. And, last but not least, the PNDC continued to use strong-arm tactics, including intimidation, force and repression.

While the PNDC had left workers some latitude in remoulding power relations in the work-place between 1982 and 1984, by the mid-1980s there was a good chance that the coercive apparatus of the state would be actively deployed on the side of management and employers in the event of a dispute. For example, in November 1985, when Cocobod wanted to lay off over 20,000 workers, the PNDC passed a special law (PNDC Law 125) that empowered the management to ignore the labour law regarding retrenchment. Protesting union leaders were summoned to the Bureau of National Investigations (BNI) (the state security agency), were held for a couple of hours and then released with a warning to behave 'if they did not want to spend Christmas in detention'. Subsequently, the government was to deploy security forces at the GTUC head-quarters to prevent the GTUC leadership from holding a mass meeting to protest against the manner of retrenchment. At the end of 1986, armed policemen arrested local labour leaders at the Assene Company in Accra, following a long wrangle over the entitlement of workers to protective clothing (Graham 1989). In mid-1987, when the GTUC intended to hold a meeting to protest against mass retrenchments and other anti-labour measures such as taxing various workers' allowances and benefits, it was refused a permit and armed police were deployed again to forestall the 'illegal' holding of the meeting. This was complemented by an attack by an armed mob on the Hall of Trade Unions, during which trade-union leaders were assaulted. In 1988, the government dismissed thirty-six union leaders and activists from the Ghana Broadcasting Corporation (GBC), dissolved the local union and banned officers of the relevant national union, the Public Services Workers' Union (PSWU), from entering GBC premises. The same kind of arbitrariness was displayed in the dismissal of over thirty union leaders and activists at the State Gold Mining

Table 15.6 Recorded labour strikes in Ghana, 1982–9

Year	Number of strikes	Number of workers involved	Working days lost
1982	104	4,707	11,690
1983	16	15,076	36,957
1984	9	10,550	17,022
1985	12	2,830	8,025
1986	19	7,459	24,936
1987	22	1,116	19,401
1988	11	2,798	7,152
1989	20	8,925	15,704

Source: Gyimah-Boadi and Essuman-Johnson 1993: 206

Corporation (SGMC) in 1988, following agitations during negotiations for a collective agreement. In 1990, the government dismissed over 200 workers at the Ghana Italian Petroleum Company over an alleged illegal strike of workers against management malpractices. The inability of the GTUC to secure reinstatement of the dismissed workers contributed to a growing loss of union influence among workers. It was a mark of the regime's ruthlessness in dealing with worker and union protests that relatively few strikes were recorded between 1983 and 1989, even though labour discontent was high (Table 15.6).

The GTUC and structural adjustment under the NDC (1992–2000)

The global trend towards political liberalization from the end of the 1980s, the new standards of Western governments and international financial institutions for capital allocation, linking structural adjustment to liberal democracy, and the growing opposition of urban civil-society organizations in Ghana to military rule contributed to the PNDC announcement in 1991 that the country would return to a multi-party system (Nugent 1995, Drah and Oquaye 1996, Ninsin 1998).

Recent research shows a large variation in the degree of intensity of the trade unions' role in the democratic transition in Africa (Konings 2000). The GTUC appears to occupy a middle position in the spectrum of trade-union involvement. After 1986, it began to move away from being limited to economic issues, and made various calls for political liberalization. No attempt, however, was made to mobilize the workers to press home these demands, out of fear that such actions would exacerbate its already antagonistic relationship with the PNDC. In 1986, for example, the GTUC appealed to the PNDC to install a People's Assembly composed of representatives of all identifiable civil-society organizations, which would allow people to make their views heard and also help the government to take generally acceptable decisions. A few years later, it called for the convening of a democratic National Constituent Assembly to formulate a constitution which would then be submitted to the people for approval, as well as for the introduction of a large measure of political liberalization. Although these demands coincided with those of the Movement for Freedom and Justice (MFJ), an opposition umbrella organization created in 1990, the GTUC refused to join this organization and support its struggle for the introduction of multi-partyism in Ghana. And, even more significantly, around the time that the campaign for multi-party elections began in the autumn of 1992, the GTUC constitution was amended to prohibit the organization from entering into alliance with, or formally supporting, any political party for the purpose of winning elections. This amendment appears to have been motivated first by the GTUC's memory of the harmful effects on the defence of workers' interests of previous alliances with political parties such as the Convention People's Party (CPP), 1958–66 and the Social Democratic Front (SDF), 1979–81; and second by the lack of confidence in the alternative constituted by the opposition coalition to Rawlings. The GTUC, therefore, had come to the conclusion that it would be in a better position to defend workers' interests if it preserved its autonomy with respect to the political parties.

During the transition period, Rawlings formed his own party, the National Democratic Congress (NDC), which pledged to continue PNDC policies. He was eventually able to win the 1992 presidential election, mainly due to the following factors: he was largely able to control the transition period, making full use of his position as head of state; he still enjoyed a considerable measure of popularity, especially in the rural areas which had benefited to a certain extent from structural adjustment (the provision of higher producer prices and infrastructural facilities); and he took advantage of the fact that the opposition parties were divided and had no clear programme. The opposition accused Rawlings of large-scale electoral fraud and of intimidating opponents, and boycotted the 1992 parliamentary elections. As a result, the first period of the Fourth Republic (1992–6) resembled a one-party state. In the 1996 presidential and parliamentary elections, Rawlings and the NDC scored a further victory. This time the opposition parties admitted that the elections had been relatively fair and they entered parliament for the second period of the Fourth Republic (1996–2000).

At first sight, there appeared to be little change between the PNDC period and the Fourth Republic. The 1992 liberal-democratic constitution provided the new president with wide-ranging powers. Rawlings continued to enjoy a large measure of autonomy in the planning and execution of policies. His party controlled parliament and he could still rely, if necessary, on a tight security apparatus. On the other hand, the Ghanaian experience had not yet disproved those who expected democratization to spur needed reforms. Not only did the Fourth Republic outlast earlier democratic interludes, it also spawned, albeit in the midst of conflict and compromize, a fragile institutionalization of some of the rules and procedures of the democratic game, manifest, among others, in a large measure of autonomy for the press and the judiciary, and the resurgence of civil society (Sandbrook and Oelbaum 1997).

From the very start, it was clear that the NDC government would experience greater difficulties than the PNDC in the implementation of the harsh SAP measures. Given the ongoing process of political liberalization, it could no longer afford to deploy the same repressive tactics to subdue labour as had its predecessor. Not unexpectedly, the country soon witnessed renewed labour militancy. The civil and public services in particular were regularly paralysed by severe and protracted strike actions – a manifestation of the workers' relative freedom to voice their long-standing grievances about low real incomes, increasing retrenchment and job insecurity, persistent government efforts to postpone or reduce end-of-service benefits which prevented workers from setting up in the informal sector, and 'flexible' management practices. On several occasions, workers invaded the office of the Minister of Finance and Economic Planning, Dr Kwesi Botchwey, who had occupied this position since 1982 and was generally perceived as one of the main architects of structural adjustment in Ghana, and threatened to harm him.

A newly emerging feature of Ghana's industrial relations scene was the use of court injunctions by workers and unions to block the liquidation or sale of state-owned enterprises. Litigation was used by the workers in the Tema Food Complex, the State Fishing Corporation and Coca Cola Ghana Limited to ensure that the government paid all benefits due to them prior to the sale of their enterprises (Panford 1997).

The mounting social discontent exploded in 1995. On 1 March, the NDC-dominated parliament approved a new value-added tax (VAT) of 17.5 per cent. The new tax was part of the IMF- and World Bank-endorsed revenue enhancement strategy adopted by the NDC. On 11 May, a group of opposition leaders, calling itself the Alliance for Change (AFC), organized a massive demonstration by workers, youth, unemployed and members of the general public to protest against the VAT. Initially, anti-VAT protests were restricted to Accra but they later spread to other regional capitals as well. The demonstrators were even more furious, as parliament had exempted the President from paying VAT. They chanted in Akan 'Kume Preko', meaning 'You might as well kill me now', to express their willingness to die rather than live under structural adjustment conditions. In many respects, these demonstrations resembled the previous anti-SAP uprisings in Zambia (from 1985 to 1987) and in Nigeria (in 1986 and 1988–9), where the revolt of the urban masses protesting against the withdrawal of subsidies and concomitant price hikes forced their governments to withdraw the SAP temporarily (Bangura and Beckman 1993, Simutanyi 1996). Although the anti-VAT demonstrations in Ghana were of a peaceful nature, participants were nevertheless attacked by members of the pro-government Association of Committees for the Defence of the Revolution (ACDR), resulting in the death of four demonstrators and numerous injuries, some critical.

Confronted with such a dangerous situation, President Rawlings recalled parliament from recess, which under a certificate of urgency reduced the VAT rate to 15.5 per cent and then repealed it completely on 11 June. The government also announced monetary compensation for the deaths and injuries caused during the demonstrations. Furthermore, the Minister of Finance and Economic Planning, Dr Botchwey, who was blamed for the ministry's failure to educate the Ghanaian population on the VAT measures, was forced to resign.

With the establishment of a political framework for constitutional democracy, trade unions acquired a larger measure of autonomy. Following the election of a more radical leadership in 1992, the GTUC began to reassert its right to promote the interests of the workers through the pursuit of collective bargaining, participation in the national decision-making process, and other ways of representing the workers, such as representations to parliament on issues that were considered vital. In 1993, the GTUC presented a memorandum to parliament that expressed its concern over aspects of a Serious Fraud Office Bill considered to be anti-democratic and unconstitutional.

Compared with during the PNDC era, the GTUC leadership now proved less reluctant to deploy the general-strike weapon to back its demands for higher wages and to denounce the NDC government's repeated attempts to violate collective agreements as well as decisions arrived at in the bilateral and tripartite fora. For instance, in January 1995, the GTUC threatened a general strike on these issues. Subsequently, the government allowed the tripartite forum to nego-tiate a new national minimum wage, and promised to implement the decisions of the tripartite meetings (Adu-Amankwah and Tutu 1997: 265–6).

The GTUC also began to explore other ways of forcing the government to respect collective-bargaining procedures. In 1993, it filed a complaint with the ILO about the government's refusal to honour agreements on procedures for lay-offs and retrenchment benefits. Again, in 1993, it went to court in an attempt to overturn an arbitrator's award that was considered to be biased, ill-founded and an abuse of process. It also went to court in 1996 to compel the government to accede to the right of unionization by senior staff in a foreign-controlled bank.

The GTUC also began to propose revisions to the SAP. It suggested a review of the unbridled trade liberalization, the free-floating foreign-exchange system, the wholesale removal of all subsidies, the retrenchment of labour and the doctrinaire privatization. As an alternative, it posed a vision of the economy where every individual had access to education and health care, and contributed to the growth of the economy through employment. With arable land, industries and abundant labour as major national resources, such an economy was to be based on agriculture, and it had to be supported to become the engine of growth and sustainable development. In 1995, the GTUC requested that the govern-ment install a national forum on the state of the Ghanaian economy, made up of the tripartite partners and important civil-society organizations.

In August 1996, the GTUC held its Quadrennial Congress at the University of Cape Coast. This important congress adopted a number of policies to meet the challenges posed by structural adjustment and democratization. The two major ones were as follows:

Strengthening the organization and internal democracy

In order to retain current members' interests, the unions had to encourage membership participation in trade-union affairs – paying particular attention to the youth and women – through consciously improving communications inside the organization, and to expand services to its membership, such as vocational training and retraining, helping workers to prepare for redeployment and to meet the uncertainties associated with loss of employment, counselling and other welfare services. To increase membership, the unions were particularly requested to intensify their efforts to unionize the rapidly expanding informal sector. Since the end of the 1980s, a number of unions had already started organizing in the informal sector. This was to be given a further boost by more conscious planning, so that appropriate organizational forms would be developed for bringing informal-sector workers and associations into the framework of union organization (Yanney 2000).

Improving workers' representation and participation

For more effective representation of workers' interests in the process of collective bargaining, the unions were asked to deepen and expand their research activities and to train officers at all levels. But, beyond more effective collective bargaining, the trade unions also had the responsibility of improving workers' participation at all levels, including in the work-place. This is why the GTUC is at present involved in a programme of research on industrial democracy and educating the rank and file on workers' participation in enterprises.

Another important initiative taken at this congress was the establishment of worker-owned enterprises (Yanney 2000). This initiative was an attempt to contribute to employment generation, to expand the base for union membership, and to improve and broaden the main source of union finances. It was also thought to have the potential to assist in creating the conditions for worker participation to gain legitimacy and acceptability in Ghana.

Conclusions

This study has attempted to fill one of the conspicuous lacunae in the growing body of literature on structural adjustment in Africa: the response of organized labour to the dramatic effects of SAPs on labour markets. While there may be a large variation in the actual roles played by African trade unions (cf. Bangura and Beckman 1993, Mihyo 1995, Schiphorst 1995, Simutanyi 1996), this case study of the Ghanaian trade unions appears to partly reject the pessimistic view that trade unions in Africa had their backs to the wall during structural adjustment and could do little for their suffering members. This view seems more relevant to the PNDC era than to the NDC era.

During the PNDC era, the government proved capable of implementing the austere SAP measures essentially on the basis of political repression and within the framework of an effective military dictatorship, earning Ghana the reputation of being the 'success story' of structural adjustment in Africa. In these circumstances, few concessions could be won by Ghanaian trade unions.

During the NDC era, the government found it hard to implement the SAP measures in an environment of political liberalization, leading to the resurgence of worker militancy and the development of increased trade-union autonomy. The latter enabled the unions to better defend workers' interests and promote trade-union rights.

The current economic and political reforms also turned out to be a source of inspiration for union leaders in their search for new and innovative ways to mobilize workers. First, they attempted to strengthen the organization by providing the rank and file with more services and more space for participation in trade-union affairs, as well as by recruiting new members from outside the traditional trade-union constituency, especially workers in the expanding informal sector and in the rural areas. Second, they tried to improve workers' participation in the national decision-making process and in the enterprises. Their drive for greater worker participation is a clear expression that trade unions are not only prepared to contribute to the emergence of a democratic culture in society but also to come to grips with forms of collective action which are supplementary to traditional (and often confrontational) collective bargaining (cf. Mihyo and Schiphorst 1995). Realizing more and more the need for restructuring, the unions appear willing to accept responsibility for improvements in efficiency and productivity in exchange for a greater say in decision-making.

References

Adesina, J. (1994) *Labour in the Explanation of an African Crisis*, Dakar: Codesria Book Series.

Adu-Amankwah, K. (1990) 'The State, Trade Unions and Democracy in Ghana, 1982–1990', Unpublished M.A. Thesis, The Hague: Institute of Social Studies.

Adu-Amankwah, K. and Tutu, K. (1997) 'Ghana: going beyond politics', in G. Kester and O.O. Sidibé (eds) *Trade Unions and Sustainable Democracy in Africa*, Aldershot: Ashgate, pp. 207–28.

Akwetey, E.O. (1994) *Trade Unions and Democratization: a Comparative Study of Zambia and Ghana*, Stockholm: University of Stockholm.

Aryeetey, E. (1996) 'Formal and informal economic activities', in S. Ellis (ed.) *Africa Now: People, Policies and Institutions*, London: James Currey, pp. 119–35.

Bangura, Y. and Beckman, B. (1993) 'African workers and structural adjustment: a Nigerian case-study', in A.O. Olukoshi (ed.) *The Politics of Structural Adjustment in Nigeria*, London: James Currey, pp. 75–91.

Bates, R. (1971) *Unions, Parties and Political Development: a Study of Mineworkers in Zambia*, New Haven: Yale University Press.

Bates, R. (1981) *Markets and States in Tropical Africa: the Political Basis of Agricultural Policies*, Berkeley: University of California Press.

Chazan, N. (1983) *An Anatomy of Ghanaian Politics: Managing Political Recession 1969–1982*, Boulder, CO: Westview.

Clark, G. and Manuh, T. (1991) 'Women traders in Ghana and the structural adjustment program', in C.A. Gladwin (ed.) *Structural Adjustment and African Women Farmers*, Gainesville: University of Florida Press, pp. 217–33.

Crisp, J. (1984) *The Story of an African Working Class: Ghanaian Miners' Struggles, 1870–1980*, London: Zed Books.

Drah, F.K. and Oquaye, M. (eds) (1996) *Civil Society in Ghana*, Accra: Friedrich Ebert Foundation.

Ferguson, J. (1999) *Expectations of Modernity: Myths and Meanings of Urban Life on the Zambian Copperbelt*, Berkeley: University of California Press.

Fokuoh, J.A. (1996) 'Employment, Unemployment and Redeployment in Ghana: the Role of the Joint Consultative Forum', Unpublished M.A. Thesis, The Hague: Institute of Social Studies.

Freund, B. (1988) *The African Worker*, Cambridge: Cambridge University Press.

Ghana Statistical Service (1989) *Ghana Living Standards Survey (First Year Report September 1987–August 1988)*, Accra: Government of Ghana.

Gibbon, P. (ed.) (1995) *Structural Adjustment and the Working Poor in Zimbabwe: Studies on Labour, Women Informal Sector Workers and Health*, Uppsala: Nordiska Afrikainstitutet.

Graham, Y. (1988) 'Ghana: the IMF's African success story?', *Race and Class*, 29(3): 41–52.

Graham, Y. (1989) 'From GTP to Assene: aspects of industrial working class struggles in Ghana 1982–1986', in E. Hansen and K.A. Ninsin (eds) *The State, Development and Politics in Ghana*, Dakar/London: Codesria Book Series, pp. 43–72.

Green, R.H. (1988) 'Ghana: progress, problematics and limitations of the success story', *IDS Bulletin*, 19(1): 7–15.

Gyimah-Boadi, E. (1991) 'State enterprises divestiture: recent Ghanaian experiences', in D. Rothchild (ed.) *Ghana: the Political Economy of Recovery*, Boulder/London: Lynne Rienner Publishers, pp. 193–208.

Gyimah-Boadi, E. and Essuman-Johnson, A. (1993) 'The PNDC and organised labour: the anatomy of political control', in E. Gyimah-Boadi (ed.) *Ghana Under PNDC Rule*, Dakar: Codesria Book Series, pp. 196–210.

Hansen, E. and Ninsin, K.A. (eds) (1989) *The State, Development and Politics in Ghana*, Dakar/London: Codesria Book Series.

Hashim, Y. (1994) 'The State and Trade Unions in Africa: a Study of Macro-Corporatism', Unpublished Ph.D. Thesis, The Hague: Institute of Social Studies.

Herbst, J. (1991) 'Labor in Ghana under structural adjustment: the politics of acquiescence', in D. Rothchild (ed.) *Ghana: the Political Economy of Recovery*, Boulder/London: Lynne Rienner Publishers, pp. 173–92.

Hutchful, E. (1989) 'From "revolution" to monetarism: the politics and economics of the structural adjustment programme in Ghana', in B.K. Campbell and J. Loxley (eds) *Structural Adjustment in Africa*, New York: St Martin's Press, pp. 92–131.

Hutchful, E. (1996) 'Ghana 1983–94', in P. Engberg-Pedersen, P. Gibbon, P. Raikes and L. Udsholt (eds) *Limits of Adjustment in Africa: the Effects of Economic Liberalization, 1986–94*, Oxford: James Currey, pp. 143–214.

Isamah, I. (1994) 'Unions and development: the role of labour under structural adjustment programmes', in E. Osaghae (ed.) *Between State and Civil Society in Africa*, Dakar: Codesria Book Series, pp. 123–52.

ISSER (1994) *The State of the Ghanaian Economy in 1993*, Legon: University of Ghana.

ISSER (1995) *The State of the Ghanaian Economy in 1994*, Legon: University of Ghana.

Jamal, V. and Weeks, J. (1993) *Africa Misunderstood*, London: Macmillan.

Jeffries, R. (1978) *Class, Power and Ideology in Ghana: the Railwaymen of Sekondi*, Cambridge: Cambridge University Press.

Jeffries, R. (1992) 'Urban popular attitudes towards the economic recovery programme and the PNDC government in Ghana', *African Affairs*, 91(363): 207–26.

Kester, G. and Sidibé, O.O. (eds) (1997) *Trade Unions and Sustainable Democracy in Africa*, Aldershot: Ashgate.

Konadu-Agyemang, K. (1998) 'Structural adjustment programs and the perpetuating of poverty and underdevelopment in Africa: Ghana's experience revisited', *Scandinavian Journal of Development Alternatives and Area Studies*, 17(2–3): 127–43.

Konings, P. (1977) 'Trade Unionism and Government Development Strategy in Ghana, 1874–1976', Unpublished Ph.D. Thesis, Tilburg: Catholic University of Brabant.

Konings, P. (1986) *The State and the Defence Committees in the Ghanaian Revolution, 1981–1984*, Lagos: Revolutionary Monographs on Culture and Society, Series 2, No. 2.

Konings, P. (1993) *Labour Resistance in Cameroon*, London: James Currey.

Konings, P. (2000) 'Trade unions and democratisation in Africa', in P. Konings, W. van Binsbergen and G. Hesseling (eds) *Trajectoires de Libération en Afrique Contemporaine*, Paris: Karthala, pp. 167–83.

Konings, P. and Meilink, H. (1998) 'Regional economic integration in sub-Saharan Africa', in A.E. Fernández Jilberto and A. Mommen (eds) *Regionalization and Globalization in the Modern World Economy*, London/New York: Routledge, pp. 128–45.

Kraus, J. (1979) 'Strikes and labour power in Ghana', *Development and Change*, 10(2): 259–86.

Kraus, J. (1991) 'The political economy of stabilization and structural adjustment in Ghana', in D. Rothchild (ed.) *Ghana: the Political Economy of Recovery*, Boulder/London: Lynne Rienner Publishers, pp. 119–55.

Lipton, M. (1977) *Why Poor People Stay Poor: Urban Bias in World Development*, London: Temple Smith.

Mihyo, P. (1995) 'Against overwhelming odds: the Zambian trade union movement', in H. Thomas (ed.) *Globalization and Third World Trade Unions*, London/New Jersey: Zed Books, pp. 201–14.

Mihyo, P. and Schiphorst, F. (1995) 'A context of sharp decline', in H. Thomas (ed.) *Globalization and Third World Trade Unions*, London/New Jersey: Zed Books, pp. 169–200.

Ninsin, K.A. (1991) *The Informal Sector in Ghana's Political Economy*, Accra: Freedom Publications.

Ninsin, K.A. (1996) 'Ghana beyond crisis and adjustment', *Africa Development*, 21(2–3): 25–42.

Ninsin, K.A. (ed.) (1998) *Ghana: Transition to Democracy*, Dakar: Codesria Book Series.

Nugent, P. (1995) *Big Men, Small Boys and Politics in Ghana*, London/New York: Pinter.

Panford, K. (1994) 'Structural adjustment, the state and workers in Ghana', *Africa Development*, 19(2): 71–95.

Panford, K. (1997) 'Ghana: a decade of IMF/World Bank's policies of adjustment (1985–1995)', *Scandinavian Journal of Development Alternatives and Area Studies*, 16(2): 81–105.

Ray, D. (1986) *Ghana: Politics, Economics and Society*, London: Frances Pinter.

Rothchild, D. (ed.) (1991) *Ghana: the Political Economy of Recovery*, Boulder/London: Lynne Rienner Publishers.

Sandbrook, R. (1982) *The Politics of Basic Needs: Urban Aspects of Assaulting Poverty in Africa*, London: Heinemann.

Sandbrook, R. and Cohen, R. (eds) (1975) *The Development of an African Working Class*, London: Longman.

Sandbrook, R. and Oelbaum, J. (1997) 'Reforming dysfunctional institutions through democratisation?: Reflections on Ghana', *Journal of Modern African Studies*, 35(4): 603–46.

Schiphorst, F. (1995) 'The emergence of civil society: the new place of unions in Zimbabwe', in H. Thomas (ed.) *Globalization and Third World Trade Unions*, London/New Jersey: Zed Books, pp. 215–32.

Simutanyi, N.R. (1996) 'Organised labour, economic crisis and structural adjustment in Africa: the case of Zambia', in O. Sichone and B.C. Chikulo (eds) *Democracy in Zambia: Challenges for the Third Republic*, Harare: SAPES Books, pp. 151–72.

Tangri, R. (1999) *The Politics of Patronage in Africa: Parastatals, Privatization and Private Enterprise*, Oxford: James Currey.

Thomas, H. (ed.) (1995) *Globalization and Third World Trade Unions: the Challenge of Rapid Economic Change*, London/New Jersey: Zed Books.

UNDP (1997) *Human Development Report 1997*, New York: Oxford University Press.

Vandermoortele, J. (1991) 'Labour market informalisation in sub-Saharan Africa', in G. Standing and V. Tokman (eds) *Towards Social Adjustment: Labour Market Issues in Structural Adjustment*, Geneva: ILO, pp. 81–113.

Waterman, P. (1975) 'The "labour aristocracy" in Africa: introduction to a debate', *Development and Change*, 6(3): 50–64.

World Bank (1995) *World Development Report 1995: Workers in an Integrated World*, Washington D.C.: World Bank.

Yanney, I.K. (2000) 'The Changing Roles of Trade Unions: the Case of Trades Union Congress of Ghana', Unpublished M.A. Thesis, The Hague: Institute of Social Studies.

Yeebo, Z. (1991) *Ghana: the Struggle for Popular Power; Rawlings: Saviour or Demagogue*, London: New Beacon.

16 The forces of globalization and labour in Africa

The case of Mali

Diana van Stijn

Introduction

After a century of battles between many ideologies, only one ideology survives: neo-liberalism, the ideology that believes in the market mechanism. Influenced by a dialectic of historical movements and events, neo-liberalism was able to evolve and finally expand into a new ideology: *globalization*.

An important feature of the globalization process is the integration of national economies into one global economy. Labour markets are central to the functioning of this global economy. Without labour, there is no production, no service, no value. In a globalized world, labour is in a disadvantageous position. In societies as poor and underdeveloped as in Africa, the position of labour and the problem of unemployment and low wage levels bring out inequality and social injustice.

This chapter places the fragile position of labour in Africa in an international historical perspective. One of the poorest countries of the continent will serve as an example: Mali. Situated at the centre of West Africa, Mali is a land-locked country with almost ten million inhabitants. Today, it is one of the poorest countries in the world. Taking Mali as an example, it becomes evident that in emerging market economies the position of workers is weak. Malian state companies are in the process of opening up capital and thereby surrendering to the market economy. Unemployment is rising and insecurity among the workforce is causing unrest in the form of strikes. The question is: who will answer the social needs of an unemployed workforce? The forces of globalization pressurize the state to withdraw, and the same forces place a heavy burden on the African civil society.

Globalization

A new ideology

The term globalization gained popular usage after the fall of world socialism in the late 1980s and early 1990s. At that time, the world economy demanded the opening up of borders as capital sought markets. James H. Mittelman (1996:

223) explains that the process of globalization came to refer to a series of structural changes in the global political economy that accelerated during the late twentieth century.

Globalization consists of various aspects, such as free movement of trade, deregulation of social affairs, weakening of the state and political power. This means that on a global level, production and therefore labour is reorganized, industries migrate across borders and financial markets spread around the globe. All these changes encompass a new order of labour relations. Of great importance in this new order is the fact that globalization is a market-induced and not a policy-led process. Kiely and Marfleet (1998: 5) note in this respect that globalization is inscribed with an ideology to promote neo-liberalism. Modern trade organizations such as the WTO, the World Bank and the IMF are seen as the promoters of globalization. Although by no means a novel process, globalization must be regarded as a stage in the history of capital whose lineage has brought together many different societies into one system.

This new order of power relations can be traced back to three important times in history. Historically, globalization took off side by side with capitalist social relations in the four previous centuries. The second important turning point can be traced back to the 1970s, when the world-wide economic crisis laid bare the change towards neo-liberal solutions in international economic relations. The final breakthrough that caused the acceleration of the process was the collapse of the Berlin Wall.

The early capitalist centuries

The period from the late fifteenth to the nineteenth century is taken here as the period when the transition to capitalism was made in Europe. Thereafter a period of industrial capitalism followed. Both periods laid the first regional patterns of economic development and of regional trade as we know it in today's world. The first contours of contradictory processes between societies and within societies also became obvious. Capitalist social relations were characterized by uneven development from the beginning. A displacement of human lives and values took place, and the changes in labour practices that came with industrial capitalism caused inequalities that the world had not seen before. Karl Polanyi (1944) conceptualized the balance between the market mechanism and the self-protection of society as the double movement. The double movement indicates that modern society needs political control as well as social protection against the negative impact of capitalism on the poor. The state had always been the institutionalization of this control.

To explain the emergence and development of capitalism and industrialism, Immanuel Wallerstein (1974) constructed an historically based theory of global economic development: the 'Modern World System' theory (MWS). This World System theory is one of the first theories in International Relations reflecting upon the world as a whole, leaving behind the Euro-centric or Anglo-American bias. The essence of Wallerstein's theory is that nations in the MWS fall into one of three distinctive zones: core, periphery and semi-periphery. Each zone has its own constellation of economic and political structures that are a function of the imperatives of the international division of labour. Wallerstein asserts that the world economic system is predicated on the perpetuation of inequalities bene-fiting the core areas (Docking 1999: 36). Since the emergence of capitalism, both Europe and Africa (or at least large zones of each) came to be incorporated into a single system, a capitalist world economy (Wallerstein 1986: 101). According to Wallerstein, the essential elements of a capitalist world economy include the creation of a single world division of labour, production for profit in this world market, and capital accumulation for expanded re-production as a key mode for maximizing profit in the long term (Wallerstein 1986: 102). Prior to this system, trade took place between various parts of Africa and various European traders. This trade that took place before 1750 fell into the category of so-called luxury goods (Wallerstein 1986: 103).

The most important difference with the experience of trade relations with Africa since it became incorporated is that trade involved no transfer of surplus at the time. When the 'New World Order' began to become apparent, it became clear to African traders that trade would no longer be on an equal exchange basis. The price for African products was no longer profitable for the South, the trader, but for the North, the buyer. Ever since the first European trading stations were established on the west coast of Africa in the fifteenth century, the region found itself in the peripheral zone. West Africa was divided between Anglophone, Francophone and Portuguese hemispheres – a regional division still active today.

After this change in trade relations took place, the 'Great Transformation' to industrial capitalism and a global market society began in the second half of the eighteenth century. In Africa, pressure to expand the geographical bounds of the capitalist world economy began to be felt from this period onwards. One of the easiest ways to expand total primary production to feed newly established indus-tries was extensive expansion and the inclusion of new areas of primary production. This involved profits of labour and land priced below world market rates, and put more pressure on the slave trade and on demand for the use of African land (Wallerstein: 1986: 105–7). Between 1815 and 1873, during Great Britain's hegemony, the African coastal regions were peripheralized completely.

After the first phase of African incorporation into the capitalist world economy, the next phase was to create sufficient cash crops to meet world needs (Wallerstein 1986: 112). Colonization did not only mean that Africa was economically implicated in the world system; it also became politically depen-dent. Many African economies can still be seen as peripheral economies today. During colonial times, the region exported primary commodities to the metropolis and in return purchased manufacturing goods. The failure of indus-trialization in Africa since independence shows that Africa never escaped this international division of labour. The reliance on a single low-value agricultural commodity remains the main characteristic of the African economy. This reliance leaves the economy extremely vulnerable to commodity prices (van der

Walle 2000: 264). The Malian economy, for example, relies on non-manufac-
tured cotton for 50 per cent of its earnings.

The crisis of the 1970s

It became more obvious how deep the capitalist structures were embedded when
the oil crisis of the 1970s rocked the world. This world-wide economic crisis
marks a new phase in the history of globalization. At the time it seemed that the
newly independent states were beginning a new and positive era. Barely used to
the idea of independence, a large number of non-Western countries, grouped
together in the Non-Aligned Movement and its economic counterpart, the
Group of 77, called for a New International Economic Order in 1964. As the
influence and power of this movement was growing, the 1970s economic crisis
wrecked the opportunity to change world trade relations. Instead of a stronger
unit, the movement fragmented and internal crises were given priority. The
essentially Keynesian approach (international economic *laissez-faire* and domestic
control) was gradually abandoned during the crisis of the 1970s, and purist
liberal principles became increasingly dominant (Hettne 1997: 238). The oil
crisis caused the impoverishment of many countries in the South, and resulted in
the debt crisis in the 1980s. Instead of accomplishing a New International
Economic Order, the newly independent countries of the South had to adjust to
the order that they were battling, and had to remain within the same international division of labour.

The economic crisis persuaded developing countries to abandon import
substitution in favour of export promotion, which also meant that they sacrificed
production for domestic consumption and satisfaction of basic needs, in favour
of earning foreign exchange. In this period, many African states experienced the
same institutional process and created a new form of employment for their citizens. Lachaud (1994) analyses how African states copied their colonizers,
through the desire to control the creation of wealth to ensure a better redistribution among the governing élites. The need to construct an institutional
infrastructure led most African states to develop a large public sector, both
productive and non-productive. This growth process, which had already been set
in motion within a basically favourable international context, allowed an
increasing number of young graduates to be absorbed into the labour market,
which would last until the impact of the world-wide crisis was evident at the end
of the 1970s. From the beginning of the 1980s, the economic transition process
in these countries slowed down considerably (Lachaud 1994: 83). The large
public sector became a heavy burden on the state's budget. The huge debts and
economic decline in this period drove African leaders into the arms of the
International Monetary Fund (IMF) and World Bank and their Structural
Adjustment Programmes.

In this period of change, Wallerstein (1986) made an interesting prediction
about the influence of capitalist structures on the different African economies.
Wallerstein's future perspective in 1986 was that the capitalist world economy

would probably see a phase of contraction and depression, during which there would be a slowdown of expansion of industrial productive capacity and a reallocation of world income to increase effective demand and create the conditions for a further significant increase in the overall world expansion of the forces of production, probably to begin again around 1990 (Wallerstein 1986: 124). In the early period of contraction, semi-peripheral areas of the world economy would be in a relatively strong position.

In Africa, the semi-peripheral areas are those with relatively important industrial infrastructures and reserves of natural resources: countries such as South Africa, the Democratic Republic of Congo (formerly Zaire), Nigeria, and possibly Algeria and Egypt. They would emerge as significant producers of industrial products, not only for their home markets but also for neighbouring countries. This increased income would represent part of the world-wide expansion of effective demand for the products of the core countries (Wallerstein 1986: 125). This same period, according to Wallerstein, would be one of acute suffering for the truly peripheral areas, whose non-essential exports would find a very weak world market, and whose internal food production could further collapse. They would bear the brunt of death from famine and major transfers of remaining populations from rural areas to ghettos. The principal consequence of the social structure would be the disintegration of the third zone, the so-called subsistence sector, clearing the land areas of farmers and largely sounding the death knell for the concept of a semi-proletarian labour force. The 'reserve army of the unemployed' would thus become visible but would also have to be kept alive by some process of social redistribution of income (Wallerstein 1986: 125). Wallerstein's prediction of fifteen years ago unfortunately seems to be too close to reality today for those truly peripheral areas in Africa. Except for the Democratic Republic of Congo, which is caught up in a devastating civil war, the other 'African Tigers' mentioned are indeed thriving. The truly peripheral areas, such as landlocked Mali and its immediate neighbours Niger and Burkina Faso are experiencing economic decline and are drifting further away from integration. Unfortunately, Wallerstein's prediction has more or less come true.

An ideological turning point

The fall of the Berlin Wall in 1989 left neo-liberalism as the single surviving ideology. The collapse of Communism meant that suddenly globalization could proceed unimpeded. Patterns already constructed during centuries could now spread to every part of the world. Socialist regimes, except for China, Cuba and a few other states, collapsed. A host of democratic transitions followed the end of the Cold War. Since then, globalization has often been represented as a finality, as the logical and inevitable culmination of the powerful tendencies of the market at work. In this sense, globalization has become an ideology.

New strategies were implemented in Africa, with even more emphasis on privatization, and priority was given to international competitiveness. At this time, the capital gained had a choice of where to locate the various stages of the production process. Several factors can be taken into account before choosing a location: differences in labour costs, environmental regulations, fiscal incentives and political stability. All of these changes have happened in a relatively short time. The fact that the world economy has changed rapidly since the 1990s has meant that inequality, which has always existed between the Western world and its former colonies, has suddenly increased tremendously. In 1960, 20 per cent of the world population living in the richest countries had 30 times the income of the poorest 20 per cent of the world. By 1995, this had increased to 82 times as much (UNDP Human Development Report 1998: 29).

Labour in a globalized world

Robert Cox (1996) has analysed how this inequality concerning labour is structured. According to Cox, the social structure of the world shaped by globalization today has taken the form of a three-part hierarchy. At the top are people who are integrated into the global economy, including everyone from the global managers down to the relatively privileged workers who serve global production and finance in reasonably stable jobs. The second level in the hierarchy includes those who serve the global economy in more precarious employment – an expanding category segmented by race, religion and gender as a result of the restructuring of production. The bottom level consists of superfluous labour, those who are excluded from the global economy and who serve it only as a potentially destabilizing force. Whole regions of Africa belong to the bottom level (Cox 1996: 26). In underdeveloped countries and especially in African countries, only tiny segments of the population are integrated into the world economic network.

This becomes obvious by looking at the contribution of Africa to world trade. By the end of colonialism, the fragmentation of the economies of African states intensified the dependence on external markets and suppliers. During the 1960s, Africa used to account for more than 5 per cent of total world trade; today this is less than 2 per cent (Van der Walle 2000: 265). African exports grew at a smaller rate than those of the rest of the world. Van der Walle concludes that rather than increasing its integration into world markets, Africa has been standing on the sidelines while the rest of the world trading system has expanded.

Globalization leans on the principles of capitalism and tends to adjust through the labour market, either by wage levels or through unemployment. To give in to the interests of labour would mean that the freedom of multinationals on this labour market would be limited. As Marx has pointed out, workers are structurally weak relative to owners of capital. Owners of capital control the means of production and are only vulnerable to labour at times of full employment. The capitalist system is based on a reserve army of unemployed that systematically limits the capacity of labour to organize and build a political power base. In societies as poor and undeveloped as African economies, workers are therefore in an extremely fragile position. Under colonial rule, and subsequent dictatorial regimes industrialization never took place and the labour force was unable to organize itself. Today, in a situation of unemployment it is hard to find a good bargaining position for organized labour. Labour is thus disadvantaged in a situation of globalization. In countries with weak economies there are no better alternatives than to work under uncertain conditions. It is as Amadou Bocoum, an unemployed sociologist, explained: 'You have to have work to be in a position to fight for employees' rights'.

States and inter-governmental organizations used to shield domestic economies from the negative effects of globalization. Since the spread of neo-liberalism in Africa, the role of the state has diminished. The unemployed can no longer count on a helping hand from the central African government. The cure for the negative effects of the market economy is generally regarded to be further globalization and the further withdrawal of the state. According to Cox, states today are instruments for adjusting national economic activities to the exigencies of global economy (Cox 1987: 254). In other words, no government can realistically provide economic stability, development and social progress within its borders on a sustained basis, unaffected by the forces of globalization.

The African states were constructed by the European powers at the conference table in Berlin in 1884–5. Now, however, although they are officially independent, they again have to give away their power to other actors, such as multinationals and international bodies. More than in any other continent, the IMF and World Bank interfere with state matters. According to Villalon and Huxtable (1998), the African state faces two realities: first, a continued crisis in the economic sphere, including the pressure from the Bretton Woods institutions to liberalize both their economies and politics in order to fight economic global marginalization, and second, a concentrated pressure from civil society for more accountability and democratization (Villalon and Huxtable 1998: 30). I will now examine these two realities using the example of Mali.

The case of Mali

Mali is a country still economically structured as a peripheral area. The economy depends largely on the two primary products: cotton and gold. Few Malian workers are integrated into the world economy of Robert Cox's social hierarchy. Democratic reforms in 1991 brought the country financial support from the international community, but no fundamental progress. Mali distinguishes itself by its relative stable democracy and dynamic civil society. But its economic performance stands in sharp contrast to its political achievements. Mali remains one of the poorest countries in the world. To place Mali in a global context, one can best start by looking at the bottom of the United Nations list of countries arranged in order of wealth. Surrounded by its neighbouring countries Burkina Faso, Niger and not far from the war-torn Sierra Leone, Mali is ninth from the bottom (166th out of 174 countries, UN/HDI 1999).

Every day that Mali is not integrated into the world economy, the gap between its economy and those of integrated economies widens. The withdrawal of the central state causes two core changes in the structure of the

Malian political–economic scenery. One involves the implications of neo-liberal-ization, the second is the growing burden of unemployment on civil society. These two major developments have had an immense impact on Malian society.

In sharp contrast to the problems of today, the history of the African empires began in West Africa. The first of these empires was that of Ghana, which from the fourth to the eleventh century controlled the trans-Saharan caravan routes. Mali reached the peak of its power and wealth during the fourteenth century, extending over almost all of West Africa and controlling virtually all of the rich trans-Saharan gold trade. It was during this period that Mali's great cities, Timbuktu and Djenné, became fabled centres of wealth. All of this changed, however, when the Portuguese reached the Gulf of Guinea by ship, bypassing and rendering obsolete the trans-Saharan trade routes. Timbuktu and Djenné faded and fell into a decline from which they have never recovered.

The end of the empire marked the conclusion of the region's history as a trading centre, the trans-Saharan trade routes quickly lost their vitality after the establishment of sea routes by Europeans. Later, the capitalist drift for expansion of trade markets took in parts of Africa. In the late nineteenth century, Mali became a French colony. The *Soudan Français*, as Mali was then known, was administered as part of the French West African federation and was used as a labour reserve for the coastal states (EIU 1999–2000). French efforts to make their colonies in West Africa yield raw materials for metropolitan industries demonstrate the beginning of the interplay of global capitalist process with local ones. Cotton production in Mali started in the latter half of the seventeenth century. Cotton became popular in Europe, resulting in capitalist transforma-tions in the cotton textile industry on the European continent. In the beginning of the nineteenth century, this led to world-wide inducements to expand cotton production and commerce (Roberts 1996). The European conquest of the African continent was driven by the needs of European industry. Besides that, new medical technology made the tropics safer for foreign visitors and new weapons made the conquest cheaper than ever before (Curtin *et al.* 1994: 399).

By 1884, the rapid pace of competitive annexation of African territories threatened the peace of Europe, leading to the Berlin Conference in 1884–5, dealing mainly with the Congo and Niger areas. Britain and France quarrelled over West Africa but came to terms with the borders of the region and also with those of Mali. The Berlin Conference did not initiate European colonization of Africa, but it did legitimate and formalize the process. In addition, it sparked new interest in Africa. Following the close of the conference, European powers expanded their claims in Africa such that, by 1900, European states had claimed nearly 90 per cent of African territory.

Over the past hundred years, the French have been one of the two (along with the British) dominant international actors in West Africa. They directed the role of labour in the region until independence in 1960, and even after indepen-dence dominated the post-colonial West African landscape with economic treaties, military co-operation agreements and aid money for almost four decades. French colonial policy, however, was never designed to promote African development in states like Mali. It was designed to maintain the dependence of those poor developing states on France. French colonial officials had a mandate from the metropolis to spread cash-crop-farming schemes, particularly the cultivation of cotton across the Sudan, with the aim of breaking French dependence on American cotton and to build a rural tax base for the colonial government. Today cotton farming takes place in Mali as it always did, requiring backbreaking labour, causing soil degradation and yielding poor financial rewards. France's influence is illustrated by the fact that the French currency is still used as the currency of payment in international trade. The foreign revenues earned through export are thus controlled by the French Treasury. This control, together with the French loans, gives France fiscal and economic leverage over its former colonies and up till now has given French companies great advantages.

Following independence in September 1960, the Malian political landscape was strongly influenced by the two socialist governments that succeeded the colonial power: that of Modibo Keita from 1960 to 1968, and that of Moussa Traoré from 1969 to 1991. These two partisans of a centralized economy administered the country with firmness, on the basis of five-year plans. Modibo Keita was an active member of the Non-Aligned Movement and, together with other African leaders, pleaded for a New International Economic Order in 1964, to lead the country to development.

On the international scene, the second wave of structural changes in the world order can be traced back to this period of early independence. The 1970s turned out to be a decade where a shift was made towards a Western orientated neo-liberal order without any form of rule. In the years and decades to follow this change would and will mean that Mali would have to survive without protection from the central national government. The 1970s were a decade of droughts and had a devastating effect on the population, livestock and agricultural production.

As in many other African states, during the first Malian independent government (under the presidency of Modibo Keita), the state became the only employer. All students were guaranteed a job after graduation. It came to a point where many people tended to have a job but no work. Throughout the crisis in the 1970s and the economic decline of the 1980s, it became clear that the central state could no longer function. President Moussa Traoré replaced Modibo Keita and accepted the strategy of adjustment towards the world economy, as external pressures mounted and indebtedness began to rise. At the same time, he had not yet dealt with the internal pressures calling for democracy. Policies were adopted to liberalize grain markets, ease price controls, encourage investment, privatize state enterprises, reduce subsidies and correct fiscal imbalances. Although this improved Mali's reputation with the IMF and the World Bank, it made Mali irreversibly dependent on the loans and ideology of those institutions.

When the last pieces of the Berlin Wall, the symbol of a bipolar world, were torn down in the summer of 1990, the first political debates about multipartyism and democracy took place in Mali. From 1989 onwards, a broad-based coalition of social and political groups demanded multi-partyism. Mass demonstrations became common practice in the capital, Bamako, in 1990. In March 1991, a series of bloody clashes between the people and the army culminated with the arrest of the president (EIU 1999–2000). Internally and externally, Mali was pushed towards structural political change.

These protests for change, arising from within the population, took place in an international environment of change. Malian protests were spurred on by the fate of dictatorial rulers elsewhere in the world. Press reports from around the world brought Mali stories of popular struggles for freedom and democracy: *glasnost, perestroika*, the Tienanmen Square protests and massacre and the subsequent fall of world socialism at the end of the 1980s. These events reached Mali as they reached the rest of the world. Among Western nations, these events caused a re-evaluation of their ties to, and support of, authoritarian leaders.

In Mali, Western-mandated SAPs during the 1980s made future loan guarantees conditional on the liberalization of grain markets, the privatizing or liquidation of non-profitable state enterprises and the downsizing of bloated bureaucracies. Public enterprises cut their staff by 25 per cent between 1979 and 1985. The government introduced a vast structural adjustment programme for the period 1988–92, which included incentives being given for voluntary departure from public service. Together with a general reorganization, this staff reduction led to a reduction of 11 per cent. When the first economic stabilization programme was introduced in 1982, the rate of unemployment in the capital rose from 8 per cent in 1976 to 16.9 per cent in 1991 (Lachaud 1994: 89–97).

Probably the most decisive influence behind the Malian protests came from the French president, François Mitterand, after the speech he made to African leaders in July 1990 at a Franco-African Summit held in La Baule. This speech marked the period of change for Francophone Africa, and changed the relationship between France and its African ex-colonies for good. At the crux of Mitterand's speech was the message that Africa's dictators could no longer count on the unconditional financial political and military support that was once accorded to certain pro-French African leaders.

The demonstrations that started out on the streets were finally translated into structural political reforms. The country held multi-party elections in 1992; they were won by the 'Alliance pour la Democratie au Mali' (Adema) under President Alpha Oumar Konaré and Konaré has led the country ever since.

It is now hard to believe that Mali once was a powerful empire in control of the most important trade routes in Africa. The more Mali was caught within the world system of trade, the more hopeless its position became. From the end of the 1970s onwards, Mali has tried to adjust according to the international 'rules'. Malian efforts to make integration work are still based on the enthusiasm of the early 1990s when the people overthrew the dictatorial regime. Ever since this 'people's' revolution of the 1990s, the favoured direction has been one of 'zations': globalization, implying liberalization, democratization, decentralization and privatization. The state is officially the main initiator of the many programmes that should bring the country closer to integration. At the same time, it is the state that has to withdraw by downsizing its enterprises and cutting jobs. The government is pressurized by the international quest for economic prosperity to open its economy. It faces a poor population in need of social services and employment prospects. But the globalization process involves the withdrawal of the government from its social responsibilities to the population.

The government, although still officially in charge, is giving in to the wishes of the international order. The more influence the government loses to the World Bank the more the state is estranged from its own policies and from its people:

> The neo-liberal reforms currently being pushed by the First World onto the Third World have assumed an ideological nature so that the 'zations' are policies seen by the West as both interrelated and imperative. African governments today thus protest or reject one or all the 'zations' at their own peril.
>
> (Docking 1999: 232)

The international neo-liberal organizations promoting the 'zations' have become a strong influence in Malian domestic affairs, but do not take full responsibility for the negative implications.

To liberalize means to privatize

> Naturally, I am principally against this movement that the Bretton Woods institutions are pushing us to take. I don't think privatization is a good thing for Mali, unfortunately I ran out of arguments to politically fight this movement. We can not deny that the state companies have been badly managed and that something should be changed.
>
> (Tiebilé Dramé, Chairman of Parena 2000)

In order to integrate, Mali is in the process of liberalization, which implies that it has to open its borders and privatize its state companies. As discussed earlier, many state companies were badly managed and corrupt, and Mali acknowledges the need to reorganize. When Mali was relieved of its debts, the government and the Bretton Woods institutions negotiated to start privatizing several state companies, including, for example, the Malian energy company EDM, the telephone company Sotelma and the airport (Gouvernement du Mali, 2000: 9). The opening up of capital in Mali may offer opportunities for consumption and production, but it demands above all that local enterprises have to improve the production process in order to offer some international competition. The implications that this will have for employment and salaries are yet to be seen (Gouvernement du Mali 1999: 12). Nevertheless, opening up capital is presented as the solution for boosting the Malian economy. It is likely that companies will be managed more efficiently, but many people are now afraid of losing their jobs or seeing their wages decrease. Many employers fear the upcoming reorganizations. It is important to realize that the loss of a job in Mali is not just the loss of one man's dinner, every man fired means ten people with empty stomachs, since one worker typically provides food for ten family members. (In 1998, out of a population of 9,790,492, with 1,633,897 households, the formal sector employed only 0.5 per cent of the economically active population, the informal sector 23 per cent, and the rural sector 76 per cent (*Recencement Géneral de la Population et de Habitat 1998*).

Neo-liberal macro-economic strategies are supposed to create a dynamic economy, attract foreign investment and enhance competition. But instead, the formal sector in Mali attracts little interest from foreign investors and is therefore of low importance for the economic activity of the country. Its influence on GDP is not even 15 per cent, and creates almost no employment. Paradoxically, this sector receives 80 to 90 per cent of the banking credits (l'Essor 2000: 32). This formal sector includes industry, transport and banks. Malian industry, for example, consists of 200 industrial units in total, each hiring an average of seventy-five people. The structure of employment has considerably transformed over the past twenty years by replacement of the dynamics of the formal sector by those of the informal one.

The informal sector has profited from the neo-liberal reforms. In this sector one finds the millet manufacturers, the small merchandisers and saleswomen; also belonging to this sector are taxi-drivers and river merchants. Bocoum (2001) states that the informal sector received a boost from the liberalization; now that the state interferes less in the market, the sector has expanded significantly. However, working in the informal sector means hard physical labour and no social security. Meanwhile the workforce is growing by 2.7 per cent per year. The pressure on the labour market will rise more in the future, and the population is predicted to increase to 20 million in twenty years, according to Bocoum (2001). Annually, 8,000 to 10,000 students enter the labour market with full qualifications. No more than 3,000 find employment in the sectors mentioned. The public sector, for example, employs about 300 to 500 people annually. In addition, another 90,000 uneducated young people enter the labour market each year. Unemployment has continued to rise since the Structural Adjustment programmes of the IMF and World Bank were implemented in the 1980s. The resulting unemployment rates are as follows: Mali has an official urban unemployment rate of 14.6 per cent and a rural unemployment rate of 1 per cent. The unofficial rate of unemployment is 20–25 per cent, as estimated by Siaka Diakité, president of the workers' union UNTM:

> The problems of unemployment are rising, together with the speed of the privatization movements. Every time a state enterprise opens up its capital, jobs will be in danger.

As Wallerstein has predicted, unemployment has become a problem for the periphery. The government has always been the main provider of stable employment, and educated people therefore still hope and expect to get a job as a functionary. The state has withdrawn from this task of providing jobs and has not been able to create alternative employment. The prospects for African countries that implemented privatization before Mali, such as Algeria and South Africa – countries with higher GDP – give a stark warning to Mali. Both of the latter countries are dealing with unemployment rates pushing 40 per cent.

The question is, knowing for a fact that unemployment is rising, whether the state should still continue to withdraw as a major employer. International experience shows that privatization usually pays off in increased production. Therefore, the Bretton Woods institutions advocate reducing the power of the state and promoting of market mechanisms. But it is doubtful that these efforts will result in growth in Mali. Many structural problems stand in the way of equal development: droughts, dependence on primary products, poor industry and corruption. The state is withdrawing at a time when it is clear that there is rising insecurity and unemployment and people need to depend on a strong social system. The consequences of the Structural Adjustment Programmes have caused major cutbacks in health and education. The Bretton Woods institutions now realize that the situation is critical and that more investment needs to be made in these two sectors. For those who are unemployed, neither the government nor the Bretton Woods institutions can offer up any solutions. To whom should they turn? 'The government and World Bank will have to come up with some sort of social safety net', says Siaka Diakité. Unemployment can be a dangerous factor in society. At the moment, many of the unemployed are still looked after by their family. But what happens when the burden becomes too great? The social security of the family is not enough. People feel abandoned by their government – instead of the state the burden falls on civil society.

The process of finding alignment with the world economy has severe consequences for national unions and civil organizations. Civil organizations are dominated by the international political agenda. Both pressures originate in the globalization process and cause a fragmentation of forces in Malian civil society and an estrangement between official civil organizations and the Malian people.

Civil society in Mali is relatively highly developed compared with other African countries. Historically, the development of a civil society was suppressed by the one-party state Mali has had before the transformation. In the 1960s, under the regime of Mobido Keita, the policy of single-party rule crippled the urban-based labour movement. At the rural level, Keita's followed Communist-style policies, which impinged on local civil society, and were met with hostility from a peasantry long suspicious of their central government (Docking 1999: 217). When the Keita regime was replaced by the Traoré dictatorship, single-party rule again served as an effective deterrent to the development of a national civil society. Nevertheless, during the late 1980s various actors from this group broke through the wall of repression surrounding the Traoré regime and sparked the popular protests of 1990–1 which eventually led to the arrest of the president and marked the beginning of Mali's transition to democracy.

Different forms of civil society can be distinguished in Mali. First, the importance of Malian traditional society should not be underestimated: the best defence against poverty is support from the family, the clan or the village. The basic needs of the poor are provided on this level, such as food and shelter. Yet even traditional solidarity has its limits. When poverty increases, the family functions as a social safety net. One unemployed member of the family can still be fed. But what if the unemployed in the family start to outnumber the employed? The burden will become too great and the family will no longer be able to provide for the basic needs of cousins and other relatives. However strong the meaning of kinship, family ties come under a lot of stress when it comes to impossible situations.

In terms of other social organizations, the trade unions play and still play an important political role, for example the student union, AEEM, and the Malian confederation of trade unions, UNTM. These unions combined to play an instrumental role in the 1991 revolution. These days the unions are under pressure from the privatization movement, and therefore can no longer protect the interest of their rank-and-file members.

The unions that were actively present during the demonstrations calling for democracy still have a symbolic status, accompanied by a certain reputation for defending the rights of the Malian people. The student union AEEM and the workers' union UNTM still have a tight grip on the government, since they have the spirit to mobilize the people. These days this is mainly by means of strikes. Strikes in Mali are common practice. The union most known for its frequent and long strikes is the student union. Basically, students can strike for at least three months a year. Education has been obstructed like this for years, with negotiations with the government often resulting in nothing. The fact that the state has no means to change the students' situation has a paralysing effect on the entire education system.

The trade union has a powerful place in government negotiations, since its members work for state companies like the telephone and energy companies. However, even though the effects of strikes can be wide-ranging, over the past few years even the more powerful unions have been slowly losing support. The AEEM and the UNTM are both losing the confidence of their rank-and-file members and are threatened with breakup. It seems that these unions have for too long cashed in on the fame achieved during the battles for transformation. While they used to be a voice of opposition, they slowly became part of the system and drifted away from their rank-and-file members. Opposition from within their own organization might change the situation. Another important union, the cotton farmers union, Sycov, also has to cope with problems from its rank and file. Sycov negotiates with the para-state CMDT and the government on the yearly price of cotton. In the year 2000 the farmers did not agree with the set price within these negotiations, and 40 per cent of all cotton farmers refused to cultivate cotton. This is a very striking example of the situation facing the Malian economy. The world prices for cotton are low – so low that the single Malian cotton company offers farmers such a low price for their cotton that farmers are forced to go on strike against the wishes of their own union. One wonders how long the Malian economy can deal with all these strikes, and for how long stability can be guaranteed.

Conclusions

Almost sixty years ago, Polanyi wrote that poverty was embedded in capitalism. Wallerstein predicted the marginalization of the periphery in 1986. These theorists could not foresee that the fall of the Berlin Wall would cause an acceleration of capitalism and neo-liberalism, and yet their analysis can still be used to predict the world-wide labour order today. The basis of today's employment problems was shaped over three different periods. Capitalism and neo-liberalism fuelled the drive for expansion of the Western market, but were never advantageous for Africa. Before capitalism was introduced, the West African economy was flourishing. By the time of French colonization, the Malian people had become a labour reserve. The analyses on Mali reveal that there is no space for a social order in the present international climate. The international pressure for economic integration is having a paralysing effect. The Malian economy is not viable in today's world, while the Bretton Woods institutions continue to press for further privatization and integration.

The social anarchy in Mali begs the question as to whether the state can permit itself to withdraw from its social task. The workforce is left to the forces of globalization, trapped between a withdrawing state and trade unions that cannot provide the necessary answers.

The unions are losing support because the battle for employment cannot be won. The solution lies at the start of this chapter, the history of ideology. The drifting off of an entire continent is the clearest sign that it is time that the ideology of globalization was resisted. A change in the economic system should presuppose a social order. Besides investing in health and education, the Bretton Woods institutions have not taken up a social order in their macro-economic policies. These promoters of globalization should realize that the market mechanism does not provide wealth for all, and should therefore be subject to change.

Bibliography

Bocoum (2001) unpublished personal interview.

Cox, R.W. (1987) *Production, Power and World Order: Social Forces in the Making of History*, New York: Colombia University Press.

—— (1996) 'A perspective on globalization', in J.H. Mittelman (ed.), *Globalization: Critical Reflections*, Boulder, CO: Lynne Rienner, pp. 21–30.

Curtin, P., Feierman, S., Thompson, L. and Vansina, J.P. (1994) *African History. Chapter 15, European Conquest*, New York: Longman.

Docking, T.W. (1999) *International Influence on Civil Society in Mali: the Case of the Cotton Farmers' Union Sycov*, New York: Bell & Howell.

Economist Intelligence Unit (1999–2000) *EIU Country Profile: Mali 1999–2000*, London: Economist Intelligence Unit.

Gouvernement du Mali (1999) *Croissance, Equité et Pauvreté, Rapport National sur le Developpement Humain Durable*, République du Mali: Gouvernement du Mali.

Gouvernement du Mali (2000) *CSLP Interimiare: Cadre Stratégique de Lutte Contre la Pauvreté*, 30 May, République du Mali: Gouvernement du Mali.

Harbeson, J.W. and Rothchild, D. (2000) *Africa in World Politics: the African State System Influx*, Boulder, CO: Westview.

Hettne, B. (1997) 'The double movement: global market versus regionalism', in R.W. Cox (ed.) *The New Realism: Perspectives on Multilateralism and World Order*, New York: St Martin's Press.

Kiely, R. and Marfleet, P. (1998) *Globalization and the Third World*, London: Routledge.

Lachaud, J.P. (1994) *The Labour Market in Africa*, Geneva: International Institute for Labour Studies.

L'Essor (2000a) *Mali. Special Edition*, Bamako, Mali: L'Essor.

L'Essor (2000b) *Hopes and Precautions*, September 22, Bamako, Mali: L'Essor.

Mittelman, J.H. (1996) *Globalization: Critical Reflections*, Boulder, CO: Lynne Rienner.

Polanyi, K. (1944) *The Great Transformation*, New York: Rinehart.

Roberts, R.L. (1996) *Two Worlds of Cotton, Colonialism and the Regional Economy in the French Soudan 1800–1946*, California: Stanford University Press.

Smith, Z.K. (1998) *Building African Democracy: the Role of Civil Society-Based Groups in Strengthening Malian Civic Community*, New York: Bell & Howell.

United Nations Development Programme (UNDP) (1998) *Human Development Report 1997*, New York: United Nations.

Villalon, L.A. and Huxtable, P.A. (1998) *The African State at a Critical Juncture, Between Disintegration and Reconfiguration*, Boulder, CO: Lynne Rienner.

Walle, N. van der (2000) 'Africa and the world economy: continued marginalization or re-engagement', in J.W. Harbeson and D. Rothchild (eds) *Africa in World Politics: the African State System Influx*, Boulder, CO: Westview.

Wallerstein, I. (1974) *The Modern World System: Capitalist Agriculture and the Origins of the European World-Economy in the Sixteenth Century*, New York: Academic Press.

Wallerstein, I. (1986) *Africa and the Modern World: the Three Stages of Africa in the World Economy*, : New York and Trenton, NJ: Africa World Press.

17 Labour and Ghana's debt burden

The democratization of dependency

Kwame Nimako

Introduction

Ghana's debt burden, which accumulated over the last two decades under the Structural Adjustment Programme (SAP), grew from around US$1 billion in 1980 to over US$6 billion in 2000, while the per capita debt burden rose from US$83 in 1980 to US$300 in 2000. With a per capita income of US$390 (in 2000), this debt burden not only constrains the country's capacity to save, which in turn restricts internal investment capacity, but it also undermines organized labour and its ability to bargain for better wages and improved labour relations. In the past decade this has been compounded by the retrenchment of the public sector and the growth of the so-called informal sector. Increasingly, Ghana's trade-union leaders are becoming dependent on foreign (i.e. Western) trade unions and NGOs for their survival. This process constitutes a democratization of dependency, namely, the spread of dependence from the top to the bottom of Ghanaian society.

In this chapter I will assess contemporary Ghanaian labour relations against the background of the debt burden and cycles in the domestic economy. I will also describe three labour-relations scenarios in order to determine the options available to organized labour, and their implications for improving the state of the Ghanaian economy. These scenarios involve wage increases, high productivity, and health and safety standards.

Context

The construction of the Ghanaian state at the beginning of the twentieth century was founded on debt. Underlying this debt was the need for British mining companies to transfer machines and equipment to appropriate geographical locations, which was necessary for mineral exploitation, as well as for the export of the minerals to Britain at a later stage. This in turn necessitated the development of an infrastructure, in the form of harbours, telecommunications, roads and railway lines to the areas in question. It has been estimated (at 1911 prices) that, by 1910, the British had invested some £10 million (i.e. £4.4 million in construction, £3.3 million in railways, and £2.5 million in machinery) in

Ghana. A large proportion of this investment was based on borrowed money, and this fact has escaped attention and analysis because the formation of the Ghanaian state was an act of British imperialism. Taking this into account, it is obvious that the state carried a debt burden from its infancy, which may explain why there has been no local solution to infrastructural development.

Subsequent expansion of railways and other infrastructure had to await high cocoa prices on the world market in the 1950s. To recoup the borrowed money, the colonial government had to devise a system of haulage discrimination, the essence being that charges on mining-related haulage, controlled by the British, tended to be generally lower than that on cocoa, controlled by Ghanaians. Thus whereas manganese ore, wood and coal destined for the British-controlled gold mines were transported by the railway at an average rate of 4 pence per imperial ton per mile, cocoa, controlled by Ghanaians, was transported at an average of 7 pence per ton per mile. In response to discriminatory and exploitative haulage practices, Ghanaian cocoa farmers shifted part of the haulage from rail to road transport, which in turn stimulated lorry transport. In 1931 the first modern labour organization, namely the Motor Drivers' Union, was formed as a consequence.

As I have argued elsewhere, the final British occupation of Ghana at the turn of the twentieth century; the subsequent investment in railways and gold mining; and the encouragement of cocoa cultivation and export and other infrastructure, all formed the basis of the first upswing in the modern Ghanaian economy (Nimako 1991, 1996). The upswing lasted for about two decades and was followed by economic crisis and decline from the mid-1920s until the end of World War II. This process of upswing and downturn constituted the first forty-year cycle in the Ghanaian economy in the twentieth century, and was followed by a second upswing, which also lasted for about two decades, from 1946 to around 1964. However, whereas the first expansion/upswing (1900–25) was occasioned by British investment in the mining sector, the second (1946–64) was aided by favourable cocoa prices on the world market, which rose from £190 per ton in 1946 to £395 per ton in 1954. This upswing did not only strengthen the development of productive forces and infrastructure, but also the country's foreign reserves were improved under both the colonial and the nationalist administrations in the 1950s. In turn, the strengthening of productive forces, infrastructural development, and the availability of foreign reserves, gave rise to economic growth. Economic growth was aided by a conscious economic and social policy by the nationalist government, designed to provide Ghanaians with 'the minimum basic services for a modern community'. This in turn expanded the labour force in the public sector (see below). Suffice it to say that the decline in cocoa prices in the 1960s led to long-term infrastructural deterioration, and remedial action helped add to the accumulation of foreign debt in the 1980s.

Whether by accident or design, the formation of trade unions followed the pattern of investment in physical infrastructure. This is all the more so since the first trade-union activity started in the railway and mining sectors. In other words, the development of infrastructure was tied to labour recruitment. In turn, labour was necessary for both economic exploitation and control of society. For the purposes of control, the army, police, civil service and a judicial apparatus were called into being, and became the major components or constitution of the colonial system.

The process of labour recruitment, including forced labour, was both inclusive and exclusive at the same time. With regard to the formation of the colonial army, the process of labour recruitment was inclusive. For instance, in addition to some 12,000 British troops, during the preparation for the final control of Ghana the British recruited 700 soldiers from the West Indies Regiment (WIR), a few hundred Nigerians, a few Mendes from Sierra Leone, Gambians, Mossis (from Burkina Faso) and Grunshis (from the north of Ghana), against the Asantes in the British–Asante War of 1873. The end of the war against the Asantes heralded the beginning of the formation of the nucleus of the Gold Coast Constabulary (GCC). By 1897, the GCC had sixteen British officers and 1,203 African recruits or non-commissioned officers (NCOs) – mostly Mossis and Grunshis. When the Asante region was formally annexed in 1901, the GCC was renamed Gold Coast Regiment (GCR); the GCR was in turn renamed the Ghana Army in the late 1950s (Haywood and Clarke 1964: 7, in Nimako 1991). By 1960, the Ghana army stood at 7,000 people and expanded to some 14,600 in 1966.

The end of the military campaigns heralded the beginning of effective policing and control of society. The police force grew from 678 in 1902 to 838 in 1912, and by 1922 it had jumped to 1,327. The police service, which at the country's political independence in 1957 numbered about 6,000, by 1966 had grown to 14,000. Increases also occurred in the civil service; from 219 in 1911 and 763 in 1921, it jumped to 4,843 in 1931, then to 6,232, and reached 20,340 in 1960.

At another level, the process of labour recruitment was exclusive because the division of labour was not only along racial lines enforced within the Army, but also along ethnic lines. This was all the more so up until the outbreak of World War II. Asantes were excluded from recruitment into the colonial army, and this went hand in hand with the systematic exclusion of other Ghanaians from important political and economic decisions affecting the country. For instance, the number of Ghanaians who held higher positions in the colonial administration dropped from 23 per cent in 1888 to 7 per cent in 1948.

Division of labour along racial and ethnic lines was also enforced in the mining sector. It will be argued below that this racial and ethnic division of labour had an impact on organized labour in post-colonial Ghana. For the moment, suffice it to say that the mines employed a total of 12,600 Ghanaians (mostly unskilled workers) and 504 Europeans (mostly 'skilled' workers) in 1905. Just as the end of the war against the Asantes led to a reduction in the number of British soldiers, so the end of construction work within the gold mines led to a decline in the numbers of British workers. By 1925, the number of British or Europeans working in the mines had declined to 266, whereas that of Ghanaians and Africans had increased to 13,200. People from the north of Ghana did much of the underground work in the mines, whereas those from the south performed much of the surface work. To a certain degree, this division of labour along racial ethnic lines existed in other branches of the state and civil service. It should be noted, however, that, with the exception of the British employees, much of this recruitment in the colonial economy and administration took place against the backdrop of imperfectly defined labour laws. The Department of Labour of the colonial administration was established in 1938; three years later, the Trade Unions Ordinance (1941) was enacted.

At one level, in spite of the systematic exclusion of Ghanaians from major political and economic decisions, the need for labour necessitated negotiations between the colonizer and the colonized at different stages and/or levels on matters of lesser political significance, pertaining to the economy and society.

At another level, the acceptance and absorption of educated Ghanaians in large numbers within the colonial establishment implied competition between Ghanaians and top British civil servants and military officers. In the long term, the exclusion of Ghanaians from senior positions within the colonial state intensified nationalist agitation. As I have demonstrated elsewhere and will argue below, the pattern of colonization, and the process and pattern of labour recruitment, helped to condition Ghanaian nationalism.

I will argue in the next section that, in recent years, Ghana has witnessed two democratization processes, namely, first from military to civilian rule, and, second, the democratization of dependency. Like the foundations or origin of Ghana's debt problem, not only has the second escaped attention, but this form of dependency is also different from classical neo-colonialism, as formulated by Nkrumah in the 1960s.

Debt burden refers to a situation in which a country has to commit a large portion of its exports to service its foreign debt. Thus the country has to borrow from the same creditors in order to service old debt, hence making the debtor dependent on the creditor. Dependency thus refers to a situation where the debtor or borrowing country (country A) needs the creditor or lender country or institution (country B) more than the other way round. The democratization of dependency refers to the spread of dependence from the top of society or government to the lower levels of society. The debt burden is essentially a direct burden on the active labour force and, indirectly, on society as a whole. This is all the more so since not every member of society belongs to the active labour force. Ghana has a population of 20 million and a labour force of around 8 million, of which about 30 per cent are considered to be unemployed or underemployed.

In the broader economy, the agricultural sector continues to absorb a large proportion of the labour force. In 1980, the agricultural sector employed some 56 per cent of the labour force; this fell to 52 per cent in 1996. The contribution of the agricultural sector to the economy also declined from 48 per cent in 1986 to 46 per cent in 1991.

The industrial sector employed 18 per cent in 1980 and 19 per cent in 1996; however, the contribution of industry to the economy remained 17 per cent between 1986 and 1991. The service sector employed 26 per cent of the labour force in 1980, and 29 per cent in 1996; however the contribution of the service sector to the economy rose slightly from 35 per cent to 37 per cent in 1991. However, the labour-force participation rate or the percentage of the population of all ages in labour force remained around 48 per cent between 1980 and 1995 (TTC/CSIR 1991, ISSER 2000).

According to the Ghana Trades Union Congress (GTUC), the current high unemployment rate is a result of macro-economic imbalances in the economy, which find expression in an overvalued currency, high inflation and interest rates. This is compounded by policies like privatization, retrenchment, and wholesale trade liberalization pursued under the Structural Adjustment Programme (SAP) (GTUC April 2001). We will pursue this observation below. For the moment suffice it to say that around 1990 there were seventeen trade unions with a total membership of 732,818 (Obeng-Fosu 1991); this amounts to 12 per cent of the working population. But, since the large majority of the active labour force does not belong to organized labour, organized labour should go beyond its traditional role of collective bargaining.

The word 'labour' is used in this chapter in both a broad and a narrow sense. In the broader sense, 'labour' is used to refer to the whole human resources of the active population in society. In the narrow sense, 'organized labour' is used to refer to trade unions and professional bodies who can exercise influence on wages and quality of work, and can initiate strike actions. In conclusion, I will provide three labour-relations scenarios in order to determine the options available to organized labour and their implications for the improvement of the Ghanaian economy. These scenarios are: wage increases, high productivity, and health and safety standards.

Labour and nationalism

The Ghanaian labour movement is linked to Ghanaian nationalism, although the latter is older than the former. The first modern nationalist movement, the Aborigines Rights Protection Society (ARPS), was formed in 1896 by a group of the Ghanaian intelligentsia in coalition with native rulers in the coastal area of the country. The immediate objective of the ARPS was to counter attempts by the British to expropriate Fante lands, through the introduction of a Lands Bill (1897), designed to transmute what the British authorities considered as 'tribal or family holdings into individual ownership'.

After successfully preventing the British from expropriating Fante lands, the ARPS became conservative, and was superseded by the United Gold Coast Convention (UGCC) in 1947. Like the formation of the ARPS, the force behind the formation of the UGCC was economic, but its instruments were political. According to the initiator of the UGCC, George Grant, the UGCC's formation was necessary partly because Ghanaian merchants 'were not being treated right, [they] were not getting the licenses for the import of goods'. In other words, underlying the formation of the UGCC were the colonial politics of exclusion and discrimination. Whether by accident or design, the first trade-union organization, the Gold Coast Railway Union (GCRU), was registered in 1943 and became active in 1947 – the same year that the UGCC was formed.

When the UGCC became radicalized and was overtaken two years later by Kwame Nkrumah's Convention People's Party (CPP) in 1949, the labour movement also became radicalized. In response to the successes of the CPP, other political groupings emerged; by the mid-1950s there were five variants of Ghanaian nationalism. This intensified, since the process of British occupation and/or colonization conditioned the pattern of nationalism(s). Four areas were colonized successively:

- the Gold Coast colony proper (i.e. the southern part, in 1874);
- the Asante (i.e. the central part, in 1901);
- the North (in 1902); and
- the Volta region (i.e. the eastern part, in 1921).

In response to the process of colonization, however, five nationalisms (i.e. four sub-nationalisms, plus holistic (or Ghana) nationalism) emerged:

Gold Coast nationalism (1897–1958);
Asante nationalism (1954–8);
northern nationalism (1954–8);
Ewe – or Volta – nationalism (1951–8); and
holistic (or Ghana) nationalism (1948 onwards).

In a nutshell, the distinctive feature of the five nationalisms and their impact on Ghanaian political culture and the labour movement is as follows. At the broader level of political culture, sub-nationalism followed the pattern of British colonization, and holistic nationalism followed the construction and development of the colonial state. The colonial state, which was the outcome of complex trade and political relations as well as (British) military occupation of the country, became the thread that held the (geographical) regions together. In a similar vein, holistic nationalism became the thread that held Ghanaians together, by uniting them in their resistance and opposition to British rule, irrespective of class and ethnic background. Unlike holistic nationalists (whose focus of opposition was British colonial rule), the primary target for the opposition of the sub-nationalists was actually the holistic nationalists! Just as the emergence of holistic nationalism presupposed the existence of British domination, so the existence of sub-nationalism presupposed British domination and the spectre and/or the existence of holistic nationalism.

The existence of the various nationalisms also gave rise to a relative diffusion of political power in society. Thus, around 1950, the probability that any of the three organized political forces in question (i.e. the colonial authorities, holistic nationalists and sub-nationalists) could carry out its own wishes in isolation was relatively low. The ability of any one of the political actors to dominate the political arena depended on a conscious and/or unconscious alliance of two of the forces, in opposition to a third party. The power of the colonial authorities depended on their control of the colonial state machinery, namely, the civil service, the police service, the judiciary, and the armed forces.

The power of the holistic nationalists was based on their ability to galvanize the masses (including organized labour) into action, and, flowing from that, by making the country ungovernable by the colonial authorities. A case in point is the way that the holistic nationalists encouraged the first general strike in Ghana's history, in 1950, which involved 40,000 workers.

The power of the holistic nationalists was not only constrained by the colonial state, but also by sub-nationalism. The power of the sub-nationalists rested on an alliance between a large section of the intelligentsia and the native rulers, and their subsequent non-co-operation with holistic nationalists, which in turn undermined the *legitimacy* of the holistic nationalists' rule. In turn, the issue of legitimacy became the basis of political instability; colonial rule was considered illegitimate by both the colonizer and the colonized, hence the need to transfer power to a legitimate nationalist government, of which more below.

At the level of the impact of nationalism on the labour movement, not only was the position of organized labour important in the political equation, but it also helps to explain the fact that after the formation of the northern sub-nationalist party, the Northern Peoples Party (NPP) in 1954, workers of northern origin refrained from taking part in a strike (encouraged by holistic nationalists), designed to put pressure on the colonial authorities to grant political independence. The northern workers, who were predominantly underground miners, had previously joined forces with workers of southern origin, who happened to be predominantly surface workers, in a strike against the management of the gold mines, in order to demand higher wages. After the formation of the NPP (whether by accident or design), a similar call by the trade-union leaders (mostly of southern origin) was not heeded by the northern workers. It was rejected not only because of the division of labour within the mines along geographical and/or ethnic lines (i.e. underground versus surface workers), but also because the surface workers happened to be supporters of the CPP – the core or holistic nationalist movement (Jeffries 1978). Division of labour along ethnic lines was thus reinforced by sub-nationalism. Nevertheless, 29,216 workers joined the 1955–6 miners' union strike.

The initial support of the labour unions for the holistic nationalists became mutually reinforcing. On the one hand, the general strike of 1950 strengthened the position of the holistic nationalists (the CPP) *vis-à-vis* the colonial authorities and sub-nationalists. On the other hand, the position of the trade unions was strengthened after Ghana gained political independence in 1957, through the introduction of the Industrial Relations Act of 1958 by that nationalist government. The nationalist government also provided the Trades Union Congress (TUC) with a building to serve as a headquarters, and facilitated the TUC's joining of the International Labour Organization (ILO) in 1958. In turn, the position of the trade unions could be strengthened because of the economic conditions in the country. The price of cocoa (Ghana's major export commodity) on the world market, jumped from £115 per ton in 1947 to £204 per ton in 1950, and reached £395 per ton in 1954.

The nationalist government's economic strategy and/or policy was based on a 'development model' framed by the colonial authorities, whose basis was an internal cocoa-price stabilization policy. Formally, the underlying assumption of the colonial development model was that, with the formation of the Cocoa Marketing Board in 1947, the domestic price of cocoa would be set lower than the world market price, so that 'a reserve fund could be built up'. This in turn could provide savings to be invested to develop the country's economy. Although designed by the colonial authorities for different reasons, the nationalist government adopted and justified this development model as follows in its programme of 'Work and Happiness':

> Imperialism–colonialism left Ghana without the accumulation of capital in private hands which assisted the Western World to make its industrial revolution. Only Government can therefore find the means to promote those basic services and industries which are essential prerequisites to intensive, diversified agriculture, speedy industrialization and increased economic productivity.
>
> (Nimako 1991)

The real impact of this colonial regime of capital accumulation, however, was that it gave rise to 'economic development' in the realm of welfare, and made 'development' almost solely the task of the government. The failure of the development policy in the 1960s led the leader of the nationalist government, Nkrumah, to conclude that Ghana was a neo-colony. In Nkrumah's formulation, the essence of neo-colonialism is that the state which is subjected to it is, in theory, independent, and has all the trappings of sovereignty. In reality, its economic system and its political policy are directed from outside.

In an attempt to transform the neo-colony, the Nkrumah government introduced economic planning in the form of the Seven Year Development Plan in 1963. Belief in the viability of the plan in turn required the government to prolong its stay in power (at least until 1970), and so contributed to declaration of a one-party state a year later. This process was compounded by the fact that the process of industrialization generates its own conflict, namely industrial conflict. There was a tendency for government-initiated and/or controlled industrialization to 'centralize' such industrial conflict. This was all the more so since management–labour relations became government–labour relations, and were thus transformed into political conflict. Strike actions thus became tied to political advocacy.

Formally, however, strike actions have taken place against the backdrop of thirteen demands. These are:

1   demands for the removal of management;
2   claims for a yearly bonus;

3 demands for wage increases;
4 protests against non-payment of wages;
5 demands for better service conditions;
6 protests against delays in the implementation of collective agreements;
7 demands for the payment of allowances;
8 demands for the payment of wages arrears;
9 demands for the payment of the minimum wage;
10 protests against dismissals and demands for the re-instatement of dismissed colleagues;
11 demands for the payment of a rent allowance;
12 protests against delays in the signing of collective agreements; and
13 protests against the delays in the Prices and Incomes Board approving signed negotiated collective agreements (Obeng-Fosu 1991: 76)

As a consequence of the colonial legacy, reinforced by the Work and Happiness project, the state became the largest employer. Since the state tended to employ educated people, the majority of these were concentrated within the state bureaucracy. The civil service, for instance, accounted for 65.7 per cent of employment in the public sector and 36.8 per cent of recorded employment in the country in 1960. Furthermore, 83 per cent of a total of about 60,000 professionals and technical workers in Ghana worked in the public sector in 1960. This implied that the most technically productive workers were working in the economically non-productive sectors of society.

The overthrow of the Nkrumah government in 1966, in a military coup, was followed by retrenchment by the National Liberation Council (NLC). Like the colonial regime, the basis of NLC power was the control of the core state structures, namely, the army, police and civil service. By the end of 1967, retrenchment measures had affected 40,000–50,000 workers. The wage gap between the lowest and highest paid increased dramatically, from 1:22 in 1966 to 1:39 by 1968. This was contrary to a TUC proposal which emphasized, first, the need for 'a living wage', and second, for the gap between the lowest and highest paid to be reduced from 1:22 to 1:10 (Kraus 1979).

The Kofi Abrefa Busia government (1969–71), which succeeded the NLC, resorted to the de-Nkrumahnization of the Ghana Trades Union Congress (GTUC), through its dissolution in the context of the Industrial Relations Act (Amendment) of 1971. These structural changes and interventions in trade-union organization went hand in hand with extensive strike action; 186 strike actions involving 90,798 workers were recorded between 1969 and 1971. Whereas workers in the manufacturing sector were the most frequent strikers between 1960 and 1965, 'no manufacturing workers joined in the major protest strikes in the September 1971 union confrontation with the Busia government. Resistance centred in the more militant dockworkers and railway unions' (Kraus 1979). This was compounded by the retrenchment policy; on the basis of the IMF's advice, government spending was cut, resulting directly in the loss of

20,000 jobs. Also, fewer jobs were being created to absorb the growing labour force: according to Ewusi's calculation,

> Ghana's labour force rose from 2,723,026 to 3,331,618 between 1960 and 1970, an increase of 22.4 percent; while total population increased at an annual rate of 2.4 percent, the labour force increased at a slightly slower rate of 2.1 percent. Productivity as measured by output per economically active as well as output per worker increased at the dizappointing rate of 0.3 percent per annum.
>
> (Ewusi 1978)

The Busia government's fanatical appeal for foreign aid and investment (which was then viewed as an excessively pro-Western stance) also revived Ghanaian nationalism. However, retrenchment of the public sector became one of the justifications for the overthrow of this government in 1972, by the National Redemption Council (NRC) led by Ignatius Kutu Acheampong. This was followed by the restoration of the Ghana Trades Union Congress, through the Industrial Relations (Amendment) Decree of 1972.

Like the colonial regime, the basis of the NRC's power was the control of the core state structures. The NRC was also blessed with higher prices for raw materials on the world market between 1972 and 1974 – the highest levels since the Korean War boom in the 1950s. We should recall that cocoa prices on the world market jumped from £204 per ton in 1950 to £395 per ton in 1954, declined to £219 per ton in 1960 and dropped to £138 per ton in 1965. Cocoa prices in 1972 were 20 per cent above the levels of the previous year; they jumped further from £270 per ton in 1972 to £585 in 1973. Following this, a trade surplus of US$124 million was recorded in 1972, as compared with a deficit of US$176 million in 1971. However, the world-wide oil-price rise (that followed the world-wide rises in the prices for raw materials) at the end of 1974, cancelled the gains in the Ghanaian economy and undermined the power of the dominant elements within the core state structures. By the middle of 1975, the NRC regime was experiencing 'repression fatigue' and had to be transformed into the Supreme Military Council (SMC). During the same period (1970–82), the volume of imports fell by one-third, whereas real export earnings fell by 52 per cent; per capita real income declined by 30 per cent. The number of strike actions per year increased from ten in 1972 under NRC rule to forty-six in 1976 under SMCI rule, and reached forty-nine in 1978 under SMCII rule.

The dilemma of the state as the largest wage employer and the 'erosion of its bureaucratic base', occasioned by the deterioration of the economy, found its expression in both mass emigration and protests/resistance simultaneously: the latter culminated in a palace coup in 1978, SMCII. This was followed by a military uprising of junior officers – the Armed Forces Revolutionary Council (AFRC) in 1979.

The civilian government of Hilla Limann, installed in 1979, lasted for only two years and was replaced by the self-styled revolutionary Provisional National

Defence Council (PNDC) government of Rawlings in December 1981. Like the colonial regime, the basis of PNDC power was control of the core state structures.

The ensuing nationalist rhetoric of the PNDC gained the sympathy of organized labour. Thus, whereas the Limann regime experienced sixty-nine strike actions in 1981, the Rawlings regime experienced only ten in 1982, although the economic conditions in both years were roughly the same. This has led one authority on Ghana's industrial relations to the conclusion that:

> It is worthy to observe that in independent Ghana strikes have been more pronounced during civilian rule than during military rule. This could partly be due to the fact that workers tend to fear possible martial action against them during military regimes and consequently tend to co-operate more with them than with civilian administrations.
>
> (Obeng-Fosu 1991: 76)

Available evidence, collected by Obeng-Fosu (1991), suggests that his observations are difficult to confirm. Let us pursue this reasoning further at four levels of analysis, namely,

- number of strikes,
- number of workers involved,
- staff-days lost, and
- economic trends.

The first issue that we should address is the relationship between regime type and the number of strikes. As can be observed from Table 17.1, there have been nine regime types in Ghana since the formation of trade unions in Ghana.

Table 17.1 Ghana: regime type and strike actions, 1944–2001

Year	Regime type	Number of strikes	Number of workers involved	Number of working days lost
1944–51	Colonial	150	150,650	639,056
1952–6	Colonial/nationalist	247	110,999	2,815,310
1957–65	Civilian	274	76,255	316,702
1966–8	Military	107	66,372	166,047
1969–71	Civilian	186	90,798	387,495
1972–9	Military	242	133,439	514,252
1979–81	Civilian	174	167,694	732,815
1982–92[a]	Military	120	62,461	140,887
1992–2001	Civilian	n.a.	n.a.	n.a.[b]

Source: Adapted and computed from Obeng-Fosu

Note: We recognise that the beginnings and ends of the regimes do not necessarily coincide with calendar years, especially for 1966, 1969 and 1979. The data should thus be treated as indicative rather than authoritative.

[a] Data cover the period 1982–9 only.

[b] n.a. = not available to the author at the time of writing.

The first regime type, the colonial regime (1944–51) saw 150 strikes; this amounts to an average of twenty-five strikes per year. The second type, the colonial/nationalist regime (1952–6) saw 247 strikes and an average of sixty-two per year. The third type, the civilian/nationalist (CPP) regime (1957–65) saw 274 strikes – an average of thirty-four per year. The fourth, the military NLC regime (1966–8) saw 107 strikes – an average of fifty-four per year. The fifth, civilian (PP) regime (1969–71) saw 186 strikes – an average of ninety-three strikes per year. The sixth, military (NRC/SMC/SMC-II/AFRC) regimes (1972–9) saw 242 strikes – averaging thirty-four per year. The seventh, civilian (PNP) regime (1979–81) saw 174 strikes and amounts to an average of eighty-seven strikes per year. The eighth, military (PNDC) regime (1982–92) saw 120 strikes, which is an average of seventeen per year.

We have noted that a proportion of the strike actions during the colonial regime were also politically motivated, i.e. designed to accelerate the attainment of political independence from Britain. If we exclude the colonial period (1944–57), we can conclude that the average number of strike actions per year was greater under the Progress Party (PP) of the Busia government (1969–72), which experienced an average of ninety-three per year. This is followed by the People's National Party (PNP) of the Limann government (1979–81), an average of eighty-seven per year, the NLC military regime (1966–8), an average of fifty-four per year, the Nkrumah regime (1957–66), an average of thirty-four per year, and the NRC military regime, an average of thirty-four per year, then the PNDC, with an average of seventeen strike actions per year (Table 17.2).

The second issue that we need to pursue in this analysis is the number of workers involved versus the number of strikes, under each type of regime. Table 17.1 shows that the colonial regime (1944–51) saw 150,650 workers involved in strikes, and this amounts to an average of 21,521 workers per year, followed by the colonial/nationalist regime (1952–6), which recorded 110,999 workers involved in strikes – an average of 27,750 workers per year. The third, the civilian/nationalist (CPP) regime (1957–65), recorded 76,255 workers involved in strikes – an average of 9,532 workers per year. The fourth, the (NLC) military regime (1966–8) recorded 66,372 workers involved in strikes – an average of 33,186 per year. The fifth, the (PP) civilian regime (1969–71) recorded 90,798 involved – an average of 45,399 per year. The NRC/SMC/SMC-II/AFRC military regimes (1972–9)

Table 17.2 Ghana: rank of regime type and strike actions per year

Rank	Regime type	Strike actions per year, 1957 –89
1	Civilian PP government	93
2	Civilian PNP government	87
3	Military NLC government	54
4	Civilian CPP government	34
4	Military NRC/SMC/SMC-II/AFRC	34
5	Military PNDC government	17

Source: Adapted and computed from Obeng-Fosu

recorded 133,439 involved – an average of 19,063 workers per year. The seventh, civilian (PNP) regime (1979–81) recorded 167,694 involved in strikes – an average of 83,847 workers per year. The eighth regime type, the military (PNDC) regime (1982–92) recorded 62,461 workers involved – an average of 8,923 per year.

Again, if we exclude the colonial period (1944–57), we find that on the issue of workers involved per year, the Limann (PNP) government (1979–81) ranks higher, followed by the Busia (PP) government (1969–72). This is then followed by the NLC military regime (1966–9), the NRC/SMC/SMC-II/AFRC military regimes (1972–9), the Nkrumah (CPP) government (1957–66), and finally the PNDC military regime (1982–92) (Table 17.3).

The third issue is number of working days lost to strikes, in relation to regime type (Table 17.4). The first, the colonial regime (1944–51) recorded 639,056 days lost in strikes – an average of 91,294 days lost per year, followed by the colonial/nationalist regime (1952–6), which recorded 2,815,310 days lost in strikes – an average of 703,828 days lost per year. The civilian/nationalist (CPP) regime (1957–65) recorded 316,702 days lost – an average of 39,588 days lost per year. The fourth, the NLC military regime (1966–8) recorded 166,702 days lost in strikes – an average of 83,351 days lost. The fifth, civilian (PP) regime (1969–71) recorded 387,495 days lost – an average of 193,748 days lost per year. The sixth regime type, the military regime (1972–9) recorded 514,252 days lost – an average of 73,465 days per year. The seventh, civilian (PNP) regime (1979–81) recorded 732,815 days lost in strikes – an average of 366,408 days per year. And the eighth, the military (PNDC) (1982–92) recorded 140,887 days lost – an average of 20,127 days per year.

The issue of working days lost gives an indication of how strike actions were handled (Table 17.4). Here too, if we exclude the colonial period (1944–57), we can see that the Limann government (1979–81) ranks higher, followed by the Busia government (1969–72), then the NLC military regime (1966–9), in third place. The NRC/SMC/AFRC military regimes (1972–9) rank fourth, followed by the Nkrumah government (1957–66), and finally, the PNDC military regime (1982–92).

Clearly the regime type, i.e. civilian or military, does not tell us enough about the propensity for strike action. One plausible explanation for strike actions is a combination of the relationship between the leadership of the GTUC and the

Table 17.3 Ghana: rank of regime type and workers involved in strike actions per year

Rank	Regime type	Workers involved per year, 1957–89
1	Civilian PNP government	83,847
2	Civilian PP government	45,399
3	Military NLC government	33,186
4	Military NRC/SMC/SMC-II/AFRC	19,063
5	Civilian CPP government	9,532
6	Military PNDC government	8,923

Source: Adapted and computed from Obeng-Fosu

Table 17.4 Ghana: rank of regime type and staff days lost in strike actions per year

Rank	Regime type	Number of working days lost per year, 1957 –89
1	Civilian PNP government	366,408
2	Civilian PP government	193,748
3	Military NLC government	83,351
4	Military NRC/SMC/SMC-II/AFRC	73,465
5	Civilian CPP government	39,588
6	Military PNDC government	20,127

Source: Adapted and computed from Obeng-Fosu

leadership of a regime – and the economic cycles – rather than the regime type. This is all the more so since, during the period of expansion between 1945 and 1965, the average recorded number of strike actions per year was thirty-four; this amounted to an average of 16,895 workers in strike actions per year. During the period of economic downturn between 1966 and 1983, an average of thirty-seven strike actions per year was recorded; this accounted for the involvement of 38,435 workers in strikes per year. Of course the workforce was larger in the 1970s and 1980s than in the 1950s and 1960s, so we should be careful in drawing conclusions. Moreover, there was a massive emigration of Ghanaians to Europe, North America and elsewhere in the 1970s and 1980s, which reduced economic pressure on the state/governments and contributed to a relative political stability. It cannot be denied, however, that much of the strike action took place under regimes that had experienced an economic downturn in the last forty-year cycle, namely, between 1964 and 1983.

Another factor that should be taken into account is the relationship between the leadership of a regime and the leadership of the GTUC. Clearly the Nkrumah (CPP), Acheampong (NRC) and Rawlings (PNDC) regimes took a pro-worker stance at the beginning of their rule. Nkrumah was able to deliver by creating jobs within his Work and Happiness project; the CPP government also provided the GTUC with a massive building for its headquarters. The Acheampong government reinstated senior public servants sacked under the previous Busia government. Rawlings, on the other hand promised and instituted worker participation in the form of Workers Defence Committees (WDC), but later abandoned this project and resorted to retrenchment. A paper sent to the PNDC government on 18 February 1985 by the Trades Union Congress (Ghana), confirmed the earlier fascination of the GTUC with the PNDC approach when it noted that:

> Indeed, we believe that the PNDC has the national and patriotic duty to reawaken the mass enthusiasm and militancy of the people, as well as offer the people consistent guidance and leadership in organising and struggling for revolutionary transformation of our neo-colonial society.
>
> (GTUC 1985: 11)

However, this optimism was turning into pessimism when the above statement was issued. Thus, among other things, the Executive Board of the TUC demanded that the PNDC addressed itself closely to the following:

> to recognize as a fundamental conflict the interests of national economic independence and development on the one hand, and foreign aid and investment on the other hand;

> to provide clear avenues for the trade unions to be involved in negotiating agreements alongside government negotiators with all external financial interests, in particular the International Monetary Fund (IMF) and the World Bank;

> to end this imposition of IMF and World Bank style of development on our economy and nation. In this connection to take steps to discuss with the trade unions democratic methods of re-training and redeployment of labour.

(GTUC 1985: 13)

Clearly, the GTUC leadership considered capital as alien or foreign when it requested the PNDC government to recognize as a fundamental conflict the interests of national economic independence and development on the one hand, and foreign aid and investment on the other. In fact, Rawlings and his associates shared this view when he stated in 1982 that '[t]he problems of Ghana stemmed from the activities of multinational [companies and his] revolution [was] meant to cut off the strangle-hold these companies have got on Ghana' (Nimako 1991). However, instead of providing clear avenues for the trade unions to be involved in negotiating agreements alongside government negotiators, as requested by the GTUC, the PNDC government resorted to the retrenchment of the public sector, which cost around 70,000 jobs between 1984 and 1989 – in response to the IMF conditions imposed on fiscal policy before the country qualifies for an IMF loan. However, this did not change the fact that the government remained the largest employer. About 80 per cent of the people working in the formal sector have been hired by government. In the 1980s, the government's expenditure on wages and salaries was 90 per cent of recurrent expenditure. Most of the members of trade unions are also government employees and this makes industrial conflict a 'political' conflict. The dependence of waged workers on the state also explains the trickle-down effect of dependency, a subject that we will now turn to.

The democratization of dependency

In recent years, Ghana has witnessed two forms of democratization processes, namely, *from military to civilian rule*, and the *democratization of dependence*. The first form of democratization process is a consequence of the legitimacy problem linked to the decolonization process.

The second form of democratization process is a consequence of the accumulation of foreign debt in the past twenty years. This has not only escaped attention, but this form of dependency also differs from classical neo-colonialism (or dependency as described by the Latin American school) as formulated by Nkrumah in the 1960s. In the classical dependency school, a nominally independent African state becomes dependent on external powers for trade, technology and military protection. Since the 1980s, however, like many African countries, Ghanaian governments have become dependent on foreign creditors or lenders, also referred to as donors, for public finance. This new dependency is also qualitatively different from the previous one (classical neo-colonialism) because the dependence on public finance has a trickle-down effect on other segments of society. Part of what has now become popularly known as civil society, including individual journalists and academics and the leadership of trade unions, has become dependent on external or donor NGOs (referred to officially as a 'partnership') for finance and subsistence, hence the democratization of dependency.

Democratization of politics

At the political level, the power struggle is not only tied to developments in the Ghanaian and world economies, but is also fuelled by the legitimacy problem, in turn linked to the nature of the Ghanaian state and how it evolved (Nimako 1996). In fact, the struggle against colonial rule was a struggle against political illegitimacy. The colonial state/government was considered by holistic nationalists as illegitimate and thus had to end. The holistic nationalist government that replaced the colonial government in the 1950s was also considered illegitimate by sub-nationalists, and had to be undermined.

Decolonization and the process of 'Ghanaianization' of the state enhanced the power of holistic nationalists and accelerated the decline of sub-nationalism; this process obliged the latter to unite against holistic nationalists and thus transformed sub-nationalists into a legitimate national political opposition party. The withering away of sub-nationalist groupings and the subsequent decline of their numbers in parliament brought the conflictual and contradictory relations between the nationalist government and the state bureaucracy to the fore. This found its expression in the latter's opposition to 'socialist development', the professed ideology of the leadership of the nationalist government, and led to the overthrow of the holistic nationalist government in a military coup in 1966, with the tacit approval of (ex-)sub-nationalists.

The military revolt, however, did not resolve the legitimacy problem. Rather it 'politicized' the armed forces and other core state structures and fuelled political and social instability. For not only did holistic nationalists refuse to recognize the NLC regime (1966–9), but also the civilian government (1969–72), a coalition of sub-nationalists that replaced the NLC, was considered as illegitimate by holistic nationalists. This is all the more so since the general elections organized by the NLC in 1969, which brought the Progress Party (PP) to power, excluded the participation of holistic nationalists. In turn, the PP government (1969–72) was undermined by holistic nationalists. This was compounded by a fanatical right-wing rhetoric in response to previous left-wing rhetoric under the regime of the holistic nationalists, and a search for ideological purification within the state bureaucracy. This in turn brought the alliance of sub-nationalists (PP) government into a confrontation with the dominant elements within the core state structures.

Like the previous confrontation between holistic nationalists and state bureaucrats, the confrontation between the Busia government and the state was resolved through a military revolt in 1972. In other words, both the 1966 (NLC) and 1972 (NRC) military coups were precipitated by confrontations between the civilian governments and the dominant elements within the core structure of the state. Just as sub-nationalists had endorsed the overthrow of holistic nationalists in 1966, so the latter endorsed the overthrow of the former in 1972, although both the nationalists of either stripe were not responsible for the coups.

Not only did the members of the Busia regime consider the NRC regime to be illegitimate, but also they initially undermined it. Later, they gained the support of (ex-)holistic nationalists and civil society at large. In response to massive opposition, the NRC broadened its appeal to the state-bureaucracy. This found its expression in the formation of the SMC, which embraced all the commanders of the armed forces and the head of the police service. This was followed by a disengagement of the rest of the ruling council from its leader in a palace coup in 1978 (SMC-II), and finally a revolt by junior army officers in a successful uprising in 1979 by the Armed Forces Revolutionary Council (AFRC).

The coalition of (ex-)sub-nationalists, (ex-)holistic nationalists and civil-society opposition to the NRC/SMC/SMC-II led to the implosion of the state and gave way to a transfer of power to civilian rule in 1979. Thus if the state bureaucracy can be said to have 'exploded' in the 1960s, then it 'imploded' in the 1970s. The 'explosion–implosion' of the state bureaucracy formed part of two decades (1964–84) of economic decline, and the deterioration of productive forces. The threat of total national disintegration obliged the state to turn to producers or civilians, through general elections in 1979.

The 1979 general elections that brought the PNP government of Limann (1979–81) to power resolved the problem of political legitimacy. For the first time in modern Ghana's political history, no organized section of the Ghanaian society questioned the legitimacy of the government in power. However, two decades of economic decline and the 1979–82 world recession undermined the new civilian government, and made the country an 'anarchist's paradise': it was uncertain as to who actually governed the country. It also explains why the Limann government ranks high on strike actions in relation to the number of workers involved. Following this, for the first time in Ghana's history, retired junior army officers, under the leadership of Rawlings, were able to organize and stage a successful coup (in December 1981), with the support of General Gadaffi of Libya. (Similar efforts had failed in the mid-1970s.) Not only was Rawlings' coup a consequence of 'state collapse', but also, in order to circumvent the problem of illegality and illegitimacy, Rawlings chose to call his coup a 'revolution'. This was justified through pre-emptive terror and repression which lasted for about three years, and the selective violence afterwards. Being illegitimate, the PNDC could not turn to mainstream Ghanaians to co-operate and solve economic, political and social problems. Thus, it turned to heavy borrowing from international financial institutions and Western governments in order to give the appearance of delivering the goods. Having taken power by force with the backing of Libya, Rawlings looked to Western governments for his survival, which intensified dependency and increased the debt burden. Foreign borrowing arrested the economic downturn and gave rise to economic growth – a third upswing. Between 1983 and 1989 there was an infusion of nearly US$3.5 billion in external assistance to the Ghanaian economy. A major component of this was a project to co-finance a US$158 million, five and a half year rehabilitation programme for the gold industry – the first major investment project in the country since 1984. Following this, the gross national investment (as a percentage of GDP), increased from 6 per cent in 1980 to 14 per cent in 1990, and reached 17 per cent in 1999; this constituted an annual average growth of 9 per cent between 1980 and 1990, and 18 per cent between 1991 and 1999. In turn this led to an average annual economic growth of 6 per cent between 1984 and 1990, and 2 per cent in 1990s. The upswing was also aided by a massive emigration of Ghanaian young people to Europe, North America and elsewhere. These sent money back to their relatives in Ghana, thus contributing to political stability.

Unlike previous growth, expansions or upswings, the recent investments have taken the form of loans, and have increased the country's external debt burden. Ghana's foreign debt increased from US$120 million in 1966 to US$400 million in 1970, then to US$895 million in 1975, and reached $1 billion in 1983. After the IMF intervention in 1983 the debt jumped to US$2.4 billion in 1986 and surpassed US$3.1 billion in 1987. By 1990 it had reached US$3.3 billion, jumped to US$6 billion in 1996, and reached US$7 billion in 1998 (Nimako 1991, 1996, African Development Bank 2000).

Thus, whereas the economic downturn was arrested (at the expense of external debt accumulation), the erosion of the bureaucratic structures of the state continues, and has found its expression in the retrenchment of the public sector in an attempt to reduce the budget deficit. As we have noted above, between 1984 and 1989 around 70,000 people lost their jobs due to retrenchment in the public sector. The overall government deficit, as a percentage of GDP (at year 2000 price levels), was reduced from 12 per cent in 1980 to 2 per cent in 1990, increased to 7 per cent in 1995, reached 8 per cent in 1998 and then declined to 6 per cent in 1999.

Another qualitative difference between the third upswing and previous upswings is that, unlike previous upswings, the third was not accompanied by improved standards of living in the country, due partly to low cocoa prices on the world market. Cocoa prices fell 48 per cent between 1986 and 1989. This partly explains the declining contribution of agriculture to GDP. Ghana's terms of trade (1995 = 100) deteriorated from 144 in 1980 to 95 in 1990, and improved slightly to 103 in 1999, but remained below the level of 1980. This economic engineering, however, did not prevent the problem of legitimacy from surfacing. Resistance to repression from society, as well as protests against military rule, obliged the PNDC regime to hold elections in 1992 and transform itself from the military PNDC to the civilian National Democratic Congress (NDC) in 1992.

The 1992 elections that precipitated the transformation of PNDC to NDC were initiated from two structurally opposing positions. On the one hand, from the position of the PNDC, it was a means to legitimize its rule so that its leaders could emerge from the 'bunkers' where they have ruled. Following this, the PNDC has attempted to be a player and referee of electoral games at the same time by manipulating the electoral process. On the other hand, from the positions of the other four major political parties, the elections were the only peaceful means of overthrowing the military regime. In other words, the opposing civilian groupings which formed the political parties sought the transfer of power from the military regime to a civilian regime. The PNDC, however, sought continuity and legitimacy.

At the end of the day, the elections were boycotted by the major political parties, due to the manipulation of the electoral process, which culminated in the rigging of the presidential elections. Thus the legitimacy problem remained unresolved after the 1992 general election, and thus reduced the major political parties to 'social movements' with the role of policing human rights. In the 1996 elections parties opposed to the NDC returned to mainstream politics; the opposition parties lost, but continued to consider the NDC to be illegitimate. However, the defeat by the Kuffour's New Patriotic Party (NPP) of the NDC in the 2000 general election has resolved the problem of legitimacy. In other words, in modern Ghanaian political history, only two governments, Limann (1979–81) and Kuffour (2001–) have been considered by all sections of organized society as legitimate. For this reason, the struggle for political democracy has been a struggle from military rule or dictatorship (i.e. state rule) to civilian rule (i.e. government rule or rule of law). Let us now turn to the new phenomena, namely, the democratization of dependency.

Democratization of dependency

We noted above that organized labour had a positive impact on de-colonization and hence democratization of society in the 1940s and 1950s. However, the same cannot be said of the role of organized labour in the democratization process in the past two decades. In fact, initially, the leadership of organized labour supported the PNDC dictatorship. This is partly because organized labour viewed capital as alien, and this explains why, among other things, the Executive Board of the GTUC demanded that the PNDC would recognize the interests of national economic independence and development on the one hand – and foreign aid and investment on the other – as a fundamental conflict. Apparently, the leadership of organized labour confused overseeing the economy with control of the economy. This also explains why the leadership of the

GTUC demanded that the PNDC

> provide clear avenues for the trade unions to be involved in negotiating agreements alongside government negotiators with all external financial interests, in particular the International Monetary Fund (IMF) and the World Bank.
>
> (GTUC 1985)

Clearly, this statement should be seen in the context of dependency. For not only does organized labour depend on the state as the largest employer, but the nationalist government also provided buildings and infrastructure for the TUC as a reward for the latter's contribution to the decolonization of Ghana. For this reason, the dependency of the state on lenders or donors easily translated itself into the dependency of the leadership of organized labour on the donor NGOs. The extent of dependency is informed by two factors:

- foreign reserves, and
- level of foreign debt servicing.

First, the capacity of the Ghanaian state to sustain its debt declined as foreign reserves dwindled. Ghana's foreign-exchange reserves stood at US$293 million in 1979, and declined to US$199.4 million in 1980. As a result of foreign loans and aid in the 1980s, they increased to US$905.9 million in 1990 and dropped to US$78.6 million in 1999 under the burden of foreign debt.

Second, as foreign debt increased, more resources tended to be allocated to service it. Ghana's foreign debt servicing increased from negligible levels in 1980 to US$248 million in 1990, and reached US$438 million in 1998. Ghana's debt stock in relation to GDP grew from 32 per cent in 1980 to 111 per cent in 2000, while debt stock relative to exports rose from 115 per cent in 1980 to 247 per cent in 2000. Asenso-Okyere, however, pointed out that the

> value of the debt to Ghana's exports, for instance stood at about 175 per cent as at the end of 2000. In liquidity terms the country's debt service burden was equivalent to 22.3 per cent of its exports. In fiscal terms, it accounted for almost 90 per cent of total government revenue without divestiture receipts and grants as at the end of 2000.

As a borrower, the central government (in 2000) accounted for about 90 per cent of total debts, with government-guaranteed borrowings by the private sector accounting for 3 per cent, and external borrowings by public corporations accounting for only 2 per cent (Asenso-Okyere 2000: 7). Clearly, most of the loans were acquired for non-productive purposes (Harrod 1992).

In turn, dwindling foreign reserves and increased foreign-debt servicing has given rise to layers of dependency, from government/state levels through civil-society organizations to society at large. Like the Ghanaian government (and for that matter many African governments), the leadership of Ghana's TUC does not depend on its members for survival. In recent years, the Rawlings (or Ghanaian) government has supported itself through dependence on foreign loans and aid, in the context of the Structural Adjustment Programme (SAP), sponsored by the IMF and World Bank. In turn, the SAP has found its expression in the Structural Adjustment Facility (SAF), Enhanced Structural Adjustment Facility (ESAF) and Programme of Actions to Mitigate the Social Cost of Adjustment (PAMSCAD) in the 1980s, and the Poverty Reduction and Growth Facility (PRGF) and Heavily Indebted Poor Countries (HIPC) programme in the 1990s and into the current century.

How a country that was praised by the IMF and World Bank in the 1980s became a heavily indebted poor country in the 1990s and beyond, is yet to be explained by its sponsors. For the moment, suffice it to say that groups of state officials, intellectuals, official women's organizations, journalists and trade-union officials support themselves through the politics of per diem. The essence of the politics of per diem is that groups of officials, intellectuals and civil-society organizations are invited by lenders or donors to the renegotiations of debt or conferences in order to reaffirm their dependence. These invitations to lender or donor countries are necessary for the donors to justify their 'aid' or loans to their taxpayers. This process not only absorbs much of the energy of state officials, but also reduces sections of the Ghanaian intellectual class to the status of research assistants. In other words, state officials spend much of their time working for the lenders or donors rather than for their taxpayers. In a similar vein, sections of the intellectual class spend their time collecting data for lenders or donors and their NGOs. Women's organizations, UN and donor women-initiated programmes serve the same purpose. For journalists, especially investigative journalists, the situation means being dependent on foreign NGOs for their wages. The dependence of journalists on donor NGOs has increased in response to the activities of Transparency International, which culminated in the conference on *Global Forum on Fighting Corruption and Safeguarding Integrity* in The Netherlands in May 2001. The cultural irony is that vested interests in the donor or developed countries objected to the word 'corruption', so the word 'integrity' had to be used for the West or donors, so that 'corruption' could apply to the developing or dependent countries.

Similarly, the leadership of the Ghana's TUC can continue to exist through the support of international agencies, foreign trade unions and donor NGOs. Underlying the democratization of dependency is the shift of international financial institutions or donor austerity programmes from conditional loans in the context of SAP in the 1980s, to good governance, civil-society programmes and advocacy in the 1990s. This shift of donor resources has benefited the leadership of organized labour, but it has not made the government and state officials any less dependent (Reardon 1997). This is likely to intensify the disconnection of the GTUC leadership from the rank and file. It should be mentioned, however, that this disconnection has a long tradition. We noted above that labour recruitment went on for more than forty years without any clearly defined rules under the colonial regime. Since senior officials in the colonial administration or economy were by definition white British people, they did not take part in trade-union activities in Ghana. The division of labour along racial and ethnic lines in the colonial period was transformed along class lines in the post-colonial period. Consequently, senior officials did not become members of trade unions. It appears, however, that Obeng-Fosu failed to make the historical–structural link that impacted on organized labour when he noted that:

> Even though there is no law in Ghana, as at present, excluding senior staff members from trade union membership under the Industrial Relations Act, 1965, and owing possibly to [a] superiority complex, senior staff members of establishments, in general, do not belong to trade unions. Instead, they have formed senior staff associations and have, in some cases, obtained the recognition of their respective establishments.
>
> (Obeng-Fosu 1991: 79)

It should be mentioned, however, that senior staff associations benefit from junior staff negotiations, since senior staff also increase their wages after the latter have obtained a wage rise, in order to maintain the wage gap.

At the level of the broader society, the dependence of the élites has led Ghanaians to fend for themselves within the natural economy, left to the vagaries of the weather and the remittances sent by Ghanaians from abroad. Ghanaians in Europe and North America remit and invest more than US$200 million in Ghana yearly. This makes remittance from the Ghanaian diaspora the fourth-largest foreign-exchange earner (after gold, tourism and cocoa). In other words, many Ghanaians have come to depend on the remittance from their friends and relatives abroad, whereas those without relatives abroad are left at the mercy of the natural environment. The dependency circle is thus complete.

The political irony is that the Ghanaian diaspora has less direct political influence on the government and élites than the donors, although the former contribute more to the economy than the latter. It will not do, however, to argue that the government, state officials, intellectuals and civil-society organizations are content with their dependence status. They complain in private, but do not protest in public, due to the politics of per diem. From the point of view of rational choice, the politics of per diem is beneficial to sections of the Ghanaian élite. The politics of per diem also appears to be the only link between the Ghanaian élite and the international community, because the local wage levels of élites are too low to allow them to travel abroad. However, the politics of per diem disconnects the Ghanaian masses from the élites, and thus does not make the government and élites accountable to their electorate.

Concluding remarks:

Repositioning organized labour

We have demonstrated above that Ghana's debt burden has its origin in the formation of the Ghanaian state and the development of the infrastructural underpinnings of the colonial economy. The development of the basic physical infrastructure, namely, harbours, telecommunications, roads and railway lines, was based on borrowed money. Since then, there has been no local solution to infrastructural development. Nevertheless, infrastructural development at the turn of the twentieth century gave rise to the first economic upswing: between 1900 and 1925. This was followed by an economic downturn between 1925 and 1945, which symbolized the first forty-year cycle in the Ghanaian economy. Ghana experienced a second economic upswing between 1946 and 1965. This was caused by high cocoa prices on the world market in the late 1940s and early 1950s. In both of the expansions or upswings (1900–25 and 1946–65), the development of productive forces and infrastructure was simultaneously accompanied by budget deficits and an improvement in the standards of living of Ghanaians, especially during the latter phase. This was followed by an economic downturn between 1965 and 1984, and the deterioration of the infrastructure. This was compounded by the 1979–82 recession in the world economy, and aggravated by the 1981–3 drought.

Not only did the 1946–65 upswing and 1965–83 downturn symbolize a second forty-year cycle, but also the resulting foreign-exchange shortages made it impossible for the government to import sufficient food to bolster the resulting shortages and revive the infrastructure. This obliged Rawlings' PNDC government to turn to the West for its survival, which in turn intensified dependency and increased the debt burden; this arrested the economic downturn and gave rise to a third upswing. Like the first upswing, the third upswing (1984–2000, and beyond(?)) was also strongly influenced by developments in the gold-mining sector; also, as in the first upswing, infrastructural development was based on external borrowing. This was because there is no local solution to infrastructural development.

We have also demonstrated that, in recent years, Ghana has witnessed two forms of democratization processes, first, from military to civilian rule, and second, the democratization of dependence. This new form of dependence is a consequence of the shifting of resources by donors – from SAP-related activities to issues related to good governance and civil-society advocacy activities; in other words the shift in resources has given rise to the democratization of dependency.

This of course raises the question of how Ghanaian (and for that matter African) élites can effectively take advantage of the international political–economic system. Clearly, economic development depends on savings, investments and access to markets. On this score, the country's debt burden blocks savings and investments, and hence further economic development. However, economic development also depends on social organization. In turn, social organization influences political conflict and the kind of marketing strategies that could be pursued. In the absence of massive foreign investment, what is left is institutional renewal to foster economic development. This implies that, apart from wage claims, issues related to productivity and safety should be incorporated into organized labour's advocacy strategy.

First, the traditional GTUC role, namely, representation and wage claims, has come to an end. Many of the thirteen reasons for strike actions are related to wage claims. However, these claims have not prevented retrenchment or deterioration of the infrastructure, including the physical infrastructure of the GTUC. Wage claims and inflation have become a vicious circle; high inflation leads to high wage claims and vice versa. This is compounded by external debt burden and high local interest rates, which also fuels inflation. In other words, high wage claims by organized labour are at a dead end. Given the structure and state of the Ghanaian economy, high wages can be met only by a government licence to print money. The reduction of Ghana's external debt burden will, however, be beneficial to Ghanaians and organized labour. Therefore, from the point of view of organized labour advocacy, it will be useful for the trade unions to plead for a moratorium on Ghana's foreign debt. A moratorium, as opposed to debt relief or cancellation, is more businesslike. However, the government may not be able to plead for a moratorium because it can be 'threatened or blackmailed' (privately) by donor or lender countries (in international 'diplomacy', what is said or agreed in private often outweighs what is said in public). The leadership of the GTUC is in a better position to influence international politics than the government. This of course leads us to another scenario. If the government can be 'blackmailed' by lenders or donors, why can donor NGOs not (whose source of income is the same donors) 'blackmail' the GTUC?

Second, the GTUC has to reposition itself to serve society as a whole, rather than its dwindling number of members. Much of organized labour is located in the public sector or the non-productive sectors of the economy. Its contribution to economic growth and development is thus indirect. The GTUC can serve as facilitators for the productive sectors of the formal and informal economy. Repositioning also means creativity: for example, they can negotiate for better working hours and transportation facilities for construction workers, which can improve the productivity and the health of the workers. It makes little sense, productivity-wise and health-wise, for construction workers to work for long periods under the blistering sun, only to record that they have worked eight hours in order to meet some 'international standards'. The same goes for civil and public servants who, on some occasions, spend more time on the road to work, due to poor wages and transportation problems, than in the work-place. In other words, the number of hours that a person spends at their work-place does not tell us about the amount of work done. Hence the need for creativity.

Finally, the issue of health-and-safety standards can be broadened beyond the work-place and incorporate other security issues (ILO 2000). It is clear that the drive for a healthy and safe work-place can lead to technological adaptation and innovation. For instance, it is not sufficient for workers in sanitation to demand more wages; it is also necessary for them to work in a healthy environment. Furthermore, through advocacy, the leadership of the GTUC can address issues like road safety and armed robbery. Both are major social and economic problems. This certainly requires a broader understanding of the dynamics of the Ghanaian economy and society in relation to the international political–economic system. It is not sufficient for the GTUC to argue that the current high unemployment rate is a result of the macro-economic imbalances in the economy, which finds expression in an overvalued currency, high inflation and interest rates. The GTUC leadership should go beyond government policy and take advantage of the international political–economic system without becoming dependent on the weakest link of the world system.

References

African Development Bank (2000) *African Development Report 2000*, Oxford: Oxford University Press.

Asenso-Okyere, K. (2001) 'HIPC for Africa with special reference to Ghana', Legon, Ghana: ISSER.

Boateng, K. (2001) *Policy Brief on the Labour Market and Human Resource Development in Ghana*, Legon, Ghana: ISSER.

Ewusi, K. (1986) *Statistical Tables on the Economy of Ghana, 1950–1985*, Legon, Ghana: ISSER.

Ghana Trades Union Congress (GTUC) (1985) *Position Paper of Executive Board of TUC on National Situation*, Accra, Ghana: GTUC.

Ghana Trades Union Congress (GTUC) (2001) *Report of Three Day TUC Workshop on Labour Market*, held at Capital View Hotel, Koforidua, 18–20 April.

Harrod, J. (1992) *Labour and Third World Debt*, Brussels: ICEF.

Institute of Statistical, Social and Economic Research (ISSER) (2000) *The State of the Ghanaian Economy in 1999*, Legon: ISSER.

International Labour Organization (2000) *World Labour Report 2000: Income Security and Social Protection in a Changing World*, Geneva: ILO.

Jeffries, R. (1978) Class, Power and Ideology in Ghana: the Railwaymen of Sekondi, Cambridge: Cambridge University Press.

Konings, P. (1980) *The Political Potential of Ghanaian Miners: a Case Study of the AGC workers at Obuasi*, African Studies Centre, Research Reports, No. 9, Leiden.

Kraus, J. (1979) 'Strikes and labour power in Ghana', *Development and Change*, 10(2): 59–86.

National Council on Women and Development (1995) *Sectoral Policy and Programme for Promotion of Employment for Women*, Accra, Ghana: National Council on Women and Development.

Nimako, K. (1991) *Economic Change and Political Conflict in Ghana, 1600–1990*, Amsterdam: Thesis Publishers.

Nimako, K. (1996) 'Power struggle and economic liberalization in Ghana', in A.E. Fernandez Jilberto and A. Mommen (eds) *Liberalization in the Developing World: Institutional and Economic Changes in Latin America, Africa and Asia*, London: Routledge: 266–84.

Obeng-Fosu, P. (1991) *Industrial Relations in Ghana: the Law and Practice*, Accra, Ghana: Ghana Universities Press.

Reardon, G. (ed.) (1997) *This is APADEP*, The Hague.

Technology Transfer Centre, Council for Scientific and Industrial Research (CSIR) (1991) *Report on Small and Medium Enterprises Sector Study*, Accra, Ghana: Council for Scientific and Industrial Research (CSIR).

Index

For Product Safety Concerns and Information please contact our EU
representative GPSR@taylorandfrancis.com Taylor & Francis Verlag GmbH,
Kaufingerstraße 24, 80331 München, Germany

Printed and bound by CPI Group (UK) Ltd, Croydon, CR0 4YY
08/05/2025
01864443-0001